Gun Crime

International Library of Criminology, Criminal Justice and Penology – Second Series
Series Editors: Gerald Mars and David Nelken

Titles in the Series:

Gender and Prisons
Dana M. Britton

Quantitative Methods in Criminology
Shawn Bushway and David Weisburd

Computer Crime
Indira Carr

Insurgent Terrorism
Gerald Cromer

Criminal Courts
*Jo Dixon, Aaron Kupchick and
Joachim J. Savelsberg*

Crime and Immigration
Joshua D. Freilich and Graeme R. Newman

Crime and Security
Benjamin Goold and Lucia Zedner

Crime and Regulation
Fiona Haines

Recent Developments in Criminological Theory
Stuart Henry and Scott A. Lukas

Gun Crime
Rob Hornsby and Dick Hobbs

The Criminology of War
Ruth Jamieson

**The Impact of HIV/AIDS on Criminology and
Criminal Justice**
Mark M. Lanier

Burglary
R.I. Mawby

Domestic Violence
Mangai Natarajan

Women Police
Mangai Natarajan

Crime and Globalization
David Nelken and Suzanne Karstedt

Surveillance, Crime and Social Control
Clive Norris and Dean Wilson

Crime and Social Institutions
Richard Rosenfeld

The Death Penalty, Volumes I and II
Austin Sarat

Gangs
Jacqueline Schneider and Nick Tilley

Corporate Crime
Sally Simpson and Carole Gibbs

Green Criminology
Nigel South and Piers Beirne

Crime, Criminal Justice and Masculinities
Stephen Tomsen

Crime and Deviance in Cyberspace
David Wall

Gun Crime

Edited by

Rob Hornsby

Northumbria University, UK

and

Dick Hobbs

London School of Economics and Political Science, UK

ASHGATE

Published by
Ashgate Publishing Limited
Gower House
Croft Road
Aldershot
Hampshire GU11 3HR
England

Ashgate Publishing Company
Suite 420
101 Cherry Street
Burlington, VT 05401-4405
USA

Ashgate website: http://www.ashgate.com

British Library Cataloguing in Publication Data
Gun Crime – (International library of criminology,
    criminal justice and penology. Second series)
    1. Firearms – Social aspects 2. Firearms and crime
    I. Hornsby, Rob II. Hobbs, Dick
    364.2

Library of Congress Cataloging-in-Publication Data
Gun Crime / edited by Rob Hornsby and Dick Hobbs
        p.cm
    Includes index
    1. Firearms – Social aspects. 2. Firearms and crime. 3. Firearms and crime –
    Research. 4. Violence. I. Hornsby, Rob. II. Hobbs, Dick.
        HV6016.G86 2008
        364–dc22   2007031501

ISBN: 978–0–7546–2585–8

Mixed Sources
Product group from well-managed
forests and other controlled sources
www.fsc.org Cert no. SGS-COC-2482
© 1996 Forest Stewardship Council

Printed and bound in Great Britain by
TJ International Ltd, Padstow, Cornwall

Contents

Acknowledgements		ix
Series Preface		xiii
Introduction		xv

PART I   YOUTH, GANGS AND GUNS

1　Paul B. Stretesky and Mark R. Pogrebin (2007), 'Gang-Related Gun Violence: Socialization, Identity, and Self', *Journal of Contemporary Ethnography*, **36**, pp. 85–114.　3

2　Scott H. Decker and G. David Curry (2002), 'Gangs, Gang Homicides, and Gang Loyalty: Organized Crimes or Disorganized Criminals', *Journal of Criminal Justice*, **30**, pp. 343–52.　33

3　Deanna L. Wilkinson and Jeffrey Fagan (1996), 'The Role of Firearms in Violence "Scripts": The Dynamics of Gun Events Among Adolescent Males', *Law and Contemporary Problems*, **59**, pp. 55–89.　43

4　Gavin Hales, Chris Lewis and Daniel Silverstone (2006), *Gun Crime: The Market In and Use of Illegal Firearms*, Findings 279, London: Home Office, pp. 1–6.　79

5　Cynthia Perez McCluskey, John D. McCluskey and Timothy S. Bynum (2006), 'Early Onset Offending and Later Violent and Gun Outcomes in a Contemporary Youth Cohort', *Journal of Criminal Justice*, **34**, pp. 531–41.　85

6　Robert H. DuRant, Alan G. Getts, Chris Cadenhead and Elizabeth R.Woods (1995), 'The Association between Weapon-Carrying and the Use of Violence among Adolescents Living in or Around Public Housing', *Journal of Adolescence*, **18**, pp. 579–92.　97

7　Rick Ruddell and G. Larry Mays (2003), 'Examining the Arsenal of Juvenile Gunslingers: Trends and Policy Implications', *Crime and Delinquency*, **49**, pp. 231–52.　111

8　Avelardo Valdez and Stephen J. Sifaneck (2004), '"Getting High and Getting By": Dimensions of Drug Selling Behaviors among American Mexican Gang Members in South Texas', *Journal of Research in Crime and Delinquency*, **41**, pp. 82–105.　133

PART II   ROBBERY AND FIREARMS

9　Bruce A. Jacobs and Richard Wright (1999), 'Stick-Up, Street Culture, and Offender Motivation', *Criminology*, **37**, pp. 149–73.　159

10 Jody Miller (1998), 'Up it Up: Gender and the Accomplishment of Street
    Robbery', *Criminology*, **36**, pp. 37–66.   185
11 Trevor Bennett and Katy Holloway (2004), 'Possession and Use of Illegal Guns
    Among Offenders in England and Wales', *Howard Journal*, **43**, pp. 237–52.   215
12 David F. Luckenbill (1981), 'Generating Compliance: The Case of Robbery',
    Urban Life, **10**, pp. 25–46.   231
13 Ian O'Donnell and Shona Morrison (1997), 'Armed and Dangerous? The Use of
    Firearms in Robbery', *Howard Journal*, **36**, pp. 305–20.   253
14 Shawn L. Schwaner (2000), '"Stick 'Em Up, Buddy": Robbery, Lifestyle, and
    Specialization within a Cohort of Parolees', *Journal of Criminal Justice*, **28**,
    pp. 371–84.   269
15 Philip J. Cook (1987), 'Robbery Violence', *Journal of Criminal Law and
    Criminology*, **78**, pp. 357–76.   283

PART III GUN CRIME, VIOLENCE AND HOMICIDE

16 Craig Perkins (2003), 'Weapon Use and Violent Crime: National Crime
    Victimization Survey, 1993–2001', *Bureau of Justice Statistics Special
    Report*, US Department of Justice: Office of Justice Programs, pp. 1–12.   305
17 Richard B. Felson and Steven F. Messner (1996), 'To Kill or Not to Kill? Lethal
    Outcomes in Injurious Attacks', *Criminology*, **34**, pp. 519–45.   317
18 Sean P. Varano, John D. McCluskey, Justin W. Patchin and Timothy S. Bynum
    (2004), 'Exploring the Drugs-Homicide Connection', *Journal of Contemporary
    Criminal Justice*, **20**, pp. 369–92.   345
19 Charis E. Kubrin and Ronald Weitzer (2003), 'Retaliatory Homicide:
    Concentrated Disadvantage and Neighborhood Culture', *Social Problems*, **50**,
    pp. 157–80.   369
20 Bruce P. Kennedy, Ichiro Kawachi, Deborah Prothrow-Stith, Kimberly Lochner
    and Vanita Gupta (1998), 'Social Capital, Income Inequality, and Firearm Violent
    Crime', *Social Science and Medicine*, **47**, pp. 7–17.   393
21 Gary Kleck and Michael Hogan (1999), 'National Case-Control Study of
    Homicide Offending and Gun Ownership', *Social Problems*, **46**, pp. 275–93. 405
22 Barbara A. Koons-Witt and Pamela J. Schram (2003), 'The Prevalence and
    Nature of Violent Offending by Females', *Journal of Criminal Justice*, **31**,
    pp. 361–71.   425
23 Graham C. Ousey and Matthew R. Lee (2004), 'Investigating the Connections
    between Race, Illicit Drug Markets, and Lethal Violence, 1984–1997', *Journal of
    Research in Crime and Delinquency*, **41**, pp. 352–83.   437
24 James Alan Fox and Alex R. Piquero (2003), 'Deadly Demographics: Population
    Characteristics and Forecasting Homicide Trends', *Crime and Delinquency*, **49**,
    pp. 339–59.   469
25 Caroline Wolf Harlow (2001) [Rev. 2/4/02], 'Firearm Use by Offenders: Survey
    of Inmates in State and Federal Correctional Facilities', *Bureau of Justice Statistics
    Special Report*, US Department of Justice, pp. 1–15.   491

PART IV STITCHING UP THE PIECES: FIREARM INJURY TRAUMA FROM CRIMINAL OFFENDING

26 Marianne W. Zawitz and Kevin J. Strom (2000), 'Firearm Injury and Death from Crime, 1993–97', *Bureau of Justice Statistics Selected Findings*, US Department of Justice, pp. 1–8.   509
27 Danielle Laraque, Barbara Barlow, Maureen Durkin, Joy Howell, Franklyn Cladis, David Friedman, Carla DiScala, Rao Ivatury and William Stahl (1995), 'Children Who Are Shot: A 30-Year Experience', *Journal of Pediatric Surgery*, **30**, pp. 1072–76.   517
28 Kathy Sanders-Phillips (1997), 'Assaultive Violence in the Community: Psychological Responses of Adolescent Victims and Their Parents', *Journal of Adolescent Health*, **21**, pp. 356–65.   523
29 I.J. Persad, R. Srinivas Reddy, M.A. Saunders and J. Patel (2005), 'Gunshot Injuries to the Extremities: Experience of a U.K. Trauma Centre', *Injury: International Journal of the Care of the Injured*, **36**, pp. 407–11.   533

Index   539

Acknowledgements

The editors and publishers wish to thank the following for permission to use copyright material.

American Society of Criminology for the essays: Bruce A. Jacobs and Richard Wright (1999), 'Stick-Up, Street Culture, and Offender Motivation', *Criminology*, **37**, pp. 149–73. Copyright © 1999 American Society of Criminology; Jody Miller (1998), 'Up it Up: Gender and the Accomplishment of Street Robbery', *Criminology*, **36**, pp. 37–66. Copyright © 1998 American Society of Criminology; Richard B. Felson and Steven F. Messner (1996), 'To Kill or Not to Kill? Lethal Outcomes in Injurious Attacks', *Criminology*, **34**, pp. 519–45. Copyright © 1996 American Society of Criminology.

Blackwell Publishing Ltd for the essays: Trevor Bennett and Katy Holloway (2004), 'Possession and Use of Illegal Guns Among Offenders in England and Wales', *Howard Journal*, **43**, pp. 237–52. Copyright © 2004 Blackwell Publishing Ltd; Ian O'Donnell and Shona Morrison (1997), 'Armed and Dangerous? The Use of Firearms in Robbery', *Howard Journal*, **36**, pp. 305–20. Copyright © 1981 Sage Publications, Inc. Copyright © 1997 Blackwell Publishing Ltd.

Copyright Clearance Center for the essays: Paul B. Stretesky and Mark R. Pogrebin (2007), 'Gang-Related Gun Violence: Socialization, Identity, and Self', *Journal of Contemporary Ethnography*, **36**, pp. 85–114. Copyright © 2007 Sage Publications; Gary Kleck and Michael Hogan (1999), 'National Case-Control Study of Homicide Offending and Gun Ownership', *Social Problems*, **46**, pp. 275–93. Copyright © 1999 Society for the Study of Social Problems, Inc; Charis E. Kubrin and Ronald Weitzer (2003), 'Retaliatory Homicide: Concentrated Disadvantage and Neighborhood Culture', *Social Problems*, **50**, pp. 157–80. Copyright © 2003 Society for the Study of Social Problems, Inc.

Crown Copyright for the essay: Gavin Hales, Chris Lewis and Daniel Silverstone (2006), *Gun Crime: The Market In and Use of Illegal Firearms*, Findings 279, London: Home Office, pp. 1–6. Copyright © 2006 Crown Copyright.

Elsevier for the essays: Kathy Sanders-Phillips (1997), 'Assaultive Violence in the Community: Psychological Responses of Adolescent Victims and Their Parents', *Journal of Adolescent Health*, **21**, pp. 356–65. Copyright © 1997 Society for Adolescent Medicine; Scott H. Decker and G. David Curry (2002), 'Gangs, Gang Homicides, and Gang Loyalty: Organized Crimes or Disorganized Criminals', *Journal of Criminal Justice*, **30**, pp. 343–52. Copyright © 2002 Elsevier Science Ltd; Cynthia Perez McCluskey, John D. McCluskey and Timothy S. Bynum (2006), 'Early Onset Offending and Later Violent and Gun Outcomes in a Contemporary

in State and Federal Correctional Facilities', *Bureau of Justice Statistics Special Report*, US Department of Justice, pp. 1–15.; Marianne W. Zawitz and Kevin J. Strom (2000), 'Firearm Injury and Death from Crime, 1993–97', *Bureau of Justice Statistics Selected Findings*, US Department of Justice, pp. 1–8.

Preface to the Second Series

The first series of the International Library of Criminology, Criminal Justice and Penology has established itself as a major research resource by bringing together the most significant journal essays in contemporary criminology, criminal justice and penology. The series made available to researchers, teachers and students an extensive range of essays which are indispensable for obtaining an overview of the latest theories and findings in this fast changing subject. Indeed the rapid growth of interesting scholarly work in the field has created a demand for a second series which like the first consists of volumes dealing with criminological schools and theories as well as with approaches to particular areas of crime criminal justice and penology. Each volume is edited by a recognised authority who has selected twenty or so of the best journal articles in the field of their special competence and provided an informative introduction giving a summary of the field and the relevance of the articles chosen. The original pagination is retained for ease of reference.

The difficulties of keeping on top of the steadily growing literature in criminology are complicated by the many disciplines from which its theories and findings are drawn (sociology, law, sociology of law, psychology, psychiatry, philosophy and economics are the most obvious). The development of new specialisms with their own journals (policing, victimology, mediation) as well as the debates between rival schools of thought (feminist criminology, left realism, critical criminology, abolitionism etc.) make necessary overviews that offer syntheses of the state of the art.

GERALD MARS
Honorary Professor of Anthropology, University College, London, UK

DAVID NELKEN
Distinguished Professor of Sociology, University of Macerata, Italy;
Distinguished Research Professor of Law, University of Cardiff, Wales;
Honorary Visiting Professor of Law, LSE, London, UK

Introduction

The concept of 'gun crime', by the very nature of divergent sovereign and legal contexts is a definitional conundrum. Yet, what is evident and pervasive is that the use of firearms in criminal acts can 'profoundly change the consequences of a violent encounter' (Blumstein, 2003, p. 657), and the very notion of gun crime is often used by politicians, law enforcement personnel and the mass media as an indicator of societal decline and moral decay. Guns are powerful tools that can temporarily afford power to the powerless. Gun crime is also a transgression engaged in by the powerful, however, and while agents of the State, although not immune to the allure of gun-play, are not the subject of this volume, it is hoped that this series might attend to this phenomena at a later date.

'Gun crime', as we employ the term in this volume, relates to an assorted range of illegal activities involving firearms including, for example, commercial and street robberies, gang-drug activities and violent and homicidal assaults. A further issue examined in this volume relates to the medical trauma often created by firearm offences. The chapters also explore the 'foreground ... criminality' (Katz, 1988, p. 3) of gun crime, and connect factors such as victimization, fear, retaliation and retribution, social and economic deprivation and criminal lifestyles, utilizing a range of social science, public health, medical and official sources, and there are of course a number of overlaps between these thematic categories of gun crime. For instance, drug dealing gang members may also commit armed robberies, may murder with guns and become the victims of shootings.

Although in the USA, there is a strong base of research which deals with a range of gun related crime (and gun control) perspectives, reflecting the extraordinary rates of violent gun crime, which are linked to the USA's frontier heritage (Bellesiles, 1996, p. 426), and is, 'as American as cherry pie' (Leonard and Leonard, 2003, p. 99), elsewhere in English speaking countries, there is a paucity of peer-reviewed academic literature. As a consequence, this volume focuses mainly, but not exclusively, upon research from the USA. The USA is the only upper-income post-industrial nation which ardently 'persists in maintaining a gun culture' (Hofstadter, 1970, p. 4). While there have been legislative attempts in the USA to make guns safer, and possessed only by 'safe' people, such measures are difficult to enforce (Sherman, 2001) when private ownership of firearms in the USA exceeds 200 million (Kleck, 1991; Weaver *et al.*, 2004), and each year approximately 4.5 million new firearms, including 2 million handguns, and a further 2 million used/second-hand firearms, are sold (US Dept of Treasury, 2000). Consequently, the US National Crime Victimization Survey (NCVS) estimated that as many as 477,040 victims experienced criminal acts perpetrated by an offender armed with a firearm (NCVS, 2005).

The use of firearms in order to facilitate violent criminal events is determined by a 'weapons effect' scenario (see, Cook, 1983, 1991; Kleck and McElrath, 1991; Weaver *et al.*, 2004). While some studies have questioned that guns used in criminal events are more deadly than knives (see, Wright *et al.*, 1983; Kleck, 1997), the annual FBI Uniform Crime Reports consistently reveal that firearms by far outweigh any other form of potentially deadly tool categories (for example, knives, hands and feet or 'other' types of weaponry) for homicides in the USA. Between 1988 and 1997, there were 233,251 homicides in the US, and 68 per cent of the victims were murdered by firearms, the majority of which were handguns (Miller *et al.*, 2002).

In the UK, firearms offences are far less significant. For example, in England and Wales during 2003, the number of all violent crimes recorded by the British Crime Survey stood at 2,715,000, and the majority of these incidents involved common assault offences (no injuries incurred by the victims). Serious injuries caused by firearms (including air weapons) totalled 572 during 2002/03, and firearms were used in just 1 per cent of violence related offences (Smith and Allen, 2004).

In the first part of this collection the chapters look into continuing concerns relating to youth, urban gangs and firearm use. Part II examines the use of firearms in robbery offences. Part III focuses upon the use of firearms in violent acts and homicide. Part IV deals with public health issues caused by gun use.

Youth, Gangs and Guns

Gang-related gun violence in the USA now has a significant history, with studies demonstrating that gang related homicides accounted for approximately 60 per cent of youth homicides in Boston (Kennedy, Piehl and Braga, 1996), and over one third of all homicides in Chicago (Block and Block, 1993). During the 1980s and 1990s, an increase in the use of guns within gang disputes led to episodes of violence which may have previously been resolved by less deadly means (Wilkinson and Fagan, Chapter 3, this volume). During that time the 'gang-problem' had been elevated to the forefront of Community, State and Federal political agendas in the USA to such a degree that inner city gangs and their increased reliance upon armed violence was considered as a 'public health' issue (Cohen and Swift, 1993; Hutson *et al.*, 1995).

As Sanchez-Jankowski (1991) has established, violence is the currency of the gang, and Sanders (1994) affords this currency its full economic worth in his examination of gang related drive-by shootings, arguing that such acts of violence are not only generally enacted as retaliatory measures between feuding gangs in order to enhance members' reputations, but also serve an economic purpose as a means to control turf in order to enhance drug-dealing activities.

Explanations for the dramatic rise in gang related armed violence during the 1980s and 1990s are varied, but often centre upon the development of the crack cocaine market (see, Williams 1989; Cohen *et. al*, 1998; Decker and Van Winkle, 1996; Fagan and Chin, 1990; Howell and Decker, 1999; Inciardi, 1986; Padilla, 1992; Klein, 1995; Klein, Maxson and Cunningham, 1991; Moore, 1990; Venkatesh, 1996). Alternative explanations have also been offered which focus upon security and protection (Horowitz, 1983; Decker, Pennell and Caldwell, 1997). Decker, Pennell and Caldwell's research found that 31 per cent of arrested gang members admitted to carrying firearms. Clearly, such reliance upon lethal weaponry in the control of turf and street-level drug disputes has consequences at the individual, community and policy levels (Braga, McDevitt and Pierce, 2006), and it is perhaps unsurprising that during the mid-1980s until the early 1990s, homicide rates among 15- to 19-year-olds increased by 154 per cent (Dahlberg, 1998, p. 259).

As to the configuration of gang membership, there are contrasting viewpoints. In one camp are those who claim that gangs are highly structured rational organizations with delineated management arrangements, in which specific roles within the organization are defined from above in facilitating drug-trafficking activities at import and street distribution level (Moore, 1991; Skolnick, 1990; Sanchez-Jankowski, 1991). Conversely, others have explained the composition of gangs as loosely-structured, chaotic and unable to compete within the complexities of major drug trafficking business operations (Klein and Maxson, 1994; Klein, Maxson and Cunningham, 1991; Decker and Van Winkle, 1996; Huff, 1996).

Street retribution and retaliation are also significant factors in increased gun use, and Jacobs and Wright (2006, p. 78) show that that lethal 'gun play' mechanisms are situated within concerns of masculinity, respect and retaliatory vengeance. Informal codes of justice amongst marginalized groups are complex, and it is clear that 'inequalities of wealth, status and prestige guarantee that the benefits of formal justice will be more available to some people than others' (Jacobs and Wright, 2006, p. 134). In Part I the chapters examine a myriad of gun crime related contexts related to youth and gang issues.

Paul Stretesky and Mark Pogrebin (Chapter 1) provide a study of gangs and their reliance upon violence and gun use. Drawing upon in-depth interviews with twenty-two incarcerated gang members, the research considers the processes of socialization of gang members and their internalizing of norms and values which are reliant upon frequent acts of armed violence. For gang members, gun related violence is considered as a required masculine attribute, where the processes of socialization to the gang and its maintenance, identity and notions of the 'self', inform us that 'guns are tools that aid in identity formation and impression management' (p. 26).

In Chapter 2, Scott Decker and David Curry's study of gang related homicides in St Louis examines variations between gang-related and non-gang-related homicides, and the social organization of such murders at the peak of the US gang wars. The research reveals marked differences between gang- and non-gang-related homicides and reinforces Cloward and Ohlin's (1960) theory that gangs are generally without unyielding structure, lacking the capacity to organize themselves effectively in the management of drugs markets and the risks associated with such illicit trading. The gangs of St Louis were poorly equipped to negotiate the violent risks involved in being gang members due to the gang's overall lack of corporate control and governance.

In Chapter 3, Deanna Wilkinson and Jeffrey Fagan argue that, while historically youth violence has always been an inherent element of delinquency (see, for example, Thrasher, 1927; Yablonsky, 1962; Valentine, 1995; Short Jr., 1997), the 'ecology of danger' (p. 46) that emerged in the inner cities of the United States during the 1980s until the mid-1990s was the context for the perturbing body count of gang members. The study locates contemporary youth gun crime within a range of structural factors which 'have reshaped both the social controls and street networks that in the past regulated violent transactions' (p. 76). Challenged by the onslaught of post-industrialization and segregation, violence is determined by socio-cultural responses to increasingly aggressive encounters within those social environments, and governed by the symbolic and instrumental meanings and outcomes of gun use within violence-prone 'scripts'.

In Chapter 4, Gavin Hales, Chris Lewis and Daniel Silverstone provide a short summary of findings from a Home Office study which examines the gun-crime perspective from a British viewpoint. In interviewing incarcerated young men involved in firearms offending, the study provides insight of UK illegal gun markets and the use of guns. Owing to the UK's rigid gun control legislation, the sources of distribution of firearms in the UK are described by the authors as illegal imports, leakages from the legal market (for example, burgled shotguns) and the conversion of imitation/replica firearms. However, due to the illegality of this market, ammunition for illicit guns is in short supply and is often manufactured in an ad hoc and impoverished manner. Guns are often passed-around within gangs, although there is evidence of the role of professional 'armourers' in supplying the market. Within the UK illegal drug markets are said to 'underpin the criminal economy and represent the most important theme in relation to the illegal use of firearms' (p. 79).

Cynthia McCluskey *et al.* (Chapter 5) evaluate initiation into the use and carrying patterns of guns by young people. Utilizing life course and criminal career perspectives of delinquency, the arrest data of 1,159 arrestees born in 1979 were analysed. It was found that there was a connection between early violent offending and firearms offences committed when older. Indeed, so correlated are these factors within this cohort, that the early age arrest of young males more than doubled the probability of later arrests for gun-crime offences. Male offenders under the age of fourteen were particularly vulnerable to transitions that would later involve the criminal use of firearms.

Chapter 6 examines the social and psychological factors associated with the regularity of adolescents' possession of firearms. Robert DuRant and his colleagues conducted a cross-sector survey of 225 black adolescents aged between 11 and 19 living in housing projects in Augusta, Georgia. They examined the number of days that a weapon (that is, gun, knife or club) had been carried during the previous 30 days, and the levels of frequency that such weapons had been carried during the previous year. The context for this study being that homicide had become the main cause of death for young black men aged 15 to 24 years of age, and that the use of firearms was a main factor in this upsurge of homicides, occurring in areas of entrenched poverty with high levels of violent crime. The study highlights that a significant minority of the cohorts had carried weapons during that 30 day period, with the number of armed young men rising when analysing the previous year data. The study correlates these data with these young men's experiences of violence and victimization, their experiences of corporal punishment and family conflict, high rates of mental depression and social and economic attainment. Another major factor in this study was that a high number of them believed that they would be dead by the age of 25. For DuRant *et al.* a lethal reliance upon conflict-ridden resolutions become a form of 'cultural transmission' (Sutherland and Cressey, 1978) that should be central to our understanding of alienated young black men, and who adopt a subculture of violence as a 'solution' to the profound disparities of the social and economic system (Anderson, 1999).

Chapter 7 deals with the moral panics linked to media and law enforcement representations of heavily-armed youth gangs with military-style assault weapons. Rick Ruddell and Larry Mays' study of firearms confiscated from juveniles in St Louis, Missouri between 1992 and 1999, found that the lethal capacity of firearms possessed by this juvenile cohort within the city had remained relatively constant during the 1990s, and that levels of fire-power had not significantly increased. This was contrary to the perception of law enforcement and policy makers that the possession by juveniles of cheap and less potent 'Saturday night special' handguns were in decline, and that more lethal forms of firepower had been adopted by sectors of the city's juvenile population. The study found that young men were generally continuing to arm themselves with lower calibre firearms.

Youth gangs in the USA are synonymous with illicit drug distribution (Decker and Van Winkle, 1996; Klein, 1995), and in the final chapter of Part I, Avelardo Valdez and Stephen Sifaneck examine a number of correlated dimensions of Mexican-American gang membership and their relationships to drug markets in a South Texan city. Concentrating on the behavioural traits of drug dealing gang members, this study provides detailed analysis of the role of violence, often gun related, in understanding the association of gang membership, drug use and the distribution of 'street' and 'drug' gangs composed of 'homeboys', 'hustlers', 'slangers' and 'ballers'. The study details the feuds that ensue when drug-dealing and territorial differences remain unresolved and where armed violence has a central role in settling those disputes.

Robbery and Firearms

Part II examines the act of armed robbery. In the USA between 1981 and 1996, 41 per cent of robberies involved firearms, whereas in England and Wales robbery offences involving firearms equated to just 5 per cent of all robberies (Langan and Farrington, 1999).

Bruce Jacobs and Richard Wright (Chapter 9) examine the decision-making processes of 86 active armed-robbers, both male and female. Need, opportunity, excitement and sensory stimulation were found to be the guiding motives of the majority of armed robbers interviewed. Street-culture and its fetish for highly-prized and ostentatious clothing, jewellery and other expensive accessories, the pursuit of high living and living for the moment by 'earning and burning money' (Katz, 1988, p. 215), with the enactment of 'life as party' (Wright and Decker, 1999, p. 155; see also, Shover and Honaker, 1992), are identified as key factors in making the decision to commit robbery to fund lifestyles embedded in expensive and self-indulgent activities. Jacobs and Wright also seek to explain the foreground dynamics and associated risk factors which predispose armed robbers to the activity. Strain, broken homes, social capital deficits, participation in street culture, the thrills of illicit action, and the focus upon hedonistic ritual in the pursuit of conspicuous consumption shape the background motivations of such offenders, while the financial desperation that often accompanies such chaotic lifestyles ultimately drives the offender's to commit robbery.

Jody Miller (Chapter 10) provides analysis of female participation in the 'gender stratified' (p. 185) world of violent street robbery. Despite evidence of an increase in female robbers representing a new dynamic in our understanding of armed robbery, Miller argues, that 'gender inequality remains a salient feature of the urban street scene' (p. 189). Miller describes three dominant ways in which women commit robberies: a) by robbing female victims with overtly confrontational physical assault; b) by luring potential male victims by appearing sexually available, and c) by committing street robberies with male associates. While strong arm tactics or knives are favoured in dealing with female targets, guns are used occasionally when committing robberies against male victims. In accompanying male robbers in their activities, usually taking supportive roles rather than the lead ones, the females were often armed with handguns. This study highlights the gendered-stratified male domination of the urban street environment, and suggests that female adoption of male orientated structural and cultural norms in the committal of violent street crime should be regarded as 'a culturally legitimate response' (p. 210).

In Chapter 11, Trevor Bennett and Katy Holloway discuss the increased possession and use of firearms in criminal activities in England and Wales. Pointing to the scarcity of UK academic studies of illegal gun ownership, they attempt to bridge this research void with a study that focuses upon offender possession and use of guns. The study found that 20 per cent of 1,570 arrestees had owned or had possession of a gun at some point in their lives, with 8 per cent having done so in the previous year. One third of the arrestee sample who possessed a handgun said that they had used the weapon in committing offences. As with other chapters in this volume the most common reason for criminal possession of handguns were explained by the cohort as self-preservation and protection.

In Chapter 12, David Luckenbill examines how armed robbers aim to generate victim compliance, a vital feature in the committal of a successful robbery. From within an interactionist framework, Luckenbill describes the act of robbery in terms of four interconnected robbery tasks. At stage one the robber establishes his presence with the victim. At stage two, the offender and victim encounter a 'common robbery frame', which aims to ensure the audience (victim/s) acceptance of the act. At this point in the drama the robber will aim to take control of victims' responses by way of force, or the threat of force, in order to consummate the transaction. During stage three, once the robbery frame has been established, the transaction proceeds with the relatively simple task of the transfer of goods from victim to offender. Finally, the offender needs to leave the scene.

In Chapter 13, Ian O'Donnell and Shona Morrison's British study examines the setting of armed robbery and the types of firearms used. The study demystifies armed robbery and examines the extent of harms associated with this form of criminal activity, the types of weapons used in committing it, and the scale of serious injuries and deaths caused. In interviewing 88 armed robbers about their choice of firearms, the data differed significantly from information published by the Home Office *Criminal Statistics for England and Wales*, and draws attention to 'the inherent difficulties' (p. 265) in interpreting official statistics on the selection of weapons used by criminals, and the characteristics of their targets for robbery. A key finding from this study is that while armed robbery has increased in recent years in the UK, 'the majority of robbers choose not to carry live firearms' (p. 265), and instead tend to select replica/imitation firearms. Taylor and Hornsby's (2000) study relates closely with the above findings, with victims of armed robbery finding it difficult to differentiate between real and replica handguns.

Shawn Schwaner (Chapter 14) examines the lifestyles of armed robbers in the USA. The study highlights that for recidivist offenders serving prison sentences for armed robbery, only a select few of 'specialist' career armed robbers were reconvicted within a three year period for further robbery offences. Schwaner argues that the offenders' 'age at first felony conviction, age of commitment to prison, and race suggest that violent crime is strongly influenced by social factors and, theoretically, economic inequality' (p. 279). Here, and in essence, Schwaner highlights that the younger the offender at the time of his first offence, and the deeper he is pushed into the criminal justice system, the more likely he is to reoffend. Released back into society and into environments where legitimate moneymaking opportunities are sparse within a culture that sustains the 'code of the street' (Anderson, 1999), a continuous cycle of robbery where 'recidivism is hinged upon several structural factors related to the development of identity and lifestyle' (p. 381), often results.

In the final chapter of Part II, Philip Cook (Chapter 15) examines patterns of robbery violence and the demographic characteristics of robbers, their victims, the locations and the choice of weapons. As Cook explains, there is often a '"Russian roulette" character' (p. 300) to being wounded or murdered in the process of a violent robbery. This, Cook argues, can be related to the victims' levels of resistance during the offence or to the assailants' momentary murderous impulses. The findings suggest that gun robberies yield far more dangerous outcomes than those featuring other types of weapons, and that the types of guns used in robberies have implications for the degree of injury and lethality.

Gun Crime, Violence and Homicide

As Beckett and Sasson (2000) neatly summarise, 'the unusually high homicide rate in America is due to the catastrophic interaction of factors, including the ubiquity of guns, high rates of economic and racial inequality (especially in the form of concentrated urban poverty), the trade in illegal drugs, and the emergence of a 'code of the streets' that encourages the use of violence' (p. 8. cited in Leonard and Leonard, 2003). The chapters in Part III examine in detail how a range of unique social, cultural and economic factors influence incidents of murder where firearms are used. In England and Wales during 2005 and 2006, there were 41 gun-crime homicides (Walker *et al.*, 2006, p. 72), and in 1996 firearms were used in 68 per cent of US murders but only in 7 per cent of English murders (Langan and Farrington, 1998).

In the opening chapter, Craig Perkins (Chapter 18) provides an overview of data collected during 1993 to 2001 from the US's National Crime Victimization Survey examining the categories of weapons used in violent crime. As these concise and neatly drawn up statistical data demonstrate, during this period of time firearm violence accounted for 10 per cent of all violent crime offences and unmistakably reveals that guns are used frequently during violent criminal events in the USA.

In Chapter 17, Richard Felson and Steven Messner examine the decision-making processes of armed offenders in deciding to kill or maim their victims. The authors argue that such actions 'sometimes appear to be purely impulsive and therefore lacking meaningful intent, we prefer to view these actions as the result of quick and sometimes careless decisions rather than involuntary behaviour' (p. 319). For Felson and Messner, where the intent to kill is planned, such decisions are often based upon the offender's concerns to do away with rivals, to dish out retribution and gain status within their peer groups.

Sean Varano and his colleagues (Chapter 18) consider the relationship between the illicit drugs market and homicide by evaluating the distinctive features of both 'peripheral' drug and intrinsically 'drug-motivated' related homicides. In the former, drugs were present at the crime scene and/or were being used by the victim or offender, yet were not the primary cause of the homicides. In the latter, drugs were found to be the primary motive for homicide. The authors reveal a strong connection between drugs violence via three causal paths created by the psychopharmacological effects of the drugs, the need to obtain money for the drugs themselves, or the systemic violence that is related to the illicit drug business. Firearms play a significant role in both peripheral and intrinsically drug-motivated homicides, and are generally selected as the primary weapon of choice in the committal of murder.

In Chapter 19, Charis Kubrin and Ronald Weitzer examine the socio-economic correlates and ecological distribution of homicide. They argue that a distinct form of murder, which they label as 'cultural retaliatory homicide', is more common in neighbourhoods that are characterized by socio-economic disadvantage and severe mistrust of the police. As a consequence, residents implement their own forms of security and codes of honour, and in these neighbourhoods retaliatory violence is implemented to settle arguments, provide status, defend honour and win respect. Such lethal cultural codes are, as the authors argue, 'collectively tolerated, endorsed, and rewarded by other residents' (p. 390). In such environments, reliance upon 'civil law' and the criminal justice system are omitted and replaced with street versions of 'natural law'. What emerges is a form of DIY street justice, where the victims of crime, their friends, family or associates adopt the primary role of delivering and administering justice and unsurprisingly a cycle of retaliatory violence ensues.

In Chapter 20, Bruce Kennedy and his colleagues discuss the correlation between social capital and firearm homicides, and underline the argument that 'poverty and income are powerful predictors of homicide and violent crime' (p. 393). Using poverty and household income data from states in the USA, the study utilizes ecological variables to predict a range of socio-environmental outcomes which impact upon high-risk urban settings. The authors argue that the erosion of social capital in poverty-stricken towns and cities provides powerful insights into the demographic macro-level determinants of violent gun crime.

Gary Kleck and Michael Hogan (Chapter 21), discuss gun ownership and homicide offending rates. The question they pose is, 'Does gun ownership increase the likelihood that a person will commit a homicide?' (p. 405). A previous study that tackled the same question found that people living in households with guns were 2.7 times more likely to become murder victims than in households where there were no firearms (Kellermann *et. al*, 1993). The results indicated a present, yet somewhat weaker relationship between gun ownership and homicide rates to that of Kellermann and his colleagues' earlier findings.

In Chapter 22, Barbara Koons-Witt and Pamela Schram examine the nature and prevalence of violent offending by females. Generally recognized as a violation of gender roles, violent female offenders have often been portrayed as 'monsters' and an affront to their gender. Using the National Incident-Based Reporting System the study examines the relationships of co-offending, types of offences and the use of weapons in those offences. The study found that dependent on the type of crime committed, whether the offender acted alone, with a co-offender or in a group, violent female offenders were more likely to use knives or physical assaults than guns. However, in co-offending with males (see Miller in Part II, Chapter 10 of this volume), female offenders were found to be more prone to use guns to carry out acts of violent offending.

In Chapter 23, Graham Ousey and Matthew Lee provide a time series analysis of race and lethal violence within the illicit drugs trade. As has been addressed in earlier chapters of this volume, during the late 1980s and into the 1990s lethal inner city drug related violence escalated dramatically in the USA, and the authors set about attempting to analyse the fluctuations of homicide rates of that era. Ousey and Lee examine aggregate-level violence connected to drug markets, finding that changes in drug markets have a positive association with both black and white homicide rates, although this association is substantially stronger for the black community. For black communities, the strongest socio-economic factor in determining the drug-related homicide rate continues to be connected to racial inequality. Whereas for whites, it is argued that this homicide connection is strongly connected to resource deprivation, highlighting a complex set of socio-economic conditions which impact upon the drug market and lethal violence.

In Chapter 24, James Fox and Alex Piquero examine the importance of demographic studies on crime rates in general, and homicide rates in particular. As discussed at various stages of this volume, criminologists have been intrigued by fluctuations in homicide rates and in particular the downward slope of homicide rates during the mid-1990s. Fox and Piquero argue that changes in demographic characteristics (that is, age, race and gender) have associations with homicide rates, and can be useful indicators for the future forecasting of homicide rates in urban areas. Their analysis yields three main conclusions. First, although law enforcement strategies and improved employment opportunities may have had beneficial impacts upon reducing homicide rates in the USA. There was a 10 per cent decline in the homicide rate attributable solely to demographic change. Second is the plateauing of young people as the most prominent age group, indicating that the downturn in homicide rates for this group might well be over. Finally, and connected to the previous finding, although rates in homicide may continue to decline in some demographic groups, the youth homicide rate, particularly for those between 14 and 25 years of age, may in fact undergo an upswing in the near future, with black on black lethal violence continuing to be a significant factor. Crucially, the authors are shrewd enough to consider the etiological factors that persist in the causation of differing demographics and their relation to homicide rates, and citing Sampson and Wilson (1995, p. 42), they note that in, 'not one city over 100,000 in the United States do blacks live in ecological equality with whites when it comes to [the] basic features of economic and family organization' (p. 484).

In the final chapter of Part III Caroline Wolf Harlow (Chapter 25) provides a summary of firearm use by offenders in the USA. During 1997, 203,300 prisoners serving time in State and Federal prisons were armed with guns when they committed the offence for which they were currently convicted. This equates to almost a fourth of all State, and one third of Federal inmates, being armed while carrying out their offences. Semi-automatic handguns, due to their firepower and easy concealment, were the firearms of choice for the majority of those offenders, with approximately 80 per cent of the sample selecting this type of weapon. In terms of offence categories, 8 per cent of drug offenders and 3 per cent of property offenders were armed when apprehended for their offences. Those inmates sentenced for violent offending reported using firearms more frequently than drug, public order or property type offenders. For violent-crime offenders (for example, physical assaults) an estimated 65 per cent had a firearm in their possession at the time of the offence. Unsurprisingly, those offenders who had committed robbery or homicides were more prone to possess firearms during their offences, with an aggregated 82 per cent reporting possession of a firearm at the homicide scene. Likewise, 75 per cent of those convicted of robbery had a firearm in their possession during their offences. Social and environmental factors featured strongly, as the author points out: 'Inmates who lived in families receiving welfare or living in publicly-subsidized housing while growing up were more likely than those who did not live under these types of government programs to be carrying a weapon' (p. 495).

Stitching Up the Pieces: Firearm Injury Trauma from Criminal Offending

Death and injury caused by guns, often as the result of criminal acts, incur a range of associated health costs. Between 1999 and 2004, it is estimated that there were 171,019 firearm-related deaths (including homicides, accidents and suicides) in the USA (WISQARS, 2006, p. 19) and during 2004 the number of firearms homicides stood at 11,250 (Miniño *et al.*, 2006, p. 19). While such lethal levels of criminal activity are obviously appalling, the picture becomes far more bloody if we also consider non-fatal violence-related firearm injuries. However, and despite the under-recording and disparities of the occurrence of firearm injuries in any given year, it is evident that victims of gun injuries are often left with severe levels of suffering that require acute levels of medical intervention. The following chapters in this final part of the volume are concerned with the physical and psychological trauma that victims experience.

In the opening chapter of Part IV, Marianne Zawitz and Kevin Strom (Chapter 26) reveal that between 1993 and 1997 there were approximately 412,000 non-fatal firearm injuries (including accidents and failed suicide attempts) dealt with in US hospital emergency departments. During the same period there were 78,620 recorded firearm homicides. The statistical analysis in this report reveals that the majority of gunshot victims are male (89 per cent), with 54 per cent of the victims of non-fatal gun injuries being black, and almost one in five of the victims of non-fatal woundings being from Hispanic backgrounds. Black males equated to 54 per cent of gunshot homicide casualties. Police officers in the US by the very nature of their employment regularly face the threat of firearm injury and fatality. During 1998, 400 US police officers were injured by firearm assaults and 58 were killed by a firearm. As we have seen elsewhere within these chapters, and as Zawitz and Strom's report confirms, handguns are the weapons that maim and kill most frequently.

Danielle Laraque and her colleagues (Chapter 27) describe the patterns of gunshot injuries to children in Harlem and the South Bronx district between 1960 and 1993. Before 1970 gunshot injury to children was a rare occurrence in Harlem but, at the time of their paper's original publication, it represented 15 per cent of all trauma admissions to Harlem Hospital, and this dramatic upsurge of violence was replicated in the neighbouring South Bronx district. Using a control group of children who were attending hospital for other medical conditions, the results demonstrate that those who had been shot had few organized extracurricular activities compared to those of the control group. Prior involvement with the criminal justice system and non-attendance at school were not significant factors within the control group, but were seen with frequency within the shot cohort. A toxicology programme was conducted on the sample, with 60 per cent of the wounded children testing positively for drug use, compared to 20 per cent of the control group. The shot children were also more likely to be living in either a one-parent or non-parent household, and were also more likely to have reported a parental death. Juvenile narcotics arrests in the area had shown a steady increase between 1986 and 1990, and this factor corresponded with increased paediatric gunshot wounds experienced in both districts during the same time-frame. This study presents a somewhat grim and violent overview of despondent street lifestyles for those children growing up in disenfranchised neighbourhoods featuring an absence of informal social controls.

In Chapter 28, Kathy Sanders-Phillips provides a review of the psychological, medical and public health literature of paediatric gunshot victims and parental responses to such traumatic events. The literature demonstrates that adolescent psychological responses to gun crime include 'high levels of stress, impaired judgment, reduced attention span, irritability, short-term memory loss, and ongoing memory deficits during recovery' (p. 526).

In the final chapter of this volume, I.J. Persad *et al.* explore suggestions by the Metropolitan Police that gun crime in London is increasing. While such research findings are abundant in the USA (see, for example, Deitch and Grimes, 1984; Ordog *et. al*, 1994), there has been a paucity of similar research in the UK, thus making Persad and his colleagues work nationally unique. The study aimed to highlight the incidences of gunshot wounds, their medical complications and the medical experience in the treatment of such trauma. Although the research team report an increase in incidents which correlated closely with the Metropolitan Force figures, the scale of correlation with police figures has some significant disparity. As the authors point out: 'While the police reported an 80 per cent nationwide increase in incidence, we have seen an approximately 200 per cent increase in incidence over five years locally' (p. 536). This clearly demonstrates that gunshot injuries committed during criminal events in the British capital are on the increase; and more so than the official statistics represent.

Conclusion

Due to the overwhelming paucity of published academic research on guns and crime elsewhere from English speaking countries, the vast majority of these chapters have placed much of the focus on studies from the USA. Overall, this collection of essays demonstrates the varying methods in which guns are commissioned to facilitate criminal acts, the choice of weaponry, the selection of victims, retaliatory responses with the social embedding of guns as 'problem solvers', and of the physical and social damage that gun crime can impact upon individuals and communities.

As we have seen in this volume, gun crime in its many guises is now 'recognized by scholars as a central violence problem in American life and culture' (Leonard and Leonard, 2003, p. 142), and continues to be of widespread concern for academic researchers (Weaver *et al.*, 2004). In the USA, there appears to have been a closer association between policy makers, law enforcement agencies and academics in attempting to tackle many of the issues raised in this volume. In the UK, we rely largely upon vague law enforcement 'sound bites', policy knee-jerk reactions, media inspired panics and the occasional Home Office report to inform us of this growing social menace where criminal offences are, as we have been led to believe, increasingly committed by armed felons.

Yet, both societies share a post-industrialized landscape where once stable communities have become increasingly fragmented. Consumerism and racialized narratives of fear and despair pose as problem-solving strategies, and the disposition of the market society has created an emphasis on individuality that makes empathy a somewhat redundant emotion. The fact that gun use makes perfect sense to an increasing number of our citizens who seek safety, respect or a fellow citizen's goods must be addressed along with the markets that have mutated to provide for such urges.

As we write this the British media are feeding on a spate of shootings that have victimized black teenagers. The clichés, no doubt familiar to North American readers, have flowed in a distinctly routine manner. Gangs, gangsters, fallen soldiers, drugs, black youth, absentee fathers and so on are tossed randomly into a mixer that proceeds to spew forth images so distorted, that the victims, their families, and their communities are transformed into a series of grotesques devoid of humanity. If nothing else, it is hoped that this sparse and no doubt inadequate volume might highlight the need to venture beyond the cliché, and humanize gun crime.

Rob Hornsby
Dick Hobbs

References

Anderson, E. (1999), *The Code of the Street: Decency, Violence, and the Moral Life of the Inner City*, New York: Norton.

Beckett, K. and Sasson, T. (2000), *The Politics of Injustice: Crime and Punishment in America*, Thousand Oaks, CA: Pine-Forge.

Belleslies, M.A. (1996), 'The Origins of Gun Culture in the United States', 1760–1865', *The Journal of American History*, **83**, pp. 425–55.

Block, R. and Block, C. (1993), 'Street Gang Crime in Chicago', *Research in Brief*, Washington, DC: US Department of Justice, National Institute of Justice.

Blumstein, A. (2003), 'Youth Violence and Guns', in Wilhelm Heitmeyer and John Hagan (eds), *International Handbook of Violence Research, Volume 1*, Kluwer Academic Press: Dordecht.

Braga, A.A., McDevitt, J. and Pierce, G.L. (2006), 'Understanding and Preventing Gang Violence: Problem Analysis and Response Development in Lowell, Massachusetts', *Police Quarterly*, **9**, pp. 20–46.

Cloward, R.A. and Ohlin, L.F. (1960), *Delinquency and Opportunity: A Theory of Delinquent Gangs*, Glencoe, IL: Free Press.

Cohen, L. and Swift, S. (1993), 'A Public Health Approach to the Violence Epidemic in the United States', *Environment and Urbanization*, **5**, pp. 50–66.

Cohen, J., Cork, D., Engberg, J., and Tita, G.E. (1998), 'The Role of Drug Markets and Gangs in Local Homicide Rates', *Journal of Homicide Studies*, **2**, pp. 241–42.

Cook, P.J. (1983), 'The Influence of Gun Availability on Violent Crime Patterns', *Crime and Justice*, **4**, pp. 49–89.

Cook, P.J. (1991), 'The Technology of Personal Violence', *Crime and Justice*, **14**, pp. 1–71.

Cook, P.J., Lawrence, B.A., Ludwig, J. and Miller, T.R. (1999), 'The Medical Costs of Gunshot Injuries in the United States', *Journal of the American Medical Association*, **282**, pp. 447–45.

Dahlberg L.L. (1998), 'Youth Violence in the United States: Major Trends, Risk Factors, and Prevention Approaches', *American Journal of Preventive Medicine*, **14**, pp. 259–72.

Decker, S., Pennell, S. and Caldwell, A. (1997), *Illegal Firearms: Access and Use by Arrestees*, Washington, DC: National Institute for Justice.

Decker, S. and Van Winkle, B. (1996), *Life in the Gang: Family, Friends, and Violence*, New York: Cambridge University Press.

Deitch, E.A. and Grimes W.R. (1984), 'Experience with 112 Shotgun Wounds of the Extremities', *Journal of Trauma*, **24**, pp. 600–03.

Fagan, J.E. and Chin, K. (1990), 'Violence as Regulation and Social Control in the Distribution of Crack', in M. De La Rosa, E.Y. Lambert, and B. Gropper (eds), *Drugs and Violence: Causes, Correlates, and Consequences*, NIDA Research Monograph 103, Rockville, MD: US Department of Health and Human Services, National Institutes of Health, National Institute on Drug Abuse.

Hofstadter, R. (1970), 'America as a Gun Culture', *American Heritage*, **21**, pp. 4–85.

Horowitz, R. (1983), *Honor and the American Dream: Culture and Identity in a Chicano Community*, New Brunswick, NJ: Rutgers University.

Howell, J. and Decker, S. (1999), *The Gangs, Drugs, and Violence Connection*, Washington, DC: US Department of Justice, Office of Juvenile Justice and Delinquency Prevention.

Huff, C. R. (ed.) (1996), *Gangs in America* (2nd edn), Newbury Park, CA: Sage.

Hutson, H.R., Anglin, D., Kyriacou, D.N., Hart, J. and Spears, K. (1995), 'The Epidemic of Gang-Related Homicides in Los Angeles County from 1979 through 1994', *Journal of the American Medical Association*, **274**, pp. 1031–36.

Inciardi, J.A. (1986), *The War on Drugs: Heroin, Cocaine, Crime, and Public Policy,* Palo Alto, CA: Mayfield.

Jacobs, B.A. and Wright, R. (2006), *Street Justice: Retaliation in the Criminal Underworld*, Cambridge: Cambridge University Press.

Katz, J. (1988), *Seductions of Crime: Moral and Sensual Attractions of Doing Evil*, New York: Basic Books.

Kellermann, A.L., Rivara F.P., Rushforth N.B., Banton J.G., Reay D.T., Francisco J.T., Locci A.B., Prodzinski J., Hackman B.B., and Somes, G. (1993), 'Gun Ownership as a Risk Factor for Homicide in the Home', *New England Journal of Medicine*, **329**, pp. 1084–91.

Kennedy, D.M., Piehl, A.M. and Braga, A.A. (1996), 'Mobilizing the Police and the Community: Youth Violence in Boston: Gun Markets, Serious Youth Offenders and a Use-Reduction Strategy', *Law and Contemporary Problems*, **59**, pp. 147–96.

Kleck, G. (1997), *Targeting Guns: Firearms and their Control*, Hawthorne, NT: Aldine de Gruyter.

Kleck, G. (1991), *Point Blank: Guns and Violence in America*, New York: Aldine de Gruyter.

Kleck, G. and McElrath, K. (1991), 'The Effects of Weaponry on Human Violence', *Social Forces*, **69**, pp. 669–92.

Klein, M.W. (1995), *The American Street Gang*, New York: Oxford University Press.

Klein, M.W. and Maxson, C.L. (1994), 'Gangs and Cocaine Trafficking', in D. MacKenzie and C. Uchida (eds), *Drugs and Crime: Evaluating Public Policy Initiatives*, Thousand Oaks, CA: Sage Publications, pp. 42–58.

Klein, M.W., Maxson, C.L. and Cunningham, L.C. (1991), 'Crack, Street Gangs and Violence', *Criminology*, **26**, pp. 623–50.

Langan, P.A. and Farrington D.P. (1998), *Crime and Justice in the United States and in England and Wales, 1981–96*, US Department of Justice, Office of Justice Programs, Bureau of Justice Statistics: http://www.ojp.usdoj.gov/bjs/pub/pdf/cjusew96.pdf (accessed 21/06/06).

Leonard, I.M. and Leonard, C.C. (2003), 'The Historiography of American Violence', *Homicide Studies*, **7**, pp. 99–153.

Miller, M., Azrael, D. and Hemenway, D. (2002), 'Household Firearm Ownership Levels and Homicide across US Regions and States, 1988–1997', *American Journal of Public Health*, **92**, pp. 1988–93.

Miniño, A.M., Heron M., Smith B.L., Kochanek, K.D. (2006), *Deaths: Final data for 2004, Health E-Stats.* Released 24 November, 2006: http://www.cdc.gov/nchs/fastats/homicide.htm (accessed 12/12/06).

Moore, J.W. (1990), 'Gangs, Drugs, and Violence', in M. De La Rosa, E.Y. Lambert and B. Gropper (eds), *Drugs and Violence: Causes, Correlates, and Consequences*, US Department of Health and Human Services, National Institutes of Health: National Institute on Drug Abuse.

Moore, J.W. (1991), *Going Down to the Barrio: Homeboys and Homegirls in Change*, Philadelphia, PA: Temple University Press.

NCVS (2005), *Firearms and Crime Statistics*: http://www.ojp.usdoj.gov/bjs/guns.htm (accessed 10/10/06).

Ordog, G.J., Wasserberger, J., Balasubramanium, S. and Shoemaker, W. (1994), 'Civilian Gunshot Wounds–Outpatient Management', *Journal of Trauma*, **36**, pp. 106–11.

Padilla, F.M. (1992), *The Gang as an American Enterprise: Puerto Rican Youth and the American Dream*, New Brunswisk, NJ: Rutgers University Press.

Sampson, R.J. and Wilson, W.J. (1995), 'Toward a Theory of Race, Crime, and Urban Inequality', in John Hagan and Ruth D. Peterson (eds), *Crime and Inequality*, Stanford, CA: Stanford University Press.

Sanchez-Jankowski, M.S. (1991), *Islands in the Street: Gangs and American Urban Society*, Berkeley, CA: University of California Press.

Sanders, W.B. (1994), *Gangbangs and Drive-Bys: Grounded Culture and Juvenile Gang Violence*, New York: Aldine de Gruyter.

Sherman, L.W. (2001), 'Reducing Gun Violence: What Works, What Doesn't, What's Promising', *Criminology and Criminal Justice*, **1**, pp. 11–25.

Short, J. Jr. (1997), *Poverty, Ethnicity and Violent Crime*, Boulder, CO: Westview Press.

Shover, N. and Honaker, D. (1992), 'The Socially Bounded Decision Making of Persistent Property Offenders', *Howard Journal of Criminal Justice*, **31**, pp. 276–93.

Skolnick, J. (1990), 'The Social Structure of Street Drug Dealing', *American Journal of Police*, **9**, pp. 1–41.

Smith, C. and Allen, J. (2004), *Violent Crime in England and Wales*: *Home Office Online Report 18/04*, London: Home Office: www.homeoffice.gov.uk/rds/pdfs05/hosb1805.pdf (accessed 16/06/06).

Sutherland, E. and Cressey, D.R. (1978), *Principles of Criminology* (10th edn), New York: J.B. Lippincott.

Taylor, I. and Hornsby, R. (2000), *Replica Firearms: A New Frontier in the Gun Market*, INFER Trust Report.

Thrasher, F. (1927), *The Gang*, Chicago: Chicago University Press.

US Department of Treasury, Bureau of Alcohol, Tobacco and Firearms (2000), *Commerce in Firearms in the United States*, (Feb.): http://permanent.access.gpo.gov/lps4006/020400report.pdf (accessed 10/10/06).

Valentine, B. (1995), *Gang Intelligence Manual*, Boulder, CO: Paladin Press.

Venkatesh, S.A. (1996), 'The Gang and the Community', in C.R. Huff (ed.), *Gangs in America* (2nd edn), Newbury Park, CA: Sage.

Walker, A., Kershaw, C. and Nicholas, S. (2006), *Crime in England and Wales 2005/06: Home Office Statistical Bulletin*: http://www.homeoffice.gov.uk/rds/pdfs06/hosb1206chap456.pdf (accessed, 10/01/07).

Weaver, G.S., Clifford Wittekind, J.E., Huff-Corzine, L., Petee, T.A. and Jarvis, J.P. (2004), 'Violent Encounters: A Criminal Event Analysis of Lethal and Nonlethal Outcomes', *Journal of Contemporary Criminal Justice*, **20**, pp. 348–68.

Williams, T. (1989), *The Cocaine Kids*, Reading, MA: Addison-Wesley.

WISQARS (2006), *1999–2004, United States Violence-Related Firearm Deaths and Rates per 100,000*: http://webappa.cdc.gov/cgi-bin/broker.exe (accessed 11/11/06).

Wright, R. and Decker, S. (1997), *Armed Robbers in Action: Stick-Ups and Street Culture*, Boston, MA: Northeastern University Press.

Wright, J.D., Rossi, P.H. and Daley, K. (1983), *Under the Gun: Weapons, Crime and Violence in America*, New York: Aldine de Gruyter.

Yablonsky, L. (1991), *The Violent Gang*, New York: John Wiley.

Recommended Further Reading

We have included below a number of books, articles, reports and edited collections which may be useful for those readers with further interest in the issue of gun crime.

Cook, P.J. (1983), 'The Influence of Gun Availability on Violent Crime Patterns', *Crime and Justice*, **4**, pp. 49–89.

Decker, S., Pennell, S. and Caldwell, A. (1997), *Illegal Firearms: Access and Use by Arrestees*, Washington, DC: National Institute for Justice.

Hales, G., Lewis, C. and Silverstone, D. (2006), *Gun Crime: The Market in and use of Illegal Firearms*, Home Office Research Study 298: http://www.homeoffice.gov.uk/rds/pdfs06/hors298.pdf

Howell, J.C. (1999), 'Youth Gang Homicides: A Literature Review', *Crime and Delinquency*, **45**, pp. 208–41.

Jacobs, B.A. and Wright, R. (2006), *Street Justice: Retaliation in the Criminal Underworld*, Cambridge University Press: Cambridge.

Kates, D. and Kleck, G. (1997), *The Great American Gun Debate: Essays on Firearms and Violence*, San Francisco, CA: Pacific Research Institute for Public Policy.

Kleck, G. (1991), *Point Blank: Guns and Violence in America*, New York: Aldine de Gruyter.

Leonard, I.M. and Leonard, C.C. (2003), 'The Historiography of American Violence', *Homicide Studies*, **7**, pp. 99–153.

Matthews, R. (2002), *Armed Robbery*, Cullompton, Devon: Willan Publishing.

May, D.C. (1999), 'Scared Kids, Unattached Kids, or Peer Pressure: Why Do Students Carry Firearms to School', *Youth and Society*, **31**, pp. 100–27.

US Deptartment of Justice (2005), *Guns Used In Crime: Firearms, Crime, and Criminal Justice*, http://www.ojp.usdoj.gov/bjs/pub/pdf/guic.pdf.

Wright J.D. and Rossi P.H. (1994), *Armed and Considered Dangerous: A Survey of Felons and Their Firearms* (Expanded Edn), New York: Aldine de Gruyter.

Part I
Youth, Gangs and Guns

[1]

Gang-Related Gun Violence

Socialization, Identity, and Self

Paul B. Stretesky
Colorado State University
Mark R. Pogrebin
University of Colorado–Denver

Few studies have examined how violent norms are transmitted in street gangs. The purpose of this research is to add to the gang-related literature by examining socialization as the mechanism between street gang membership and violence. To explore this issue, we draw upon in-depth interviews with twenty-two inmates convicted of gang-related gun violence. We find that the gangs are important agents of socialization that help shape a gang member's sense of self and identity. In addition, inmates reported to us that whereas guns offered them protection, they were also important tools of impression management that helped to project and protect a tough reputation. Our findings provide greater insight into the way gang socialization leads to gun-related violence and has implications for policies aimed at reducing that violence.

Keywords: *gang socialization; gang violence; gun use; gang identity; reputation; masculinity; respect*

This study considers how gangs promote violence and gun use. We argue that socialization is important because it helps to shape a gang member's identity and sense of self. Moreover, guns often help gang members project their violent identities. As Kubrin (2005, 363) argues, "The gun becomes a symbol of power and a remedy for disputes." We examine the issue of gang socialization, self, and identity formation using data derived from face-to-face qualitative interviews with a sample of gang members who have been incarcerated in Colorado prisons for gun-related violent crimes. Our findings, although unique, emphasize what previous studies have found—that most gangs are organized by norms that support

Authors' Note: We are grateful to Scott Hunt and the anonymous reviewers for their suggestions and encouragement, but note that we alone bear any responsibility for errors remaining in the article. Please direct all correspondence to Paul Stretesky, Department of Sociology, Colorado State University, Fort Collins. CO 80523.

the use of violence to settle disputes, achieve group goals, recruit members, and defend identity.

Prior to our analysis of gang members, we briefly review the literature on the relationship between gangs, crime, guns, and violence. In that review, we emphasize the importance of socialization and the impact of gangs on identity and self. We explain how guns help gang members shape and convey their identity. Finally, in our discussion we relate our findings to the relative efficacy of different intervention strategies that are focused on reducing gang violence.

Gangs and Violence

Research suggests that gang members are more likely than non-gang members to engage in crime—especially violent crime (Gordon et al. 2004). According to Thornberry et al. (1993, 75), the relationship between gang affiliation and violence "is remarkably robust, being reported in virtually all American studies of gang behavior regardless of when, where, or how the data were collected." Whereas the relationship between gangs and violence is pervasive, "little is known about the causal mechanisms that bring it about" (Thornberry et al. 1993, 76). Do gangs attract individuals who are predisposed to violence or do they create violent individuals? The debate in the literature about these explanations of gang violence is rather extensive.

Thornberry et al. (1993) point out that there are three perspectives that inform the debate concerning the relationship between gangs and violence. First, the selection perspective argues that gang members are individuals who are delinquent and violent prior to joining the gang. Thus, gang members are individuals who are likely to engage in violent and deviant behavior even if they are not gang members (Gerrard 1964, Yablonsky 1962). From this perspective, what makes gang members more criminal than non-gang members is that criminal individuals have self-selected or been recruited into gangs. The second perspective is known as the social facilitation perspective. This perspective argues that gang members are no different from non-gang members until they enter the gang. Therefore, the gang serves a normative function. In short, the gang is the source of delinquent behavior because new gang members are socialized into the norms and values of gang life, which provides the necessary social setting for crime and violence to flourish. The enhancement perspective is the third explanation for the relationship between gang and crime (Thornberry et al. 1993). The enhancement perspective proposes that new gang members are recruited from a pool of individuals who show propensity to engage in crime and violence, but their level of violence intensifies once they enter the gang because the gang provides a structure that encourages crime and violence (see also Decker and Van Winkle 1996).

According to McCorkle and Miethe (2002, 111) the second and third explanations for gang-related crime are the most popular explanations in the literature because both perspectives rely on the assumption that social disorganization increases socialization into the gang subculture, which produces crime. Recent criminological research suggests that the enhancement perspective is the most likely explanation for the association between gang involvement and criminal behavior. For instance, Gordon et al. (2004) discovered that individuals who join gangs are, in general, more delinquent than their peers *before* they join the gang. However, Gordon et al. also found that violent behavior among individuals who join a gang significantly increases *after* they become gang members. Although Gordon et al.'s work provides some answers concerning the potential causal mechanisms of gang violence, it still leaves open the question about why gang members increase their violent behavior after they join a gang. It is for that reason that we focus our research on the concept of socialization as a mechanism that leads to gang-related gun violence.

Gang Socialization

Research on gang socialization—the process of learning the appropriate values and norms of the gang culture to which one belongs—suggests that group processes are highly important (Sirpal 1997, Vigil 1988, Miller and Brunson 2000). In addition, Moore (1991) believes that many city gangs have become quasi-institutionalized. In these cities, gangs have played a major role in ordering individuals' lives at the same time that other important social institutions such as schools and families play less of a normative role (see also Blumstein 1995; Bowker and Klein 1983; Bjerregaard and Lizotte 1995; Vigil 1988). Vigil (1988, 63) has found that gangs help to socialize "members to internalize and adhere to alternative norms and modes of behavior and play a significant role in helping . . . youth acquire a sense of importance, self-esteem, and identity." One way to attain status is to develop a reputation for being violent (Anderson 1999). This reputation for violence, however, is likely to develop (at least to some degree) after an individual joins a gang.

The reasons individuals join gangs are diverse (Decker and Van Winkle 1996). According to Decker and Van Winkle (1996), the most important instrumental reason for joining a gang is protection. In addition to instrumental concerns, a large portion of all gang members indicate that their gang fulfills a variety of more typical adolescent needs—especially companionship and support, which tend to be more expressive in nature. That is, the gang is a primary group. The idea that the gang is a primary group into which individuals are socialized is not new. For instance, long ago Thrasher (1927, 230) pointed out,

> [The gang] offers the underprivileged boy probably his best opportunity to acquire status and hence it plays an essential part in the development of his personality. In striving to realize the role he hopes to take he may assume a tough pose, commit feats of daring or vandalism, or become a criminal.

Thus, gang violence may often be viewed as expressive in nature. The value of masculinity as a form of expression plays an important role in gang socialization (Miller and Decker 2001). Oliver (1994) argues that gang violence is often a method of expressing one's masculinity when opportunities to pursue conventional roles are denied. Acts of manhood, note Decker and Van Winkle (1996, 186), are "important values of [a member's] world and their psyches—to be upheld even at the cost of their own or others' lives." Katz (1988) also believes violence plays an important and acceptable role in the subculture of people living in socially isolated environments and economically deprived areas because violence provides a means for a member to demonstrate his toughness, and displays of violent retaliation establish socialization within the gang.

According to Short and Strodtbeck (1965; see also Howell 1998), a good portion of all gang violence can be attributed to threats to one's status within the gang. Gang membership, then, helps to create within-group identity that defines how group members perceive people outside their formal organizational structure. By way of altercasting (i.e., the use of tactics to create identities and roles for others), gangs cast nonmembers into situated roles and identities that are to the gang's advantage (Weinstein and Deutschberger 1963). Altercasting, then, is an aggressive tactic that gangs often use to justify their perception of other gangs as potentially threatening rivals, and it is used to rationalize the use of physical violence against other gangs. If the objective of a gang is to be perceived by the community, rival gangs, law enforcement officials, and others in a particular way, then their collective group and individual identities will be situated in these defining situations. Even though there is a good deal of research examining the important relationship between violence and status within the gang as it relates to socialization, little is known about the specific ways that status impacts gang violence.

Socialization into the gang is bound up in issues of identity and self. Identity, according to Stone (1962), is the perceived social location of the person. Image, status, and a host of other factors that affect identity are mostly created by group perceptions of who we are and how we define ourselves. "People see themselves from the standpoints of their group and appropriate action in relation to those groups becomes a source of pride" (Shibutani 1961, 436). Berger (1963, 92) notes that "identities are socially bestowed, socially maintained, and socially transformed."

Moore (1978, 60) has suggested that "the gang represents a means to what is an expressive, rather than an instrumental, goal: the acting out of a male role of competence and of 'being in command' of things." The findings of Decker and Van Winkle (1996) and Moore suggest that although instrumental reasons for joining a gang are important, once a member joins a gang they largely see the gang as an important primary group that is central to their lives and heavily influences their identity and personality. Because this is a primary group, the approval of gang peers is highly important. It is this expressive reason for remaining in a gang that may help to explain gang crime and violence, especially as it relates to socialization. Hughes and Short (2005) provide insight into the area of identity and gang violence. Specifically, they find that when a gang member's identity is challenged, violence is often a result—especially if the challenger is a stranger. If a gang member does not comply with gang role expectations when they are challenged, the result may be a loss of respect. It is important to project a violent reputation to command respect and deter future assaults. Walking away from conflict is risky to one's health (Anderson 1999). Gang members must by necessity make efforts to show a continued commitment to role expectations to the group (Lindesmith and Strauss 1968). From this perspective, it appears that character traits that are a consequence of being socialized into street gangs may result in youthful acts of violence through transformations in identity (Vigil 1996).

Initiation rights are one important aspect of identity formation (Hewitt 1988, Vigil 1996). Initiation rights that new gang members are obligated to go through demonstrate commitment to the gang and attest to an individual's desire to gain official membership in the organization. Hewitt (1988) argues that these types of acts help create a "situated self," where a person's self can be defined and shaped by particular situations. Thus, notions of identity formation are highly consistent with notions of gang violence as a function of social facilitation and enhancement perspectives in that they explain why gang members may increase their levels of crime and violence once they join the gang. Moreover, research suggests that the more significant the relationship to

90   Journal of Contemporary Ethnography

a gang is, the more committed an individual is to a gang identity (Callero 1985; Stryker and Serpe 1982). In short, gangs provide a reference group for expected role behavior and shape a member's identity and sense of self (Callero 1985). The greater the commitment a person has to a gang identity, the more frequently that person will perform in ways that enact that identity, ways that include acts of violence (Stryker and Serpe 1982).

Guns also play an important role in many gangs and are often reported to be owned for instrumental reasons (Decker and Van Winkle 1996). Gang members who perceive a threat from rival gangs are believed to carry guns to protect themselves and their neighborhoods (Decker and Van Winkle 1996; Horowitz 1983; Lizotte et al. 1994; Wright and Rossi 1986). Gang membership "strongly and significantly increases the likelihood of carrying a gun" (Thornberry et al. 2003, 131). However, the reason that gang members carry guns is sill unclear. It is likely that in addition to instrumental reasons for carrying a gun, gang members carry guns for expressive reasons (Sheley and Wright 1995). That is, guns provide gang members with a sense of power, which may be extremely important in identity formation. Guns help gang members project a tough image. Thornberry et al. (2003, 125) report that gang members who carry guns may feel "emboldened to initiate criminal acts that they may otherwise avoid."

Sociologists have long recognized that symbols are important indicators of identity. This is especially true of gangs (Decker and Van Winkle 1996; Vigil 2003). Gang members often display symbols of gang membership, and this is part of being socialized into the role of a gang member:

> Wearing gang clothes, flashing gang signs, and affecting other outward signs of gang behavior are also ways to become encapsulated in the role of gang member, especially through the perceptions of others, who, when they see the external symbols of membership respond as if the person was a member (Decker and Van Winkle 1996, 75).

Bjerregaard and Lizotte (1995, 42) argue that it is plausible that "juveniles are socialized into the gun culture by virtue of their gang membership and activity."

Although there is some indication that gang members are more likely to own guns than non-gang members prior to joining a gang, gang membership also clearly appears to increase the prevalence of gun ownership. Bjerregaard and Lizotte (1995) believe that future research needs to focus on why gang membership encourages gun ownership. In this vein, Sanders's (1994) research on drive-by shootings provides some insight into why gang membership may encourage gun ownership. Drawing on Goffman's (1961) notion of realized resources, Sanders argues that gangs are organizations that provide the necessary context for drive-bys. Sanders is clear when he states that guns and cars are the least important resource in producing drive-bys. However, it is also true that guns are necessary for drive-bys to occur and as such are an important part of gang culture to the extent that drive-bys help gang members "build an identity as having heart" (Sanders 1994, 204). Thus, notions of character and identity provide a way to look at drive-by shootings as a product of the gang structure, where guns are important instruments in building identity. Given the importance of guns to a gang member's identity, it is interesting to note that little research exists that examines the relationship between guns and gangs in terms of identity formation.

Methods

The interviews in this study of twenty-two gang members were taken from a larger qualitative study of seventy-five Colorado prison inmates who used a firearm in the commission of their most recent offense. Inmates were asked general questions about their families, schools, peer groups, neighborhoods, prior contact with the criminal justice system, and experiences with firearms. They were also asked a series of questions surrounding the circumstances that lead up to the crime for which they were currently incarcerated. It was from this vantage point that we began to see the importance of gang socialization, self, and identity as important aspects of violence and gun use.

Inmates we interviewed were located in eleven different correctional facilities scattered throughout Colorado and were randomly selected by means of a simple random sample from a list of all inmates incarcerated for a violent crime in which a firearm was involved. The overall sample was composed of 39.1% whites, 40.6% African Americans, 15.6% Hispanics, and 4.7% Asians and Middle Easterners. Eight percent of our subjects were female. The demographics of the inmates in our study correspond closely to the demographics of inmates incarcerated in Colorado prisons (see Colorado Department of Corrections 2005).

We used official inmate case files located at the Colorado Department of Corrections to verify that the twenty-two self-identified gang members were likely to have actually been gang members prior to their incarceration. That validity check substantiated what our subjects said—they did indeed appear to be gang members. Case files were also used to gain information about offenders' past criminal records to determine the validity of each inmate's responses with respect to previous offending patterns as well as characteristics associated with their most current offense.

During the interview process, we made every effort to ensure that inmates understood that our conversations were both voluntary and confidential. We told each inmate that only we would be able to identify their answers and that any information they provided to us would be used only for research-related purposes. Moreover, we informed inmates that if they were uncomfortable with any of the topics of discussion, they could simply tell us that they felt uncomfortable and we would proceed to other topics of interest. Finally, we emphasized that we did not want any details that might compromise an inmate's pending legal case. It is important to point out that we did discover— through our conversations with inmates—that those subjects who refused to be interviewed were mainly concerned about legal repercussions associated with our interviews. Still, we have good reason to believe that the inmates we did interview were surprisingly open and honest about their past behavior. Again, we are confident in the validity of our data because inmates often gave answers that closely matched available information recorded in their official inmate files. Finally, we should point out that a few inmates who felt uncomfortable with a particular line of questioning asked the interviewer to momentarily turn off the tape recorder so that their responses were not recorded. These brief, unrecorded conversations were often focused on a particular aspect of an inmate's crime and are largely inconsequential to the current research.

The appendix lists the characteristics of the inmates in our gang sub-sample. The median age of the twenty-two gang members in our sample was 25 years old, though their age at the commission of the crime was considerably younger. Thirteen of the inmates were black, five were white, one was Asian, and three were Hispanic. Six of the inmates we interviewed were convicted of murder or nonnegligent manslaughter, four were convicted of attempted murder, two were convicted of robbery, eight were convicted of assault, and two were convicted of kidnapping. At the time of the interviews, our subjects had been incarcerated for an average of 4.7 years. All but one of the inmates in our sample of gang members were male, and all subjects used a handgun in the commission of their most recent violent crime.

In order to arrange times to interview inmates, we sent a letter to the case worker of each inmate we selected into our sample. The purpose of these letters was to (1) identify the inmates selected for inclusion in our study, (2) explain the nature of the study, and (3) indicate that inmate participation in the study was voluntary. Correctional case workers were asked to provide inmates with information about the study, tell them that their participation was voluntary, and inform them of the dates that the researchers would be at the prison to conduct interviews. We also informed subjects that as an incentive to participate in the interview, we would put five dollars into their inmate account.

Prison officials were notified of our visits prior to our arrival, and they helped us locate the inmates in our sample and arrange for a place for the interviews to be conducted. All interviews were conducted in the prison in private conference rooms, vacant staff offices, and empty visitation rooms. Each interview was tape-recorded with the subjects' consent and lasted between 60 and 120 minutes. A semistructured format was used that relied on sequential probes to pursue leads provided by the inmates. This technique allowed subjects to identify and elaborate important domains they perceived to characterize their life histories. Generally, these included their gang experience, engagement in violent encounters throughout their life, and their involvement with a firearm in those situations.

The interview tapes were transcribed for qualitative data analysis, which involves scanning and identifying general statements about relationships among categories of observations. We looked for explanations concerning gang members' perceptions about how they learned to become gang members and their perceptions of the importance of guns in that process. Thus, we used an inductive-methods approach where the inmates' responses directed our empirical generalizations and conclusions. As Schatzman and Strauss (1973, 110) note, "the most fundamental operation in the analysis of qualitative data is that of discovering significant classes of things, persons, and events and the properties which characterize them." Our face-to-face interviews allowed our subjects to elaborate on important domains they perceived to characterize their criminal life history as it related to their perceptions of gang involvement.

It is important to point out that although we would have preferred to conduct and establish a long-term relationship with our subjects and observe their behavior as they went about their daily lives, such an approach is, unfortunately, highly unrealistic in the case of the most violent gang members. This is important as there are some researchers who believe that ethnography excludes qualitative research approaches where the researcher has not spent a long period of time observing study participants in the field in order to become sufficiently knowledgeable of the setting being studied (Glaser and Strauss, 1967). We, however, agree with Lofland and Lofland (1995, 18) that the distinction between participant observation and intensive interviewing is "overdrawn and any invidious comparisons are [typically] unwarranted." Moreover,

94   Journal of Contemporary Ethnography

Hobs and May (1993) suggest that in-depth interviews are the best way to gather data that could never be obtained just by observing the activities of people. Given the fact that intensive interviews are often part of participant observation, we argue that they are sufficient to draw conclusions regarding gang socialization and the creation of a gang identity among the gang members in our sample—those who find themselves incarcerated for violent crimes.

One potential methodological issue that could be interpreted as cause for concern has to do with the generalizability of our sample. The gang members we talked with were probably more highly integrated into their gang than the typical gang member. We believe this because our subjects were incarcerated for gang-related violence, which we interpreted as a sign of high commitment to their group. Thus, we should expect that our subjects' gang experiences are quite different from gang members in general who have not displayed similar levels of violence. Such selection bias might be problematic if the purpose of the study is to generalize our findings to all gang members. The purpose of this research, however, is more modest in nature. We are interested in the experiences of violent gang members in our sample precisely because they are likely to be the most committed to the gang and because that commitment is likely to be translated into gang-related gun violence. As studies of gang violence indicate, a large percentage of gang violence is committed by a small percentage of gang members. (Piehl, Kennedy, and Braga 2000, 100). The gang members in our study, then, are likely to have the most to offer in terms of their gang and gun experiences, and their stories are likely to be the most useful in thinking about policy-related issues surrounding gang- and gun-related violence.

Findings

We divide our findings into four sections. First, we focus on our subjects' socialization into the gang and the impact that socialization has on their self and identity. Second, we explore the importance of gang commitment as reinforcing a gang member's self and identity. Third, we focus on masculinity as a central value among gang members. During our discussions of masculinity, gang members often referred to notions of respect and reputation. Reputation is a way that gang members can project their image of masculinity to others. Respect was often referenced when their masculine identity was challenged. Finally, we focus on the importance of guns as instruments central to the lives of our gang members in the sense that they help project and protect masculine identities.

Gang Socialization, Self, and Identity

Goffman (1959) argues that as individuals we are often "taken in by our own act" and therefore begin to feel like the person we are portraying. Baumeister and Tice (1984) describe this process as one where initial behaviors are internalized so that they become part of a person's self-perception. Once initial behaviors are internalized, the individual continues to behave in ways consistent with his or her self-perception. Related to the current study, the socialization process of becoming a gang member required a change in the subject's self-perception. That is, who did our gang members become as compared with who they once were? Social interaction is highly important in the process of socialization because it helps create one's identity and sense of self, as Holstein and Gubrium (2003, 119 [emphasis added]) point out:

> As personal as they seem, our selves and identities are extremely social. They are hallmarks of our inner lives, *yet they take shape in relation to others. We establish who and what we are through social interaction.* In some respects, selves and identities are two sides of the same coin. Selves are the subjects we take ourselves to be; identities are the shared labels we give to these selves. We come to know ourselves in terms of the categories that are socially available to us.

Most inmates we interviewed appeared to indicate that their socialization into the gang began at a relatively young age:

> At about fifteen, I started getting affiliated with the Crips. I knew all these guys, grew up with them and they were there. . . . I mean, it was like an influence at that age. I met this dude named Benzo from Los Angeles at that time. He was a Crip and he showed me a big wad of money. He said, "Hey man, you want some of this?" "Like yeh! Goddamn straight. You know I want some of that." He showed me how to sell crack, and so at fifteen, I went from being scared of the police and respecting them to hustling and selling crack. Now I'm affiliated with the Crips; I mean it was just unbelievable.

Another inmate tells of his orientation in becoming a member of a gang. He points out the glamour he associated with membership at a very impressionable age:

> I started gang banging when I was ten. I got into a gang when I was thirteen. I started just hanging around them, just basically idolizing them. I was basically looking for a role model for my generation and ethnic background; the

96　Journal of Contemporary Ethnography

main focus for us is the popularity that they got. That's who the kids looked up to. They had status, better clothes, better lifestyle.

One of our black study participants residing with his father in a predominantly white, suburban community felt estranged from the minority friends he had in his former neighborhood. He discussed his need to be among his former peers and voluntarily moved back to his old neighborhood.

A lot of the people that lived where my father was staying were predominantly white. I mean, not to say I didn't get along with white kids but, you know, it was just two different backgrounds and things of that nature.

His racial and socioeconomic identification in the white community, where he resided with his father, offered little opportunity for him to fit in. When he returned to the city, he became involved with a gang quite rapidly.

I started getting charged with assaults. Gang rivalry, you know, fighting, just being in a gang.

Because he was better educated and did not use street vernacular as his peers did, our participant claims he had to continually prove his racial proclivity to his peers.

Other kids would call me "white wash" because I spoke proper English. Basically, I wanted to be somebody, so I started hanging around with gang bangers. I was planning on being the best gang member I can be or the best kind of criminal I can be or something like that.

Consistent with Goffman's (1959) observations, once our subjects became active gang members, their transformation of identity was complete. That is, consistent with the notion of social facilitation and enhancement perspectives (Thornberry et al. 1993), the self-perceptions and identity of the subjects in our study appear to have changed from what they were prior to joining the gang. Shibutani (1961, 523) explains such changes by claiming that

a person's self-perception is caused by a psychological reorientation in which an individual visualizes his world and who he thinks he is in a different light. He retains many of his idiosyncrasies, but develops a new set of values and different criteria of judgment.

Violent behavior appeared to play an important role in this transformation of identity and self. Most gang members noted that they engaged in violent behavior more frequently once they joined the gang.

> At an early age, it was encouraged that I showed my loyalty and do a drive-by . . . anybody they (gangster disciples) deemed to be a rival of the gang. I was going on fourteen. At first, I was scared to and then they sent me out with one person and I seen him do it. I saw him shoot the guy. . . . So, in the middle of a gang fight I get pulled aside and get handed a pistol and he said, "It's your turn to prove yourself." So I turned around and shot and hit one of the guys (rival gang members). After that, it just got more easier. I did more and more. I had no concern for anybody.

A further illustration of situated identity and transformation of self is related by another inmate, who expresses the person he became through the use of violence and gun possession. Retrospectively, he indicates disbelief in what he had become.

> As a gang banger, you have no remorse, so basically, they're natural-born killers. They are killers from the start. When I first shot my gun for the first time at somebody, I felt bad. It was like, I can't believe I did this. But I looked at my friend and he didn't care at all. Most gang bangers can't have a conscience. You can't have remorse. You can't have any values. Otherwise, you are gonna end up retiring as a gang banger at a young age.

The situations one finds themselves in, in this case collective gang violence, together with becoming a person who is willing to use violence to maintain membership in the gang, is indicative of a transformed identity. Strauss (1962) claims that when a person's identity is transformed, they are seen by others as being different than they were before. The individual's prior identity is retrospectively reevaluated in comparison with the present definition of a gang member. Such a transformation was part of the processional change in identity that our prisoners/gang members experienced.

Commitment to the Gang

"As a creature of ideas, man's main concern is to maintain a tentative hold on these idealized conceptions of himself, to legitimate his role identities" (McCall and Simmons 1966, 71). Commitment to the gang also serves individual needs for its members. We found that gang identification and loyalty to the group was a high priority for our subjects. This loyalty to

98   Journal of Contemporary Ethnography

the gang was extreme. Our subjects reported that they were willing to risk being killed and were committed to taking the life of a rival gang member if the situation called for such action. That is, gang membership helped our subjects nourish their identity and at the same time provided group maintenance (Kanter 1972). As Kanter (1972) points out, the group is an extension of the individual and the individual is an extension of the group. This notion of sacrifice for the group by proving one's gang identification is expressed by an inmate who perceives his loyalty in the following terms:

> What I might do for my friends [gang peers] you might not do. You've got people out their taking bullets for their friends and killing people. But I'm sure not one of you would be willing to go to that extreme. These are just the thinking patterns we had growing up where I did.

Another inmate tells us about his high degree of identity for his gang:

> If you're not a gang member, you're not on my level . . . most of my life revolves around gangs and gang violence. I don't know anything else but gang violence. I was born into it, so it's my life.

The notion of the gang as the most important primary group in a member's life was consistently expressed by our study subjects. Our subjects often stated that they were willing to kill or be killed for the gang in order to sustain their self-perception as a loyal gang member. This extreme degree of group affiliation is similar to that of armed services activities during wartime. The platoon, or in this case, the local gang, is worth dying for. In this sense, the notion of the gang as a protector was an important part of gang life. All members were expected to be committed enough to aid their peers should the need arise. The following gang member points to the important role his gang played for him in providing physical safety as well as an assurance of understanding.

> That's how it is in the hood, selling dope, gang bangin', everybody wants a piece of you. All the rival gang members, all the cops, everybody. The only ones on your side are the gang members you hang with.

For this particular member, his gang peers are the only people he perceives will aid him from threatening others. The world appears full of conflicting situations, and although his gang affiliation is largely responsible for all the groups that are out to harm him in some way, he nevertheless believes his fellow gang members are the only persons on whom he can depend.

Violence against rival gangs was a general subject that the majority of the inmates interviewed discussed freely. However, only a few of our study participants focused on this subject compared with the less violence-prone gang-affiliated inmates. The violent gang members perceived other gangs as ongoing enemies who constantly presented a threat to their safety. As our literature review suggests, there is some debate about whether gang members would be violent without belonging to a gang, or if formal membership in the group provided them with the opportunity to act out this way. However, we find clarity in the inmate accounts that a gang member's identity provided the context necessary to resort to violence when confronted with conflicting events, as the following inmate notes

> I have hate toward the Crips gang members and have always had hate toward them 'cuz of what they did to my homeboys. . . . I never look back. I do my thing. I always carry a gun no matter what. I am a gang member, man! There are a lot of gang members out to get me for what I done. I shot over forty people at least. That's what I do.

This perception of being a person who is comfortable with violence and the perception of himself as an enforcer type characterizes the above inmate's role within his gang. Turner (1978) suggests that roles consistent with an individual's self-concept are played more frequently and with a higher degree of participation than roles that are not in keeping with that individual's self-concept. Our study subject in this situation fits Turner's explanation of role identity nicely. His hatred for rival gangs and his willingness to retaliate most likely led to his incarceration for attempted murder.

Masculinity, Reputation, and Respect

For those gang members we interviewed, socialization into the gang and commitment to the gang appear to be central to the notion of masculinity. That is, all gang members we interviewed spoke of the importance of masculinity and how it was projected (though the creation of a reputation) and protected (through demands for respect). The notion of masculinity was constantly invoked in relation to self and identity. In short, masculinity is used to communicate to others what the gang represents, and it is used to send an important signal to others who may wish to challenge a gang's collective identity. A gang member's masculine reputation precedes him or her, so to speak. On an individual level, similar attributes apply as well.

100   Journal of Contemporary Ethnography

> Whatever an individual does and however he appears, he knowingly and
> unknowingly makes information available concerning the attributes that might
> be imputed to him and hence the categories in which he might be placed. . . .
> The physical milieu itself conveys implications concerning the identity of
> those who are in it (Goffman 1961, 102).

According to Sherif and Wilson (1953), people's ego attitudes define
and regulate their behavior toward various other groups and are formed in
concert to the values and norms of that person's reference group. They formulate an important part of their self-identity and their sense of group identification. For our gang member study population, the attributes that the
gang valued consisted of factors that projected a street image that was
necessary to sustain. It was a survival strategy.

Masculinity. "Every man [in a gang] is treated as a man until proven different. We see you as a man before anything." This comment by a gang
member infers that masculinity is a highly valued attribute in his gang. The
idea of manhood and its personal meanings for each interviewed prisoner was
a subject consistently repeated by all participants. It usually was brought up
in the context of physical violence, often describing situations where one
had to face danger as a result of another's threatening behavior or testing of
one's willingness to use physical force when insulted by someone outside
of the group.

> Even if you weren't in one [gang], you got people that are going to push the
> issue. We decide what we want to do; I ain't no punk, I ain't no busta. But it
> comes down to pride. It's foolish pride, but a man is going to be a man, and
> a boy knows he's going to come into his manhood by standing his ground.

Establishing a reputation coincides with becoming a man, entering the
realm of violence, being a stand-up guy who is willing to prove his courage
as a true gang member. This strong association between a willingness to
perpetrate violence on a considered rival, or anyone for that matter, was a
theme that defined a member's manhood. After eight years in the gang, the
following participant was owed money for selling someone dope. After a
few weeks of being put off by the debtor, he had to take some action to
appease his gang peers who were pressuring him to retaliate.

> I joined the gang when I was eleven years old. So now that I'm in the gang
> for eight years, people are asking, "What are you going to do? You got to
> make a name for yourself." So we went over there [victim's residence] and

they were all standing outside and I just shot him. Everybody was happy for me, like "Yea, you shot him, you're cool," and this and that.

A sense of bravado, when displayed, played a utilitarian role in conflicting situations where a gang member attempts to get others to comply with his demands by instilling fear instead of actually utilizing violent means. Having some prior knowledge of the threatening gang member's reputation is helpful in preventing a physical encounter, which is always risky for both parties involved. Again, the importance of firearms in this situation is critical.

> The intimidation factor with a gun is amazing. Everybody knows what a gun can do. If you have a certain type of personality, that only increases their fear of you. When it came to certain individuals who I felt were a threat, I would lift my shirt up so they would know I had one on me.

In this case, the showing of his firearm served the purpose of avoiding any altercation that could have led to injury or even worse. Carrying a gun and displaying it proved to be an intimidating, preventative factor for this gang member. The opposite behavior is noted in the following example of extreme bravado, where aggressive behavior is desired and a clear distinction (based on bravery) between drive-by shootings and face-to-face shootings is clear.

> If someone is getting shot in a drive-by and someone else gets hit, it is an accident. You know, I never do drive-bys. I walk up to them and shoot. I ain't trying to get anyone else shot to take care of business.

A final example of masculinity and bravado, as perceived by this particular study participant, illustrates his commitment to being a stand-up guy, a person who will face the consequences of gang activity. The situation he discussed had to do with his current incarceration. Here he explains how he adhered to the gang value of not being a snitch, and refused to provide information about rival gang members' involvement in two homicides to the police, which could have helped in his prosecution for murder.

> I know what I did [gang war murder], you know what I mean? I'm not gonna take the easy way out [snitch on rival gangs for two homicides]. I know what I did. I'm facing my responsibility.

An interesting note in this scenario has to do with the above inmate's continued loyalty to the values of his gang when he was outside of prison. His information on the rival gang's homicides most likely could have had the criminal charges against him reduced and subsequently he would have received a lesser prison sentence. We are taking into consideration that the inmate's cultural code is similar if not the same as the gang code, and our study participant was simply adhering to the same value system.

The image of toughness fits well under masculinity and bravado as an attribute positively perceived by gang members we interviewed. Its importance lies in projecting an image via reputation that conveys a definition of who the collective group is and what physical force they are willing to use when necessary. A clear explanation of this attribute is related by the following subject.

> Everybody wants to fight for the power, for the next man to fear him. It's all about actually killing the mother fuckers and how many mother fuckers you can kill. Drive-by shootings is old school.

The implication here is that having a collective reputation for being powerful motivates this prisoner. He notes that the tough image of shooting someone you are after instead of hiding behind the random shooting characterized by drive-bys projects an image of toughness and power.

There are others who prefer to define their toughness in terms of physical fighting without the use of any weapons—though it was often noted that it was too difficult to maintain a tough reputation under such conditions. For instance, the predicament the following gang member found himself in is one where rival gangs use guns and other lethal instruments, and as a result of this, his reputation as an effective street fighter proved to be of little value. In short, his toughness and fighting skills were obsolete in life-threatening encounters.

> Like my case, I'm a fighter. I don't like using guns. The only reason I bought a gun was because every time I got out of the car to fight, I'd have my ribs broken, the back of my head almost crushed with a baseball bat. I was tired of getting jumped. I couldn't get a fair fight. Nobody wanted to fight me because I had a bad reputation. Then I decided, why even fight? Everybody else was pulling guns. It's either get out of the car and get killed or kill them.

The fact that this prisoner had good fighting skills ironically forced him to carry a gun. The rules of gang fighting found him outnumbered and unarmed, placing him in a very vulnerable position to defend himself. The proliferation of firearms among urban street gangs is well documented by Blumstein (1995) and others. Lethal weapons, mainly firearms, have drastically changed the defining characteristics of gang warfare in the late 1980s and 1990s, when most of our study subjects were active gang members in the community.

Reputation. On a collective group level, developing and maintaining the gang's reputation of being a dangerous group to deal with, especially from other groups or individuals who posed a threat to their drug operations, was important. The following inmate points out the necessity of communicating the gang's willingness to use violent retaliation against rivals. Guns often played an important role in the development and maintenance of reputation, though they were rarely utilized in conflicting situations:

> We had guns to fend off jackers, but we never had to use them, 'cause people knew we were straps. People knew our clique, they are not going to be stupid. We've gotten into a few arguments, but it never came to a gun battle. Even when we werne gang bangin', we didn't use guns, we only fought off the Bloods.

Aside from a collective reputation, the group serves the identifying needs of its individual members (Kanter 1972). Our study participants related their need to draw upon the reputation of the gang to help them develop their own reputation, which gave them a sense of fulfillment. People want to present others with cues that will enhance desired typifications of who they are. They desire to present who they are in ways that will cause those they interact with to adhere to their situated claims (Hewitt and Stokes 1975). The following participant discusses the way gang affiliation enhanced his reputation as a dangerous individual, a person not to be tested by others.

> There are people that know me: even ones that are contemplating robbing me know of me from the gang experience. They know if you try and rob me [of drugs and money], more than likely you gonna get killed. I was gonna protect what was mine. I'll die trying.

Another study subject perceives gang membership differently. He attained a reputation through gang activity, and guns clearly played an important role in that process.

> Fear and desire to have a reputation on the streets made me do it. When I got into the streets, I saw the glamour of it. I wanted a reputation there. What better way to get a reputation than to pick up a pistol? I've shot several people.

104   Journal of Contemporary Ethnography

Although each prisoner/gang member interviewed expressed a desire to be known in the community for some particular attribute, there were some gang members who simply wanted to be known, sort of achieving celebrity status.

> You basically want people to know your name. It's kind of like politicians, like that, you wanna be known. In my generation you want somebody to say, "I know him, he used to hang around with us."

Respect. One constantly associates the subject of disrespect in gang vernacular with retaliatory violence. Interactions with rivals stemming from an affront to one's self-image often became the excuse to use a gun to redeem one's reputational identity. Strauss (1969) argues that anger and withdrawal occur when a person is confronted with a possible loss of face. For our subjects, this anger was apparent when rivals challenged their self-identity (i.e., when our subjects were disrespected).

According to the gang members we talked to, disrespect, or rejection of self-professed identity claims by others, often was the cause of violence. Violence is even more likely to be the result of disrespect when no retaliatory action may lead to a loss of face. The following inmate relates his view on this subject in general terms.

> Violence starts to escalate once you start to disrespect me. Once you start to second guess my manhood, I'll fuck you up. You start coming at me with threats, then I feel offended. Once I feel offended, I react violently. That's how I was taught to react.

The interface of their manhood being threatened seems to be directly associated with Strauss's (1962) concept of identity denial by an accusing other. This threat to one's masculinity by not recognizing another's status claims is apparently an extremely serious breach of gang etiquette.

> When someone disrespects me, they are putting my manhood in jeopardy. They are saying my words are shit, or putting my family in danger. . . . Most of the time, I do it [use violence] to make people feel the pain or hurt that I feel. I don't know no other way to do it, as far as expressing myself any other way.

Hickman and Kuhn (1956) point out that the self anchors people in every situation they are involved in. Unlike other objects, they claim that the self is present in all interactions and serves as the basis from which we all make judgments and plans of reaction toward others that are part of a given situation.

When being confronted by gang rivals who have been perceived as insulting an opposing gang member, the definition of street norms calls for an exaggerated response. That is, the disrespectful words must be countered with serious physical force to justify the disrespected individual's maintenance of self (or manhood). A prime example of feeling disrespected is discussed in terms of territory and the unwritten rules of the street by one gang member who told us of an encounter with a rival gang who disrespected him to the point that he felt he was left with no other alternative choice of action but to shoot them.

> So, as we were fighting, they started saying that this was their neighborhood and started throwing their gang signs. To me, to let somebody do that to me is disrespect. So I told them where I was from.

A little while later the gang members in question showed up in our study subject's neighborhood and shot at him as he was walking with his two small children to a convenience store to get ice cream. He continues to recite the tale:

> I was just so mad and angry for somebody to disrespect me like that and shoot. We got a rule on the street. There is rules. You don't shoot at anybody if there is kids. That's one of the main rules of the street. They broke the rules. To me that was telling me that they didn't have no respect for me or my kids. So, that's how I lost it and shot them. I was so disrespected that I didn't know how to handle it.

The notion of disrespect is analogous to an attack on the self. Because many of the inmates in our sample reported that masculinity is an important attribute of the self, they believed any disrespect was a direct threat to their masculinity. For those brought up in impoverished high-crime communities, as these study population participants were, there are limited alternatives to such conflicting situations (Anderson 1999). Retaliation to redeem one's self-identity in terms of his internalized concept of manhood precludes a violent reaction to all actions of insult. To gang members caught in those confrontational encounters, there is a very limited course of action, that of perpetrating violence toward those who would threaten their self-concept of who they believe they are.

Gangs and Guns

The perceived necessity by gang participants to carry handguns became a reality for our study group. They collectively expressed the danger of their life on the street, whether it was selling narcotics, committing a robbery, being a provocateur against rivals, or being the recipient of violent retaliation on the part of perceived enemies. They viewed their world fraught with potential danger, thus the need for the possession of guns. It is necessary, then, to take the person's definition of the situation into account in explaining their unlawful conduct (Hewitt 1988). Often, the interviewed prisoners emphasized the importance of the gun as an attribute that communicated their masculinity in some situations but was protection in others. Quite often, both definitions of the situation existed simultaneously.

Our analysis of the interview data dichotomized those gun-using encounters as expressions of either power or protection, based on each participant's perceived definition of the situation.

Carrying a firearm elicits various feelings of power.

> When I have a gun, I feel like I'm on top of it, like I'm Superman or something. You got to let them know.

Another participant explains that the larger the gun, the more powerful he felt:

> I was fifteen at that point in time and I had a fascination with guns. It was like the more powerful impact the gun had, the more fascinated I got and the more I wanted it.

The actual use of a firearm is described in a situation that most lethally expressed the power of guns in an attempt to injure those belonging to rival gangs. In this situation, our subject points out that they were not trying to injure or kill anyone for personal reasons but rather to display a sense of willingness to commit a lethal act for purposes of dominance.

> When I was younger, we used to do drive-bys. It didn't matter who you were. We didn't go after a specific person. We went after a specific group. Whoever is standing at a particular house or wherever you may be, and you're grouped up and have the wrong color on; just because you were in a rival gang. You didn't have to do anything to us to come get you, it was a spontaneous reaction.

When not being involved in collective gang violence, individual members find themselves being involved in gun-use situations as instigators when confronting rivals on one's own.

> My cousin told me if you pull it you better use it. So you gotta boost yourself. When the time came I was just shooting.

Our findings showed that in the vast majority of gang member–related shootings, most of these violent gun-using situations involved individuals as opposed to large numbers of gangs confronting each other with firearms. Yet, we were told that in gang representation, either on an individual basis or in a small group, whether it be in a protective or retaliatory mode, gang members needed to display a power position to those confronting them to maintain their reputations, and guns were important in that respect.

The issues surrounding gun possession often have to do with interpersonal conflict as opposed to collective gang situations. The fear of being physically harmed within their residential environment, coupled with the relative ease in which a person can attain a firearm, has resulted in a proliferation of weapons in the community. Growing up in such high-crime neighborhoods and then joining a gang can shape a minority teen's perceptions of his or her social world.

> There's a lot of brutality, there is a lot of murder around us. There is a lot of violence, period. There are enemies and all. A lot of pressure, you know. If you're not going to do this, then they're going to do it to you. I'd rather get caught with a gun than without.

The perceived fear for potential harm caused this female gang member to carry a gun with her outside her home. When she expresses the violence that is prevalent in her environment, she is also telling us how random threats can often occur and sees the necessity to harm rivals before they harm her.

Individually or collectively, rival gang members constantly pose a physical threat according to the next inmate. He also discusses the need for protection and how drug sales caused him to be a target for those who would try and rob him.

> I carried a gun because I knew what I was doing, especially since I was in a gang. Other gangs are gonna try and come after us. So I used it [gun] against those gangs and to make sure that my investments in the drugs was protected. I don't want nobody to take money from me.

Last, one study subject relates the need to carry a gun all the time to protect his jewelry, which he openly displays as a symbol of his monetary success through the use of illegal means.

> I basically carried a gun for protection. Just like you have a best friend. You and your best friend go everywhere. I got over ten thousand dollars of jewelry

on me. People see all this jewelry and may try and beat me up. There may be two or three and just myself.

For our prisoner/gang member study population, the descriptive attributes they related all played an important role in shaping their individual gang identity. The roles they learned to play through their processional development into bona fide gang participants were accomplished by group socialization. Their acting upon those perceived valued attributes resulted in their transformed identity. Once the socializing process is complete, the novice gang member has to sustain his reputation and status personally as well as collectively with the formal group.

> An individual who implicitly or explicitly signifies that he has certain social characteristics ought in fact to be what he claims he is. In consequence, when an individual projects a definition of the situation and thereby makes an implicit or explicit claim to be a person of a particular kind, he automatically exerts a moral demand upon others, obliging them to value and treat him in the manner that persons of his kind have a right to expect. (Goffman 1959, 1-5)

For Goffman, the claims (attributes) our sample of gang members desired to convey to others of just who they perceived themselves to be directly affected their sense of self.

Discussion and Conclusion

Gangs not only fulfill specific needs for individuals that other groups in disadvantaged neighborhoods may fail to provide, but as our interviews suggest, they are also important primary groups into which individuals become socialized. It is not surprising, then, that self-concept and identity are closely tied to gang membership. Guns are also important in this regard. We propose that for the gang members in our sample, gang-related gun violence can be understood in terms of self and identity that are created through the process of socialization and are heavily rooted in notions of masculinity. Thus, our analysis provides insight into the way gang socialization can produce violence—especially gun-related violence.

We find that related to the issue of gun violence, the possession and use of guns among gang members is relatively important because, in addition to protecting gang members, guns are tools that aid in identity formation and impression management. As many of our subject narratives suggest, guns were often connected in some way to masculine attributes. Gang members reported to us that they could often use guns to project their reputation or reclaim respect. We believe that the consequences of our findings regarding gang violence and guns are important for public policy for three reasons.

First, because our sample only consisted of those gang members who committed the most severe forms of violence (i.e., they were incarcerated for relatively long periods of time for their gun-related violence), there may be some interest in targeting individuals like the ones in our sample early in their criminal careers to "diminish the pool of chronic gang offenders" (Piehl, Kennedy, and Braga 2000, 100). We believe this may be one potential method for reducing gang-related violence because the gang members in our sample often had extensive violent histories. Moreover, in studies of gang violence, researchers have generally found that a small number of offenders commit most of the crime. For instance, Kennedy, Piehl and Braga (1996) found that less than one percent of Boston's youth were responsible for nearly sixty percent of the city's homicides. Thus, identifying the rather small pool of chronic gang members may be a useful approach to reducing gang violence because they are the ones engaged in most of the violence. This approach, however, is somewhat problematic because identifying chronic offenders is both difficult and controversial (Walker 1998). Moreover, Spergel and Curry (1990), who studied the effectiveness of various gang-related intervention strategies, argue that law enforcement efforts seem to be one of the least effective methods for reducing gang-related problems.

Second, our research suggests that policies aimed at reducing gang violence should take gang socialization into account. Simply reducing gun availability through law enforcement crackdowns on violent gang members is probably not sufficient (see Piehl, Kennedy, Braga 2000). In addition, our interviews suggest that guns are probably far more important to the daily lives and identities of gang members than most policy makers might imagine, precisely because they help project a reputation and create respect. Thus, it might be pointed out that if gang culture could be changed through the resocialization of gang members, gun-related gang violence might significantly decrease. Indeed, studies of gun initiatives such as the Boston Gun Project suggest that gang violence is reduced when gang culture is changed. As Piehl, Kennedy, and Braga (2000, 100) point out, one reason homicides in Boston decreased as a result of the Boston Gun Project was because that initiative focused on "establishing and/or reinforcing nonviolent norms by increasing peer support for eschewing violence, by improving young people's handling of potentially violent situations."

Overall, however, the strategy of focusing on gang socialization, however, falls most closely in line with social intervention perspectives that have not proved to be highly successful in various situations (Shelden, Tracy, and Brown 2001). In short, altering the values of gang members to make gang-related violence less likely may not be the most promising approach to reducing gang violence. As Klein (1995, 147) recently noted, "Gangs are by-products of their communities: They cannot long be controlled by attacks on symptoms alone; the community structure and capacity must also be targeted." Whether gang violence can be reduced by the resocialization of gang members appears to remain open to debate, but it is clearly one avenue of intervention that requires further attention in the research.

Third, it is not clear from our research whether simply eliminating or reducing access to guns can reduce gun-related gang violence. For example, studies like the Youth Firearms Violence Initiative conducted by the U.S. Department of Justice's Office of Community Oriented Policing Services does suggest that gun violence can be reduced by focusing, at least in part, on reducing access to guns (Dunworth 2000). However, that study also indicates that once these projects focusing on access to guns end, gang violence increases to previous levels. Moreover, our interviews suggest that there is little reason to believe that gang members would be any less likely to look to gangs as a source of status and protection and may use other weapons— though arguably less lethal than guns—to aid in transformations of identity and preserve a sense of self. Thus, although reduction strategies may prevent gang-related violence in the short-term, there is little evidence that this intervention strategy will have long-term effects because it does not adequately deal with gang culture and processes of gang socialization.

Overall, our findings suggest that gang socialization produces gang-related gun violence through changes to identity and self. Although the problems of gang-related violence appear to play out at the microlevel, the solutions to these problems do not appear to be overwhelmingly situated at this level. Instead, we believe that intervention efforts must reside at the macrolevel and impact socialization processes at the microlevel. We agree with Short (1997, 181) that "absent change in macro level forces associated with [gang violence], vulnerable individuals will continue to be produced" (see also Shelden, Tracy, and Brown 2001). Thus, it may be more fruitful to focus on intervention efforts aimed at improving the economic and social environments that create gangs.

Appendix
Characteristics of Inmates in Sample

ID	Age	Sex	Race/ Ethnicity	Education (Years)	Offense	Sentence (Years)	Years Served	No. Previous Felonies
1	28	M	Hispanic	11	Attempted first degree murder	16	7	0
2	21	M	Black	7	Second degree kidnapping	16	3	1
3	20	M	Black	11	Attempted first degree murder	21	3	3
4	21	M	Hispanic	11	Second degree assault	3	2	2
5	21	M	Black	12	First degree murder	Life	2	2
6	48	M	White	12	Second degree assault	14	6	7
7	33	M	Black	12	Attempted first degree murder	16	9	2
8	22	M	Black	9	Second degree assault	25	5	4
9	38	M	Black	12	Manslaughter	22	9	1
10	28	M	White	12	Second degree murder	30	8	2
11	25	M	Black	11	First degree murder	Life	4	2
12	23	M	Black	12	First degree assault	14	2	3
13	24	M	White	10	Aggravated robbery	20	5	2
14	32	M	Black	12	First degree murder	40	16	0
15	29	M	Hispanic	12	Second degree assault	5	4	1
16	25	M	Black	12	First degree assault	3	1	1
17	32	M	Black	10	Attempted first degree murder	20	3	2
18	20	M	Asian	9	Second degree kidnapping	40	3	0
19	26	F	Black	11	Aggravated robbery	8	4	0
20	43	M	White	12	First degree assault	9	0	2
21	33	M	Black	12	Second degree murder	35	5	0
22	23	M	White	11	First degree assault	45	5	1

References

Anderson, Elijah. 1999. *Code of the street: Decency, violence, and the moral life of the inner city*. NewYork: W.W. Norton.

Baumeister, Roy, and Dianne Tice. 1984. Role of self-presentation and choice in cognitive dissonance under forced compliance. *Journal of Personality and Social Psychology* 46:5-13.

Berger, Peter. 1963. *Invitation to sociology: A humanistic perspective*. Garden City, NY: Doubleday.

112   Journal of Contemporary Ethnography

Bjerregaard, Beth, and Alan Lizotte. 1995. Gun ownership and gang membership. *Journal of Criminal Law and Criminology* 86:37-58.

Blumstein, Alfred. 1995. Violence by young people: Why the deadly nexus? *National Institute of Justice Journal* 229:2-9.

Bowker, Lee, and Malcolm Klein. 1983. The etiology of female juvenile delinquency and gang membership: A test of psychological and social structural explanations. *Adolescence* 18:739-51.

Callero, Peter. 1985. Role identity salience. *Social Psychology Quarterly* 48:203-15.

Colorado Department of Corrections. 2005. *Statistical report, fiscal year 2004*. Colorado Springs: Office of Planning and Analysis.

Decker, Scott, and Barrik Van Winkle. 1996. *Life in the gang: Family, friends, and violence*. New York: Cambridge University Press.

Dunworth, Terence. 2000. *National evaluation of youth firearms violence initative. Research in brief*. Washington, DC: U.S. Department of Justice, Office of Justice Programs, National Institute of Justice.

Gerrard, Nathan. 1964. The core member of the gang. *British Journal of Criminology* 4:361-71.

Glaser, Barney, and Anselm Strauss. 1967. *The discovery of grounded theory: Strategies for qualitative research*. New York: Doubleday.

Goffman, Erving. 1959. *The presentation of self in everyday life*. Garden City, NY: Doubleday.
———. 1961. *Encounters: Two studies in the sociology of interaction*. Indianapolis, IN: Bobbs-Merrill.

Gordon, Rachel, Benjamin Lahey, Kriko Kawai, Rolf Loeber, Magda Stouthamer-Loeber, and David Farrington. 2004. Antisocial behavior and youth gang membership: Selection and socialization. *Criminology* 42:55-88.

Hewitt, John. 1988. *Self and society*. Boston: Allyn and Bacon.

Hewitt, John, and Randall Stokes. 1975. Disclaimers. *American Sociological Review* 40:1-11.

Hickman, C. Addison, and Manford Kuhn. 1956. *Individuals, groups, and economic behavior*. New York: Dryden.

Hobs, Dick, and Tim May. 1993. Forward. In *Interpreting the field accounts of ethnography*, ed. Dick Hobbs and Tim May (vii-xviii). New York: Oxford University Press.

Holstein, James, and Jaber Gubrium. 2003. *Inner lives and social worlds*. New York: Oxford University Press.

Horowitz, Ruth. 1983. *Honor and the American dream*. New Brunswick, NJ: Rutgers University Press.

Howell, James. 1998. Youth gangs: An overview. *Juvenile Justice Bulletin* August 1998. Washington DC: U.S. Department of Justice, Office of Juvenile Justice and Delinquency Prevention.

Hughes, Lorine, and James Short. 2005. Disputes involving youth street gang members: Micro-social contexts. *Criminology* 43:43-76.

Kanter, Rosabeth. 1972. *Commitment and community: Communes and utopias in sociological perspective*. Cambridge, MA: Harvard University Press.

Katz, Jack. 1988. *Seductions of crime: Moral and sensual attractions in doing evil*. New York: Basic Books.

Kennedy, David, Ann Morrison Piehl, and Anthony Braga. 1996. *Youth gun violence in Boston: Gun markets, serious youth offenders, and a use reduction strategy*. Research in Brief. Washington, DC: U.S. Department of Justice, Office of Justice Programs, National Institute of Justice.

Klein, Malcolm. 1995. *The American street gang*. New York: Oxford University Press.

Kubrin, Charis. 2005. Gangstas, thugs, and hustlas: Identity and the code of the street in rap music. *Social Problems* 52:360-78.

Lindesmith, Alfred, and Anslem Strauss. 1968. *Social psychology*. New York: Holt, Rinehart and Winston.

Lizotte, Alan, James Tesoriero, Terence Thornberry, and Marvin Krohn. 1994. Patterns of adolescent firearms ownership and use. *Justice Quarterly* 11:51-74.

Lofland, John, and Lyn H. Lofland. 1995. Analyzing social settings: A guide to qualitative observation and analysis. Belmont, CA: Wadsworth.

McCall, George, and Jerry Simmons. 1966. *Identities and interactions: An examination of human associations in everyday life*. New York: Free Press.

McCorkle, Richard, and Terance Miethe. 2002. *Panic: The social construction of the street gang problem*. Upper Saddle River, NJ: Prentice Hall.

Miller, Jody, and Rod Brunson. 2000. Gender dynamics in youth gangs: A comparison of males' and females' accounts. *Justice Quarterly* 17:419-48.

Miller, Jody, and Scott Decker. 2001. Young women and gang violence: Gender, street offender, and violent victimization in gangs. *Justice Quarterly* 18:115-40.

Moore, Joan. 1978. *Homeboys: Gangs, drugs, and prison in the barrios of Los Angeles*. Philadelphia: Temple University Press.

———. 1991. Going down to the barrio: *Homeboys and homegirls in change*. Philadelphia: Temple University Press.

Oliver, William. 1994. *The violent world of black men*. New York: Lexington.

Piehl, Anne Morrison, David Kennedy, and Anthony Braga. 2000. Problem solving and youth violence: An evaluation of the Boston gun project. *American Law and Economics Review* 2:58-106.

Sanders, William. 1994. *Gang-bangs and drive-bys: Grounded culture and juvenile gang violence*. New York: Walter de Gruyter.

Schatzman, Leonard, and Anselm Strauss. 1973. *Field research strategies for a natural sociology*. Englewood Cliffs, NJ: Prentice Hall.

Shelden, Randall, Sharon Tracy, and William Brown. 2001. *Youth gangs in American society*. Belmont, CA: Wadsworth.

Sheley, Joseph, and James Wright. 1995. *In the line of fire: Youth, guns and violence in America*. New York: Aldine de Gruyter.

Sherif, Muzafer, and Milbourne Wilson. 1953. *Group relations at the crossroads*. New York: Harper.

Shibutani, Tomatsu. 1961. *Society and personality: An interactionist approach to social psychology*. Englewood Cliffs, NJ: Prentice Hall.

Short, James. 1997. *Poverty, ethnicity, and violent crime*. Boulder, CO: Westview Press.

Short, James, and Fred Strodtbeck. 1965. *Group processes and gang delinquency*. Chicago: University of Chicago Press.

Sirpal, Suman K. 1997. Causes of gang participation and strategies for prevention in gang members' own words. *Journal of Gang Research* 4:13-22.

Spergel, Irving, and G. David Curry. 1990. Strategies perceived agency effectiveness in dealing with the youth gang problem. In *Gangs in America*, ed. C. Ronald Huff (288-309). Newbury Park, CA: Sage.

Stone, Gregory. 1962. Appearance and self. In *Human behavior and social processes*, ed. Arnold Rose (86-118). Boston: Houghton Mifflin.

Strauss, Anselm. 1962. Transformations of identity. In *Human behavior and social processes: An interactional approach,* ed. Arnold Rose (63-85). Boston: Houghton Mifflin.

————. 1969. *Mirrors and masks: The search for identity.* New York: Macmillan.

Stryker, Sheldon, and Richard Serpe. 1982. Commitment, identity salience and role behavior. In *Personality, roles and social behavior,* ed. William Ikes and Eric Knowles (199-218). New York: Springer-Verlag.

Thornberry, Terence, Marvin Krohn, Alan Lizotte, and Debra Chard-Wierschem. 1993. The role of juvenile gangs in facilitating delinquent behavior. *Journal of Research in Crime and Delinquency* 30:75-85.

Thornberry, Terence, Marvin Krohn, Alan Lizotte, Carolyn Smith, and Kimberly Tobin. 2003. *Gangs and delinquency in developmental perspective.* Cambridge, England: Cambridge University Press.

Thrasher, Frederick. 1927. *The gang.* Chicago: University of Chicago Press.

Turner, Ralph. 1978. The role and the person. *American Journal of Sociology* 84:1-23.

Vigil, James. 1988. *Barrio gangs.* Austin: University of Texas Press.

————. 1996. Street baptism: Chicago gang initiation. *Human Organization.* 55:149-53.

————. 2003. Urban violence and street gangs. *Annual Review of Anthropology* 32:225-42.

Walker, Samuel. 1998. *Sense and nonsense about crime and drugs.* Belmont, CA: Wadsworth.

Weinstein, Eugene, and Paul Deutschberger. 1963. Some dimensions of altercasting. *Sociometry* 26:454-66.

Wright, James, and Peter Rossi. 1986. *Armed and considered dangerous: A survey of felons and their firearms.* New York: Aldine de Gruyter.

Yablonsky, Lewis. 1962. *The violent gang.* New York: Macmillan.

Paul B. Stretesky is an associate professor of sociology at Colorado State University in Fort Collins. His research interests are in the areas of criminology and environmental justice. He is currently studying the structural and organizational covariates associated with the level of corporate self-reporting of environmental violations under the Environmental Protection Agency's audit policy.

Mark R. Pogrebin is a professor and director of criminal justice at the University of Colorado at Denver. He has recently published two edited books titled *Qualitative Approaches to Criminal Justice: Perspectives from the Field* (Sage, 2003) and *About Criminals: A View of the Offender's World* (Sage, 2004). His scholarly interests are in the areas of qualitative methods, symbolic interaction, and corrections. He has published five books and more than fifty articles in peer-reviewed journals.

[2]

Gangs, gang homicides, and gang loyalty: Organized crimes or disorganized criminals

Scott H. Decker*, G. David Curry

527 Lucas Hall, Department of Criminology and Criminal Justice, University of Missouri-St. Louis, 8001 Natural Bridge Road, St. Louis, MO 63121-4499, USA

Abstract

Gang members contribute disproportionately to homicide. This article examines gang homicide during its peak in the mid-1990s in St. Louis, a city with high homicide rates and large gang problems. The article addresses two related questions, the differences between gang and non-gang homicides, and the social organization of gang homicide. Marked differences between gang and non-gang homicides were found. These differences centered primarily on guns and the similarity of victim and offender characteristics. Gang homicides most often occurred within gang factions rather than between factions. Gangs were unable to organize homicides in an effective manner, which reflected the disorganized character of gangs and the neighborhoods in which they reside. The findings of this article raised important questions about the cohesiveness of gangs.

Introduction

... my boy Victor got shot a while, well not even a while back. It hurt me so bad because this is by another Crip. They, they had, they was beefin' about something that happen between them. So Loc Man shot Victor so Victor's set went shootin' at Loc Man. I mean, and it was Crip against Crip and that hurt me so bad. I was like, "It ain't even supposed to be like this." Columbus (OH) gang member

Gang members account for a disproportionate amount of violence. That fact is well known, but the way that gang violence is organized is not well understood. As the quote above illustrates, some gang violence occurs within gangs, rather than between

* Corresponding author. Tel.: +1-314-516-5038; fax: +1-314-516-5048.

E-mail address: c1911@umsl.edu (S.H. Decker).

rival gangs. This is inconsistent with the dominant popular and law enforcement image of gangs as oppositional groups whose organizational structure leads them to violence with rivals. In addition, the dominant law enforcement view of gangs as well-organized groups suggests that most gang violence occurs between rivals rather than among members of the same gang grouping (Conly, 1993; Jackson & McBride, 1985).

Despite considerable attention to the study of gang crime, the analysis of gang homicide in particular and gang violence in general has not paid attention to the role of gang rivalries in homicide. That is, the extant research literature has largely ignored the issue of whether gang violence occurs within or between gangs. The implications of such a study are important, as they have a direct bearing on the role of the organizational structure of gangs. This study used the results of an analysis of gang homicides to provide insight into the role of one aspect of gang organization—gang cohesion and solidarity—on gang homicides.

344   *S.H. Decker, G.D. Curry / Journal of Criminal Justice 30 (2002) 343–352*

The involvement of gang members in violence has been a topic of concern since Thrasher (1927). Contemporary research has emphasized the role of firearms (Bjerregaard & Lizotte, 1995; Kennedy, Braga, & Peihl, 1997), threat and contagion (Decker, 1996), the spatial concentration of gang violence (Block, 1991, 1996; Cohen & Tita, 1999; Kennedy et al., 1997; Rosenfeld, Bray, & Egley, 1999), and the role of drugs (Block, 1996; Kennedy et al., 1997; Klein & Maxson, 1994) in gang violence.

One of the elements central to the discussion of gang violence is defining what counts as a gang homicide. This significance of definitional issues is demonstrated by a comparison of Chicago and Los Angeles Police Department definitions of gang crimes. In Chicago, a crime must be motivated by gang concerns to be counted as a gang crime. This definition is more strict than that used in Los Angeles, resulting in far fewer "gang" crimes. For Los Angeles, a gang crime includes a wider range of behavior. This more permissive definition includes all crimes that are "gang related"; that is, any crime is counted as a gang crime if it involves a gang member or a gang motive. The differences were made clear by the Maxson and Klein (1990) analysis, which applied the two definitions to Los Angeles homicides. They found that the Los Angeles definition yielded twice as many gang crimes as did the Chicago definition, underscoring the salience of definitions for understanding the problem of gang homicide.

One goal of research was to ask increasingly specific questions made possible by more sophisticated measurement, better data, improved analysis tools, or some combination of the three. This research expanded the understanding of gang violence specifically, and gang homicide more broadly, by conducting a microanalysis of gang homicides that included the gang affiliation—if any—of victims and perpetrators in St. Louis homicides for the years 1994–1996.[1] By knowing the gang affiliation of perpetrators and victims of homicide, one could speculate about the ability of the gang as an organization to control and target the behavior of its members.

St. Louis was labeled as an "emerging" gang city by Spergel and Curry (1993, p. 262) in the 1988 OJJDP National Youth Gang Survey. The term "emerging" was applied to cities that had developed gang problems since 1980. In contrast, the survey staff identified a set of cities with more long-term gang problems as "chronic." In addition to having identified gang problems prior to 1980, chronic cities had at least some gangs that were organized and engaged in serious criminal activities. As noted below, most research on gang homicide had been conducted in the cities that Spergel and Curry identified as chronic, particularly Los Angeles and Chicago. By examining

gang homicides in a city where gang problems emerged in the late 1980s and became more lethal in the 1990s, patterns of gang homicide that might have been similar to or different from those observed in chronic gang cities could be identified.

The goal of this article is to examine the nature of gang homicides in an emerging gang city to determine how well violence is organized within gangs. The hypothesis that guides this analysis is that well-organized gangs (e.g., groups that function in corporate-like fashion) will engage in relatively few acts of homicide against their own members, preserving group solidarity and cohesion. For such groups, cohesion, solidarity, and leadership mitigate against internecine violence. Correspondingly, gangs with low levels of internal organization are expected to experience higher levels of intragang homicide. It is likely that the inability of these groups to control the behavior of their members may reflect a lower level of organization and control. The results of this analysis have important implications for the understanding of the nature of gang organization particularly for understanding the nature of gang crime.

Gang violence and homicide

The significance of gang homicide

It is important to understand gang homicide for a number of reasons. First, the precipitous increase in homicides in urban America in the early 1990s occurred at about the same time as the increase in the number of gangs, gang members, and gang-related crimes (Klein, 1995; Miller, 2001). Separating the contribution of gangs to the overall increase in homicide was an important contribution to our understanding of the rise in homicides. In this context, gang homicides were important because they might spark corresponding increases in violence, particularly retaliatory violence. Second, and closely related, was the apparent contribution of the drug–gun–diffusion process (Blumstein, 1995; Blumstein & Wallman, 2000) to the growth in homicide, and the obvious links to gangs. Blumstein and Wallman specified a temporal model in which relatively disorganized street drug sales—primarily crack cocaine—generated the need for protection in the form of guns. As more guns were drawn to urban drug markets, they eventually became diffused throughout the youthful population and contributed to the sudden spike in youth homicide recorded between 1990 and 1994. Despite debate about the extent to which gangs control drug markets, the extensive participation of gang members in drug sales has been well documented by a number of observers (Decker & Van Winkle, 1996; Fagan, 1989;

S.H. Decker, G.D. Curry / Journal of Criminal Justice 30 (2002) 343–352 345

Hagedorn, 1994; Maxson & Klein, 1985; Padilla, 1992; Vigil, 1988). Thus, gangs might play an important role in facilitating drug sales and the concomitant need for protection. A final reason to examine gang homicide as a separate category of fatalities was the proportion of fatal events that such offenses represented. In Chicago (Block, 1996), gang-motivated homicides represented approximately one-quarter of all homicides between 1993 and 1995, and gang-motivated homicides accounted for 45 percent of all homicides in Los Angeles County between 1994 and 1995 (Maxson, 1999). Clearly, gang homicides had contributed disproportionately to the dramatic increases in homicide recorded during the early 1990s. Yet, it was often difficult to disentangle gang homicides from the modal category of all homicides, those in which young, minority males were killed by firearms. In addition, the nature of gang affiliation might provide important insights about the extent to which gang homicides involved rivals or non-gang members.

Characteristics of gang homicide

It is important to understand why gang homicide should be studied as a special subcategory of homicides. Gang homicides can be distinguished from other homicides by virtue of a number of characteristics. These characteristics include: (1) spatial concentration; (2) weapon use; (3) race of victim and perpetrator; (4) location; (5) drug involvement; (6) age; (7) sex; and (8) victim–offender relationship.

Unlike Los Angeles and Chicago, Boston was not a chronic gang city. The findings regarding gang homicides in Boston (Kennedy et al., 1997), however, were consistent with those reported by Block for Chicago and Maxson (1999) for Los Angeles. Kennedy et al. (1997) reported an especially strong spatial concentration among gang homicides. These events disproportionately involved gun assaults, weapons, and drugs. This finding was similar to that reported by Rosenfeld et al. (1999) for St. Louis, as well as by Cohen, Cork, Engberg, and Tita (1998) and Cohen and Tita (1999). The correspondence across chronic and emerging gang cities suggested that a similar underlying process was at work in these cities, regardless of gang status. While these studies did not represent the nation, their consistency was rather striking. The role of firearms in gang-related homicides had been documented for a number of other cities (Bjerregaard & Lizotte, 1995; Decker, Pennell, & Caldwell, 1996) and remained one of the strongest correlates of gang homicide.

Maxson, Gordon, and Klein (1985) examined over 700 homicides from the Los Angeles Sheriff and Police departments between 1978 and 1982. They found that gang homicides were more likely to occur between members of the same ethnic group and involve younger offenders and victims than non-gang homicides. In addition, gang homicides were more likely to have multiple participants, occur on the street, and involved the use of automobiles. Perhaps the most prominent feature of gang homicides, however, was the use of firearms. Gang homicides were significantly more likely to involve the use of firearms than other homicides, perhaps the most important finding from their research.

Chicago, another "chronic" gang city with serious levels of gang violence, had also been the site of research on gang homicides. Carolyn Block had tracked the pattern of homicides in Chicago over the last thirty years, documenting and examining the correlates of such events. Her examination of gang homicides (1991) revealed a pattern not dissimilar from that reported by Maxson et al. in Los Angeles. Specifically, Block (1991, 1996) found that gang homicides had a strong spatial concentration, and that the risk of being a victim or perpetrator peaked between the ages of fifteen and nineteen. The Chicago homicide data supported the conclusion that most gang-related homicides involved the use of firearms. Finally, Block reported that intragang violence was more common than might be expected. This finding was noteworthy, as most gang research (Maxson, 1999) reported a strong intergang character to gang violence. This contrast provided the central focus for the current analysis.

Theories of gang homicide

Despite the level of gang homicide, there have been few attempts to develop theoretical explanations for this behavior. The dominant explanations have followed two distinct approaches: (1) community explanations and (2) explanations that emphasize the role of collective behavior. Explanations based on community characteristics pointed to the role of community structure and other social correlates, including correlates of community social control, in the generation of patterns and trends in homicide. Those explanations that emphasize collective behavior pointed to the role of social processes such as retaliation. The former approach emphasized the spatial distribution of individual and neighborhood characteristics, while the latter highlighted dynamic social processes.

Curry and Spergel (1988) provided a community explanation for gang homicide. They examined both homicide and gang delinquency among Latinos and African Americans in Chicago. They concluded that gang homicides had a significantly different ecological pattern than did non-gang homicides. In addition, Curry and Spergel (1988) concluded that gang homicides conformed to classic models of social disorganization and poverty. They argued that viewing gang groups as a function of mobility patterns was a productive conceptual means of understanding gang homicides. The strong spatial concentration of gang homicides in neighborhoods characterized by poverty and social change was a consistent theme throughout the literature (Block, 1991; Kennedy et al., 1997; Wilson, 1987).

Decker (1996) emphasized the role of collective behavior in explaining gang violence, especially the spikes in violence that were observed over time. Decker argued that "threat" played a central role in the explanation of gang homicides, especially the retaliatory character of many gang homicides. This perspective grew from the work of Short (1989), who identified a process by which gang violence could be seen as a group phenomenon rather than acts of individuals. From this perspective, gang violence could escalate rapidly, as one event precipitated another. Such an approach emphasized the dynamic social processes that resembled collective behavior among informal groups and led to retaliatory violence between gangs and gang members.

Klein and Maxson (1987, p. 219) and Maxson (1999) provided support for the "escalation hypothesis." From this perspective, gang violence could best be understood as a series of reciprocal actions between rival gangs. This reciprocity was largely a function of the rivalries that existed between gangs. Such rivalries were the consequence of a number of factors (drug turf, neighborhood dominance, symbolic ascendance, etc.) that over time were sublimated to the more immediate need to dominate turf, a rival, or both. Klein and Maxson also reported that gangs had weak internal structures and generate little cohesion among members. As such, they were generally ineffective mechanisms for generating compliance among members. It should be noted that these findings were drawn from a chronic gang city, Los Angeles.

Taken together, these studies suggested that gangs were not well organized and had weak control over their members, and that rivalries could lead to violence within and between gangs. In addition, these studies pointed to the transitory nature of gang membership, reinforcing the notion that gangs might not be organizations capable of controlling the behavior of their members. This leds to the conclusion that gangs were not effective organizations for carrying out the mission of a group of individuals.

The conceptual argument

Typically, examinations of gang homicide in chronic cities have examined differences between gang and non-gang events. Such analyses highlighted the gang status of victims and perpetrators. In this analysis, a dimension in the social organization of gang homicide was considered, which had not been examined in prior research, the choice of victims by gang perpetrators and the gang status of offenders and victims.

Prior research on St. Louis gangs suggested a pattern of gang activity that was not organized (Decker, 1996; Decker & Van Winkle, 1996). As less organized groups, gangs in St. Louis were characterized as lacking effective leadership, with little internal discipline and few well-defined roles, and failed to invest profits from gang-related crime into the gang. This behavior was characterized as collective behavior, subject to the dynamics of contagion with considerable variation over time. It is not well understood at present whether gang homicides in an emerging gang city with loosely organized gangs are committed primarily against rival gang members, against gang members more generally (including members of one's own gang), or against a variety of individuals, both gang and non-gang members.

Two specific questions formed the basis of this analysis. First, the extent to which gang homicides shared characteristics with other "youth homicides" was examined. Here, the correlates of gang homicides were compared with other youth homicides. This was important as a premise to the argument that gang homicides were indeed different from other forms of homicide, particularly youth homicide. Next, the social organization of gang homicide was analyzed. Four categories of gang homicide framed this part of the analysis: (1) homicides committed by members of one gang against members of rival gangs; (2) homicides committed by members of one gang against members of their own or allied gangs; (3) homicides committed by gang members against non-gang members; and (4) homicides committed by non-gang members against gang members.

The implications of such an analysis were important to understanding the variation in urban street gangs specifically, and patterns of youth violence more generally. A strong pattern of gang homicides between rival groups indicated that the divisions between gangs were quite distinct and provided a potent mechanism for governing the behavior of gang members. Such a pattern would strengthen the argument that the organizational structure of the gang was effective in generating loyalty and creating discipline among its members. When members of the same gang kill each other or their allies, such a pattern indicated far different things about the nature of gang organization, loyalties, and discipline within the gang. If the perpetrators of gang homicides committed their offenses against a broader range of individuals, including members of their own gang, it was

S.H. Decker, G.D. Curry / Journal of Criminal Justice 30 (2002) 343–352 347

more difficult to conclude that the gang effectively controlled the behavior of its members. A pattern in which non-gang members were chosen as victims, or in which gang members were killed by non-gang members, suggested that gang homicide, as a special category of offenses, did not have as much theoretical or operational validity in cities where gangs and gang membership were not especially stable for any length of time.

The conceptualization of gangs as groups occupying particular locations in a socially evolving environment found support in the approach of environmental ecology (Vila, 1994). Gang problems in St. Louis emerged in the late 1980s. In that period, gangs often emerged and developed in response to neighborhood rivals, typically based on a collective awareness of other developing gangs. This led field researchers (Decker & Van Winkle, 1996) to identify perceived "threat" from other gangs as the key element in gang emergence and expansion in St. Louis. Members were drawn to gangs by their individual-level perceptions of threat from other gangs, just as gangs as organizations used conflict and the potential for intergang violence as principles around which to organize and recruit. This emergence was compatible with the view of gangs as loosely organized groups with shifting leadership, loyalty, and membership. Gangs formed and grew in response to collective threats of violence from other gangs. It was little wonder that researchers had found that violence, in thought and deed, pervaded almost every aspect of gang activity (Decker, 1996).

It was important to understand organizations such as gangs in the context of their environments, particularly in the amount and nature of resources that could be collectively mobilized by such organizations. Levels of organization within communities themselves played a special part (Bursik & Grasmick, 1993) in the emergence and nature of gangs and gang violence. The presence of gangs in neighborhoods was associated with weak network ties, either among individual residents or between residents and institutions. Especially noteworthy among youths who became involved in gangs were deficits in social capital (Coleman, 1988; Decker & Van Winkle, 1996; Short, 1990). This lack of social capital was linked to the well-documented marginality of gang members (Hagedorn, 1998; Vigil, 1988) and their inability to access the resources and relationships available to them. Gangs represented collective responses to perceived threats and were organizationally infused with the capacity to engage in violence, where there was already a deficit of personal and collective resources to develop social structure and resolve conflicts in a nonlethal manner. These deficits reflected the environment in which most urban gang members found themselves, poor underclass neighborhoods. The objective character-

istics of such neighborhoods accounted for the loose, fluid organization of gangs reported by most researchers (Hagedorn, 1998; Klein, 1995; Spergel, 1995). A community foundation of weak social structure should correspond to comparably weak correlations between stated organizational goals and outcomes among groups in such communities, particularly groups with little social capital. In the context of the gang and gang violence, such actions might not reflect stated group goals—such as the protection of and loyalty to the group—and would often occur within the gang and external to the gang, as well as between rival gang groups. Such a perspective was consistent with the dynamic and conflict-ridden nature of urban life for many of the individuals who join gangs and might be involved in a broad pattern of offending. In short, it was expected that disorganized communities would produce disorganized behavior among the members of those communities, particularly the adolescents of those communities.

In this research, the homicide event was used as the unit of analysis. Following the advice of James F. Short (1998), a measure of the gang as a group was used: the gang affiliation of victims or perpetrators in gang homicides. This theoretical and methodological commitment was particularly relevant in St. Louis, where the universal cultural currency of gangs as collective activity was the conflict between Crips and Bloods. An enmity borrowed from California gangs, either through migration or media, the Crips-versus-Bloods distinction provided a special vitality to accounts offered by St. Louis gang members describing their commitments, rivalries, and behavior (Decker & Van Winkle, 1996). Though the declaration of hostility to the opposing faction was ubiquitous among gang members of both Crip and Blood gangs, if gang structures were weak and ineffective mechanisms for insuring the compliance of their members, the outcomes of gang violence might be quite different. Characterized by low social capital and organizations with weak ties to social institutions, gangs appeared to be ineffective mechanisms for controlling the most fundamental behavior of their members—violence.

Data and methods

St. Louis was an appropriate site for the current analysis. It was a city that experienced high rates of violent crime, consistently ranking among the U.S. cities with the five highest rates of homicide and robbery. For example, in 1993, the city of St. Louis recorded a total of 261 homicides resulting in a homicide rate just under seventy per 100,000 citizens, compared to the U.S. rate of just over nine per

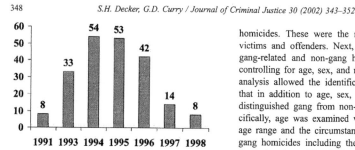

Fig. 1. Gang-related homicides in St. Louis for selected years.

100,000. Since St. Louis is a quite compact city, comprising only sixty-one square miles, it therefore intensified the spatial concentration of the violent crime problem. The city had experienced many of the conditions common to Midwest industrial cities, a fleeing middle class, eroding tax base, declining employment in the industrial sector, and substantial population loss. Law enforcement surveys indicated that there were approximately 33 gangs and 1,300 gang members in 1991 (Curry, Ball, & Fox, 1994) and 70 gangs and 4,000 gang members in 1997 (National Youth Gang Center, 1999).

The data for this study were drawn from the case files of the St. Louis Metropolitan Police Department Homicide Division and verified with the Gang Intelligence Unit that originated in 1989. Units within law enforcement agencies are always subject to variations in crime problems and resources dedicated in response to the assessments of such problems, as well as the transfer or retirement of key personnel. Details on victim–offender relationships and demographics were available in the Homicide Division's case records. The University of Missouri-St. Louis Homicide Project had converted the Homicide Division's records from 1970 to present into a computerized data set. One variable in that data set was whether or not the homicide was "gang related." The Homicide Division did not record the specific gang affiliation of offenders or victims. That was available from the Gang Intelligence Unit.

The analysis proceeded in several steps. First, the basic trend in gang homicides in the 1990s in St. Louis was reviewed. Following that, gang and non-gang homicides for the years 1994–1996 were examined in greater detail using the data from the Homicide Division. These years were selected for two reasons. First, these were the peak years of gang-related homicide in St. Louis, and second, these were the years for which both Homicide Division and Gang Intelligence Unit data on homicides were available.[2] Three primary demographic factors dominated the distinction between gang and non-gang

homicides. These were the race, age, and sex of victims and offenders. Next, comparisons between gang-related and non-gang homicides were made, controlling for age, sex, and race of offenders. This analysis allowed the identification of those factors that in addition to age, sex, and race of offenders distinguished gang from non-gang homicides. Specifically, age was examined within this diminished age range and the circumstances of gang and non-gang homicides including the method of inflicting death, location of homicide, whether or not it was drug related, and victim–offender relationship. Finally, using the offender–victim gang affiliation data from the Gang Intelligence Unit, this analysis examined the extent to which gang homicides involved rival gang members as perpetrators and victims, occurred between members of the same or allied gangs, or represented conflicts between gang members and non-gang members.

Findings

Gang homicide has become a significant problem in St. Louis. Following the pattern of many Midwest cities with an emerging gang problem, the early and mid-1990s was the period of most intense gang violence. This pattern is reflected in Fig. 1, which presents the number of gang-related homicides by year, and the fraction of city homicides accounted for by gang homicides for the years 1991 through 1998. As Figs. 1 and 2 depict, there was a rather dramatic growth in the number and fraction of gang-related homicides from 1991 to the peak year, 1994. In 1994, gang homicides achieved a brief stability, representing approximately one-quarter of all homicides in the city. In 1997 and 1998, gang homicide declined somewhat more rapidly than the general decline in homicides.[3]

Table 1 compares gang and non-gang homicides as identified by the UMSL Homicide Project's data

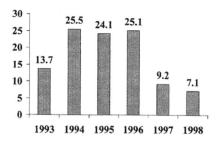

Fig. 2. Gang-related homicides as % of all homicides in St. Louis for selected years.

S.H. Decker, G.D. Curry / Journal of Criminal Justice 30 (2002) 343–352 349

Table 1
Gang versus non-gang homicides

| | Homicide type | | | | | |
| | Non-gang | | Gang | | | |
	n	%	n	%	Significance	Total n
Suspect: African American	394	90.8	77	100	.01	511
Victim: female	84	15.6	9	11.3	n.s.	617
Victim: White	82	15.3	1	1.3	.001	617
	Mean	n	Mean	n	Significance	Total n
Mean age of victim	31.9	534	22.7	80	0.001	614
Mean age of suspect	26.7	431	20.1	79	0.001	511
Mean number of suspects	1.4	432	1.5	79	n.s.	511

coded from the case files of the St. Louis Metropolitan Police Department Homicide Division. At first, a number of distinct differences appeared to exist. In gang homicides, the suspect and the victim were significantly more likely to be African Americans. Similarly, the offender and the victim were on the average younger than offenders and victims in non-gang homicides. All of the gang homicide suspects were males.

Since offenders in gang homicides were more likely to be African American, male, and younger, for the comparison group, gang and non-gang homicides in which the suspects were African American males under age twenty-five were chosen. The comparison of gang and non-gang homicides for this subset of all homicides are shown in Table 1.

Differences between the two types of homicides narrowed once this subset of homicides was examined, but statistically significant differences still remained. Non-gang homicide victims were significantly older. Though the difference narrowed considerably, gang homicide offenders were still younger than non-gang homicide offenders. There was a perfect correlation between the use of a gun and the classification of a homicide as gang related by the Gang Intelligence Unit. Gang homicide offenders and victims were slightly more likely to know one another. These characteristics underscored both the distinctive nature of gang homicide, as well as the fact that gang homicides shared many correlates with typical homicides in St. Louis: Both categories were dominated by young, African American males who killed their victims with guns. These data were consistent with the findings reported by Block in Chicago, Maxson and Klein in Los Angeles, and Kennedy et al. in Boston (Table 2).

The next issue examined in the analysis was a key for this research: the extent to which gang homicides occurred between rival gangs, within gangs or gang alliances, or involved non-gang members. In this

analysis, the data on gang-related homicides provided by the St. Louis Police Department Gang Intelligence Unit were used to assess homicides. Gang affiliation of offender and victim were recorded for only seventy-two homicides in comparison to the seventy-seven gang-related homicides recorded from the Homicide Division data used in Table 1. In St. Louis in the mid-1990s, there were two main gang divisions, Bloods and Crips (Decker & Van Winkle, 1996), and Crip gang members outnumbered Blood members by at least a two-to-one margin. Here, data that reflected the extent to which gang homicides

Table 2
Homicide African American male suspects 25 and under

| | Non-gang | | Gang | | |
	Mean	n	Mean	n	Significance
Mean victim age	28.1	238	22.7	72	.001
Mean suspect age	20.3	239	19.2	72	.001
Mean number of suspects	1.6	239	1.5	72	n.s.
	n	%	n	%	Significance
Victim: female	30	12.0	8.0	11.7	n.s.
Location					
Inside	45	18.8	7	9.7	n.s.
Outside	134	56.1	38	52.8	
Automobile	51	21.3	20	27.8	
Other	9	3.80	7	9.72	
Weapon					
% Gun	208	89.3	70	100.0	.01
Victim–offender relationship					
% Stranger	52	26.8	13	22.4	.05
% Acquaintance	26	18.3	3	5.2	
% Intimate	110	56.7	34	58.6	
% Unknown	6	3.1	8	13.8	
Drug related	125	52.3	33	43.1	n.s.

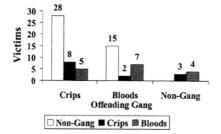

Fig. 3. Gang-related homicides by status of offender and victim 1994–1996 (*n* = 72).

victims, were killed by other Crips. Non-gang victims were more likely to be killed by Crips (65.1 percent) than by Bloods.

The picture offered by these data did not support a vision of gang homicide in which gangs deliberately targeted rival gang members, and offended in a highly patterned manner. Indeed, quite the opposite view was suggested by the data. The overwhelming majority of gang members were killed by non-gang members, and when gang members were killed by another gang member, it was most likely to be by someone from their own gang faction. These conclusions had implications for the way gang homicide was viewed, particularly in cities that had high rates of lethal violence. It might be that in such cities, gang status failed to add significantly to the risk for violence. Alternatively, gang membership might involve members in activities that placed them at risk for violent victimization as a consequence of activities related to gang membership, such as drug sales or other offenses, which were likely to draw the attention of active offenders in the neighborhood. The differences between gang and non-gang homicides are examined below.

occurred within Crip and Blood factions, between the two factions, or involved non-gang members were presented. The data to support this analysis are presented in Fig. 3.

Fig. 3 clearly reveals a picture of gang homicide at odds with the view that gangs control the pattern of violence that their members engage in. More Blood gang members (sixteen) were killed than Crips, and the largest portion of them (nine; 43.8 percent) were killed by non-gang members. Crips were more likely to be killed by other Crips than by members of their main rivals, the Bloods. This did not present a picture of gang homicide in which loyalty to fellow gang members controlled the choice of targets and victims for violence. Similar findings emerged for homicides involving Blood gang members. The majority of Crip gang victims (eight) or 61.5 percent of all Crip

The final part of the analysis looked only at gang-related homicides in order to compare the gang affiliations of offenders and victims. Table 3 shows the differences to be few across the four types of homicides considered. Non-gang members who killed gang members were significantly older than gang members who were offenders in gang-related homicides identified by the Gang Intelligence Unit.

Table 3
Gang homicide characteristics by gang affiliation

	Intrafaction	Interfaction	Attack on nonaffiliate	Attacked by nonaffiliate	Total	Significance
n	15	7	43	7	72	
Age of suspects	18.9	20.0	19.7	24.7	20.0	.05
Age of victims	20.6	23.8	23.8	19.9	22.7	n.s.
Number of suspects	1.60	1.29	1.56	1.00	1.49	n.s.
% Female (victims)	6.3	25.0	11.6	12.5	12.0	n.s.
Location						
% Inside	6.3	25.0	9.3	25.0	12.0	n.s.
% Outside	68.8	62.5	51.2	25.0	53.3	
% Automobile	18.8	12.5	30.2	37.5	26.7	
% Other location	6.3	0.0	9.3	12.5	8.0	
Weapon						
% Gun	100.0	100.0	97.6	87.5	97.3	n.s.
Victim–offender relationship						
% Stranger	0.0	20.0	34.3	0.0	22.4	n.s.
% Acquaintance	7.7	0.0	5.7	0.0	5.2	
% Intimate	61.5	40.0	54.3	100.0	58.6	
% Unknown	30.8	40.0	5.7	0.0	13.8	
Drug-related incident	18.8	37.5	58.1	62.5	48.0	.05

S.H. Decker, G.D. Curry / Journal of Criminal Justice 30 (2002) 343–352 351

Intrafaction gang killings were more likely to involve male offenders while females were more likely to be killed in interfactional incidents. Neither of the two types of homicides that involved gang members as offenders and victims were as likely to be classified as drug related by the Homicide Unit of the St. Louis Police Department as the homicides that involved violence between gang members and nonmembers. This could be interpreted to indicate that there was not as much overlap between gang conflicts and drug conflicts as some researchers have suggested. At least, this was the case in St. Louis.

Discussion

Cloward and Ohlin (1960) argued that gangs lack the structure and corporate capability to coordinate activities effectively. This observation had not been effectively challenged by empirical research in the forty years since it was made. The research presented here supports that conclusion, despite claims about more organized gangs. Gangs have been characterized in the research literature (Klein, 1995) as loosely organized confederations that coalesce irregularly over issues that emerge and vanish from the streets. That patterns of gang violence reflect the structural characteristics of gang membership is only logical.

Hagedorn (1998) concluded that the escalation of gun ownership in gang neighborhoods had implications that extended far beyond drug sales. As such, it was reasonable to expect that the presence of firearms led to lethal violence in circumstances that might otherwise have been settled with less-than-lethal means (Cook, 1991). As Rosenfeld et al. (1999) pointed out, gang members were involved in a variety of crimes that were not motivated by membership, but rather reflected the concerns and activities of young, urban offenders. The recent review of gang homicide research by Maxson (1999) found that the correlates of gang and non-gang homicides had narrowed over time. Taken together, this research provided support for the conclusions regarding the corporate structure and control of gang violence. To put a fine point on these findings, individuals at risk for violence were likely to engage in violence. When such individuals were gang members, that risk was elevated.

The fact that St. Louis gang members committed homicides within their own gang affiliation lends credibility to the view that gangs lack the characteristics of effective social organizations. Gang members were more likely than others to have access to the means of inflicting lethal violence, motives for doing so, and the opportunities to commit homicides. The fact that members of their own gang were most often the victims of their violence reflects the lack of

corporate control, restrictions of geography and age, and proximal nature of most youthful conflict.

Notes

1. While many studies have examined patterns in gang homicide, few have examined the micro-characteristics of homicides.
2. The Gang Unit participated in the U.S. DOJ Anti-Gang Initiative in 1994–1997.
3. The numbers of gang-related homicides for years 1991, 1993, 1997, and 1998 used to construct Figs. 1 and 2 were taken from St. Louis Police Department responses to national gang surveys of law enforcement agencies (Curry, Ball, & Decker, 1996; Curry et al., 1994; National Youth Gang Center, 1999).

Acknowledgments

We gratefully acknowledge the cooperation of the St. Louis Metropolitan Police Department for providing the data for this study. Sergeants Terry Sloan, Gary Hill, and Robert Ogilve are to be commended for their work in this regard, as is the Director of Planning, Larry Pattison. We also acknowledge our colleague, Jody Miller, for her insightful contributions to this article. Her contributions have meant more to us than she knows. This project was supported in part by funding by the Office of Community Oriented Policing Anti-Gang Initiative. The opinions expressed here are those of the authors and are not necessarily those of the funding or cooperating agencies.

References

Bjerregaard, B., & Lizotte, A. J. (1995). Gun ownership and gang membership. *Journal of Criminal Law and Criminology, 86,* 37–57.

Block, C. R. (1991). Gang homicide in Chicago: patterns over time, area of city, and type of victim. Presented to the Midwestern Criminal Justice Association. Chicago, Illinois.

Block, C. R. (1996). *Street gangs and crime. Research bulletin.* Chicago, IL: Illinois Criminal Justice Information Authority.

Blumstein, A. (1995). Youth violence, guns, and the illicit-drug industry. *Journal of Criminal Law and Criminology, 86,* 10–36.

Blumstein, A., & Wallman, J. (2000). The recent rise and fall of American violence. In A. Blumstein & Wallman J. (Eds.), *The crime drop in America* (pp. 1–12). New York: Cambridge.

352   *S.H. Decker, G.D. Curry / Journal of Criminal Justice 30 (2002) 343–352*

Cohen, J., Cork, D., Engberg, J., & Tita, G. E. (1998). The role of drug markets and gangs in local homicide rates. *Journal of Homicide Studies, 2,* 241–262.

Cohen, J., & Tita, G. E. (1999). Spatial diffusion in homicide: an exploratory analysis. *Journal of Quantitative Criminology, 15,* 451–493.

Conly, C. (1993). *Street gangs: current knowledge and strategies.* Washington, DC: National Institute of Justice.

Cook, P. J. (1991). The technology of personal violence. In M. Tonry (Ed.), *Crime and Justice vol. 14* (pp. 1–7). Chicago: University of Chicago Press.

Curry, G. D., Ball, R. A., & Fox, R. J. (1994). *Gang crime and law enforcement record keeping. Research in brief.* Washington, DC: National Institute of Justice.

Curry, G. D., & Spergel, I. A. (1988). Gang homicide, delinquency, and community. *Criminology, 26,* 381–405.

Decker, S. H. (1996). Collective and normative features of gang violence. *Justice Quarterly, 13,* 243–264.

Decker, S. H., Pennell, S., & Caldwell, A. (1996). *Arrestees and guns: monitoring the illegal firearms market.* (Final report). Washington, DC: National Institute of Justice.

Decker, S. H., & Van Winkle, B. (1996). *Life in the gang: family, friends and violence.* New York: Cambridge.

Fagan, J. E. (1989). The social organization of drug use and drug dealing among urban gangs. *Criminology, 27,* 633–669.

Hagedorn, J. M. (1994). Neighborhoods, markets and gang drug organization. *Journal of Research in Crime and Delinquency, 32,* 264–294.

Hagedorn, J. M. (1998). *People and folks: gangs, crime and the underclass in a Rustbelt City.* Chicago: Lakeview Press.

Jackson, R. K., & McBride, W. D. (1985). *Understanding street gangs.* Sacramento, CA: Custom Publishing.

Kennedy, D. M., Braga, A. A., & Piehl, A. M. (1997). The unknown universe: mapping gangs and gang violence in Boston. In D. Weisburd, & J. T. McEwenx (Eds.), *Crime mapping and crime prevention* (pp. 219–262). New York: Criminal Justice Press.

Klein, M. W. (1995). *The American street gang.* New York: Oxford.

Klein, M. W., & Maxson, C. L. (1987). Street gang violence.

In M. E. Wolfgang, & N. Weiner (Eds.), *Violent crime, violent criminals* (pp. 198–234). Beverly Hills, CA: Sage.

Klein, M. W., & Maxson, C. L. (1994). Gangs and crack cocaine trafficking. In D. L. MacKenzie & C. D. Uchida (Eds.), *Drugs and crime* (pp. 42–58). Thousans Oaks, CA: Sage.

Maxson, C. L. (1999). Gang homicide. In D. Smith & M. Zahn (Eds.), *Homicide studies: a sourcebook of social research* (pp. 239–254). Newbury Park, CA: Sage.

Maxson, C. L., Gordon, M. A., & Klein, M. W. (1985). Differences between gang and nongang homicides. *Criminology, 23,* 209–222.

Maxson, C. L., & Klein, M. W. (1990). Street gang violence: twice as great, or half as great? In C. R. Huff (Ed.), *Gangs in America, vol. 1.* Newbury Park, CA: Sage.

Miller, W. B. (2001). *The growth of youth gang problems in the United States: 1970–1998.* Washington, DC: OJJDP.

Padilla, F. M. (1992). *The gang as an American enterprise.* New Brunswick: Rutgers.

Rosenfeld, R.B, Bray, T., & Egley, H. A., Jr. (1999). Facilitating violence: a comparison of gang-motivated, gang-affiliated, and non-gang youth homicides. *Journal of Quantitative Criminology, 15,* 495–516.

Short, J. F. (1998). The level of explanation problem revisited: the American Society of Criminology 1997 Presidential address. *Criminology, 36,* 3–36.

Short, J. F., Jr. (1989). Exploring integration of theoretical levels of explanation: notes on gang delinquency. In S. F. Krohn, M. D. Krohn, & A. E. Liska (Eds.), *Theoretical integration in the study of deviance and crime: problems and prospects* (pp. 243–260). Albany, NY: State University of New York Press.

Short, J. F., Jr. (1990). Gangs, neighborhoods, and youth crime. *Criminal Justice Research Bulletin, 5,* 1–11.

Thrasher, F. (1927). *The gang.* Chicago: University of Chicago Press.

Vigil, D. (1988). *Barrio gangs.* Austin, TX: University of Texas Press.

Vila, B. (1994). A general paradigm for understanding criminal behavior: extending evolutionary ecological theory. *Criminology, 32,* 311–360.

[3]

THE ROLE OF FIREARMS IN VIOLENCE "SCRIPTS": THE DYNAMICS OF GUN EVENTS AMONG ADOLESCENT MALES

Deanna L. Wilkinson* and Jeffrey Fagan**

I

INTRODUCTION

In recent years, the use and deadly consequences of gun violence among adolescents has reached epidemic proportions. At a time when national homicide rates are declining, the increasing rates of firearm deaths among teenagers is especially alarming. Deaths of adolescents due to firearm injuries are disproportionately concentrated among nonwhites, and especially among African-American teenagers and young adults. Only in times of civil war have there been higher within-group homicide rates in the United States. There appears to be a process of self-annihilation among male African-American teens in inner cities that is unprecedented in American history. Unfortunately, few studies have examined these sharp increases in gun fatalities among young males.

This article attempts to contribute to the scant literature by examining the role of firearms in violent events among adolescent males. First, using an event-based approach, it suggests a framework for explaining interactions that involve adolescents and firearms. Events are analyzed as "situated transactions," including rules that develop within specific contexts, the situations where weapons are used, the motivations for carrying and using weapons, and the personality "sets" of groups where weapons are used. There are "rules" that govern how disputes are settled, when and where firearms are used, and the significance of firearms within a broader adolescent culture. This approach does not deny the importance of the individual attributes that bring people to situations, but it recognizes that once in the situation, other processes shape the outcomes of these events.

This article describes how violence "scripts" are invoked, how scripts may limit the behavioral and strategic options for resolving disputes, and how the presence of firearms may influence which scripts are invoked. Because violence generally is a highly contextualized event, this article also focuses on how specific contexts shape decisions by adolescents to carry or use weapons, and

* Doctoral candidate, School of Criminal Justice, Rutgers University; staff associate, Center for Violence Research and Prevention, Columbia University.

** Visiting Professor, School of Public Health, Columbia University; Professor, School of Criminal Justice, Rutgers University.

how violence "scripts" are developed and shaped through diffusion within closed social groups.

This article then reviews the patterns of firearm use among adolescents over time and in specific eras and identifies factors that seem to have contributed to the recent escalation and the present day crises. It then provides an analysis of recent, influential surveys. The literature on guns and adolescents is characterized by broad surveys that gauge how often students bring weapons to school, and how their outlooks have been affected by the presence of firearms.[1] Most of these studies suffer from selection biases by excluding dropouts and institutionalized youths with higher rates of violence and weapons use.[2] Research on inner-city adolescents has often confounded firearm use with other forms of adolescent violence (for example, physical and sexual assault or robbery) or co-morbid problem behaviors (for example, substance use, school dropout, or teenage pregnancy). But there is no evidence that firearm use by adolescents is part of a generalized pattern of adolescent violence or a maladaptive developmental outcome. In fact, few studies have distinguished adolescents who are violent from those violent adolescents who carry or use firearms.

Perhaps most importantly, no studies have examined the specific role of firearms in violent events.[3] The 1993 survey by LH Research suggests that the number of events where guns are used are a small fraction of the number of events where guns are present.[4] Although several studies attribute violence to the dynamics and contingencies in contexts such as gang conflicts, drug markets, domestic disputes, or robberies, few studies have addressed the dynamics or antecedents of firearm use in inner cities among adolescents or young males, especially the mechanisms that escalate gun possession to gun use.[5] That is,

---

1. *See, e.g.*, JOSEPH F. SHELEY & JAMES D. WRIGHT, NAT'L INSTITUTE OF JUSTICE, GUN ACQUISITION AND POSSESSION IN SELECTED JUVENILE SAMPLES (Dec. 1993); LH Research, A Survey of Experiences, Perceptions, and Apprehensions About Guns Among Young People in America (1993) (on file with School of Public Health, Harvard University).

2. Jeffrey Fagan et al., *Violent Delinquents and Urban Youths*, 24 CRIMINOLOGY 445 (1986).

3. These studies often confound firearms with other weapons, and confound weapons use generally with other forms of violence. *See, e.g.*, DELBERT S. ELLIOTT ET AL., MULTIPLE PROBLEM YOUTH: DELINQUENCY, DRUGS, AND MENTAL HEALTH PROBLEMS 1 (1989). Moreover, the low base rates of violence in these studies limits efforts to explain the use of firearms or other weapons. Violence in these studies is more often concentrated in inner-cities, leading to a potential confounding of individual characteristics with social area effects. Robert J. Sampson & William J. Wilson, *Race, Crime and Urban Inequality*, in CRIME AND INEQUALITY 37-54 (John Hagan and Ruth D. Peterson eds., 1995).

4. LH Research, *supra* note 1.

5. Philip J. Cook, *A Strategic Choice Analysis of Robbery*, in SAMPLE SURVEYS OF THE VICTIMS OF CRIME 186 (W. Skogan ed., 1976) (finding that guns are a means to pursue more lucrative targets for victimization); Jeffrey Fagan, *Set and Setting Revisited: Influences of Alcohol and Illicit Drugs on the Social Context of Violent Events*, in ALCOHOL AND INTERPERSONAL VIOLENCE: FOSTERING MULTIDISCIPLINARY PERSPECTIVES 161, 163, 169-72 (Susan E. Martin ed., 1993). The social and cultural landscape of inner-city neighborhoods described by Anderson provides further support for research focused on situational transactions. Elijah Anderson, *The Code of the Streets*, THE ATLANTIC MONTHLY, May 1994; ELIJAH ANDERSON, STREETWISE: RACE, CLASS, AND CHANGE IN AN URBAN COMMUNITY (1990); GEOFFREY CANADA, FIST, KNIFE, STICK, GUN: A PERSONAL HISTORY OF VIOLENCE IN AMERICA (1995). Social networks within neighborhoods where these events are likely

research on adolescent firearm use has not yet analyzed the interactions of the individual characteristics involved, the interpersonal transactions and interactions between the parties, or how the presence of guns affects the outcomes of these interactions. And no studies have focused on specific social or neighborhood contexts that also shape the outcomes of putative violent events. Such an approach seems necessary to explain the increase in firearm fatalities among young African-Americans and to locate the problem in the specific contexts where these events occur.

This article then presents an analysis of our research, applying an event-based approach to provide a conceptual framework. The preliminary results of the research will demonstrate the role weapons have in adolescent violence, and how the presence of firearms contributes to increasingly alarming homicide rates among inner-city adolescents. We will then follow the presentation of our analysis with a section discussing ideas for prevention and intervention to curb gun-related violence among inner-city males.

II

THEORIES OF VIOLENT EVENTS: TOWARD AN INTEGRATED FRAMEWORK

Violence researchers have come to understand dispute-related violent events as a process of social interactions with identifiable rules and contingencies.[6] Numerous studies have applied this framework with respect to violence focusing on the interactional dynamics of situated transactions.[7] The processual nature of violent, interpersonal transactions is both rule oriented and normative.[8] It is through these processes and contingencies that individual characteristics such as "disputatiousness" are channeled into violent events. Violent behavior can

---

to occur are adaptive organizational responses to specific social and cultural contexts. The social exchanges within these networks provide specific motivations and social values that may limit the range of behavioral choices once conflicts arise. Anderson, *The Code of the Streets, supra,* at 82.

6. Felson distinguishes "predatory" violence from dispute-related violence, suggesting that there are processual factors in dispute-related violence that are not evident in "predatory" assaults. Richard B. Felson, *Predatory and Dispute-Related Violence: A Social Interactionist Approach, in* 5 ROUTINE ACTIVITY AND RATIONAL CHOICE, ADVANCES IN CRIMINOLOGICAL THEORY 104-05 (Ronald V.Clarke & Marcus Felson eds., 1993). Predatory violence is defined as physical aggression committed without provocation while dispute-related violence involves a reaction to some alleged wrong. *Id.* However, Katz suggests that even the most seemingly irrational violent acts have a logical and predictable sequence. JACK KATZ, SEDUCTIONS OF CRIME: MORAL AND SENSUAL ATTRACTIONS OF DOING EVIL 9-10 (1988). There may be disputes involved between the aggressor and the victim, but there appears to be no interaction between the two parties preceding the violent act. In these cases, the victim may be a proxy, surrogate or symbolic target for the other disputant. *Id.*

7. Richard B. Felson & Henry J. Steadman, *Situational Factors in Disputes Leading to Criminal Violence,* 21 CRIMINOLOGY 59-60 (1983); David F. Luckenbill, *Criminal Homicide as a Situated Transaction,* 25 SOC. PROBLEMS 176 (1977); Richard B. Felson, *Impression Management and the Escalation of Aggression and Violence,* 45 SOC. PSYCHOL. Q. 245 (1982); ANNE CAMPBELL, THE GIRLS IN THE GANG: A REPORT FROM NEW YORK CITY 28-32 (1984); David F. Luckenbill & Daniel P. Doyle, *Structural Position and Violence: Developing a Cultural Explanation,* 27 CRIMINOLOGY 422-23 (1989); WILLIAM OLIVER, THE VIOLENT SOCIAL WORLD OF BLACK MEN 138-40 (1994).

8. Derek Cornish, Crimes as Scripts, presented at the Second Annual Seminar on Environmental Criminology and Crime Analysis (May 26-28, 1993) (unpublished manuscript, on file with the author).

be viewed as a method of communicating social meanings within contexts where such action is either expected or at least tolerated.

This article argues that the presence of firearms presents a unique contingency that shapes decisionmaking patterns of individuals. The presence of firearms influences decisions both in social interactions with the potential for becoming disputes and also within disputes that have already begun.[9] The influence on decisionmaking is compounded by the social contexts in which firearm injuries are concentrated: inner-city neighborhoods characterized by extensive "resource deprivation."[10] The article specifies two socialization processes that have converged in these areas to create a unique influence of firearms: the emergence of a "street code" that shapes perceptions of grievances and the norms of their resolution,[11] and an "ecology of danger" where social interactions are perceived as threatening or lethal, and where individuals are normatively seen as harboring hostile intent and the willingness to inflict harm. The latter is the product of three successive generations in inner cities who grew up in epochs of high rates of homicide and firearm injuries.

A. Symbolic Interactionism and Social Interaction

Symbolic interactionism offers a useful perspective for examining transactional aspects of violent behavior among two or more individuals. According to Herbert Blumer, "human interaction is mediated by the use of symbols, by interpretation, or by ascertaining the meaning of one another's actions."[12] Human action is processual and begins with observation/sensation that results in an "indication to the self," which is noted and interpreted in order to construct a proper response. It is through this process of self-indication that an individual digests information and begins to formulate a decision for his or her future action. One of the central ideas of symbolic interactionism is "taking each other into account." Blumer has stated that

> taking another person into account means being aware of him, identifying him in some way, making some judgement or appraisal of him, identifying the meaning of his action, trying to find out what he has on his mind or trying to figure out what he intends to do. Such awareness of another person in this sense of taking him and his acts into consideration becomes the occasion for orienting oneself and for the direction of one's own conduct. One takes the other person and his action into account not merely at the point of initial contact, but actually throughout the period of interaction. . . . Perceiving, defining and judging the other person and his action and organizing oneself in terms of such definitions and judgements constitute a continuing or running process.[13]

---

9. *See* Jeffrey Fagan & Deanna L. Wilkinson, *Situational Contexts of Gun Use Events Among Young Males in the Inner City* (proposal submitted to the National Science Foundation) (on file with authors).

10. Kenneth Land et al., *Structural Covariates of Homicide Rates*, 95 AM. J. SOC. 922, 951 (1990).

11. *See, e.g.*, Anderson, *The Code of the Streets*, *supra* note 5, at 82.

12. HERBERT BLUMER, SYMBOLIC INTERACTIONISM: PERSPECTIVE AND METHOD 79 (1969).

13. *Id.* at 109.

Blumer has further noted that an individual also takes his or her own actions into account and makes interpretations.[14]

In his work, Erving Goffman offers many insights into the dynamic social processes of human interaction. Early in his career, Goffman studied the ways in which a person presents an image of himself to others and develops a view of others as social actors.[15] In addition, he studied the ritualistic aspects of social interaction in a variety of different social contexts. Defining interaction as "the reciprocal influence of individuals upon one another's actions when in one another's immediate physical presence," Goffman concluded that the actor could manipulate the impression received by projecting a certain definition of the situation he enters.[16] Goffman explained that "first impressions" were crucial for determining the next stage in most interactions. Other participants in the situations will most often confirm the original definition of the situation consistent with how others around them react or register the event. Under this theory, individual behavior is "scripted" to the extent that scripts are used to convey the kind of impression (or situational identity) an actor wants others to perceive. The importance of status and reputation in this social context influences the scripts an individual may choose when confronted with a dispute on the streets. One could argue that based on whatever limited knowledge is available at the start of the event, an individual will choose a script that casts him or her in the best light.

Goffman later began to focus on linking the micro-dynamics of social interaction with the macro-level forces working to structure such interactions. People create meaning in face-to-face interactions by drawing on local agreements, definitions, and understandings that are upheld during an event.[17] The lesson of an event may continue into the future as the parties have future contact. In an inner-city context, the scope of the repertoire available for the actor is quite limited.[18] The code of the streets operates both at the micro and macro levels through social interaction, cumulative definitions of conflict situations, and replication support for the code.[19]

B. Violence and the Social Interactionist Perspective

The social interactionist perspective also emphasizes the role of social interaction over other "personality" explanations in aggressive behavior.[20] It

---

14. *Id.* at 111.
15. Goffman describes the concepts of "character contests" and "impression management." ERVING GOFFMAN, INTERACTION RITUAL 218-19, 238-57 (1967).
16. ERVING GOFFMAN, THE PRESENTATION OF SELF IN EVERYDAY LIFE 15 (1959).
17. Erving Goffman, *The Interaction Order*, 48 AM. SOC. REV. 1-17 (1983).
18. This is described in detail by Anderson. Anderson, *The Code of the Streets, supra* note 5, at 86-88.
19. *Id.* at 80, 86.
20. See, e.g., Fagan, *supra* note 5 at 179-180, on the influence of set and setting on the outcomes of disputes where the actors have been drinking. Felson also explains different outcomes of barroom disputes (brawls versus crying in one's beer) as the interaction of personality "set" of the actors and

interprets all aggressive behavior as goal oriented or instrumental, that is, as an attempt to achieve what is valued. Social interaction is examined in terms of a rational choice or decisionmaking model. Three main goals of aggressive actions have been identified: (1) to compel and deter others; (2) to achieve a favorable social identity; and (3) to obtain justice.[21] An interactionist perspective is concerned with the actor's point of view. The interactionist approach focuses on describing the factors that produce conflict and those that inhibit it.

According to James Tedeschi and Richard Felson, all violence is goal-oriented behavior, and such behavior is either motivated by the desire to achieve some outcome (terminal values) or is a means of acting (procedural values).[22] It is the valued outcome (goal) that motivates the use of violence and not some involuntary response to aversive stimuli. Tedeschi and Felson explain that the means of achieving the goal are also valued and play a part in fulfilling the objectives of the actor.[23]

Felson and Tedeschi articulate three assumptions of the social interactionist perspective: (1) harm-doing and the threat of harm are motivated by the desire to achieve personal goals; (2) situational factors should be emphasized, including interpersonal relationships between actors, the social interchange between actors, and third parties; and (3) the perceptions, judgments, expectations, and values of the perpetrator need to be examined.[24] Consistent with the rational choice perspective, they argue that a violent action involves a sequence of decisions and that an actor evaluates alternatives before carrying out a violent action. Four elements of decisions were outlined: the value of the outcome; the expectations of success in reaching the goal; the value of the costs; and the expectations of the costs.[25] Costs and the presence of third parties can inhibit violence.[26] The actor makes a choice to engage in violent behavior because it seems to be the best alternative available in the situation.

Felson and Tedeschi also explain that a decisionmaker is typically operating under some type of decision rule. They described two rules: the "minimax" principle (maximum benefits and minimize costs) and the "satisficing" principle (good enough).[27] A decisionmaking framework thus examines what goes on

---

the social control mechanisms present in the "setting." Richard B. Felson et al., *Barroom Brawls: Aggression and Violence in Irish and American Bars, in* VIOLENT TRANSACTIONS 153, 163-65 (Anne Campbell & John Gibbs eds., 1986).

21. KATZ, *supra* note 6, at 18-19; Felson, *supra* note 6, at 105.

22. JAMES T. TEDESCHI & RICHARD B. FELSON, VIOLENCE, AGGRESSION, AND COERCIVE ACTIONS 22 (1994) (departing greatly from previous work in the area of violence research primarily because of the claim that all violent behaviors (coercive actions) are instrumental or goal-oriented behavior).

23. *Id.*

24. Richard B. Felson & James T. Tedeschi, *A Social Interactionist Approach to Violence: Cross-cultural Applications, in* INTERPERSONAL VIOLENT BEHAVIORS: SOCIAL AND CULTURAL ASPECTS 153-54 (Ruback Barry & Neil Alan Weiner eds., 1995).

25. *Id.* at 154-55.

26. *Id.* at 154, 162.

27. TEDESCHI & FELSON, *supra* note 22, at 182.

in the actor's mind during a violent event in terms of weighing the rewards and costs of an action while in pursuit of a desired outcome. If an actor determines that the benefits outweigh the costs of a violent action, then he chooses to engage in the action.[28] This decisionmaking process thus becomes extremely complicated in a social environment where the choices in handling a situation may be limited to "takin' care of your business" (with a gun) or losing face on the street.[29]

C. Violence as Situated Transactions

David Luckenbill and Daniel Doyle have argued that interpersonal disputes are the products of three successive events: "naming," "claiming," and "aggressing."[30] At the naming stage, the first actor identifies a negative outcome as an injury caused by the second actor (assigning blame).[31] At the claiming stage, the injured party expresses his grievance and demands reparation from the adversary. It is the final stage that determines whether or not the interaction is transformed into a dispute. According to Luckenbill and Doyle, "disputatiousness" is defined as the likelihood of naming and claiming, and aggressiveness is defined as the willingness to preserve and use force to settle the dispute. They claim that violence is triggered by norms of the code of personal honor and that differential disputatiousness and aggressiveness would depend on the situation.[32] This article argues that increased availability of guns, especially among adolescents, changes these processes in important ways that are not fully understood at this time. The stages of violent events are altered by the presence, expectancies, and lethal nature of firearms in specific social contexts.

Later research has used a similar event-centered approach to examine the interactive processes leading to criminal violence.[33] Using official data from 159 incidents of homicide and assault (where suspects were incarcerated), Felson and Steadman developed a detailed action-unit coding scheme for the data. They found that the incidents tended to follow systematic patterns, beginning with identity attacks, followed by attempts and failures to influence the

---

28. Felson & Tedeschi, *supra* note 24, at 154-55.
29. *Id.* at 156.
30. Luckenbill & Doyle, *supra* note 7, at 419, 423 (*relying on* Luckenbill, *supra* note 7).
31. *Id.*
32. *Id.* at 425. This conceptualization closely resembles Goffman's "character contest" used by Luckenbill to examine violent transactions resulting in homicide. Luckenbill, *supra* note 7, at 177. According to Luckenbill and Doyle, a character contest goes something like this:

> [O]ne begins by attacking another's identity, challenging his or her claim to a valued position in a situation. The other defines the attack as offensive and retaliates, attempting to restore identity either by threatening to injure the challenger if he or she does not back down or by using force to make the challenger if he or she does not withdraw or by using limited force to make the challenger withdraw. Rather than back down and show weakness, the challenger maintains or intensifies the attack. Fearing a show of weakness and loss of face, and recognizing that peaceful or mildly aggressive means have failed to settle the dispute, one or both mobilize available weapons and use massive force, leaving one dead or dying.

Luckenbill & Doyle, *supra* note 7, at 423.
33. Felson & Steadman, *supra* note 7, at 60.

opponent, then verbal threats, and finally, ending in physical attack. Retaliation, escalation, and aggressiveness of the victim were found to be important factors. This study, albeit limited methodologically, illustrates the usefulness of a processual analysis of violent events. Detailed narratives on incidents, offered voluntarily without prejudicial motive, both discovered by law enforcement and those that go unnoticed, may provide insights that previous research using official data could not.

An even later study used detailed narratives of violent confrontations between black males in bars and bar settings.[34] In a study of forty-one adult African-American males, a five-stage sequence of events was observed that is similar to Felson and Steadman's previous classification. The first stage was characterized by a perception that an antagonist committed an act that represented a potential threat to the respondent's manhood, physical safety, and/or reputation.[35] The second stage involved an attempt to clarify the antagonist's intentions. This step also included an attempt to confirm one's definition of the situation. Stage three was the development of a plan of action and the actual physical confrontation. The fourth stage was the conclusion of the confrontation.[36] The final stage of the sequence of events was described as post-incident aftermath including psychological and behavioral adjustments. This analysis once again illustrates the importance of situational factors.[37]

Although the study did not specifically focus on gun-use events, many of the events described involved the use of weapons. Older respondents (men in their thirties to forties), explained that weapons had changed the dynamics of interpersonal violence. Fighting on the street was characterized as being unfair because of the power of guns, and carrying a weapon resulted from a lack of closure in an on-going interpersonal conflict. The study concluded that respondents packed a weapon because they anticipated violence or retaliation in the future and/or they knew from previous transactions that the antagonist had a weapon.[38]

Equally important in the study of situated transactions are the techniques of avoidance and dispute diffusion. Previous studies have looked exclusively at completed actions that resulted in some sort of criminal justice involvement.[39] Other examinations have been similarly one-sided and may have distorted our understanding of situated transactions more generally. Little is known about events that do not end in physical fights or the firing of a weapon.[40]

---

34. OLIVER, *supra* note 7, at 3-4, 43-47.
35. *Id.* at 153.
36. *Id.* at 138. The conclusion included three types of endings: symbolic; overt; and internal. *Id.*
37. *Id.* at 139-40, 151-52.
38. *Id.* at 130-32.
39. *See, e.g.,* Luckenbill, *supra* note 7, at 176-77; *Criminal Homicide as a Situated Transaction,* 25 SOCIAL PROBLEMS 176-77 (1977); David F. Luckenbill, *Patterns of Force in Robbery,* 1 DEVIANT BEHAVIOR 361-378 (1980); Felson & Steadman, *supra* note 7, at 61.
40. We are currently gathering information on diffused and "squashed" events to better understand the realm of possible scripts existing in the world of active gun users. *See* Fagan & Wilkinson, *supra*

D. The Code of the Streets

Firearm violence represents an extreme on a continuum of violence in the dynamics of inner-city youths. "Fair fights" have always been the most elementary form of interpersonal violence among inner-city youths, and perceived insults or transgressions typically have been grounds for fighting.[41] Until the 1960s, fatalities were rare, whether by firearm or any other weapon, and the circumstances that called for fighting generally were confined to territorial disputes, ritual displays of toughness, or family and ethnic solidarity. Rising homicide rates among inner-city adolescents in recent years suggest sharp changes in this social and behavioral landscape.

Yet, few studies have examined the current social worlds of young inner-city males in depth.[42] Elijah Anderson's study of inner-city Philadelphia is perhaps the most detailed description of violence and inner-city life.[43] According to Anderson, the causes of inner-city violence are both structurally and situationally determined.[44] He proposes that there are two types of normative systems operating within the inner-city context: the "decent" (locked into middle class values) families and the "street" (opposed to mainstream society) families.[45] He argues that while the majority of inner-city residents are of the "decent" orientation, the street orientation has come to govern the normative system regarding human behavior in public spaces, especially among the young. Thus community norms on the street are regulated and enforced by the smaller minority who possess the street orientation.

The street code has a strong influence over the behaviors of young children, adolescents, and young adults. Accordingly, children growing up in this environment learn the "code of the streets" by navigating their way through interpersonal situations that often involve violent encounters. The street code provides rules for how individuals are to communicate with one another, how respect is to be earned, how and when respect is to be granted, and what should

---

note 9.

41. *See, e.g.,* ELIJAH ANDERSON, A PLACE ON THE CORNER (1978); RICHARD A. CLOWARD & LLOYD E. OHLIN, DELINQUENCY AND OPPORTUNITY: A THEORY OF DELINQUENT GANGS 3, 14, 178 (1960); JAMES F. SHORT & FREDERICK L. STRODTBECK, GROUP PROCESS AND GANG DELINQUENCY 251-54 (1965); GERALD D. SUTTLES, THE SOCIAL ORDER OF THE SLUM: ETHNICITY AND TERRITORY IN THE INNER CITY 323-52 (1968); FREDERICK M. THRASHER, THE GANG: A STUDY OF 1,313 GANGS IN CHICAGO (1927); WILLIAM F. WHYTE, STREET CORNER SOCIETY: THE SOCIAL SUBCULTURE OF AN ITALIAN SLUM 5-6 (1981); JAMES D. VIGIL, BARRIO GANGS: STREET LIFE AND IDENTITY IN SOUTHER CALIFORNIA 129 (1988).

42. *But, see* Anderson, *The Code of the Streets, supra* note 5; CANADA, *supra* note 5; MERCER L. SULLIVAN, "GETTING PAID": YOUTH CRIME AND WORK IN THE INNER CITY 1-18 (1989); Fagan & Wilkinson, *supra* note 9.

43. Anderson, *The Code of the Streets, supra* note 5, at 80-94.

44. *Id.* at 81. "The inclination to violence springs from the circumstances of life among the ghetto poor—the lack of jobs that pay a living wage, the stigma of race, the fallout from rampant drug use and drug trafficking, and the resulting alienation and lack of hope for the future." *Id.*

45. *Id.* at 83.

happen when someone disrespects or "disses" you.[46] Violence and other types of domination are tools in promoting one's self-image, in other words, conquering others is one way of achieving higher levels of status.[47]

Anderson is mostly silent on the issue of lethal violence by firearms. Although he states that possessing a willingness to "pull the trigger" is an important part of an individual's quest for respect, he does not analyze the implications of gun use in the code of the streets.[48] The availability of guns in the inner-city has undoubtedly raised the stakes even higher. It seems that "nerve," "toughness," and being a "punk" would take on new meanings within a climate regulated by lethally armed actors. This increased availability of guns in our inner-cities and the corresponding problems they pose have the subject of concern beginning in the late eighties.[49]

E. Violence as Scripted Behavior

Script theory offers a way of generalizing, organizing, and systematizing knowledge about the processual aspects and requirements of crime commission. The theory borrows heavily from cognitive psychology and was first articulated by Robert Abelson in 1976.[50] According to Abelson, a script is a cognitive structure or framework that, when activated, organizes a person's understanding of typical situations, allowing the person to have expectations and to make conclusions about the potential result of a set of events.[51] He explains:

> The script concept raises and sketchily addresses a number of fundamental psychological issues: within cognitive psychology, the nature of knowledge structures for representing ordinary experience; within social psychology, the way in which social reality is constructed and how constructions of reality translate into social behavior through action rules; in learning and developmental psychology, how and what knowledge structures are learned in the course of ordinary experience; in clinical psychology, how resonances between present situations and past schemata can preempt behavior maladaptively.[52]

The concept of "procedural scripts" was introduced in a recent theoretical paper on offender's decisionmaking processes.[53] Studying crimes as *scripts*

---

46. *Id.* at 82.
47. *Id.* at 88-89.
48. *Id.* at 92.
49. SULLIVAN, *supra* note 42, at 112. Sullivan reported that there were more guns on the streets and that they were more frequently in the hands of younger offenders. *Id.*
50. Robert P. Abelson, *Script Processing in Attitude Formation and Decision-making, in* COGNITION AND SOCIAL BEHAVIOR 33 (J.S. Carroll & J. W. Payne eds., 1976).
51. Robert P. Abelson, *Psychological Status of the Script Concept,* 36 AM. PSYCHOL. 717 (1981).
52. *Id.* at 727.
53. Cornish, *supra* note 8, at 7-10. Cornish's conception of "scripts" and scripted behavior varies slightly from the type of script discussed by Tedeschi and Felson. TEDESCHI & FELSON, *supra* note 22, at 181-83. Cornish's "script" focuses in detail on the step-by-step procedures of committing crime that are learned, stored in memory, and enacted when situational cues are present. Tedeschi and Felson's use of the concept of scripts is as a way of explaining behavior that is seemingly impulsive (nonrational) as habitual learned responses to situational cues, which involves a limited number of decisions over which script is most cost effective in a given situation. While different in emphasis, both usages should be explored in the future research in this area. Derek Cornish, *The Procedural Analysis of Offending,*

provides another useful framework for understanding the decisionmaking process involved in gun-use events.[54]

Research on child and adolescent violence suggests several ways in which script theory can explain violent events: (1) scripts are ways of organizing knowledge and behavioral choices;[55] (2) individuals learn behavioral repertoires for different situations;[56] (3) these repertoires are stored in memory as scripts and are elicited when cues are sensed in the environment;[57] (4) choice of scripts varies between individuals, and some individuals will have limited choices;[58] (5) individuals are more likely to repeat scripted behaviors when the previous experience was considered successful;[59] and (6) scripted behavior may become "automatic" without much thought or weighing of consequences.[60]

The application of script theory to adolescent gun events as "situated transactions" may provide a level of understanding to a complex process that is not well understood. Adolescents are likely to look to the streets for lessons on the rules of gun fighting, learn from experience in conflict situations, and practice moves they have observed others performing in handling disputes on the street.[61] The processes of learning and diffusion of this sort of gun "knowledge" remain unstudied and unknown.

What is needed are studies that will analyze interactions that involve young males and firearms using an event-based approach. This approach does not deny the importance of the individual attributes that bring people to situations, such as "disputatiousness," but recognizes that once there, other processes shape the outcomes of these events.[62] Events are analyzed as "situated transactions," including rules that develop within specific socio-cultural contexts, the situations and contexts where weapons are used, the motivations for carrying and using weapons, and the personality "sets" of groups where weapons are used. There are "rules" that govern how disputes are settled, when and where firearms are used or avoided, and the significance of firearms within a broader adolescent culture. We need to understand these processes in order to have any hope of

---

in 3 CRIME PREVENTION STUDIES 151-196 (R.V. Clarke ed., 1994).

54. *See* Cornish, *supra* note 8; Cornish, *supra* note 53, at 151-96 ("The unfolding of a crime involves a variety of sequential dependencies within and between elements of the action: crimes are pushed along or impeded by situational contingencies—situated motives; opportunities in terms of settings; victims and targets; the presence of co-offenders; facilitators, such as guns and cars.").

55. Abelson, *supra* note 50, at 35-36.

56. RICHARD SCHANK & ROBERT ABELSON, SCRIPTS, PLANS, GOALS AND UNDERSTANDING: AN INQUIRY INTO HUMAN KNOWLEDGE STRUCTURE 36-37 (1977); TEDESCHI & FELSON, *supra* note 22, at 181; Abelson, *supra* note 51, at 717; Rowell L. Huesmann, *An Information Processing Model for the Development of Aggression*, 14 AGGRESSIVE BEHAV. 14-16 (1988).

57. TEDESCHI & FELSON, VIOLENCE, *supra* note 22, at 182; Abelson, *supra* note 51, at 716-17, 719; Kenneth A. Dodge & Nicki Crick, *Social Information Processing Bases of Aggressive Behavior in Children*, 16 PERSONALITY & SOC. PSYCHOL. BULL. 8, 12-14 (1990); Huesmann, *supra* note 56, at 14-16.

58. Dodge & Crick, *supra* note 57, at 14-15.

59. SCHANK & ABELSON, *supra* note 56, at 55-64; TEDESCHI & FELSON, *supra* note 22, at 181.

60. TEDESCHI & FELSON, *supra* note 22, at 181; Abelson, *supra* note 51, at 717.

61. Anderson, *supra* note 5, at 86; CANADA, *supra* note 5, at 21, 35.

62. Luckenbill & Doyle, *supra* note 7, at 422-23.

intervening in future potentially explosive situations. Thus, research must examine both the symbolic and instrumental meanings of firearms in the lives of young males. We are currently engaged in a qualitative study of this nature to reconstruct the stages and transactions within gun events among inner-city adolescent males.[63] Preliminary findings of this study are presented below.

III

FIREARMS AND ADOLESCENT VIOLENCE: HISTORICAL PERSPECTIVES

The use of firearms by adolescents is part of several recurrent delinquency problems. First, delinquent groups and street gangs in the United States have been involved in struggles to dominate urban areas for well over two centuries. Luc Sante describes the sometimes deadly and oftentimes comical struggles between early street gangs of New York City to control territory and assert their authority.[64] In the late eighteenth century, gangs such as the Fly Boys, the Smith's Vly gang, and the Bowery Boys were well known in the streets of New York City. As European immigration increased in the early nineteenth century, gangs such as the Kerryonians (from County Kerry in Ireland) and the Forty Thieves formed in the overcrowded slums of the Lower East Side.[65] These gangs warred regularly over territory with weapons including stones, hobnail boots (good for kicking), and early versions of the blackjack. Guns were rarely mentioned until the era following the Draft Riots of 1863, when gangs fought with every weapon then available including pistols, muskets, and (rarely) canons.[66] As smaller and more portable guns were developed, they became an important part of the milieu of gangs and street groups over the ensuing decades. Guns played a strategic role in settling conflicts and asserting dominance in matters of honor, territory, and business.

Historians are quick to point out that many of the perceived social sources of violence and homicide in the post-modern United States were as common in the late nineteenth and early twentieth centuries as they are today: rapid urbanization, population mobility, ethnic tensions, abuse of intoxicants, class conflicts, and the spread of cheap handguns.[67] Yet, for much of the nineteenth century, homicide rates were declining.[68] With the advent of concealable handguns around 1850, homicide rates rose slightly but not enough to offset a long downward trend that had begun early in the nineteenth century.[69] These declines were part of a 150-year historical trend where violence reached its ebb

---

63. Fagan & Wilkinson, *supra* note 9.
64. LUC SANTE, LOW LIFE: LURES AND SNARES OF OLD NEW YORK 219 (1991).
65. *Id.*
66. *Id.* at 201.
67. ROGER LANE, VIOLENT DEATH IN THE CITY: SUICIDE, ACCIDENT AND MURDER IN NINETEENTH-CENTURY PHILADELPHIA 6-10 (1979); Roger Lane, *On the Social Meaning of Homicide Trends in America, in* VIOLENCE IN AMERICA, PART I, 55-79 (Ted R. Gurr ed., 1989).
68. Ted R. Gurr, *Historical Trends in Violent Crime: A Critical Review of the Evidence, in* 3 CRIME AND JUSTICE: AN ANNUAL REVIEW OF RESEARCH 324-27 (Michael Tonry & Norval Morris eds., 1981).
69. *Id.* at 316.

as the twentieth century began. The urbanization and modernization of the coming century offered new economic opportunities to both immigrants and migrants to the cities from rural areas which in turn fostered social controls.

Firearms played a prominent role in the growth of organized crime groups, beginning in the 1920s. These groups employed teenagers and street gangs in a variety of support roles, from running numbers to serving as lookouts for illegal gambling operations or liquor distribution points.[70] Bootlegging and gambling provided a career ladder for teenagers. Of seventy-two "important" bootleggers identified by law enforcement authorities in the 1920s, most were young men in the later teenage years or early twenties.[71] Firearms were a prominent part of the security system used to protect liquor shipments, and documents from bootleggers and smugglers claim there was more danger from "rum pirates" than from other bootleggers or the police. However, despite the involvement of adolescents in street gangs and emerging organized crime groups, there is little evidence that this led to the use of guns by teenagers.

During this time, problems of youth crime were serious enough to prompt the creation of juvenile courts in nearly every state in the United States.[72] However, the crimes that motivated these reforms rarely involved violence or weapons.[73] Even in this era when youth gangs were increasingly a part of the urban landscape, there was little mention of adolescent use of firearms in homicides or robberies.[74] Nationwide, Uniform Crime Report data reveals that homicides increased from the turn of the century into the early 1930s, and then declined from 1933 to the early 1960s.[75] The majority of local studies on homicides confirmed this trend. Throughout this period, differentials in homicide death rates between African-Americans and whites were quite pronounced.[76] Yet, none of these studies examined adolescent rates separately from adult rates. Their silence must indicate either no noticeable differences between adolescents and adults, or that the base rates among adolescents were so small that they were not worth mentioning.

Nor was there much discussion of firearms in studies of delinquency from the Chicago School beginning in the 1920s. For nearly forty years, violence

---

70. Mark H. Haller, *Bootlegging: The Business and Politics of Violence, in* VIOLENCE IN AMERICA, PART I, 146-62 (Ted R. Gurr ed., 1989).

71. *Id.* at 148.

72. STEVEN SCHLOSSMAN, LOVE AND THE AMERICAN DELINQUENT: THE THEORY AND PRACTICE OF "PROGRESSIVE" JUVENILE JUSTICE, 1825-1920 (1977).

73. James Bourdouris, Trends in Homicide, Detroit, 1926-1968 (1970) (unpublished Ph.D. dissertation, Wayne State University) (on file with author).

74. *See id.* For example, the analysis by Bourdouris of homicides in Detroit from 1926-68 does not mention adolescents. The data provide a composite picture of homicides as the product of quarrels between family members, lovers, or two males. Murders during robberies were rare. *Id.*

75. *See* Margaret Zahn, *Homicide in the Twentieth Century United States, in* HISTORY AND CRIME: IMPLICATIONS FOR CRIMINAL JUSTICE POLICY 28-63 (James Inciardi & Charles Faupel eds., 1980).

76. *See, e.g.,* MARVIN WOLFGANG & FRANCO FERRACUTI, THE SUBCULTURE OF VIOLENCE: TOWARD AN INTEGRATED THEORY IN CRIMINOLOGY 263-64 (1967).

among youth gangs involved fighting.[77] While both common and makeshift weapons were used strategically in gang fights, firearms were extremely rare.[78] Throughout this era, fighting was integral to the group identification of gangs and a central part of group interaction. Behavioral norms developed around fighting, and fighting had several meanings in gang life.[79]

By the 1960s, discussions of firearms in the literature on youth violence were more frequent, but not central in the delinquency literature. Although guns were prevalent in "streetcorner life," there were distinct situations where they were used and there were rules governing their use. They had a symbolic meaning in addition to their instrumental value, and generally represented a threshold of commitment to street life. Guns were rarely used by adolescents outside these contexts. Several studies of streetcorner life casually mentioned the presence of firearms and their use in settling interpersonal disputes.[80] R. Lincoln Keiser's portrait of the Vice Lords also showed that weapons were not central to gang life, but were used selectively and strategically in conflicts with other gangs and in gang "business."[81] Among both gangs and "near groups," guns were valued as defensive weapons but sometimes also for offensive purposes.[82]

Guns often were carried for show, with little intention to use them.[83] Guns were used for impression management—that is, to convey to others that someone with a gun "means business" and is a person to be taken seriously. In some groups, people carrying guns, or even threatening to use them, could be easily dissuaded from shooting if face-saving alternatives were presented.[84]

Gun use also was confined to specific situations and contingencies. In one reported incident, an important figure in a leadership clique brandished a weapon to break up a fight among gang members and then shot three gang

---

77. *See* THRASHER, *supra* note 41; Jeffrey Fagan, *The Social Organization of Drug Use and Drug Dealing Among Urban Gangs,* 27 CRIMINOLOGY 633, 634 (1989); Jeffrey Fagan, *Gangs, Drugs, & Neighborhood Change, in* GANGS IN AMERICA 39, 41, 44-45 (Ronald Huff ed., 2nd ed. 1996).

78. Through the important works of the 1950s, firearms again were not mentioned as part of the everyday life of gang members or other delinquent youths. *See* ALBERT COHEN, DELINQUENT BOYS: THE CULTURE OF THE GANG (1955); CLOWARD & OHLIN, *supra* note 41, at 198. While some youths no doubt had and used weapons, firearms had a limited role in the social processes of delinquency.

79. LEWIS YABLONSKY, THE VIOLENT GANG 175-83 (1962); Irving A. Spergel, *Violent Gangs in Chicago: In Search of Social Policy,* 58 SOC. SCI. REV. 199-225 (1984); Walter B. Miller, Violence By Youth Gangs and Youth Groups as a Crime Problem in Major American Cities, Address to the National Institute for Juvenile Justice and Delinquency Prevention (1975) (on file with author).

80. ANDERSON, A PLACE ON THE CORNER, *supra* note 41; ULF HANNERZ, SOULSIDE: INQUIRIES INTO GHETTO CULTURE AND COMMUNITY (1969); ELLIOT LIEBOW, TALLEY'S CORNER: A STUDY OF NEGRO STREETCORNER MEN (1967); SUTTLES, *supra* note 41, at 198-201.

81. R. LINCOLN KEISER, THE VICE LORDS: WARRIORS OF THE STREETS 29-30, 34-36 (1969).

82. *Id.* at 31-34.

83. Walter Bernstein, *The Cherubs are Rumbling, in* GANG DELINQUENCY AND DELINQUENT SUBCULTURES 36, 45 (James F. Short, Jr. ed., 1968) (describing life in a gang of about 35 Italian-American teenagers in the Park Slope neighborhood of Brooklyn). In Bernstein's account, guns were carried by only a very few members of the Cherubs, and almost never used. *Id.* at 36, 45, 48.

84. *Id.* at 37.

members when the incident unfolded in a way that challenged his authority.[85] The decision to shoot has been characterized as a complex decision, reflecting elements of cognitive mediation of the risks and reward of alternative outcomes, which is a function of a utility-risk paradigm where choices are contingent on in situ evaluations of these risks and rewards.[86] The actor was motivated by the threat to his leadership status.[87] Guns were used as a last resort, primarily because of the risks of arrest; but the risks of not using the gun to his status in the gang and in the neighborhood were also quite high.[88] Finally, though it appears that the threat of retaliatory gun use was not evident in this incident.

In that era, guns were a minor part of street scenes of delinquent youths, and usually only within the province of the "toughest" youths or the leadership of delinquent groups. Guns were more often shown than used, their use was contingent and episodic, and gun episodes primarily were defensive or status conferring. Motivations for carrying and using guns often revolved around status concerns, and only after alternate outcomes had narrowed were guns actually fired.

In contrast to the rare but serious discussions of guns in the gang literature in the 1960s, similar discussions of guns in the 1970s gang literature were more frequent and their influence on interpersonal violence was more widespread. The presence of guns had become an important influence on trends in violence in central cities.[89] In addition to violence toward other gangs, gun violence was also used to redress grievances against businesses and resolve personal disputes over women or drugs.[90]

IV

FIREARMS IN CONTEXT

Several studies on specific contexts of violence (for example, gangs, drug markets, robberies) suggest that gun use is infrequent and contingent, part of a context of a *"situated transaction."*[91] In fact, many of these studies are somewhat casual in reporting the presence of guns, merely noting that they are

---

85. *See* Fred L. Strodtbeck & James F. Short, Jr., *Aleatory Risks Versus Short-Run Hedonism in Explanation of Gang Action, in* GANG DELINQUENCY AND DELINQUENT SUBCULTURES 277-78 (James F. Short, Jr. ed., 1968).

86. *Id.* at 279-82.

87. *Id.* at 279.

88. There was cultural value to the action, as well, that enhanced the leader's status. He did not carry the weapon. In that incident, it was passed to him. The expectation of using guns was fairly high for specific types of conflicts. Beyond gangs and near groups, the fear of guns and community support for their use reflected what Strodtbeck and Short described as the widespread fear of sudden violence and the inability of police to stop it. *Id.* at 283-84. Guns were status conferring, and a valuable asset in a context where disputes are common, where they tend to be settled by violence, and where demonstrations of "toughness" are appropriate.

89. JOAN MOORE, HOMEBOYS 40 (1978) (describing how behavior patterns were accelerated by each successive generation of *klikas*).

90. VIGIL, *supra* note 41, at 130-36.

91. Luckenbill, *supra* note 7, at 184-85; Felson, *supra* note 6.

common features of these scenes.[92] One consequence is that the influence of guns has not been carefully examined.

For example, although gangs have always been a venue where weapons were prevalent, but the presence and types of weapons have changed the stakes and calculus of gang violence. One study reported that 40.8 percent of incidents of gang violence in San Diego in 1988 were drive-by shootings, up from 23.7 percent in 1981.[93] Although drive-bys were favored by gangs over twenty years ago, the increase in the use of manufactured guns has de-emphasized the importance of fist-fighting in resolving gang conflicts.[94] If gangs are an important context of gun use, the growing number of gangs and gang youths may have increased market demand for guns. As gangs emerge in cities and new gangs form, and consequently more adolescents join gangs, the simple probability of a conflict between gangs and gang members grows.[95] If guns proscribe the rules and nature of settling gang conflicts, the likelihood of disputes settled by guns increases, as does the frequency of conflict.

Although drug markets are another context where gun possession is common, the precise relationship between drugs and guns is uncertain. Homicides by and of young males continue to rise or remain stable even as drug markets contract.[96] Many homicides seem to be unrelated or tangential to drugs, involving material goods or personal slights.[97] While the increase in homicides may have at one time reflected the expansion of the drug market, homicides may now—nearly a decade after the emergence of crack markets—reflect the residual effects of those markets. That is, guns that entered street networks during the expansion of drug markets remained part of the street ecology even as the drug economy subsided.[98]

Firearm use in robbery is the paradigm instrumental violent crime in the American consciousness. Because of its unpredictability and the threat of serious harm, it is one of the most feared crimes. Especially among adolescents, robberies often are unplanned or hastily planned events, the result of the instantaneous confluence of motivation and opportunity.[99] Guns provide a tactical advantage in robberies, even beyond the advantage first created by the selection of time and circumstances. The choice of "coercive lethal resources"

---

92. *See, e.g.,* Luckenbill, *supra* note 7, at 184-85.
93. WILLIAM SANDERS, GANGBANGS AND DRIVEBYS: GROUNDED CULTURE AND JUVENILE GANG VIOLENCE 67 (1994).
94. Miller, *supra* note 79.
95. Jeffrey Fagan, *Drug Selling and Illicit Income in Distressed Neighborhoods: The Economic Lives of Street-level Drug users and Dealers, in* DRUGS, CRIME AND SOCIAL ISOLATION: BARRIERS TO URBAN OPPORTUNITY 99-142 (George Peterson & Adelle Harrell eds., 1992).
96. UNDERSTANDING AND PREVENTING VIOLENCE 188 (Albert J Reiss, Jr. & Jeffrey A. Roth eds., 1993).
97. Fagan, *Gangs, Drugs, & Neighborhood Change, supra* note 77, at 44.
98. ANSLEY HAMID, BEAMING UP 1-40 (1994).
99. Franklin E. Zimring & James Zuehl, *Victim Injury and Death in Urban Robbery: A Chicago Study,* 15 J. LEGAL ISSUES 1-40 (1986).

(weapon or no weapon) determines the offenders opening move and the subsequent patterns of behavior in the robbery event.[100]

In reality, the increased availability and lethal nature of firearms has resulted in offenders taking on "risky or harder" targets, anticipating little or no resistance when using a lethal weapon and relying upon threat of force, which may or may not be followed up by use of force.[101] Offenders can do more with lethal weapons and be successful at it.[102] In robberies, victims are more likely to be injured by unarmed (non-gun) offenders than by offenders with a gun.[103] Victims are sufficiently intimidated by the weapon to comply more readily with the offender's demands.[104] However, Philip Cook notes that the presence of a firearm does open the way for a robbery to become a homicide.[105]

While firearms may often be present during robberies, their use in the course of a robbery reflects other contingencies, such as "recreational violence."[106] There are predictable stages for the robbery event, and when responses fail to meet the robber's expectations, threatened violence may become actual to gain compliance or to get the event back on its planned course.[107] Difficulties are introduced in robbery situations when victims (or third parties) do not adhere to the robbery "script." At that point, the offender is faced with the decision to back up his lethal threats with action. This stage in the event may be complicated by the young offenders' limited reasoning ability. Adolescence is a developmental stage when abstract reasoning about the consequences of using guns and cognitive capacities to read social cues are incomplete.[108] The choices in these situations may be seen as "black and white" or "all or nothing" for the adolescent robber. During the course of a robbery, the teenager armed with a gun (presumably inexperienced) becomes an unstable actor in a scenario whose outcomes are dependent on a predictable set of interactions between the robber and his victim. It is when the initial definition of the situation strays from robbery to a threat, personal slight, or conflict (in the wake of resistance) that seemingly irrational violence occurs. When guns are present, the violence often results in death.

---

100. Luckenbill, *supra* note 39, at 367 (concluding that "based on the observations of the interviewed offenders, that offenders with lethal resources open the transformation process with a threat of force, whereas offenders with nonlethal resources open with incapacitating force").

101. Wesley Skogan, *Weapon Use in Robbery*, *in* VIOLENT CRIME: HISTORICAL AND CONTEMPORARY ISSUES 68 (James A. Inciardi & Ann E. Pottieger eds., 1978).

102. *Id.*

103. Philip J. Cook, *Reducing Injury and Death Rates in Robbery*, 6 POLICY ANALYSIS 36-37 (1980).

104. *Id.* at 36.

105. *Id.* at 42.

106. Zimring & Zuehl, *supra* note 99.

107. Skogan, *supra* note 101, at 64-65; Floyd Feeney, *Robbers as Decision Makers*, *in* THE REASONING CRIMINAL: RATIONAL CHOICE PERSPECTIVES ON OFFENDING 53, 66-71 (Ronald V. Clarke & Derek B. Cornish eds., 1986).

108. JEROME KAGAN, UNSTABLE IDEAS: TEMPERAMENT, COGNITION, AND SELF 10-15 (1989).

Once again, these studies illustrate the highly contextualized patterns of gun use by young males, and the importance of guns as part of the contingencies of violence in disputes. They suggest that guns are part of the ecology in inner cities, and have become a variable in event decisionmaking during disputes. The symbolic and instrumental meanings of violent behavior develop in a specific socio-cultural context, and we will expect that they will reflect the physical and social isolation that young people experience in inner-cities. This context may shape how young males develop a range of behavioral styles and evaluate the contingencies of behavioral choices. Advanced segregation[109] and social isolation[110] of inner-city communities create social boundaries that effectively seal off adolescent networks from potentially moderating influences of other social contexts. In these circumstances, cultural diffusion transmits such views and behavioral norms quite efficiently.[111] High levels of exposure to violence, including witnessing or participating in the death of peers, friends, family members, or neighbors, has become a way of life for too many inner-city adolescents. Thus, these adolescents are exposed to a limited set of problem-solving techniques and when conflict or threatening situations occur, violence is often one of the few options available. Adolescents simply do what they know in these situations. The handling of one situation by using violence feeds into the next situation, and so on. The costs of violence to the offender, including death by gunfire, are rated very low in this context, especially compared to his criminal goals.[112] Futures, especially for males, are seen as tenuous both in terms of survival into adulthood and any hope of being successful in life.

> Lacking an attainable future, or at least the belief in one, and absent models of deferred gratification and conventional success, it is all too easy to see how life can quickly become a quest for the immediate gratification of present impulses, a moment-to-moment existence where weighing the consequences of today's behavior against their future implications is largely pointless.[113]

Thus, what may appear as a problem of impulsive violence may in fact reflect a calculation of the benefits of restraint compared to the short term payoffs from high-risk acts of violence.[114]

---

109. DOUGLAS S. MASSEY & NANCY A. DENTON, AMERICAN APARTHEID: SEGREGATION AND THE MAKING OF THE UNDERCLASS 160-62 (1993).

110. Sampson & Wilson, *supra* note 3, at 37-54.

111. *See, e.g.*, Marta Tienda, *Poor People and Poor Places: Deciphering Neighborhood Effects on Poverty Outcomes*, in MACRO-MICRO LINKAGES IN SOCIOLOGY 244, 249-50 (Joan Huber ed., 1991).

112. ALEXANDER KOTLOWITZ, THERE ARE NO CHILDREN HERE (1991); Anderson, *The Code of the Streets*, *supra* note 5, at 92.

113. JOSEPH SHELEY & JAMES WRIGHT, IN THE LINE OF FIRE: YOUTH, GUNS, AND VIOLENCE IN URBAN AMERICA 160 (1995).

114. In this context driven by fear, young people believe that life is dangerous, that anything (fatal) can happen at any time, and that having a gun is a necessary, if not attractive, option. LH Research, *supra* note 1, at ix. The more that guns are present within their social networks, the more they seem normative and the more inured kids become to the realities of guns. In a world where they see themselves as having no power or control over the dangers and fears they evoke, guns provide a means to reduce fear and regain some defense against ever-present threats and enemies. Some young males

V

CHARACTERISTICS AND RISK FACTORS OF ADOLESCENT GUN VIOLENCE

Most of what we know about young people and guns comes either from newspaper and magazine features or a very small number of student surveys. The surveys typically measure student attitudes, behaviors, and opinions about guns in the school environment, and attempt to locate characteristics and attitudes of youths who carry or use firearms.

A. The LH Survey

The most recent survey, by LH Research, questioned 2,508 adolescents in ninety-six randomly selected elementary, middle, and senior high schools.[115] The results showed that handguns were a significant part of their everyday social ecology. About one in seven (fifteen percent) reported carrying a handgun in the past thirty days, and four percent reported taking a handgun to school during the year.[116] Nine percent of the students reported shooting a gun at someone else, while eleven percent had been shot at during the past year.[117] Thirty-nine percent of the youths reported that they personally knew someone who had been either killed or injured from gun fire.[118] Twenty-two percent reported that carrying a handgun would make them feel safer if they were going to be in a physical fight.[119] More than fifty percent (fifty-nine percent) could get a handgun if they so desired.[120]

The presence of guns also affected the students' emotional well being, including fear and shortened life expectancies. For example, forty-two percent said they worry about "being wiped out from guns" before reaching adulthood.[121] Not surprisingly, those who worry most and those who carry guns often are the same individuals. Guns also affected the routine activities of both gun-carrying and gun-avoiding students: forty percent reported behavioral changes to cope with violence including decisions on where they go, where they

---

may decide that the option of defense through gun use is too attractive to pass up, especially when weighed against the social and mortality costs of not carrying it. *Id.*

115. *Id.* at iii. The survey was a simple random sample of classrooms in public, private, non-Catholic, and Catholic schools. The self-administered anonymous questionnaires included questions on gun ownership, carrying firearms, using guns, injury, and perceptions of safety. The sample was divided among central city schools (30%), suburban schools (46%), and schools in small towns or rural communities (24%). The recipients of the survey were predominantly caucasian (70%), with a significant number of African-American students (16%), Latino students (15%), and Asian or Native American students (4%). Most students (87%) attended public schools, with small samples from private non-Catholic schools (8%), and attended Catholic schools (5%). *Id.* at iv.

116. *Id.* at vi.

117. *Id.*

118. *Id.*

119. *Id.*

120. *Id.* Of those who knew where to get a firearm, two-thirds could obtain one within 24 hours. *Id.*

121. *Id.*

stop on the street, night time activities, what neighborhoods they walk in, and what friends they choose.[122]

There are several important limitations of the study, however, and in the end it fails to address the disproportionate rates of gun fatalities among African-American youths. The school-based sample under-represents young African-American males who are at the highest risk of mortality from guns and have the highest concentration of risk factors.[123] Dropouts, frequent absentees, and institutionalized youths are also excluded, a source of bias since these groups have higher rates of both violence and the risk factors for violence.[124] The analyses of gun possession and carrying by subgroups (area, gender, or ethnicity) was limited and selective, and the general population sample would likely yield cells too small for reliable comparisons when such controls are introduced. Nevertheless, the LH study suggests the pervasive influence of guns on the everyday decisions of young people in schools.

B.   The Sheley, Wright, and Smith Survey

Some of the limitations in the LH survey were later addressed by others, including research by Joseph Sheley and by Sheley and James Wright.[125] They interviewed 835 male inmates in three juvenile correctional institutions in four states, complemented by surveys of 758 male high school students from ten inner-city public schools in the largest cities in each state.[126] Both student and inmate samples were voluntary, and non-incarcerated dropouts were not included. Most (eighty-four percent) of the inmate sample reported that they had been threatened with a gun or shot at, and eighty-three percent owned a gun prior to incarceration.[127] More than one in three inmates (thirty-eight percent) reported shooting a gun at someone.[128] More than half owned three or more guns, and the age of first acquisition was fourteen.[129]

Both the inmate and student samples described in more detail the ecology of guns within the social organization of their neighborhoods. They claimed that firearms were widely available at low costs.[130] Distribution was informal, with guns bought and sold through family, friends, and street sources.[131] Among incarcerated young males, forty-five percent reported that they "had bought, sold, or traded 'lots' of guns."[132] Stealing guns and using surrogate buyers in gun shops were common methods of obtaining guns. Motivation for

---

122. *Id.* at ix.
123. Fagan et al., *supra* note 2 at 439, 447-48.
124. *Id.*
125. SHELEY ET AL., *supra* note 1, at 2-3; SHELEY & WRIGHT, *supra* note 113, at xi-xii, 15.
126. SHELEY ET AL., *supra* note 1, at 1.
127. *Id.* at 4.
128. *Id.*
129. *Id.* at 5.
130. *Id.* at 5-6.
131. *Id.* at 6.
132. *Id.* at 7-8.

owning and carrying guns was reported to be more for self-protection than for status. The drug business was a critical context for gun possession: eighty-nine percent of inmate drug dealers and seventy-five percent of student dealers had carried guns.[133] So too was gang membership: sixty-eight percent of inmates and twenty-two percent of students were affiliated with a gang or quasi-gang, and seventy-two percent of inmates were involved in the instrumental use of guns.[134]

Although one of the studies focused on inner cities, the voluntary samples raise concerns regarding selection bias and other measurement error. The Sheley and Wright study sampled disproportionately from states and cities with concentrations of gang activity,[135] perhaps overstating the importance of gangs as a context for gun use. Like the LH survey, this study did not focus on events where guns were used, only on individuals and their patterns of gun possession and gun use.

C. Other Adolescent Studies

Other studies have examined the prevalence of gun or weapon possession, but with little specificity. One group interviewed 611 youths in inner-city neighborhoods in Miami as part of a study on crack cocaine and "street crime."[136] They reported that 295 (forty-eight percent) carried guns in the year preceding the interview.[137] However, they do not report the percentage that used them or in what contexts they had been carried (drug deals, robbery, or homicide). The National Youth Survey is generally silent on the question of weapons.[138] Based on 1,203 student surveys and interviews with dropouts in three cities with high gang concentrations, Jeffrey Fagan reported that 42.5 percent of gang males and 17.6 percent of non-gang males carried weapons.[139] But his findings made no distinction between guns and other weapons (for example, knives). Also, Allan Lizotte and others examined the role of peers, social networks, and lifestyles on the carrying and use of firearms, using data from the Rochester Youth Survey.[140] They found that individuals who possessed firearms for the purpose of "sport" were socialized into gun use primarily within the family while youth who possessed guns for "self-protection" purposes were socialized into gun use within their peer networks.[141]

---

133. *Id.* at 8.
134. *Id.* at 9.
135. SHELEY & WRIGHT, *supra* note 113, at xi, 15.
136. JAMES A. INCIARDI ET AL., STREET KIDS, STREET DRUGS, STREET CRIME: AN EXAMINATION OF DRUG USE AND SERIOUS DELINQUENCY IN MIAMI 162 (1993).
137. *Id.*
138. *See, e.g.,* ELLIOTT ET AL., *supra* note 3, at 1-2.
139. Jeffrey Fagan, *Social Processes of Delinquency and Drug Use Among Urban Gangs, in* GANGS IN AMERICA 183-219 (C. Ronald Huff ed., 1990).
140. Allan J. Lizotte et al., *Patterns of Adolescent Firearms Ownership and Use,* 11 JUST. Q. 51, 61-62 (1994).
141. *Id.*

These studies are not very helpful in explaining the use of firearms by young males or the procedural dynamics of such events. They typically confound firearm use with firearm possession, and also with other forms of adolescent violence (such as physical and sexual assault, robbery) or poor developmental outcomes such as drug use, dropout, or adolescent pregnancy.[142] Few studies have distinguished adolescents who are violent from those violent adolescents who carry or use firearms. They often fail to distinguish firearms from other weapons, despite important strategic differences. There also is little information on nonlethal firearm use, virtually no information from gunshot victims, and little research on the situations and contexts in which adolescents carry or use guns.[143]

D. Gender, Firearms and Youth Violence

Our research focuses upon male firearm use because the growing presence of firearms has had minimal influence on female adolescents. Historically, female offenders have not used weapons, but they may carry weapons for males.[144] Homicide data also show the rare involvement of both gang and non-gang females in lethal violence.[145] Bjerregaard and Lizotte omitted girls from their analysis of gun ownership among inner-city youths because "girls rarely own guns, whether for sport or protection."[146]

Survey data also indicate low rates of gun or other weapon use by female adolescents. The rate of female high school students who carried a firearm to school was reported to be about one percent.[147] And, though Sheley and Wright state that nine percent of the female respondents reporting having owned a revolver at some time in their lives, five percent had owned an automatic or semiautomatic weapon, and fewer than five percent owned other

---

142. *E.g.* ELLIOTT ET AL., *supra* note 3, at 5-86.

143. Only homicide research has examined the contexts surrounding firearm use, but most of these studies have focused on specific contexts such as spousal violence, gangs, or drug exchanges. *See, e.g.,* Paul J. Goldstein et al., *Crack and Homicide in New York City, 1989: A Conceptually-Based Event Analysis*, 16 CONTEMP. DRUG PROBS. 651-687 (1989); Cheryl L. Maxson et al., *Differences Between Gang and Nongang Homicides*, 23 CRIMINOLOGY 209, 216-218 (1985).

144. VIGIL, *supra* note 41, at 98-103; JOAN MOORE, *supra* note 89; JOHN QUICKER, HOMEGIRLS: CHARACTERIZING CHICANA GANGS (1983); BETTY-LOU VALENTINE, HUSTLING AND OTHER HARD WORK: LIFE STYLES IN THE GHETTO (1978).

145. Cheryl L. Maxson & Malcolm W. Klein, *Street Gang Violence, in* PATHWAYS TO CRIMINAL VIOLENCE (Marvin E. Wolfgang & Neil A. Weiner eds., 1989); IRVING A. SPERGEL, THE YOUTH GANG PROBLEM: A COMMUNITY APPROACH 58 (1995) (reporting that only one of 345 gang homicide offenders in Chicago between 1978 and 1981 was female; only six of 204 gang homicide victims were female). Between 1988 and 1990, two of 286 gang homicide offenders were females; three of 233 gang homicide victims in this period were females. Spergel concludes that "the youth gang problem in its violent character is essentially a male problem." *Id.*

146. B. Bjerregaard and Alan Lizotte, *Gun Ownership and Gang Membership*, 86 J. CRIM. L. & CRIMINOLOGY 43 (1995).

147. L. Sadowski et al., *Firearm Ownership Among Nonurban Adolescents*, 1434 AMERICAN JOURNAL OF DISEASE OF CHILDREN 1410-13 (1989); C.M. Callahan & F.P. Rivera, *Urban High School Youth and Handguns*, 267 JAMA 3039-3042 (1992).

types of firearms,[148] fewer than three percent carried weapons to school, and only eight percent carried them outside the home.[149]

Our current research attempts to reconstruct the stages and transactions within gun events among inner-city adolescent males.[150] Lengthy interviews with young men who have been involved in gun violence are generating data on the dynamic exchanges within gun events, including those where violence ensued and others where violence was avoided. The young men are asked to reconstruct three violent events: one where guns were present and they were used; one where guns were present but they were not used; and one where guns were not present. The sample consists of young men (aged sixteen to twenty-four) who were released from Rikers Island Academy between April 1995 and May 1996, and who entered a membership program called Friends of Island Academy, Guys' Insight on Imprisonment for Teenagers ("G.I.I.F.T.").[151] The analysis of the interview narratives will focus on the presence of "scripts," the various forms and types of scripts that are employed in specific contexts, how they are employed in different circumstances or contexts, and the roles of contexts and circumstances in shaping the outcomes of violent events.

Several caveats should be considered. The data presented here are drawn from thirty of eighty cases. These analyses, while computer aided, are very preliminary. While we suspect that further analysis will be consistent with these preliminary findings, additional themes will emerge and patterns will become more salient as the sample size increases. The themes and patterns identified in this paper, and therefore the quotations used, represent consistency across at least five cases.[152] Although our findings are consistent with other recent studies, the level of insight gained through these detailed qualitative narratives on adolescent gun use goes beyond previous studies.

VI

THE SYMBOLIC AND INSTRUMENTAL MEANINGS OF FIREARMS

Today, there seems to be an increase in the number of situations and contexts in which conflicts arise that may escalate to lethal violence. The use of violence may reflect an apparent lowering of the thresholds for using

---

148. SHELEY & WRIGHT, *supra* note 113, at 123.

149. *Id.*

150. This research is supported by grants from the Centers for Disease Control and Prevention, the National Institute of Justice, and the National Science Foundation. Developmental and pilot research was supported by the Harry Frank Guggenheim Foundation.

151. For a detailed discussion of the methodology for this study, *see* Deanna L. Wilkinson et al., Using Peer Interviewers to Enhance Data Collection Efforts in a Study of Gun Use Among Young Males in the Inner City: Tales from the Field, presented at the Academy of Criminal Justice Sciences Annual Meeting (Mar. 15, 1996) (on file with author).

152. We decided that patterns that held up across five different individuals in this data set could be considered strong enough for consideration and discussion. As noted in the text, many of the themes were found across nearly all of the subjects, however, there were also many other apparent themes that failed to meet the five-case minimum cut-off point.

weapons to resolve conflicts. Individuals can have a variety of different experiences with guns, including owning, carrying, buying, selling, trading, stealing, having access to, borrowing, threatening someone with a gun, beating someone with a gun, firing for play, firing to injure, and firing to kill. It appears that gun use has become a central part of status and identity formation within the "street-oriented" world of the inner-city. Guns have both symbolic and instrumental meanings within this context. Below we discuss some of the recurrent themes emerging from our data on adolescent gun use events in the inner city.

A. The Role of Guns in Identity Formation and Status Attainment

Social identity is extremely important within inner-city neighborhoods. As described above, impression management, reputation, and image are necessary for daily survival.[153] Our preliminary analysis suggests that gun violence is the ultimate tool in forming and sustaining positive social identities within the neighborhood. One subject explained:

> Interviewer D: So umm, why is it important to have a reputation? G-58:[154] 'Cause if you ain't got no rep . . . ; it's gonna be like this if you ain't got no rep, everybody is gonna pick on you . . . ; they gonna be like oh that nigga pussy, he don't do nothing, they gonna try to pick you as a herb, you coming up the block niggas be trying to bump you, look at you, ice grill you look at you up and down . . . like you nobody. D: Yeah. G-58: So that when you gotta go all out, man, you know? D: What you mean by "go all out"? G-58: You gotta go all out, you go "lace" 'em . . . ; have a fight with duke or whatever, pull out a gun and blast 'em . . . ; you gotta be, niggas ain't gonna fuck with you if you shoot a nigga . . . ; just lace 'em, and niggas will say "yo that nigga don't play, he lace something in a heartbeat."

Projecting the "right image" may have consequences for personal safety, social acceptance, and self-esteem among individuals.

> Interviewer R: What about image or a reputation on the streets? G-61: Image? Well, a image is something, is a very, it's important on the streets . . . ; we just show how we come out and show themselves as somebody they not, then people, some people could look and see a fake person between a real person. A real person is the person that . . . I see is that don't take no shit, just do anything that he wanna do or whatever or he gets down for whatever . . . . A fake nigga is a nigga who talk about it but when its time to get down, he got excuses, he got to do this or come up with an excuse or all he do is politic about, talk about. They never really get in the mix . . . , he just talk about it. [I]t's just, you know, you gotta, you just like, you look at you people as your son, daughter, you got to look out for them, and they gotta do the same for you . . . . That comes with my other thing, 'cause you gotta, if you gotta problem I'm there and if I got a problem you there . . . ; and another thing when, in the streets police is mostly hated, . . . they are least involved with anything, . . . they got, they familiar what's goes on, but people do not want them involved with them. R: Why? G-61: I don't know. They feel more safer without the police than with the police.

---

153. *See* Anderson, *The Order of the Streets*, *supra* note 5, at 80, 82, 86-89; CANADA, *supra* note 5, at 38-39. *But, see*, SHELLEY & WRIGHT, *supra* note 113, at 64-65 (surveyed sample rejected statement that gun ownership was important for image and respect).
154. The G-58 or any other number following the "G" refer to the interviewee being quoted.

Thus, building a reputation is something that young males take seriously and into which they put effort. A reputation can be won via several routes, which are all connected by the threat or use of violent force. One subject explained how it works:

> Interviewer R: How you get a rep, you know? You know how some brothers, sometimes brothers just go out there looking to get a rep. Be the man. G-42: Those are called like new comers . . . ? Like a person that moves into a new community he's like, he's like damn you know "nigga's out here is cool and they real I got to show these niggas I ain't no punk yo." So when he hangs out with them, he see any of them about to get into a "scrobble" he be like "yo step back money I'll handle this for you yo" . . . he's only doing it for a rep cause it's not like that's your brother and you like "Nah, yo you ain't going to fight my brother. For that you fight me." R: Nigga's is just doing it to get a name? G-42: Doing so people could look at him and be like "oh word that nigga bust that nigga's ass yo word." I don't know that's the way I look at it.

Social interaction is regulated through a strict adherence to a proscribed dominance hierarchy where there are only a limited number of desirable statuses to attain. Displays of respect are expected by those who have higher levels of status on the street. However, shows of disrespect or "dissing" is often an intended or unintended attack on someone else's identity and, according to the "code of the street," be addressed aggressively.

> G-61: Getting dissed? Interviewer R: Is that deep or what? G-61: That's deep, according to the street that's really deep, 'cause if a nigga diss you, he feel you dissed everything, he just ran over you like a mop, just walked over you like a mat. If somebody disrespect you everybody will, that's why there be a lot of killing in the neighborhoods today, niggas ain't trying to get disrespected. R: But why do words have to end in death? G-61: Just, it's not like it used to be, most of the time some people just talk it out, or fight it out. R: Yeah. G-61: But now since there are so much guns, people ask "why should I scuffle my knuckles out or bruise up my face when I can use some that will take care of the problem in less than five minutes?" Most people just say fuck fighting. R: That's taking a life, man. G-61: Most people don't look at it like that; they be like "that's one less problem in life I got to worry about."

Subjects often talked about verbal attacks on one's mother and how that type of attack could not be tolerated. As one subject described:

> Interviewer M: Why you fired, what was the situation? G-56: Well somebody played themself in trying, try to disrespect my moms, so I had to handle my business. May he rest in peace black.

Doing time (in jail or prison) and having a lot of guns were described by several young men as being important ways to attain status.

> Interviewer W: Can you describe the importance of image and reputation on the street? What is reputation mean? G-33: Reputation? W: Have rep.? G-33: Nowadays is, some people look at it as a because they got locked up, they come home you know, he got a rep, and like that, you know. "Oh, that's the man right there, he did a 5 bid or he did a 10 bid." And the truth is nigga was ass in there. People look at it like that. W: Is it the same for all guys? G-33: No, you know for some who chillin' in the better rhine. Who got the more guns. You know, whatever. Stupid things. Like me I don't care if I . . . . To some people it is. To me it's got no importance, it holds no weight.

80   LAW AND CONTEMPORARY PROBLEMS   [Vol. 59: No. 1

As shown above, violence is a central tool in gaining or losing respect. Having a strong reputation can protect young men from attacks or robberies by others.

> G-44: Yeah. You make money, if you make money it's just gonna come. Interviewer R: If you make money then you get your props? G-44: You'll get your respect then everybody gonna want to be down with you instead of robbing . . . instead of robbing you, everybody think "yo why should I rob him" you know what I'm saying he show, if he could show me something, he could show me how to make mine. R: True. G-44: They, while they robbing him they going home getting a certain amount of money, but he making more, he making the money that he lost. And everybody want that everybody want to make the money that they lost and not stress. I'm saying "he stole like five G's from us already. Don't stress it I'm making more money, I'm make it again next week."

Within the context of status and identity posturing, ordinary conflicts that occur over personal slights, looks, insults, or playful threats may turn to murder in a matter of minutes.

> Interviewer R: Did you ever shoot anyone? G-61: Yeah. R: When? Before you got shot or after? G-61: After, after I got shot. I shot somebody, we had this conflict, this kid, I don't know him but we was just sitting next, and he exchanged words with my friend, so he told, he came to the kid, the kid came to my friend and told him to move . . . ; so my man was like "move, what you mean move, man, the word is excuse me," he was like "no move," . . . some rude boy. So he was like, I heard them, so I turned around and said, "yo what the fuck is going on, yo," the kid talking about "what you gonna do," so I said "what you mean what I'm gonna do," so I shot 'em . . . . R: Where you shoot 'em? G-61: I don't know where I shot 'em at, I shot 'em up in the face. R: What you just shot 'em and left. So umm, you left? G-61: Yeah. R: So what happened you ain't hear what happened? G-61: I heard he was dead. R: Oh, so umm, how that made you feel? G-61: Fine. But then again it made me feel like, after that I felt like I was still on my mission, I was like fuck that. He ain't mean nothing to me . . . ; he wasn't nobody to me so, he ain't mean nothing to me . . . . R: Did you feel like your life was threatened like? G-61: I ask myself that question all the time, I be saying to myself "damn, did I make the right decision? Was that the right decision or not. . . ." And I haven't come up with an answer yet.

B. Toughness

"Toughness" has been central to adolescent, masculine identity in American life. Physical prowess, emotional attachment, and the willingness to resort to violence to resolve interpersonal conflicts are hallmarks of adolescent masculinity.[155] While these terms have been invoked recently to explain high rates of interpersonal violence among nonwhites in central cities, "toughness" has always been highly regarded and a source of considerable status among adolescents in a wide range of adolescent subcultures, from streetcorner groups to gangs.[156] In some cases, displays of toughness are aesthetic: Facial expression, symbols and clothing, physical posture and gestures, car styles, graffiti, and unique speech are all part of "street style" that may or may not be complemented by

---

155. Elijah Anderson, *The Code of the Streets, supra* note 5, at 80, 89-92; CANADA, *supra* note 5, at 40.

156. CANADA, *supra* note 5, at 21-22; GOFFMAN, *supra* note 16, at 83-84; Whyte, *supra* note 41, at 4; WOLFGANG & FERRACUTI, *supra* note 76, at 305; William Oliver, *Black Males and the Tough Image: A Dysfunctional Adaptation*, 8 W. J. BLACK STUD. 199, 200-01 (1984).

physical aggression. While changing over time with tastes, these efforts at "impression management" to convey a "deviant aesthetic" and "alien sensibility" have been evident across ethnicities and cultures.[157] Toughness requires young males to move beyond symbolic representation to physical violence.[158] Firearms often are used to perpetuate and refine the aesthetic of "toughness," and to claim the identity of being among the toughest.

In our data, "toughness" and "being the man" were two strong concepts for all subjects and most of the violent events they described. Again, our data show that guns are an important part of these social processes. Guns are equated with status and with a certain level of respect.

> Interviewer M: What makes somebody tough or a big man in your neighborhood? G-56: What make 'em tough? M: Yeah. G-56: When they got guns. When they got when they got a whole lot of friends know the guys back. Of course he gon say he the big man, nobody could touch him. He got prop, he got juice.

Another subject explained that violent behavior and guns are important for defining manhood for young pre-teens and adolescent males.

> Interviewer R: How is manhood defined? G-40: Manhood now it's like gunhood. If you got a gun you the man (laughing). Ain't no more manhood it's gunhood.

C. Power and Dominance

Power and dominance were also salient themes in our preliminary data. Previous research suggests that "bad asses," robbers and other fighters, seem to gain much pleasure from violence, including the use of guns and other weapons.[159] There are several possible explanations, from the feelings of power and security that weapons may provide, to the pleasures of dominance and unrestrained "ultimate" aggression that guns provide. One subject describes why he got a gun and how it made him feel to have it.

> Interviewer D: When did you get your first gun you know? At what age? G-51: What age. I got my first gun at age of I think was sixteen. D: Why why'd you get it? G-51: 'Cause I wanted to be bad. D: You wanted to be bad huh? G-51: I wanted to be like I had a reputation to keep so maybe with a gun would have boost it up a little bit more. D: Have you ever fired a gun ? . . . G-51: Yes. D: How'd it feel firing a gun, how'd it . . . ? G-51: It felt, it felt good.

The use of weapons may reflect a total identity that is geared to dominate if not humiliate adversaries. Some adversaries are created in order to express this dominance. Another subject reported how his identity as being "trigger happy" gave him status and also brought him into many additional conflicts.

> G-61: Yeah it might turn out tragic . . . . Interviewer R: So when you shot the guy you shot, when you shot him, or when you found out he was dead or something, how did that make you feel, did that give you, did that boost you up? G-61: It ain't hype me;

---

157. KATZ, *supra* note 6, at 88-89.
158. This does not suggest merely any physical action. It also requires a display of pleasure beyond the instrumental purposes of the act, and well beyond whatever calculation followed an initial dispute. Thus, domination, and its payoffs in pleasure as well as status, supplant the instrumental goals of physical violence.
159. *See* KATZ, *supra* note 6, at 80-113, 193-236.

> it didn't make me feel like going out there and doing it again; it just made me feel like . . . I just gotta stripe; that's how that made me feel, I got a stripe. R: Did you get a reputation after that? G-61: Well, I kept a reputation but, . . . 'cause I was into a lot of stuff, . . . and thing I did came to where I was like one of the people, I was like one of the most people they would come and get when it was time for conflict, then anybody . . . that I really be around, when there beef, when it's beef time they know who to come get and outta those people, I was one of the top ones they would come and get . . . 'cause they always known me . . . for being trigger happy and . . . .

While this from of violence has a long history, its recent manifestation as "senseless" violence may in fact simply reflect the changes brought about by the availability of weapons and the meanings ("scripts") attached to them. The perpetuation of the sense of self and the image in the minds of others also is an instrumental goal of much weapon use. There is a very low threshold for the use of violence for these ends. Some subcultures or networks may also reflect norms where excessive violence, including weapons use, is valued, gains social rewards, and gives great personal pleasure. For example, this is true in some gang contexts where "locura" acts of violence establish one's status in the gang. It is senseless only in the fact that the violence is an end unto itself. The use of weapons, especially guns, has elevated the level of domination. Guns can be used tactically to disable an opponent, or to humiliate an opponent by evoking fear (begging, tears, soiling his pants, etc.), even if there is little advantage gained by using the weapon.

Adolescent gathering locations are "hot spots" of violence where weapons are part of the scenario of fighting. What characterizes these locations is a combination of individual personality "sets," their expectancies about what might happen in that locale (at what time of the day), and the absence of social controls (restraints) in those spaces. These places are flashpoints for conflict, posturing, imaging, and impression management. Carrying weapons is an expressive part of this world. Carrying a gun also may alter an individual's perception of safety within different locations. As one subject explained, with a gun "you could go places you wouldn't go."

> Interviewer R: Through selling drugs I know you had to maybe like experience guns? G-42: Yeah. I had my experience with guns but I never and I thank god I never had to shot nobody but I pulled out on somebody before, I slap somebody with a gun before. R: Why is that? Tell me about those times? G-42: Alright umm. One time boom I was kind of young too I was like fifteen. My cousin had a lot of guns I asked him to let me hold it and I just held it and at that time. R: That was the first time you ever held a gun? G-42: Yeah. Never had a gun so I was kind of happy. R: What kind was it? G-42: It was a little thirty eight the one that revolve. I use to try to go on the bus with it and I use to just carry it for protection but I never had to use it to protect myself. R: What, you say you was carrying it for protection. Do you know what you was protecting yourself from? G-42: Nothing. . . . That's what I was beginning to figure out I was like "yo I don't need a gun." I be carrying this heavy thing and I don't even need it. If anything it would cause me to get into more trouble, than bring me trouble. . . . I brought myself more trouble with it cause I endanger myself ever time I have it on me I see a cop I get kind of nervous I be like "damn I wonder if he know I got this joint on me?" Or, how about if I even if I'm on the train cause I hear stories yo word yo this nigga took my chain on the train yo psss. Next thing you be like I dare a nigga try to take my shit cause I ain't having it boy I let that nigga know "bloow bloow" I kind of wanted the gangster, I was on the

> gangster mentality for a little while I'm kind of glad I grew out of it. R: With that gun it kind of like gave you . . . . G-42: Yeah. I went places I wouldn't go, I did, I felt more bolder I would hop a cab with no reason I be like yo I could get anywhere I want to go with this. "This is my Visa."

Physical and social locations also present reasons for concern about one's personal safety. Street corners, subway and bus stops, corner stores, night clubs, house parties, and certain buildings were all mentioned as places where conflict is likely to escalate into violence or evening shootouts. According to our subjects, safety in most settings was uncertain and, therefore, "being prepared" for the worst was important. Facing a gun or other type of violent situation seemed inevitable to many of our subjects.

> Interviewer W: Why did you do what you did? G-38: With the gun? W: Yeah. G-38: To protect myself. To protect my peers. W: What were you thinking at the time? G-38: I say we going to this club. Whatever happens, happens. Let's just be ready because people ain't fighting no more like I said. Everybody shooting and I'm not trying to get shot for nothing. For nobody. I don't got no problems with nobody. I'm very humble.

Popular culture has served as a transmitter, amplifier, and interpreter of gun-related violence.[160] The celebration of gun possession as a symbol of safety and power is commingled with the dress and speech codes that characterize the behaviors and contexts where violence carries a positive value. This includes conceptions of manhood that place a high value on the willingness to "take a bullet" or otherwise engage in acts of extreme violence.[161]

D. Self-defense or Protection

Much of the recent survey-based research has shown that offenders and high school students alike report "self-defense" as the most important reason for carrying firearms.[162] "Self-defense" has a number of different meanings, including defense against other youth in increasingly hostile and unsafe environments, as well as self-defense from law enforcement officials during the course of illegal activity.[163] Our subjects provided examples of how weapons were needed for protection and self-defense, what "self-protection" meant to them, and alternative means of avoiding violent situations.

> Interviewer R: How did you use to feel when you had a gun? G-41: Had a gun? . . . [W]hen I felt, when I had a gun I felt . . . if anything come up I'll be able to protect myself. And if I want to get some money I go get some.

---

160. Michel Marriott, *Hard-Core Rap Lyrics Stir Black Backlash*, N.Y. TIMES, Aug. 15, 1993, at A1, A42.

161. Bob Herbert, *Kids Know the Real Deal*, N.Y. TIMES, Feb. 6, 1994, at § 4, 17.

162. LH Research, *supra* note 1, at 12; David Kennedy, *Guns and Youth: Disrupting the Market* (1993) (unpublished manuscript, on file with the John F. Kennedy School of Government, Harvard University); SHELEY & WRIGHT, *supra* note 113, at 67. Defense of "self" seems to be recurrent theme is the stories of young inner-city males. *See* Fagan & Wilkinson, *supra* note 9; Anderson, *supra* note 5, at 89-92; Donald Black, *Crime as Social Control*, 48 AM. SOC. REV. 34, 35-38 (1983).

163. JAMES D. WRIGHT & PETER H. ROSSI, ARMED AND CONSIDERED DANGEROUS: A SURVEY OF FELONS AND THEIR FIREARMS 14-15 (expanded ed. 1994).

All thirty subjects included in the analysis mentioned either "protection" or "defense" of self, peers, family members, and girls. Subjects perceived a variety of sources of attack on self: for example, identity or status attacks, attacks on their physical well-being, attacks on their material possessions, attacks on their relationships with others, and attacks on their freedom from incarceration. Many subjects talked about the dual role that guns played for them: as a means of protection and as a means of facilitating robberies.

> Interviewer R: So after that did guns become a repeated thing in your life dealing with guns like I mean you still carry a gun now and I mean so now you carry a gun for what protection? G-44: Protection. R: You have beef what? G-44: For protection or if like or if you want to do robberies and stuff. I mean I don't rob people on the street and stuff like that. I'm talking about some big money type project. R: Drug dealers? G-44: Yeah. Yeah.

Gun use for "protection" among individuals heavily involved in hustling or drug selling was very common. The need for "protection" often followed some type of violent conflict or being victimized.

> Interviewer W: After the fight did you do anything extra to protect yourself? G-32: In ways. I may, I may have like . . . , just to be on the safe side I might have carried my joint down with me. W: Was it necessary to do that? G-32: Yeah. W: Why was it necessary to do anything extra. G-32: 'Cause after I came out I had a feeling that I was gonna see this kid again. Just for the simple ass whipping he caught I felt he was gonna come back and blast me. [Later in the interview] W: After the shootout did you do anything extra to protect yourself? G-32: Yeah. Everyday after that day. W: Why was it necessary to do that? G-32: 'Cause I didn't want to be in that position again of being caught unprepared. Of being stop without a ghat. Being near fucking death is not the way. I don't fucking tell nobody pack a gun, but if you feel like your life is definitely in that path yo, pack on. Throw them guns in the air.

Another subject had a similar experience.

> Interviewer M: After the fight you did anything extra to protect yourself? G-56: Oh yes, no doubt, no doubt I'm saying. The only thing I did was to get my gun. M: Why was it necessary to do that? G-56: Why? 'Cause you never know who the next man, what's on the next man mind. You don't know what he gon do to you. Got to worry 'bout the man creep up on you, busting you first.

E.   How Guns have Changed the Script

The presence of weapons may alter the scenarios that govern conflicts and the natural rules of their resolution. Repeatedly, subjects described how things have changed on the street and how guns have taken over in handling beefs or conflicts. Weapons, especially guns, represent a quick and oftentimes final resolution to conflicts. One subject described the continuum of weapons available on the street and how situations are managed with each type of weapon. His description supports the notion that there has been a historical change and that the "interaction order" has been altered by guns. The outcome of these violent events is often perceived as justified or deserved because the other actor made the wrong move or played out the situation in the wrong way.

> Interviewer M: All right. What about knives and bottles and stuff like that. What kind of code defines these situations? G-56: Yo anything you use you ain't got no weapon if it's a bottle crack, if if it could hurt your opponent I'm saying, for you to

take him out for he gon take you out, do what you got to do. Crack the bottle, stick him in his neck, do ever. Knife, if you got to stab a man to death I'm saying, fear for your life, you got to handle it. M: So it's always to say that it's expected that that a guy uses gun to handle his beef? G-56: Yes. It was like that now. See you was back in '83 be a fair a fair fight, hand to hand, but it ain't like that no more. As a old, as the years get older the more the world get violent. M: All right. Let's say you and this guy arguing and he he flash a gun what you gon do? G-56: Well. If I, if I know he got to draw me first I'm saying, I'm say to him talk my way out of it I'm saying. As soon as he turn his back on me that's the wrong move, 'cause I'm gon put one right in his head. I'm gon make sure I empty the whole clip. M: So that's what you suppose to do in that situation? G-56: No doubt. Talk your way out until you I'm saying til' he let down his guard. And then you do what you got to do 'cause you can't let the man live, 'cause yo if man pull a gun on you and let you live he a fool. He deserve to die.

Guns are also the most efficient route to obtaining money or material possessions by illegal means. Accordingly, gun homicides by adolescents reflect a variety of social learned cues motivating the use of weapons. First-hand accounts offer a number of motivations for carrying weapons.

Interviewer M: All right. Who's carrying these guns in your neighborhood like ah what's the ages? . . . G-59: [L]ike fifteen to to at least twenty-five, twenty-four. M: For what? Why they carry . . . why they got that? G-59: For they got they got a little a lot of beefs going around and a lot lot of bad reputation they like they they need that gun 'cause so much dirt they did since . . . buying the gun they do mad dirt just because they have a gun. They got to put the use for it or is to be robbing somebody, showing it out, shooting it out, or just having a victim to shoot him.

If a gun is available, these accounts suggest that it will be the weapon of choice, since it maximizes the possibilities of surviving or managing a violent situation.

VII

IMPLICATIONS FOR PREVENTION AND INTERVENTION

For many adolescents in urban areas, violence has had a pervasive influence on their social and cognitive development.[164] Coupled with high adolescent mortality and firearm injury rates, the presence of firearms in their immediate social contexts perpetuates their perceptions of risk and danger in the most common activities of everyday life. Even when not immediately present, the diffusion of violence and danger through popular culture and urban "legends" enhances the perceptions of personal risk. Rituals of mourning and burial, whether real or mythologized, have become cultural touchstones that are reinforced and internalized in normative beliefs and attitudes about the inevitability of violence. Guns have become an important part of the discourse of social interactions, with both symbolic meaning (power and control) as well as strategic importance. Expressions of shortened life expectancies reflect processes of anticipatory socialization based on the perceived likelihood of victimization from lethal violence. Conversely and perversely, carrying firearms

---

164. John E. Richter & Pedro Martinez, *The NIMH Community Violent Project: I. Children as Victims of and Witnesses to Violence*, PSYCHIATRY: INTERPERSONAL & BIOLOGICAL PROCESSES, Feb. 1993, at 7.

seems to enhance feelings of safety and personal efficacy among teenagers.[165] The result is a developmental "ecology of violence," where beliefs about guns and the dangers of everyday life may be internalized in early childhood and shape the cognitive frameworks for interpreting events and actions during adolescence. In turn, this context of danger, built in part around a dominating cognitive schema of violence and firearms, creates, shapes and highly values scripts skewed toward violence. In turn, it also underscores the central role of guns in achieving the instrumental goals of aggressive actions or defensive violence in specific social contexts.

Interventions that adopt this perspective should naturally focus on the development of behavioral scripts, the contingencies within scripts that lead to violence, and the role of firearms in both scripts themselves and the contingencies that evoke them. Focusing on the role of guns within scripts assumes that guns may alter scripts in several ways. For example, guns may change the contingencies and reactions to provocations or threats, and change strategic thinking about the intentions and actions of the other person in the dispute. The presence of guns in social interactions may also produce "moral" judgments that justify aggressive, proactive actions. Accordingly, the development of interventions should be specific to the contexts and contingencies of *gun* events, rather than simply interpersonal conflicts or disputes.

A variety of conflict-resolution and violence prevention curricula have been developed that focus on social competence, problem-solving, and anger management skills. Many are school-based, focusing on the development of an awareness of violence problems and attitudes about the desirability of violence to solve conflicts.[166] These classroom-based preventive efforts also focus on self-esteem, co-morbid problem behaviors such as substance use, and techniques for problem solving and conflict resolution. Evaluations suggest that these efforts often improve students' social skills as measured by verbal responses to hypothetical conflict situations about the self-reported likelihood of violent behavior.[167]

One reason for the limited success of these efforts is the limited range of situational contexts and motivations implicit in the violent events they address. Few directly address the contexts in which firearms are present, and the potential effects of firearms in the unfolding of disputes. For example, scripts involving firearms often are effected under conditions of angry arousal and intensified emotional states.[168] Decisionmaking behaviors modeled in classrooms may not anticipate the changes in cognition that occur under these

---

165. LH Research, *supra* note 1, at 10, 12; SHELEY & WRIGHT, *supra* note 113, at 67.
166. *See, e.g.*, DEBORAH PROTHROW-STITH, DEADLY CONSEQUENCES 173-75 (1991).
167. Devon D. Brewer et al., *Preventing Serious, Violent and Chronic Juvenile Offending: A Review of Evaluations of Selected Strategies in Childhood, Adolescence, and the Community, in* A SOURCEBOOK ON SERIOUS, VIOLENT AND CHRONIC JUVENILE OFFENDERS 73-74 (J.C. Howell et al., eds., 1995).
168. Jeffrey Fagan & Deanna Wilkinson, *The Function of Adolescent Violence, in* VIOLENCE IN AMERICAN SCHOOLS (Delbert S. Elliott & Beatrix Hamburg eds., forthcoming 1997) (manuscript on file with author); Wilkinson et al., *supra* note 151.

conditions of emotional and physiological arousal. And the early reports from our research suggest that in many cases, firearms introduce complexity in decisionmaking introduced by the actions of third parties, or the longstanding nature of disputes that erupt periodically over many months. In other cases, firearms simply trump all other logic.

Preventive interventions must address the growing reality of firearms in the environmental contexts of development, and the internalization of firearms in the development of scripts. Firearms present a level of danger—or strategic certainty—that is unequaled in events involving other weapons or in "fair fights." Interventions should be specific to developmental stages. At early developmental stages, preventive efforts must recognize that for many youngsters with high exposure to lethal violence, the anticipation of lethal violence influences the formation of attitudes favorable to violence and scripts that explicitly incorporate lethal violence. At later developmental stages, the incorporation of strategic violence via firearms alters the course of disputes and narrows options for non-violent behavioral choices.

Classroom methods rely on methods that fail to approximate the conditions on the street where conflicts unfold, including those where guns are present.[169] They fail to address the role of bystanders and other contextual factors, and do not incorporate the cognitive and emotional states of the disputants. They do not recognize the social embeddedness of disputants in peer networks where the presentation of self carries enormous weight that outweighs other forms of self perception and status.[170] These curricula do not incorporate the strategic dimension that firearms introduce into the decisionmaking of disputants. They do not recognize how violent *discourse* often can translate into violent *action*, and that violence as a symbol often is transformed into violence as substantive action designed to redress grievances or protect one's physical person.

These attributes of conflict, including the presence of guns and their effects on cognition and decisionmaking, should inform the design of preventive efforts and interventions. Contingencies in a variety of contexts should be included: schools, parties, street corner life, the workplace, and in dating situations. The within-event contingencies suggest that interventions be built around stages and sequences of actions, as well as the scripts that individuals bring to events. Firearms can profoundly alter the event dynamics of disputes, and should be explicitly incorporated into prevention activities. Interventions for adolescents should include theater and role play, and employ methods where facilitators "unpack" the stages of events in contexts where the provocative and steering behaviors of bystanders and other third parties are included. Efforts to increase the salience of the training events are needed through provocation and arousal of participants to simulate the fear, anger, and complexity of disputes or

---

169. *See, e.g.*, D. Bretherton et al., *Dealing with Conflict: Assessment of a Course for Secondary School Students*, 28 AUSTRALIAN PSYCHOL. 105-111 (1993); D. Webster, *The Unconvincing Case for School-Based Conflict Resolution Programs for Adolescents*, 12 HEALTH AFFAIRS 126-141 (1993).

170. Anderson, *The Code of the Streets*, *supra* note 5, at 86-92.

situations where firearms are present. Interventions also should teach non-combatants how their behaviors as bystanders can increase the risks of lethal violence for young men facing off on the street. Interventions for younger children should increase their recognition of their own (and others') scripts.

Evaluations of these efforts also should include a focus on events to determine the effects of interventions on decisionmaking and event outcomes. Evaluations that address only attitudes about violence or self-reports of likely violent behaviors risk validity threats from social desirability in students' responses, and short-term follow-ups that do not take into account intervening experiences. Incremental gains from interventions can be detected when interaction patterns are analyzed to assess how scripts may be altered, events may be analyzed in a new or different framework, and ultimately how the risks and likelihood of violence can be reduced.

VIII

CONCLUSION

This article has attempted to examine the role of firearms in violent events among adolescent males in the inner city. By comparing the pattern of firearm use among adolescents across historical periods, factors could be identified that seem to have contributed to the recent escalation and the present day crises. Structural changes in communities and neighborhoods have preceded the rise in adolescent weapons use, as have the nature and density of illegal markets as well as the availability and firepower of weapons themselves. These changes have reshaped both the social controls and street networks that in the past regulated violent transactions. There are a number of antecedents and factors contributing to the current crisis that we are only beginning to understand.

Explanations of firearms use among adolescents requires several levels of analysis: the sources of weapons, the nature of everyday life that gives rise to conflicts that turn lethal, the "scripts" of adolescent life that lead to escalation (and the factors that underlie those scripts), the motivations for carrying/using weapons, and the role of weapons in the decisionmaking processes of adolescents when they engage in disputes or even predatory violence. The presence of firearms is not an outcome of other processes, but part of a dynamic and interactive social process where they alter the decisions leading to violence and the outcomes of violent events.

Using an event-based approach, the article suggests a conceptual framework for explaining interactions that involve adolescents and firearms. This approach does not deny the importance of the individual attributes that bring people to situations, but recognizes that once there, other processes shape the outcomes of these events. Events are analyzed as "situated transactions," including rules that develop within specific contexts, the situations and contexts where weapons are used, the motivations for carrying and using weapons, and the personality "sets" of groups where weapons are used. There are "rules" that govern how disputes are settled, when and where firearms are used, and the significance of firearms within a broader adolescent culture. Violence "scripts" often are invoked. These scripts may limit the behavioral and strategic options for resolving disputes, and the presence of firearms influences which scripts are invoked. Several theories from criminology, cognitive psychology, symbolic interactionism, and social psychology are brought to bear on the issue of the study of violent events. Because violence generally is a highly contextualized event, we have discussed the ways in which specific contexts shape decisions by adolescents to carry or use weapons, and how scripts are developed and shaped through diffusion within closed social groups. Finally, to advance the study and to prevent violent events involving adolescents, interventions, research and methodological innovation must reflect specificity about guns and their effects on cognition, moral development, and behavior.

[4]

Gun crime: the market in and use of illegal firearms

Gavin Hales, Chris Lewis and Daniel Silverstone

Crimes involving the use of firearms comprise around 0.4 per cent of all recorded offences in England and Wales and have doubled since the mid- to late-1990s (Povey and Kaiza, 2006). However, relatively little is known about criminal attitudes towards and the market in illegal firearms and the relationship, if any, between gun crime, illegal drug selling, gangs and a supposed 'gun culture'. This limits the development of policy, policing practice and an understanding of the impact of firearms legislation. Therefore, this research addresses these gaps by presenting evidence from interviews with 80 imprisoned male Firearms Act offenders aged 18 to 30. It also identifies potential interventions and deterrence strategies.

Key points

The market in illegal firearms and ammunition

● The source of firearms described by offenders included illegal importation, 'leakage' from legitimate sources (e.g. burgled shotguns) and the conversion of widely-available imitation firearms. Ammunition is relatively scarce and may be improvised or illegally manufactured. Some offenders were concerned about the risk of obtaining a gun used in a previous offence.

● Criminal contacts were pre-eminent in determining firearm availability. Specialist criminal 'armourers' were mentioned by at least 12 of the interviewees. Illegal firearms were circulated, particularly within gangs and other collectives.

● Prices varied by firearm type, quality and provenance. They ranged from £20 for an imitation firearm, £50 for a shotgun, £1,000+ for a 'new' purpose-built lethal handgun and £800–£4,000 for an automatic firearm.

The possession and use of illegal firearms

● Illegal drug markets underpin the criminal economy and represent the most important theme in relation to the illegal use of firearms. Firearms possession was reported in relation to robberies of drug dealers, territorial disputes, personal protection and sanctioning of drug market participants.

● In addition to drug dealer robbers, four other groups of armed robber were identified: specialist armed robbers, mixed offending robbers, opportunists and debtors. Armed robberies were committed with realistic imitation firearms by those who lacked contacts to obtain real firearms.

● Conflict formed part of the social relations of many offenders, notably including disputes related to status and respect. Even trivial disputes may result in shootings as guns elevate threat levels and a 'shoot or be shot' scenario precipitates pre-emptive violence. Gang or crew structures serve to escalate and perpetuate violence. Rivals may encounter each other in shared social spaces such as nightclubs where status may be publicly challenged.

● The illegal use of firearms is a complex problem. There are some clear recommendations, such as greater efforts to tackle the availability and conversion of highly realistic imitation firearms. However, most problems are more challenging and require social and economic rather than technical solutions.

The views expressed in these Findings are those of the authors, not necessarily those of the Home Office (nor do they reflect Government policy)

Offenders interviewed

The 80 offenders included 36 who described themselves as White, 28 Black, 11 mixed race, four Asian and one Chinese; their average age was 24 years. Of the 80 offenders, 59 reported a disrupted family life, including 35 who had grown up in a single-parent household; 43 had been excluded from school, 22 permanently (only 15 reported any post-16 education); ten offenders had never worked; 49 only in unskilled or manual occupations.

Gang or crew membership

Around half of the interviewees indicated they had been in a gang or crew; most knew of other such groups. Although reported gang or crew cultures and structures varied considerably, four 'ideal type' collective structures were identified (Box 1).

Box 1 Four types of gang or crew

- Close friendship groups: a social focus, offering safety in numbers and physical backup.

- Associates: known to each other but not close friends, typically interacting socially, sharing spaces such as housing estates, and engaged in low-level criminality; an important interface with local criminal cultures.

- Criminal crews: focussed on activities like controlling local drugs markets and, for some, conducting armed robberies and other offending.

- Organised crime networks: almost always engaged in drug market participation, e.g. middle-market level activities, in addition to offending such as more serious armed robberies and quasi-legitimate enterprises such as door security.

Offending

Half the offenders had been convicted of robbery as their primary current offence, 25 of firearm possession, eight of violence, two each of burglary, drugs and false imprisonment and one of theft. Fifty-eight had previous convictions, at least six for firearms offences.

Victimisation

For most interviewees the distinction between offender and victim was significantly blurred (see Table 1). However, typically the police only knew about victims in the case of fatalities or serious injury. Interviewees reported a preference for personal retribution and a fear of being labelled a 'grass' (police informant).

First contact with firearms

Almost half of the offenders first experienced firearms in the context of crime, notably associating with criminal friends.

Table 1   Different experiences of violence reported by interviewees (n=80)

Type of violence experienced	No.
Had previously been threatened with guns	40
Shot at	29
Had been shot	8
Had been stabbed	28
Injured with other weapons	17
Had been robbed	34
Had been kidnapped	3
Reported friends/family shot and injured	26
Reported friends/family shot dead	26

Another quarter first experienced airguns and airsoft/BB guns, typically in their early teens (BB guns usually refer to low-powered imitation firearms that discharge plastic pellets). Six had first used guns in legitimate contexts and a further six had encountered them during violence in their countries of origin.

The market in illegal firearms and ammunition

Interviewees provided a range of insights into the market in illegal firearms and ammunition. Nevertheless, questions remain that would require further research, e.g. concerning international sources of illegal firearms. Table 2 shows the types of firearms used for 76 offenders.

Table 2   Different types of firearms used including the different types of 'real' firearms

Type of firearm used	No.
'Real' firearms	71
Handguns	41
Shotguns	20
Automatic weapons	6
Stun guns	3
CS gas canister	1
Imitations	13
BB guns	6
Converted imitation firearms	4
Blank firers	4
Air guns	2
Deactivated firearms	1
Reactivated firearms	1
Unspecified type	4
Total no. firearms used	106

Notes: A total of 106 firearms were involved in the offences of 76 offenders (4 claimed no firearm was present).

Firearm supply, procurement and disposal

Firearms came to be possessed and/or used illegally through various methods. These include firearms illegally imported into the UK, misappropriated legally-owned firearms (e.g. burgled shotguns) and legally purchased imitation and deactivated firearms and airguns illegally converted to fire live ammunition.

Firearm availability is pre-eminently determined by criminal contacts under predominantly closed market conditions. At least 12 offenders described individuals who specialised in supplying firearms ('armourers'), including several who specialised in converting imitation firearms.

Choice was generally limited, although a well-connected minority reported having access to a range of firearms.

Reported prices varied, sometimes markedly, but there was some consistency. Price was determined by a combination of: firearm type and availability; 'leakage' from legal sources; location; firearm quality; firearm provenance; criminal contacts; how quickly the gun is required; whether the seller is a dependent drug user; and ammunition availability. See Box 2 for details of firearm types and cost.

Only four offenders described always keeping their gun with them; generally guns were kept at home, buried or otherwise accessible – typically being minded by third parties. In many cases used guns are sold on, keeping them in circulation and obscuring their provenance, something that was consistently mentioned as a cause for concern.

> '... you have to be very careful, cos you can buy a gun that killed people... you can get life for that, for things that you haven't even done.' (London)

The possession and use of illegal firearms

Development of a criminal career

The broader socio-economic context described by the offenders can be summarised as follows. Social pressures to attain a conspicuously material lifestyle in the context of economic hardship are reconciled by some through involvement in the criminal economy, in many cases facilitated by the availability of criminal opportunities. This is reinforced by the presence of criminal role models and other visibly 'successful' criminals demonstrating the viability of criminal careers that in some cases are more lucrative, at least in the short-term, than the likely legitimate alternatives.

Box 2 Choice of firearms and costs

Shotguns

Shotguns, particularly 'sawn-off', tend to be chosen for their availability and significant intimidatory value and are the weapon of choice for more serious armed robbers. Prices appear to be very low, around £50 to £200 (although some at £700 to £800 were mentioned). The low price appears to result from ongoing leakage from legitimate sources and ammunition is relatively easy to obtain.

Converted imitation firearms

Converted firearms are more widely available and cheaper than purpose-built firearms, although they are considered inferior and indeed dangerous to use. New prices were reported to range from £400 to £800, with .38″ revolvers at the lower end.

Automatic weapons

Five offenders had been caught with automatic weapons, in all cases related to violent conflict. The symbolic value, overwhelming power and often indiscriminate aim of these guns seems to conform to a 'gangster' stereotype not aspired to by the majority. Costs ranged from £800 to £4,000.

Imitation firearms

Imitation firearms were reported to be readily available and often very realistic. Costs ranged from £20 to £110 from legitimate outlets.

Purpose-built lethal handguns

Handguns are more concealable than shotguns, making them ideal for individuals who possess firearms for their own protection.

> 'Yeah, it's easier to conceal innit. The last thing you want is a fucking shotgun if you're going out or something.' (London)

The reported prices varied considerably, from around £150 to £200 for a gun known to have been used in a crime, to a typical £1,000 to £1,400 for a new 9mm model. They are generally sold with one full load of ammunition included.

Ammunition procurement

Ammunition is generally bought in small quantities with a gun and priced as a package. Ammunition is relatively scarce and harder to obtain than firearms, with the exception of shotgun cartridges. In some cases, criminals are exploiting a legal loophole to manufacture ammunition themselves, or else are using improvised ammunition such as blank firing ammunition combined with a ball bearing. Prices varied widely, from £2,000 to £3,000 for a box of .45″ ammunition to £0.50 a bullet for a .38″.

Ancillary items

Three offenders were convicted of offences relating to stun guns, with one also being convicted of possessing CS gas. There were ten references to bulletproof vests, four to sound moderators ('silencers') and one to night vision goggles.

'It's the whole rat race thing, you know. We're living in that age now, where if you ain't, like, wearing Nike Shox for example, then you know, you're a tramp... a lot of people can't afford it, but they see it, and if they ain't got em, they ain't part of it...' (West Midlands)

'Like, in the poor areas, yeah they look up to them [drug dealers]. They see them with like nice cars, superbikes, like um, chains, jewellery, lots of money, they see that and they want to be just like them. And that's really educating the kids really, it ain't the schools, it's really them.' (London)

Illegal drug markets

Illegal drug markets were found to underpin the criminal economy and represent the single most important theme in relation to the illegal use of firearms, characterised by systemic violence that appears to increase towards the street (retail) end of the market. Firearms possession was reported in relation to robberies of drug dealers, territorial disputes, personal protection and sanctioning of drug market participants.

'...when you are making that much money, a lot of people try to rob you... And because people were hearing about the money that I was making, that is why I bought the gun and started carrying it... solely for protection.' (London)

Robbery and burglary

In addition to drug dealer robberies, four types of armed robber were identified:

- specialists, most demonstrating a degree of target preference
- mixed offending robbers who committed robberies alongside other offences
- opportunists, including individuals who had obtained imitation firearms that facilitated serious offending and individuals associating with criminals who involved them in unplanned robberies
- debtors, who used armed robbery to try and pay off debts, typically owed to other criminals, sometimes under duress.

The ready availability of realistic imitation firearms enables robberies to be committed by individuals who lack the criminal contacts necessary to obtain real firearms.

Violence including gangs or crews

Conflict forms a significant part of the social relations of many offenders, especially disputes related to status and respect – so-called 'beef'. Even quite trivial disputes may result in shootings as the presence of firearms elevates threat levels and the so-called 'shoot or be shot' scenario precipitates pre-emptive violence.

'...you just have to bust [shoot] in their face before they bust at you.' (West Midlands)

Gang or crew structures escalate and perpetuate violence, which may transcend individual incidents and become generalised.

Nightclubs and other public social venues are significant here. Violence can escalate in shared social spaces where rivals meet. An individual's status may be publicly challenged which necessitates retaliation. Where such individuals are engaged in armed criminality, trivial disputes may quickly escalate into fatal violence. Access to firearms and a public audience both raise the stakes.

'Because you're raving, you're round other gangs; you are round other people like you aren't you? There are people like you and you could step on someone's shoe and they'd want to fight you... If you go raving and you want to feel safe, you want to feel alright, you've got to have a gun on you.' (London)

Meanwhile, those involved in the door security industry may be drawn into these conflicts, or even targeted by rival firms seeking access to potentially lucrative security contracts.

Possession offences

Of the 25 offenders caught in possession of firearms, eight were minding them for other criminals. The main 'other reasons' stated included protection – typically in the context of drug markets or violence – and offences in which a firearm was retrieved about which the offender denied any prior knowledge. The highly constrained legislation concerning firearms possession raises several issues. For example, accused persons facing the mandatory minimum sentence appear to have no incentive to enter an early guilty plea or co-operate with wider investigations. Also, individuals may be set up (e.g. by rivals).

Gun culture?

Two types of criminal gun culture were identified:

- an instrumental criminal gun culture in which guns are used only for offensive criminal purposes such as armed robbery
- a complex criminal gun culture in which the role of firearms is more generalised, including offensive, defensive and symbolic functionality.

The latter type of gun culture is more recent and appears to reflect changing criminal cultures. It is becoming increasingly significant. It is underpinned by three consistent themes, often hand-in-hand:

- the ascendancy of criminal role models
- the market in illegal drugs
- cultures of gang or crew membership.

Increasingly, firearms have become a normal part of the systemic violence found in the street-level criminal economy. They have assumed a symbolic significance as they have become associated with criminal affluence resulting from activities such as drug dealing and robbery, and have been conflated with respect, status and violent potential. The extent to which this symbolism may be attributed to popular cultural sources such as the urban music industry and media more generally is unclear, but on balance appears peripheral.

Preventing gun crime

A number of intervention and deterrence strategies are discussed below.

Tackling the market in illegal firearms

- Ongoing efforts are required to tackle the manufacture and sale of convertible imitation firearms and the conversion process. It may be possible to exploit criminals' concerns about the dangers of using converted imitation firearms to limit their sale and use.

- Consideration should be given to further controls on realistic imitation firearms.

- The legal loophole allowing criminals to lawfully obtain ammunition components and tools should be closed and further controls on blank ammunition considered. Also, the loophole allowing shotgun ammunition to be transferred to and possessed by non-certificated individuals should be closed.

- It may be possible to exploit criminals' concerns about buying firearms that have previously been used in crime.

- Enabling discretion in relation to mandatory sentencing may offer some benefits. For example, it may provide an incentive for individuals caught minding guns for other criminals to co-operate with police investigations into the origins of those guns.

- Further amnesties should be considered to try and reduce the existing stock of illegal or unwanted firearms.

- Publicity could be used to make offenders and others aware of the likely consequences of getting involved with illegal firearms, particularly in relation to conflict escalation.

Criminal justice system

- The five-year mandatory minimum sentence for possession of a firearm was well known (but those interviewed were serving prison sentences). Longer sentences might bring about counter-productive outcomes, such as offenders trying to 'shoot their way out' if challenged by the police.

- Greater availability of witness protection resources could be beneficial, as could greater use of independent intermediaries such as Crimestoppers.

- Expanding the use of Independent Advisory Groups should help police to understand the communities they are policing better.

- There may be scope for increasing the use of Anti-Social Behaviour Orders (ASBOs) and Acceptable Behaviour Contracts (ABCs) to disrupt gangs, criminal networks and drug dealing.

Diversion from crime

- Further research could explain the economics of drug dealing and empirical evidence could produce a means or lever with which to deter young people from entering drug dealing.

- Publicity, targeted at young people, should highlight successful convictions and criminal asset confiscation to undermine criminal role models.

- There may be greater scope for promoting the advantages of legitimate employment to young people and educating them about their options, particularly outside their immediate area.

- Greater provision of youth services should be supported, particularly in deprived inner-city communities.

- Gang or crew disruption and mediation programmes may be beneficial in some areas.

Harm reduction in the criminal economy

- A public health/harm reduction approach would seek to minimise levels of violence within the criminal economy.

Conclusions

The illegal use of firearms is not a singular problem but is complex, entrenched and poses significant challenges to communities, police and policy makers. Some findings point to clear recommendations, such as greater efforts to tackle the availability and conversion of highly realistic imitation firearms. Most, however, are more challenging and require social and economic rather than technical solutions.

The emergence of a complex gun culture in which firearms have become embedded within broader criminal lifestyles suggests significant limitations to interventions which are based on a rational choice understanding of offending. It highlights the need to address the social and cultural significance of offending behaviour such as gang conflict, armed robbery and drug dealing. Furthermore, the relationship between illegal firearms and crime is constantly changing. Consequently, ongoing efforts are required to keep abreast of changes to ensure that they are responded to appropriately.

A number of areas for further research are proposed, including further research on the origins of purpose-built lethal firearms in the criminal economy and the role of women in relation to the possession and use of illegal firearms.

Methodological note

This qualitative research study is based on in-depth interviews with 80 imprisoned and recently convicted male Firearms Act offenders aged 18 to 30, focussing on London, Greater Manchester, Nottinghamshire and the West Midlands. The sample is broadly in line with the national picture for gun crime in England and Wales (Povey, D. and Kaiza, P., 2006). Further details on the methodology can be found in Hales et al. (2006).

Reference

Povey, D. and Kaiza, P. (2006) 'Recorded crimes involving firearms'. Chapter 3 in K. Coleman, C. Hird and D. Povey (Eds.) *Violent Crime Overview, Homicide and Gun Crime 2004/2005* (Supplementary Volume to Crime in England and Wales 2004/2005) (pp 71–93). Home Office Statistical Bulletin 02/06. London: Home Office. See: www.homeoffice.gov.uk/rds/pdfs06/hosb0206.pdf

For a more detailed report see *Gun Crime: the market in and use of illegal firearms* by Gavin Hales, Chris Lewis and Daniel Silverstone (2006). Home Office Research Study No. 298. London: Home Office. Copies are available from the Home Office website http://www.homeoffice.gov.uk/rds/

Gavin Hales, Chris Lewis and Daniel Silverstone are at the University of Portsmouth, Institute of Criminal Justice Studies.

[5]

Early onset offending and later violent and gun outcomes in a contemporary youth cohort

Cynthia Perez McCluskey [a,*], John D. McCluskey [a], Timothy S. Bynum [b]

[a] *Department of Criminal Justice, University of Texas at San Antonio, 501 West Durango Boulevard, San Antonio, TX, 78259, United States*
[b] *School of Criminal Justice, Michigan State University, East Lansing, MI 48824, United States*

Abstract

Currently there is great concern regarding the high homicide rate and persistent weapon carrying among urban youth. Criminal career research has offered criminology an opportunity to understand offending as a process that has a beginning, middle, and end. Using that framework, the current study examined a contemporary cohort of arrestees and estimated the extent to which age of first arrest predicts future violent and gun offending. Net of demographic and offending variables, the results indicated that early onset was a significant predictor of serious violent offenses and weapon involvement. Theoretical and policy implications of these findings are discussed.

Introduction

Delinquency in a Birth Cohort (Wolfgang, Figlio, & Sellin, 1972) represented a seminal advancement of criminological research and helped spark thinking about crime in a dynamic fashion across a career (e.g., Blumstein, Cohen, Roth, & Visher, 1986). The examination of juveniles from the first Philadelphia birth cohort of 1948 (Wolfgang et al., 1972) and follow-up cohort of 1958 (Tracy, Wolfgang, & Figlio, 1990) identified several factors that led to a variety of delinquency outcomes. In particular, early entrance into official delinquency, prior to age fourteen, was found to be associated with later serious and chronic delinquency. Recently this research finding had been explored by the Study Group on Very Young Offenders, chaired by Rolf Loeber and David Farrington, and was the impetus for

* Corresponding author. Tel.: +1 210 458 2623; fax: +1 210 458 2680.
  E-mail address: Cynthia.McCluskey@utsa.edu (C.P. McCluskey).

the development of early intervention strategies (Butts & Snyder, 1997; Welsh, 2001). Understanding the impact of early official offending is imperative for drawing the attention of policymakers to develop effective interventions for an often-overlooked group (Howell, 2001).

Contemporary youth violence and gun involvement

The issue of gun involvement, especially for youthful offenders, has taken on recent urgency as a research question (Blumstein, 1995; Cook & Laub, 1998; Fingerhut, Ingram, & Feldman, 1992). Rising gun homicides by and against youths in cities such as Boston, have led to intensive intervention efforts (Kennedy, Braga, & Piehl, 2001). The proliferation of guns in the hands of urban youths has been well documented in schools, institutional settings, and among other samples (Myers, McGrady, Marrow, & Mueller, 1997; Sheley & Wright, 1995; Vaughn et al., 1996; Webster, Gainer, & Champion, 1993). Decker, Pennell, and Caldwell (1997) used the Drug Use

532   *C.P. McCluskey et al. / Journal of Criminal Justice 34 (2006) 531–541*

Forecasting Survey of seven thousand arrestees in eleven large cities, collected in 1995, to explore patterns of gun use and found that 14 percent of arrestees reported carrying guns most or all of the time and among juvenile male arrestees the percentage carrying guns rose to 20 percent.

Initiation into usage and carrying patterns for firearms represents an important focal point for current research. Lizotte and Sheppard (2001), Lizotte, Tesoriero, Thornberry, and Krohn (1994), and Tesoriero (1998) conducted extensive research on gun carrying of city youths in Rochester, New York. Overall, these studies indicated that a small proportion of youthful males were at risk for carrying weapons for both defense (protection) and offense (committing crimes).

That research, combined with the career criminal approach of Blumstein et al. (1986), gives rise to the charge of identifying those most likely to initiate a gun using or gun carrying component to their delinquent career. Previous studies suggested that the youngest initiates or early starters are most at risk to have future arrests for gun carrying or use in a crime (see e.g., Myers et al., 1997). Similarly, the literature indicated that males were most likely to be gun-involved (Lizotte, Krohn, Howell, Tobin, & Howard, 2000; Sheley & Wright, 1995; Tesoriero, 1998). Other research indicated that youths that adopted early onset to weapon carrying had elevated levels of later self-reported weapon-related acts (Tesoriero, 1998, p. 284). The relationship between early initiation into offending and later juvenile involvement, particularly among contemporary cohorts, is still being examined. Data analyzed by Krohn, Thornberry, Rivera, and LeBlanc (2001) indicated that there was a consistent link between early onset and more serious outcomes (not necessarily gun outcomes) for delinquents in Rochester and Montreal, as well as nearly all of the studies they reviewed in that research. Thus far, studies revealed that youthful males–those that carried weapons early in adolescence in particular–were at greatest risk for later gun involvement.

As such, this study utilized official arrest histories for those born in 1979 and arrested as a juvenile in a mid-sized urban area to assess the impact of early onset offending on later violent behavior. The consequences of early arrest for youth on violent outcomes were examined, including later arrests for violent and gun offenses. There were two purposes for the current study: first, using current data, the strength of the relationship between early onset and violent outcomes was examined in a contemporary cohort coming of age in the modern drug–gun–violence "period" discussed by Cook and Laub (2002) (also see Braga, 2003; Cork, 1999). Cook and Laub (2002) argued that the availability of guns and the motivation of crack markets were among period specific effects that drove youth ho-

micide in the early 1990s. Consonant with concerns about changing patterns in youth violence (compare Cook & Laub, 1998, 2002), the link between early onset and future violent offending was examined in this context. Second, the preoccupation with juvenile weapon involvement is currently a national public health concern (Braga, 2003; Webster et al., 1993; Wintemute, 2000); therefore, the specific impact of early onset offending on later gun offenses was also examined.

Official data, self-report data, and contemporary youth violence

While the initial birth cohort studies were used to examine offending patterns and provided much information about delinquency, data from the 1948 and 1958 Philadelphia birth cohorts and other early studies were unlikely to generalize to current conditions of youth violence and weapon involvement (see e.g., Blumstein, 1995; Braga, 2003; Cook & Laub, 1998, 2002; Zimring & Hawkins, 1997, pp. 91–105). Of particular concern was the nature of the relationship between early onset and participation in serious violence, a problem which crosses the disciplines of criminology (Krohn et al., 2001; Piquero & Buka, 2002; Tolan & Gorman-Smith, 1998) and public health (Dahlberg, 1998; Ellickson & McGuigan, 2000). This article offers a view of a contemporary cohort of youth, born in 1979, which provides a more current understanding of the nature of their initial and future contacts with a central city police department. Using this birth year/arrest cohort provides insight into current consequences of youthful behavior established by the classic data collected in the Philadelphia birth cohort and other studies.

Farrington (1998) has noted that official data are limited in the utility for uncovering the panoply of risk factors that may be associated with violent offending. Alternatively, one can opt to study self-reported outcomes in a prospective longitudinal design such as those fielded by the Rochester, Pittsburgh, and Denver efforts on uncovering the causes and correlates of delinquency. Self-reported data, however, suffer from potential validity problems (Farrington, 1998; Hindelang, Hirschi, & Weis, 1981), especially with regard to the reporting of more serious crimes. Cohen, Kasen, Smailes, and Fagan (2002) found, for example, that in self-report data collected on a sample of 663 subjects, twenty–two violent crimes were officially recorded, sixteen self-reported, and only four overlapped in the sample. This yielded a concordance measure of kappa=.19, indicating very weak association (see Landis & Koch, 1977). The authors noted that this could be associated with methodological issues, but the kappa concordance statistics

C.P. McCluskey et al. / Journal of Criminal Justice 34 (2006) 531–541 533

reported for other crimes (DUI, property, simple assault, drug-associated charges, and miscellaneous offenses) reflected a higher concordance level. In addition, relatively low base rates of serious mis-behavior accrue in self-report samples (Loeber, Farrington, & Waschbusch, 1998; Tolan & Gorman-Smith, 1998). In a general population sample, involvement in serious violent offending is likely to be rare. At the same time, such studies are unlikely to include school dropouts or chronic truants who are likely to be high rate and potentially serious or violent offenders (Farrington, 1998). For example, Lizotte and Sheppard (2001) analyzed data on gun ownership, carrying, and use in crimes on a sample of one thousand Rochester adolescents who were in the seventh or eighth grade in 1987–1988. They reported that 1.3 percent of non-gun owners ($n=548$), 3.7 percent of sport gun owners ($n=27$), and 30 percent of those who owned for protection ($n=40$), also reported that they were involved in gun crime in the six months preceding interviews during the ages fourteen to fifteen. Thus, out of 615 males interviewed, 20 reported involvement in gun crime. It is important to also note that no females were included because the girls rarely owned or used guns (Lizotte & Sheppard, 2001, p. 2).

The advantage of self-report data obtained through interviews is that it allows for ordering of life events and psychological measures for complex theory testing (e.g., Thornberry, 1987) and allows for the discovery of hidden, undetected delinquency (Huizinga, 1991; Wright & Decker, 1997). For assessing the relationship between race, gender, age of onset of official delinquency, and violent and gun outcomes, contemporary arrest data, though limited, offer valuable insight into offending patterns. This article provides a current examination of early onset and violence that could not be found with older birth cohorts, particularly since the nature and extent of youth violence had changed over time (Cook & Laub, 2002). The utility of official data in estimating the relationship between age of onset and serious and violent offending was supported by the work of Krohn et al. (2001), which revealed the largest differences in outcomes between early and late groups when an official onset variable was used over a self-report measure of onset.

Theoretical framework

Early onset and subsequent outcomes

For those who begin their offending careers early, the literature has cited a variety of negative outcomes. Most recently, Moffitt, Caspi, Harrington, and Milne (2002) described the consequences of early antisocial behavior among life-course persistent offenders in adulthood. Such outcomes include increased involvement and frequency of general criminality and violence, and interpersonal relationships characterized by conflict, economic disadvantage, and mental health problems. In terms of offending patterns, the literature on childhood delinquency suggests that those with an early age of onset are more likely to be at risk for later serious, violent, and chronic offending (for a review, see Krohn et al., 2001).[1] For example, in describing a three-stage trajectory of child antisocial behavior and juvenile offending, Patterson, Forgatch, Yoerger, and Stoolmiller (1998) identify a predominant path between child antisocial behavior, early arrest, and chronic juvenile offending.

This article focuses specifically on violent outcomes for early starters. The likelihood and frequency of later arrests for violence and gun offenses were examined among those first arrested between the ages of nine and thirteen (early starters) and those first arrested at fourteen to sixteen years of age. As longitudinal research has revealed, early delinquency has consequences for serious and violent behavior in adolescence and adulthood (Bartusch, Lynam, Moffitt, & Silva, 1997; Krohn et al., 2001; Moffitt et al., 2002; Tolan & Gorman-Smith, 1998; Tolan & Thomas, 1995).

In a recent review of early onset and criminal career patterns, Krohn et al. (2001) provided empirical support for the link between early offending and later seriousness. In their analysis, they examined three separate onset groups in place of a common early/late dichotomy to represent an age of onset continuum. The earliest onset group of the Rochester Youth Development Study (RYDS) was found to have the highest prevalence and frequency of serious offending of all onset groups and had a higher prevalence of violent offending than the middle onset group. In predicting violence in early adulthood, Krohn et al. (2001) found the earliest onset group to have the highest prevalence for both serious and violent offending, but found no significant group differences in the frequency of self-reported violence. In their examination of 1970 and 1990 cohorts from Montreal, the relationship between early onset and serious and violent outcomes was also supported. Notably, the official measure of onset produced the greatest group differences in outcomes. When official data were used, the earliest onset group was found to have the highest rates of official serious and violent offending (Krohn et al., 2001). Among females in the 1990 Montreal cohort, the relationship between early onset and violence was found with the middle onset group. Through the inclusion of females, a refined distinction of onset groups, and multiple outcomes, this article addressed shortcomings of earlier research.

Other studies have cited the lack of gender and ethnic diversity in longitudinal studies of criminal careers (Moffitt, Caspi, Rutter, & Silva, 2001; Tolan & Gorman-Smith, 1998; Tolan & Thomas, 1995). In an analysis of nationally representative and high-risk samples of youth, Tolan and Gorman-Smith (1998) found a relationship between age of onset and serious and violent offending in the National Youth Survey (NYS). In the high-risk sample of African Americans and Latinos in the Chicago Youth Development Study (CYDS), findings related to early onset were not consistent (Tolan & Gorman-Smith, 1998). While it was unclear whether differences in early onset across samples were due to the high-risk nature of the CYDS sample or differences in behavioral patterns among minority youth compared to the general population, the study by Tolan and Gorman-Smith (1998) drew attention to the importance of examining patterns of behavior across diverse youth. Similarly, Tolan and Thomas (1995) examined the influence of early onset among males and females of the National Youth Survey. They found that for both groups early onset "relates to more serious offending and greater involvement in serious offenses, in a more stable manner, over a longer period of time" (Tolan & Thomas, 1995, p. 175). The influence of early onset persisted once psychosocial factors were controlled in the model.

In recent examinations of the Dunedin Multidisciplinary Health and Development Study, adolescent and adult outcomes were assessed among life-course persistent (LCP) and adolescence-limited (AL) offender types (Moffitt, 1993). Early antisocial behavior, as demonstrated by LCP offenders, was found to predict convictions for violent offenses at age eighteen (Bartusch et al., 1997; Moffitt, Caspi, Dickson, Silva, & Stanton, 1996). At age twenty-six, LCP offenders demonstrated a greater likelihood of violent behavior according to self-report, informant, and official data, along with a higher mean number of offenses overall, including drug offenses and violence. In addition, the LCP group had a significantly higher prevalence and frequency of convictions for violence (Moffitt et al., 2002).

In a meta-analysis of risk factors for violent and serious delinquency, Lipsey and Derzon (1998) examined findings from thirty-four distinct longitudinal studies. Among childhood and adolescent predictors of violent or serious delinquency in late adolescence/early adulthood were antisocial behavior and social relationships. General offending and early substance use emerged as the predominant childhood predictors of adult violence. In adolescence, the strongest predictor of later violence was peer relationships, although general offending was also a strong predictor (Lipsey & Derzon, 1998). Findings related to early onset and violence persisted, even after controlling for study characteristics. As demonstrated by Lipsey and Derzon (1998) and Moffitt et al. (2002), the consequences of early onset, including violent offending, continue into adulthood. Overall, longitudinal research has revealed that early delinquency can result in serious and violent behavior that extends into adolescence and adulthood.

Purpose of current study

This study was undertaken from life-course and criminal career perspectives of delinquency which recognize that the early onset of offending can lead to negative outcomes, including future offending. This study was similar to the second Philadelphia Birth Cohort Study (Tracy et al., 1990), although data through adulthood were not available for inclusion and the residency restriction available in that study was not applicable here. Instead, the current cohort (1979) allowed for the examination of juvenile and early adulthood trends (seventeen to nineteen years) in official offending for males and females. Comprehensive arrest histories were generated for those born in 1979 and arrested before twenty years of age. Official data from 1989 through 1998 were included in the analysis of early onset offending and later violent outcomes in adolescence and early adulthood. To obtain an understanding of the relationship between early onset and violence, serious violent offenses were included such as homicide, assault, robbery, and rape. This was particularly important since previous studies of early onset and later offense seriousness typically included serious property offenses and minor violent acts.

Site and sample

The Lakeside Police Department is a mid-sized police agency that served a population that grew from 190,000 in 1990 to nearly 200,000 in 2000. Approximately 10 percent of the city's population are living in poverty. The Lakeside Police Department has grown from approximately 250 in the early 1990s to nearly 400 in 1999. The records kept by the agency are in an electronic format that allows one to assemble arrest histories for youths from those data.[2]

Official arrest records from the city of Lakeside were utilized in the analysis. Electronic arrest records were compiled for the years 1989 through 1998 and included a unique identifier, race, gender, offense type, and offense date. Individual arrest histories were calculated based on that information.

C.P. McCluskey et al. / Journal of Criminal Justice 34 (2006) 531–541   535

Table 1
Sample description: independent measures and onset timing

	Total sample	Late onset	Early onset
Number of cases	1,159	813 (70%)	346 (30%)
Gender			
Male*	820 (71%)	548 (67%)	272 (79%)
Female	339 (29%)	265 (33%)	74 (21%)
Race			
White	587 (51%)	414 (51%)	173 (50%)
African American	572 (49%)	399 (49%)	173 (50%)
Average age (standard deviation in parentheses)	14.67 (1.70)	15.58 (.83)	12.52 (1.23)

*Note: gender differences are statistically significant across groups ($p < .05$, two tail test).

A total of 1,159 arrestees born in 1979 were included in the analysis (see Table 1). Thus, individuals were between ten and nineteen years of age during the study period. The sample included males and females (71 and 29 percent, respectively), and allowed the opportunity to examine the impact of early onset and violent offending by gender, which had not always been feasible in previous studies (Wolfgang et al., 1972, for example). In addition, the sample was evenly distributed by race, with 51 percent White arrestees and 49 percent African American.

Measures and analysis

Defining early onset

In the analysis, early onset was defined as official contact with police prior to age fourteen. In contrast, arrests at age fourteen or older were considered late onset. The categorization of early onset in this study was consistent with previous studies on the onset of offending (Mazerolle, Brame, Paternoster, Piquero, & Dean, 2000; Moffitt, 1993). For example, Moffitt's life-course persistent offenders are described as those who initiate offending prior to age fourteen. Of those in the 1979 birth cohort of arrestees included in the analysis, 30 percent ($n = 346$) were arrested for the first time before the age of fourteen and were considered early onset offenders. Those arrested for the first time at age fourteen or later were coded as late onset ($n = 813$).

Outcome variables

To assess the consequences of early onset offending, later offending patterns were examined using official arrest histories. Literature has suggested that early onset is

associated with later serious and violent offending. In the study, early and late onset groups were examined with respect to the likelihood of future violent and gun offenses. Since data through 1998 were utilized, outcome variables captured offending in adolescence and early adulthood (through age nineteen).[3] This represented a minimum three-year follow-up period for late starters.

In the current analysis, violent crime included arrests for serious violent offenses such as homicide, assault, robbery, and rape. Less serious violence was excluded from the analysis to allow for the examination of the most serious violent behavior. In previous studies of the relationship between early onset and future offense seriousness, outcomes typically included serious property offenses and minor violent acts. Therefore, to obtain a better understanding of the relationship between early onset and violence, serious violent offenses were included. Three separate variables were included which assessed the prevalence, frequency, and rate of violent offending as outcomes. A dichotomous variable was constructed to estimate the prevalence of serious violent offenses following onset (0 = no serious violent offenses; 1 = any serious violent offenses). In addition, the number of serious violent arrests was calculated to generate the frequency of serious violent offending following onset (range 0–5). In an effort to control for follow-up time for early and late groups, an individual violent offending rate (lambda) was calculated. For each individual, the number of violent offenses was divided by the number of years following first arrest to calculate a yearly offending rate (λ; range 0–1.13). Specifically, the number of days between December 31, 1998 (last day of data collection) and the onset date (first arrest recorded) was computed and divided by 365.25 to generate the denominator for each lambda computation.

Gun offenses included weapons violations such as carrying a concealed weapon (CCW) and any violent crime that records indicated was committed with a firearm (such as armed robbery and assault with a weapon). A dichotomous variable was constructed to estimate the prevalence of gun-related arrests following onset (0 = no gun offense; 1 = any arrest for gun offense). In addition, the frequency of gun arrests following onset was calculated (range from 0–3), as well as the individual rate (λ) of gun offenses (range 0–.82). Since only four females were arrested for gun-related offenses, the analysis was conducted with males only ($n = 820$).

Control variables

Demographic characteristics were included in the study in estimating the impact of early onset on later

Table 2
Prevalence and frequency of violent outcomes

Dependent variables	Total sample ($n=1{,}159$)	Late onset ($n=813$)	Early onset ($n=346$)
Serious violent offenses			
Any violent offenses	14%	10%	25%*
Total number of violent offenses	242	104	138
Mean number of violent offenses	0.21	0.13	0.40[a]
Mean violent offending rate	0.04	0.03	0.06[a]

	Males only ($n=820$)	Late onset ($n=548$)	Early onset ($n=272$)
Gun offenses			
Any gun offenses	12%	10%	18%*
Total number of gun offenses	141	66	75
Mean number of gun offenses	0.17	0.12	0.28[a]
Mean gun offending rate	0.03	0.03	0.04[a]

*$p<.05$ chi-squared test.
[a]$p<.05$ *t*-test.

violent outcomes. Specifically, gender (0 = female; 1 = male) and race (0 = White; 1 = African American) were included in multivariate analyses. In addition, the type of first offense was included in regression models via four dichotomous variables that indicated whether the first arrest was for a disorderly, drug, property, or violent offense (contrasted with status offenses). In each of the dichotomous variables, specific offense type was coded 1 and all others were coded 0.

Findings

The purpose of this study was to explore the impact of early onset offending on later offending patterns. To that end, those arrested prior to age fourteen were compared with those whose first arrest occurred at age fourteen or later on several dimensions of later violent offending. The prevalence and frequency of future arrests for violent crime or arrests for gun offenses. As a first step in estimating violent outcomes of early arrest, the prevalence and frequency of violent and gun arrests following onset were assessed. Descriptive statistics for the total sample and onset groups are presented in Table 2.

Across the total sample, 14 percent were arrested for a subsequent violent arrest and 12 percent of males were arrested for a gun offense by age nineteen. As expected, the prevalence rates for the early onset group were significantly higher for both violent and gun offenses. One-quarter of early onset offenders were arrested for a later serious violent offense compared with 10 percent of the late onset

group. Additionally, the prevalence rate of gun arrests was nearly twice as large for early onset males compared to the late onset group (18 versus 10 percent, respectively).

In terms of frequency, the early onset group was responsible for 138 violent arrests following onset, while the late onset group comprised 104 violent arrests. Groups differed significantly in their average number of violent offenses (.40 for early compared to .13 for late onset). Similarly, early onset males had a significantly higher mean frequency of gun arrests than the late onset group (.28 compared to .12). Therefore, those arrested prior to the age of fourteen had a greater prevalence and frequency of subsequent violent and gun arrests than those arrested for the first time at age fourteen or later.

Since the frequency of offending was calculated for both groups through 1998, there was an unequal amount of follow-up time. Early onset arrestees had a minimum of five-year follow-up time in the analysis (maximum of nine years), while late onset arrestees had a follow-up time that ranged from three to five years. To control for follow-up time, individual offending rates, or lambda, were calculated for each arrestee. The average offending rate in both violent ($\lambda = .06$ for early starters compared to .03 for late onset) and gun offenses ($\lambda = .04$ early versus .03 for late onset) was significantly different across groups, even after controlling for follow-up time.

To examine the impact of age of onset on violent outcomes, multivariate regression analyses were conducted predicting the prevalence, frequency, and individual rate of offending. In each estimation, a dichotomous onset variable was included (0 = late, 1 = early) along with

Table 3
Logistic regression equations predicting *prevalence* of violence and gun outcomes

Variable	Violence prevalence ($n=1{,}159$)		Gun prevalence– males only ($n=820$)	
	Unstandardized coefficient	Odds ratio	Unstandardized coefficient	Odds ratio
Early onset	1.01* (.19)	2.7	0.71* (.23)	2.0
African American	0.78* (.18)	2.2	0.87* (.23)	2.4
Disorderly first offense	0.02 (.30)	1.0	0.11 (.38)	1.1
Drug first offense	−0.01 (.50)	1.0	−0.34 (.66)	0.7
Property first offense	−0.01 (.25)	1.0	0.15 (.32)	1.2
Violent first offense	0.36 (.31)	1.4	−0.26 (.41)	1.3
Male	0.99* (.24)	2.7	–	–
Intercept	−3.43* (.31)		−2.83 (.32)	
Model improvement χ^2	78.73*		23.31*	

*$p<.001$ (two-tailed test), standard errors in parentheses.

C.P. McCluskey et al. / Journal of Criminal Justice 34 (2006) 531–541   537

Table 4
Negative binomial regression equations predicting *frequency* of violence and gun offenses

Variable	Violence frequency ($n = 1,159$)		Gun frequency–males only ($n = 820$)	
	Unstandardized coefficient	Standard error	Unstandardized coefficient	Standard error
Early onset	1.04*	.17	0.78*	.22
African American	0.63*	.17	0.75*	.22
Disorderly firstoffense	−0.15	.28	0.27	.36
Drug first offense	−0.07	.47	−0.57	.70
Property first offense	−0.06	.24	0.08	.32
Violent first offense	0.12	.29	0.42	.39
Male	0.98*	.22	–	–
Intercept	−3.12*	.28	−2.65*	.31
Overdispersion parameter	2.14*	.45	2.55*	.70
Model improvement X^2	79.16*		40.2*	

*$p < .001$ (two-tailed test).

race, gender, and the type of first offense. First offense type was controlled to estimate whether the seriousness of first offense was indicative of future seriousness and potentially mediated the impact of age of onset.

In a logistic regression equation predicting serious violence for the total sample and gun offense prevalence for males (see Table 3) early onset significantly predicted the likelihood of participation in future violence (as indicated by arrest). Early starters were nearly three times as likely ($\text{Exp}(b) = 2.7$) to be arrested for a violent crime compared to late starters, and males with early onset were twice as likely to be arrested for a future gun crime ($\text{Exp}(b) = 2.0$). In the violence prevalence model, race and gender significantly predicted prevalence of violent offending, with African Americans and males more likely to have an arrest for a serious violent offense. In the model predicting gun offending, race was also significant. Finally, the type of first offense did not significantly predict the prevalence of either future outcome. Those with a disorderly, drug, property, or violent first offense were no more likely than those with a status offense to be arrested for a future violent or gun crime.

In predicting the extent of involvement in violent and gun offenses following onset, a set of negative binomial regression equations was estimated predicting the frequency of offending (see Table 4). Since the data for both dependent variables are in the form of counts, Poisson or negative binomial models are superior to ordinary least squares regression. Overdispersion of data would suggest that negative binomial models would be superior. The variance of both dependent variables exceeds the means, which is a threshold test for determining whether negative binomial regression is preferred. In addition, tests suggested by Cameron and Trivedi (1998) were conducted to determine whether the variables were overdispersed, and the *t*-values associated with that test

affirmed the use of negative binomial models.[4] Early onset, race, gender, and first offense type variables were included as predictors in the negative binomial model for serious violent offending and all but type of first offense significantly predicted the frequency of later violent arrests. Similarly, early onset and race significantly predicted the frequency of gun offending for males. Controlling for background factors, early onset was found to have a direct and statistically significant impact on the frequency of arrests for serious violence among males and females and gun offending among males. Since the frequency measure did not take into account follow-up time, a set of OLS equations predicting individual offending rates, or lambda, was estimated (see Table 5). Findings were consistent with those generated in previous analyses. Early onset significantly predicted the rate of arrest for violent offenses, once race, gender, and type of first offense were held constant. Additionally, African Americans and males were found to have significantly higher rates of serious violence than their White and female counterparts. With respect to rate of gun involvement, African American males had significantly higher rates of gun offending than White males, however, age of onset did not significantly predict the rate of future gun offending.

Additional analyses

To estimate violent outcomes of early onset by race, 587 White and 572 African American arrestees were examined. Early and late onset groups were compared within each racial group to determine whether patterns observed for the total sample were consistent by race and whether early onset within each racial group had the same consequences for later violent offending. Early and late onset groups were compared within each racial category on later violent offending patterns, including the

Table 5
OLS regression equations predicting *offending rate* of violence and gun offenses

Variable	Violence offending rate (λ) ($n=1,159$)		Gun offending rate (λ)–males only ($n=820$)	
	Unstandardized coefficient	Standard error	Unstandardized coefficient	Standard error
Early onset	0.02*	.01	0.01	.01
African American	0.02*	.01	0.02*	.01
Disorderly first offense	−0.00	.01	0.01	.01
Drug first offense	0.01	.02	−0.02	.02
Property first offense	−0.00	.01	0.00	.01
Violent first offense	0.01	.01	0.02	.01
Male	0.03*	.01	–	–
Intercept	0.00	.01	0.02	.01
F-ratio	6.27*		2.71*	
R^2	0.04		0.02	

*$p<.05$ (two-tailed test).

prevalence, frequency, and rate of violent offending. Later gun offenses were observed among males only (White males $n=427$; African American males $n=393$). Overall, African Americans had a higher prevalence of serious violence and gun offending. Within each racial group, a pattern similar to the total sample held for violent offending among early and late starters, where the prevalence and frequency of later arrests for violent crime were higher for early onset groups. Within each racial category, the pattern based on age of onset held. For example, African Americans arrested before age fourteen were at increased risk for a later violent and gun offense; of those in the early onset category, 33 percent had an arrest for a later violent offense (murder, aggravated assault, robbery), and 20 percent of males had an arrest for

a gun offense. Among African American late starters, 13 and 9 percent were arrested for similar offenses following onset (respectively). Among Whites, 16 and 10 percent of early starters had a later violent and gun arrest, compared to 8 and 4 percent of late starters. In multivariate regression equations (see Table 6) predicting prevalence and frequency of later violence and gun offending using logistic and negative binomial model estimations, early onset was a statistically significant predictor among Whites and African Americans. In predicting individual offending rate (λ), early onset significantly predicted later violent offending for African Americans only; early onset did not significantly predict rate of later gun offending for males, regardless of race. This finding may suggest an interaction between early onset and one's social

Table 6
Unstandardized regression coefficients by race (males only subsamples used in predicting gun outcomes)

Variable	Violent offending ($n=572$, Black; $n=587$, White)						Gun offending–males only ($n=427$, White; $n=393$, Black)					
	Logistic		Negative binomial[a]		OLS		Logistic		Negative binomial[a]		OLS	
	Prevalence		Frequency		Rate		Prevalence		Frequency		Rate	
	Black	White	Black	White	Black	White	Black	White	Black	White	Black	White
Early onset	1.15*	0.80*	1.19*	0.89*	0.04*	0.01	0.70*	0.74*	0.82*	0.76	0.02	0.01
Disorderly first offense	−0.28	0.54	−0.56	0.60	−0.02	0.02	−0.07	0.56	−0.05	1.05	−0.01	0.03
Drug first offense	−0.08	0.11	−0.35	0.71	−0.01	0.02	−0.67	0.72	−0.92	0.41	−0.03	0.01
Property first offense	−0.17	0.30	−0.29	0.48	−0.01	0.01	0.12	0.34	−0.04	0.51	0.00	0.01
Violent first offense	0.38	0.41	−0.13	0.68	0.00	0.02	0.07	0.67	0.26	0.91	0.02	0.02
Male	1.10*	0.80*	1.00*	0.84*	0.04*	0.02*	–	–	–	–	–	–
Constant	−2.69*	−3.43*	−2.37*	−3.44*	0.02	0.00	−1.88*	−3.11*	−1.78	−3.12*	0.04*	0.01
Model fit statistics												
Model improvement chi-square	48.20*	16.22*					9.53*	5.38				
Likelihood ratio chi-square			53.41*	18.78*					13.70*	6.36		
F-ratio					4.10*	1.69					1.16	1.01

*$p<.05$, two tailed tests.
[a]Each negative binomial model had a significant alpha component, indicating Poisson models would be inappropriate.

C.P. McCluskey et al. / Journal of Criminal Justice 34 (2006) 531–541   539

environment affecting later violence. This is, however, a post hoc interpretation that would require further analysis.

Discussion

A consistent relationship between the age of onset for first arrest and violent outcomes was found in this study, which was congruent with the findings of previous studies. The influence of early arrest on serious violent behavior and gun offending persisted once gender, race, and seriousness of first offense were controlled. In fact, an early arrest translated into more than a two-fold increase over later onset in the prevalence of later violence and gun offending (among males), holding all else constant.

Although findings were consistent with other studies, this research represented advancement in the understanding of criminal careers among a contemporary youth cohort. Additionally, the focus of the research was on violent crime and firearms offending, which represents a class of crime that had not been examined in previous research, particularly self-report studies, given the low base rate of violent offending.

A limitation of the data set was the lack of self-report data to estimate participation and frequency of offending that is not captured by the criminal justice system. Further research might examine other dimensions of criminal careers, such as time between offenses using self-report and official data simultaneously. An additional limitation to the official data set employed in this research was the unequal follow-up time for both groups. There are various approaches to addressing this particular issue. In the analysis, violence and gun offending rates were calculated for each subject, which controls for follow-up time and calculates the number of offenses per year. Also, of primary theoretical importance to the current analysis was the influence of onset on subsequent juvenile offenses. While three years of adult data were included for the 1979 birth cohort in the study, the primary interest was adolescent outcomes, which was consistent with other research (Fergusson, Horwood, & Nagin, 2000; Patterson et al., 1998). Therefore, a shorter follow-up time for late onset offenders was expected.

Another data concern relates to the use of official records from a single city. Aside from potential validity and reliability threats that coincide with official record keeping (related to citizen reporting behavior and police recording practices), there is the potential that members of the 1979 birth cohort who were arrested for the first time in Lakeside may have had subsequent arrests in other locations. Since data are from a single city, arrests that occurred in other places are missing.

Although the relationship between early onset and later offending emerged in the current study, it is unclear whether age of onset has a causal influence on future violent behavior or whether both phenomena represent manifestations of an underlying trait. This issue had been raised in previous research (see Krohn et al., 2001; Tolan & Thomas, 1995). Once other risk factors were controlled, age of onset had an independent and statistically significant influence on violence and gun offending. Since the study utilized official data, individual variables were not included in the analysis beyond demographic characteristics. Given the findings of Tolan and Thomas (1995), it is expected that the relationship would persist once psychosocial factors are introduced. It is possible that early onset sets in motion a series of events that lead to future violent behavior, which was described by Moffitt (1993) as cumulative continuity. At the same time, it is possible that early onset offending and later violence have similar underlying causes that Moffitt (1993) describes as contemporary continuity. Continued analysis of longitudinal studies and additional research is required to better understand the specific mechanisms by which early onset offending is linked with violent outcomes.

Additionally, little remains known about the outcomes of early onset by gender and ethnicity. Since very few females committed gun offenses (consistent with larger national patterns of firearm use), they were not included in the firearms analysis. The gender disparity was consistent with the observations of Lizotte et al. (1994) that urban gun carrying, especially with regard to criminal pursuits, is largely a male phenomenon. To further develop this line of research on early onset and gender, detailed information on the careers of diverse youth must be collected and examined.

Aside from onset, there are other dimensions of a criminal career which may also relate to violent outcomes, including the frequency of offending. Previous studies on violent outcomes have drawn attention to the relationship between chronic offending and participation in violence. In a study of childhood aggression and later violence, Farrington (1991) found that violent offenders could not be distinguished from nonviolent offenders once the frequency of offending was controlled. In their replication of Farrington's study, Capaldi and Patterson (1996) also found a relationship between chronic and violent offending. These findings suggested an overlap between frequent and violent offending, such that frequent offenders were likely to engage in violent offending as a consequence of their involvement in many offenses. Capaldi and Patterson (1996) also concluded that chronic and violent offending had the same underlying causes, with the predominant risk factor being early antisocial behavior. Future analyses of onset and violent offending might consider chronicity of offending as well.

The findings of the current research suggest that the gun offending and violence crisis experienced in the 1990s differentially involved youths that likely entered into delinquency relatively early in their lives. Offenders under fourteen appear to be particularly prone to making transitions into officially recorded events involving violence and gun use compared to their adolescent peers.

Although gun offending was relatively rare in this sample (12 percent of male arrestees) as it was in other studies, findings indicate that gun offending was not evenly distributed among early and later onset offenders. This comports with Howell's (2001) contention that resources ought to be focused on very young offenders to steer their trajectories towards pro-social paths. Exposure to gangs, gun-carrying peers, and gun sales have been identified as important avenues into gun carrying (Decker et al., 1997; Lizotte et al., 2000; Sheley & Wright, 1995); this suggests that those risk factors be examined particularly among very early offenders. Gun recovery efforts aimed at juveniles, such as the St. Louis Consent-to-Search program, would also serve to reduce the opportunity for youth to possess guns (Decker & Rosenfeld, 2004). Such programs in general ought to reduce the density of guns in a youthful offender's immediate environment and might diminish the opportunity for future gun violence.

Notes

1. In examining behavioral outcomes of early onset, Krohn et al. (2001) provided a detailed description and analysis of key studies. They described research findings on the age of onset and dimensions of future criminal careers, including frequency, duration, and seriousness.

2. Errant data entry represented the only threat to the data, and efforts were made by the research team to clean cases with misassigned identifiers.

3. In the state of Michigan, the minimum for adult criminal offending is seventeen; therefore, three years of adult arrest histories were included in the study.

4. A key assumption of Poisson models is that the data have equal mean and variance, or equidispersion. Violations of this assumption are likely to affect standard errors and t-statistics, producing doubt regarding the utility of significance tests of coefficients obtained from Poisson models of overdispersed data (Cameron & Trivedi, 1998, p. 77). The overdispersion parameter in the negative binomial model corrects for this shortcoming in the Poisson models. One should also note that the negative binomial model is reduced to the Poisson model when the overdispersion parameter equals zero (Cameron & Trivedi, 1998).

References

Bartusch, D. R. J., Lynam, D. R., Moffitt, T. E., & Silva, P. A. (1997). Is age important? Testing a general versus developmental theory of antisocial behavior. *Criminology, 35,* 13–48.

Blumstein, A. (1995). Youth violence, guns, and the illicit-drug industry. *Journal of Criminal Law and Criminology, 86,* 10–36.

Blumstein, A., Cohen, J., Roth, J. A., & Visher, C. A. (1986). *Criminal careers and "career criminals."* Washington, DC: National Academy Press.

Braga, A. A. (2003). Serious youth gun offenders and the epidemic of youth violence in Boston. *Journal of Quantitative Criminology, 19,* 33–54.

Butts, J. A., & Snyder, H. N. (1997). *The youngest delinquents: Offenders under age 15.* Washington, DC: U.S. Department of Justice, Office of Juvenile Justice and Delinquency Prevention.

Cameron, A., & Trivedi, P. (1998). *Regression analysis of count data.* Cambridge, UK: Cambridge University Press.

Capaldi, D. M., & Patterson, G. R. (1996). Can violent offenders be distinguished from frequent offenders: Prediction from childhood to adolescence. *Journal of Research in Crime and Delinquency, 33,* 206–231.

Cohen, P., Kasen, S., Smailes, E., & Fagan, J. (2002). *Childhood antecedents of adolescent and adult crime and violence.* Washington, DC: U.S. Department of Justice.

Cook, P. J., & Laub, J. H. (1998). The unprecedented epidemic in youth violence. In M. Tonry (Ed.), *Youth violence* (pp. 27–64). Chicago: University of Chicago Press.

Cook, P. J., & Laub, J. H. (2002). After the epidemic: Recent trends in youth violence in the United States. In M. Tonry & N. Morris (Eds.), *Crime and Justice: An Annual Review.* (Vol. 29 pp. 1–37) Chicago: University of Chicago Press.

Cork, D. (1999). Examining space-time interaction in city-level homicide data. *Journal of Quantitative Criminology, 15,* 379–406.

Dahlberg, L. L. (1998). Youth violence in the United States: Major trends, risk factors, and prevention approaches. *American Journal of Preventive Medicine, 14,* 259–272.

Decker, S. H., Pennell, S., & Caldwell, A. (1997). *Illegal firearms: Access and use by arrestees.* Washington, DC: U.S. Department of Justice, National Institute of Justice.

Decker, S. H., & Rosenfeld, R. (2004). *Reducing gun violence: The St. Louis Consent-to-Search program.* Washington, DC: U.S. Department of Justice, National Institute of Justice.

Ellickson, P. L., & McGuigan, K. A. (2000). Early predictors of adolescent violence. *American Journal of Public Health, 90,* 566–572.

Farrington, D. P. (1991). Childhood aggression and adult violence: Early precursors and later-life outcomes. In D. J. Pepler & K. H. Rubin (Eds.), *The development and treatment of childhood aggression* (pp. 5–29). Hillsdale, NJ: Lawrence Erlbaum Associates.

Farrington, D. P. (1998). Predictors, causes, and correlates of male youth violence. In M. Tonry (Ed.), *Youth violence* (pp. 421–475). Chicago: University of Chicago Press.

Fergusson, D. M., Horwood, L. J., & Nagin, D. S. (2000). Offending trajectories in a New Zealand birth cohort. *Criminology, 38,* 525–551.

Fingerhut, L. A., Ingram, D. D., & Feldman, J. J. (1992). Firearm and nonfirearm homicide among persons 15 through 19 years of age. *Journal of the American Medical Association, 267,* 3048–3053.

Hindelang, M. J., Hirschi, T., & Weis, J. G. (1981). *Measuring delinquency.* Beverly Hills, CA: Sage.

Howell, J. C. (2001). Juvenile justice programs and strategies. In R. Loeber & D. P. Farrington (Eds.), *Child delinquents: Development, intervention, and service needs* (pp. 305–321). Thousand Oaks, CA: Sage.

Huizinga, D. (1991). Assessing violent behavior with self-reports. In J. S. Milner (Ed.), *Neuropsychology of aggression* Boston: Kluwer.

Kennedy, D. M., Braga, A. A., & Piehl, A. M. (2001). *Reducing gun violence: The Boston Gun Project's Operation Ceasefire.* Washington, DC: U.S. Department of Justice, National Institute of Justice.

Krohn, M. D., Thornberry, T. P., Rivera, C., & LeBlanc, M. (2001). Later delinquency careers. In R. Loeber & D. P. Farrington (Eds.), *Child delinquents: Development, intervention, and service needs* (pp. 67–93). Thousand Oaks, CA: Sage.

Landis, J. R., & Koch, G. G. (1977). The measurement of observer agreement for categorical data. *Biometrics, 33,* 159–174.

Lipsey, M. W., & Derzon, J. H. (1998). Predictors of violent or serious delinquency in adolescence and early adulthood: A synthesis of longitudinal research. In R. Loeber & D. P. Farrington (Eds.), *Serious and violent juvenile offenders: Risk factors and successful interventions* (pp. 86–105). Thousand Oaks, CA: Sage.

Lizotte, A. J., Krohn, M. D., Howell, J. C., Tobin, K., & Howard, G. J. (2000). Factors influencing gun carrying among young urban males over the adolescent-young adult life course. *Criminology, 38,* 811–835.

Lizotte, A. J., & Sheppard, D. (2001). *Gun use by male juveniles: Research and prevention.* (Juvenile Justice Bulletin, NCJ 188992). Washington, DC: U.S. Department of Justice, Office of Justice Programs, Office of Juvenile Justice and Delinquency Prevention.

Lizotte, A. J., Tesoriero, J. M., Thornberry, T. P., & Krohn, M. D. (1994). Patterns of adolescent firearms ownership and use. *Justice Quarterly, 11,* 51–73.

Loeber, R., Farrington, D. P., & Waschbusch, D. A. (1998). Serious and violent juvenile offenders. In R. Loeber & D. P. Farrington (Eds.), *Serious and violent juvenile offenders: Risk factors and successful interventions* (pp. 13–29). Thousand Oaks, CA: Sage.

Mazerolle, P., Brame, R., Paternoster, R., Piquero, A. R., & Dean, C. (2000). Onset age, persistence, and offending versatility: Comparisons across gender. *Criminology, 38,* 1143–1172.

Moffitt, T. E. (1993). Adolescent-limited and life-course persistent antisocial behavior: A developmental taxonomy. *Psychological Review, 100,* 674–701.

Moffitt, T. E., Caspi, A., Dickson, N., Silva, P., & Stanton, W. (1996). Childhood-onset versus adolescent-onset antisocial conduct problems in males: Natural history from ages 3 to 18 years. *Development and Psychopathology, 8,* 399–424.

Moffitt, T. E., Caspi, A., Harrington, H., & Milne, B. J. (2002). Males on the life-course-persistent and adolescence-limited antisocial pathways: Follow-up at age 26 years. *Development and Psychopathology, 14,* 179–207.

Moffitt, T. E., Caspi, A., Rutter, M., & Silva, P. A. (2001). *Sex differences in antisocial behaviour: Conduct disorder, delinquency, and violence in the Dunedin longitudinal study.* Cambridge, UK: Cambridge University Press.

Myers, G. P., McGrady, G. A., Marrow, C., & Mueller, C. W. (1997). Weapon carrying among Black adolescents: A social network perspective. *American Journal of Public Health, 87,* 1038–1040.

Patterson, G. R., Forgatch, M. S., Yoerger, K. L., & Stoolmiller, M. (1998). Variables that initiate and maintain an early-onset trajectory for juvenile offending. *Development and Psychopathology, 10,* 531–547.

Piquero, A. R., & Buka, S. L. (2002). Linking juvenile and adult patterns of criminal activity in the Providence cohort of the National Collaborative Perinatal Project. *Journal of Criminal Justice, 30,* 259–272.

Sheley, J. F., & Wright, J. D. (1995). *In the line of fire: Youth guns and violence in urban America.* New York: Aldine De Gruyter.

Tesoriero, J. T. (1998). *A longitudinal study of weapon ownership and use among inner-city youth.* Ann Arbor, MI: UMI.

Thornberry, T. P. (1987). Toward an interactional theory of delinquency. *Criminology, 25,* 863–891.

Tolan, P. H., & Gorman-Smith, D. (1998). Development of serious and violent offending careers. In R. Loeber & D. P. Farrington (Eds.), *Serious and violent juvenile offenders: Risk factors and successful interventions* (pp. 68–85). Thousand Oaks, CA: Sage.

Tolan, P. H., & Thomas, P. (1995). The implications of age of onset for delinquency risk II: Longitudinal data. *Journal of Abnormal Child Psychology, 23,* 157–181.

Tracy, P. E., Wolfgang, M. E., & Figlio, R. M. (1990). *Delinquency careers in two birth cohorts.* New York: Plenum Press.

Vaughn, R. D., McCarthy, J. F., Armstrong, B., Walter, H. J., Waterman, P. D., & Tiezzi, L. (1996). Carrying and using weapons: A survey of minority junior high school students in New York City. *American Journal of Public Health, 86,* 568–572.

Webster, D. W., Gainer, P. S., & Champion, H. R. (1993). Weapon carrying among inner-city junior high school students: Defensive behavior versus aggressive delinquency. *American Journal of Public Health, 83,* 1604–1608.

Welsh, B. C. (2001). Economic costs and benefits of early developmental prevention. In R. Loeber & D. P. Farrington (Eds.), *Child delinquents: Development, intervention, and service needs* (pp. 339–355). Thousand Oaks, CA: Sage.

Wintemute, G. (2000). Guns and gun violence. In A. Blumstein & J. Wallman (Eds.), *The crime drop in America* (pp. 45–96). New York: Cambridge University Press.

Wolfgang, M. E., Figlio, R. M., & Sellin, T. (1972). *Delinquency in a birth cohort.* Chicago: University of Chicago Press.

Wright, R. A., & Decker, S. H. (1997). *Armed robbers in action.* Boston: Northeastern University Press.

Zimring, F. E., & Hawkins, G. (1997). *Crime is not the problem: Lethal violence in America.* New York: Oxford University Press.

[6]

The association between weapon-carrying and the use of violence among adolescents living in or around public housing

ROBERT H. DuRANT, ALAN G. GETTS, CHRIS CADENHEAD AND
ELIZABETH R. WOODS

The study examined social and psychological factors associated with the frequency of weapon-carrying by Black adolescents living in a community where there is extensive poverty and a high level of violent crime. Using a cross-sectional anonymous survey design adolescents ($N=225$; males= 44%) ages 11 to 19 years living in or around nine HUD housing projects in Augusta, Georgia were administered an anonymous questionnaire. The dependent variables were the number of days that a weapon, such as a gun, knife, or club was carried in the previous 30 days and the frequency that a hidden weapon was carried in the last year. Carrying a weapon during the previous 30 days was significantly ($p<0.05$) associated with previous exposure to violence and victimization, age, corporal punishment scale, depression, family conflict, purpose in life, and the self-appraised probability of being alive at age 25, and was higher among males. Based on multiple regression analysis, previous exposure and victimization to violence, gender, age, and self-appraised probability of being alive at age 25 explained 17 per cent of the variation in frequency of weapon-carrying. The exposure to violence and victimization scale, school grade, and probability of being alive at age 25 explained 12·1 per cent of the variation in frequency of carrying a hidden weapon in the last year. The two indicators of weapon-carrying were not associated with family structure, religious behavior, or any other demographic variable.

INTRODUCTION

Homicide is the leading cause of death for Black men ages 15 to 24 years, with 61 per cent of these homicides occurring during non-felony activity as a means

Reprint requests and correspondence should be addressed to R. H. DuRant, Division of Adolescent/Young Adult Medicine, Children's Hospital, Harvard Medical School, 300 Longwood Ave, Boston, MA 02115, U.S.A.

Supported in part by Project MCT-MA 259195 from the Maternal and Child Health Bureau (Title V, Social Security Act), Health Resources and Services Administration, Department of Health and Human Services.

580   R. H. DuRANT *ET AL.*

to resolve conflict (Mercy and Fenley, 1991). Among 15- to 19-year-old Black men, the 1988 homicide rate (76·78 per 100,000) was over nine times greater than White men from the same age group (Guyer, 1992). Although male adolescents engage in more violent behavior than females (DuRant *et al.*, 1994 *a,b*), female adolescents also engage in violent behavior in order to resolve conflict (Mercy and Fenley, 1991; Prothrow-Stith, 1991; Prothrow-Stith and Spivak, 1992; DuRant *et al.*, 1994 *a,b*).

Much of the increase in morbidity and mortality among lower socio-economic minority youth is associated with use of firearms and other weapons (Fingerhut *et al.*, 1987, 1992; Callahan and Rivara, 1992). In 1991, 41 per cent of male and 11 per cent of female high school students reported that they had carried a weapon such as a gun, knife, or club in the previous 30 days (CDC, 1992). Among those who carried a weapon, 11 per cent reported that they carried a hand gun most often. Adolescents who carry guns, and who are members of families where males carry guns, are more likely to become victims of gun-related violence (Sheley *et al.*, 1992). Although a variety of theoretical (Smith *et al.*, 1978; Sutherland and Cressey, 1978) and public health (Runyan and Gerken, 1989; Fulginiti, 1992; Koop and Lundberg, 1992; Mason and Proctor, 1992; Novello *et al.*, 1992; Rosenberg *et al.*, 1992) approaches have been proposed to explain adolescents' use of weapons to resolve conflict, there have been few empirical tests of these theories. DuRant *et al.* (1994) recently proposed cultural transmission theory to explain adolescent fighting behavior. This theory proposes that crime and delinquency are learned in interaction with other people, largely within intimate primary groups such as families and peer groups (Sutherland and Cressey, 1978). There is extensive evidence that many children and adolescents are continually exposed to high levels of violence throughout their lives and that this socialization may be having a significant effect on the increase in violent behavior observed over the last 40 years (Centerwall, 1992). This includes witnessing violence on the television and in movies, in the community, and in the home (Gladstein and Slater, 1988; Widom, 1989 *a,b*; Shakoor and Chalmers, 1991; Martinez *et al.*, 1992). In further support of cultural transmission theory, compelling evidence suggests that being a victim of violence, severe corporal punishment, and early physical abuse are all strongly linked to the development of aggressive behaviors, delinquency, and suicidal attempts (Fagan and Gersten, 1986; American Association for Protecting Children, 1987; Cavaiola and Schiff, 1988; Holmes and Robins, 1988; Powers and Eckenrode, 1988; Widom, 1989 *a,b*; Richters and Martinez, 1990; Riggs *et al.*, 1990; Bayatpour *et al.*, 1992; Bishop *et al.*, 1992). Also, as adolescents witness their peers carrying weapons and using them to resolve conflicts, substantial attitude changes toward the acceptability of carrying weapons are likely to occur (Collohan and Rivara, 1992; Fingerhut *et al.*, 1992 *a,b*; Sheley *et al.*, 1992). Not all adolescents who live in communities with high levels of poverty and unemployment, and who are exposed to or are victims of violence, carry and use weapons. Other social and psychological factors such as family structure, religious behavior, involvement in school and athletics, depression, emotional distress, etc. have been associated with adolescents' involvement in other problem behaviors and may add to our understanding of weapon-carrying (Rutter, 1987; Werner, 1989, 1992; Masters *et al.*, 1990; Garmezy, 1991; Jessor, 1992; Kagan, 1992; Prothrow-Stith, 1992; DuRant *et al.*, 1994 *a,b*). These findings support the social psychological theory of resiliency which proposes that certain characteristics of the individual and/or his or her environment transactions make an adaptive outcome more likely, despite "negative odds" or the presence of multiple risk factors (Rutter, 1987; Warner, 1989, 1992; Masters *et al.*, 1990; Garmezy, 1991; Jessor, 1992). These characteristics, combined with external support systems, provide the individual with a belief in system by which to live. Resiliency is associated with a sense of hope or purpose that negative odds can be overcome, especially if the origin of that hope is in some defined religious faith or belief system (Jessor, 1992). Drawing upon a conceptual framework from both cultural transmission and resiliency theories this study examined the relationships between exposure to or being a victim of violence, other social and psychological factors, and weapon-carrying among Black adolescents living in communities characterized by high levels of poverty, unemployment and violence.

METHODS

Participants

The study was conducted on 225 Black adolescents living in or around nine HUD housing projects in Augusta, Georgia (DuRant *et al.*, 1994 *a*). The participants ranged in age from 11 to 19 years ($\bar{x}14\cdot4\pm2\cdot2$). Ninety-nine (44%) of the participants were male. The majority of the adolescents lived with a female head of household (84·9%) with a mean educational level of 12·5 grades completed.

Procedures

The study protocol was approved by the Human Assurance Committee of the Medical College of Georgia and has been described in two previous reports from these data (DuRant *et al.*, 1994 *a,b*). Eight adolescents living in the targeted housing projects were enlisted to help recruit participants. They were asked to contact as many adolescents in their project area as was possible by delivering to the youth a parental and youth-informed consent form along with information as to when and where the questionnaires were to be administered. The recruiters were paid one dollar for each participant who completed a questionnaire. The use of a non-random convenience sample may have resulted in excluding adolescents engaging in high levels of violent behavior. Questionnaires were administered in the housing project community centers, a local school during a summer enrichment program, an area high school holding summer school, and in the conference room of the Georgia Children and Youth Project which provides health care to children and adolescents living in HUD housing projects. There were no differences among sites or the recruiters in the dependent or demographic variables. Written parental and subject-informed consent was obtained and the participant's name was not placed in the questionnaire.

To control for differences in reading levels, the questionnaire was read aloud by trained interviewers to groups of participants ranging in size from 3 to 40 and took between 45 and 60 minutes to administer, depending upon the size of the group and the number of questions asked by the participants. While one interviewer read the questions, two other interviewers roamed the room to help participants stay on task. In no cases were adolescents' parents present when the questionnaire was administered. Participants were paid $5·00 for completing the questionnaire. Two questionnaires completed by mentally handicapped youths were discarded.

Questionnaire

The questionnaire was constructed from several standardized measures described in the following sections. The questionnaire contained 171 items. The questionnaire was assessed for 1 week test–retest reliability on 12 of the 225 participants. Each constructed scale underwent item analysis and was tested for internal consistency with Cronbach's alpha. The psychometric analyses of the questionnaire have been reported previously (DuRant *et al.*, 1994 *a,b*). In general, for most variables the test–retest reliability coefficients were >0·85 and Cronbach's alpha values ranged from 0·58 to 0·86. The means and standard deviations of these scales are reported in Table 1.

Adolescent weapon-carrying was measured with items from the Denver Youth Study Self-Reported Delinquency Questionnaire (Huizinga *et al.*, 1991) and items from the CDC's Youth Risk Behavior Survey (1991). The first question assessed the number of days that a weapon, such as a gun, knife, or club was carried in the previous 30 days ($\bar{x}=0\cdot63$, s.d.$=1\cdot26$, skewness$=1\cdot86$). The responses were measured on a 5-point ordinal scale ranging from 0 to 6 or more days. The second question assessed the frequency that a hidden weapon was carried during the last year ($\bar{x}=2\cdot4$, s.d.$=9\cdot1$, skewness$=7\cdot3$). This question was open-ended and responses ranged from 0 to 100 times.

Table 1. *Means and standard deviations for the social and psychological scales*

	$\bar{x}$	S.D.
Desired SES	2·9	1·6
Anticipated SES at age 25	3·5	1·9
Church attendance	3·5	1·5
Corporal punishment	0·9	1·3
Conflict tactics scale (Family conflict)	34·9	9·9
Exposure to and victim of violence	4·2	22·6
Children's depression inventory	7·8	6·0
Hopelessness scale for children	2·4	2·3
Purpose in life	81·2	12·9
Alive at age 25 years	3·8	0·9

Being exposed to and victimized by violence in the community was assessed with questions from Richter and Martinez's (1990) Survey of Exposure to Community Violence. This survey measures the frequency of exposure to or being a victim of 27 types of violence such as gang violence, selling drugs, burglary, police arrests, assaults, physical threats, sexual assaults, weapon carrying, firearm use, intentional injuries such as stabbings, gunshots, suicides, murders, etc. Each item is scored on a scale ranging from never (0) to almost every day (8). Based on item analyses, questions measuring exposure to violence had high internal consistency with questions assessing being victims of crime and violence.

Exposure to domestic conflict and violence was assessed through a modified version of the Conflict Tactics Scale (Straus, 1979). Each item was scored on a 4-point scale ranging from never (1) to often (4). This 20-item scale has good concurrent validity when correlated with other measures of parental psychosocial distress. In the present study, one item was found to have poor internal consistency with the other 19 items and was discarded. The revised scale ranged from 19 indicating low domestic conflict to 71 representing high conflict. The scale had a Cronbach's alpha of 0·86, and a test–retest reliability of 0·97.

The Home Environment Interview, Version II, was employed to assess disciplinary activity in the home (Holmes and Robins, 1988). This 6-item scale was modified slightly to measure current rather than retrospective patterns of corporal punishment. The scale assessed severity of physical punishment, such as being punched or hit with a belt, being punished so hard the adolescent had to see a physician, etc. Each item was scored as a 0 (no) or 1 (yes). The scale ranged from zero to six (high disciplinary activity) and had a Cronbach's alpha of 0·58. However, the test–retest reliability was only 0·24.

584   R. H. DuRANT *ET AL.*

The Children's Depression Inventory (CDI) was used to measure a variety of symptoms of depression (Kovacs, 1985). This 27-item self report measure has been found to have good scale reliability and to correlate well with other similar psychological scales. Each item has three possible responses scored as either 0, 1 or 2. The CDI has a potential range of 0 to 54, with 54 suggesting the maximum level of depression. In this sample, the scale ranged from 0 to 31, had a Cronbach's alpha of 0·82, and a test–retest reliability of 0·84.

The Hopelessness Scale for Children (HSC) was employed to measure subjects' negative expectations about the future (Kuzdin *et al.*, 1986). Each item was scored as either true (like you) or false (not like you). This 16-item scale ranged from 0, indicating low hopelessness to 12 indicating a high level of hopelessness. The scale had a Cronbach's alpha of 0·64 and a test–retest reliability coefficient of 0·61.

The Purpose in Life (PIL) test was designed to measure the level of perceived meaning in one's life (Crumbaugh and Maholick, 1964; Crumbaugh, 1977). The PIL has been found to measure a construct distinctly different from locus of control (Waters and Klein, 1980). Each of the 14 items was scored on a seven point scale so that the minimum ("worst") score is 14 and the maximum is 98. The participants' scores ranged from 35 to 98, and the scale had a Cronbach's alpha of 0·86 and a test–retest reliability coefficient of 0·61.

A 5-point scale was created to determine the subjects' certainty of being alive at age 25 (DuRant *et al.*, 1994 *a,b*). The choices ranged from "I am absolutely sure that I will live to be 25 years of age", scored as a 1, to "I am absolutely sure that I won't live to be 25 years of age", scored as a 5. This item had a test–retest reliability of 1·0. Subjects' religious activity was assessed with two questions. The first question asked whether the participant was a member of any church or religious organization. The second was a 5-point scale used to determine frequency of church attendance or religious activity. Test–retest reliability was 0·82 for the first question and 0·60 for the second.

Four questions were asked to assess family structure. These included the total number of people in the home, whether the participant lived with a parent or adult relative, the subject's birth order, and the head of the participant's household. All of these questions had a test–retest reliability of 0·89 or better.

Future aspirations were assessed with two questions (DuRant *et al.*, 1994 *a,b*). Participants were asked, "If you could do whatever you wanted, what type of job or profession do you want to have when you grow up?" The answers are scored on a 7-point ordinal scale based on the educational level needed to achieve the professional goal (with one (1) being the highest educational level). At a separate point in the questionnaire the participants were asked what kind of job they saw themselves doing when they were 25 years of age. This question was scored identically to the preceding question. Test–retest correlation for these questions was 0·91. Parent(s)' socio-economic status was based on the expected educational level needed to qualify the parents' for their current job or profession (DuRant *et al.*, 1994 *b*). This was scored on a 7-point ordinal scale with one (1) indicating the highest socio-economic status level (professional job requiring a doctoral degree), six (6) indicating employment not requiring a high school education, and seven (7) indicating unemployed.

Statistical analysis

Interval and ordinal data are summarized as the mean±standard deviation (S.D.). Bivariate analyses were conducted with Spearman Ranked correlation Coefficients (rho), and chi-square tests (for categorical data). Variables found to be significantly ($p \leq 0.05$) associated with adolescents' weapon-carrying were analysed with stepwise multiple regression analysis. The regression models were computed by first entering all independent variables into the equation and then removing the variable with the largest probability of F larger than 0·10. The equation is then recomputed without the removed variable, and the evaluation process is repeated until no more independent variables can be removed. Then, the independent variable that was the smallest probability of F and is not in the equation, is entered, if the probability value is smaller than 0·05 and if the variable passes the tolerance tests of 0·01. The tolerance test is the proportion of a variable's variance not accounted for by other independent variables in the equation. Minimum tolerance associated with a given variable not in the equation is the smallest tolerance any variable already in the equation would have, if the given variable were included. Next, all variables are again examined for removal. This process continues until no variables in the equation need to be removed, and no variables not in the equation are eligible for entry.

RESULTS

Almost 25 per cent of these adolescents reported carrying a weapon during the month prior to the interview, with over 12 per cent carrying weapons for 4 or more days. Similarly, 26·9 per cent stated that they had carried a hidden weapon during the previous year.

Recent weapon carrying was significantly correlated with greater previous exposure to violence and victimization, higher depression, more severe corporal punishment, older age, higher family conflict, lower purpose in life, and a lower self-appraised probability of being alive at age 25 years and was higher ($p <$ 0·001) among males than females (Table 2). Number of days of weapon-carrying was not associated with religious behavior, family structure, or any other demographic variable. When analysed with multiple regression, previous exposure to violence and victimization, gender, age, and the self-appraised

Table 2. *Spearman correlation coefficients between Black adolescents' frequency of weapon-carrying and social and psychological variables*

	Frequency			
	Carried weapon in previous 30 days		Carried hidden weapon in past 12 months	
	rho	*p*	rho	*p*
Age	0·18	0·006	0·20	0·003
School grade	0·11	n.s.*	0·16	0·02
Number of brothers	0·05	n.s.	0·02	n.s.
Total members of family	−0·02	n.s.	0·06	n.s.
Age at first coitus	−0·04	n.s.	−0·09	n.s.
Future SES	0·10	n.s.	0·13	0·053
Alive at age 25 years	−0·13	0·054	−0·16	0·014
Corporal punishment	0·18	0·007	0·04	n.s.
Family conflict	0·15	0·029	0·16	0·017
Exposure to violence	0·28	0·0001	0·32	0·0001
Depression	0·18	0·009	0·19	0·006
Purpose in life	−0·14	0·044	−0·08	n.s.
Hopelessness	0·06	n.s.	0·01	n.s.

*n.s.=*p*>0·05.

Table 3. *Multiple regression analysis of the number of days that adolescents carried a weapon for during the previous month*

Variable	Beta	Partial correlation	R^2 change	F	*p*
Exposure to violence	0·0145	0·275	0·118	26·01	0·0001
Gender	−0·5444	−0·231	0·030	16·94	0·0001
Age	0·0931	0·174	0·021	13·21	0·0001
Probability of being alive at age 25	−0·2233	−0·170	0·024	11·58	0·0001
Constant	0·3135	0·194	0·178		

probability of being alive at age 25 explained 17·8 per cent of variation in the frequency that these adolescents carried weapons during the previous 30 days (Table 3). When the linear effects of the other independent variables were removed from each independent variable and weapon-carrying, previous exposure to violence explained the most variation in frequency of weapon-carrying, following in order by gender, age and the self-appraised probability of being alive at age 25 years. The frequency that a hidden weapon had been carried during the previous year was positively correlated with greater previous exposure to violence and victimization, older age, higher depression, higher school grade, higher family conflict scale, and negatively correlated with the

Table 4. *Multiple regression analysis of the frequency of carrying a hidden weapon during the past year by adolescents*

Variable	Beta	Partial correlation	R^2 change	F	p
Exposure to violence	0·0642	0·244	0·079	17·22	0·0001
School grade	0·4851	0·203	0·031	12·39	0·0001
Probability of being alive at age 25	−1·0299	−0·162	0·024	10·24	0·0001
Constant	−0·8602	0·134	0·121		

probability of being alive at age 25 years (Table 2). Based on multiple regression analysis, three of these variables explained 13·4 per cent of the variation in the frequency a hidden weapon had been carried (Table 4). In order of magnitude of the partial correlation coefficients, these variables were previous exposure to violence and victimization, school grade, and the probability of being alive at age 25 years.

DISCUSSION

Although leaders in public health have recently called for increased efforts aimed at stemming the epidemic of violence (Mason, 1992; Novello *et al.*, 1992), it must be remembered that violence is a multi-faceted public health problem for which there does not exist any prevention program whose efficacy has been tested with randomized controlled designs (Rosenberg *et al.*, 1992). Koop and Lundberg (1992) state that the solutions to violence are very complex and that research into the causes, prevention, and cures of violence is needed. In response to this need, DuRant *et al.* (1994*a*) recently reported that three variables accounted for 32 per cent of the variation in a scale measuring a wide variety of violent behaviors: previous exposure to and being a victim of violence, depression and male gender. In a follow-up to this study, DuRant *et al.* (1994 *b*) found that 16 per cent of the variation in these adolescents' frequency of fighting was accounted for by previous exposure to and being a victim of violence, school grade and number of sexual partners. The purpose of this report was to examine another aspect of this form of adolescent problem behavior from the same data set reported above, frequency of weapon-carrying. The CDC (1992) has reported that 26 per cent of high school students nationally, and 27 per cent of Georgia's students, carried a weapon such as a gun, knife, or club in the 30 days prior to the 1991 Youth Risk Behavior Survey. This is probably an over-estimation of the frequency these adolescents carry weapons for self-defence or violence, since the survey was conducted during the school year and did not control for students who carried a gun for hunting, skeet-shooting, target practice, etc. In comparison, we found that 24·4 per cent of our sample of 11- to 19-year-old youth living in or around public housing responded that they had carried a weapon within the last 30 days, when asked in the summer months when there was not a hunting season. We also found that the number of days that these adolescents reported carrying a weapon during the previous month was significantly correlated with three indicators of previous exposure to violence: the previous exposure to violence and victimization scale, degree of family conflict, and severity of corporal punishment and discipline. Similarly, the frequency that a hidden weapon was carried during the previous year was associated with the previous exposure to violence and victimization scale and family conflict. Because these data are correlational analyses, causation between multiple exposures to violence and adolescents' weapon carrying cannot be inferred. These relationships may be co-variational in nature, with viewing violence in the community, personally experiencing violence and crime, witnessing violence and conflict among family members in the home, being a victim of severe corporal punishment, and carrying a weapon such as a gun or knife, dynamically interacting with one another as these events co-occur (Sheley *et al*., 1992). These data support the cultural transmission theory that has proposed that adolescents' use of violence is learned within intimate primary groups such as families, peer groups, and other sources for modeling such as gangs (Sutherland and Cressey, 1978; DuRant *et al*., 1994 *b*). These data also support previous theoretical and empirical work suggesting that experiencing or being a victim of violence will increase the risk that an adolescent will be prepared to use violence against others by carrying a weapon (Runyan and Gerken, 1989; Bishop *et al*., 1992; Sheley *et al*., 1992).

Similarly to previous reports of other analyses from this data set (DuRant *et al*., 1994 *a,b*), adolescents with higher levels of depression were more likely to report carrying weapons. Because these are cross-sectional data, care must be taken not to assume that depressed adolescents are more likely to carry weapons. It could easily be argued that exposure to high levels of violence and being prepared to engage in violent activity by carrying weapons could result in higher levels of depression among youth.

Although these adolescents were living in a community characterized by high levels of poverty, unemployment, and criminal activity, and 84 per cent had reported engaged in at least one form of violent behavior, only a quarter of these youth reported that they had carried a weapon in the past. Two variables were found to be associated with adolescents' resiliency to the temptations to carry deadly weapons despite the presence of multiple risk factors. In agreement with our previous studies (DuRant *et al*., 1994 *a,b*), adolescents who reported higher scores on the purpose in life scale and who thought there was a higher likelihood that they would be alive at age 25 years were less likely to report carrying weapons. When analysed with a multiple regression analysis, the perceived probability of being alive at age 25 years continued to explain significant amounts of additional variation in both weapon-carrying variables, after the influence of the previous exposure to violence and victimization scale was accounted for. Despite living in an environment that would be expected to facilitate feelings that there was little chance for successfully changing their life situations and a chance that they may not live to be adults, many of these adolescents felt the opposite and correspondingly did not carry weapons.

The social psychological theory of resiliency states that certain characteristics of the individual and/or his environmental transactions make an adaptive outcome more likely despite "negative odds" or the presence of multiple risk factors (Rutter, 1987; Weiner, 1989, 1992; Masters *et al.*, 1990; Garmezy, 1991; Jessor, 1992). Jessor (1992) has outlined a model of the acquisition of adolescent problem behaviors which included "protective" resiliency factors. Some factors extrinsic to the individual are quality schools, cohesive family, neighborhood resources, interested adults, models for conventional behavior, high community controls against deviant behavior, church attendance, and involvement in school and voluntary clubs. Some intrinsic to the individual are high intelligence, value on achievement, value on health, and intolerance of deviance. Also, a sense of hope is necessary for resiliency (Warner, 1989, 1992). However, variables such as hopelessness, family structure, parental socio-economic status, religious behavior, and parental employment status were not associated with weapon-carrying in this sample of adolescents. These findings may partially be explained by one of the weaknesses of this study, the lack of variation in the family structure, parental socio-economic and employment status variables. An additional limitation of the study design is that the sample consisted of volunteers of only Black youth from one small city in the Southeast of the U.S.A. Thus, our ability to generalize these findings is limiting. However, few studies to date have examined correlates of adolescent weapon-carrying.

For many adolescents coming of age in the 1990s, violence is a daily reality. They experience it in their homes and communities, and witness the irresponsible portrayal of violence on prime time television and in movies (Fulginiti, 1992; DuRant *et al.*, 1994 *b*). Among minority youth living in lower socio-economic urban areas, the hopelessness of social immobility and a lack of modeling of non-violent conflict resolution skills in their homes and communities provides scenarios in which there are neither incentives nor skills to avoid the use of violence. Whether weapon-carrying or weapon availability is associated with increased likelihood of using violence to resolve a conflict is uncertain, and has been debated. However, it is clear that the availability of a lethal weapon changes the dynamics of interpersonal conflict by introducing the power to kill. Our data suggest that weapon-carrying by adolescents, while not strictly a violent behavior, is associated with the same set of risk factors that are linked with the use of interpersonal violence, and thus may be considered to be a part of a behavioral risk profile of aggression and violence.

REFERENCES

American Association for Protecting Children. (1987). *Highlights of Official Child Abuse and Neglect Reporting* 1986. Denver: American Humane Association.

Bayatpour, M., Wells, R. D. and Holford, S. (1992). Physical and sexual abuse as predictors of substance use and suicide among pregnant teenagers. *Journal of Adolescent Health*, **13**, 128–132.

Bishop, V., Woodward, K. and D'Angelo, L. (1992). Health risk behavior in urban youth. *Journal of Adolescent Health*, **13**, 65.

Callahan, C. M. and Rivara, F. P. (1992). Urban high school youth and handguns: a school based survey. *Journal of the American Medical Association*, **267**, 3038–3042.

Cavaiola, A. A. and Schiff, M. (1988). Behavioral sequelae of physical and/or sexual abuse in adolescents. *Child Abuse and Neglect*, **12**, 181–188.

Centers for Disease Control. (1992). Behaviors related to unintentional and intentional injuries among high school students—United States, 1991. *Morbidity and Mortality Weekly Report*, **41**, 760–762.

Centerwall, B. S. (1992). Children, television, and violence. *Report of the Twenty-third Ross Roundtable on Critical Approaches to Common Pediatric Problems*. Columbus: Ross Laboratories, pp. 87–94.

Crumbaugh, J. C. (1977). The seeking of noetic goals test: a complimentary scale to the purpose in life test. *Journal of Clinical Psychology*, **3**, 900–907.

Crumbaugh, J. C. and Maholick, L. T. (1964). An experimental study in existentialism: the psychometric approach to Frankl's neogenic neurosis. *Journal of Clinical Psychology*, **29**, 200–207.

DuRant, R. H., Cadenhead, C., Pendergrast, R. A., Slavens, G. and Linder, C. W. (1994a). Factors associated with the use of violence among black adolescents. *American Journal of Public Health*, **84**, 612–617.

DuRant, R. H., Pendergrast, R. A. and Cadenhead, C. (1994b). Exposure to violence and victimization and fighting behavior among urban black adolescents. *Journal of Adolescent Health*, **15**, 311–318.

Fingerhut, L. A., Ingram, D. D. and Feldman, J. J. (1992a). Firearm and nonfirearm homicide among persons 15 through 19 years of age: differences by level of urbanization, United States, 1979 through 1989. *Journal of the American Medical Association*, **267**, 3048–3053.

Fingerhut, L. A., Ingram, D. D. and Feldman, J. J. (1992b). Firearm homicide among black teenage males in metropolitan counties. *Journal of American Medical Association*, **267**, 3054–3058.

Fulginiti, V. A. (1992). Violence and children in the United States. *American Journal of Diseases in Children*, **146**, 671–672.

Garmezy, N. (1991). Resilience in children's adaptation to negative life events and stressed environments. *Pediatric Annals*, **20**, 459–466.

Gladstein, J. and Slater, E. J. (1988). Inner city teenagers' exposure to violence: a prevalence study. *Maryland Medical Journal*, **37**, 951–954.

Guyer, B. (1992). An epidemiological overview of violence among children. *Report of the Twenty-third Ross Roundtable on Critical Approaches to Common Pediatric Problems*. Columbus: Ross Laboratories.

Holmes, S. K. and Robins, L. N. (1988). The role of parental disciplinary practices in the development of depression and alcoholism. *Psychiatry*, **51**, 24–36.

Huizinga, D., Esbensen, F. A. and Weiber, A. W. (1991). Are there multiple paths to delinquency? *Journal of Criminal Law and Criminology*, **82**, 83–118.

Jessor, R. (1992). Risk behavior in adolescence: a psychosocial framework for understanding and action. *Journal of Adolescent Health*, **12**, 597–605.

Kagan, J. (1992). Etiologies of adolescents at risk. *Journal of Adolescent Health*, **12**, 591–596.

Kazdin, A. E., Rodgers, A. and Colbus, D. (1986). The hopelessness scale for children: psychometric characteristics and concurrent validity. *Journal of Consulting and Clinical Psychology*, **54**, 241–245.

Koop, C. E. and Lundberg, G. D. (1992). Violence in America: a public health emergency. *Journal of American Medical Association*, **267**, 3076–3076.

Kovacs, M. (1985). The children's depression inventory (CDI). *Psychopharmacology Bulletin*, **21**, 995–998.

Martinez, P., Richters, J. E. and Benoit, M. (1992). The NIMH community violence project: II. Children's distress symptoms associated with violence exposure. *Psychiatry*.

Mason, J. and Proctor, R. (1992). Reducing youth violence—the physician's role. *Journal of American Medical Association*, **267**, 3003.

Masters, A. S., Best, K. M. and Garmezy, N. (1990). Resilience and development: contributions from the study of children who overcame adversity. *Deviant Psychopathology*, **2**, 425–444.

Mercy, J. A. and Fenley, M. A. (1991). Forum on youth violence in minority communities: setting the agenda for prevention, summary of the proceedings. *Public Health Reports*, **106**, 225–279.

Novello, A. C., Shasky, J. and Froehike, R. (1992). A medical response to violence. *Journal of the American Medical Association*, **67**, 3007.

Powers, J. L. and Eckenrode, J. (1988). The maltreatment of adolescents. *Child Abuse and Neglect*, **12**, 189–199.

Prothrow-Stith, D. and Spivak, H. R. (1992). Homicide and violence in youth. In *Principles and Practices of Student Health*, Vol. 1, Wallace, H. M., Patrick, K., Parcel, A. S. and Igol, J. P. (Eds). Oakland: Third Party.

Prothrow-Stith, D. and Weissman, M. (1991). *Deadly Consequences*. New York: Harper-Collins.

Richters, J. E. and Martinez, P. (1990). *Survey of Exposure to Community Violence, Self-report Version*. Rockville: National Institute of Mental Health.

Riggs, S., Alario, A. J. and McHorney, C. (1990). Health risk behaviors and attempted suicide in adolescents who report prior maltreatment. *Journal of Pediatrics*, **116**, 815–821.

Roseberg, M. L., O'Carroll, P. W. and Powell, K. E. (1992). Let's be clear: violence is a public health problem. *Journal of the American Medical Association*, **267**, 3071–3072.

Runyan, C. W. and Gerken, E. A. (1989). Epidemiology and prevention of adolescent injury, a review and research agenda. *Journal of the American Medical Association*, **262**, 2273–2279.

Rutter, M. (1987). Psychosocial resilience and protective mechanisms. *American Journal of Orthopsychiatry*, **57**, 316–331.

Shakoor, B. H. and Chalmers, D. (1991). Co-victimization of African-American children who witness violence: effects on cognitive, emotional, and behavioral development. *Journal of the National Medical Association*, **83**, 233–238.

592   R. H. DuRANT *ET AL.*

Sheley, J. F., McGee, Z. T. and Wright, J. D. (1992). Gun-related violence in and around inner-city schools. *American Journal of Diseases in Children*, **146**, 677–682.

Simcha-Fagan, O. and Gersten, J. C. (1986). Early precursors and concurrent correlates of illicit drug use in adolescents. *Journal of Drug Issues*, **60**, 7–28.

Smith, D. L., DuRant, R. and Carter, T. J. (1978). Social integration, victimization and anomie. *Criminology*, **16**, 395–402.

Straus, M. A. (1979). Measuring intrafamily conflict and violence: the conflict tactics (CT) scales. *Journal of Marriage and Family*, **41**, 75–88.

Sutherland, E. H. and Cressey, D. R. (1978). *Criminology* (10th Edn). Philadelphia PA: Lippincott.

Walters, L. H. and Klein, A. E. (1980). A cross-validated investigation of the Crumbaugh purpose-in-life test. *Educational and Psychological Measurement*, **40**, 1065–1071.

Werner, E. E. (1989). High risk children in young adulthood: a longitudinal study from birth to 32 years. *American Journal of Orthopsychiatry*, **52**, 72–81.

Werner, E. E. (1992). The children of Kauai: resiliency and recovery in adolescence and adulthood. *Journal of Adolescent Health*, **13**, 262–268.

Widom, C. S. (1989*a*). Does violence beget violence? a critical review of the literature. *Psychological Bulletin*, **106**, 3–28.

Widom, C. S. (1989*b*). The cycle of violence. *Science*, **244**, 160–165.

[7]

Examining the Arsenal of Juvenile Gunslingers: Trends and Policy Implications

Rick Ruddell
G. Larry Mays

Using the National Institute of Justice body armor threat-level scale, this study classified 1,055 firearms confiscated by police officers from juveniles in St. Louis, Missouri, from 1992 to 1999. The authors found that for this city, the lethal capacity of juveniles' firearms has remained relatively constant over time. Examination of the different types of firearms recovered also found that the sophistication of firearms used by juveniles did not increase throughout the 1990s. By disaggregating firearm types, the authors were able to demonstrate that the police are likely to confiscate relatively unsophisticated firearms from juveniles, such as Saturday night specials, .22 caliber and nonpowder weapons. In St. Louis, juveniles were very unlikely to have an assault weapon confiscated. More troubling, however, were the relatively high numbers of illegally sawed-off rifles and shotguns recovered from youths.

Keywords: juvenile gun use; youth violence

Our perceptions about juvenile firearms possession and use are inextricably linked with media depictions of youth gang activities and accounts of school shootings. The general public may believe that youths have access to sophisticated military-style assault weapons that have a high capacity for lethality. Police officials tend to reinforce these perspectives by reporting that youths are gaining access to increasingly sophisticated firearms over time (Bjerregaard & Lizotte, 1995). These images of juvenile gunslingers with assault weapons largely have displaced our fear of juveniles using Saturday night specials, the inexpensive and easily concealed handguns that fire less powerful cartridges (Cook, 1991; Funk, 1995; Shine, 1998).

RICK RUDDELL: California State University, Chico. **G. LARRY MAYS:** New Mexico State University.

This study was completed with the support of the Social Sciences and Humanities Research Council of Canada dissertation grant award 752-00-0357. An earlier version of this paper was presented at the 2001 annual meeting of the American Society of Criminology. The authors would like to thank Yolanda Kenton, Planning and Development Division, St. Louis Metropolitan Police Department, for her assistance in compiling crime statistics. The authors would also like to thank the editor and reviewers for their comments and suggestions.

232   **CRIME & DELINQUENCY / APRIL 2003**

Juveniles and young adults made a significant contribution to the increases in homicide rates throughout the 1980s and 1990s (Cole, 1999; Fingerhut, Ingram, & Feldman, 1998), and whereas rates of violent juvenile crime have decreased, there is a significant positive association between youth gun violence and homicide (Cherry, Annest, Mercy, Kresnow, & Pollock, 1998; Wintemute, 2000; Zimring, 1998). Juveniles were responsible for approximately one third of the increase in murders during the 1985 to 1994 period (Snyder, Sickmund, & Poe-Yamagata, 1996), but increases in homicides are not attributable to young persons alone. Analysis of the FBI Supplemental Homicide Reports found that the homicide commission and victimization rates for 13- to 17-year-old and 18- to 24-year-old males during the late 1980s and early 1990s were similar (Cook & Laub, 1998). From 1983 to 1992, the Violent Crime Index arrest rate increased among all age groups (Snyder & Sickmund, 1995, p. 112), and the increase was larger (66%) among 30- to 49-year-olds than among any other age group, including teenagers (Males, 1997).

Often the presence of a firearm in the hands of a juvenile increases the lethality of confrontations that otherwise may be resolved by alternative means (Wilkinson & Fagan, 1996). Youths who are involved in illicit drug markets or gangs are also more likely to possess or use firearms, and these activities increase the potential for lethal violence (Bjerregaard & Lizotte, 1995; Blumstein & Cork, 1996; Hemenway, Prothrow-Stith, Bergstein, Ander, & Kennedy, 1996; Lizotte, Krohn, Howell, Tobin, & Howard, 2000).

Irrespective of other factors, the calibers of weapons that offenders use are likely to influence the homicide rate (Zimring, 1972). Koper (1995) observed that "criminologists have long recognized the importance of determining the impact of weapon types on the volume, patterns, and lethality of violence" (p. 1). It has been hypothesized, for instance, that the growing use of semiautomatic handguns and handguns of larger calibers have a direct positive association with increases in homicides (Block & Block, 1993; McGonigal et al., 1993; Wintemute, 1996, 2000). In his analysis of crime-guns confiscated from Kansas City, Missouri, offenders from 1985 to 1993, Koper found that the use of firearms with larger bore sizes significantly influences the homicide rate: Weapon caliber is a better predictor of lethality than whether a firearm is a revolver, semiautomatic or single shot. Consistent with these observations, Caruso, Jara, and Swan (1999) used autopsy data to establish that the average caliber of bullets in fatal shootings has been increasing over time.

Concerns over youth gun violence have resulted in a number of policy initiatives, including the expansion of federal, state, and municipal legislation to increase the consequences for illegal firearm acquisition and use (Kopel, 1994). A number of innovative harm-reduction strategies to reduce the use by youngsters also have been introduced (Bureau of Alcohol, Tobacco and Firearms [BATF], 1999b; Kennedy, 1997; Kennedy, Piehl, & Braga, 1996; Rosenfeld & Decker, 1996; Scales & Baker, 2000). It is our contention that interventions should be based on demonstrable research results about juvenile gun offenses rather than anecdotal information or media portrayals.

Most of our knowledge about juvenile firearms use is a product of interviews with incarcerated juvenile offenders (Birkbeck et al., 1999; Callahan, Rivara, & Farrow, 1993; Limber & Pagliocca, 1998; Sheley & Wright, 1993) or samples drawn from youths in the community (Bjerregaard & Lizotte, 1995; Hemenway et al., 1996; Sadowski, Cairns, & Earp, 1989; Sheley & Brewer, 1995; Sheley & Wright, 1998). The BATF also has traced firearms used in juvenile offenses in 27 metropolitan areas at the request of local police departments. Previous research strategies, however, might not be representative of the actual types of firearms the average juvenile offender is likely to possess or use. As a result of these limitations, this study examines 1,055 firearms confiscated by the police department in St. Louis, Missouri, from January 1, 1992, to December 31, 1999, to determine whether juveniles are using more sophisticated firearms over time. We also examined several subtypes of firearms including Saturday night specials, assault weapons, and inherently illegal firearms: rifles or shotguns that have their barrels or stocks illegally sawed off or any firearm that has its serial number altered or defaced in violation of the 1934 National Firearms Act (NFA).

YOUTH GUN USE

Previous studies of confiscated firearms generally have disaggregated them into broad classifications such as handguns, rifles, and shotguns (BATF, 1977; Brill, 1977; Little & Boyen, 1990; Wachtel, 1998). This research typically has found that handguns are more likely to be seized by the police than either rifles or shotguns. Additionally, these studies have demonstrated the widespread confiscation of Saturday night specials (BATF, 1977; Little & Boyen, 1990) and the relative scarcity of assault weapons (Kopel, 1994; Koper, 1995). Recent evidence from Los Angeles, however, suggests that there are trends in firearms use, and that most law-abiding citizens, as well as their criminal counterparts, prefer large-caliber semiautomatic handguns such as the 9mm (Wachtel, 1998). Examination of firearm industry trends also demonstrates that the production of larger caliber semiautomatic handguns has increased substantially over the past two decades (Wintemute, 2000).

One limitation of the firearms literature to date is that scholars have not examined trends in firearms confiscated from individuals legally defined as juveniles but, instead, have included all persons younger than 21 years of age, classifying them as young adults (Kennedy et al., 1996). This approach has some basis in legislation, given that the Gun Control Act of 1968 made handgun sales to those younger than 21 illegal, but such designations do not help us understand gun use of persons legally defined as juveniles. In an attempt to better understand juvenile gun acquisition and use, the BATF (1999b) traced juvenile crime-guns in 27 metropolitan areas and found that these guns represented 11.3% of all firearms traced nationally. In addition to finding that there are regional differences in juvenile firearms use, the BATF reported that the modal juvenile crime handgun throughout the nation is a semiautomatic pistol.

A number of self-report surveys and interviews also have increased our understanding of juvenile gun possession. Drug Use Forecasting survey information has been utilized by Rosenfeld and Decker (1996) to examine firearms use in a sample of one hundred twenty-eight 12- to 16-year-old detention residents, and 53% of this group reported possessing a firearm at some point. From these data, Rosenfeld and Decker estimated that

> Some 26 percent of African-American males aged 12 to 16 years have owned or possessed a firearm in their lifetime; fourteen percent have possessed a firearm during the previous month; six percent always carry a gun, seven percent have used a gun to commit a crime, and eight percent have stolen a gun. (p. 209)

Survey research suggests that these samples may be representative of national youth gun use (Hemenway et al., 1996; Sadowski et al., 1989; Sheley & Wright, 1998).

Although interviews of youths in detention or custody facilities may provide some insights into the reasons why youngsters possess or carry guns, there are some methodological weaknesses in attributing the firearm experiences of persistent or serious offenders to all youths. Data from 380 incarcerated youths in New Mexico, for instance, suggest that a number of juveniles carry firearms for self-defense or aggression rather than to enhance their status (Birkbeck et al., 1999). Sheley and Wright (1993) also interviewed incarcerated youths and found that

> Inmates are more likely to have owned guns, to have carried guns and have had ready access to guns, to own assault-style weapons, to have owned sawed-off shotguns and have owned semi-automatic pistols. (p. 64)

A review of firearms involved in crimes, however, demonstrates that military-style assault weapons are used in less than 1% of all firearms offenses (Kopel, 1994). Accordingly, one can extrapolate that some juveniles may be exaggerating their involvement with such weapons.

Traces of 152 juvenile crime-guns in St. Louis established that semiautomatic pistols and revolvers are commonly encountered, representing 35.8% and 27% of all crime-guns, respectively, and the modal juvenile crime-gun in St. Louis was a Smith and Wesson .38 Special caliber revolver (BATF, 1999a). Of these St. Louis juvenile crime-guns, 61.8% were involved in firearms offenses, 18.4% in narcotics offenses, 10% in robberies, 8% in assaults, and none in homicides. A significant weakness of tracing only these crime-involved guns, however, is the fact that these firearms are not randomly selected, and police requests to trace firearms potentially reflect some degree of selection bias.

Using a sample of 8,290 firearms confiscated in St. Louis from 1992 to 1994, Ruddell (2000) compared adult and juvenile gun use and found that juveniles are likely to possess less sophisticated firearms than their adult counterparts. Whereas the police were likely to recover large-caliber handguns, rifles, and shotguns from adults, juveniles were more likely to possess nonpowder firearms (BB guns and pellet guns), Saturday night specials, and illegally sawed-off rifles and shotguns. This study used the National Institute of Justice (NIJ) body armor rating scale to classify the threat level of these seized firearms and demonstrated how this scale can be used to study trends in firearms use.

The current research expands our understanding of juvenile firearms use by examining two questions. First, over time, have juveniles started carrying more lethal firearms? The NIJ threat-level scale is used as a method of classifying the capacity of lethality for these seized firearms. Second, this study classifies firearms into commonly used categories such as Saturday night specials, assault weapons, and illegally sawed-off rifles and shotguns to assess whether police are likely to recover more sophisticated weapons from juveniles over time.

RESEARCH DESIGN

Between January 1, 1992, and December 31, 1999, 1,055 firearms were confiscated from persons legally defined as juveniles by the St. Louis, Missouri, Metropolitan Police Department. Juvenile firearms possession is an offense, so any firearm used by a juvenile without adult supervision is likely to be confiscated by the police. Nonpowder firearms, such as BB and pellet guns, also are included in the analysis as they are typically recovered from youths (Ruddell, 2000). The dates for this research were determined by the availability of data. One of the major limitations in operationalizing firearms trend research is that few jurisdictions have collected such data over time, and fewer have disaggregated these data into categories of juveniles and adults. Although the St. Louis data help us understand the types of firearms recovered from juveniles, they also are limited because we have no information about the demographic characteristics of the juveniles other than the fact that the weapons were seized from persons under the age of 17 years. As a result, we cannot determine from these data whether these firearms were seized from younger or older juveniles, their race, gender, or the seriousness of their alleged offenses.

The capacity for lethality of firearms in this research is categorized using the NIJ (1998) body armor classification ratings. Body armor, typically called "bullet proof vests," distributed in the United States is rated on a five-level scale for its ability to withstand penetration by different cartridges.[1] We added one additional classification—for weapons with a very low capacity for injury—to the lower end of the scale to account for BB and pellet guns. We believe we have employed a conservative approach in classifying threat levels. Where a caliber was listed in two threat-level classifications due to different types of ammunition or longer barrel lengths that increased the velocity of the bullet, it was placed in the higher classification. The .38 Special cartridge, for instance, is rated in both the Type I and Type IIa body armor classifications, so it was placed in the higher classification. The .45 Automatic Colt Pistol (ACP) cartridge, categorized as a Type IIa threat by the NIJ, was also placed in a higher classification due to its widely acknowledged lethality (Kleck, 1991; Wintemute, 1996, 2000).[2] Table 1 outlines how the NIJ scale has been adapted to classify the capacity for injury or lethality into six threat levels. A review of the literature finds that classification of cartridges into categories using a modified NIJ scale is consistent with observations about cartridge lethality made by Kleck (1991) and Wintemute (1996, 2000). Koper's (1995) analysis of the lethality of firearms suggests that irrespective of other factors, a weapon's caliber has the greatest influence on lethality.

We recognize that adapting the NIJ scale to assess the threat of firearm cartridges offers a somewhat simplistic solution to a complex issue. The lethality of wounds from firearms is related to a variety of factors, including the design of the bullet used (e.g., a full metal jacket bullet that is less likely to expand than a hollow point bullet), the velocity of the bullet (a product of both the barrel length and the amount of powder used), the weight of the bullet (Di Maio,

TABLE 1: Modified National Institute of Justice (NIJ) Threat-Level Scale

Level 1	Pellet and BB firearms.
Level 2	(Type I) Smaller handgun rounds, including .25 and .32 calibers. This classification includes the .22 rimfire, in either handguns or rifles.
Level 3	(Type II-A) Medium-caliber handgun rounds, including the .38 Special, .380 automatic and, 9 × 18 Makarov.
Level 4	(Type II) Medium-caliber, high-velocity handgun rounds, including the 9mm, .357 magnum, .40 Smith and Wesson, .44 special, and .45 Automatic Colt Pistol.
Level 5	(Type III-A) Large-caliber, high-velocity handgun rounds, such as the .41 and .44 magnums.
Level 6	(Type III) High-powered rifle calibers, such as the .223 Remington and 7.62 × 39mm. As rifled shotgun slugs were in this classification, all shotgun gauges, from .410 to 10 gauge, are included in this threat level.

1985), and bullet placement. There is very little agreement, however, in the wound ballistics literature about the lethality of handgun cartridges (Fackler, 1999; Marshall & Sanow, 1996; Van Maanen, 1999). Again, our data were limited somewhat as there was no information about the type of cartridge that was recovered with the firearms. Hence, a .357 magnum revolver could be loaded with .38 Special ammunition that has a lower threat level. To account for the variation in the type of cartridges chambered in these firearms, we assumed that the most lethal cartridges were used in any firearm recovered by police when classifying the threat levels.

As a result of the wide disagreement in the wound ballistics literature about the nature of threat posed by various handgun cartridges, two other measures of threat were also examined in this study: muzzle energy and Marshall and Sanow's (1996) stopping power classification. Muzzle energy refers to the kinetic energy created by the velocity and weight of the bullet. Marshall and Sanow, by contrast, based their ratings on the percentage likelihood of a single bullet's ability to incapacitate an individual if hit in the torso. Their data have an intuitive appeal as they are based on actual reports of shootings, but this approach has been widely criticized for methodological weaknesses (Fackler, 1999; Van Maanen, 1999).

The appendix outlines how Marshall and Sanow's (1996) stopping power data, the muzzle energy statistics, and the NIJ threat scale are very highly correlated; the apparent differences are further reduced when only handgun cartridges are examined.[3]

The NIJ scale does not account for issues of firearms design, and all other factors being equal, a semiautomatic pistol or rifle that has a magazine capacity of 15 rounds theoretically poses a greater potential threat than a single-shot firearm that must be reloaded after every shot. In addition, more expensive weapons that are both more accurate and mechanically reliable are potentially more threatening than their cheaper and less reliable counterparts. To account for differences in firearm design, the present study also examined the types of firearm seized. We broadly classified these firearms into rifles, shotguns, and handguns, then disaggregated these three types into commonly used classifications, such as Saturday night specials or assault firearms.

Data from the St. Louis Metropolitan Police Department are limited somewhat by the type of information collected and their accuracy. Several cases that were missing data were excluded from the analysis, as were toy firearms or blank pistols. Data were coded, and some precision was lost due to rounding (e.g., barrel lengths were rounded to the nearest quarter inch).

Additionally, recent examination of juvenile crime-guns has found that firearms less than 3 years old are more likely to be involved in crimes (BATF, 1999b). However, the ages of the firearms seized were not available, making it impossible to determine whether the firearms seized were recently sold or whether they were part of the existing 220 to 250 million firearms currently in circulation in the United States.

Table 2 illustrates that there was a significant variance in the annual number of firearms recovered by the police. Throughout the decade, juvenile gun confiscation decreased annually. From 1992 to 1994, for instance, the average number of firearms recovered by the police was 201 per year. By contrast, between 1996 and 1999, the average number of recovered firearms had decreased to 54 per year. There are two major reasons why the number of firearms seized from juveniles may have decreased over time. First, gun crimes, for both juveniles and adults, decreased in the United States throughout the 1990s. In St. Louis, for instance, the number of aggravated assaults with guns dropped substantially during the era of this study. Consistent with national trends, the annual number of St. Louis homicides dropped as well. Table 2 demonstrates how aggravated assaults with firearms dropped by more than 50% during the era of this study. There was also a corresponding decrease in homicides in St. Louis. It is also likely that reductions in funding to the St. Louis Police Department's Mobile Reserve also contributed to these decreases in the number of firearms seized, because a primary mission of this unit is firearms suppression.

RESULTS

Examination of firearms confiscated from juveniles from 1992 to 1999 shows variation in their threat level over time. When all firearms are consid-

TABLE 2: Trends in Threat Levels of Firearms Confiscated from St. Louis, Missouri, Juveniles, 1992-1999

| | Threat Levels of Firearms Confiscated from St. Louis, Missouri, Juveniles, 1992-1999 | | | | | | | | |
	1992	1993	1994	1995	1996	1997	1998	1999	Mean
Guns confiscated	183	238	183	169	110	65	59	48	131.80
Average	2.71	2.53	2.68	2.76	2.80	2.77	3.15	2.27	2.70
Average (less airguns)	3.02	2.69	2.88	2.96	3.15	3.09	3.40	2.69	2.93
Average (less Threat Level 6[a])	2.21	2.25	2.39	2.30	2.29	2.32	2.50	2.11	2.29

| Threat Levels of Firearms Confiscated From St. Louis Juveniles, 1992-1999 | | | | | |
Level 1	Level 2	Level 3	Level 4	Level 5	Level 6
134	504	204	95	4	114

| | Aggravated Assaults With Firearms and Total Homicides: St. Louis, 1992-1999 | | | | | | | |
	1992	1993	1994	1995	1996	1997	1998	1999
Aggravated assaults with firearms	3,501	4,320	4,062	3,045	2,308	2,266	1,822	1,651
Total homicides	231	267	248	204	166	153	113	130

a. Most of the firearms that were Threat Level 6 were shotguns (69 of the 95 recovered were illegally sawed-off).

ered, the average threat level ranged from a low of 2.25 in 1999 to a high 3.15 in 1998. Despite the fact that there was a significant variation, there was no overall systematic trend.[4] When the firearms were classified using two alternative measures—muzzle energy and stopping power (Marshall & Sanow, 1996)—the results were very similar, and these scales also demonstrated that there was no significant trend over time. The lack of a significant trend was apparent after nonpowder firearms were removed from the analysis.

Annual threat level means were also assessed when Threat Level 6 firearms were removed from the analysis and the variance was no longer statistically significant. From these findings, we can conclude that the number of Threat Level 6 firearms, which are generally sawed-off shotguns, confiscated in any year, drives the variance: When these firearms are removed from the analysis, there is no significant difference in threat level between the years.

Handguns are the type of firearm most likely to be confiscated from juveniles. The mean threat level for all cartridge sizes of handguns was assessed, excluding nonpowder firearms, rifles, and shotguns from this analysis. Once these types of firearms were removed, the average threat level of handguns remained almost constant over the 8 years. Again, these findings were consistent after we classified these firearms based on the muzzle energy their cartridges produced or Marshall and Sanow's (1996) stopping power data. Table 2 illustrates that the modal firearm confiscated from juveniles over this 8-year period was in Threat Level 2; this classification includes the .22 long rifle, .25 automatic, and .32 automatic cartridges. Youth crime-gun research in St. Louis previously found that the modal category of youth crime-gun was a .38 Special caliber handgun (BATF, 1999a), yet Table 2 shows that these higher threat-level firearms represent less than 20% of all the firearms recovered. In contrast with the BATF (1999a) data, after rifles, shotguns, and nonpowder firearms were removed from the sample, the modal handgun in this analysis was classified in Threat Level 2. In fact, of the 821 handguns recovered by police, 435 were Threat Level 2 weapons.

According to the BATF (1999a), a majority of the juvenile crime-guns traced in St. Louis were semiautomatic pistols. However, of the 734 cartridge handguns recovered from juveniles over 8 years, revolvers were more likely to be recovered: There were 379 revolvers and 331 semiautomatic pistols. The remaining 24 firearms were black powder guns, single shots or derringers, all of which are fairly antiquated firearms designs. Accordingly, the present study demonstrates that the BATF crime-gun statistics might not be representative of the handguns juveniles are likely to possess.

This finding also tends to affirm the ability of the NIJ scale as a measure of threat. As most cartridge handguns seized from juveniles in this sample have the capacity to fire more than one round, whether the firearm is a semiautomatic pistol or a revolver is relatively unimportant distinction. Semiautomatic pistols typically can hold more cartridges, and the shooter is normally able to fire a semiautomatic more rapidly than a revolver. Kleck (1991), however, correctly noted that the magazine capacity does not significantly influence the outcome of most police encounters with offenders, as relatively few shots are ever fired. As previously noted, Koper (1995) found that the caliber of firearm, rather than the design of the weapon used in a shooting, most often determines the lethality of a gun assault.

Consistent with previous research (BATF, 1977; Little & Boyen, 1990), Saturday night specials were defined as firearms of .32 caliber or less and having a barrel length of 3.1 inches or less (Funk, 1995).[5] These firearms are generally inexpensive—their retail price often ranges from $100.00 to $150.00—easily concealed, and widely distributed (Wintemute, 2000). Therefore, they may be more popular with youths who may have fewer opportunities to purchase more desirable semiautomatic firearms that fire

TABLE 3:   Firearms Confiscated From St. Louis, Missouri, Juveniles by Type, 1992-1999

Total firearms	1,055
Handguns	821
Saturday night specials[a]	301
Higher lethality handguns[b]	98
Nonpowder handguns[c]	86
All other cartridge handguns	330
Assault weapons[d]	6
Rifles	139
Sawed-off rifles[e]	27
Nonpowder rifles	48
Other cartridge rifles	64
Assault weapons	0
Shotguns	95
Sawed-off shotguns	69
Other shotguns	26

a. .32 caliber or less, with a barrel length of less than 3.1 inches.
b. All 9mm, .40 Smith & Wesson, .357 magnum, .45 Automatic Colt Pistol, .41 and .44 magnum revolvers and pistols.
c. Typically BB or pellet guns.
d. Assault weapons consist of 19 firearms banned in the 1994 Omnibus Crime Bill.
e. Sawed-off rifles and shotguns defined as per the 1934 National Firearms Act.

9mm or .45 ACP rounds and may have a retail value approaching $600.00.[6] The Saturday night special was the modal category of handgun confiscated in this sample, and Table 3 illustrates how 301 of the total 821 handguns recovered were Saturday night specials. Handguns with a greater threat level, by contrast, were classified separately.

Of the total 821 handguns recovered by police, 98 had the greatest threat level. These weapons chambered cartridges in 9mm, .40 Smith and Wesson, .357 magnum, .45 ACP, and .41 and .44 magnums. Typically, these firearms are better made, more reliable, and more expensive than Saturday night specials. Table 4 illustrates how handguns with the greatest threat level ranged from 5.8% to 12.3% of the annual firearms recovered by the police, but these guns were no more likely to be seized in 1999 than 1992.

The NFA made several types of firearms illegal, including rifles or shotguns that have sawed-off barrels or serial numbers altered or obliterated. Of the entire sample of firearms, 144, or 13.4%, of the weapons recovered by the police were inherently illegal firearms. Due to their illegal status, increased threat level, and ease of concealment, sawed-off rifles and shotguns represent a substantial threat to the police and public safety, and they appear to be commonly encountered. Of the 95 shotguns recovered, for instance, 69 had ille-

242   CRIME & DELINQUENCY / APRIL 2003

TABLE 4:   Firearm Types Seized From St. Louis, Missouri, Juveniles, 1992-1999
(in percentages)

	1992	1993	1994	1995	1996	1997	1998	1999
Sawed-off rifles and shotguns (*n* = 96)	12.0	6.7	8.2	11.2	10.0	10.8	10.0	6.0
High threat handguns (*n* = 98)	10.3	5.8	11.5	8.3	12.3	10.8	8.5	8.3
Defaced serial numbers (*n* = 45)	2.2	4.6	6.6	3.0	7.3	4.6	1.7	2.0
Saturday night specials (*n* = 301)	42.0	15.8	24.5	23.6	30.9	24.6	13.6	35.4

gally sawed-off barrels. Again, Table 4 demonstrates how the percentage of sawed-off firearms recovered annually remained relatively stable over the period of this study.

There is considerable public and political concern about the criminal use of assault weapons due to their perceived threat (Kopel, 1994; Roth & Koper, 1999; Wintemute, 1996; Zimring, 1989). In this study, assault weapons were defined using the firearms banned for importation in the 1994 Omnibus Crime Bill.[7] Nevertheless, there is some ambiguity over definitions of assault weapons (Kopel, 1994; Koper, 1995; Wintemute, 1996; Zimring, 1989), and semiautomatic firearms are sometimes labeled as assault weapons based solely on cosmetic reasons such as the presence of a bayonet lug, flash suppressor, or pistol grip (Wachtel, 1998). Regardless of definitions, assault weapons were rarely confiscated: A total of 6 were recovered from juveniles during the 8 years examined. Even if one broadened the classification to include the SKS rifle, a commonly encountered military-style, semiautomatic rifle, the number of assault weapons would only increase by 10, bringing the total to 16.

In stark contrast to the assault weapons, one of the most commonly confiscated firearms is the nonpowder firearm: typically called a BB or pellet gun. Although these firearms are considered to have relatively little capacity for injury, the medical literature has documented some cases of death and serious injury (American Academy of Pediatrics, 1987; Lawrence, 1990; Schein, Enger, & Tielsch, 1994). Of the entire St. Louis sample of firearms, 134, or 12.7%, were nonpowder firearms.

DISCUSSION

Much of our knowledge about juvenile firearms use is a product of sensationalized media accounts and anecdotal information from emergency room physicians and police officers. In addition, the entertainment industry portrays juvenile gunslingers increasingly carrying a range of sophisticated firearms. Fortunately, many of these depictions are inaccurate.

The present study, by contrast, finds that youths are more likely to have pellet guns, .22 caliber firearms, and Saturday night specials confiscated by the police. We also found that although there has been a statistically significant variation in the capacity of lethality of firearms seized from persons legally defined as juveniles in St. Louis, Missouri, from 1992 to 1999, there was no trend indicating that these firearms were becoming more lethal over time. By eliminating firearms classified within Threat Level 6, which are primarily sawed-off shotguns, the mean variance between years became insignificant. Overall, most firearms seized from juveniles by the police have a low threat level.

Contrary to most media accounts, the recovery of assault weapons from youngsters is a relatively rare event. In the 96-month period of this research, only six assault weapons were confiscated. On a more ominous note, youths were likely to possess illegally sawed-off rifles or shotguns. As a vast majority of these sawed-off firearms are shotguns (69 of the 96 sawed-off guns), they have both a high capacity for lethality and they are easily concealed: Many of these firearms had an overall length of less than 16 inches. Stolzenberg and D'Alessio (2000) found that such illegal firearms, represented by the number of stolen weapons in circulation, are likely to influence rates of firearms violence. Therefore, it is possible that the inherently illegal status of sawed-off rifles and shotguns make them more likely to be involved in criminal offenses.

The widespread use of firearms classified as illegal by the NFA in this sample of juveniles may be one unanticipated consequence of reducing firearms availability. Interviews of adult offenders completed by Wright and Rossi (1986) and Knox et al. (1994) indicated that sawed-off rifles and shotguns are widely used by adult offenders. Shortening the barrel or stock of a firearm to increase the ease of concealment appears to be one manner of responding to the lack of handgun availability. One unanticipated drawback of this practice, however, is that these weapons have a high capacity for lethality compared to Saturday night specials. As Di Maio (1985) has observed, "At close range, the shotgun is the most formidable and destructive of all small arms" (p. 182). In this sample, the percentage of sawed-off firearms recovered remained relatively stable over time; these firearms ranged from 6% to 12% of the number of weapons seized annually, and no trends were evident.

It is important that we not minimize the seriousness of youths' illegally possessing or carrying any firearm. Wounds from pellet guns can cause painful and permanent as well as lethal injuries to victims (American Academy of Pediatrics, 1987; Lawrence, 1990; Schein et al., 1994). Alternatively, despite their diminutive size, the .22 long rifle and similar small calibers can be exceedingly lethal cartridges (Di Maio, 1985; Swistounoff, 1999). As one example of this, of the 599 police officers killed in the United States from 1985 to 1996, 75 were killed by firearms with a caliber of .32 or less (NIJ, 1998).

POLICY IMPLICATIONS

Juveniles and young adults made a significant contribution to increases in American homicide rates throughout the 1980s and 1990s (Cole, 1999; Fingerhut et al., 1998; Suffredini, 1994). Wintemute (2000) for instance, noted that "weapons-related offenses among juveniles (age 17 or less) more than doubled from 1985 to 1993, whereas those among all adults taken together increased a relatively modest 33 percent" (p. 51). Although this study demonstrates that juveniles are likely to possess firearms that are not very sophisticated, any illegally used firearm represents a threat to the police and public safety. Sherman (2001) observed how juvenile gun violence is a product of the gun density in a small number of inner city neighborhoods that are responsible for half of the nation's homicides. Stolzenberg and D'Alessio (2000) found that increases in the numbers of illegally obtained and carried firearms in these neighborhoods are positively associated with violent crime. Therefore, the gun density in a neighborhood may be a less reliable predictor of lethal violence than the types of guns circulating.

A number of innovative programs have attempted to reduce gun density in inner city urban areas, especially when they target high risk offenders or illegally carried weapons. The St. Louis Metropolitan Police Department developed a firearms suppression program where police received parental consent-to-search the homes of high-risk juveniles and confiscate firearms—with no legal consequences for the youths or parents—if a gun was found. While this program eventually was disbanded, it represents one method of reducing gun density for the highest-risk juveniles in the highest-risk neighborhoods (Rosenfeld and Decker, 1996).

Such high-risk youths typically are gang-involved, and gang involvement has been positively associated with increases in the juvenile and young adult homicide rates in the 1980s and 1990s (Howell, 1999). Gangs are more likely to recruit adolescents who own illegal firearms, and gang members are more than twice as likely than non–gang members to own a gun for protection, more likely to have peers who own guns for protection, and more likely to carry their firearms outside the home (Bjerregaard & Lizotte, 1995). In addition, gang involvement has been positively associated with illegal gun carrying in urban adolescents until age 16 and drug trafficking afterwards (Lizotte et al., 2000).

Like many inner-city urban areas, St. Louis has a significant gang problem, and these gangs are responsible for importing firearms into the city (Decker & Van Winkle, 1996). In addition, firearms are commonly exchanged, at a fraction of their retail value, for money or drugs in the routine street activities of crime-involved juveniles and adults in urban areas (Decker & Ruddell, n.d.). Therefore, any successful intervention to reduce the proliferation of firearms in these urban areas must address the twin problems of gang ownership of firearms as well as the use of firearms as a medium of exchange in the street culture.

Two well-documented experiments used uniformed police patrols to reduce the proliferation of illegally carried firearms in high-risk Kansas City, Missouri (Sherman, Shaw, & Rogan, 1995), and Indianapolis, Indiana, neighborhoods (McGarrell, Shermak, & Weiss, 1999). These short-term experiments demonstrated that homicides could be reduced through targeted police interventions. In a nation like the United States, with a gun density of nearly one firearm per person, the confiscation of illegally carried firearms in urban areas can lead to a significant reduction in lethal violence.

Taking a more intermediate and integrated orientation, Boston's Cease Fire Project has been touted as one example of violent crime reduction through cooperative enforcement strategies between prosecutors, and municipal and federal law enforcement agencies concurrent with the implementation of community-based interventions. By using these cooperative law enforcement interventions to reduce violence by chronic gang offenders, youth homicide was reduced significantly (Kennedy, 1997). It is important to note, though, that juvenile violence, particularly homicide, was dropping throughout the country during the era when these programs were introduced. Related to this, Table 2 demonstrates that St. Louis homicides and aggravated assaults with firearms followed these national trends.

A number of other jurisdictions have used similar problem-solving approaches to reduce youth firearms use. Lizotte and Sheppard (2001), for instance, examined a number of gun violence prevention programs. A com-

246   CRIME & DELINQUENCY / APRIL 2003

mon theme in these successful firearms suppression programs was their reliance on multiple strategies most often directed at high-risk residential areas and high-risk populations such as gang members. Law enforcement strategies were supported by community-based initiatives that offered positive opportunities, such as academic, vocational, or after-school programs. In addition, public information campaigns and mobilization of community leaders in these high-risk residential areas sought to enhance resiliency in these neighborhoods (Lizotte & Sheppard, 2001).

Despite the relative success of these different types of firearms intervention initiatives, however, perhaps long-term changes in public perceptions will be the most successful method of reducing firearms crimes over time. Sherman (2001) has argued that public attitudes toward illegally carrying concealed weapons need to change. He has advocated using sentencing policies as a starting point for changing public perceptions about the seriousness of firearms offenses. Through stricter punishments for offenders, we may be able to reduce illegally carried firearms in a manner similar to the way driving while intoxicated was discouraged throughout the 1980s and 1990s. Certainly, increasing awareness about school shootings has resulted in a number of youngsters contacting the police when their peers are planning such acts of violence. Despite the intuitive appeal of these changes in culture and attitude, however, youths who carry firearms because they fear lethal violence may be resistant to abandoning their weapons, fearing their peers or gangs more than fearing legal sanctions.

One of the clearest points of possible intervention is a school-based program aimed at problem solving and conflict resolution. Already, programs such as DARE and GREAT offer curriculum components designed to address the issue of conflict (see, for example, Winfree, Peterson-Lynskey, & Maupin, 1999). These programs could be expanded to deal explicitly with the carrying and use of firearms by juveniles.

Confronting the issue of safe schools involves a cluster of social problems such as drugs, gangs, and firearms (Loeber, Kalb, & Huizinga, 2001; Wasserman, Miller, & Cothern, 2000). However, as Pollack and Sundermann (2001) noted,

> School safety is not about one method of control: metal detectors, surveillance systems, or swift punishment. Nor is it about any single risk factor such as dysfunctional homes and inadequate schools. We have learned that we cannot identify with certainty those students who, for reasons clear only to themselves, will assault their teachers and peers. We now understand that safe schools require broad-based efforts on the part of the entire community, including educators, students, parents, law enforcement agencies, businesses, and faith-based organizations. (p. 13)

Although this quote is especially insightful in regards to school-based violence (including firearms use), two very important points remain. First, as Pollack and Sundermann (2001, p. 20) concluded, even the most thorough planning for safe schools will not eliminate all acts of violence on school property. Second, and perhaps even more critical for educators and law enforcement agencies, not all of the youngsters charged with weapons violations are in schools where they can be exposed to violence prevention education: Some schools do not offer such courses, some of these youngsters have graduated, but unfortunately, a number have dropped out or have been expelled. Therefore, other interventions will be necessary.

It has been suggested that there are technological solutions to the problem of illegally carried firearms in high-risk neighborhoods. Wilson (1998) has advocated the use of portable scanning devices similar to radar units that the police could use unobtrusively to identify whether illegally concealed firearms are being carried. The NIJ has supported research and development of these types of technological interventions that could reduce illegally carried weapons or contraband. Although there are many technological and perhaps legal barriers to implementing such innovations (Paulter, 2001), such technologies offer one potential long-term solution to illegally carried firearms. Although such approaches have clear civil-liberties implications, an added benefit of these unobtrusive measures is that they reduce the chance of negative citizen-police confrontations inherent in "stop and frisk" programs.

CONCLUSIONS

The development of harm-reduction strategies to reduce youth gun possession, consideration of further legislation, and the development of police tactics and training should be driven by research, not rhetoric. When considering such strategies, we have to understand the factors that motivate youngsters to possess or use a Saturday night special, pellet gun, or sawed-off rifle or shotgun. Youths who carry firearms as a status symbol or to impress their friends (Keene, 1997) more than likely have different motivations than youths who carry firearms for protection from real or perceived threats (Lizotte et al., 2000; Lizotte, Howard, Krohn, & Thornberry, 1997; May, 1999). Accordingly, future studies of juvenile firearms use should explore the motivations for use.

Clearly, further research is needed to determine how adolescents choose the weapons they possess and whether their decisions are motivated by price, availability, style, or size (Kennedy et al., 1996), the status it can offer a young person (Birkbeck et al, 1999; Keene, 1997), or whether the firearm is new and cannot be linked to any crime. In addition, there are very little data that address the type of cartridges that offenders are likely to use. For instance, do juveniles use the cheapest and typically least lethal cartridges or more expensive and lethal bullets? Such research might also inform selection and use of body armor, police tactics, legislation, and emergency room practices. Scholars who study trends in firearms use suggest that expensive semiautomatic handguns that chamber larger cartridges are becoming more widely manufactured and distributed (Watchel, 1998; Wintemute, 2000). These firearms commonly are depicted in movies and television programs, and they may be very desirable to youths as well. Regardless of their popularity, however, this study finds that these types of weapons were no more likely to be confiscated by the police in 1999 than they were in 1992, at least in St. Louis, Missouri.

APPENDIX

Correlation Between the National Institute of Justice (NIJ) Threat-Level Scale, Marshall and Sanow Stopping Power Data (M&S), and Muzzle Energy (ME) of Firearms Seized From St. Louis Juveniles, 1992-1999

	All 1,055 Firearms			821 Handguns		
	NIJ	*M&S*	*ME*	*NIJ*	*M&S*	*ME*
Modified NIJ threat level	1.00	.860*	.848*	1.00	.903*	.863*
M&S	.860*	1.00	.651*	.903*	1.00	.854*
ME	.848*	.651*	1.00	.863*	.854*	1.00

SOURCE: M&S data from Dale Towert's Stopping Power Web page: http://www.evanmarshall/daletowert/stoppingpower.htm; ME data from Ballistics Data, http:web4.integraonline.com/~bbroadside/Ballistic_Info.html.
NOTE: Because nonpowder firearms were not included in M&S, the stopping power of a pellet firearm was reported as 1/2 the stopping power of a .22 rimfire. Stopping power of the .38 Special was averaged for 2- and 4-inch barrels. All figures represent the greatest stopping power ammunition for the caliber. Because nonpowder firearms were not included in ME, the muzzle energy of a 10-grain pellet at a velocity of 1,000 feet per second was used.
*$p < .01$.

NOTES

1. Although body armor can withstand penetration of a projectile, there is still a risk of serious injury or mortality due to blunt trauma injury. The National Institute of Justice (NIJ) threat rating has been criticized as having overly conservative classifications. See Jason and Fackler's (1991) analysis of body armor standards.

2. Placing the .45 Automatic Colt Pistol (ACP) in a higher classification had no measurable impact on the findings as these firearms were rarely confiscated from juveniles.

3. For researchers interested in comparing the modified NIJ scale, Marshall and Sanow's (1996) Stopping Power data, and Muzzle Energy data used in this sample, these data are available from the first author.

4. Examination of the yearly means was completed using an ANOVA analysis, and we found a statistically significant variation between the annual threat level means ($p = .031$). When nonpowder firearms were removed from the analysis, the variance remained statistically significant ($p = .009$), but this variance became insignificant once Threat Level 6 firearms were removed.

5. As there was no measure of value of the firearm in the data, Saturday night specials are coded on the basis of barrel length and caliber: Classical definitions of Saturday night specials have usually included a dollar value. Recent classifications have also included melting point of the frame—a reflection of the cheaper materials used in some of these firearms.

6. Wintemute (2000) has identified a number of inexpensive firearms made by six manufacturers in Southern California as "Ring of Fire" guns and suggested that these firearms are disproportionately involved in violent crime. An examination of this sample found that of the 735 cartridge handguns recovered, 99 were made by these firms. There was no clear change in the recovery of these firearms over the 8-year period of this study, ranging from 4.4% to 15.3% of the sample.

7. The 19 firearms banned from further importation include the AK-47 and its variants, the UZI and Galil, Beretta AR-70, Colt AR-15, FN/FAL, FN/LAR and FNC, the SWD M-10, M-11, M-11/0 and M-12, Steyr AUG, TEC-9, TEC-DC9 and TEC 22, and the Street Sweeper and Striker 12 shotguns. Of the 6 assault weapons confiscated by St. Louis police, all were TEC-9 or TEC-22 firearms.

REFERENCES

American Academy of Pediatrics. (1987). Injuries related to 'toy' firearms. *Pediatrics, 79,* 473-474.

Birkbeck, C., LaFree, G., Gabaldon, L., Bassin, A., Wilson, N., Fernandez, M., et al. (1999). Controlling New Mexico juveniles' possession and use of firearms. *Justice Research and Policy. 1,* 25-49.

Bjerregaard, B., & Lizotte, A. (1995). Gun ownership and gang membership. *Journal of Criminal Law and Criminology, 86,* 37-58.

Block, C., & Block, R. (1993). *Street gang crime in Chicago-Research in brief.* Washington, DC: National Institute of Justice.

Blumstein, A., & Cork, P. (1996). Linking gun availability to youth gun violence. *Law and Contemporary Problems, 59,* 5-24.

Brill, S. (1977). *Firearm abuse: A research and policy report.* Washington, DC: Police Foundation.

Bureau of Alcohol, Tobacco and Firearms. (1977). *Concentrated urban enforcement: An analysis of the initial year of operation CUE in the cities of Washington D.C., Boston, Mass., Chicago, Ill.* Washington, DC: U.S. Department of the Treasury.

Bureau of Alcohol, Tobacco and Firearms. (1999a). *Crime gun trace analysis report: The illegal youth firearms market in St. Louis, Missouri.* Washington, DC: U.S. Department of the Treasury.

250   CRIME & DELINQUENCY / APRIL 2003

Bureau of Alcohol, Tobacco and Firearms. (1999b). *Crime gun trace analysis reports: The illegal youth firearms markets in 27 communities.* Washington, DC: U.S. Department of the Treasury.

Callahan, C., Rivara, F., & Farrow, J. (1993). Youth in detention and handguns. *Journal of Adolescent Health, 14,* 350-355.

Caruso, R., Jara, D., & Swan, K. (1999). Gunshot wounds: Bullet caliber is increasing. *Journal of Trauma, 46,* 462-465.

Cherry, D., Annest, J., Mercy, J., Kresnow, M., & Pollock, D. (1998). Trends in nonfatal and fatal firearm-related injury rates in the United States 1985-1995. *Annals of Emergency Medicine, 32,* 51-59.

Cole, T. (1999). Ebbing epidemic: Youth homicide at a 14-year low. *Journal of the American Medical Association, 281,* 25-26.

Cook, P. (1991). The Saturday night special: An assessment of alternative definitions from a policy perspective. *Journal of Criminal Law and Criminology, 72,* 1735-1745.

Cook, P., & Laub, J. (1998). The unprecedented epidemic of youth violence. In M. Tonry & M. Moore (Eds.), *Youth violence* (pp. 27-64). Chicago: University of Chicago Press.

Decker, S., & Ruddell, R. (n.d.). *Tools of the trade: A routine activities approach to gun acquisition.* Unpublished manuscript.

Decker, S., & Van Winkle, B. (1996). *Life in the gang: Family, friends and violence.* New York: Cambridge University Press.

Di Maio, V. (1985). *Gunshot wounds: Practical aspects of firearms, ballistics and forensic techniques.* New York: Elsevier.

Fackler, M. (1999). Undeniable evidence. *Wound Ballistics Review, 4,* 15-16.

Fingerhut, L., Ingram, D., & Feldman, J. (1998). Homicide rates among U.S. teenagers and young adults—Differences by mechanism, level of urbanization, race and sex, 1987-1995. *Journal of the American Medical Association, 280,* 423-427.

Funk, T. (1995). Gun control and economic discrimination: The melting-point case-in-point. *Journal of Criminal Law and Criminology, 85,* 764-793.

Hemenway, D., Prothrow-Stith, D., Bergstein, J., Ander, R., & Kennedy, B. (1996). Gun carrying among adolescents. *Law and Contemporary Problems, 59,* 39-53.

Howell, J. (1999). Youth gang homicides: A literature review. *Crime & Delinquency, 45,* 208-241.

Jason, A., & Fackler, M. (1991). Body armor standards: A review and analysis. *Wound Ballistics Review, 1,* 22-25.

Keene, L. (1997, July 20). Study takes look at why young people carry guns. *Seattle Times.* Retrieved February 13, 2003, from http://archives.seattletimes.nwsource.com

Kennedy, D. (1997). *Juvenile gun violence and gun markets in Boston—Research preview.* Washington, DC: National Institute of Justice.

Kennedy, D., Piehl, A., & Braga, A. (1996). Youth violence in Boston: Gun markets, serious youth offenders and a use-reduction strategy. *Law and Contemporary Problems, 59,* 147-196.

Kleck, G. (1991). *Point blank: Guns and violence in America.* New York: Aline de Gruyter.

Knox, G., Houston, J. Laskey, J, McCurrie, T, Tromanhauser, E., & Laske, D. (1994). *Gangs and guns.* Chicago: National Gang Crime Research Center.

Kopel, D. (1994). Rational basis analysis of assault weapon prohibition. *Journal of Contemporary Law, 20,* 381-417.

Koper, C. (1995). *Gun lethality and homicide: Gun types used by criminals and the lethality of gun violence in Kansas City, Missouri, 1985-1993.* Unpublished doctoral dissertation, University of Maryland.

Lawrence, H. (1990). Fatal non-powder firearm wounds: Case report and review of the literature. *Pediatrics, 85,* 177-181.

Limber, S., & Pagliocca, P. (1998). *Firearm possession and use among youth: Findings from a survey of incarcerated juveniles in South Carolina.* Columbia, SC: Institute for Families in Society.

Little, R., & Boyen, M. (1990). Facing the gun: The firearms threat to police officers. *Journal of Police Science and Administration, 17,* 49-53.

Lizotte, A., Howard, G., Krohn, M., & Thornberry, T. (1997). Patterns of illegal gun carrying among young urban males. *Valparaiso University Law Review, 31,* 375-393.

Lizotte, A., Krohn, M., Howell, J., Tobin, K., & Howard, G. (2000). Factors influencing gun carrying among young urban males over the adolescent-young adult life course. *Criminology, 38,* 811-834.

Lizotte, A., & Sheppard, D. (2001). *Gun use by male juveniles: Research and prevention.* Washington, DC: U.S. Department of Justice, Office of Juvenile Justice and Delinquency Prevention.

Loeber, R., Kalb, L., & Huizinga, D. (2001). *Juvenile delinquency and serious injury victimization.* Washington, DC: U.S. Department of Justice, Office of Juvenile Justice and Delinquency Prevention.

Males, M. (1997, winter). Distorting youth violence. *Juvenile and Family Justice Today, 1,* 21-22.

Marshall, E., & Sanow, E. (1996). *Street stoppers: The latest handgun stopping power street results.* Boulder, CO: Paladin.

May, D. (1999). Scared kids, unattached kids, or peer pressure. *Youth & Society, 31,* 100-127.

McGarrell, E., Shermak, S., & Weiss, A. (1999). *Targeting firearms through directed patrols.* Indianapolis, IN: Hudson Institute.

McGonigal, M., Cole, J., Schwab, C., Kauder, D., Rotondo, M., & Angood, P. (1993). Urban firearm deaths: A five-year perspective. *Journal of Trauma, 35,* 532-537.

National Institute of Justice. (1998). *Selection and application guide to police body armor.* Rockville, MD: U.S. Department of Justice.

Paulter, N. (2001). *Guide to the technologies of concealed weapon and contraband imaging and detection.* Rockville, MD: U.S. Department of Justice.

Pollack, I., & Sundermann, C. (2001). Creating safe schools: A comprehensive approach. *Juvenile Justice, 8,* 13-20.

Rosenfeld, R., & Decker, S. (1996). Consent to search and seize: Evaluating an innovative youth firearm suppression program. *Law and Contemporary Problems, 59,* 197-220.

Roth, J., & Koper, C. (1999). *Impacts of the 1994 assault weapons ban, 1994-96—Research in brief.* Washington, DC: National Institute of Justice.

Ruddell, R. (2000, October). *Using the NIJ threat level scale to evaluate the capacity for lethality of juvenile firearms.* Paper presented at the Midwestern Criminal Justice Association annual meeting, Chicago.

Sadowski, L., Cairns, R., & Earp J. (1989). Firearm ownership among nonurban adolescents. *American Journal of Diseases of Children, 143,* 1410-1413.

Scales, B., & Baker, J. (2000). *Seattle's effective strategy for prosecuting juvenile firearm offenders.* Washington, DC: Office of Juvenile Justice and Delinquency Prevention.

Schein, O., Enger, C., & Tielsch, J. (1994). The context and consequences of ocular injuries from air guns. *American Journal of Ophthalmology, 117,* 501-506.

Sheley, J., & Brewer, V. (1995). Possession and carrying of firearms among suburban youth. *Public Health Reports, 110,* 18-26.

Sheley, J., & Wright, J. (1993). *Gun acquisition and possession in selected juvenile samples— Research in brief.* Washington, DC: National Institute of Justice.

252   CRIME & DELINQUENCY / APRIL 2003

Sheley, J., & Wright, J. (1998). *High school youths, weapons and violence: A national survey—Research in brief.* Washington, DC: National Institute of Justice.

Sherman, L. (2001). Reducing gun violence: What works, what doesn't, what's promising. In *Perspective on crime and justice 1999-2000 lecture series.* Rockville, MD: National Institute of Justice.

Sherman, L., Shaw, J. W., & Rogan, D. (1995). *The Kansas City gun experiment—Research in brief.* Washington, DC: National Institute of Justice.

Shine, E. (1998). The junk gun predicament: Answers do exist. *Arizona State Law Journal, 30,* 1183-1207.

Snyder, H., & Sickmund, M. (1995). *Juvenile offenders and victims: A national report.* Washington, DC: U.S. Department of Justice, Office of Juvenile Justice and Delinquency Prevention.

Snyder, H., Sickmund, M., & Poe-Yamagata, E. (1996). *Juvenile offenders and victims: 1996 update on violence.* Washington, DC: U.S. Department of Justice, Office of Juvenile Justice and Delinquency Prevention.

Stolzenberg, L., & D'Alessio, S. (2000). Gun availability and violent crime: New evidence from the national incident-based reporting system. *Social Forces, 78,* 1461-1482.

Suffredini, B. R. (1994). Juvenile gunslingers: A place for punitive philosophy in rehabilitative juvenile justice. *Boston College Law Review, 35,* 885-906.

Swistounoff, V. (1999). Comparison of the terminal performance of the .22 long rifle hollow point bullets. *Wound Ballistics Review, 4,* 36-46.

Van Maanen, M. (1999). Discrepancies in the Marshall and Sanow data base: An evaluation over time. *Wound Ballistics Review, 4,* 9-13.

Wachtel, J. (1998). Sources of crime guns in Los Angeles, California. *Policing: An International Journal of Police Strategies and Management, 21,* 220-239.

Wasserman, G., Miller, L., & Cothern, L. (2000). *Prevention of serious and violent juvenile offending.* Washington, DC: U.S. Department of Justice, Office of Juvenile Justice and Delinquency Prevention.

Wilkinson, D., & Fagan, J. (1996). Understanding the role of firearms in violence "scripts": The dynamics of gun events among adolescent males. *Law and Contemporary Problems, 59,* 55-90.

Wilson, J. Q. (1998). Hostility in America: A book review of crime is not the problem. *University of Colorado Law Review, 69,* 1207-1216.

Winfree, L. T., Jr., Peterson-Lynskey, D., & Maupin, J. (1999). Developing local police and federal law enforcement partnerships: G.R.E.A.T. as a case study of policy implementation. *Criminal Justice Review, 24,* 145-168.

Wintemute, G. (1996). The relationship between firearm design and firearm violence. *Journal of the American Medical Association, 275,* 1749-1753.

Wintemute, G. (2000). Guns and gun violence. In A. Blumstein & J. Wallman (Eds.), *The crime drop in America* (pp. 45-96). Cambridge: Cambridge University Press.

Wright, J., & Rossi, P. (1986). *Armed and considered dangerous: A survey of felons and firearms.* New York: Aldine De Gruyter.

Zimring, F. (1972). The medium is the message: Firearm caliber as a determinant of death from assault. *Journal of Legal Studies, 1,* 97-123.

Zimring, F. (1989). The problem of assault firearms. *Crime & Delinquency, 35,* 538-545.

Zimring, F. (1998). *American youth violence.* New York: Oxford University Press.

[8]

"GETTING HIGH AND GETTING BY": DIMENSIONS OF DRUG SELLING BEHAVIORS AMONG AMERICAN MEXICAN GANG MEMBERS IN SOUTH TEXAS

AVELARDO VALDEZ
STEPHEN J. SIFANECK

This article discerns the role that Mexican American gang members play in drug markets, and the relationship between gang members' drug use and drug selling in South Texas. A four-part typology based on the two dimensions of gang type and gang member emerged from this qualitative analysis of 160 male gang members: Homeboys, Hustlers, Slangers, and Ballers. Major findings include the following: (1) many gang members are user/sellers and are not profit-oriented dealers, (2) gangs commonly do extend "protection" to drug-selling members, and (3) proximity to Mexican drug markets, adult prison gangs, and criminal family members may play important roles in whether these gang members have access and the profit potential to actually deal drugs. This research contributes to our complex intersections between gangs, drug using, and drug selling.

Keywords: gangs; drug selling and dealing; Mexican Americans

Research on gangs and drug dealing has generally found it difficult to discern the role that gangs and gang members play in drug markets, and the relationship between gang members' drug use and drug selling behaviors (Howell and Gleason 1999). Studies have reportedly found that most gangs' major illegal activity is associated with the marketing of drugs, especially in low-income urban minority communities (Moore 1978; Covey, Menard, and Franzese 1992; Chin 1995; Spergel 1995). The degree, however, to which gangs are involved is found to vary from one community to another, often

Direct all correspondence to Avelardo Valdez, University of Houston, Graduate School of Social Work, Office for Drug and Social Policy Research, 237 Social Work Building, Houston, Texas 77204-4013. We would like to thank Charles D. Kaplan, Joan Moore, and David Desmond for consultation and comments; Richard Arcos, Ramon Vasquez, and Alice Cepeda for research assistance. This research was supported by the National Institute on Drug Abuse grant R01 DA086.

times among gangs within the same neighborhood (Hagedorn 1988; Padilla 1992a; Morales 2001). Most studies, however, have found that even though drug selling is common among individual gang members, it is not a primary focus of the street gang itself (Klein 1995). Rather, drug sales develop almost as an unintended consequence of drug use by gang members as it does among other drug users. This article addresses the various roles of gang members in drug sales, the structure and function of the gangs, and the relationship to other actors in the drug market, especially adult prison gangs. The purpose here is to address an important gap in our knowledge of the gang's participation in drug market in relationship to other actors.

MEXICAN AMERICAN ILLEGAL DRUG MARKET

In South Texas, the geographic context of this article, marijuana and heroin account for more than half of the total seizures of these drugs in the United States (ONDCP 2002). The Office of National Drug Control Policy (ONDCP) pursuant to the Anti-Drug Abuse Act of 1988 designated the Southwest Border, which encompasses the entire 2,000 mile border one to two counties deep, as a High Intensity Drug Traffic Area (HIDTA). These are areas that are identified as having the most critical drug trafficking problems that adversely impact the United States. Within the Southwest, South Texas is identified as a primary staging area for large-scale, bi-national, narcotic trafficking operations and a common source of marijuana, cocaine, and heroin.

The business of illegal drugs in South Texas is similar in its structure to those in other regions of the United States (Johnson et al. 1990; Adler 1993). Considering the proximity of Mexico (a few hours drive from several large southwestern U.S. cities) trafficking operations are, however, somewhat different from distribution operations in other regions of the U.S. Drug dealing operations typically involve a bi-national hierarchic structure comprising of Mexican Americans and Mexicans. Mexican Americans living near the U.S./ Mexico border and involved in drug distribution have more direct access to primary illegal drug sources than others who must go through multiple layers of middle-men, which decreases profits and increases risks. Cultivating a drug connection in Mexico may also be easier for a Mexican American who may be more acceptable to a Mexican dealer since they share a common ethnic background. This type of access for persons in the Southwest makes it unnecessary for them to develop an organizational hierarchy to traffic in drugs as opposed to those residing in cities and towns located in other areas of the U.S. These factors result in highly decentralized drug markets in the Southwest characterized by multiple small-time drug entrepreneurs with ties to Mexican distributors along with larger international cartels.

One other factor that has begun to characterize the drug market in Mexican American communities in the Southwest is the presence of Chicano prison gangs. Few studies that describe the role of prison gangs in drug sales and their relationship to juvenile and adult gangs outside the prison either in Mexican American communities or others. Jacob's (1974) study is one of the few to address the prison/street nexus. In that study, however, he describes how inmate culture is actually imported from the outside by street gangs into the prison. What seems to be occurring in U.S. Mexican communities is actually the opposite, adult prison gangs are influencing the community's illegal activities from inside the prison. The participation of "pintos" (a term used in the barrio by Mexican Americans to describe ex-convicts) in the drug market was initially described in Moore's Homeboys (1978). At that time in Los Angeles, (and we speculate throughout the Southwest), prison gangs were selling drugs on " a relatively small-scale" and did "see their business as a lifetime commitment to a deviant role" (Moore 1978:149). Their role in the drug market in states like California and Texas seems to have substantially increased over the last two decades based on reports from law enforcement in these two states (although there is little information on these groups in the academic literature). In the Texas prison system, gang membership grew substantially during the 1990s (Cornyn 1999). As members of these prison gangs were released (paroled) from penal institutions, they began to organize themselves into a criminal network engaged in drug dealing and other illegal activities. This same pattern has been reported in California and other states with large concentrations of incarcerated Mexican Americans.

JUVENILE GANGS, DRUG DISTRIBUTION, DEALING, SELLING, AND ORGANIZATION

The term *youth gang* is used in this study to refer to groups of adolescents[1] who engage in collective acts of delinquency and violence, and are perceived by others and themselves as a distinct group. Moreover, the group has a structured hierarchy with rituals, symbols (colors, signs, etc.) and is associated with a territory. Research in the past twenty years has yielded a large amount of data on youth gangs and their role in the distribution of drugs (Fagan 1996; Hagedorn 1994a; 1994b; Klein 1995; Padilla 1992b; Taylor 1990; Venkatesh 1997; Waldorf 1993; Hagedorn, Torres, and Giglio 1998). Dolan and Finney (1984), Moore (1978) and Spergel (1995) have all suggested that youths involved in gang activities are more likely to be involved in the drug trade than other adolescents. During the crack epidemic of the late 1980s and early 1990s, the distribution of this drug was often linked to juvenile drug gangs or "crews" in large U.S. cities like New York and Chicago (Miezkowski 1986; Padilla 1992a; Sullivan 1989; Williams 1989). Taylor (1990) and others have suggested that the growth of gang membership is due to resources made available through the gang's connection to drug markets. Declining economic conditions in many minority urban communities increased juvenile involvement in illegal drug markets (Hagedorn 1988). In the case of New York City, drug suppliers often used juveniles to retail their wares and avoid the risk of harsh sentences adults faced under the Rockefeller drug laws (Williams 1989).

Many researchers such as Skolnick et al. (1990) have argued that drug dealing by gangs is carried out by highly structured organized crime units. As well, Jankowski (1991:131-32) proposed that gangs were cohesive and structured organizations which all had a relationship with organized crime. Applying contingency theory from the literature on organizations, Hagedorn et al. (1998) explores the relationship between gangs and drug selling among minorities in Milwaukee. His findings show that a gang whose drug sales were limited to people within the neighborhood, i.e. their low-income neighbors, are likely to be less organized as a drug gang than those gangs who sell to people outside the neighborhood, especially to middle-class and affluent Whites.

Most contemporary literature reports youth gangs to be rarely involved in large-scale drug distribution activities as an organized gang function (Decker and Van Winkle 1996; Klein 1995). As described by Howell and Gleason (1999:2), "Distribution implies organizational management and control, as opposed to individual involvement in selling drugs directly to individual buyers." Waldorf and Lauderback's (1993) study found Latino and African-American street gangs in San Francisco to be loosely organized with individuals engaged in freelance, rather than organized, drug distribution entities. Skolnick et al. (1990) did find that African-American gangs are more likely to be "instrumental" and vertically organized than "cultural" Latino gangs. In his description, the instrumental gangs are more dedicated to the organized sale of drugs and the cultural gangs are closer to the classic notion of neighborhood corner groups. Mieczkowski (1986) has argued, as well, that crack in Detroit was distributed by small entrepreneurs rather than a large organization.

DRUG USE, DRUG SELLING BEHAVIORS, DRUG DEALING, AND DISTRIBUTION

Research over three decades has established the intersection between different types of illegal drug use and drug selling (Hunt 1990; Hunt, Lipton, and Spunt 1984; Preble and Casey 1969). Users who serve as intermediaries for other users in drug transactions seem to be a consistent phenomenon. This has been observed with some consistency across the different types of illegal drug markets (marijuana, crack, cocaine, heroin) in varied geographic contexts for over 30 years (Andrade, Sifaneck and Neaigus 1999; Furst et al. 1997). For insistence, Sifaneck (1996) has observed a relationship between chronic marijuana users in New York City who played various roles in the distribution, some essentially becoming "subsistence dealers" of the drug in order to pay for their own use.

There have been few noninstitutionalized, or community-based studies of Mexican American drug use and selling/ dealing especially among gang members (Bullington 1977; Moore 1978; Sanders 1994). In Moore's (1978:85) study of East Los Angeles' drug market, she states "drug dealers did employ members of their own barrios in a hierarchy that included non-addicted dealers, addicted dealers (who in turn would supply addict-pushers who sold heroin for use rather than profit), and finally the consumer addict." Individual gang members who dealt drugs operated in the same manner. A consistent finding in these few published studies is that users often paid for their drugs, as Preble and Casey (1969) found among New Yorkers, "by taking care of business," that is, with involvement in drug sales.

In this study we identify and describe the different types of drug use, selling behaviors, and dealing found among members of 26 active gangs in a large metropolitan area in South Texas. We explore the different dimensions of relationships that are involved in constructing a typology of Mexican American gang membership, and the distribution and use of drugs in the Mexican American illegal drug market. Finally, we discuss the implications of current public policies pertaining to gang formation and drug distribution.

METHOD

This research evolved from a study of Mexican American gangs in South Texas, whose focus was to identify and distinguish the relationship between gang violence and drug use among male gangs. The study used multiple methods, including ethnographic field observations, focus groups, and life history /intensive interviews with 160 male gang members sampled in a large Southwestern city (see Yin et al. 1996). The study was delimited to two areas of the city's Mexican American population, encompassing centers of commerce and residency for this group. These areas also have the highest concentration of delinquent behavior and Mexican American gang activity as well as underclass characteristics (Kasarda, 1993). This delimitation was based on secondary data such as the U.S. Census, criminal justice data, public housing statistics, and previous published governmental reports and studies.

After identifying two study areas, two indigenous field workers began the social mapping of these communities, using systematic field observations and recording extensive field notes. Using Wiebel's (1993) indigenous outreach model, fieldworkers were selected based on their knowledge and familiarity with the targeted community and their ability to provide entrée to groups of Mexican American juvenile gang members. The social mapping stage of the study lasted approximately six months, although field work was a continuous process lasting a total of four years. Social mapping assisted us in the identification of gangs and where the target groups congregate, such as public parks, public housing spaces, playgrounds, recreational centers, downtown areas, neighborhood businesses and specific neighborhoods. In conducting this initial fieldwork, field workers were able to establish "an ethnographic presence" (Sifaneck and Neaigus 2001) and maintain a high visibility within the targeted community to help legitimize the project in the community. After this was accomplished, the field workers began to make contacts with the gang members, gain their trust, and obtain access to their social networks. The primary goals of the field workers were to establish rapport with the gang members, maintain nonjudgmental attitudes, and to promote candid and accurate reporting by respondents during data collection and the interview process.

After gaining access, rapport, and trust, field workers began to collect observational data based on gang hangouts mentioned previously. Results of this fieldwork were recorded in daily field notes that were shared and discussed with the research team. All efforts were made not to use information from school officials or police agencies in order to avoid associating the project with these authorities. Attention was focused on the primacy of developing and maintaining networks and a research presence in these communities and among the gangs in these areas.

The fieldwork resulted in identifying all 26 active juvenile gangs and their respective rosters in this area whose cumulative membership totaled 404 persons. The validity and accuracy of gang rosters were checked using at least three of four collateral sources: "gatekeepers", gang member contacts, key respondents , and field workers' observations. Gatekeepers control access to information, other individuals and places (Hammersley and Atkinson 1995, LeCompte and Schensul 1999). Fieldworkers were able to acquire information for initially classifying membership (leader, core, peripherals), gang type, and to delineate the gang's territory (neighborhood). Using this information, we designed a stratified sample that generated the 160 gang members interviewed for this study. A monetary incentive of $50 was provided to the gang member for participating in the interview. In order to protect the identities of the study participants, actual names of the gangs and gang members were known only to the field workers and the project administrator. Any reference to individual members or organizations was based on pseudonyms or identification number assigned by the administrator. As well, fictitious names were given to all geographic and other physical locations.

For the purpose of this paper emphasis will be on drug selling and drug use pattern information elicited from respondents at various times during the life history/intensive interview. Scenario questions provided the respondents' gangs' two major illegal activities (Page 1990). This scenario included specifics on the activity such as the individual in charge, the subject's participation and the distribution of profits. Additionally, a closed-ended question elicited data on the gangs' frequency of dealing during the last year. Individual level data was also collected by asking respondents their frequency of drug selling during the last year as well as the characteristics of their customers. The field note and life history /intensive interview data were combined into an electronic qualitative database. The data was then analyzed and contextualized for themes and commonalities. After the analysis of the data, we developed a typology based on distinct themes.

Dimensions of Drug Selling Behaviors and
Drug Dealing Among Gang Members

Based on the analysis of our qualitative data gathered during field observations and life history interviews, two dimensions have emerged (see Figure 1) that shape and influence behavior associated with drug use and dealing among gang members. These are dimensions, not absolute points, and there is room for overlap between categories (Bailey 1994).

The first dimension focuses on to what extent the gang as an organization is a drug dealing criminal enterprise. At one extreme are gangs who are not involved as a gang in drug dealing activity. These street gangs are traditional, territory-based gangs located in diverse neighborhoods ranging from public housing projects to single-family residential neighborhoods. Nineteen of the 26 gangs in this study were identified as street gangs. They encompass the various types of youth gangs described in the literature, but exclude criminal gangs which overlap with our drug gang category (Morales 2001). Street gangs generally are not hierarchical, although they adhere to some gang rituals such as identification with distinct colors, hand signs, and gang "placas" or symbols. They are involved in "cafeteria-style" crimes including auto theft, burglary, robbery, vandalism, criminal mischief, and petty crime. These crimes tend to be more individual and less organized. The gang member demonstrates more individual agency in his own activities and behavior. Violent behavior tends to be more random and personal rather than purposeful. The gang does offer protection from rival gangs or others in the community who threaten them. This protection is extended to those members who are involved in drug selling and dealing activities.

At the other end of this dimension are those gangs that are organized, criminal, drug dealing enterprises. These drug gangs, that comprised 7 out of the 26 gangs, usually function as a hierarchy with a clearly defined leadership that shares in the profits generated among all gang members involved in the business. Klein (1995:130) suggests these gangs exist in communities where there are "an adequate market of users, a sufficiently uncontrolled neighborhood, and connections with at least mid-level distributors." They may consist of several independent cliques that function under the protective umbrella of a gang. These gangs are distinct from other gangs in that they are not concerned with territorial issues or "turf violations," and do not engage in random acts of violence such as drive-by shootings. Violence among these gangs tends to be more systemic, i.e. related to drug distribution (Goldstein 1985). For instance, little importance is placed on identifying their territory with gang tags, even when other gangs tag their neighborhoods. Members are discouraged from engaging in more expressive acts of violence such as drive-by shootings, random assaults, and personal fights. According to several members, these types of violent acts draw unnecessary attention from the police, which could lead to exposure of covert drug dealing operations. Not all members of these gangs are involved in dealing drugs, some may be involved in other criminal enterprises such as auto theft and fencing stolen goods. Others, especially the younger members, may simply be involved in the gang "socially" without engaging in any criminal activity except occasional fights with rival gang members.

The second dimension identified by our analysis is based on an individual gang member's role in selling and dealing drugs within the gang. The one extreme of this dimension is the user-seller who is primarily buying drugs for personal consumption, and selling a portion of the drugs to offset the costs associated with his drug use. This behavior tends to occur among users who are in the early stages of drug using careers or who have established a relatively controlled regular (daily or weekly) drug use pattern. A user-seller is typically a young gang member who smokes marijuana on a daily basis with friends and acquaintances in the context of socializing. Marijuana purchased by these types of members is usually a quarter ounce that sells for $20 to $30 in a typical barrio neighborhood. An average daily user may purchase a quarter ounce every 3 to 4 days. This does not necessarily mean that the person is smoking the entire quarter ounce himself, since marijuana is a drug that is generally shared with other users. Any profits generated by such a transaction are usually in the form of the drug involved. This pattern of marijuana use and purchasing behavior is common among most gang members in this community.

The other extreme of this dimension includes the dealers, gang members who deal drugs (marijuana, cocaine, and heroin) for their own profit. These persons are connected with criminal networks that provide easy or reliable access to the drug market. They are either dealing as an individual, or with a group of other gang members, or with individuals outside the gang. Profits generated by dealers vary from a highly lucrative business that may afford a newer model car, jewelry, stereo, and other accruements of wealth in the barrio, to barely enough money to sustain or distinguish the person from other nondealing "homeboys." Drug use among these members varies from not using any drugs at all to those that have become heavy users of cocaine and heroin. The crossclassification of the subjects by the two dimensions result in a two-fold typology (see Figure 1).

Homeboys: Drug User/Sellers in Nondealing Gangs

Homeboys are gang members who belong to a street gang whose criminal behavior tends to be more individual, less organized, and less gang directed. Violent behavior tends to be more random and personal as opposed to more purposeful such as physically injuring someone because of an unpaid debt. Except for gang turf disputes, most violence is centered on interpersonal fights and random situational acts of violence often associated with male bravado. Most of these user-sellers usually buy just what they are going to use to get "high" and sell small remaining quantities to reduce the costs associated with their own consumption. Drug selling behaviors exhibited by these homeboys are essentially independent and separate from any formal link to a collective gang activity. These members usually "score" small amounts for themselves, friends and other associates. They may act as a middleman for members who may not have access to a connection. But, the primary feature of this user is that his drug selling is motivated more by the desire for pharmacological effects of a drug than desire to make a profit. One heroin sniffer stated, "Yeah, I am selling drugs, but only so I can get my own stuff. The gang don't have shit to do with this."

The Circle is a gang whose members exemplify this individualized selling/buying activity.[2] Members of the Circle are like many of the other gang members in this study, they smoked marijuana on a daily basis and stayed high most of the day. Most gang members in the Circle, like other members in this category, tend to sell small amounts of marijuana. They would usually sell marijuana to other gang members, friends and acquaintances in the neighborhood. The quantity they sold was usually $10 bags. They would also occasionally sell cocaine in a similar fashion in $10 and $20 units.

A gang member commenting on selling and dealing in his gang said, "None of them deal, they mostly just buy it and smoke it or sniff it or

	Street Gang	Drug Gang
User-Seller	Homeboy	Slanger
Dealer	Hustler	Baller

Figure 1: **A Typology of Drug Dealers and User-Sellers in Street and Drug Gangs**

whatever." Even though the gang is not a drug dealing gang, in most cases, there is usually a "veterano" who is the source for the user/seller gang members. Veterano literally translates to veteran in English, and in Chicano street jargon is reserved for an older experienced criminal drug user. The primary source for the Circle was "Fat Boy" an older gang member who was marginally affiliated with the gang. He was linked through relatives to one of the prison gangs in the area who had connections to higher level dealers. Fat Boy operated with full knowledge of the gang leadership that consisted of a leader and two seconds. The leadership themselves had neither interest in dealing nor the profits generated by Fat Boy. The Circle was territorial, and involved in activities associated with protecting their turf, while drug dealing was not a primary interest.

The majority of the gang members buying from Fat Boy were relatively young, averaging from 15 to 18 years old, and had few dependable drug connections. As some of Fat Boy's customers got a little wiser they started to develop their own connections outside the gang. For instance, Julio was sent to an alternative school after being expelled from his high school. At the alternative school he met someone who introduced him to a cocaine connection. Julio eventually began to use this connection rather than Fat Boy.

Another nondealing gang is the Invaders. This gang is located in a low-income, residential area characterized by modest and older single-family homes. The neighborhood is accessible by car only through a couple of major streets, making it difficult for rival gang members or anyone else to enter the area unobtrusively. The gang consists of approximately twenty members ranging in age from 14 to 18. Their primary illegal activity is "gang banging."

This includes protecting the gang's turf from rival gangs, drive-by shootings, fights and assaults. The Invaders also have a reputation as a party gang known for heavy use of marijuana, cocaine, and alcohol. The members seem to fall in the user/seller category with the majority involved in small-time drug selling, primarily marijuana sales.

Up in the Sky (UIS) is a gang that in the initial months of the research project had been classified as a "tagging crew." This is a group of individuals whose major activity focuses on spray-painting walls, alleyways, street signs, and buildings in a highly individualistic style described as "graffiti art." The general public, and school and police authorities often confuse tagging crew art for gang graffiti. In fact, tagging crew art is much more elaborate than gang graffiti, which is primarily used to mark off territory. These tagging crews are often in competition with each other for the most elaborate tags and the best location. Prestige is bestowed on those that display their art in the highest places (i.e., tops of buildings, freeway crossings).

Members of tagging crews vary according to the roles played in the organization's tagging functions such as "bombers" and "crew members." Bombers are members who actually create the works identified as graffiti art, while the crew provide support as assistants or lookouts. There are also members who are the "partyers." They are attracted to the gang because of the group's social activities, which include the frequent use of marijuana and alcohol, and the occasional use of cocaine. The leader of the UIS was a charismatic 19-year-old whose father was a police officer. In an interview, the leader stated, "In the beginning we didn't let in anyone into the gang that wasn't a tagger. But, as we started to get shit from other gangs we let them in." These nontaggers were attracted to the gang because of the party aspect of the group, but did have to meet gang obligations like fighting rivals.

The members of this gang were primarily homeboys. A few of the gang members, including the leader, had a connection with an older acquaintance from whom he bought 1/2 to 1 ounce of marijuana at a time. He would resell the drug to the other members at a slightly higher cost than he purchased it to cover the cost of the marijuana he used. Other members of this crew were involved in a similar practice. According to the leader, "No one was making any money off the stuff." However, as tension mounted between UIS members and other rivals they began to organize themselves more as a gang. As the crew began to diversify, the group's activities expanded to more profit-oriented drug dealing by certain homeboys. The crew's identity as a gang was solidified when they successfully defended themselves in a gang fight with one of the most notorious gangs in the area.

Hustler: Drug Dealers in Nondealing Gangs

Gang members identified as hustlers deal drugs for profit within a street gang that is not characterized as a drug dealing organization. However, it does provide protection to hustlers within the territory controlled by the gang. Protection is extended to those persons because they are members of the organization rather than because of their drug selling activities. Profits generated by these hustlers are their own and are not used to support the collective activities of the street gang.

The Chicano Dudes are one of the largest and most violent street gangs on the city's West Side. There were approximately 59 members in the gang at the time of the study. Its territory is one of the largest public housing projects in the Mexican American community. The neighborhoods they dominate are filled with the gang's tags on building walls, commercial billboards, and traffic signs.

The leader of the Chicano Dudes is Mark Sanchez who took over the gang after the previous leader was sent to prison for attempted murder. Most of the gang's drug selling is controlled by Mark as an individual, not as leader of the gang. The dealers do not, and are not expected to share profits with the gang. The gang serves a lucrative drug market within a geographic territory they control, although Mark, "his boys" and the other hustlers sell outside this territory. It is the public housing territory, however, that the gang protects through intimidation and violence. Members are expected to support and defend the gang's collective interests, often through violence, and may be required to participate in a drive-by shooting, an assault, or a gang fight. Violating this expectation could have serious repercussions, as one field worker's notes recount:

> Last night Jesse, an ex–Chicano Dude who turned Vida (an adult prison gang) got an order to jump on a Chicano Dude who broke a car window of a sister who is still a Chicano Dude, with him. He did his job, and roughed up Tony, the one who broke the window. The Chicano Dude who went along, Robert, did not do anything but observe the situation. This all happened around 9:00 p.m. till 11:00 p.m. Mark the head of Chicano Dudes sent a group of seven boys to find Jesse, and beat him. They also found Robert, and beat him for watching.

Mark Sanchez maintained the loyalty of a close-knit group of gang members who were primarily older gang members (OGs). Some of these members were involved in his drug dealing and others were not. They were used by Mark as his "backup" (protection) to deal with clients who were giving him trouble or not paying their drug debts. This selective group was given special treatment by Mark such as being provided a lawyer and bond if arrested. If members were incarcerated, he was also known to provide protection while "locked up."

As Mark's drug dealing operation expanded, he began to sell drugs to other gangs on the West Side of San Antonio. When asked if this conflicted with his obligations as leader of the Chicano Dudes, one community researcher stated, "No, the dealing was seen as separate from the gang's business such as protecting its turf. But, Mark would use gang members to back up his business." Toward the end of the study Mark's dealing operations were even expanding outside the gang community into other criminal social networks that put him in conflict with one of the adult prison gangs.

There were other members of the gang selling and dealing drugs that were not part of Mark's clique and operated independently. One of these was a young charismatic gang member named Sparks who was the leader of a set within the Dudes comprised of the gang's pee wees. "I really love these little guys, and try to take care of them," he commented to us in an interview conducted by one of the authors of this paper. "I try and make sure they don't get into too much trouble, especially staying away from the 'brown' (heroin)." Over the years of the study, as the Dudes evolved into primarily a drug dealing gang under the tyrannical control of Mark, Sparks stayed loyal to the principles of the gang. However, Sparks was dealing marijuana, cocaine and heroin to other gang members and people outside the gang. With profits from these deals he was able to purchase marijuana for his own use (which he smoked on daily basis) and support himself economically.

"Biggie" was another member of the Chicano Dudes who was dealing independently. He was the leader of set or clique within the gang located in a different section of the "courts" (public housing projects) they controlled. According to our fieldworkers, he sold ounces of cocaine and heroin. What made Biggie different from the other hustlers is that used his leadership of a major sub-set of the Chicano Dudes as front for his drug business. "He would even give out gang v's (violations) for late payments and members who were getting addicted to heroin." According to several sources, other gang members loyal to Biggie fatally beat one of Biggie's crew for a violation. Biggie was given the leeway in these matters by Mark, as long as he remained loyal to him.

One of the distinctions of the Chicano Dudes was its independence from Vida Loca, an adult prison gang that operated in the same area as his gang. Over the years the prison gang had attempted to control the Chicano Dudes, particularly its drug trade. Mark Sanchez was one of the few gang leaders to stand up to them. He did this through his own violent behavior and the loyalty of several OGs who were not intimidated by these adults. Only recently did this independence begin to weaken when a rival gang associated with Vida Loca seriously injured Sanchez in an aborted attempt on his life. His vulnerability to the prison gang and personal accumulation of wealth started to affect the loyalty of many of his members to the gang and his leadership. Over the course of this study, this gang became to transform itself more into a dealing gang as its dealing activities became its primary activity.

Slanger: Drug User/Sellers in Drug-Dealing Gangs

Gang members in this category are characterized as user/sellers in gangs that are organized as drug dealing enterprises. Slangers are members who either chose not to participate in the higher levels of the gang's organized drug dealing activities or who are excluded from those circles for various reasons. However, the slangers continue to use and sell drugs at an individual level mostly to help off-set costs associated with their drug use and to support themselves economically. In the vernacular of the gangs, these members are dealing to "get high and get by." The slangers stand in contrast to the hardcore dealer members in the drug gang who are heavily involved in the gang's higher level organized drug distribution activities.

Varrio La Paloma (VLP) is a gang that is located in San Miguel Public Housing Project, one of the oldest courts on the Westside. The gang's activities have recently expanded to a working-class suburban subdivision outside the barrio after public housing authorities displaced many project families to this location. There are approximately 100 hard-core and 80 marginal members in this gang. Organizationally, this dealing gang has several sets or subgroups of members. Each of the sets has a head that is under the command of a leader. VLP is an older established gang and one of the few gangs whose former members were parents and other relatives who have in the past participated in this same gang.

The distribution of drugs by the VLP was controlled by the leader of the gang and his closest gang associates, primarily older hard core members, including two of his brothers. There were several cliques of members who were responsible for different tasks or functions associated with the gang's drug business. VLP leadership had connections to wholesale drug distributors who were associated with independent adult criminals with ties to Mexico. The actual drug distribution in the barrios was conducted by slangers. The slangers were "fronted" drugs by the gang's leadership for retail sale. Fronting is a form of credit or consignment in the drug culture given to sellers who agree to pay for the drugs within an agreed upon time. Amount of profits accrued by the slangers depends on their mode of distribution. One report from the field stated,

> How much money a slanger made, depended on how you cut it, or whether you
> resold it in smaller qualities. If one of the guy's in the crew got an eight ball (3 ½
> grams) of cocaine from Leo for $100, he might mix it with a gram of cut for
> about a $50 profit if he sold the whole amount . Or, he could make more profits
> if he bagged it up in smaller quantities and sold it that way like 10s and 20s bags
> (dollars).

Selling in smaller units entails higher risks because of the higher volume of customers needed to get rid of the "batch."

Interestingly, the VLP's status as a drug dealing gang is a relatively recent phenomena and is in response to the emergence of the prison gangs in the community during the last 10 years. They became involved in a serious conflict with the adult prison gang, which was attempting to enforce its diez porciento (10%) take from VLP's total sales. At that time, drug dealing was conducted on an individual basis by gang members. In order to protect their share of the drug market, the gang's dealers began to organize their drug business around the gang. This allowed them to use the gang's organization to protect themselves from the prison gang attempting to control the drug market in their community.

This conflict culminated when two adult prison gang members were murdered by a VLP member when he refused to cooperate with him. One of our fieldworkers described the time he met the VLP member soon after the shoot-out incident:

> Georgie walked with the help of two crutches as he approached the car. Vida
> put out a contract on him because he refused to pay the 10% commission on his
> drug sales. Georgie had started out selling dime bags of heroin. Shortly thereaf-
> ter, he was selling three to four ounces of heroin and coke a week. That's when
> Vida started asking for their 10%. He said, "They sent two hit men. The men
> shot first hitting me in the thigh and the knee. I was shooting on the way down
> and killed them both. I gave the gun to Ray-Ray, who stashed it before the po-
> lice got there." Georgie was upset because none of the VLP got down for him.

Eventually, after serious threats of retaliation from both sides, the VLP and the prison gang reached a compromise. The VLP would be allowed to sell cocaine and marijuana, but the heroin trade would be the exclusive right of the prison gang even within the San Miguel Courts.

As previously mentioned, slangers are those members on the lower end of the gang's dealing hierarchy. Slangers may include many of the younger members who were excluded from more serious drug dealing operations because of the legal risks and violence associated with these activities. This protective attitude was even stronger if the younger member was a sibling of the older veteranos drug dealers. One of these types told us, "There was no way my carnalito (younger brother) was going to get involved." However, these members continued to engage in user-seller behavior to economically supplement their recreational drug use. What distinguishes these slangers from other user-sellers is the high-level protection and reputation of the drug gang. In fact, outsiders often treated them as full-fledged "ballers" (described in the following section) because of their drug dealing gang affiliation.

Another category of slangers in the VLP were gang members who voluntarily decided not to participate in the gang dealing activities, although to continue user/seller behavior. These often included VLP members on probation and parole. In these types of cases, the person fears that an arrest for drug dealing could result in a long prison term. This threat is often a deterrent to becoming involved in the gang's organized drug dealing. In other cases, the veterano may be experiencing a process of maturing out of the gang life style. In these situations the member is often emotionally attached to a woman whose child he may have fathered. He may have also found a job that offered a good salary and some stability. At this point in his life, the veterano may be considering dropping out of the gang scene. However, he may still be using drugs, especially marijuana, and since he has solid connections to drug dealers, he will continue to sell to a few trusted customers to compensate for his own drug use. As one of these slangers put it, "I am selling enough to cover my own huesos (bones)."

Ballers: Drug Dealers—Drug-Dealing Gangs

As discussed, drug gangs are those organized as a criminal enterprise with profits distributed either to the gang as an entity or equally among the gang members active in the organization. Ballers are the individuals within these gangs who control the drug distribution business. One gang member commented, "These are the batos (guys) making all the feria (money), jewelry, and fancy cars. They have the big connections." The ballers usually sit atop the gang's hierarchy and comprise a leadership structure that provides protection to members against rival gangs and predatory adult criminals. Among these gang members, heroin use was generally discouraged, although as the gangs began to deal heroin, many ballers began shabanging (noninjection) and/or picando (injecting), and some subsequently became addicted. One of the distinctions of ballers from seller-dealers, slangers and homeboys is their generally lower visibility and the higher volume of drugs they deal. "You don't see these guys on the street selling drugs like those others," an older gangster (OG) member mentioned to us in an interview. Furthermore, they avoid ostentatious aggressive behavior that attracts law enforcement like drive-by shootings. Violence among ballers is also more purposeful and revolved around business transactions as discussed in Goldstein's drug-nexus typology (1985).

The Nine-Ball Crew (NBC) is a dealing gang located in La Luna Courts, another large city housing project. This gang was distinct from other youth gangs in its direct ties to Vida Loca. This prison gang controlled the heroin trade in this community by imposing the 10 percent rule that it enforced through violence and intimidation. The gang leader's stepfather was one of the heads of the prison gang. Over the last few years, they have recruited several gangs, and subsequently their members, to distribute heroin for them. Although, the relationship between a youth gang and the adult prison gang is initially based on drug distribution, the youth gang often becomes a subsidiary of the prison gang. The control of Vida Loca over the NBCs is their most successful example of this process. During the course of the study, a Nine-Baller shot the leader of the Chicano Dudes for refusing to pay the adult prison gang a percentage of his profit. The hit was an attempt by the adult prison gang to solidify their control of the drug trade in this area.

The Nine-Ball Crew is highly organized with a leader and two second-heads or lieutenants, a hard-core membership of 20 members and approximately 30 others. The leader of this gang is Juan, a baller, who tightly rules the gang. He is 23 years old and has been described as "cold-blooded and vicious." His control of the gang is solidified by the support of his five brothers who are active in the gang. The NBC drug market is primarily in the La Luna Courts and nearby vicinity, where there is little competition from other sellers and dealers. The selling of drugs is coordinated by one of Juan's brothers and another member identified as an original gangster (OG). The gang's hardcore membership, under the direct supervision of the two heads, is responsible for the distribution and sale of the drugs. Ballers, such as Juan and his OGs, are the primary sources of drugs for other slangers, hustlers, homeboys, and other drug sellers in the community. When one of the NBC members was asked about Juan, he said

> Yeah, he's the main guy that controls the drugs. He says who is going to sell and who ain't going to sell. If you're selling without permission and don't bring money to him you're going to get in trouble, get a v.

Another well recognized baller was Pio Gomez who operated out of a public-housing complex on the near West Side. What distinguished him from some of the other ballers was that he was not a member of one of the drug gangs. He was actually a childhood friend of a leader of the Chicano Dudes. This widely acknowledged relationship among gangs members and the community allowed him to run his drug business as if he was a high-ranking member of a drug gang. This provided him the "street muscle" to deal with those who tried to interfere in his business or refused to pay their debts to him and his crew. Through independent adult dealers and other dealing gangs, including Mark from the Chicano Dudes, he would acquire kilos of cocaine and ounces of heroin. Pio broke these larger quantities into ounces, half ounces, quarter ounces and eight-balls (3 1/2 grams) that he fronted to his crew. His crew, which consisted of gang members and other young men, distributed the drugs to slangers in the courts and the surrounding neighborhoods. Over the course of the study, Pio generated a great deal of money, spending it in a very conspicuous manner. One gang member stated, "Everyone considered Pio a baller. He bought a brand new silver Eclipse. He had gold chains, expensive watches that stood out like a sore thumb. But, he never got busted. Some of his crew did, but not him."

During the period of this study there were gang members who moved from one category of the typology to another. El Gato, the leader of the Deep West, transformed himself from a slanger to baller, and finally was recruited as a "soldier" by Vida Loca. El Gato used his gang members as runners in an area on the western outskirts of the Mexican American community. At the height of his dealing career, he was distributing large amounts of cocaine and heroin. When El Gato was finally arrested, it was for possession with intent to distribute 6 ounces of cocaine and 4 ounces of heroin, an amount he would sell through his crew 2 or 3 times a week. Most of these drugs were fronted to other gang members or other independent drug sellers. To make sure that his gang members stayed loyal and in his services, he was known for giving away $10 to $20 bags of heroin to them. As result, many of his hard-core slangers became addicted and were less useful to his operation especially in collection efforts. As El Gato started to lose key members to heroin addiction and increased police pressure, he started to create alliances with the prison gang that eventually recruited him as a full-fledged member.

Although many of the dealing gangs, and subsequently the ballers were generating large amounts of money, others were not. One informant told us, "the VLP as a gang wasn't selling nothing compared to a couple of guys (a set) associated with the Chicano Dudes." He went on to explain how the VLP were really small-time in the larger drug market in the community, although, the VLP did manage to control through violence a corner of that market in the courts. "These guys were not driving around in new cars, and flashing money around. These guys were small time, many couldn't even pay their utility bills." However, even those ballers and hustlers like Mark Sanchez that were perceived as " making money" were not wealthy enough to invest in legitimate businesses like more successful criminals such as those in larger illegitimate enterprises.

DISCUSSION AND CONCLUSION

We have attempted to develop a framework for describing and understanding the relationships among drug use, gang membership, and drug distribution and gang membership in the context of a Mexican American community in South Texas. We constructed this framework along two dimensions: (1) the gang's organizational structure defined by involvement in drug dealing; and (2) the individual gang member's role in using, selling and dealing drugs. The analysis of the two dimensions resulted in a fourfold typology. The typology encompasses a wide range of connections and intersections between gangs, their individual members, and the selling of illegal drugs within the wider distribution system.

Malcolm Klein (1995:132) asserts that a clear distinction exists between street and drug gangs (Howell and Gleason 1999). He posits that few gangs are involved as an organization in drug distribution in entrepreneurial marketing of drugs because of key structural limitations. For example, drug dealing requires a hierarchical and cohesive organization, dependable leadership, a business focus, and avoidance of opportunistic "cafeteria style" crimes. Our findings generally corroborate Klein's theory as applied to the Mexican Americans in South Texas. However, our data suggests that Klein underestimates the extent to which street gangs and gang members are fluid in their drug dealing roles and are susceptible to existing, adult based drug distribution systems.

Findings from this study suggest that gang members' involvement in selling and dealing is influenced by the presence of adult criminals in key members' social network. Many of the gang members are related by family ties to adult criminals who are prison gang members active in drug distribution. Moore (1994) similarly described the importance of the "cholo" family in sustaining a wide array of delinquent and criminal behavior among Mexican Americans in Los Angeles (Vigil 1988 and Moore 1994). This "intergenerational closure" provides a social cohesiveness to the street gang that sharply contrasts to that in Chicago that has been related to positive social outcomes (Sampson, Morenoff, and Earls 1999). Nonetheless, the capacity of adult criminal family relationships to influence and intervene in the lives of young males provides a marker for distinguishing the Mexican American gangs in this study.

The inclusion of the second dimension pertaining to drug user-seller and dealer roles in the construction of our typology provides a more comprehensive understanding of gangs and the drug distribution system. The appreciation of the subtle yet complex roles played by individual gang members in this system has been overlooked by some gang researchers. An exception has been the work of Spergel (1995) who recognized a fluidity and similarity in the roles of members in street and drug gangs. Our typology contributes to this recognition by explicating the multiplicity of roles that individual gang members play in the drug distribution system that is not necessarily dictated by gang structure, i.e. street vs. drug gang.

The role of gang members in this system is often obscured because of the fact that most gang members are more frequent users and sellers of drugs compared to other non-gang youth. But as Spergel (1995) concludes, this does not mean that the majority of gang members are dealers as we have defined them by our typology nor that the gangs they belong to are necessarily criminal drug organizations. What emerges from our data is that some gangs have nothing to do with the dealing of drugs. This was clearly illustrated by the "tagging crew" who spent their time, energy and money on elaborate, although illegal, displays of public art, and not the selling of illegal drugs.

Another important finding of this study is that drug selling and dealing is not only related to extended family networks but also to the larger social context of the gang. Thus, the gang can offer to drug sellers and dealers protection in exchange for their commitment and obligation to the gang. As a result, the role of the gang in the distribution of drugs in the community is difficult to discern and is obscured to most outsiders. For instance, protection may often misperceived by police as evidence that a gang is a drug dealing enterprise when in reality members may be operating independently from the gang. Often law enforcement personnel indiscriminately extend this flawed perception to all Mexican American youth living in these neighborhoods. This misconception may lead to continual harassment, shakedowns and detainment of many innocent youth.

A serious consequence of this perception is very often drug law enforcement that indiscriminately arrests and prosecutes offenders without distinguishing the differences that constitute our four distinct types. Even those "homeboys" arrested for minor violations of drug laws, such as possession of small amounts of marijuana, get caught up in a criminal justice system that often treat them like "ballers," leading to serious lifelong consequences. Our typology suggests that a more variegated law enforcement and balanced social intervention policy is needed to address the complexity of the situation.

The analysis presented here suggests the need for police, judges and district attorneys to understand the relationship between the use of illegal drugs by poor youth and the diverse operative roles these youth may play in the distribution of these drugs. Police need to be trained in recognizing the differences in the "homeboy" user/seller who is affiliated with a street gang from "slangers" and "ballers" who are the persons really dealing drugs. Judges also need more discretion in the sentencing of those who violate drug laws.

Mandatory sentencing minimums need to be balanced with social work and treatment options for "homeboys," and in certain cases "hustlers" and "slangers." These changes in policy would shift the emphasis away from a wholesale punishment approach, usually in the form of incarceration, to a refined rehabilitation approach involving creative applications of drug treatment, job training, and probationary social work.

In closing, the methodological limitations of our study need to be acknowledged. Common with other ethnographic and qualitative studies, the generalizability of the results is limited to other communities. Ethnographic studies of drug dealing often arrive at seemingly contradictory findings in relatively similar communities (Hagedorn 1988; Taylor 1990). South Texas, with its proximity to Mexican trafficking operations, may present so special a context that replication of our gang drug dealing typology without essential modifications would be problematic. However, confidence in the generalizability of our typology is increased in that we were able to find and distinguish street and drug gangs and membership behavior in South Texas as has been widely done elsewhere. This is complemented by the inclusion in our analysis of the mechanism of intergenerational closure to help explain the variation we discovered. A deeper and more extended program of qualitative research needs to be initiated in cities in diverse regions and with gang members of other ethnicities in order to further evaluate the significance of the findings from this single study.

NOTES

1. In the literature there are very different definitions of what constitutes an adolescent gang (Klein 1971; Miller 1975; Moore 1978; Yablonsky 1962) often based on the researcher's relationship to the gang and source of information. The definition used in study is based on our experiences in working with gangs in San Antonio.

2. All the names of gangs and gang members are aliases. Some of the descriptive characteristics have been altered to prevent identification of the actual participants, gangs, and neighborhoods.

3. *Shabanging* is a term used by these youth to describe intranasal use of heroin, typically via a plastic nasal spray bottle. The heroin is diluted with water and sprayed into the nasal cavity with the plastic device.

REFERENCES

Adler, Patricia A. 1993. *Wheeling and Dealing: An Ethnography of an Upper-Level Drug Dealing and Smuggling Community.* New York: Columbia University Press.

Andrade, Xavier, Stephen J. Sifaneck, and Alan Neaigus. 1999. "Dope Sniffers in New York City: An Ethnography of Heroin Markets and Patterns of Use." *Journal of Drug Issues* 29:271-98.

Bailey, Kenneth B. 1994. *Typologies and Taxonomies: An Introduction to Classification Techniques.* Thousand Oaks, CA: Sage.

Bullington, Bruce. 1977. *Heroin Use in the Barrio.* Lexington, MA: Lexington Books.

Chin, Ko-Lin. 1995. "Chinese gangs and extortion." Pp. 46-52 in *The Modern Gang Reader,* edited by M. W. Klein, C. L. Maxson, and J. Miller. Los Angeles, CA: Roxbury.

Cornyn, John. 1999. "Gangs in Texas: 1999." Austin, TX: Office of the Attorney General, State of Texas. Retrieved August 15, 2003 from http://www.oag.state.tx.us/AG_Publications/ pdfs/1999gangs.pdf.

Covey, Herbert C., Scott Menard, and Robert J. Franzese. 1992. *Juvenile Gangs.* Springfield, IL: Charles C. Thomas.

Decker, Scott and Barrik Van Winkle. 1996. "Slinging Dope: The Role of Gangs and Gang Members in Drug Sales." *Justice Quarterly* 11:583-604.

Dolan, Edward F. and Shan Finney. 1984. *Youth Gangs.* New York: Julian Messner.

Fagan, Jeffery. 1996. "Gangs, Drugs, and Neighborhood Change." Pp. 39-74 in *Gangs in America,* edited by C. R. Huff. Newbury Park, CA: Sage.

Furst, Terry R., Richard S. Curtis, Bruce D. Johnson, and Douglas S. Goldsmith. 1997. "The Rise of the Street Middleman/Woman in a Declining Drug Market." *Addiction Research* 5:1-26.

Goldstein, Paul J. 1985. "The Drugs/Violence Nexus: A Tripartite Conceptual Framework." *Journal of Drug Issues* 15:493-506.

Hagedorn, John. 1988. *People and Folks: Gangs, Crime and the Underclass in a Rust Belt City.* Chicago: Lake View Press.

―――. 1994a. "Neighborhoods, Markets, and Gang Drug Organization." *Journal of Research in Crime and Delinquency* 31:264-94.

―――. 1994b. "Homeboys, Dope Fiends, Legits, and New Jacks." *Criminology* 32:197-219.

Hagedorn, John, Jose Torres, and Greg Giglio. 1998. "Cocaine, Kicks, and Strain: Patterns of Substance Use in Milwaukee Gangs." *Contemporary Drug Problems* 25:113-45.

Hammersley, Martyn and Paul Atkinson. 1995. *Ethnography, Principles in Practice.* London: Routledge.

Howell, James C. and Debra K. Gleason. 1999. *Youth Gang Drug Trafficking.* Washington, DC: US Department of Justice, Office of Justice Programs, Office of Juvenile Justice and Delinquency Prevention.

Hunt, Dana E. 1990. "Drugs and Consensual Crimes: Drug Dealing and Prostitution." Pp. 159-202 in *Crime and Justice: An Annual Review of Research, vol. 13: Drugs and Crime,* edited by J.Q.W.A.M. Tonry. Chicago: University of Chicago Press.

Hunt, Dana E., Douglas S. Lipton, and Barry Spunt. 1984. "Patterns of Criminal Activity Among Methadone Clients and Current Narcotics Users Not in Treatment." *Journal of Drug Issues* 14:687-702.

Jacobs, James B. 1974. "Street Gangs Behind Bars." *Social Problems* 21:395-409.

Jankowski, Martín Sánchez. 1991. *Islands in the Street: Gangs and American Urban Society.* Berkeley: University of California Press.

Johnson, Bruce D., Terry Williams, Kojo A. Dei, and Harry Sanabria. 1990. "Drug Abuse in the Inner City: Impact on Hard-Drug Users and the Community." Pp. 9-30 in *Drugs and Crime,* vol. 13, edited by M. Tonry, N. Morris, and N.I.O. Justice. Chicago: The University of Chicago Press.

Kasarda, John D. 1993. *Urban Underclass Database: An Overview and Machine-Readable File Documentation.* New York: Social Science Research Council.

Klein, Malcolm. 1971. *Street Gangs and Street Workers.* Englewood Cliffs, NJ: Prentice Hall.

―――. 1995. *The American Street Gang.* New York: Oxford Press.

LeCompte, Margaret D. and Jean J. Schensul. 1999. *Designing & Conducting Ethnographic Research, Ethnographer's Toolkit, Vol. 1.* Walnut Creek, CA: Altamira Press.

Mieczkowski, Thomas. 1986. "Geeking Up and Throwing Down: Heroin Street Life in Detroit." *Criminology* 24:645-65.

Miller, Walter B. 1975. *Violence by Youth Gangs and Youth Groups As a Crime Problem in Major American Cities*. Washington, DC: Department of Justice.

Moore, Joan. 1978. *Homeboys: Gangs, Drugs, and Prison in the Barrios of Los Angeles*. Philadelphia: Temple University Press.

———. 1994. "The Chola Life Course: Chicana Heroin Users and the Barrio Gang." *The International Journal of the Addictions* 29:1115-26.

Morales, Armando T. 2001. "Urban and Suburban Gangs: The Psychosocial Crisis Spreads." Pp. 397-433 in *Social Work: A Profession of Many Faces*, 9th ed., edited by A. T. Morales and B. W. Sheafor. Boston, MA: Allyn & Bacon.

Office of National Drug Control Policy, High Intensity Drug Trafficking Areas. 2002. "Southwest Border HIDTA South Texas Partnership." Retrieved August 15, 2003 from http://www.whitehousedrugpolicy.gov/hidta/frames_stex.html.

Padilla, Felix M. 1992a. *The Gang As an American Enterprise*. New Brunswick, NJ: Rutgers University Press.

———. 1992b. *Becoming a Gang Member: The Gang As an American Enterprise*. New Brunswick, NJ: Rutgers University Press.

Page, Bryan. 1990. "Shooting Scenarios and Risk of HIV-1 Infection." *The American Behavioral Scientist* 33:478.

Preble, Edward and John J. Casey. 1969. "Taking Care of Business—The Heroin User's Life on the Street." *The International Journal of the Addictions* 4:1-24.

Sampson, Robert J., Jeffery D. Morenoff, and Felton Earls. 1999. "Beyond Social Capital: Saptial Daynamic of Collective Efficacy for Children." *American Sociological Review* 64:633-60.

Sanders, William B. 1994. *Gangbangs and Drive-by*. New York: Aldine de Gruyter.

Sifaneck, Stephen J. 1996. "Regulating Cannabis: An Ethnographic Analysis of the Sale and Use of Cannabis in New York City and Rotterdam." Unpublished Ph.D. Dissertation. City University of New York (CUNY), New York.

Sifaneck, Stephen J. and Alan Neaigus. 2001. "The Ethnographic Accessing, Sampling and Screening of Hidden Populations: Heroin Sniffers in New York City." *Addiction Research and Theory* 9:519-43.

Skolnick, Jerome H., Theodore Correll, Elizabeth Navarro Navarro, and Roger Rabb. 1990. "The Social Structure of Street Drug Dealings." *American Journal of Police* 9:1-41.

Spergel, Irving A. 1995. *The Youth Gang Problem: A Community Approach*. New York: Oxford University Press.

Sullivan, Mercer L. 1989. *Getting Paid: Youth Crime and Work in the Inner City*. Ithaca, NY: Cornell University Press.

Taylor, Carl. 1990. *Dangerous Society*. East Lansing: Michigan State University Press.

Venkatesh, Sudhir A. 1997. "The Social Organization of a Street Gang Activity in an Urban Ghetto." *American Journal of Sociology* 103:82-111.

Vigil, Diego. 1988. *Barrio gangs*. Austin: University of Texas Press.

Waldorf, Dan. 1993. *When the Crips Invaded San Francisco: Gang Migration- Homeboy Study*. Alameda, CA: Institute for Scientific Analysis.

Waldorf, Dan and David Lauderback. 1993. *Gang Drug Sales in San Francisco: Organized or Freelance?* Alameda, CA: Institute for Scientific Analysis.

Wiebel, Wayne. 1993. *The Indigenous Leader Outreach Model: Intervention Manual*. Rockville, MD: National Institute on Drug Abuse.

Williams, Terry. 1989. *The Cocaine Kids: The Inside Story of a Teenage Drug Ring*. Redding, MA: Addison-Wesley.

Yablonsky, Lewis. 1962. *The Violent Gang.* New York: McMillan.
Yin, Zenong, Avelardo Valdez, Alberto G. Jr. Mata, and Charles Kaplan. 1996. "Developing a
Field-Intensive Methodology for Generating a Randomized Sample for Gang Research."
Free Inquiry-Special Issue: Gang, Drugs and Violence 24:195-204.

*Avelardo Valdez is currently a professor at the University of Houston, Graduate School of
Social Work and director of the Office for Drug and Social Policy Research. He has been
a recipient of several federally funded research projects on Mexican American drug use,
violence, and gangs. His more recent publications include research on street gangs, female drug users, and sex workers on the U.S./Mexico border. He is currently a principal
investigator on a National Institutes of Health, National Institute on Drug Abuse (NIDA)
grant that focuses on Mexican American noninjecting heroin use.*

*Stephen J. Sifaneck, Ph.D., is presently a project director/coinvestigator in the Institute
for Special Populations Research (IPSR) at National Development and Research Institutes (NDRI) Inc. in New York City. His publications include articles and chapters about
the sale and use of marijuana, heroin and prescription drugs, ethnographic research
methodologies, and subcultural urban issues.*

Part II
Robbery and Firearms

[9]

STICK-UP, STREET CULTURE, AND OFFENDER MOTIVATION*

BRUCE A. JACOBS
RICHARD WRIGHT

Motivation is the central, yet arguably the most assumed, causal variable in the etiology of criminal behavior. Criminology's incomplete and imprecise understanding of this construct can be traced to the discipline's strong emphasis on background risk factors, often to the exclusion of subjective foreground conditions. In this article, we attempt to remedy this by exploring the decision-making processes of active armed robbers in real-life settings and circumstances. Our aim is to understand how and why these offenders move from an unmotivated state to one in which they are determined to commit robbery. Drawing from semistructured interviews with 86 active armed robbers, we argue that while the decision to commit robbery stems most directly from a perceived need for fast cash, this decision is activated, mediated, and shaped by participation in street culture. Street culture, and its constituent conduct norms, represents an essential intervening variable linking criminal motivation to background risk factors and subjective foreground conditions.

Motivation is the central, yet arguably the most assumed, causal variable in the etiology of criminal behavior. Obviously, persons commit crimes because they are motivated to do so, and virtually no offense can occur in the absence of motivation. Though the concept inheres implicitly or explicitly in every influential theory of crime, this is far from saying that its treatment has been comprehensive, exhaustive, or precise (but see Tittle, 1995). In many ways, motivation is criminology's dirty little secret—manifest yet murky, presupposed but elusive, everywhere and nowhere. If there is a bogeyman lurking in our discipline's theoretical shadows, motivation may well be it.

Much of the reason for this can be located in the time-honored, positivistic tradition of finding the one factor, or set of factors, that accounts for

* The research on which this article is based was funded jointly by the Harry Frank Guggenheim Foundation, the National Institute of Justice (N.I.J. Grant 94–IJ–CX–0030), and the National Consortium on Violence Research (NCOVR Grant 98–1SDRP). Points of view or opinions expressed are those of the authors and do not necessarily reflect the position of the funding agencies. Each author contributed equally to the article. Our names appear in alphabetical order. We would like to thank Scott Decker, Richard Felson, Janet Lauritsen, Rick Rabe, Rick Rosenfeld, and this journal's anonymous reviewers for their helpful comments and criticisms.

150   JACOBS AND WRIGHT

it. Causality has been called criminology's "Holy Grail" (Groves and Lynch, 1990:360), the quest for which makes other disciplinary pursuits seem tangential, sometimes inconsequential. The search typically revolves around identification of background risk factors (Katz, 1988)—behavioral correlates—that establish nonspurious relationships with criminal behavior (Groves and Lynch, 1990:358). A panoply of such factors have been implicated over many decades of research—spanning multiple levels, as well as units, of analyses. They include, among other things, anomie, blocked opportunities, deviant self-identity, status frustration, weak social bonds, low self-control, social disorganization, structural oppression, unemployment, age, gender, class, race, deviant peer relations, marital status, body type, IQ, and personality (see e.g., Akers, 1985; Becker, 1963; Chambliss and Seidman, 1971; Cloward and Ohlin, 1960; Cohen, 1955; Cornish and Clarke, 1986; Felson, 1987; Hirschi, 1969; Merton, 1938; Miller, 1958; Quinney, 1970; Sampson and Laub, 1992; Shaw and McKay, 1942; Sutherland, 1947).

Common to all such factors, however, is their independent status from the "foreground" of criminal decision making—the immediate phenomenological context in which decisions to offend are activated (see also Groves and Lynch, 1990; Katz, 1988). Though background factors may predispose persons to crime, they fail to explain why two individuals with identical risk factor profiles do not offend equally (see e.g., Colvin and Pauly, 1983), why persons with particular risk factors go long periods of time without offending, why individuals without the implicated risk factors offend, why persons offend but not in the particular way a theory directs them to, or why persons who are not determined to commit a crime one moment become determined to do so the next (see Katz, 1988:3–4; see also Tittle, 1995, on "theoretical precision"). Decisions to offend, like all social action, do not take place in a vacuum. Rather, they are bathed in an "ongoing process of human existence" (Bottoms and Wiles, 1992:19) and mediated by prevailing situational and subcultural conditions.

In this article we attend to these important foreground dynamics, exploring the decision-making processes of active armed robbers in real-life settings and circumstances. Our aim is to understand how and why these offenders move from an unmotivated state to one in which they are determined to commit robbery. We argue that while the decision to commit robbery stems most directly from a perceived need for fast cash, this decision is activated, mediated, and channeled by participation in street culture. Street culture, and its constituent conduct norms, represents an essential intervening variable linking criminal motivation to background risk factors and subjective foreground conditions.

STREET CULTURE AND MOTIVATION 151

METHODS

The study is based on in-depth interviews with a sample of 86 currently active robbers recruited from the streets of St. Louis, Missouri. Respondents ranged in age from 16 to 51. All but 3 were African-American; 14 were female.[1] All respondents had taken part in armed robberies, but many also had committed strong-arm attacks. Respondents did not offend at equal rates, but all (1) had committed a robbery within the recent past (typically within the past month), (2) defined themselves as currently active, and (3) were regarded as active by other offenders. Sixty-one of the offenders admitted to having committed 10 or more lifetime robberies. Included in this group were 31 offenders who estimated having done at least 50 robberies. Seventy-three of the offenders said that they typically robbed individuals on the street or in other public settings, 10 reported that they usually targeted commercial establishments, and 3 claimed that they committed street and commercial robberies in roughly equal proportions.

Though "total" institutions afford the chance to obtain data from armed robbers without the risk of harm associated with "street" interviews (Agar, 1973), collecting valid and reliable data may not be possible there because incarcerated offenders "do not behave naturally" (Wright and Decker, 1994:5; see also Polsky, 1967:123; Sutherland and Cressey, 1970:68). Studies of incarcerated robbers also are susceptible to the charge of being based on "unsuccessful criminals, on the supposition that successful criminals are not apprehended or are at least able to avoid incarceration" (McCall, 1978:27). Traditional methods, such as household surveys, likely would not be able to identify such persons in the first place because they "cannot produce reliable samples," they are inefficient, and because most hidden populations (such as active armed robbers) are "rare" (Heckathorn, 1997:174).

Respondents were located using a snowball sampling strategy. Probably the most difficult aspect of researching active offenders using this technique is making the initial contacts. The first study participants were recruited by a specially trained "street ethnographer" (Weppner, 1977). This person, an ex-offender who had retired from crime after being shot and paralyzed in a gangland-style execution attempt, earlier had supported himself for many years as a highly skilled thief. He had been arrested just a few times and was never convicted. As a thief, he had acquired a solid

---

1. Using the same sample reported here, Miller (1998) compared male and female accounts of motivations to commit robbery. She found no differences, arguing that—when it comes to motivation—robbery is more a case of gender similarity than anything else (see p. 44). We therefore make no distinction between male and female responses in this study.

reputation among his fellow criminals for both toughness and integrity. Trading on his reputation, he initiated the recruitment process by approaching former criminal associates. Some of these contacts still were committing crimes; others either had retired or remained involved only peripherally. After explaining the project to them, and stressing that the police were not involved, he asked them to provide referrals of active robbers. Informants were paid $10 for each successful referral.

In an attempt to construct a more representative sample, we recruited respondents through a variety of contacts, thereby reducing the chances of tapping into only one or two networks of criminals. Respondents also were questioned extensively about their knowledge of other offenders to guard against having a sample of highly atypical robbers. Such measures are not foolproof, and offenders outside of the penetrated networks inevitably will remain unknown. This is to say nothing of the fact that the representativeness of a sample of active offenders can never be determined conclusively because the parameters of the population are impossible to estimate (Glassner and Carpenter, 1985). The most that we can reasonably claim is that the sample appears to be broadly representative of the population of active offenders known to the interviewees.

The interviews were semistructured and conducted in an informal manner. They revolved around a basic set of questions that focused on the offenders' thoughts and actions before, during, and after their crimes. As with all such research, other promising areas of inquiry presented themselves throughout the study period. Every attempt was made to follow up on these areas in subsequent interviews, even though this meant that only a subsample of offenders would have an opportunity to comment. The nature of open-ended qualitative interviewing is such that not all topics can be anticipated and all offenders asked the same questions about issues that emerge later, often serendipitously, during the research process (Henslin, 1972:52). The fact that responses became repetitious indicated sufficient topical covering, though this could have been an artifact of the sampling design. The sample's purposive design prevents us from claiming to have achieved theoretical saturation.

Interviews typically lasted between one and two hours, were tape-recorded, and transcribed verbatim. Considerable time was devoted to explaining questions and probing answers. The truthfulness of what the offenders said was monitored by questioning vague or inconsistent responses. Some of the interviewees went to great lengths to back up their claims with hard evidence—for example, by bringing parole papers or newspaper clippings with them to the interview or by revealing recently acquired bullet wounds. Though skeptical at first, most interviewees relaxed and opened up soon after the interview began. A number of offenders seemed to enjoy speaking with someone "straight" about their criminal experiences, as it may have provided some sort of outlet for them to disseminate their expertise and teach "squares" a thing or two about street life. The secrecy of criminal work "means that offenders have few opportunities to discuss their activities with anyone besides associates, a matter which many find frustrating"(Wright and Decker, 1994:26). Active offenders have certain skills and knowledge that researchers lack (Berk and Adams, 1970:107), and this asymmetry may empower them to open up or open up sooner than they otherwise would. The fact that respondents may see something in the research that benefits them, or an opportunity to correct faulty impressions of what it is they actually do (Polsky, 1967), only facilitates openness (for a comprehensive discussion of the interview process, see Wright and Decker, 1997).

The internal validity of our data warrants comment. Here, we were intruding into the lives of individuals engaged in felonies for which they could receive hard time. How could we know they were giving us the "straight story"? How could it have been in their best interest to give incisive, accurate comments about their lives, when divulging such details might ultimately undermine their success as criminals? As others have noted, "interviewees are people with a considerable potential for sabotaging the attempt to research them" (Oakley, 1981:56) since "every researcher could be a cop" (Yablonsky, 1966:vii). Though street criminals have a stereotypical image of lying or avoiding the truth to a greater extent than others, there is little evidence to support this claim (Maher, 1997:223). The validity and reliability of self-report data have been carefully assessed by a number of researchers, all of whom conclude that self-reports are among the best, if not the best, source of information about serious criminality (Ball. 1967; Chaiken and Chaiken, 1982; Hindelang et al., 1981). Indeed, the most accurate self-report designs are said to be those that ask questions about serious offenses and those that involve face-to-face data collection, our technique, rather than surveys administered impersonally (see Huizinga and Elliott, 1986). This is not to say that offenders' reports are immune from "exaggerations, intentional distortions. lies, self-serving rationalizations, or drug-induced forgetfulness" (Fleisher, 1995:80). Rather, it is to suggest that they appear to be less susceptible to inaccuracy than some might think.

MONEY, MOTIVATION, AND STREET CULTURE

FAST CASH

With few exceptions, the decision to commit a robbery arises in the face of what offenders perceive to be a pressing need for fast cash (see also Conklin, 1972; Feeney. 1986; Gabor et al., 1987; Tunnell, 1992). Eighty of 81 offenders who spoke directly to the issue of motivation said that they did robberies simply because they needed money. Many lurched from one financial crisis to the next, the frequency with which they committed robbery being governed largely by the amount of money—or lack of it—in their pockets:

> [The idea of committing a robbery] comes into your mind when your pockets are low; it speaks very loudly when you need things and you are not able to get what you need. It's not a want, it's things that you need, . . . things that if you don't have the money, you have the artillery to go and get it. That's the first thing on my mind; concentrate on how I can get some more money.

> I don't think there is any one factor that precipitates the commission of a crime, . . . I think it's just the conditions. I think the primary factor is being without. Rent is coming up. A few months ago, the landlord was gonna put us out, rent due, you know. Can't get no money no way else; ask family and friends, you might try a few other ways of getting the money and, as a last resort, I can go get some money [by committing a robbery].

Many offenders appeared to give little thought to the offense until they found themselves unable to meet current expenses.

> [I commit a robbery] about every few months. There's no set pattern, but I guess it's really based on the need. If there is a period of time where there is no need of money . . ., then it's not necessary to go out and rob. It's not like I do [robberies] for fun.

The above claims conjure up an image of reluctant criminals doing the best they can to survive in circumstances not of their own making. In one sense, this image is not so far off the mark. Of the 59 offenders who specified a particular use for the proceeds of their crimes, 19 claimed that they needed the cash for basic necessities, such as food or shelter. For them, robbery allegedly was a matter of day-to-day survival. At the same time, the notion that these offenders were driven by conditions entirely beyond their control strains credulity. Reports of "opportunistic" robberies confirm this, that is, offenses motivated by serendipity rather than basic human need:

> If I had $5,000, I wouldn't do [a robbery] like tomorrow. But [i]f I got $5,000 today and I seen you walkin' down the street and you look like you got some money in your pocket, I'm gonna take a chance and see. It's just natural. . . . If you see an opportunity, you take that opportunity. . . . It doesn't matter if I have $5,000 in my pocket, if I see you walkin' and no one else around and it look like you done went in the store and bought somethin' and pulled some money out of your pocket and me or one of my partners has peeped this, we gonna approach you. That's just the way it goes.

STREET CULTURE AND MOTIVATION 155

Need and opportunity, however, cannot be considered outside the open-ended quest for excitement and sensory stimulation that shaped much of the offenders' daily activities. Perhaps the most central of pursuits in street culture, "life as party" revolves around "the enjoyment of 'good times' with minimal concern for obligations and commitments that are external to the . . . immediate social setting" (Shover and Honaker, 1992:283). Gambling, hard drug use, and heavy drinking were the behaviors of choice:

I [have] a gambling problem and I . . . lose so much so I [have] to do something to [get the cash to] win my money back. So I go out and rob somebody. That be the main reason I rob someone.

I like to mix and I like to get high. You can't get high broke. You really can't get high just standing there, you got to move. And in order to move, you got to have some money . . . Got to have some money, want to get high.

While the offenders often referred to such activities as partying, there is a danger in accepting their comments at face value. Many gambled, used drugs, and drank alcohol as if there were no tomorrow; they pursued these activities with an intensity and grim determination that suggested something far more serious was at stake. Illicit street action is no party, at least not in the conventional sense of the term. Offenders typically demonstrate little or no inclination to exercise personal restraint. Why should they? Instant gratification and hedonistic sensation seeking are quite functional for those seeking pleasure in what may objectively be viewed as a largely pleasureless world.

The offenders are easily seduced by life as party, at least in part because they view their future prospects as bleak and see little point in long-range planning. As such, there is no mileage to be gained by deferred gratification:

I really don't dwell on [the future]. One day I might not wake up. I don't even think about what's important to me. What's important to me is getting mine [now].

The offenders' general lack of social stability and absence of conventional sources of support only fueled such a mindset. The majority called the streets home for extended periods of time; a significant number of offenders claimed to seldom sleep at the same address for more than a few nights in a row (see also Fleisher, 1995). Moving from place to place as the mood struck them, these offenders essentially were urban nomads in a perpetual search for good times. The volatile streets and alleyways that criss-crossed St. Louis's crime-ridden central city neighborhoods provided their conduit (see also Stein and McCall, 1994):

I guess I'm just a street person, a roamer. I like to be out in the street

156   JACOBS AND WRIGHT

... Now I'm staying with a cousin ... That's where I live, but I'm very rarely there. I'm usually in the street. If somebody say they got something up ... I go and we do whatever. I might spend the night at their house or I got a couple of girls I know [and] I might spend the night at their house. I'm home about two weeks out of a month.

KEEPING UP APPEARANCES

The open-ended pursuit of sensory stimulation was but one way these offenders enacted the imperatives of street culture. No less important was the fetishized consumption of personal, nonessential, status-enhancing items. Shover and Honaker (1992:283) have argued that the unchecked pursuit of such items—like anomic participation in illicit street action—emerges directly from conduct norms of street culture. The code of the streets (Anderson, 1990) calls for the bold display of the latest status symbol clothing and accessories, a look that loudly proclaims the wearer to be someone who has overcome, if only temporarily, the financial difficulties faced by others on the street corner (see e.g., Katz, 1988). To be seen as "with it," one must flaunt the material trappings of success. The quest is both symbolic and real; such purchases serve as self-enclosed and highly efficient referent systems that assert one's essential character (Shover, 1996) in no uncertain terms.

You ever notice that some people want to be like other people ...? They might want to dress like this person, like dope dealers and stuff like that. They go out there [on the street corner] in diamond jewelry and stuff. "Man, I wish I was like him!" You got to make some kind of money [to look like that], so you want to make a quick hustle.

The functionality of offenders' purchases was tangential, perhaps irrelevant. The overriding goal was to project an image of "cool transcendence," (Katz, 1988) that, in the minds of offenders, knighted them members of a mythic street aristocracy. As Anderson (1990:103–104) notes, the search for self-aggrandizement takes on a powerful logic of its own and, in the end, becomes all-consuming. Given the day-to-day desperation that dominates most of these offenders' lives, it is easy to appreciate why they are anxious to show off whenever the opportunity presents itself (particularly after making a lucrative score). Of course, it would be misleading to suggest that our respondents differed markedly from their law-abiding neighbors in wanting to wear flashy clothes or expensive accessory items. Nor were all of the offenders' purchases ostentatious. On occasion, some offenders would use funds for haircuts, manicures, and other mundane purchases. What set these offenders apart from "normal citizens" was their willingness to spend large amounts of cash on luxury items to the detriment of more pressing financial concerns.

STREET CULTURE AND MOTIVATION 157

Obviously, the relentless pursuit of high living quickly becomes expensive. Offenders seldom had enough cash in their pockets to sustain this lifestyle for long. Even when they did make the occasional "big score," their disdain for long-range planning and desire to live for the moment encouraged spending with reckless abandon. That money earned illegally holds "less intrinsic value" than cash secured through legitimate work only fueled their spendthrift ways (Walters, 1990:147). The way money is obtained, after all, is a "powerful determinant of how it is defined, husbanded, and spent" (Shover, 1996:104). Some researchers have gone so far as to suggest that through carefree spending, persistent criminals seek to establish the very conditions that drive them back to crime (Katz, 1988). Whether offenders spend money in a deliberate attempt to create these conditions is open to question; the respondents in our sample gave no indication of doing so. No matter, offenders were under almost constant pressure to generate funds. To the extent that robbery alleviated this stress, it nurtured a tendency for them to view the offense as a reliable method for dealing with similar pressures in the future. A self-enclosed cycle of reinforcing behavior was thereby triggered (see also Lemert, 1953).

WHY ROBBERY?

The decision to commit robbery, then, is motivated by a perceived need for cash. Why does this need express itself as robbery? Presumably the offenders have other means of obtaining money. Why do they choose robbery over legal work? Why do they decide to commit robbery rather than borrow money from friends or relatives? Most important, why do they select robbery to the exclusion of other income-generating crimes?

LEGAL WORK

That the decision to commit robbery typically emerges in the course of illicit street action suggests that legitimate employment is not a realistic solution. Typically, the offenders' need for cash is so pressing and immediate that legal work, as a viable money-making strategy, is untenable: Payment and effort are separated in space and time and these offenders will not, or cannot, wait. Moreover, the jobs realistically available to them—almost all of whom were unskilled and poorly educated—pay wages that fall far short of the funds required to support a cash-intensive lifestyle:

> Education-wise, I fell late on the education. I just think it's too late for that. They say it's never too late, but I'm too far gone for that . . . I've thought about [getting a job], but I'm too far gone I guess . . . I done seen more money come out of [doing stick-ups] than I see working.

158   JACOBS AND WRIGHT

Legitimate employment also was perceived to be overly restrictive. Working a normal job requires one to take orders, conform to a schedule, minimize informal peer interaction, show up sober and alert, and limit one's freedom of movement for a given period of time. For many in our sample, this was unfathomable; it cramped the hedonistic, street-focused lifestyle they chose to live:

> I'm a firm believer, man, God didn't put me down on this earth to suffer for no reason. I'm just a firm believer in that. I believe I can have a good time every day, each and every day of my life, and that's what I'm trying to do. I never held a job. The longest job I ever had was about nine months . . . at St. Louis Car; that's probably the longest job I ever had, outside of working in the joint. But I mean on the streets, man, I just don't believe in [work]. There is enough shit on this earth right here for everybody, nobody should have to be suffering. You shouldn't have to suffer and work like no dog for it, I'm just a firm believer in that. I'll go out there and try to take what I believe I got comin' [because] ain't nobody gonna walk up . . . and give it to me. [I commit robberies] because I'm broke and need money; it's just what I'm gonna do. I'm not going to work! That's out! I'm through [with work]. I done had 25 or 30 jobs in my little lifetime [and] that's out. I can't do it! I'm not going to!

The "conspicuous display of independence" is a bedrock value on which street-corner culture rests (Shover and Honaker, 1992:284): To be seen as cool one must do as one pleases. This ethos clearly conflicts with the demands of legitimate employment. Indeed, robbery appealed to a number of offenders precisely because it allowed them to flaunt their independence and escape from the rigors of legal work.

This is not to say that every offender summarily dismissed the prospect of gainful employment. Twenty-five of the 75 unemployed respondents claimed they would stop robbing if someone gave them a "good job"—the emphasis being on good:

> My desire is to be gainfully employed in the right kind of job . . . If I had a union job making $16 or $17 [an hour], something that I could really take care of my family with, I think that I could become cool with that. Years ago I worked at one of the [local] car factories; I really wanted to be in there. It was the kind of job I'd been looking for. Unfortunately, as soon as I got in there they had a big layoff.

Others alleged that, while a job may not eliminate their offending altogether, it might well slow them down:

> [If a job were to stop me from committing robberies], it would have to be a straight up good paying job. I ain't talkin' about no $6 an hour . . . I'm talkin' like $10 to $11 an hour, something like that. But as far

STREET CULTURE AND MOTIVATION 159

as $5 or $6 an hour, no! I would have to get like $10 or $11 an hour, full-time. Now something like that, I would probably quit doing it [robbery]. I would be working, making money, I don't think I would do it [robbery] no more . . . I don't think I would quit [offending] altogether. It would probably slow down and then eventually I'll stop. I think [my offending] would slow down.

While such claims may or may not be sincere, it is unlikely they will ever be challenged. Attractive employment opportunities are limited for all inner-city residents and particularly for individuals like those in our sample. Drastic changes in the post World War II economy—deindustrialization and the loss of manufacturing jobs, the increased demand for advanced education and high skills, rapid suburbanization and out-migration of middle class residents (Sampson et al., 1997)—have left them behind, twisting in the wind. The lack of legal income options speaks to larger societal patterns in which major changes in the U.S. economy have reduced the number of available good-paying jobs and created an economic underclass with unprecedented levels of unemployment and few options—beyond income-generating crime—to exercise (Wilson, 1987). Governmental directives, such as changes in requirements and reductions in public transfer payments, decidedly reduce the income of already marginalized persons in inner-city communities (Johnson and Dunlap, 1997)—those at highest risk for predatory crime. This only intensifies their economic and social isolation (Sampson et al., 1997), makes their overall plight worse, and their predisposition to criminality stronger.

Most offenders realized this and, with varying degrees of bitterness, resigned themselves to being out of work:

I fill out [job] applications daily. Somebody [always] says, "This is bad that you got tattoos all over looking for a job." In a way, that's discrimination. How do they know I can't do the job? I could probably do your job just as well as you, but I got [these jailhouse] tattoos on me. That's discriminating. Am I right? That's why most people rob and steal because, say another black male came in like me [for a job], same haircut, same everything. I'm dressed like this, tennis shoes, shorts and tank top. He has on [a] Stacy Adams pair of slacks and a button-up shirt with a tie. He will get the job before I will. That's being racist in a way. I can do the job just as well as he can. He just dresses a little bit better than me.

Clearly, these offenders were not poster children for the local chamber of commerce or small business association. By and large, they were crudely mannered and poorly schooled in the arts of impression management and customer relations. Most lacked the cultural capital (Bourdieu, 1977) necessary for the conduct of legitimate business. They were not "nice" in the

160   JACOBS AND WRIGHT

conventional sense of the term; to be nice is to signal weakness in a world where only the strong survive.

Even if the offenders were able to land a high-paying job, it is doubtful they would keep it for long. The relentless pursuit of street action—especially hard drug use—has a powerful tendency to undermine any commitment to conventional activities (Shover and Honaker, 1992). Life as party ensnares street-culture participants, enticing them to neglect the demands of legitimate employment in favor of enjoying the moment. Though functional in lightening the burdensome present, gambling, drinking, and drugging—for those on the street—become the proverbial "padlock on the exit door" (Davis, 1995) and fertilize the foreground in which the decision to rob becomes rooted.

BORROWING

In theory, the offenders could have borrowed cash from a friend or relative rather than resorting to crime. In practice, this was not feasible. Unemployed, unskilled, and uneducated persons caught in the throes of chronically self-defeating behavior cannot, and often do not, expect to solve their fiscal troubles by borrowing. Borrowing is a short-term solution, and loans granted must be repaid. This in itself could trigger robberies. As one offender explained, "I have people that will loan me money, [but] they will loan me money because of the work [robbery] that I do; they know they gonna get their money [back] one way or another." Asking for money also was perceived by a number of offenders to be emasculating. Given their belief that men should be self-sufficient, the mere prospect of borrowing was repugnant:

> I don't like always asking my girl for nothing because I want to let her keep her own money . . . I'm gonna go out here and get some money.

The possibility of borrowing may be moot for the vast majority of offenders anyway. Most had long ago exhausted the patience and goodwill of helpful others; not even their closest friends or family members were willing to proffer additional cash:

> I can't borrow the money. Who gonna loan me some money? Ain't nobody gonna loan me no money. Shit, [I use] drugs and they know [that] and I rob and everything else. Ain't nobody gonna loan me no money. If they give you some money, they just give it to you; they know you ain't giving it back.

When confronted with an immediate need for money, then, the offenders perceived themselves as having little hope of securing cash quickly and legally. But this does not explain why the respondents decided to do robbery rather than some other crime. Most of them had committed a wide

STREET CULTURE AND MOTIVATION 161

range of income-generating offenses in the past, and some continued to be quite versatile. Why, then, robbery?

For many, this question was irrelevant; robbery was their "main line" and alternative crimes were not considered when the pressing need for cash arose:

> I have never been able to steal, even when I was little and they would tell me just to be the watch-out man . . . Shit, I watch out, everybody gets busted. I can't steal, but give me a pistol and I'll go get some money. . . . [Robbery is] just something I just got attached to.

When these offenders did commit another form of income-generating crime, it typically was prompted by the chance discovery of an especially vulnerable target rather than being part of their typical modus operandi:

> I do [commit other sorts of offenses] but that ain't, I might do a burglary, but I'm jumping out of my field. See, I'm scared when I do a burglary [or] something like that. I feel comfortable robbing . . .., but I see something they call "real sweet," like a burglary where the door is open and ain't nobody there or something like that, well. . .

Many of the offenders who expressed a strong preference for robbery had come to the offense through burglary, drug selling, or both. They claimed that robbery had several advantages over these other crimes. Robbery took much less time than breaking into buildings or dealing drugs. Not only could the offense be committed more quickly, it also typically netted cash rather than goods. Unlike burglary, there was no need for the booty "to be cut, melted down, recast or sold," nor for obligatory dealings with "treacherous middlemen, insurance adjustors, and wiseguy fences" (Pileggi, 1985:203). Why not bypass all such hassles and simply *steal* cash (Shover, 1996:63).

> Robbery is the quickest money. Robbery is the most money you gonna get fast . . . Burglary, you gonna have to sell the merchandise and get the money. Drugs, you gonna have to deal with too many people, [a] bunch of people. You gonna sell a $50 or $100 bag to him, a $50 or $100 bag to him, it takes too long. But if you find where the cash money is and just go take it, you get it all in one wad. No problem. I've tried burglary, I've tried drug selling . . . the money is too slow.

Some of the offenders who favored robbery over other crimes maintained that it was safer than burglary or dope dealing:

> I feel more safer doing a robbery because doing a burglary, I got a fear of breaking into somebody's house not knowing who might be up in there. I got that fear about house burglary . . . On robbery I can select my victims, I can select my place of business. I can watch and see who all work in there or I can rob a person and pull them around

> in the alley or push them up in a doorway and rob them. You don't got [that] fear of who . . . in that bedroom or somewhere in another part of the house.
>
> [I]f I'm out there selling dope somebody gonna come and, I'm not the only one out there robbing you know, so somebody like me, they'll come and rob me . . . I'm robbin' cause the dope dealers is the ones getting robbed and killed you know.

A couple of offenders reported steering clear of dope selling because their strong craving for drugs made it too difficult for them to resist their own merchandise. Being one's own best customer is a sure formula for disaster (Waldorf, 1993), something the following respondent seemed to understand well:

> A dope fiend can't be selling dope because he be his best customer. I couldn't sell dope [nowadays]. I could sell a little weed or something cause I don't smoke too much of it. But selling rock [cocaine] or heroin, I couldn't do that cause I mess around and smoke it myself. [I would] smoke it all up!

Others claimed that robbery was more attractive than other offenses because it presented less of a potential threat to their freedom:

> If you sell drugs, it's easy to get locked up selling drugs; plus, you can get killed selling drugs. You get killed more faster doing that.
>
> Robbery you got a better chance of surviving and getting away than doing other crimes . . . You go break in a house, [the police] get the fingerprints, you might lose a shoe, you know how they got all that technology stuff. So I don't break in houses . . . I leave that to some other guy.

Without doubt, some of the offenders were prepared to commit crimes other than robbery; in dire straits one cannot afford to be choosy. More often than not, robbery emerged as the "most proximate and performable" (Lofland, 1969:61) offense available. The universe of money-making crimes from which these offenders realistically could pick was limited. By and large, they did not hold jobs that would allow them to violate even a low-level position of financial trust. Nor did they possess the technical know-how to commit lucrative commercial break-ins, or the interpersonal skills needed to perpetrate successful frauds. Even street-corner dope dealing was unavailable to many; most lacked the financial wherewithal to purchase baseline inventories—inventories many offenders would undoubtedly have smoked up.

The bottom line is that the offenders, when faced with a pressing need for cash, tend to resort to robbery because they know of no other course of action, legal or illegal, that offers as quick and easy a way out of their

STREET CULTURE AND MOTIVATION 163

financial difficulties. As Lofland (1969:50) notes, most people under pressure have a tendency to become fixated on removing the perceived cause of that pressure "as quickly as possible." Desperate to sustain a cash-intensive lifestyle, these offenders were loathe to consider unfamiliar, complicated, or long-term solutions (Lofland, 1969:50–54). With minimal calculation and "high" hopes, they turned to robbery, a trusted companion they could count on when the pressure was on. For those who can stomach the potential violence, robbery seems so much more attractive than other forms of income-generating crime. Contemplating alternative offenses becomes increasingly difficult to do. This is the insight that separates persistent robbers from their street-corner peers:

> [Robbery] is just easy. I ain't got to sell no dope or nothing, I can just take the money. Just take it, I don't need to sell no dope or work . . . I don't want to sell dope, I don't want to work. I don't feel like I need to work for nothing. If I want something, I'm gonna get it and take it. I'm gonna take what I want . . . If I don't have money, I like to go and get it. I ain't got time [for other offenses]; the way I get mine is by the gun. I don't have time to be waiting on people to come up to me buying dope all day . . . I don't have time for that so I just go and get my money.

DISCUSSION

The overall picture that emerges from our research is that of offenders caught up in a cycle of expensive, self-indulgent habits (e.g., gambling, drug use, and heavy drinking) that feed on themselves and constantly call for more of the same (Lemert, 1953). It would be a mistake to conclude that these offenders are being driven to crime by genuine financial hardship; few of them are doing robberies to buy the proverbial loaf of bread to feed their children. Yet, most of their crimes are economically motivated. The offenders perceive themselves as needing money and robbery is a response to that perception.

Though background risk factors, such as pressing financial need, predispose persons to criminality, they fail to provide comprehensive, precise, and deep explanations of the situational pushes, urges, and impulses that energize actual criminal conduct (Tittle, 1995). Nor do such factors identify the "necessary and sufficient" conditions for criminal motivation to eventuate in criminal behavior. Focusing on the foreground attends to these problems. A foreground analytic approach identifies the immediate, situational factors that catalyze criminal motivation and transforms offenders from an indifferent state to one in which they are determined to commit crime.

164   JACOBS AND WRIGHT

Though the theoretical priority of the criminological foreground is unrivaled, one would scarcely know this from its extant treatment (but see e.g., Gibbons, 1971; Hagan and McCarthy, 1997; Katz, 1988). The dearth of attention is emblematic of criminology's positivistic bent, which holds paramount the study of "background and developmental variables" (Hagan and McCarthy, 1997:81) to the virtual exclusion of precipitating foreground influences. Sutherland (1947:77) may have set the precedent for this in his seminal, persuasive, and widely disseminated statement in which he insisted that background risk factors determine the way in which persons define situations and act on them through deviance. Briar and Piliavin (1965) and Gottfredson and Hirschi (1990) echoed the same sentiment years later. Indeed, the most popular, prominent, and influential paradigms of our discipline attest to the extent to which Sutherland's lead has been followed by scholars who shun the foreground in favor of more parsimonious, though less precise, explanations of criminal motivation (but see Tittle, 1995).

To be sure, strain, anomie, subcultural, labeling, radical, and conflict theories specify some motivating forces but not the majority, nor even the most important ones (see Empey and Stafford, 1991; Tittle, 1995). Such approaches also drip with determinism by assuming that criminal behavior is preordained by developmental background factors that accumulate over time (see Hagan and McCarthy, 1997:81). Social learning/reinforcement theories are contingent upon assumptions of positively reinforced, crime-favorable messages being internalized as deviant propensities, as well as "preexisting distributions of potentially reinforcing elements" (see Tittle, 1995:47)—distributions that are not explained well within the theory. Rational choice and routine activities theories assume rather than account for motivation, and they fail to recognize contingencies and reciprocal relationships that moderate, mediate, or mitigate predicted outcomes (see Tittle, 1995). Biological and psychological theories are notoriously tautological, a consequence of their inability to discuss or measure deviant motivation independently of deviant behavior (see Gottfredson and Hirschi, 1990). Transcendence theory (Katz, 1988) places justifiable emphasis on the foreground of offender decision making, but it locates deviant motivation in the seductiveness of crime to the exclusion of other, equally germane explanations (especially material concerns—see McCarthy, 1995). Control theory is arguably the only "honest" paradigm with regard to deviant motivation by dismissing it altogether: Criminal/deviant motivation (i.e., propensity) inheres in all of us to varying degrees; only those with weak social bonds become offenders (Gottfredson and Hirschi, 1990;

STREET CULTURE AND MOTIVATION 165

Hirschi, 1969; Kornhauser, 1978).[2]

Although the streets were a prime focus of much early criminological work, the strong influence of street culture on offender motivation has largely been overlooked since (but see Baron and Hartnagel, 1997; Fleisher, 1995; Hagan and McCarthy, 1992, 1997). Below, we attempt a conceptual refocusing by exploring the criminogenic influence of street culture and its constituent conduct norms on offender decision making (see also Hagan and McCarthy, 1997). In doing so, we do not wish to make a Katzian attempt to "outgun positivism" with a sensually deterministic portrait of crime (see Groves and Lynch, 1990:366). Our goal rather is to highlight the explanatory power and conceptual efficiency of street culture participation as a mediating foreground factor in the etiology of armed robbery.

Street culture subsumes a number of powerful conduct norms, including but not limited to, the hedonistic pursuit of sensory stimulation, disdain for conventional living, lack of future orientation, and persistent eschewal of responsibility (see Fleisher 1995:213–214). Street culture puts tremendous emphasis on virtues of spontaneity; it dismisses "rationality and long-range planning . . . in favor of enjoying the moment" (Shover and Honaker, 1992:283). Offenders typically live life as if there is no tomorrow, confident that tomorrow will somehow take care of itself. On the streets, "every night is a Saturday night" (Hodgson, 1997), and the self-indulgent pursuit of trendy consumerism and open-ended street action becomes a means to this end.

The pursuit of fast living is more than symbolic or dramaturgical, it cuts to the very core of offenders' perceptions of self-identity. To be cool, hip, and "in," one must constantly prove it through conspicuous outlays of cash. The fetishized world of street-corner capitalism dictates that fiscal responsibility be jettisoned and money burned on material objects and illicit action that assert in no uncertain terms one's place in the street hierarchy. Carefree spending creates the "impression of affluence" (Wright and Decker, 1994:44) by which offenders are judged; it serves to demonstrate that they have indeed "made it"—at least for the time. On the streets, the image one projects is not everything, it is the only thing (see Anderson, 1990). To not buy into such an approach is to abandon a source of recognition offenders can get nowhere else (see Liebow, 1967) or, worse, to stare failure full in the face. It is not hard to fathom why many offenders in our sample regarded a lack of funds as an immediate threat to their social standing.

---

2. It should be noted that many of the more recent integrated theories fail similarly in largely ignoring the role of foreground factors in the etiology of criminal behavior (see e.g., Braithwaite, 1989; Colvin and Pauly, 1983; Elliott et al., 1985).

166   JACOBS AND WRIGHT

The problem becomes one of sustenance; the reputational advantages of cash-intensive living can be appreciated and enjoyed to their fullest "only if participants moderate their involvement in it" (Shover and Honaker, 1992:286). This requires intermittent and disciplined spending, an anomalous and ultimately untenable proposition. Offenders effectively become ensnared by their own self-indulgent habits—habits that feed on themselves and constantly call for more of the same (Lemert, 1953; Shover, 1996). These habits are expensive and create a pressing and pervasive need for cash—a need remedied through robbery but only temporarily, since the proceeds of any given robbery merely "enable" more action (Shover, 1996).[3] The seductive attractions of street life appear to take on a powerful logic of their own (Hagan and McCarthy, 1997); offenders burn money only to create (albeit inadvertently) the conditions that spark their next decision to rob. This self-enclosed cycle of reinforcing behavior (see also Lemert, 1953) is depicted schematically in Figure 1. Predisposing background risk factors also are represented (see Hagan and McCarthy, 1997, for a comprehensive discussion of these factors as they relate to street-culture participation).

Figure 1
Etiological Cycle of Robbery

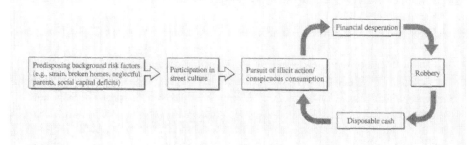

As much as these offenders sought liberation through the hedonistic, open-ended pursuit of sensory stimulation, such a quest ultimately is both self-defeating and subordinating. Those hooked on street action may never see it this way, but objective assessments of reality are difficult to render when rationality is as severely bounded (Walsh, 1986) as it is here.

---

3. The idea that these offenders are acting to restore "control balance" (Tittle, 1995) is questionable. They seem rather to be going from deficit to surplus, and back again, without ever pausing to assess their current state of equilibrium.

STREET CULTURE AND MOTIVATION   167

Suffice it to say that, for those in our sample, the "choice" to rob occurs in a context in which rationality not only is sharply bounded, it barely exists. If one takes the influence of context seriously, most offenders "decide" to commit robbery in a social and psychological terrain bereft of realistic alternatives (Shover, 1996). Street-culture participation effectively obliterates, or at least severely circumscribes, the range of objectively available options, so much so as to be almost deterministic. Offenders typically are overwhelmed by their own predicament—emotional, financial, pharmacological, and otherwise—and see robbery as the only way out. Chronic isolation from conventional others and lifestyles only reinforces their insularity (Baron and Hartnagel, 1997:413–414), driving them deeper and deeper into a "downward life trajectory" of ever-increasing criminal embeddedness (see Hagan and McCarthy, 1997; see also Ekland-Olson et al., 1984, on "role engulfment").

That our respondents typically perceived themselves to be in a situation of pressing need at the time of actually contemplating their offenses has a number of powerful implications for rational choice theory. It suggests a mind-set in which offenders are seeking less to maximize their gains than to deal with a present crisis. It also indicates an element of emotional desperation that undoubtedly weakens the influence of threatened sanctions. Glazed by the anomic pursuit of street action, threats of legal sanctions become "remote and improbable contingencies" (Shover, 1996:102). Offenders are increasingly likely to "dispense with [care] and proceed quickly at high risk" (Letkemann, 1973:143). This is to say nothing of the fact that thoughts about getting caught are typically dismissed anyway during the course of many crimes (Bennett and Wright, 1984; Feeney, 1986; Tunnell, 1992; Wright and Decker, 1994)—a function of perceptions of invincibility, superoptimism (Walters, 1990:145), or beliefs that since the risk of offending is quick, the threat of detection is over "in a flash" and thus not something over which to fret (Felson, 1987). Even if offenders are caught, periodic bouts of prison time are regarded by many as a welcome respite from the "dog-eat-dog" world of the streets (see Fleisher, 1995, on jails as "sanctuaries"; Tunnell, 1992). Finally, the experiential effects (Minor and Harry, 1982) on which offenders can draw (as a result of being caught) and iatrogenic influences (Klein, 1992) accrued from prison life result in increasingly refined techniques for avoiding detection and capture in the future (see Shover, 1996: Ch. 6). Taken together, all of these factors systematically undermine the deterrent power of legal sanctions and seemingly enhance rather than inhibit criminal behavior.

Being a street robber is more than a series of offenses that allow one to meet some arbitrarily specified inclusion criteria; it is a way of behaving, a

168   JACOBS AND WRIGHT

way of thinking, an approach to life (see e.g., Fleisher, 1995:253). Stopping such criminals exogenously—in the absence of lengthy incapacitation—is not likely to be successful. Getting offenders to "go straight" is analogous to telling a lawful citizen to "relinquish his history, companions, thoughts, feelings, and fears, and replace them with [something] else" (Fleisher, 1995:240). Self-directed going-straight talk on the part of offenders more often than not is insincere—akin to young children talking about what they're going to be when they grow up: "Young storytellers and . . . criminals . . . don't care about the [reality]; the pleasure comes in saying the words, the verbal ritual itself brings pleasure" (Fleisher, 1995:259). Gifting offenders money, in the hopes they will reduce or stop their offending (Farrington, 1993), is similarly misguided. It is but twisted enabling and only likely to set off another round of illicit action that plunges offenders deeper into the abyss of desperation that drives them back to their next crime.

REFERENCES

Agar, Michael
    1973   Ripping and Running: A Formal Ethnography of Urban Heroin Addicts. New York: Seminar Press.

Akers, Ronald L.
    1985   Deviant Behavior: A Social Learning Approach. 3d ed. Belmont, Calif.: Wadsworth.

Anderson, Elijah
    1990   Streetwise. Chicago: University of Chicago Press.

Ball, John C.
    1967   The reliability and validity of interview data obtained from 59 narcotic drug addicts. American Journal of Sociology 72:650–654.

Baron, Stephen and Timothy Hartnagel
    1997   Attributions, affect, and crime: Street youths' reactions to unemployment. Criminology 35:409–434.

Becker, Howard S.
    1963   Outsiders. New York: Free Press.

Bennett, Trevor and Richard Wright
    1984   Burglars on Burglary: Prevention and the Offender. Aldershot: Gower.

Berk, Richard A. and Joseph M. Adams
    1970   Establishing rapport with deviant groups. Social Problems 18:102–117.

Bottoms, Anthony and Paul Wiles
    1992   Explanations of crime and place. In David Evans, Nigel Fyfe, and Derek Herbert (eds.). Policing and Place: Essays in Environmental Criminology. London: Routledge.

Bourdieu, Pierre
    1977   Outline of a Theory of Practice. Cambridge: Cambridge University Press.

STREET CULTURE AND MOTIVATION 169

Braithwaite, John
 1989   Crime, Shame, and Reintegration. Cambridge: Cambridge University
         Press.

Briar, Scott and Irving Piliavin
 1965   Delinquency, situational inducements, and commitment to conformity.
         Social Problems 13:35–45.

Chaiken, Jan M. and Marcia R. Chaiken
 1982   Varieties of Criminal Behavior. Santa Monica, Calif.: Rand Corporation.

Chambliss, William J. and Robert Seidman
 1971   Law, Order, and Power. Reading, Mass.: Addison-Wesley.

Cloward, Richard A. and Lloyd E. Ohlin
 1960   Delinquency and Opportunity. New York: Free Press.

Cohen, Albert K.
 1955   Delinquent Boys. New York: Free Press.

Colvin, Mark and John Pauly
 1983   A critique of criminology: Toward an integrated structural-Marxist theory
         of delinquent production. American Journal of Sociology 89:513–551.

Conklin, John
 1972   Robbery. Philadelphia: JB Lippincott.

Cornish, Derek B. and Ronald V. Clarke (eds.)
 1986   The Reasoning Criminal: Rational Choice Perspectives on Offending.
         New York: Springer-Verlag.

Davis, Peter
 1995   Interview. "If You Came This Way." All Things Considered, National
         Public Radio, October 12.

Ekland-Olson, Sheldon, John Lieb, and Louis Zurcher
 1984   The paradoxical impact of criminal sanctions: Some microstructural
         findings. Law & Society Review 18:159–178.

Elliott, Delbert S., David Huizinga, and Suzanne S. Ageton
 1985   Explaining Delinquency and Drug Use. Beverly Hills, Calif.: Sage.

Empey, LaMar T. and Mark C. Stafford
 1991   American Delinquency. 3d ed. Belmont, Calif.: Wadsworth.

Farrington, David P.
 1993   Motivations for conduct disorder and delinquency. Development and
         Psychopathology 5:225–241.

Feeney, Floyd
 1986   Robbers as decision-makers. In Derek B. Cornish and Ronald V. Clarke
         (eds.), The Reasoning Criminal: Rational Choice Perspectives on Offend-
         ing. New York: Springer-Verlag.

Felson, Marcus
 1987   Routine activities in the developing metropolis. Criminology 25:911–931

Fleisher, Mark S.
 1995   Beggars and Thieves: Lives of Urban Street Criminals. Madison:
         University of Wisconsin Press.

170   JACOBS AND WRIGHT

Gabor, Thomas, Micheline Baril, Maurice Cusson, Daniel Elie, Marc LeBlanc, and
    Andre Normandeau
    1987   Armed Robbery: Cops, Robbers, and Victims. Springfield, Ill.: Charles
             C Thomas.

Gibbons, Donald L.
    1971   Observations on the study of crime causation. American Journal of
             Sociology 77:262–278.

Glassner, Barry and Cheryl Carpenter
    1985   The feasibility of an ethnographic study of adult property offenders.
             Unpublished report prepared for the National Institute of Justice.

Gottfredson, Michael and Travis Hirschi
    1990   A General Theory of Crime. Stanford, Calif.: Stanford University Press.

Groves, W. Byron and Michael J. Lynch
    1990   Reconciling structural and subjective approaches to the study of crime.
             Journal of Research in Crime and Delinquency 27:348–375.

Hagan, John and Bill McCarthy
    1992   Streetlife and delinquency. British Journal of Sociology 43:533–561.
    1997   Mean Streets: Youth Crime and Homelessness. Cambridge: Cambridge
             University Press.

Heckathorn, Douglas D.
    1997   Respondent-driven sampling: A new approach to the study of hidden
             populations. Social Problems 44:174–199.

Henslin, James M.
    1972   Studying deviance in four settings: Research experiences with cabbies,
             suicides, drug users, and abortionees. In Jack Douglas (ed.), Research on
             Deviance. New York: Random House.

Hindelang, Michael J., Travis Hirschi, and Joseph Weis
    1981   Measuring Delinquency. Beverly Hills, Calif.: Sage.

Hirschi, Travis
    1969   Causes of Delinquency. Berkeley: University of California Press.

Hodgson, James F.
    1997   Games Pimps Play. Toronto: Canadian Scholars' Press.

Huizinga, David and Delbert S. Elliott
    1986   Reassessing the reliability and validity of self-report delinquency meas-
             ures. Journal of Quantitative Criminology 2:293–327.

Johnson, Bruce D. and Eloise Dunlap
    1997   Crack Selling in New York City. Paper presented at the 49th Annual
             Meeting of the American Society of Criminology, San Diego.

Katz, Jack
    1988   Seductions of Crime: Moral and Sensual Attractions in Doing Evil. New
             York: Basic Books.

Klein, Malcolm W.
    1992   Personal communication, University of Southern California, Los Angeles.

Kornhauser, Ruth R.
    1978   Social Sources of Delinquency. Chicago: University of Chicago Press.

STREET CULTURE AND MOTIVATION 171

Lemert, Edwin
    1953   An isolation and closure theory of naive check forgery. Journal of Criminal Law, Criminology, and Police Science 44:296–307.

Letkemann, Peter
    1973   Crime as Work. Englewood Cliffs, N.J.: Prentice-Hall.

Liebow, Eliot
    1967   Tally's Corner. Boston: Little, Brown.

Lofland, John
    1969   Deviance and Identity. Englewood Cliffs, N.J.: Prentice-Hall.

Maher, Lisa
    1997   Sexed Work. Oxford: Clarendon Press.

McCall, George
    1978   Observing the Law. New York: Free Press.

McCarthy, Bill
    1995   Not just for the thrill of it: An instrumentalist elaboration of Katz's explanation of sneaky thrill property crimes. Criminology 33:519–538.

Merton, Robert K.
    1938   Social structure and anomie. American Sociological Review 3:672–682.

Miller, Jody
    1998   Up it up: gender and the accomplishment of street robbery. Criminology 36:37–66.

Miller, Walter B.
    1958   Lower class culture as a generating milieu of gang delinquency. Journal of Social Issues 14:5–19.

Minor, W. William and Joseph Harry
    1982   Deterrent and experiential effects in perceptual deterrence research: A replication and extension. Journal of Research in Crime and Delinquency 19:190–203.

Oakley, Annie
    1981   Interviewing women: A contradiction in terms. In Helen Roberts (ed.), Doing Feminist Research. London: Routledge & Kegan Paul.

Pileggi, Nicholas
    1985   Wiseguy. New York: Simon & Schuster.

Polsky, Ned
    1967   Hustlers, Beats, and Others. Chicago: Aldine.

Quinney, Richard
    1970   The Social Reality of Crime. Boston: Little, Brown.

Sampson, Robert J. and John H. Laub
    1992   Crime and deviance in the life course. Annual Review of Sociology 24:509–525.

Sampson, Robert J., Stephen W. Raudenbush, and Felton Earls
    1997   Neighborhoods and violent crime: A multilevel study of collective efficacy. Science 277:918–924.

172 JACOBS AND WRIGHT

Shaw, Clifford R. and Henry D. McKay
    1942   Juvenile Delinquency and Urban Areas. Chicago: University of Chicago Press.

Shover, Neal
    1991   Burglary. In Michael Tonry (ed.), Crime and Justice: A Review of Research. Chicago: University of Chicago Press.
    1996   Great Pretenders: Pursuits and Careers of Persistent Thieves. Boulder, Colo.: Westview.

Shover, Neal and David Honaker
    1992   The socially-bounded decision making of persistent property offenders. Howard Journal of Criminal Justice 31:276–293.

Stein, Michael and George McCall
    1994   Home ranges and daily rounds: Uncovering community among urban nomads. Research in Community Sociology 1:77–94.

Sutherland, Edwin
    1947   Principles of Criminology. 4th ed. Philadelphia: JB Lippincott.

Sutherland, Edwin and Donald Cressey
    1970   Criminology. 8th ed. Philadelphia: JB Lippincott.

Tittle, Charles R.
    1995   Control Balance: Toward a General Theory of Deviance. Boulder, Colo.: Westview.

Tunnell, Kenneth D.
    1992   Choosing Crime: The Criminal Calculus of Property Offenders. Chicago: Nelson-Hall.

Waldorf, Dan
    1993   Don't be your own best customer: Drug use of San Francisco gang drug sellers. Crime. Law, and Social Change 19:1–15.

Walsh, Dermot
    1986   Victim selection procedures among economic criminals: The rational choice perspective. In Derek B. Cornish and Ronald V. Clarke (eds.), The Reasoning Criminal: Rational Choice Perspectives on Offending. New York: Springer-Verlag.

Walters, Glenn
    1990   The Criminal Lifestyle. Newbury Park, Calif.: Sage.

Weppner, Robert
    1977   Street Ethnography. Beverly Hills, Calif.: Sage.

Wilson, William J.
    1987   The Truly Disadvantaged. Chicago: University of Chicago Press.

Wright, Richard T. and Scott H. Decker
    1994   Burglars on the Job. Boston: Northeastern University Press.
    1997   Armed Robbers in Action. Boston: Northeastern University Press.

Yablonsky, Lewis
    1966   The Violent Gang. New York: Macmillan.

Bruce Jacobs is an Assistant Professor of Criminology and Criminal Justice at the

STREET CULTURE AND MOTIVATION   173

University of Missouri–St. Louis. His research focuses on the dynamics and processes relevant to street-level drug markets. He is author of the forthcoming book, *Dealing Crack: The Social World of Streetcorner Selling* (Boston: Northeastern University Press, 1999).

Richard Wright is a Professor in the Department of Criminology and Criminal Justice, University of Missouri–St. Louis and a Fellow in the National Consortium on Violence Research. Currently, he is co-principal investigator (with Bruce Jacobs) of a field-based study of active drug robbers.

[10]

UP IT UP: GENDER AND THE ACCOMPLISHMENT OF STREET ROBBERY*

JODY MILLER
University of Missouri-St. Louis

Attempts to understand women's participation in violence have been plagued by a tendency either to overemphasize gender differences or to downplay the significance of gender. The goal of this research is to reconcile these approaches through an examination of the experiences of female and male street robbers in an urban setting. Based on in-depth interviews with active offenders, the study compares women's and men's accounts of why they commit robbery, as well as how gender organizes the commission of the crime. The research suggests that while women and men articulate similar motives for robbery, their enactment of the crime is strikingly different—a reflection, in part, of practical choices women make in the context of a gender-stratified street setting.

With the exception of forcible rape, robbery is perhaps the most gender differentiated serious crime in the United States. According to the Federal Bureau of Investigation's Uniform Crime Report for 1995, women accounted for 9.3% of robbery arrestees, while they were 9.5%, 17.7%, and 11.1% of arrestees for murder/manslaughter, aggravated assault, and burglary, respectively (Federal Bureau of Investigation, 1996). And while recently there has been considerable attention among feminist scholars to the question of why males are more violent than females, there have been few attempts to examine women's participation in these "male" crimes. Though their numbers are small, women who engage in violent street crime have something significant to teach us about women's place in the landscape of the urban street world.

Simpson (1989:618; see also Kelly, 1991; White and Kowalski, 1994) recently noted that feminist scholars' "reticence [to address issues concerning women's criminality] leaves the interpretive door open to less critical perspectives." Nowhere is this more the case than with the issue of

* Thanks to Richard Wright and Scott Decker for so generously allowing me to re-read their data with a feminist eye; to Richard Wright for his feedback throughout the writing process; and to the anonymous reviewers at *Criminology* for their helpful suggestions on an earlier draft. The research on which the article is based was funded jointly by the Harry Frank Guggenheim Foundation and the National Institute of Justice (NIJ grant 94-IJ-CX-0030). Opinions expressed are those of the author and do not necessarily reflect those of the funding agencies.

38   JODY MILLER

women's participation in violent street crime. Sensational accounts of the
"new violent female offender" (e.g., Sikes, 1997; see Chesney-Lind, 1993),
which draw heavily on racial imagery of young women of color, must be
countered with accurate, nuanced accounts of women's use of violence in
the contexts of racial and economic inequalities. This research compares
the experiences of male and female robbers active in an urban underclass
environment with the goal of expanding understanding of women's use of
violence in nondomestic street settings.

MASCULINITIES AND CRIME: ROBBERY AS GENDER ACCOMPLISHMENT

In the late 1980s, feminist sociologists began theorizing about gender as
situated accomplishment (West and Fenstermaker, 1995; West and Zimmerman, 1987). According to these authors, gender is "much more than a
role or an individual characteristic: it is a mechanism whereby situated
social action contributes to the reproduction of social structure" (West and
Fenstermaker, 1995:21). Women and men "do gender" in response to normative beliefs about femininity and masculinity. These actions are "the
interactional scaffolding of social structure" (West and Zimmerman,
1987:147) such that the performance of gender is both an indication and a
reproduction of gendered social hierarchies.

This approach has been incorporated into feminist accounts of crime as
a means of explaining differences in women's and men's offending (Messerschmidt, 1993, 1995; Newburn and Stanko, 1994; Simpson and Elis,
1995). Here, violence is described as "a 'resource' for accomplishing gender—for demonstrating masculinity within a given context or situation"
(Simpson and Elis, 1995:50). Further, it is suggested that although some
women may engage in violent behavior, because their actions transgress
normative conceptions of femininity, they will "derive little support for
expressions of masculine violence from even the most marginal of subcultures" (Braithwaite and Daly, 1994:190).

Several authors suggest that robbery epitomizes the use of crime to construct masculine identity (Katz, 1988; Messerschmidt, 1993). Messerschmidt argues as follows:

> The robbery setting provides the ideal opportunity to construct an
> "essential" toughness and "maleness"; it provides a means with which
> to construct that certain type of masculinity—hardman. Within the
> social context that ghetto and barrio boys find themselves, then, rob-
> bery is a rational practice for "doing gender" and for getting money
> (Messerschmidt, 1993:107).

UP IT UP   39

Moreover, given the disproportionate use of robbery by African-American versus white men (Federal Bureau of Investigation, 1996), the masculinity that robbery constructs may be one that fits particularly well in urban underclass settings, which are unique from areas in which poor whites live (see Sampson and Wilson, 1995). Katz, in fact, suggests that "for some urban, black ghetto-located young men, the stickup is particularly attractive as a distinctive way of being black" as well as male (1988:239).

Examining violence as masculine accomplishment can help account for women's lack of involvement in these crimes, just as this approach offers explanation for women's involvement in crime in ways scripted by femininity (e.g., prostitution). However, it leaves unexplained women's participation in violent street crime, except as an anomaly. Perhaps this is because femininity in this approach is conceived narrowly—specifically "within the parameters of the white middle class (i.e., domesticity, dependence, selflessness, and motherhood)" (Simpson and Elis, 1995:51). Given urban African-American women's historical patterns of economic self-sufficiency and independence, this passive feminine ideal is unlikely to have considerable influence and is "much more relevant (and restrictive) for white females" (Simpson and Elis, 1995:71).

Messerschmidt himself has recently recognized this oversight. Given that urban African-American females are involved in violent street crime at higher rates than other females, he suggests that "theory must not universalize female crime" (1995:171) and must consider significant women's involvement in presumably "male" crime. Simpson (1991:129; see also White and Kowalski, 1994) concludes: "The simplistic assertion that males are violent and females are not contains a grain of truth, but it misses the complexity and texture of women's lives."

WOMEN'S VIOLENCE AS RESISTANCE TO MALE OPPRESSION

Feminist scholars who address the use of street violence by women often suggest that women's violence differs from that of men's—women use violence in response to their vulnerability to or actual victimization in the family and/or at the hands of men (Campbell, 1993; Joe and Chesney-Lind, 1995; Maher, 1997; Maher and Curtis, 1992; Maher and Daly, 1996). In her ethnography of a Brooklyn drug market, Maher notes that women adopt violent presentations of self as a strategy of protection. She explains, "'Acting bad' and 'being bad' are not the same. Although many of the women presented themselves as 'bad' or 'crazy,' this projection was a street persona and a necessary survival strategy" (1997:95; see also

40   JODY MILLER

Maher and Daly, 1996). These women were infrequently involved in violent crime and most often resorted to violence in response to threats or harms against them. She concludes that "unlike their male counterparts, for women, reputation was about 'preventing victimization'" (Maher, 1997:95–96; see also Campbell, 1993). In this account, even when women's aggression is offensive, it can still be understood as a defensive act, because it emerges as resistance to victimization.

Maher's research uncovered a particular form of robbery—"viccing"—in which women involved in the sex trade rob their clients. Although the phenomenon of prostitutes robbing tricks is not new, Maher's work documents the proliferation of viccing as a form of resistance against their greater vulnerability to victimization and against cheapened sex markets within the drug economy. Comparing viccing with traditional forms of robbery, Maher and Curtis conclude, "The fact that the act [of viccing] itself is little different to any other instrumental robbery belies the reality that the motivations undergirding it are more complex and, indeed, are intimately linked with women's collective sense of the devaluation of their bodies and their work" (1992:246). However, it is likely that not all of women's street violence can be viewed as resistance to male oppression; instead, some women may be motivated to commit violent crimes for many of the same reasons some men are. In certain contexts, norms favorable to women's use of violence may exist, and they are not simply about avoiding victimization, but also result in status and recognition.

RACE, CLASS AND GENDER: WOMEN'S VIOLENCE AS SITUATED ACTION

It is necessary to consider that some of women's participation in violent street crime may stem from "the frustration, alienation, and anger that are associated with racial and class oppression" (Simpson, 1989:618). The foregrounding of gender is important; however, there are structural and cultural underpinnings related to racial and economic inequalities that must simultaneously be addressed when one considers women's involvement in violent street crime (Simpson, 1991).

Research suggests that urban African-American females are more likely to engage in serious and violent crime than their counterparts in other racial groups and/or settings (Ageton, 1983; Hill and Crawford, 1990; Laub and McDermott, 1985; Mann, 1993). Ageton's analysis of the National Youth Survey found little difference across race or class in girls' incidence of crimes against persons, but she reports that "lower class females report . . . the greatest involvement in assaultive crime . . . [and] a consistently higher proportion of black females are involved in crimes against persons for all five years surveyed" (1983:565). This is not to suggest that African-

American women's participation in these offenses parallel or converge with that of urban African-American males (see Chesney-Lind and Shelden, 1992:21-24; Laub and McDermott, 1985). Rather, my point is to highlight the contexts in which these women negotiate their daily lives. Violence is extensive in the lives and communities of African-American women living in the urban underclass. As a result, some women in these circumstances may be more likely than women who are situated differently to view violence as an appropriate or useful means of dealing with their environment. As Simpson (1991:129) notes,

> Living daily with the fact of violence leads to an incorporation of it into one's experiential self. Men, women, and children have to come to terms with, make sense of, and respond to violence as it penetrates their lives. As violence is added to the realm of appropriate and sanctioned responses to oppressive material conditions, it gains a sort of cultural legitimacy. But not for all.

Evidence of the significance of the link between underclass conditions and African-American women's disproportionate involvement in violence may be found in recent research that examines factors predicting women's criminal involvement. Hill and Crawford (1990) report that structural indicators appear to be most significant in predicting the criminal involvement of African-American women, while social-psychological indicators are more predictive for white women. They conclude that "the unique position of black women in the structure of power relations in society has profound effects not shared by their white counterparts" (Hill and Crawford, 1990:621). In fact, Baskin et al. (1993:413) suggest that "women in inner city neighborhoods are being pulled toward violent street crime by the same forces that have been found to affect their male counterparts. As with males, neighborhood, peer and addiction factors have been found to contribute to female initiation into violence."

This is not to suggest, however, that gender does not matter. Gender remains a salient aspect of women's experiences in the urban street milieu, and must remain—along with race and class—at the forefront of attempts to understand their involvement in violent crime. Some research that stresses race and economic oppression as factors in women's criminality overlooks the significance of gender oppression in these contexts. For instance, Baskin et al. (1993:415) argue that "women's roles and prominence have changed in transformed neighborhoods" such that there exist "new dynamics of crime where gender is a far less salient factor" (p. 417).

However, there is overwhelming evidence that gender inequality remains a salient feature of the urban street scene (Anderson, 1994; Maher, 1997; Maher and Curtis, 1992; Maher and Daly, 1996; Oliver, 1994; Steffensmeier, 1983; Steffensmeier and Terry, 1986; Wilson, 1996). As

42   JODY MILLER

Maher notes, for scholars who suggest that gender has lost its relevance, women's "activity is confused with [their] equality" (1997:18). Research that examines women's participation in violent street crime without paying sufficient attention to the gendered nature of this participation or the ways in which "gendered status structures this participation" (Maher, 1997:13) cannot adequately describe or explain these phenomena.

The strength of the current study is its comparative analysis of women's *and* men's accounts of the accomplishment of one type of violent crime—street robbery. In comparing both the question of *why* women and men report engaging in robbery, and *how* gender organizes the commission of robbery, this research provides insight into the ways in which gender shapes women's involvement in what is perhaps the typification of "masculine" street crime. As such, it speaks to broader debates about women's place in the contemporary urban street world.

METHODOLOGY

The study is based on semistructured in-depth interviews with 37 active street robbers. The sample includes 14 women and a comparative sample of 23 men, matched approximately by age and age at first robbery.[1] The respondents range in age from 16 to 46; the majority are in their late teens to mid-twenties.[2] All of the men are African-American; 12 of the women are African-American and 2 are white.[3] See the appendix for a fuller description of each respondent.

Respondents were recruited on the streets through the use of snowball sampling (Watters and Biernacki, 1989) in impoverished urban neighborhoods in St. Louis, Missouri. An ex-offender was hired to serve as a street ethnographer; he culled from his former criminal associates in order to generate the initial respondents for the study (see also Decker and Van Winkle, 1996; Wright and Decker, 1994). These respondents were then

---

1.   The original study (Wright and Decker, 1997) contained 86 interviews, 72 of which were with males. From these, the matched sample of males for the current study was drawn prior to data analysis to avoid sampling biases.

2.   This age distribution differs from that of the larger sample, which included a sizable number of older male robbers. Eighteen of the males in the current sample were under 25 (78%), while only 35 of the 72 males in the larger sample (49%) were under 25.

3.   One white male was interviewed for the original study but was excluded from this analysis because he didn't fit the matching criteria (age, age at first robbery) and had only committed one robbery, which was retaliatory in nature. He was 30 years old and had recently been ripped off by someone, whom he robbed in order to get his money back. Notably though, the physicality of his style in committing the robbery—"I had my left hand on his neck and the gun on his cheekbone"—paralleled the predominant style of the male robbers included.

asked to refer other friends or associates who might be willing to be interviewed, and the process continued until an appropriate sample was built.

Criteria for inclusion in the sample included the following: the individual had committed a robbery in the recent past, defined him- or herself as currently active, and was regarded as active by other offenders.[4] Though it is not possible to determine the representativeness of this sample of active offenders (see Glassner and Carpenter, 1985), the approach nonetheless overcomes many of the shortcomings associated with interviewing ex-offenders or offenders who are incarcerated (see Agar, 1977). In fact, in the current study snowball sampling allowed for the purposive oversampling of both female and juvenile robbers.

Perhaps the greatest limitation of the sample is the overrepresentation of African-American robbers and the near absence of white offenders. According to the St. Louis Metropolitan Police Department's (1994) *Annual Report*, whites were 18% of robbery arrestees in that year. As Wright and Decker (1997:11) explain,

> No doubt the racial composition of our sample is a reflection of the social chasm that exists between blacks and whites in the St. Louis underworld. Black and white offenders display a marked tendency to "stick to their own kind" and seldom are members of the same criminal networks. Successfully making contact with active black armed robbers proved to be of almost no help to us in locating white offenders.

This problem was exacerbated because the hired street ethnographer was African-American and was unable to provide any initial contacts with white robbers. In fact, both of the white females interviewed in the study were referred by their African-American boyfriends.

Each respondent was paid $50 for participation in the research and was promised strict confidentiality.[5] Respondents were paid an additional $10

---

4. All but five of the respondents reported that they had committed at least one robbery within the month prior to being interviewed. These five included three men (Woods, C-Loco, and Tony Wright) and two women (Quick and Kim Brown). All nonetheless considered themselves active robbers.

5. Because the project was partially supported by funds from the National Institute of Justice, respondents' confidentiality was protected by federal law. In addition, completed interviews were kept in a locked file cabinet. For a fuller discussion of human subjects' protections, see Wright and Decker (1997). In regard to confidentiality, one clarification is in order. One of the young women (Tish) was referred by her boyfriend, who had previously been interviewed for the project. They insisted that he be present during her interview, and he occasionally interjected to offer his own clarifications of her responses. Though his presence may have made her more hesitant or self-conscious in answering, his own comments were illuminating regarding the gendered nature of their robberies, as both of them downplayed the seriousness of her involvement.

44   JODY MILLER

for each successful referral (i.e., a cooperative participant who was currently an active robber). Interviews lasted one to two hours and included a range of questions about the respondents' involvement in robbery, with particular focus on "their thoughts and actions during the commission of their crimes" (Wright and Decker, 1997:8). Respondents were asked to describe their typical approach when committing robbery, as well as to describe in detail their most recent offense; the goal was to gain a thorough understanding of the contexts of these events (see Wright and Decker, 1997, for a full discussion of the research process).

Because this research is concerned with the situational accomplishment of robbery, it does not provide a means to explore fully the contexts of offending as they relate to respondents' life circumstances. Nonetheless, it is worthwhile to situate their discussions with a brief description of the milieu from which they were drawn. As noted above, respondents were recruited from impoverished urban neighborhoods in St. Louis. St. Louis typifies the midwestern city devastated by structural changes brought about by deindustrialization. With tremendous economic and racial segregation, population loss, and resulting social isolation, loss of community resources, and concentrated urban poverty among African-Americans, the neighborhoods the respondents were drawn from are characteristic of "underclass" conditions (Sampson and Wilson, 1995; Wilson, 1996). These conditions no doubt shape respondents' offending through the interactive effects of structural barriers and resulting cultural adaptations (see Sampson and Wilson, 1995). Thus, they should remain in the foreground in examining the accomplishment of robbery.

MOTIVATIONS TO COMMIT ROBBERY

In this study, active robbers' articulation of the reasons they commit robbery is more a case of gender similarities than differences. What they get out of robbery, why they choose robbery instead of some other crime, why particular targets are appealing—the themes of these discussions are overlapping in women's and men's accounts. For both, the primary motivation is to get money or material goods. As Libbie Jones notes, "You can get good things from a robbery." For some, the need for money comes with a strong sense of urgency, such as when the individual is robbing to support a drug addiction—a situation more prevalent among older respondents than younger ones. But for the majority of women and men in this sample, robberies are committed to get status-conferring goods such as gold jewelry, spending money, and/or for excitement.[6] For instance, T-

---

6. This pattern is somewhat different from that of the larger sample of 86 active robbers, more of whom described robbing with a greater sense of desperation for money (Wright and Decker, 1997). This difference results from the differences in age

Bone says he decides to commit robberies when he's "tired of not having money." When the idea comes about, he is typically with friends from the neighborhood, and he explains, "we all bored, broke, mad." Likewise, CMW says she commits robberies "out of the blue, just something to do. Bored at the time and just want to find some action." She explains, "I be sitting on the porch and we'll get to talking and stuff. See people going around and they be flashing in they fancy cars, walking down the street with that jewelry on, thinking they all bad, and we just go get 'em." For both males and females, robberies are typically a means of achieving conspicuous consumption.

If anything, imperatives to gain money and material goods through robbery appear to be stronger for males than females, so that young men explain that they sometimes commit robberies because they feel some economic pressure, whereas young women typically do not. Masculine street identity is tied to the ability to have and spend money, and included in this is the appearance of economic self-sufficiency. Research has documented women's support networks in urban communities, including among criminally involved women (see Maher, 1997; Stack, 1974). This may help explain why the imperative for young men is stronger than for young women: Community norms may give women wider latitude for obtaining material goods and economic support from a variety of sources, including other females, family members, and boyfriends; whereas the pressure of society's view of men as breadwinners differentially affects men's emotional experience of relying on others economically. This may explain why several young men specifically describe that they do not like relying on their parents in order to meet their consumer needs. As Mike J. notes, "My mother, she gives me money sometimes but I can't get the stuff like I want, clothes and stuff . . . so I try to get it by robbery." Though both males and females articulate economic motives for robbery, young men,

---

structure of the current sample compared to the original sample. Because the majority of female respondents were teenagers or young adults (10 of the 14), the matched sample of males drawn for this study was younger than the larger sample of males (see note 2). Older robbers were more likely to be supporting drug habits and were more likely to have children or family that they made efforts to provide for.

Sommers and Baskin's (1993) study of female robbers offers much the same conclusion regarding motivation. In their study of 44 female robbers, 89% describe committing the crime for money, and 11% for noneconomic reasons such as excitement or vengeance. Of women who committed robbery for money, 81% did so to support drug habits, and only 19% did so to get commodities such as jewelry and clothes. These differences are likely the case because their sample is older than the current sample and because they were incarcerated at the time of the interview, and thus likely represent less successful robbers (perhaps because of their drug habits). In fact, when giving life-history accounts, two-thirds of Sommers and Baskin's sample reported that their initial reasons for committing robbery were less economic and more oriented toward thrill seeking and excitement.

46   JODY MILLER

more than young women, describe feeling compelled to commit robberies because they feel "broke."

Asked to explain why they commit robberies instead of other crimes with similar economic rewards, both women and men say that they choose robberies, as Cooper explains, because "it's the easiest." Libbie Jones reports that robbery provides her with the things she wants in one quick and easy step:

> I like robbery. I like robbery 'cause I don't have to buy nothing. You have a herringbone, I'm gonna take your herringbone and then I have me a herringbone. I don't have to worry about going to the store, getting me some money. If you got some little earrings on I'm gonna get 'em.

The ease with which respondents view the act of robbery is also reflected in their choice of victims—most frequently other street-involved individuals, who are perceived as unlikely to be able to go to the police, given their own criminal involvement. In addition, these targets are perceived as likely to have a lot of money, as well as jewelry and other desirable items. Less frequently, respondents report targeting individuals who are perceived as particularly easy marks, such as older citizens. However, most robberies, whether committed by females or males, occur in the larger contexts of street life, and their victims reflect this—most are also involved in street contexts, either as adolescents or young adults who hang out on the streets and go to clubs, or as individuals involved (as dealers and/or users) in the street-level drug economy. Because of this, it is not uncommon for robbers to know or at least know of their victims (for more on target selection, see Wright and Decker, 1997:Ch. 3).

In addition to the economic incentives that draw the respondents toward robbery, many also derive a psychological or emotional thrill from committing robberies. Little Bill says, "when my first robbery started, my second, the third one, it got more fun . . . if I keep on doing it I think that I will really get addicted to it." Likewise, Ne-Ne's comment illustrates the complex dynamics shaping many respondents' decisions to commit robberies, particularly the younger ones: "I don't know if it's the money, the power or just the feeling that I know that I can just go up and just take somebody's stuff. It's just a whole bunch of mixture type thing." Others describe a similar mixture of economic and emotional rewards. Buby notes, "you get like a rush, it be fun at the time."

When individuals on the street are perceived as "high-catting" or showing off, they are viewed by both male and female robbers as deserving targets. Ne-Ne describes the following dialogue between herself and a young woman she robbed: "[The girl] said 'if you take my money then I'm gonna get in trouble because this is my man's money.' He told you to keep it, not showboat. You talking 'nigger I got $800 in my pocket,' pulling it out. Yeah, you wanted us to know." Likewise, describing a woman he robbed at a gas station, Treason Taylor says, "really I didn't like the way she came out. She was like pulling out all her money like she think she hot shit." A few respondents even specifically target people they don't like, or people who have insulted or hurt them in the past.

For both women and men, then, motivations to commit robbery are primarily economic—to get money, jewelry, and other status-conferring goods, but they also include elements of thrill seeking, attempting to overcome boredom, and revenge. Most striking is the continuity across women's and men's accounts of their motives for committing robbery, which vary only by the greater pressure reported by some young men to have their own money to obtain material goods. As discussed in the next sections, there are clear differences in the accomplishment of robbery by gender; however, these differences are apparently not driven by differences in motivation.

MEN'S ENACTMENTS OF STREET ROBBERY

Men accomplish street robberies in a strikingly uniform manner. Respondents' descriptions of their robberies are variations around one theme—using physical violence and/or a gun placed on or at close proximity to the victim in a confrontational manner. This is reflected in Looney's description of being taught how to commit his first robbery, at the age of 13, by his stepbrother:

> We was up at [a fast food restaurant] one day and a dude was up there tripping. My stepbrother had gave me a .22 automatic. He told me to walk over behind him and put the gun to his head and tell him to give me all his stuff. That's what I did. I walked up to him and said man, this is a jack, man, take off all your jewelry and take you money out of your pockets, throw it on the ground and walk off. So that's what he did. I picked up the money and the jewelry and walked away.

By far the most common form of robbery described by male respondents entails targeting other men involved in street life—drug dealers, drug users, gang members, or other men who look "flashy" because of their clothes, cars, and/or jewelry. Twenty-two respondents (96%) report committing robberies in these contexts, which involve accosting people on the streets or accosting them in their cars. Only Little Bill, who is an addict, does not describe engaging in these types of robberies. Instead, he only targets non-street-involved citizens, whom he feels safer confronting.[7]

---

7. This may be a low estimate. Sometimes it is difficult to discern whether victims are street involved; robbers simply view them as an individual likely to have money

48   JODY MILLER

Seven men (30%) describe robbing women as well as men.

All of the men in this sample report using guns when they rob, though not everyone uses a gun every time.[8] The key is to make sure that the victim knows, as Syco says, "that we ain't playing." This is accomplished either through the positioning of the gun or by physically assaulting the victim. If the victim appears to resist, the physical assault is more severe, a shot is fired in the air or to the side of the victim, or the victim is shot—typically in the foot or the leg. Again, what is striking across men's interviews is the continuity of their approach toward street robberies. Upon spotting a target, they swiftly run up on the victim and physically confront him or her, telling the victim "up it up," "come up off it," or some similar phrase. These robberies frequently are committed with partners, but sometimes are committed alone.

For many male robbers, cooperation is achieved simply by the presence and positioning of the gun. Bob Jones confronts his victims by placing the gun at the back of their head, where "they feel it," and says, "give it up, motherfucker, don't move or I'll blow your brains out." Explaining the positioning of the gun, he says, "when you feel that steel against your head . . . that pistol carries a lot of weight." Describing one of his robberies, Looney says, "I creeped up behind him, this time I had a 12 gauge, I pointed it to the back of his head, told him to drop it." Big Prod notes that he will "have the gun to his head, can't do nothing but respect that." Likewise, Treason Taylor explains that he will "grab [the victim] by the neck and stick the gun to they head. Sometimes I don't even touch them I just point the gun right in front of they face. That really scares people." Prauch says, "I don't even have to say nothing half the time. When they see that pistol, they know what time it is."

A number of respondents report using some measure of physical confrontation, even when using a weapon, in order to ensure the victim's cooperation and/or the robber's getaway. Cooper says, "you always got to either hit 'em, slap 'em or do something to let them know you for real." T-Bone says, "I just hit them with the gun and they give it up quick." Likewise, Mike J. says, "you might shake them a little bit. If there is more than one of you, you can really do that kind of stuff like shake them up a little bit to show them you're not messing around." Sometimes physical confrontation is simply part of the thrill. Damon Jones says that while he typically doesn't physically assault his victims, a friend he often robs with "always do something stupid like he'll smash somebody with the pistol,

---

because of their physical appearance, dress, and jewelry. In the larger sample, Wright and Decker estimated that 30 of the 86 robbers (35%) targeted citizens.

   8.   In the larger sample, approximately 90% of respondents used guns to commit robberies.

UP IT UP 49

you know what I'm saying. He'll hit them in the head or something just, I guess, just to do it."

When the victim hesitates or is seen as uncooperative, the respondents describe using a variety of physical measures to ensure the completion of the robbery. The mildest version is described by Carlos Reed: "If I have a revolver, I'll cock it back, that will be the warning right there. If I run up to you like this and then you hesitate I'm gonna cock it back." Others use physical violence to intimidate the victim. Redwood says, "if they think I'm bullshitting I'll smack them up in they motherfucking head." Likewise, Tony Wright notes, "you would be surprised how cooperative a person will be once he been smashed across the face with a .357 Magnum." Other respondents describe shooting the gun, either past the victim or in the leg or foot, in order to ensure cooperation. Prauch says, "one gun shot, they ass in line. If I hit them a couple of times and that don't work, one gun shot by they ear and they in line." And Cooper notes, "If I see he just trying to get tough then sometimes I just straight out have to shoot somebody, just shoot 'em."

Though most robberies involve the use of a weapon, several men also report engaging in strong-arm robberies, sometimes when an opportunity presents itself and there is no time to retrieve a weapon. These robberies involve a great deal of physical violence. Taz says, "if it's a strong-arm, like I'll just get up on them and I'll just hit 'em and [my partner] will grab them or like he will hit them and I'll grab 'em and we keep on hitting them until they fall or something . . . we just go in his pockets, leave him there, we gone." Likewise, Swoop describes a strong-arm robbery he was involved in:

> Me and my two partners saw this dude and he had on a lot of jewelry. I wanted them chains and my partner wanted the rings. We didn't have a weapon. We strong-armed him. . . He was coming from off the lot [at a fast food restaurant], he actually was going to his car so I ran up on him . . . and I hit him in the face. He tried to run. My partner ran and kicked him in the mouth. He just let us, I took the chains off of him, my partner took his rings, my partner took his money, we split the money and that was all it took.

Seven men describe robbing women as well as men. However, male respondents—both those who have robbed women and those who have not—clearly state that robbing women is different from robbing men. Robbing women is seen as less dangerous, and women are believed to be less likely to resist. The following dialogue with Looney is illustrative:

> Interviewer: Do you rob men or women more?
> Looney: I rob men.
> Interviewer: Why?

Looney: They got money.

Interviewer: Do men behave differently than women?

Looney: Nope. Men gonna try to act like the tough guy, when they
see the gun, then they give it up quick. But a lady, I just tell them
to give it up and they give me they whole purse or whatever they
got.

While physical violence is often used in men's robberies of other men,
respondents do not describe assaulting women routinely, typically only if
they are seen as resisting. It appears not to be deemed a necessary part of
the transaction with female victims. Taz, whose robberies of men typically
involve a great deal of physical violence (see above), says, "I did a girl
before but I didn't hurt her or nothing, we just robbed her. She was too
scared." Having women present is also seen as making male targets more
vulnerable. Swoop explains: "If he like by himself or if he with a girl then
that's the best time, but if he with two dudes, you know they rolling
strapped so you wait." Unlike when a street-involved target is with other
males and needs to maintain an air of toughness, Swoop says "you know
they ain't gonna try to show off for the little gals, they gonna give it all
up."

It is notable that women are widely perceived, as C-Loco says, as "easy
to get," and yet as a rule they are not targeted for street robberies. Partly
this is because women are perceived as less likely to have a lot of money
on them. Moreover, women are not viewed as real players in the action of
the streets; they are peripheral, and thus not typically part of the masculine game of street robbery. Antwon Wright sums this up in the following
dialogue about the use of physical violence:

Interviewer: Do you hit everybody?

Antwon Wright: It depends. It depends on who is there and how
many. If it's a dude and a gal we might hit the dude and leave the
girl.

Interviewer: Why?

Antwon Wright: 'Cause a girl is no threat for real to us. A girl is no
threat. We just worry about dudes. Girls is no threat. But if it's
about six dudes, man we gonna hit everybody. We gonna get everybody on the ground, bam, bam. Then if they want to get back up
we just keep on hitting.

Male robbers, then, clearly view the act of robbery as a masculine
accomplishment in which men compete with other men for money and
status. While some rob women, those robberies are deviations from the
norm of "badass" against "badass" that dominates much of men's discussions of street robbery (see Katz, 1988). The routine use of guns, physical

contact, and violence in male-on-male robberies is a reflection of the masculine ideologies shaping men's robberies. Women's enactment of robbery is much more varied than that of men's and provides a telling contrast about the nature of gender on the streets.

WOMEN'S ENACTMENTS OF STREET ROBBERY

The women in the sample describe three predominant ways in which they commit robberies: targeting female victims in physically confrontational robberies, targeting male victims by appearing sexually available, and participating with males during street robberies of men. Ten women (71%) describe targeting female victims, usually on the streets but occasionally at dance clubs or in cars. Seven (50%) describe setting up men through promises of sexual favors, including two women who do so in the context of prostitution. Seven (50%) describe working with male friends, relatives, or boyfriends in street robberies; three (21%) report this as their exclusive form of robbery.

ROBBING FEMALES

The most common form of robbery reported by women in the study is robbing other females in a physically confrontational manner. Ten of the 14 female respondents report committing these types of offenses. Of those who do not, three only commit robberies by assisting men, whose targets are other males (see below), and one only robs men in the context of prostitution. Typically, women's robberies of other females occur on the streets, though a few young women also report robbing females in the bathrooms or parking lots of clubs, and one robs women in cars. These robberies are sometimes committed alone, but usually in conjunction with one or several additional women, but not in conjunction with men. In fact, Ne-Ne says even when she's out with male friends and sees a female target, they don't get involved: "They'll say 'well you go on and do her.'"

Most robberies of females either involve no weapon or they involve a knife. Four women report having used a gun to rob women, only one of whom does so on a regular basis.[9] Women are the victims of choice because they are perceived as less likely to be armed themselves and less likely to resist or fight back. CMW explains, "See women, they won't

---

9. This is Yolanda Smith, who robs older women by offering to give them rides in her car. Describing a typical robbery, she says: "I asked her did she need a ride. I said 'if you give me one dollar for gas I'll take you to work.' So she jumped in the car. I took her about three or four blocks and then I said 'do you have any more money?' She had this necklace on so I put a gun up to her head and said 'give it up.'" Her approach was unlike any other woman's in the sample, both in terms of how she approached the victim and in her routine use of a firearm.

52 JODY MILLER

really do nothing. They say, 'oh, oh, ok, here take this.' A dude, he might try to put up a fight." Yolanda Smith reports that she only robs women because "they more easier for me to handle." Likewise, Libbie Jones says, "I wouldn't do no men by myself," but she says women victims "ain't gonna do nothing because they be so scared." The use of weapons in these assaults is often not deemed necessary. Quick explains that she sometimes uses a knife, "but sometimes I don't need anything. Most of the time it be girls, you know, just snatching they chains or jewelry. You don't need nothing for that." Quick has also used a gun to rob another female. She and a friend were driving around when they spotted a young woman walking down the street with an expensive purse they liked. "We jumped out of the car. My friend put a gun up to her head and we just took all of her stuff." However, this approach was atypical.

On occasion, female victims belie the stereotype of them and fight back. Both Janet Outlaw and Ne-Ne describe stabbing young women who resisted them. Janet Outlaw describes one such encounter:

> This was at a little basketball game. Coming from the basketball game. It was over and we were checking her out and everything and she was walking to her car. I was, shit fuck that, let's get her motherfucking purse. Said let's get that purse. So I walked up to her and I pulled out the knife. I said "up that purse." And she looked at me. I said "shit, do you think I'm playing? Up that purse." She was like "shit, you ain't getting my purse. Do what you got to do." I was like "shit, you must be thinking I'm playing." So I took the knife, stabbed her a couple of times on the shoulder, stabbed her on the arm and snatched the purse. Cut her arm and snatched the purse. She just ran, "help, help." We were gone.

Ne-Ne describes a similar incident that occurred after an altercation between two groups of young women. When one young woman continued to badmouth her, she followed the girl to her car, pulled out a knife, "headed to her side and showed the bitch [the knife]." The girl responded, "I ain't giving you shit," and Ne-Ne said, "please don't make me stick you." Then, "She went to turn around and I just stuck it in her side. . . She was holding her side, just bleeding. And so when she fell on the ground one of my partners just started taking her stuff off of her. We left her right there."

As with pulling guns on women, stabbing female victims is a rare occurrence. Nonetheless, women's robbery of other women routinely involves physical confrontation such as hitting, shoving, or beating up the victim. Describing a recent robbery, Nicole Simpson says, "I have bricks in my purse and I went up to her and hit her in the head and took her money." Kim Brown says that she will "just whop you and take a purse but not really put a gun to anybody's face." Libbie Jones says she has her victims throw their possessions on the ground, "then you push 'em, kick 'em or whatever, you pick it up and you just burn out." Likewise, CMW describes a recent robbery:

I was like with three other girls and we was like all walking around . . . walking around the block trying to find something to do on a Saturday night with really nothing to do and so we started coming up the street, we didn't have no weapons on us at the time. All we did was just start jumping on her and beating her up and took her purse.

According to Janet Outlaw, "We push 'em and tell them to up their shit, pushing 'em in the head. Couple of times we had to knock the girls down and took the stuff off of them." She explains the reason this type of physical force is necessary: "It's just a woman-to-woman thing and we just like, just don't, just letting them know like it is, we let them know we ain't playing." As discussed below, this approach is vastly different from women's approaches when they rob men, or when they commit robberies with males. It appears to be, as Janet Outlaw says, "a woman-to-woman thing."

As noted above, sometimes female-on-female robberies occur in or around night clubs, in addition to on the streets. Libbie Jones explains, "you just chill in the club, just dance or whatever, just peep out people that got what you want. And then they come out of the club and you just get them." Likewise, Janet Outlaw says, "we get a couple of drinks, be on the blow, party, come sit down. Then be like, damn, check that bitch out with all this shit on." Libbie Jones came to her interview wearing a ring she had gotten in a robbery at a club the night before, telling the interviewer, "I like this on my hand, it looks lovely." She describes the incident as follows:

This girl was in the bathroom. I seen the rings on her hands. Everybody was in there talking and putting their makeup on, doing their hair. So I went and got my godsister. She came back with her drink. She spilled it on her and she was like, "oh, my fault, my fault." She was wiping it off her. I pulled out my knife and said "give it up." The girl was taking the rings off her hand so when we got the rings we bounced up out of the club.

Though most of the women who rob females are teenagers or young adults and rob other young women, two women in the sample—Lisa Wood and Kim Brown—also describe targeting middle-aged or older citizens. It is notable that both are older (in their late 30s) and that both describe robbing in order to support drug habits, which make them more

54   JODY MILLER

desperate.[10] As with the younger women who choose to rob other young women because they believe them unlikely to resist, both of these women choose older targets because they won't fight back. Lisa Wood says sometimes they accomplish these robberies of non-street-involved citizens by getting victims to drop their guard when they are coming out of stores. She describes approaching the person, "say 'hi, how you doing,' or 'do you need any help?' A lot of times they will say yeah. They might have groceries to take to they car and get it like that." She says once they drop their guard she will "snatch they purse and take off running."

To summarize, notable elements of women's robberies of other women are that they most frequently occur within street-oriented settings, do not include male accomplices, and typically involve physical force such as hitting, shoving and kicking, rather than the use of a weapon. When weapons are used, they are most likely to be knives. In these contexts, women choose to rob other females rather than males because they believe females are less likely to fight back; they typically do not use weapons such as guns because they perceive female targets as unlikely to be armed.

SETTING UP MALES BY APPEARING SEXUALLY AVAILABLE

Women's robberies of men nearly always involve guns.[11] They also do not involve physical contact. Janet Outlaw, who describes a great deal of physical contact in her robberies of other women (see above), describes her robberies of men in much different terms: "If we waste time touching men there is a possibility that they can get the gun off of us, while we wasting time touching them they could do anything. So we just keep the gun straight on them. No touching, no moving, just straight gun at you." The circumstances surrounding the enactment of female-on-male robberies differ as well. The key, in each case, is that women pretend to be sexually interested in their male victims, whose guard drops, providing a safe opportunity for the crime to occur. Two women—Jayzo and Nicole Simpson—rob men in the context of prostitution. The other five typically choose a victim at a club or on the streets, flirt and appear sexually interested, then suggest they go to a hotel, where the robbery takes place. These robberies may involve male or female accomplices, but they are just as likely to be conducted alone.

Nicole Simpson prostitutes to support her drug habit, but sometimes she

---

10. These two are also the only women who report having had male accomplices when robbing women in this way.

11. The only exception to this pattern was Nicole Simpson, who used a knife to rob tricks in the context of prostitution. These findings parallel those of Sommers and Baskin (1993:147), who found that women were not likely to rob men without weapons, but were likely to rob other women without them.

"just don't be feeling like doing it," and will rob her trick rather than complete the sexual transaction. Sometimes she does this alone, and other times has a female accomplice. She chooses tricks she feels will make safe victims. She explains, "like I meet a lot of white guys and they be so paranoid they just want to get away." When Nicole Simpson is working alone, she waits until the man is in a vulnerable position before pulling out her knife. As she explains, "if you are sucking a man's dick and you pull a knife on them, they not gonna too much argue with you." When she works with a female partner, Nicole Simpson has the woman wait at a designated place, then takes the trick "to the spot where I know she at." . She begins to perform oral sex, then her partner jumps in the car and pulls a knife. She explains, "once she get in the car I'll watch her back, they know we together. I don't even let them think that she is by herself. If they know it's two of us maybe they won't try it. Because if they think she by herself they might say fuck this, it ain't nothing but one person." Jayzo's techniques parallel those of Nicole Simpson, though she uses a gun instead of a knife and sometimes takes prospective tricks to hotels in addition to car dating.

Young women who target men outside the context of prostitution play upon the men's beliefs about women in order to accomplish these robberies—including the assumptions that women won't be armed, won't attempt to rob them, and can be taken advantage of sexually. Quick explains, "they don't suspect that a girl gonna try to get 'em. You know what I'm saying? So it's kind of easier 'cause they like, she looks innocent, she ain't gonna do this, but that's how I get 'em. They put they guard down to a woman." She says when she sets up men, she parties with them first, but makes sure she doesn't consume as much as them. "Most of the time, when girls get high they think they can take advantage of us so they always, let's go to a hotel or my crib or something." Janet Outlaw says, "they easy to get, we know what they after—sex." Likewise, CMW and a girlfriend often flirt with their victims: "We get in the car then ride with them. They thinking we little freaks . . . whores or something." These men's assumptions that they can take advantage of women lead them to place themselves at risk for robbery. CMW continues: "So they try to take us to the motel or whatever, we going for it. Then it's like they getting out of the car and then all my friend has to do is just put the gun up to his head, give me your keys. He really can't do nothing, his gun is probably in the car. All you do is drive on with the car."

Several young women report targeting men at clubs, particularly dope dealers or other men who appear to have a lot of money. Describing one such victim, Janet Outlaw says she was drawn to him because of his "jewelry, the way he was dressed, little snakeskin boots and all. . . I was like, yeah, there is some money." She recounts the incident as follows:

56   JODY MILLER

I walked up to him, got to conversating with him. He was like, "what's up with you after the club?" I said "I'm down with you, whatever you want to do." I said "we can go to a hotel or something." He was like "for real?" I was like, "yeah, for real." He was like, "shit, cool then." So after the club we went to the hotel. I had the gun in my purse. I followed him, I was in my own car, he was in his car. So I put the gun in my purse and went up to the hotel, he was all ready. He was posted, he was a lot drunk. He was like, "you smoke weed?" I was like, "yeah shit, what's up." So we got to smoking a little bud, he got to taking off his little shit, laying it on a little table. He was like, "shit, what's up, ain't you gonna get undressed?" I was like "shit, yeah, hold up" and I went in my purse and I pulled out the gun. He was like "damn, what's up with you gal?" I was like, "shit, I want your jewelry and all the money you got." He was like, "shit, bitch you crazy. I ain't giving you my shit." I said, "do you think I'm playing nigger? You don't think I'll shoot your motherfucking ass?" He was like, "shit, you crazy, fuck that, you ain't gonna shoot me." So then I had fired the thing but I didn't fire it at him, shot the gun. He was like "fuck no." I snatched his shit. He didn't have on no clothes. I snatched the shit and ran out the door. Hopped in my car.

Though she did this particular robbery alone, Janet Outlaw says she often has male accomplices, who follow her to the hotel or meet her there. While she's in the room, "my boys be standing out in the hallway," then she lets them in when she's ready to rob the man. Having male backup is useful because men often resist being robbed by females, believing that women don't have the heart to go through with what's necessary if the victim resists. Janet Outlaw describes one such incident. Having flirted with a man and agreed to meet him, she got in his car then pulled her gun on him:

I said "give me your stuff." He wasn't gonna give it to me. This was at nighttime. My boys was on the other side of the car but he didn't know it. He said "I ain't gonna give you shit." I was like, "you gonna give me your stuff." He was like "I'll take that gun off of your ass." I was like, "shit, you ain't gonna take this gun." My boy just pulled up and said, "give her your shit." I got the shit.

In the majority of these robberies, the victim knows that the woman has set him up—she actively participates in the robbery. Ne-Ne also describes setting up men and then pretending to be a victim herself. Her friends even get physical with her to make it appear that she's not involved. She explains:

I'll scam you out and get to know you a little bit first, go out and eat and let you tell me where we going, what time and everything. I'll go in the restroom and go beep them [accomplices] just to let them know what time we leaving from wherever we at so they can come out and do their little robbery type thing, push me or whatever. I ain't gonna leave with them 'cause then he'll know so I still chill with him for a little while.

Only Ne-Ne reports having ever engaged in a robbery the opposite of this—that is, one in which her male partners flirted with a girl and she came up and robbed her. She explains:

I got some [male friends] that will instigate it. If I see some girl and I'm in the car with a whole bunch of dudes, they be like "look at that bitch she have on a leather coat." "Yeah, I want that." They'll say "well why don't you go get it?" Then you got somebody in the back seat [saying] "she's scared, she's scared." Then you got somebody just like "she ain't scared, up on the piece" or whatever and then you got some of them that will say well, "we gonna do this together." It could be like two dudes they might get out like "what's up baby," try to holler at her, get a mack on and they don't see the car. We watching and as soon as they pulling out they little pen to write they number, then I'll get out of the car and just up on them and tell them, the dudes be looking like, damn, what's going on? But they ain't gonna help 'cause they my partners or whatever.

STREET ROBBERIES WITH MALE ROBBERS

As the previous two sections illustrate, women's accomplishment of robbery varies according to the gender of their victims. As a rule, women and men do not rob females together, but do sometimes work together to set up and rob males. In addition, half of the women interviewed describe committing street robberies—almost always against males—with male accomplices. In these robberies, women's involvement either involves equal participation in the crime or assisting males but defining their role as secondary. Three women in the sample—Buby, Tish, and Lisa Jones—describe working with males on the streets as their only form of robbery, and each sees her participation as secondary. The rest engage in a combination of robbery types, including those described in the previous two sections, and do not distinguish their roles from the roles of male participants in these street robberies.

Lisa Jones and Tish each assist their boyfriends in the commission of robberies; Buby goes along with her brother and cousins. Lisa Jones says "most of the time we'll just be driving around and he'll say 'let's go to this neighborhood and rob somebody.'" Usually she stays in the car while he approaches the victim, but she is armed and will get out and assist when necessary. Describing one such incident, she says, "One time there was two guys and one guy was in the car and the other guy was out of the car and I seen that one guy getting out of the car I guess to help his friend. That's when I got out and I held the gun and I told him to stay where he was." Likewise Buby frequently goes on robberies with her brother and cousins but usually chooses to stay in the car "because I be thinking that I'm gonna get caught so I rather stay in the back." She has never done a robbery on her own and explains, "I know what to do but I don't know if I could do it on my own. I don't know if I could because I'm used to doing them with my brother and my cousins." Though her role is not an active one, she gets a cut of the profits from these robberies.

Tish and Lisa Jones are the only white respondents in the study. Each robs with an African-American boyfriend, and—though they commit armed robberies—both reject the view of themselves as criminals. Lisa Jones, for instance, downplays her role in robberies, as the following dialogue illustrates:

Interviewer: How many armed robberies have you done in your life?
Lisa Jones: I go with my boyfriend and I've held the gun, I've never actually shot it.
Interviewer: But you participate in his robberies?
Lisa Jones: Yeah.
Interviewer: How many would you say in your whole life?
Lisa Jones: About fifteen.
Interviewer: What about in the last month?
Lisa Jones: Maybe five or six.
Interviewer: What other crimes have you done in your life, or participated with others?
Lisa Jones: No, I'm not a criminal.

It is striking that this young woman routinely engages in robberies in which she wields a weapon, yet she defines herself as "not a criminal." Later in the interview, she explains that she would stop participating in armed robberies "if I was to stop seeing him." She and Tish are the only respondents who minimize the implications of their involvement in armed robbery, and it is probably not coincidental that they are young white women—their race and gender allow them to view themselves in this way.

Both also describe their boyfriends as the decision makers in the robberies—deciding when, where, and whom to rob. This is evident in Tish's interview, as her boyfriend, who is present in the room, frequently interjects to answer the interviewer's questions. The following dialogue is revealing:

Interviewer: How do you approach the person?
Tish: Just go up to them.

UP IT UP 59

Interviewer: You walk up to them, you drive up to them?

Boyfriend: Most of the time it's me and my partner that do it. Our gals, they got the guns and stuff but we doing most of the evaluating. We might hit somebody in the head with a gun, go up to them and say whatever. Come up off your shit or something to get the money. The girls, they doing the dirty work really, that's the part they like doing, they'll hold the gun and if something goes wrong they'll shoot. We approach them. I ain't gonna send my gal up to no dude to tell him she want to rob him, you know. She might walk up to him with me and she might hit him a couple of times but basically I'm going up to them.

These respondents reveal the far end of the continuum of women's involvement in robbery, clearly taking subordinate roles in the crime and defining themselves as less culpable as a result. Tish's boyfriend also reveals his perception of women as secondary actors in the accomplishment of robbery. For the most part, other women who participate in street robberies with male accomplices describe themselves as equal participants. Older women who rob citizens to support their drug habits at times do so with male accomplices. For instance, Lisa Woods sometimes commits her robberies with a male and female accomplice and targets people "like when they get they checks. Catch them coming out of the store, maybe trip 'em, go in they pocket and take they money and take off running." Among the younger women, robberies with male accomplices involve guns and typically come about when a group of people are driving around and spot a potential victim. Janet Outlaw describes a car jacking that occurred as she and some friends were driving around:

Stop at a red light, we was looking around, didn't see no police, we was right behind them [the victims]. . . So one of my boys got out and I got out. Then the other boy got up in the driver's seat that was with them. My boy went on one side and I went on the other side and said "nigger get out of the car before we shoot you." Then the dudes got out. It was like, shit, what's up, we down with you all. No you ain't down with us, take they jewelry and shit off. It was like, damn, why you all tripping? Then my boy cocked the little gun and said take it off now or I'm gonna start spraying you all ass. So they took off the little jewelry, I hopped in, put it in drive and pulled on off.

Likewise, Ne-Ne prefers committing street robberies with males rather than females. She explains:

I can't be bothered with too many girls. That's why I try to be with dudes or whatever. They gonna be down. If you get out of the car and if you rob a dude or jack somebody and you with some dudes then you know if they see he tryin' to resist, they gonna give me some

60   JODY MILLER

help. Whereas a girl, you might get somebody that's scared and might drive off. That's the way it is.

It is not surprising, then, that Ne-Ne is the only woman interviewed to report having ever committed this type of street robbery of a male victim on her own. Her actions parallel those of male-on-male robbers described above. Ne-Ne explicitly indicates that this robbery was possible because the victim did not know she was a woman. Describing herself physically, she says, "I'm big, you know." In addition, her dress and manner masked her gender. "I had a baseball cap in my car and I seen him. . . I just turned around the corner, came back down the street, he was out by himself and I got out of the car, had the cap pulled down over my face and I just went to the back and upped him. Put the gun up to his head." Being large, wearing a ballcap, and enacting the robbery in a masculine style (e.g., putting a gun to his head) allowed her to disguise the fact that she was a woman and thus decrease the victim's likelihood of resisting. She says, "He don't know right now to this day if it was a girl or a dude."

DISCUSSION

Feminist scholars have been hesitant to grapple with the issue of women's violence, both because a focus on women's violence draws attention away from the fact that violence is a predominantly male phenomenon and because studying women's violence can play into sensationalized accounts of female offenders. Nonetheless, as this and other studies have shown, "gender alone does not account for variation in criminal violence" (Simpson, 1991:118). A small number of women are involved in violent street crime in ways that go beyond "preventing victimization," and appear to find support among their male and female peers for these activities. To draw this conclusion is not to suggest that women's use of violence is increasing, that women are "equals" on the streets, or that gender does not matter. It does suggest that researchers should continue developing feminist perspectives to address the issue.

What is most notable about the current research is the incongruity between motivations and accomplishment of robbery. While a comparison of women's and men's motivations to commit robbery reveals gender similarities, when women and men actually commit robbery their enactments of the crime are strikingly different. These differences highlight the clear gender hierarchy that exists on the streets. While some women are able to carve out a niche for themselves in this setting, and even establish partnerships with males, they are participating in a male-dominated environment, and their actions reflect an understanding of this.

To accomplish robberies successfully, women must take into account the gendered nature of their environment. One way they do so is by targeting other females. Both male and female robbers hold the view that females are easy to rob, because they are less likely than males to be armed and because they are perceived as weak and easily intimidated. Janet Outlaw describes women's robbery of other women as "just a woman to woman thing." This is supported by Ne-Ne's description that her male friends do not participate with her in robberies of females, and it is supported by men's accounts of robbing women. While women routinely rob other women, men are less likely to do so, perhaps because these robberies do not result in the demonstration of masculinity.

At the same time that women articulate the belief that other women are easy targets, they also draw upon these perceptions of women in order to rob men. Two of the women describe committing robberies much in keeping with Maher's (1997) descriptions of "viccing." In addition, a number of women used men's perceptions of women as weak, sexually available, and easily manipulated to turn the tables and manipulate men into circumstances in which they became vulnerable to robbery—by flirting and appearing sexually interested in them. Unlike women's robberies of other women, these robberies tend not to involve physical contact but do involve the use of guns. Because they recognize men's perceptions of women, they also recognize that men are more likely to resist being robbed by a female, and thus they commit these robberies in ways that minimize their risk of losing control and maximize their ability to show that they're "for real."

West and Zimmerman (1987:139) note that there are circumstances in which "parties reach an accommodation that allow[s] a woman to engage in presumptively masculine behavior." In this study, it is notable that while both women and men recognize the urban street world as a male-dominated one, a few of the women interviewed appear to have gained access to male privilege by adopting male attitudes about females, constructing their own identities as more masculine, and following through by behaving in masculine ways (see also Hunt, 1984). Ne-Ne and Janet Outlaw both come to mind in this regard—as women who completed robberies in equal partnerships with men and identified with men's attitudes about other women. Other women, such as Lisa Jones and Tish, accepted not only women's position as secondary, but their own as well. While Ne-Ne and Janet Outlaw appeared to draw status and identity from their criminality in ways that went beyond their gender identity, Lisa Jones and Tish used their gender identity to construct themselves as noncriminal.

In sum, the women in this sample do not appear to "do robbery" differently than men in order to meet different needs or accomplish different goals. Instead, the differences that emerge reflect practical choices made in the context of a gender-stratified environment—one in which, on the whole, men are perceived as strong and women are perceived as weak.

62   JODY MILLER

Motivationally, then, it appears that women's participation in street violence can result from the same structural and cultural underpinnings that shape some of men's participation in these crimes, and that they receive rewards beyond protection for doing so. Yet gender remains a salient factor shaping their actions, as well as the actions of men.

Though urban African-American women have higher rates of violence than other women, their participation in violent crime is nonetheless significantly lower than that of their male counterparts in the same communities (Simpson, 1991). An important line of inquiry for future research is to assess what protective factors keep the majority of women living in underclass settings from adopting violence as a culturally legitimate response. While research shows that racial and economic oppression contribute to African-American women's greater participation in violent crime, they do not ensure its occurrence. Daly and Stephens (1995:208) note: "Racism in criminological theories occurs when racial or cultural differences are overemphasized or mischaracterized *and* when such differences are denied." Future research should strive to strike this balance and attend to the complex issues surrounding women's participation in violence within the urban street world.

REFERENCES

Agar, Michael H.
    1977   Ethnography in the streets and in the joint: A comparison. In Robert S. Weppner (ed.), Street Ethnography: Selected Studies of Crime and Drug Use in Natural Settings. Beverly Hills, Calif.: Sage.

Ageton, Suzanne S.
    1983   The dynamics of female delinquency, 1976-1980. Criminology 21(4):555—584.

Anderson, Elijah
    1994   The code of the streets. Atlantic Monthly 273:81—94.

Baskin, Deborah, Ira Sommers, and Jeffrey Fagan
    1993   The political economy of violent female street crime. Fordham Urban Law Journal 20:401—417.

Braithwaite, John and Kathleen Daly
    1994   Masculinities, violence and communitarian control. In Tim Newburn and Elizabeth A. Stanko (eds.), Just Boys Doing Business? New York: Routledge.

Campbell, Anne
    1993   Men, Women and Aggression. New York: Basic Books.

Chesney-Lind, Meda
    1993   Girls, gangs and violence: Anatomy of a backlash. Humanity & Society 17(3):321—344.

UP IT UP 63

Chesney-Lind, Meda and Randall G. Shelden
1992   Girls, Delinquency and Juvenile Justice. Pacific Groves, Calif.: Brooks/ Cole.

Daly, Kathleen and Deborah J. Stephens
1995   The "dark figure" of criminology: Towards a black and multi-ethnic feminist agenda for theory and research. In Nicole Hahn Rafter and Frances Heidensohn (eds.), International Feminist Perspectives in Criminology: Engendering a Discipline. Philadelphia: Open University Press.

Decker, Scott and Barrik Van Winkle
1996   Life in the Gang. New York: Cambridge University Press.

Federal Bureau of Investigation
1996   Crime in the United States, 1995. Washington, D.C.: U. S. Government Printing Office.

Glassner, Barry and Cheryl Carpenter
1985   The feasibility of an ethnographic study of adult property offenders. Unpublished report prepared for the National Institute of Justice, Washington, D.C.

Hill, Gary D. and Elizabeth M. Crawford
1990   Women, race, and crime. Criminology 28(4):601—623.

Hunt, Jennifer
1984   The development of rapport through the negotiation of gender in field work among police. Human Organization 43(4):283—296.

Joe, Karen A. and Meda Chesney-Lind
1995   Just every mother's angel: An analysis of gender and ethnic variations in youth gang membership. Gender & Society 9(4):408—430.

Katz, Jack
1988   Seductions of Crime. New York: Basic Books.

Kelly, Liz
1991   Unspeakable Acts. Trouble and Strife 21:13—20.

Laub, John H. and M. Joan McDermott
1985   An analysis of serious crime by young black women. Criminology 23(1):81—98.

Maher, Lisa
1997   Sexed Work: Gender, Race and Resistance in a Brooklyn Drug Market. Oxford: Clarendon Press.

Maher, Lisa and Richard Curtis
1992   Women on the edge of crime: Crack cocaine and the changing contexts of street-level sex work in New York City. Crime, Law and Social Change 18:221—258.

Maher, Lisa and Kathleen Daly
1996   Women in the street-level drug economy: Continuity or change? Criminology 34(4):465—492.

Mann, Coramae Richey
1993   Sister against sister: Female intrasexual homicide. In C.C. Culliver (ed.), Female Criminality: The State of the Art. New York: Garland Publishing.

64   JODY MILLER

Messerschmidt, James W.
    1993   Masculinities and Crime. Lanham, Md.: Rowman & Littlefield.
    1995   From patriarchy to gender: Feminist theory, criminology and the challenge
            of diversity. In Nicole Hahn Rafter and Frances Heidensohn (eds.), International Feminist Perspectives in Criminology: Engendering a Discipline.
            Philadelphia: Open University Press.

Newburn, Tim and Elizabeth A. Stanko (eds.)
    1994   Just Boys Doing Business? New York: Routledge.

Oliver, William
    1994   The Violent Social World of Black Men. New York: Lexington Books.

Sampson, Robert J. and William Julius Wilson
    1995   Toward a theory of race, crime, and urban inequality. In John Hagan and
            Ruth D. Peterson (eds.), Crime and Inequality. Stanford, Calif.: Stanford
            University Press.

Sikes, Gini
    1997   8 Ball Chicks: A Year in the Violent World of Girl Gangsters. New York:
            Anchor Books.

Simpson, Sally
    1989   Feminist theory, crime and justice. Criminology 27(4):605—631.
    1991   Caste, class and violent crime: Explaining difference in female offending.
            Criminology 29(1):115—135.

Simpson, Sally and Lori Elis
    1995   Doing gender: Sorting out the caste and crime conundrum. Criminology
            33(1):47—81.

Sommers, Ira and Deborah R. Baskin
    1993   The situational context of violent female offending. Journal of Research on
            Crime and Delinquency 30(2):136—162.

St. Louis Metropolitan Police Department
    1994   Annual Report—1993/1994.

Stack, Carol B
    1974   All Our Kin: Strategies for Survival in a Black Community. New York:
            Harper & Row.

Steffensmeier, Darrell J.
    1983   Organization properties and sex-segregation in the underworld: Building a
            sociological theory of sex differences in crime. Social Forces 61:1010—1032.

Steffensmeier, Darrell J. and Robert Terry
    1986   Institutional sexism in the underworld: A view from the inside. Sociological
            Inquiry 56:304-323.

Watters, John and Patrick Biernacki
    1989   Targeted sampling: Options for the study of hidden populations. Social
            Problems 36:416—430.

West, Candace and Sarah Fenstermaker
    1995   Doing difference. Gender & Society 9(1):8—37.

West, Candace and Don H. Zimmerman
    1987   Doing gender. Gender & Society 1(2):125—151.

UP IT UP   65

White, Jacquelyn W. and Robin M. Kowalski
   1994   Deconstructing the myth of the nonaggressive woman: A feminist analysis.
            Psychology of Women Quarterly 18:487-508.

Wilson, William Julius
   1996   When Work Disappears: The World of the New Urban Poor. New York:
            Alfred A. Knopf.

Wright, Richard T. and Scott Decker
   1994   Burglars on the Job: Streetlife and Residential Break-Ins. Boston: North-
            eastern University Press.
   1997   Armed Robbers in Action: Stickups and Street Culture. Boston: Northeast-
            ern University Press.

Jody Miller is Assistant Professor of Criminology and Criminal Justice at the University
of Missouri-St. Louis. She is currently completing a book based on her research about
gender dynamics in youth gangs.

66   JODY MILLER

Appendix. List of Interviewees (N = 37)

Name*	Sex	Race	Age (years)	Age at 1st Robbery (years)
CMW	Female	African-American	16	14
Buby	Female	African-American	17	17
Libbie Jones	Female	African-American	18	12
Tish	Female	White	18	17
Lisa Jones	Female	White	18	17
Quick	Female	African-American	19	15
Ms. Berry	Female	African-American	19	17
Janet Outlaw	Female	African-American	20	15
Ne-Ne	Female	African-American	20	16
Yolanda Smith	Female	African-American	22	19
Nicole Simpson	Female	African-American	26	17
Lisa Wood	Female	African-American	37	18
Kim Brown	Female	African-American	37	28
Jayzo	Female	African-American	43	27
Syco	Male	African-American	17	12
Cooper	Male	African-American	17	13
Taz	Male	African-American	17	14
Swoop	Male	African-American	17	16
K-Money	Male	African-American	17	16
Looney	Male	African-American	18	13
Beano	Male	African-American	18	16
Mike J.	Male	African-American	18	17
Woods	Male	African-American	18	17
Redwood	Male	African-American	19	14
Antwon Wright	Male	African-American	19	14
T-Bone	Male	African-American	19	16
Big Prod	Male	African-American	19	18
C-Loco	Male	African-American	20	14
Little Bill	Male	African-American	20	18
Damon Jones	Male	African-American	21	19
Treason Taylor	Male	African-American	22	18
Carlos Reed	Male	African-American	24	15
Prauch	Male	African-American	36	22
C.K.	Male	African-American	36	28
Bob Jones	Male	African-American	39	17
Tony Wright	Male	African-American	43	25
Wyman Danger	Male	African-American	46	21

* Pseudonyms supplied by respondents.

[11]

Possession and Use of Illegal Guns Among Offenders in England and Wales[1]

TREVOR BENNETT and KATY HOLLOWAY

Trevor Bennett is Professor of Criminology and Director, Centre for Criminology, University of Glamorgan; Katy Holloway is Research Fellow, Centre for Criminology, University of Glamorgan

Abstract: There is a growing concern about the extent of gun possession and use among criminals. Despite this concern, relatively little is known about gun ownership in the offender population. This article aims to help fill this gap by drawing on the results of interviews with arrestees conducted in 16 locations in England and Wales as part of the NEW-ADAM (New English and Welsh Arrestee Drug Abuse Monitoring) programme. In order to monitor gun crime and to take effective action, it is important to increase current knowledge about the possession and use of guns among offenders.

There is a growing concern about the extent of gun possession and use among criminals in the UK. This has been fuelled in part by the prominence given to this topic by the media. Widely publicised reports include the case of two young women killed in Birmingham who were believed to have been the victims of crossfire between rival gangs (Barker 2003). They also include a report of a 'drive-by' shooting in Harlesden in 2003 in which the police estimate that over a dozen shots were fired (Casciani 2003). However, these concerns are not confined to mass media sources. A report from the National Criminal Intelligence Service (NCIS) reported that criminal possession and use of firearms had increased between 2000 and 2002 and estimated that there could be anything from 200,000 to four million illegal firearms in circulation. The authors believe that there is concern among the police and the public about possession and use of firearms and note their own concern about the high cost of criminal firearm use for the judicial, prison, health and police services (NCIS 2002).

The NCIS report argues that some of the variation in estimates of gun involvement among offenders is a result of the current lack of consistent data on firearms. There are some national data on the use of firearms in recorded crime and data on seizures relating to firearm offences and subsequent arrests. However, there are no national statistics on the number of illegal guns in circulation or the number of criminals who possess illegal guns. As a result, little is known about firearm use within the offender population.

There are two main sources of information on the illegal use of firearms in England and Wales. These data focus mainly on offences rather than offenders. However, they provide some indirect evidence on the criminal use of guns. The first source is government official statistics that cover police recorded crime data, stop-and-search under suspicion of gun possession, and arrest data relating to firearm offences. The second source is individual research studies that cover firearm possession in specific populations, specific areas, and specific offences.

Official Statistics

The most detailed source of information on gun involvement in crime is the official police statistics on crimes in which firearms were reported to have been used. The word 'firearms' in this context means real and imitation weapons and the attribution can be based on the subjective assessment of victims or witnesses. It includes air weapons as well as conventional firearms. The word 'used' in these reports means being fired, used as a blunt instrument, or as a threat. The most recent data cover the period 2001 and 2002 and show that 0.4% of all recorded crime involved firearms (including air weapons) (Flood-Page and Taylor 2003). This proportion rose to 3.5% of all violent offences (excluding homicide) and to 4.5% for all robberies. While the percentage of offences involving firearms might appear low, the statistics show that the proportion has been increasing in recent years. Over the previous twelve months, the number of offences involving firearms other than air weapons increased by 35% and the number of offences involving handguns increased by 46%. However, a recent supplementary note from the Home Office indicates that the annual rate of increase of firearm offences fell in 2002/2003 to 3% (RDS 2003).

A second source of published official information on gun possession and use is data on the use of firearms in homicide. These data tell us that during the period 1991 to 2000/2001 the proportion of male victim homicides involving shooting as the method of killing remained in a fairly narrow range just above or just below 10%. In 2001/2002, this increased to 15%. This represents a 41% increase over the previous year and the highest proportion over the previous ten years (Flood-Page and Taylor 2003). Interestingly, at the same time, the proportion of female victim homicides involving shootings as a method of killing decreased from 6% in 1991 to 2% in 2001/2002.

The official reports on homicides provide limited information on the use of firearms as a method of killing. However, some additional data have been published based on further analysis of the Homicide Index database (Brookman and Maguire 2003). The authors report that over 40% of all homicides involving firearms were undetected (compared with under 10% of homicides as a whole). During the period 1995 to 1999, homicides involving firearms were predominantly male on male and in over a quarter of cases both the victim and the offender were black. The authors concluded that young, black males are heavily over-represented in fatal shootings as both offenders and victims.

A third data source is the official statistics for searches made under Section 1 of the Police and Criminal Evidence Act 1984 and the arrests that result from them. In 2001/2002, 8,600 searches were made in which the reason for the search was suspected firearms (Ayres, Perry and Hayward 2002). This represented an increase of 9% over the previous year and a threefold increase since 1991. In the same period, the number of arrests made in relation to searches for firearms also rose by 9% over the previous year and more than doubled since 1991.

Official data generate a rough picture of the extent and nature of involvement of guns in crime. The data sources are consistent in suggesting an increase in the use of firearms in crime over the last few years. They also tend to show that the use of firearms in certain violent crimes is reaching notable and (according to NCIS 2002) worrying proportions. However, official data are limited and only indirectly address the problem of gun possession and use among the criminal population. Little can be determined from these data about the extent of gun possession and use among offenders or the characteristics of offenders who possess and use them.

Research Studies

Smaller-scale research studies covering specific offender populations, areas and offences have the potential to provide more detail on the nature of gun possession and use among offenders.

Offender-based surveys
One method of investigating the offender population is through national or large-scale surveys of prisoners. This is a common method used in the United States. The 1991 national survey of state prison inmates based on over 13,000 inmate interviews found that 43% of prisoners had possessed a firearm at some time in their lives and 34% said that they had owned a handgun. Sixteen per cent of inmates said that they had a gun with them while committing the offence for which they were incarcerated (Beck *et al.* 1993). Unfortunately, there have been no similar national surveys of prisoners in the United Kingdom that have included questions on the commission of crime. The first national survey of prisoners in England and Wales conducted in 1991 did not include any questions of gun possession or use among offenders (Dodd and Hunter 1992).

The offender population can also be investigated through surveys of arrestees. The only surveys of arrestees conducted in England and Wales, which address the issue of gun ownership, are those conducted as part of the NEW-ADAM (New English and Welsh Arrestee Drug Abuse Monitoring) programme. Some information on gun possession among arrestees was published from the results of the pilot stage of the programme. Surveys of arrestees were conducted in four police custody suites. These showed that 36% of all arrestees reported that they had 'owned' or 'had easy access' to a gun at some time in their lives and 24% had done so in the previous twelve months (Bennett 2000). The main findings from the NEW-ADAM programme will be presented in this current article.

It should be noted that the question: 'have you ever owned or had easy access to a gun?' used in the pilot stage covers a slightly broader set of concepts than the issue of personal possession. It could be interpreted to mean, for example, the proximity of guns owned by family and friends. Following the pilot study, the question was rephrased to address possession more directly by asking arrestees whether they had ever owned a gun or had got hold of a gun for personal use.

There have been similar surveys of arrestees conducted as part of the ADAM (Arrestee Drug Abuse Monitoring) programme in the United States that have asked questions about possession and use of guns. The results are relevant to the current research because of the similarities of the methods used. A survey of over 4,000 arrestees conducted in eleven cities in 1995 showed that 39% of arrestees reported ever owning a firearm (Decker and Pennell 1995). Fifteen per cent of the sample reported that they carried a gun all or most of the time. Juvenile arrestees, gang members, and arrestees who reported selling drugs were more likely than other arrestees to report carrying a gun. Interestingly, there was no association between testing positive for illegal drugs and reported possession of a firearm.

Area-based surveys
Some information on gun possession and use among offenders can be found in research studies based in particular locations. One of the most recent research studies describes gun possession and crime in Greater Manchester (Bullock and Tilley 2002). In those divisions for which there were relevant data, the study showed that 0.8% of all recorded crimes involved firearms. This was approximately double the national rate. During the period 1998 to 2000, the number of crimes involving firearms and the proportion of crimes involving firearms both increased. Some additional information on gun possession and use among offenders was provided from the results of interviews with 15 gang members. According to the report, one-fifth of the gang members interviewed admitted gun carrying and half of them said that they had friends who did so. Information provided by the police on known shootings estimated that 60% of shootings in Manchester involved gang members, either as a victim, the offender, or both. While shootings attributable to non-gang members reduced over the study period, shootings attributable to gang members increased.

Another area-based study by Rix, Walker and Ward (1998) conducted in three rural and three metropolitan police forces investigated incidents known to the police in which a firearm was used. The study was based on 1,373 verified incidents involving firearms. They found that firearm incidents were most common in relation to the offence of robbery (about a quarter of all firearm incidents were associated with robbery or attempted robbery). The most common firearms used in robbery offences were handguns (49%) and shotguns (26%). Fifteen per cent involved replica guns.

Offence-based studies

Some additional information about gun possession and use among offenders can be found in research on specific offences. Smith (2003), for example, in a survey of more than 2,000 personal robberies in seven basic command unit areas and two British Transport Police areas, found that guns were displayed in 3% of personal robberies. This compares with less than 0.5% for all offence types.

Morrison and O'Donnell (1994) interviewed 88 armed robbers in Prison Service establishments in England. All of the interviewed robbers were asked about the type of gun they had used in the commission of their first armed robbery. Thirty-seven per cent said that they had used a replica gun that was incapable of discharging live rounds and 23% said that they merely intimated that they possessed a gun but produced nothing. The remainder possessed real guns that could discharge live rounds. The most common guns used by armed robbers were sawn-off shotguns (24%) and handguns (17%).

Research Problem

The preceding review has shown that there is some official data in England and Wales on the use of firearms in crime and some research data on the use of guns in relation to particular areas and particular offences. However, there remains little information on the possession and use of guns in the offender population. In other words, we know something about guns and offences, but we know little about guns and offenders. In particular, there is limited information on the proportion of offenders who possess illegal guns, on the use of guns in crime, and on the characteristics of offenders who possess and use guns.

The issue of gun use among offenders is of policy relevance as it affects both the police and the public and a number of other agencies, including the prison and health services. It is also important because gun crime increases the probability of serious injury of death to the victim, offender, or general public as bystanders. It would aid understanding of how to respond to gun crime if more were known about gun possession and use among offenders. A better knowledge of the level of involvement of offenders in gun crime and the characteristics of these offenders would help in designing targeted intervention strategies.

Aims

The aim of the article is to help fill the gap in research knowledge about illegal gun possession among active offenders by drawing on the offender's perspective. We aim to do this by providing new information on gun ownership and use among arrestees currently held in police custody suites.

241

Methods

Data on illegal guns were collected as part of the New English and Welsh Arrestee Drug Abuse Monitoring (NEW-ADAM) programme. This was a three-year, rolling programme of surveys, covering 16 custody suites in England and Wales, conducted during the period 1999 to 2002. Arrestees were selected for interview over a 24-hour period for seven days a week during the survey period (approximately 30 days). The surveys aimed to sample 100% of arrestees considered eligible for interview. Arrestees were deemed ineligible if they were unfit for interview, unable to comprehend the interview or provide informed consent, a potential danger to the interviewer, or under the age of 17 years. Arrestees were also excluded if they had been in custody for more than 48 hours or if they were not at liberty prior to entering the custody suite.

The following analysis is based on the results of interviews conducted in the second and third years of the programme, covering the period 2000 to 2002. A total of 9,499 arrestees were processed through the 16 custody suites during the periods covered by the research. About 60% of these (5,628) were deemed eligible for interview. Approximately 64% of eligible arrestees (3,618) were approached for interview. Eighty-seven per cent of arrestees approached (3,135) were actually interviewed. The majority of arrestees interviewed were male (86%) and aged 25 or older (51%).

A team of four contract researchers was used to interview the arrestees. Each arrestee was interviewed using an interviewer-administered questionnaire. The questionnaire comprised two parts: (i) a core questionnaire (which included questions on recent and past drug consumption, and (ii) two follow-up questionnaires (versions A and B) containing additional questions on gun ownership or drug markets. All interviewees completed the core questionnaire and were randomly allocated to complete one of the two follow-up questionnaires. This article focuses on the 1,570 arrestees who answered follow-up questionnaire A on gun ownership.

Results

About one-quarter of arrestees selected for questionnaire A said that they had 'owned or got hold of' (henceforth 'possessed') a gun at some point in their lives and about one-tenth had done so in the previous twelve months (see *Table 1*). Gun possession was defined as 'illegal' when the stated reasons for possessing the gun included illegal reasons (for example, for protection, to impress people, use in a criminal activity and other reasons deemed to be illegal). Gun possession was defined as 'legal' when the stated reasons included only legal uses (for example, hunting, target shooting or as part of military training). Using these criteria, the results show that 20% of arrestees possessed an illegal gun in their lifetime and 8% had done so in the previous twelve months.

Type of Gun

All arrestees who reported gun possession at some point in their lives were asked about the type of gun owned. The most common 'illegal' gun

TABLE 1

Prevalence of Legal and Illegal Gun Possession Among Arrestees

		Ever		In the previous 12 months	
		%	n	%	n
Gun possession		23	352	8	127
	Illegal gun possession*	20	300	8	118
	Legal gun possession†	3	52	1	9
No gun possession		77	1,176	92	1,400
Total‡		100	1,528	100	1,527

(*Notes:* *Gun possession is classified as 'illegal' when the stated reasons for possessing the gun included illegal reasons (e.g. for protection, to impress people, use in a criminal activity, and other reasons deemed to be illegal). It includes arrestees who reported both illegal and legal gun possession.
†Gun possession is classified as 'legal' when the stated reasons for possessing the gun was only for legal use (e.g. hunting, target shooting or as a legitimate part of their job [e.g. military use]). It excludes arrestees who also reported illegal gun possession.
‡Some missing values. Maximum n = 1,570)

TABLE 2

Type of Illegal Gun Possessed Ever

	n of arrestees who possessed a named gun type (either alone or with other gun types) n	% of arrestees who possessed an illegal gun who possessed a named gun type %
Airgun	73	25
Handgun	177	60
Shotgun	90	30
Rifle	19	6
Replica	21	7
Other	25	8
Total	297	100

(*Note:* Multiple responses are possible and the results do not add to 100%. Responses are not shown over the previous 12 months as the breakdown might result in small cell sizes and potentially misleading results. The table is based on arrestees who possessed an illegal gun only (n = 300). Some missing values)

possessed was a handgun. This was reported by 60% of arrestees who said that they had owned or got hold of a gun for illegal reasons. Thirty per cent of arrestees who reported possessing a gun said that they had possessed a shotgun and one-quarter reported that they had possessed an airgun. Rifles, replica guns, and 'other' guns were cited less frequently (between 6% and 8% of those reporting gun possession) (see *Table 2*).

In order to get some idea about multiple gun ownership, the responses were aggregated across individuals. On average, arrestees who possessed guns tended to specialise in just one gun type. Nearly three-quarters of respondents reported owning just one gun type. The mean number of gun types possessed across all gun-possessing arrestees was 1.4. A small number of arrestees (about 7% of all those who reported possessing an illegal gun) reported owning three or more gun types.

Reasons for Gun Possession

Arrestees who reported possessing an illegal gun were asked about their reasons for owning one. The most common reason given, reported by more than one-third of arrestees, was protection or self-defence (see *Table 3*). About one-fifth said that they obtained a gun to use for criminal activity. Others said that they wanted a gun to impress people.

More than one-quarter of arrestees who possessed illegal guns gave additional reasons that were coded as 'other'. These arrestees were asked to specify the other reasons. Other reasons included holding or 'passing on' a gun to others (n = 15), for 'fun' (n = 14), to 'intimidate' (n = 9), and 'selling on' or 'renting' (n = 8).

In a supplementary question, the respondents were asked specifically whether their reasons had 'anything to do with drugs'. About one-third of those who said that they possessed an illegal gun said that their reasons for doing so had something to do with drugs. The largest proportion of arrestees (about one-third of those who gave a reason) said that they possessed an illegal gun for protection when dealing drugs. Others said that they obtained a gun to intimidate others when dealing drugs or carried a gun when dealing without specifying whether it was for

TABLE 3
Reasons for Possessing an Illegal Gun Ever

	%	n
What were your reasons for owing or getting hold of a gun?		
Protection	36	108
To impress people	7	21
To use on an offence	21	62
Other	27	82
Total n	–	300
Did your reason for owning or getting hold of a gun have anything to do with drugs?		
Yes	32	95
No	68	205
Total n	–	300

(*Note:* Multiple responses are possible and the results do not add to 100%. Responses are not shown over the previous 12 months as the breakdown might result in small cell sizes and potentially misleading results. The table is based on arrestees who possessed an illegal gun only (n = 300))

TABLE 4
Percentage of Arrestees who Used an Illegal Gun on an Offence

	n of arrestees who had taken a gun with them on an offence		% of arrestees who possessed an illegal gun who had taken a gun with them on an offence		% of all arrestees n = 1,570	
	Ever	Previous 12 months	Ever	Previous 12 months	Ever	Previous 12 months
Used on offence*	76	25	26	23	5	2
Not used on an offence	213	82	74	77	14	5
Total†	289	107	100	100	19	7

(*Notes:* *The term 'used' refers here to possession of a gun during the commission of a crime.
†Some missing values. Maximum 'ever' n = 300, 'previous 12 months' n = 118)

protection or intimidation. Some arrestees mentioned using a gun to commit crimes relating to drugs. These included robbery for money for drugs and robbery of drug dealers for drugs or cash. Other reasons mentioned were using a gun as currency to trade for drugs and using a gun to take revenge against drug dealers.

Gun Carrying on Offences

All arrestees who reported possessing an illegal gun were asked if they had ever had a gun with them when they had committed an offence. Over a quarter of arrestees (26%) who had ever possessed a gun said that they had carried a gun on an offence during this period. A similar proportion (23%) of arrestees who had possessed a gun in the previous twelve months said that they carried one on an offence. In total, 5% of all arrestees in the study sample said that they had taken a gun with them on an offence at some time in their lives, and 2% had done so in the previous twelve months (see *Table 4*).

The most common type of gun ever taken on an offence was a handgun (80%) followed by a shotgun (50%). Few arrestees said that they carried an airgun at the time of an offence (13%) and even fewer reported using a replica gun (9%), a rifle (4%), or 'other' types of gun (4%) (see *Table 5*). The type of guns carried on an offence had a similar distribution to the type of guns possessed. However, handguns were slightly over-represented (60% of all guns possessed and 80% of all guns used on an offence) and airguns were slightly under-represented (25% of all guns possessed and 13% of all guns used on an offence). Another way of looking at this is to compare the proportion of arrestees who owned a specific gun type with the proportion using it on an offence. About one-third of arrestees who

TABLE 5
Type of Illegal Guns Ever Used on an Offence

	n of arrestees who possessed an illegal gun	n of arrestees who used an illegal gun on an offence	% of all arrestees who possessed an illegal gun who used it on an offence	% of arrestees who possessed an illegal gun who used it on an offence	% of all arrestees who were interviewed who used a particular gun on an offence
Airgun	73	10	13	14	1
Handgun	177	61	80	34	4
Shotgun	90	38	50	42	2
Rifle	19	3	4	16	<1
Replica gun	21	7	9	33	<1
Other gun	25	3	4	12	<1
Total n	300	76	76	–	1,528

(*Note:* Multiple responses are possible and the results do not add to 100%. Responses are not shown over the previous 12 months as the breakdown might result in small cell sizes and potentially misleading results. The table is based on arrestees who possessed an illegal gun only (n = 300). The term 'used' refers here to possession of a gun during the commission of a crime)

said that they owned a handgun said that they had used it on an offence, compared with 13% of arrestees who said that they owned an airgun. Hence, handgun owners are at greater risk than airgun owners of using a gun on an offence. In total, 4% of all arrestees in the study said that they had taken a handgun with them on an offence.

Who Possesses Guns?

As mentioned earlier, there is little official information available on the characteristics of people who possess and use illegal guns. Research conducted in the United States suggests that juveniles, ethnic minorities, and males might be over-represented in terms of gun possession. However, there is little evidence of this kind in the United Kingdom.

The current research shows that a higher proportion of males than females reported illegal gun possession ever and in the previous twelve months. This difference was statistically significant at $p < 0.05$ for the whole lifetime, but just fell short of significance at this level for the previous twelve months. However, this difference was significant at the lower probability level of $p = 0.07$ (see *Table 6*).

There is some evidence from the table that younger arrestees were more likely than older arrestees to possess illegal guns. The relationship between gun possession and age is statistically significant in relation to the twelve-month results. The relationship was not significant over the whole lifetime. One explanation for this difference is that there has been an increase in gun possession among young people over time.

TABLE 6

Prevalence of Illegal Gun Possession Among Arrestees by Demographic Characteristics

		Ever			Previous 12 months		
		%	n	Sig.	%	n	Sig.
Gender							
	Males	21	1,308		8	1,305	
	Females	9	220	p < 0.001	5	222	p = 0.07
Age							
	17–19	23	358		14	356	
	20–24	19	400		8	397	
	25–29	21	280		7	281	
	30 or more	17	490	ns	4	493	p < 0.001
Ethnic group							
	White	20	1,228		8	1,207	
	Other groups	18	299	ns	8	319	ns
Total		18	1,528		8	1,527	

(*Note:* Some missing values. % based on valid cases only)

The final comparison in *Table 6* shows the relationship between ethnic group status and gun possession. There is no evidence from the table of a statistical association between gun possession and ethnic minority status in either their whole lifetime or in the previous twelve months.

Guns, Drugs and Crime

Studies of gun possession among arrestees in the United States have shown some connection between gun possession and gang membership, violent crime, and involvement in the sale of drugs (Decker and Pennell 1995). However, there is less evidence that there is a connection between use of drugs and gun possession. This final section looks at the links between gun possession, drugs and crime among the NEW-ADAM arrestees.

The bivariate comparisons show that there is a strong correlation between drug use and gun possession. Six per cent of non-drug users reported gun possession, compared with 17% of users of drugs other than heroin, crack, and cocaine and 30% of users of heroin, crack and cocaine (see *Table 7*). All differences were statistically significant. There was also a strong correlation between criminal behaviour and gun possession. Four per cent of self-reported non-offenders said that they possessed a gun, compared with 14% of low-rate offenders and 29% of high-rate offenders.

The connection between gun possession and criminal behaviour varied slightly by type of offence committed. The highest prevalence of gun possession was among arrestees who reported that they had ever committed robbery (44%) and lowest among arrestees who reported that

247

TABLE 7

Prevalence of Illegal Gun Possession Ever Among Arrestees by Drug Use and Crime Ever

Drugs and crime ever		Illegal gun possession ever			
		%	n	Sig.#	Sig.†
Drug use					
	Non drug users	6	190		
	Non-HCC drugs only	17	454	***	
	Heroin	25	583	***	**
	Crack	26	601	***	**
	Cocaine	27	649	***	***
	Heroin, crack, and cocaine	30	352	***	***
Criminal behaviour					
	Non offender	4	286		
	Low-rate offender	14	480		
	High-rate offender	29	759		
	Robbery	44	170	***	
	Theft person	43	112	***	
	Drug supply	39	370	***	
	Burglary non-dwelling	36	361	***	
	Burglary dwelling	33	340	***	
	Theft motor vehicle	33	481	***	
	Fraud	32	366	***	
	Taking motor vehicle	34	502	***	
	Handling	29	699	***	
	Shoplifting	21	946	***	
	Current gang member‡	52	48	***	
	Past gang member	43	136	***	
	Non-gang member	15	1,127		
Total		20	1,528		

(*Notes:* Some missing values. % based on valid cases only. Responses are not shown over the previous 12 months as the breakdown might result in small cell sizes and potentially misleading results. 'HCC' = heroin, crack and cocaine. Chi-square test corrected for continuity. *** = p < 0.001; ** = p < 0.01; * = p < 0.05

#Significance test comparison based on non-drug users in the 'drug use' section and non-offenders in the 'criminal behaviour' section

†Significance test comparison based on non-HCC drug users

‡Significance test comparison based on non-gang members. The gang question was asked in 14 of the 16 sites included in the survey)

they had committed shoplifting (21%). These results discussed above are similar to those reported in the United States that show an association between gun carrying, violence, and drug supply offences.

The table gives further support to the US findings by showing that gang members were significantly more likely than non-gang members to possess a gun. As part of the NEW-ADAM survey, arrestees in 14 of the 16 locations were asked if they were currently or had ever been a gang member. The question included a preamble that provided some indication of the meaning of the term. Specifically, they were told: 'In some areas, there are local gangs that sometimes have names or other means of identification and cover a particular geographic area or territory'. They were then asked: 'Do you belong to, or have you ever belonged to, a local gang of this kind?'. A fuller discussion of variations in the definition of gang membership in the research literature and problems of interpretation is included in Bennett and Holloway (forthcoming). The results showed that half of current gang members reported gun possession.

The relationship was also investigated using multivariate analysis. A number of logistic regression analyses were conducted to determine whether individual factors, criminal behaviour, gang membership and drug use could independently explain gun possession.

Table 8 shows that the only individual level variable to predict gun possession was gender. Males were three times as likely as females to report possessing a gun. There was no significant relationship between age or

TABLE 8

Odds Ratios of Likelihood of Gun Possession Ever

Characteristic	Comparison	Odds ratio Ever
Variables in either or both equations		
Gender	Males compared with females	3.0
Criminal behaviour	Violent crime compared with no violent crime	2.8
	Property crime compared with no property crime	2.7
	Drug sales compared with no drug sales	1.8
Gang membership	Current gang members compared with non-gang members	5.3
Variables in neither equation		
Age	Ages 17-19 compared with ages 20 and above	ns
Ethnic group	White compared with other ethnic groups	ns
Drug use	Use of heroin, crack or cocaine compared with non-use of these drugs	ns
Nagelkerke R^2*		
n = 1,175		0.18

(*Notes:* All odds ratios shown are statistically significant at $p < 0.05$. 'ns' = not statistically significant. Responses are not shown over the previous 12 months as the breakdown might result in small cell sizes and potentially misleading results
*The Nagelkerke R^2 is the non-parametric test equivalent of the parametric test R^2 in that it provides an estimate of the proportion of the variance explained by the model)

ethnic group status and gun ownership, once other factors had been taken into account. The table also shows that involvement in criminal behaviour independently explained gun possession. Violent offenders were 2.8 times as likely as non-violent offenders to report possessing a gun. Property offenders were also more likely than non-property offenders to admit to illegal gun possession. However, the overall strongest predictor of gun possession was gang membership. Gang members were 5.3 times as likely as non-gang members to report owning a gun.

In line with US research, the current study shows that heroin, crack, and cocaine use (as opposed to supply) was not related to gun possession, once other factors had been taken into account. Hence, the bivariate connection between drug use and gun possession discussed earlier is likely to be a product of factors associated with drug use, such as involvement in frequent criminal behaviour and lifestyle factors associated with drug dealing.

Discussion

The article has argued that there is growing concern about the possible expansion of possession and use of illegal guns among criminals. Despite this concern, relatively little is known about gun ownership among offenders. This is because the main official data primarily concern guns and offences. There are no national statistics on the population of criminals who have access to a gun or have used a gun on an offence. Independent studies that have investigated gun possession among offenders have been largely confined to specific offences, offenders or locations. It is important that more is known about illegal gun possession among offenders in order to understand the phenomenon and to take effective action against it. In particular, it would be helpful to know more about the possession and use of guns from the offender's perspective. This includes better information on who carries guns, the types of guns carried, offenders' reasons for carrying guns, and their use of guns in criminal activity.

Some of the above questions have been addressed in the current research. The survey showed that about one-quarter of arrestees interviewed said that they had owned or got hold of a gun at some point in their lives and about one-tenth had done so in the previous twelve months. The most common illegal gun possessed was a handgun and the most common reason for possessing a gun was protection. One reason for wanting the protection of a gun was during drug dealing or drug purchasing. Over one-third of arrestees who possessed a handgun said that they had used it on an offence. Male arrestees were more likely than female arrestees to possess a firearm and younger arrestees were more likely than older arrestees to do so. Gun possession was most common among high-rate offenders, violent offenders, those involved in drug supply offences, and gang members.

While accepting that the number of arrestees answering the questions on gun ownership is fairly small, the results of the interviews conducted as part of the NEW-ADAM programme are similar to those obtained from the

ADAM surveys in the United States. These show that firearm ownership is most common among juveniles, gang members, and those who reported selling drugs. These characteristics reflect the broader characteristics of the new forms of youth crime that developed in the United States during the 1980s and 1990s. The main features of this development were an expansion in gang membership, greater gun involvement, an increase in drug misuse, and an increase in youth violence (Zimring 1998). It has been argued that youth crime in the United Kingdom shares some of the features of youth crime in the United States. Shropshire and McFarquhar (2002), for example, note the increased incidence of 'turf wars' among rival gangs, 'drive-by shootings', 'rites-of-passage' violence, and 'retaliatory' violence. NCIS have also noted similar elements of violent crime in the United Kingdom such as 'black-on-black firearm crime', use of guns 'to enforce drug debts' and use of guns 'to punish perceived disrespect' (NCIS 2002).

There is a growing body of evidence that suggests that use of firearms among criminals is increasing. In order to monitor this process and to take effective action, it is important to increase current knowledge about the possession and use of guns among offenders. There are a number of potential intervention strategies that can be used to target gun possession and use of guns in criminal activity, such as education programmes, gun amnesties, gang-suppression programmes, community organising, and zero-tolerance policing (Decker and Van Winkle 1996). However, in order to implement these programmes effectively, it is important to develop a broad knowledge base of the extent, nature and purpose of gun possession among offenders.

Note

1 The findings reported in this article derive from the NEW-ADAM (New English and Welsh Arrestee Drug Abuse Monitoring) programme, which was funded by the UK Home Office. The opinions expressed in the article are not the official view of the Home Office and should not be considered an indication of Home Office policy.

References

Ayres, M., Perry, D. and Hayward, P. (2002) 'Arrests for notifiable offences and the operation of certain police powers under PACE', *Home Office Statistical Bulletin, 12/02, 7 November,* London: Home Office.

Barker, P. (2003) 'Break this murderous fashion', *The Guardian, 7 January,* (available at website: *www.guardian.co.uk/comment/story/0,3604,869917,00.html*)

Beck, A., Gilliard, D., Greenfeld, L., Harlow, C., Hester, T., Jankowski, L., Snell, T., Stephen, J. and Morton, D. (1993) *Survey of State Prison Inmates, 1991,* Washington, DC.: US Department of Justice, Office of Justice Programs, Bureau of Justice Statistics.

Bennett, T.H. (2000) *Drugs and Crime: The Results of Second Developmental Stage of the NEW-ADAM Programme* (Home Office Research Study No.205), London: Home Office.

Bennett, T.H. and Holloway, K.R. (forthcoming) 'Gang membership, drugs and crime in the UK', *British Journal of Criminology.*

Brookman, F. and Maguire, M. (2003) *Reducing Homicide: A Review of Possibilities* (Online Report 01/03), London: Home Office.

Bullock, K. and Tilley, N. (2002) *Shootings, Gangs and Violent Incidents in Manchester: Developing a Crime Reduction Strategy* (Crime Reduction Research Series Paper 13), London: Home Office.

Casciani, D. (2003) 'Did the gun amnesty work?', 30 April, BBC News, UK Edition, (available at website: *news.bbc.co.uk/1/hi/uk/2988157.stm*).

Decker, S. and Pennell, S. (1995) *Arrestees and Guns: Monitoring the Illegal Firearms Market* (Research Preview, September), Washington, DC.: US Department of Justice, Office of Justice Programs, National Institute of Justice.

Decker, S.H. and Van Winkle, B. (1996) *Life in the Gang: Family, Friends, and Violence*, New York, NY.: Cambridge University Press.

Dodd, T. and Hunter, P. (1992) *The National Prison Survey 1991*, London: HMSO.

Flood-Page, C. and Taylor, J. (2003) 'Crime in England and Wales 2001/2002', *Home Office Statistical Bulletin 01/03*, London: Home Office.

Morrison, S. and O'Donnell, I. (1994) *Armed Robbery: A Study in London* (Occasional Paper No.15), Oxford: University of Oxford, Centre for Criminological Research.

NCIS (2002) *UK Threat Assessment 2002: The Threat from Serious and Organised Crime*, London: National Criminal Intelligence Service.

RDS (2003) 'Gun crime latest trends', Supplementary note to *Statistical Bulletin 13/06. Crime in England and Wales: Quarterly Update to June 2003*, London: Home Office.

Rix, B., Walker, D. and Ward, J. (1998) *The Criminal Use of Firearms* (Ad hoc Policing and Reducing Crime Unit Publications, No.AH255), London: Home Office.

Shropshire, S. and McFarquhar, M. (2002) *Developing Multi-Agency Strategies to Address the Street Gang Culture and Reduce Gun Violence Among Young People* (Briefing No.4), Manchester: Steve Shropshire and Michael McFarquhar Consultancy Group.

Smith, J. (2003) *The Nature of Personal Robbery* (Home Office Research Study No.254), London: Home Office.

Zimring, F.E. (1998) *American Youth Violence*, New York: Oxford University Press.

Date submitted: December 2003
Date accepted: February 2004

[12]

GENERATING COMPLIANCE
The Case of Robbery

DAVID F. LUCKENBILL

ONE OF THE CENTRAL ideas in interactionist social psychology is that coorientation is vital for concerted action (Mead, 1934; Shibutani, 1961: 40-48; Scheff, 1967). When individuals are cooriented, they operate from a common definition of the situation, a common frame for interaction. When individuals operate from a common frame, they can coordinate their respective actions to form a joint act. While coorientation usually has been studied in situations of cooperation, it also must appear in situations of conflict, such as coercion (Simmel, 1950; 182-185; Schelling, 1963: 83).

Coercion requires two roles, a source and a target. In coercion, the source exacts compliance from the target, despite a conflict of interests, by means of actual or threatened punishment. A problem for social psychologists is to determine how the source manages to get the target, to adopt a particular coercive frame and act in a manner consistent with it (compare Horai and Tedeschi, 1969; Miller et al., 1969; Tedeschi et al., 1971; Tedeschi et al., 1973: 53-83). What must the source do to generate the

AUTHOR'S NOTE: I wish to thank John Baldwin, Donald R. Cressey, and Tamotsu Shibutani for their instructive comments on the larger work of which this article is a part. I also wish to thank Reynaldo Baca and Joel Best for their assistance.

EDITOR'S NOTE: David Luckenbill focuses on robbery performances as a resource for understanding the conditions under which compliance is generated in coercion target's compliance? How must the source communicate the coercive frame, and how must the source manipulate punitive resources to exact compliance? Put differently, under what conditions will the target reject the proposed frame and comply with the source's demands? Conversely, under what conditions will the target reject the proposd frame and oppose the source? This paper seeks to determine the conditions under which the source generates the target's compliance in a particular type of interpersonal coercion.

Research on this problem had been limited to certain types of coercion. It has focused on situations where the source uses the deprivation of existing resources or expected gains as the means for exacting compliance. Research generally has ignored situations where the source employs noxious stimulation to generate compliance. This is especially true when noxious stimulation takes the form of physical force, the actual or threatened infliction of bodily pain (see Goode, 1972; Wrong, 1976: 183-195). This limitation probably stems from the fact that most research on coercion uses laboratory experimentation. To be sure, experimentation is a useful method, providing substantial control over causal and extraneous conditions (Scheff, 1967b). However, there are limits to the punitive resources which sources can use in laboratory experimentation. Researchers can provide subjects with resources for inflicting either severe yet imaginary punishment, e.g., depriving targets of a large amount of play money, or real yet mild, noncorporal punishment, e.g., depriving targets of relatively small earnings from task performances. For ethical reasons, researchers cannot provide subjects with resources for inflicting genuine, severe punishment, causing targets physical injury.

based on physical force. Luckenbill suggests that the coercive frame is a collective transaction consisting of four time-ordered stages, each of which involves an important task which offender and victim accomplish together. Drawing from the robbery data, Luckenbill offers several hypotheses regarding the conditions under which voluntary compliance is generated in coercion based on force.

This investigation tries to determine the conditions under which the source generates the target's compliance in coercion based on physical force. Given a lack of research addressing this problem, my task is to develop hypotheses from the comparative analysis of actual cases of coercion. Although several types of transactions could be used as the data base, robbery is used to study the generation of compliance in coercion.[1] After describing the stages of joint action in robbery, some hypotheses about coercion are developed.

METHODOLOGICAL STRATEGY

Robbery is a transaction in which an offender (operating as the source) unlawfully takes goods from the possession of a victim (operating as the target), against his/her will, by means of force.[2] Two principal types of robbery are distinguished in the criminal law: "Aggravated robbery" means that the offender employs a weapon, while "robbery" signifies that the offender is unarmed. In this study, robbery refers to both types.

The data were drawn from cases of robbery and attempted robbery over a one-year period in one Texas city. Sampling was of a multistage design. Between February 1976 and March 1977, 732 cases of robbery and attempted robbery were reported to the police. Cases occurring in alternate months of that period were selected for analysis. For these six months, a roster of 354 cases was constructed. Of these cases, 93 were then excluded; 54 cases because the police had determined that the event was not a robbery or attemptd robbery, and 39 cases because there was too little information on the event. The remaining 261 cases comprised the sample for investigation; 179 cases were successful robberies, and 82 cases were attempted robberies.

28   URBAN LIFE   APRIL 1981

To understand the dynamics of robbery these transactions were reconstructed. Two types of information were used to reconstruct cases. First, official documents, including police field reports, detective follow-up reports, victim and witness statements, and, when available, offender statements, provided information on the central participants, who said and did what to whom, the chronology of action, and the orientations of the victim, bystanders, and, when available, offender. In reconstructing the event, each individual document was scrutinized for information regarding its development. This information was used to prepare separate accounts of the transaction. When all of the documents for a case were exhausted, a summary account was constructed, using the individual accounts as primary resources.[3] Second, for some of the cases, the account was augmented with in-depth interviews with one or both opponents. Interviews with 35 victims regarding 39 cases and 16 incarcerated offenders regarding 38 cases were conducted. All of the offenders spoke at length about the cases in which they were apprehended and convicted, and five offenders also discussed 22 cases in which they were not apprehended.

DYNAMICS OF THE ROBBERY PERFORMANCE

Employing analytic induction, a sequential model of robbery was developed from a comparative analysis of the cases. In this model, the robbery transaction consists of four stages, each involving an important task which the offender and victim usually accomplish together. First, the offender establishes co-presence with the victim. Second, the offender and victim develop coorientation toward a common robbery frame. Third, one or both opponents transfer the material goods. Fourth, the offender leaves the setting. Accomplishing all four tasks constitutes robbery: the offender obtains goods from the victim without apprehension during the operation.

STAGE 1

After selecting a victim, the offender moves into co-presence with the victim.[4] Co-presence is established in a particular manner. The offender moves into striking range, into a position where he/she can attack, without arousing suspicion and provoking unmanageable opposition.

The offender employs one of two strategies to establish co-presence. In 91 cases (35%), the offender used speed and stealth to rush the unwitting victim. Here, the offender locates behind "lurk lines," points behind which the victim's senses cannot penetrate (Goffman, 1971: 293), and prepares for the strike. Then, without advance warning, the offender quickly moves into the victim's presence with punitive resources at the ready:

> *Case 403.* The offender walked to the side of the gas station and saw the attendant helping several customers. He walked back to the rear of the station to wait for the customers to leave. The customers left a few minutes later. The offender donned a ski mask, pulled a handgun from his pocket, and walked to the side office window. He peered inside and saw the attendant sitting behind the desk reading. The offender crept up to the office door and pointed his handgun at the attendant. In a harsh tone of voice, the offender announced, "This is a stick up, man. Give me the money."

Although alarmed, the victim is not given the opportunity to launch an effective defense.

In 170 cases (65%), the offender established co-presence by managing a normal appearance, attempting to behave as someone the victim would see as an ordinary, legitimate part of the setting (see Goffman, 1971: 238-333). In a grocery store, for instance, the offender enters under the guise of a customer intent on purchasing goods:

> *Case 113.* The offender entered the convenience store and moved to the cooler, getting a carton of milk. He then walked to the cashier's counter where the lone clerk was located

30   URBAN LIFE   APRIL 1981

and placed the carton on the counter. The clerk noted the price of the milk and began to ring up the sale. Before the clerk hit the last register key, the offender stuck his hand in his pocket and said, "I've got a gun. Give me all the money in the register." The clerk was startled by the demand.

Or on a street in the late evening, the offender stops a passerby, making a legitimate request for information.

Both strategies require the victim's unawareness of the offender's intention. For the offender to successfully rush the victim, the victim should not spot the offender's preparations or approach. Similarly, for the offender to successfully manage a normal appearance, the victim should be convinced that the offender is the kind of person he/she claims to be (see Goffman, 1971: 268-284). Generally, the victim is unaware of the offender's operation until co-presence is firmly established; the victim is oblivious to the offender until the rush is accomplished, or the offender's presentation of self is convincing. In 48 cases (18%), however, the offender alarmed the victim, and the victim responded by laying low, consulting the offender about the grounds for alarm, or opposing the offender by attacking or fleeing from the setting.

When the offender fails to establish co-presence without alarming the victim and provoking strong opposition, the robbery is jeopardized. In two cases (1%), the robbery broke down because the offender failed to establish co-presence before alarming the victim: The victim fled before the offender moved into striking range. In two other cases (1%), the robbery broke down even though the offender established co-presence: The victim outwardly expressed alarm and prepared to attack. Certainly, given a relatively weak victim, the offender will continue with the robbery. But a seemingly capable victim, ready to attack, can cause the offender to forfeit the venture:

Case 61. The victim, an off-duty but uniformed police officer who was working part-time for a local business, walked up to the bank's night deposit drawer and dropped the deposit bag inside. He then heard someone running toward him from behind. He turned around and saw the hooded offender, wielding a tire iron, standing behind him. The victim, fearing impending robbery, reared back to strike the offender. The offender appeared surprised to see this particular person making the regular night deposit. The offender shouted, "Oh shit," dropped his tire iron, and tried to run past the victim. The victim managed to strike the offender with his fist. But unhurt, the offender ran from the scene.

STAGE II

After establishing co-presence, a task accomplished in 257 cases, the offender and victim reorient their interaction, transforming their encounter to a common robbery frame. The robbery frame consists of two elements: (1) To avoid death or injury, the victim should suppress opposition and permit the offender to take his/her goods. (2) To obtain the victim's goods, the offender should control the victim's conduct by means of force and make or supervise the transfer. When the opponents establish and act in terms of a common robbery frame, robbery usually is consummated.

Two variants of the transformation process appeared in the cases. In one variant, involving 80 cases (31%), the offender cast the victim in an acquiescent role; the victim was expected to not interfere while the offender took the goods. In a second variant, involving 177 cases (69%), the offender cast the victim in a participatory role; the victim was expected to assist the offender in the transfer.

In either case, the transformation process involves a succession of moves between the offender and victim. The offender opens the process with a move designed to provide the victim with the robbery frame. In 56 cases (22%), the offender opened with incapacitating force—bodily pain which debilitates or immobilizes the victim for a time. In the remaining 201 cases (78%), the offender opened with a command for compliance backed with a threat of punish-

32   URBAN LIFE   APRIL 1981

ment. The offender's choice of opening depends on two conditions. First, in deciding between incapacitating force and a command backed by a threat of force, the offender considers the victim's likely response to a threat given the strength of the offender's punitive resources. When the offender has what he/she considers to be lethal resources,[5] such as a firearm or knife, he/she envisions that a command backed with a threat will intimidate the victim into immediate compliance:

> *Offender #2:* You know, if somebody came up to me and said, "Give me your money," and he had a gun or machete, I'd give him everything. I mean, it would scare the hell out of me. It would scare the hell out of anybody.

Believing the victim will comply if threatened with lethal resources, the offender opens with a command backed by a threat of force. In every case where the offender had a gun or knife, he/she opened with a command backed by a threat.

When the offender has what he/she considers to be nonlethal resources,[6] such as a club or bare hands, he/she envisions that a command backed by a threat will bring opposition, for nonlethal resources will not intimidate the victim into submission:

> *Offender #7:* In strongarms, you have to put him out of commission for a few minutes. When you haven't got a gun or knife, he won't do anything. He'll tell you to go to hell or turn on you. So all you can do is knock him out.

Believing the victim will oppose if threatened with nonlethal resources, the offender opens with incapacitating force. In 78% of the cases where the offender possessed a club or bare hands, he/she opened with incapacitating force.

A second condition is the victim's value to the transaction. The victim may be necessary, either to sustain the fiction before outsiders that the offender and victim are involved in a respectable activity, or because the victim has knowledge and skill needed for the robbery:

> *Offender #7:* (The victim is) really important. He knows how to open the safe and he can open the registers. It's funny. You got to have him, but you can't let him think you need him. . . . You want to make him think you'd just as soon kill him as anything else, you know, that you don't need him. But you really do. If he won't open the safe, you're dead. You might as well leave.

When the victim is considered unnecessary, the offender opens with incapacitating force or a command backed by a threat of force, depending on the strength of his/her punitive resources. When the victim is cast in an acquiescent role, there is a strong relationship between the mode of opening and the strength of the offender's resources: if the offender has lethal resources, he/she always opens with a command backed by a threat of force; if the offender has nonlethal resources, he/she almost always opens with incapacitating force. But when the victim is considered necessary, the offender always opens with a command backed by a threat of force, independent of the strength of his/her punitive resources. In cases where the victim is cast in a participatory role, there is no relationship between the mode of opening and the strength of the offender's resources.

Except for one case (1%) where the robbery broke down because the offender and victim did not share a common language, and 28 cases (11%) where the victim was felled, the opening move surprised the victim. The move violates the expected tenor of action which the victim normally experiences in the setting. Momentarily shocked and disoriented, the victim delays routine action in order to determine whether the move should be taken as a sign of a prank or exploitation. Thus, attention focuses on the tenability of the robbery frame (see LeJeune and Alex, 1973).

34   URBAN LIFE   APRIL 1981

In reassessing the situation, the victim may ask the offender if he/she is serious. The offender responds in ways which indicate that he/she is serious and the proposed frame should be adopted: the offender states that he/she is serious, repeats the command, or uses force. The victim also looks for cues in assessing the tenability of the proposed frame, such as the offender's appearance, armament, and comportment. When the offender appears cold and hardened or tense and nervous, when he/she is armed, or when he/she uses force or acts as though force is imminent, the victim suspends doubts and considers the proposed frame believable.

Accepting the robbery frame as tenable, the victim adjusts, either accepting or challenging the frame. In 151 cases (66% of the 228 remaining cases), the victim complied; in 77 cases (34%), the victim opposed. In 28 of the latter cases, the victim noncomplied, refusing to adopt the role in which he/she had been cast; in 49 cases, the victim resisted, trying to block or overcome the offender.

The manner in which the victim responds depends on two conditions. First, the victim considers the offender's capacity to inflict death or serious injury. The offender is considered capable when he/she appears to possess lethal resources and to be in a position to use them, and when the victim cannot mobilize resources for opposition. Second, the victim evaluates the offender's intent regarding the use of force—whether the offender intends to inflict punishment only for opposition or regardless of opposition. If the offender appears capable of inflicting severe punishment and the use of force seems contingent on opposition, the victim complies:

Victim #4: I wasn't going to try anything because he had a pistol. When he's got a piece, you give him the money. That's all there is to it. If you try anything, he might shoot you.

When the offender appears incapable of inflicting serious injury, the victim resists:

> *Victim, Case 429:* He stuck his hand in his shirt and told me, "I'm sorry too but this is a holdup." I asked him, "Where's the gun?" I wasn't going to give him any money if he didn't have a gun. Sometimes robbers try to bluff you. They just say they have a gun, but they really don't. If he showed a gun, I would have given him the money. He never showed a gun, so I never gave him money.

And when the victim believes the offender intends to use force regardless of the victim's response, the victim also resists. However feasible its success may seem, resistance offers a chance for avoiding death or injury:

> *Case 401:* The offender pulled a hunting knife from his pocket, walked to the cashier's counter, and stated, "I want all your money." The clerk stood motionless behind the counter. The offender responded to such inaction by raising the knife over his head and shouting, "I'm going to kill you and take the money." Fearing impending death, the clerk grabbed the offender's arm and tried to take away the knife.

The victim's response provides the offender with feedback. When the victim complies, then he/she ratifies the robbery frame. But when the victim opposes or appears to oppose, the frame is in doubt.[7] The offender can respond to opposition in any of several ways: in 31 cases (36% of the 85 remaining cases), the offender issued a warning against further opposition; in 8 cases (9%), the offender coupled a command for compliance with prodding force—bodily pain short of debilitating or immobilizing the victim; in 20 cases (24%), the offender used incapacitating force; and in 26 cases (31%), the offender forfeited the robbery.

The way the victim opposes affects the offender's response. When the victim does not try to block or overcome the offender, then salvaging the robbery is the most feasible

Gun Crime

response, adopted in almost every case. But, when the victim resists and seems capable of overcoming the offender, then salvaging the robbery is not feasible; in half of these cases, the offender forfeited the robbery.

How the offender salvages the robbery depends on the same conditions involved in opening the transformation. When the offender has lethal resources, he/she will warn or prod the victim in order to demonstrate capacity and determination and thereby intimidate the victim:

> *Offender #7:* I wouldn't kill anybody. But sometimes I'd hit them. Like this one guy, you know, was stalling around, saying he didn't know the combination of the safe. So I just smacked him on the side of the head with the gun and said, "Open it." So he suddenly remembers the combination. I guess he figured I'd waste him if he kept stalling.

But when the offender has nonlethal resources, he/she will use additional force to exact compliance:

> *Offender #10:* So we hit him on the head, you know, to knock him out. . . . But I guess we didn't hit him hard enough because he started fighting back. He fought pretty good. I guess he thought he was fighting for his life. So we just hit him harder, you know, to take him out.

In addition, when the victim is considered unnecessary, the offender attempts to salvage the robbery by warning, prodding, or incapacitating the victim, depending solely on the strength of his/her resources. But when the victim is considered necessary, the offender tries to salvage the robbery by warning or prodding the victim, independent of the strength of his/her resources.

Except for 16 cases in which the victim eventually was felled, the offender's salvaging attempt usually provides the victim with information questioning the utility of the victim's preceding move. On the one hand, when the offender warns or prods the victim for intentional opposition, he/she typically brandishes a weapon, moves into striking range, informs the victim that only opposition will bring punishment, or takes charge of the victim's allies, thereby altering the conditions which the victim considers in organizing action. Such alterations bring a redefinition of the offender's capacity or intent and a shift from opposition to compliance:

> *Case 139:* The offender stated, "You see this bag? Well pick it up and give me only the cash." The clerk stared at him. The offender said, "I have a gun. If you make a sound, I'll shoot you." The clerk did not see a gun and thought the offender was bluffing. She responded, "The cash register is locked and I don't know how to open it." The offender responded, "You know how to open it. I saw you open it." The clerk stood silent, thinking about what to do. The offender pulled out a pistol, pointed it at her and stated, "Stop fucking around or I'll shoot you." The clerk spotted the pistol and feared that the offender might kill her for further opposition. She opened the cash register and give him $280.

On the other hand, when the offender prods the victim for a move which the victim deems compliance but the offender considers noncompliance, the victim believes that the offender will use force indiscriminately, and shifts from compliance to resistance. In cases where the victim shifts to or maintains opposition, the offender eventually forfeits the robbery.

When the offender and victim orient themselves toward a common robbery frame, movement toward the transfer is facilitated. But when the victim is not oriented toward the frame, and the offender fails to promote its acceptance, movement toward the transfer breaks down. In 11 cases (4% of the 257 cases entering Stage II) where the victim refused to acquiesce, and in 33 cases (13%) where the victim refused to adopt the participatory role, the robbery collapsed:

> *Case 157:* The two offenders walked up to the cashier's counter where the victim was standing. Offender #2 pulled out a small pistol, pointed it at the victim, and stated, "Hand

38   URBAN LIFE   APRIL 1981

over all the money." The victim looked at the gun and realized that the two men intended to rob her. Angered, the victim said sharply, "I'll give you nothing, you son-of-a-bitch." Before either offender could respond, the victim turned, rapped on the front window behind her, and caught the attention of two friends walking by. She yelled, "Get the police. I'm being robbed." One of the friends saw offender #2 holding a pistol on the victim. To scare the offenders, the friend rapped on the window, pointed to the parking lot, and shouted, "There's a police car over there." The offenders quickly ran out the front door.

STAGE III

After the offender and victim establish a common robbery frame, a task accomplished in 213 cases, one or both accomplish the transfer. This is a relatively simple task in which valued goods are excavated and transferred from the victim to the offender.

The transfer takes two forms. In 85 cases (40%), it seemed to follow a predetermined design; the offender wanted particular goods, leaving others untouched. For example, the victim is ordered to turn over the paper currency but not the coin change or merchandise. In 128 cases (60%), the transfer appeared to follow a search-and-seizure design; the offender took whatever valuables he/she discovered.

The role in which the victim is cast becomes important in this stage. In the 69 cases (32%) where the victim was cast in an acquiescent role, the offender used his/her knowledge and skill to make the transfer alone. But in the 144 cases (68%) where the victim was cast in a participatory role, the victim gave the goods to the offender. When the victim performs a participatory role, the offender supervises the transfer. In all cases, the offender surveyed the victim's operation, offering an implicit or explicit threat of punishment should the victim have failed to fulfill the role. In 112 cases (78% of the 144 cases), the offender also instructed the victim on how to make the transfer, e.g., to place the money in a paper bag. In 36 cases (25%), the offender attempted to certify that the victim delivered the full stock of requested goods, e.g., ordering the victim to open the second, unused cash register to see whether it has additional money.

Several obstructions can hinder the transfer and disrupt the robbery. First, the victim may not hold to the robbery frame. When the offender shifts attention from the victim to the transfer, he/she may move outside striking range or drop armed surveillance of the victim. Detecting an opening, the victim may launch an attack or attempt to flee. The offender may reinstitute the frame by moving back into striking range or warning the victim. But in 5 cases (2% of the 213 cases entering Stage III), the offender forfeited the robbery. Second, the entrance of outsiders can disrupt the robbery. When women or children (who may be defined as nonthreatening) enter the setting, the offender orders them to acquiesce and turns to the transfer. In 6 cases (3%), however, police officers or men entered the setting, and the offender fled. Third, the offender or victim may not have the knowledge and skill needed to make the transfer. When a victim who has been cast in a participatory role is unable to secure the goods, the offender usually adjusts the demand, requesting those goods which the victim can provide. But in 4 cases (2%), the offender simply forfeited the venture. When a victim has been cast in an acquiescent role and the offender lacks the knowledge and skill to secure the goods, the transfer falters. If the victim has been debilitated, the offender can recast the victim in a participatory role and enlist his/her aid. In 3 cases (1%), however, the victim's aid could not be enlisted, for he/she had been debilitated. Consequently, the transfer collapsed:

Case 443: Hearing the buzzer signaling a customer's entrance, clerk #1 walked to the front of the store. He saw offender #1 standing behind the cashier's counter. Spotting

40   **URBAN LIFE   APRIL 1981**

clerk #1, offender #1 moved toward him and, without saying a word, hit him on the head with a club. Clerk #1 fell to the floor unconscious. In the meanwhile, offender #2 moved to the back room. Spotting clerk #2 in the open rest room, offender #2 moved up behind him and struck him on the head with a club. Clerk #2 fell unconscious. The offenders then moved behind the cashier's counter and attempted to open the cash register. They were unsuccessful, even though they had depressed the main key six times (as shown by the register tape). The offenders left the store empty handed.

STAGE IV

Once the goods are transferred, a task accomplished in 195 cases, the offender leaves the setting. This involves one task, of course, but in most cases, two tasks are involved: the offender physically moves away from the victim; and the offender separates personal from situated identity, attempting to avoid identification by those who observed the event. Failure to leave the setting in either sense can lead to apprehension.

To facilitate leaving, the offender employs one or more of several strategies. He/she may adhere to a plan for expedient and stealthy departure. For instance, before entering the store, the offender parks the getaway car outside the victim's view; after the robbery the offender dashes from the store and runs for the car. By the time the victim gets outside and looks for the offender, the offender is gone. A second strategy is concealing personal identity from the victim. The offender may wear a mask or alter his/her physical appearance. One offender, for instance, would shield his brunette hair with a blond wig. A third strategy is containing the victim. In 170 cases (87%), the offender tried to hinder the victim's possible pursuit. In 94 of these cases, the offender verbally contained the victim, warning against attempts to follow, observe the getaway, or contact anyone before he/she could leave:

Case 414: The offender announced, "Okay, I'm leaving. Don't try anything because my friend is outside and he will blow your head off if you try anything." He cut the phone cord with a pocket knife. He then moved to the front door, looked back at the two clerks, and walked out. The clerks, fearing they may be killed if they attempted to pursue or observe the offender, held their positions behind the cashier's counter for several minutes. One of the clerks then went next door to phone the police.

In another 76 cases, the offender physically contained the victim. The offender bound the victim's hands and feet, placed the victim in a closet, or used force to preclude pursuit:

> *Case 400:* The clerk bent down, grabbed the money, and handed it to the offender. The offender took the money and, as the clerk started to stand up, hit her on top of the head with the butt of the pistol. She fell to the floor, startled by the blow but not injured. As soon as he had hit the clerk, the offender turned and walked from the office and out the front door, some fifty feet away. The clerk laid on the floor for what seemed like hours, trembling and afraid to get up and summon aid.

When the offender fails to move away from the victim, apprehension is likely. In 3 cases (2% of the 195 cases entering Stage IV), the victim or a coalition convened by the victim pursued and corralled the offender for the police. When the offender fails to conceal his/her personal identity, apprehension is possible. In 13 cases (7%), the victim or opposing coalition pursued the offender and learned his/her personal identity; this information was given to the police, and the offender was subsequently captured.

DISCUSSION

Robbery transactions usually involve the joint contribution of the offender and victim in accomplishing four tasks. First, the offender establishes co-presence with the victim, moving into striking range without the victim's awareness or readiness to defend against robbery. Second, the offender and victim transform their encounter toward a common robbery frame. Third, one or both opponents transfer the victim's goods. Fourth, the offender leaves the setting. Achievement of all four tasks results in robbery, while failure to accomplish any one task may result in disintegration of the transaction.

Using data on robbery, particularly on the second and third stages of the transaction, several generalizations can be advanced regarding the conditions necessary for generating voluntary compliance in coercion based on force.[8] First, the generation of compliance requires effective communication between the source and target (see Schelling, 1963). In order to assess the source's intent and respond to that assessment, the target requires understandable information. The source must communicate coherently, completely, and in a common language. Communication failing in any of these respects brings discussion over the meaning of the source's action. When discussion fails, the transaction collapses:

> *Case 2:* The offender entered the bank and moved directly to the teller's cage occupied by teller #1. The offender, his hand in his pocket, gave teller #1 a note written in Spanish. Teller #1 took the note and examined it. She announced, "I can't read Spanish. What do you want?" The offender, apparently unable to speak English, started to tremble. He looked furtively about the setting, turned around, and walked out. Teller #1 took the note to teller #2. Teller #2, fluent in Spanish, stated that the note was an order to give the offender all of her money or she would be killed.

Second, compliance requires the target to define the particular coercive frame as tenable. On the one hand, this means the target must approach the situation with a cognitive perspective amenable to defining the source's action as an indication of coercion (see Emerson, 1970). On the other hand, this requires the source to manage an appearance consistent with the particular coercive frame. The target is likely to define the frame as tenable when the source appears serious. In robbery, the offender is considered serious when he/she appears cold and hardened or tense and nervous and manipulates punitive resources in a threatening manner. If the target does not interpret the source's action as an indication of impending coercion, then he/she will not orient self to act according to that frame:

> *Case 91:* Leaning against the counter, holding a pistol, and sporting a broad grin, the offender said casually, "Be cool. This is a robbery." Spotting the pistol yet noting the offender's wide smile, clerk #1 turned to clerk #2, who was stocking shelves, and announced, humorously, "Hey, we're being robbed." Clerk #2 laughed and then stated, "Is that right?" At this point, the offender raised his pistol and told clerk #1 in a loud, harsh, voice, "Look, goddamn it, this is a robbery. Put all the money in a bag or I'll blow your fucking head off." Both clerks realized the offender was serious.

Third, the generation of compliance requires the source to manipulate punitive resources in a way that demonstrates the capacity to punish yet a judiciousness in the administration of punishment. To be sure, the level of force used to exact compliance is shaped by two conditions. One is the strength of the source's punitive resource's: the greater the strength of the source's resources, the more likely the source will use limited force, such as a threat or prodding force; the lesser the strength of the source's resources, the more likely the source will use massive force, such as incapacitating force. The relation between resource strength and level of force used is constrained by a second contingency, the value of the target to the transaction: When the target is deemed necessary to the source's goal achievement, the source is confined to using limited force, independent of the strength of his/her resources; when the target is not considered necessary, the source will use limited or massive force, depending on the strength of his/her resources.

However, to generate compliance, the source must manipulate punitive resources in a way that imparts at least two kinds of information to the target. First, the source must convey to the target that he/she has the capacity to inflict

44   URBAN LIFE   APRIL 1981

threatened punishment, that he/she possesses superior resources and can convert them into punishment (see Singer, 1958; Tedeschi, 1970; Baldwin, 1971; Michener et al., 1973). Assuming the victim could not convene an opposing coalition, when the victim believed the offender possessed lethal resources and was positioned within striking range, he/she complied. However, when the victim believed the offender did not have lethal resources or was not in the position to use them, he/she resisted. Thus, compliance is facilitated when the source manages an appearance of superior strength and advantageous position. Second, the source must convey that punishment is contingent on opposition. This information is effectively transmitted by issuing a clear threat or warning that punishment will only follow opposition. When the offender issued a threat or warning, the victim believed that the offender intended to punish only opposition. Given this judgement, the victim either complied or opposed, depending on the capacity of the offender to inflict punishment. But when the offender verbally suggested an intent to injure the victim or used prodding force in response to a move which the victim considered compliance, the victim believed that the offender planned to inflict punishment independent of the victim's action. Given this judgement, the victim opposed; opposition offered a chance for avoiding harm. Thus, compliance is facilitated when the source makes it the most attractive and profitable line of action.

NOTES

1. Robbery, like some other forms of criminal violence, is illicit coercion, typically involving strangers. These features may restrict its usefulness in generalizing to other types of coercion based on physical force. In licit coercion, such as some instances of parental control of children, the source is confined to the use of limited force. To employ massive force is to render the transaction illicit. However, when the source plans to exploit the target illegally, massive force may be acceptable to the source. In coercion involving family and friends, the source may

be restricted to limited force, for massive force would jeopardize the intimacy of the relationship. But such a restriction may not be present in such transactions as police capture of felons, skyjacking, and robbery, for these usually involve strangers who do not wish to build an intimate relationship.

2. The roles of offender and victim can each be filled by one or more individuals.

3. Parties to the transaction sometimes gave differing accounts of the event. For the most part, these discrepencies centered on the specific dialogue. Accounts were consistent with respect to the basic development of the event.

4. Because robbery generally involves only the offender and victim, and is usually designed in this way, my focus is on their activities. The behavior of bystanders will be examined only in passing.

5. Firearms and knives may be considered as "lethal" resources, for, as the interviewed offenders claimed, the offender defines them, and thinks the victim also defines them, as deadly. (See Conklin 1972: 112-119.) In 21% of the cases, the victim did not see the firearm or knife, but was informed by the offender that he/she possessed such a weapon. In some cases, the offender concealed a genuine weapon so as not to alarm bystanders, but in other cases, the weapon may have been a fiction. Whether the weapon was real or not appears to matter little, for the offender operated in the same fashion: He/She sought to intimidate the victim by claiming that he/she had the capacity to inflict death or serious injury.

6. Clubs and bare hands may be considered as "nonlethal" resources, for, as the interviewed offender claimed, the offender defines them, and believes the victim defines them, as nondeadly. (see Conklin 1972: 112-119.)

7. In 8 cases where the victim intended to comply, the offender defined the victim's move as noncompliance. In these cases, the victim qualified a part of the robbery frame, explaining that while he/she would provide whatever was available, he/she could not satisfy all of the offender's demands because of obstacles beyond control.

8. These generalizations pertain to situations in which the target has the opportunity to consciously select a course of action; they ignore cases where the target is incapacitated.

REFERENCES

BALDWIN, D. (1971) "Thinking about threats," J. of Conflict Resolution 15: 71-78.

CONKLIN, J. (1972) Robbery and the Criminal Justice System. Philadelphia: J. B. Lippincott.

EMERSON, J. (1970) "Nothing unusual is happening," in T. Shibutani (ed.) Human Nature and Collective Behavior. New Brunswick: Transaction Books.

GOFFMAN, E. (1971) Relations in Public. New York: Harper & Row.

GOODE, W. (1972) "The place of force in human society," Amer. Soc. Rev. 37: 507-519.

46   URBAN LIFE   APRIL 1981

HORAI, J. and J. TEDESCHI (1969) "The effects of threat credibility and magnitude of punishment upon compliance," J. of Personality and Social Psychology 12: 164-169.

LeJEUNE, R. and N. ALEX (1973) "On being mugged: the event and its aftermath," Urban Life and Culture 2: 259-287.

MEAD, G. (1934) Pp. 42-51 in C. Morris (ed.) Mind, Self and Society, Chicago: Univ. of Chicago Press.

MICHENER, H., E. LAWLER, and S. BACHARACH (1973) "Perception of power in conflict situations," J. of Personality and Social Psychology 28: 155-162.

MILLER, N., D. BUTLER, and J. McMARTIN (1969) "The ineffectiveness of punishment power in group interaction," Sociometry 32: 24-42.

SCHEFF, T. (1967a) "Toward a sociological model of consensus," Amer. Soc. Rev. 32: 32-46.

——— (1967b) "A theory of social coordination applicable to mixed-motive games," Sociometry 30: 215-234.

SCHELLING, T. (1963) The Strategy of Conflict. Cambridge, MA: Harvard Univ. Press.

SHIBUTANI, T. (1961) Society and Personality: An Interactionist Approach to Social Psychology. Englewood Cliffs, NJ: Prentice-Hall.

SIMMEL, G. (1950) The Sociology of Georg Simmel, K. Wolff (ed.) New York: Macmillan.

SINGER, J. (1958) "Threat-perception and the armament-tension dilemma," J. of Conflict Resolution 2: 90-105.

TEDESCHI, J. (1970) "Threats and promises," in P. Swingle (ed.) The Structure of Conflict. New York: Academic Press.

——— B. SCHLENKER and T. BONOMA (1973) Conflict, Power and Games. Chicago: Ave.

TEDESCHI, J., T. BONOMA and R. BROWN (1971) "A paradigm for the study of coercive power," J. of Conflict Resolution 15: 197-224.

WRONG, D. (1976) Skeptical Sociology. New York: Columbia Univ. Press.

DAVID F. LUCKENBILL is Assistant Professor, Department of Criminal Justice and Sociology, University of Illinois, Chicago Circle. He is engaged in research on interpersonal coercion, deviance and social organization, and deviant careers.

[13]

Armed and Dangerous? The Use of Firearms in Robbery

IAN O'DONNELL and SHONA MORRISON

Ian O'Donnell is Research Officer, University of Oxford Centre for Criminological Research and Fellow of Linacre College
Shona Morrison is Senior Officer at the Office of Strategic Crime Assessments, Canberra

Abstract: Recent years have witnessed substantial and sustained increases in the number of armed robberies recorded in England and Wales. Drawing upon an analysis of police records and interviews with convicted armed robbers, this study explores the circumstances in which such offences take place and the extent to which the guns used in robbery are actually capable of discharging lethal shot. It is hoped that this investigation will increase understanding of the phenomenon of firearm use in crime and that it will contribute to a rational consideration of what would constitute appropriate responses by potential victims, the police and other agencies of the criminal justice system.

Brief Overview of Recent Trends in the Criminal Use of Firearms

Although there is widespread concern about the criminal use of firearms, and the popular perception is of an epidemic in armed offending, it is salutary to note that the use of firearms in crime, although increasing, is still comparatively rare in England and Wales. According to the Home Office (1994) *Criminal Statistics England and Wales 1993*, about 0.3% of recorded notifiable offences involved a firearm. In this year there were 74 offences of homicide involving firearms, and firearms were reported to have been used in about 6% of attempted murders and other acts endangering life, and in 10% of robberies. The association between gun use and robbery has become firmly established. Indeed, if offences involving air weapons are excluded, robberies accounted for 75% of all armed crime. Furthermore, the average annual number of recorded armed robberies has increased greatly over the past quarter of a century – from 800 in the 1970s, to almost 2,400 during the 1980s, to more than 5,000 for the first four years of the current decade.[1]

Traditionally most robberies involving firearms have taken place in London, although recent years have witnessed substantial increases outside the capital. The annual number of robberies with firearms in the Metropolitan Police District (MPD) in 1993 was almost double what it had been a decade previously. However, in the rest of England and Wales, over the same time period, there was a fivefold increase. In 1983, 65% of all recorded robbies with firearms took place in the MPD, but by 1993 this had dropped to 42%[2].

In the country as a whole, there has been some change in recent years in the frequency with which different types of gun have been used in robbery. For example, we know that in 1993 the principal weapon used in 61% of armed robberies was reported to have been a pistol (compared with 52% in 1983); that long-barrelled shotguns were used in 7% of incidents (14% in 1983); sawn-off shotguns in 10% (17% in 1983); and 'supposed' firearms in 15% (5% in 1983)[3]. The remainder involved rifles, air weapons and miscellaneous other firearms.

However, any attempt at a definitive classification of weapon types is highly problematic. This is because apart from those rare occasions where a firearm is discharged during an offence, or recovered afterwards by the police, there is no way of knowing whether it was capable of discharging live rounds, and its categorisation must be based entirely upon the descriptions provided by victims or other witnesses.

Therefore, it is likely that a proportion of the guns which were believed to have been real on the basis of witness statements, were in fact imitations. This could be true particularly in the case of handguns because some replica pistols are so realistic that it is difficult, even for firearms experts, to distinguish them from the genuine article on the basis of their appearance alone. Thus, it would not be surprising if lay persons assumed them to be real, especially when one considers that they were seen, probably for a matter of seconds, in the highly charged context of an armed robbery. It is also possible, of course, that some of the guns used in these robberies, even if real, were unloaded or had been de-activated[4]. In other words, using existing sources of data, it is not possible to estimate the extent to which the firearms described by witnesses were genuine or imitation, loaded or unloaded.

In this context of an increasing use of firearms in robbery, together with the dearth of information about the circumstances in which armed robberies take place, and especially about the frequency with which real guns are used, the Home Office Research and Planning Unit commissioned the Oxford Centre for Criminological Research to undertake the study reported here. The aims of this study were twofold: to describe, through an analysis of police records, the nature of recorded incidents of armed robbery which occurred in the Metropolitan Police District during 1990; and through interviews with convicted armed robbers to explore the decisions they made in respect of their selection and use of firearms.

The purpose of this paper is not to analyse the relationship between gun control legislation or the availability of firearms and the incidence of armed crime (for this debate see Greenwood 1972; Kleck 1991; Kopel 1992). Nor is it to present a psychological profile of the armed robber or to explore the phenomenology of violence. The characteristics of the armed offender and the extent to which his actions may be understood within a rational choice perspective on crime have been described in detail elsewhere, and a number of commentators have begun to examine how violence more generally is learned and manifested (see Archer 1994; Feeney 1986; Gill and Matthews 1994; Haran and Martin 1984; Harding and Blake 1989; Kapardis 1988; Katz

1988, 1991; Morrison and O'Donnell 1996; Wright and Rossi 1986). Nor indeed is it primarily to advise on the prevention of robbery, although a number of potential preventive strategies will be alluded to (for such advice see Austin 1988; Ekblom 1987; Health and Safety Executive 1993; Hibberd and Shapland 1993).

Rather this paper has the modest, but not unimportant, aim of demystifying the crime of armed robbery. Its intentions are to illustrate its diversity, the extent of the harms associated with it, the kinds of weapons used to perpetrate it, and the degree to which serious injuries and deaths are caused. In this way it is hoped that it might contribute to a more sophisticated interpretation of the official statistics for armed crime and clearer thinking about how best to tackle this growing problem.

Sources of Data and Method of Data Collection

All incidents of robbery and attempted robbery which take place in the MPD and are known, or believed, to have involved a firearm[5] or imitation firearm[6], are subject to special recording procedures. When such offences are reported to the police a document called a *specrim* (report of a *spe*cially interesting *crime*), which gives a brief outline of where and when the offence took place and details of any suspects, should be sent within 24 hours from the police division where the offence occurred to the General Registry, which is the Metropolitan Police repository for files concerning serious crimes. If the incident involved an attack on a security company, bank, building society, post office, betting shop or jewellers' shop, then a *specrim* should also be sent to the Central Robbery Squad (more commonly known as the Flying Squad) at New Scotland Yard.

Detailed case files are built up for every offence which generates a *specrim*. Using these files data were collected for a total of 1,134 incidents of robbery and attempted robbery which occurred in 1990 and where a firearm, *or* what appeared to be a firearm, had been produced by the offender, *or* where the offender had given the impression, through his actions and the contents of written or verbal demands, that he possessed a gun, even though one had not actually been seen by witnesses. The vast majority of incidents for which files were available concerned the more serious robberies investigated by the Flying Squad (n=992). Few files were available for other categories of target such as for example supermarkets, public houses or bureaux de change (n=142), and it is likely that in this small number of cases a *specrim* had been produced only because the offence was considered to be particularly severe in its consequences[7].

Anyone who had been convicted of an armed robbery or attempted armed robbery which was recorded in the MPD in 1990, and who was still in custody between October 1992 and June 1993 when the fieldwork for this study was being carried out, was traced and spoken to in person by one of the authors. Eventually, exactly 100 prisoners were approached. Nine of these interviews were later discarded, usually because the interviewee maintained that he had been wrongly convicted or because he appeared to be suffering from psychiatric problems and was unable to offer any useful

information. Only five robbers refused to participate in the study, although
in two of these cases it was possible to substitute an alternative member of the
same robbery team who consented to the interview. This resulted in a final
sample of 88 completed interviews and a successful response rate of 95%[8].

The Characteristics of Recorded Armed Robberies

The incidents included in this study, classified according to the type of
target attacked, are shown in *Table 1*. The potential yield from each category
of target varied considerably. Average (median) financial losses resulting
from armed robberies ranged from just over £400 in the case of betting
shops to £20,000 for security vehicles. The minimum loss from any type of
target was less than £60 and the maxima ranged from £3,000 stolen from a
betting shop to £2,000,000 taken from a security vehicle. In the case of
jewellers' shops the figures refer to the total value of cash and jewellery
stolen. Attempted robberies have been excluded from these calculations. If
such incidents, where no money was taken, were included, the average losses
would obviously be much lower.

The number of completed armed robberies by each category of target is
also shown in *Table 1*. A robbery was considered to have been completed if
the robbers managed to breach the target's defences and escape with money
or goods, even if they were arrested shortly afterwards. The completion rate
was highest for betting offices where 90% of attacks resulted in an immediate cash loss, and for jewellers' shops where 86% of attacks achieved their
objective. Interestingly, there was substantial variation in the extent to which
robberies were completed within individual categories of target. In the case
of building societies, 69% of all attacks were successfully completed.
However, this was true for only 22% of attacks on branches of one well-known

TABLE 1
Characteristics of the Armed Robberies Included in this Study

Target	Number in sample	Median loss per completed attack (£)	Range (£)	Completed attacks
Security van	140	20,000	47-2,000,000	74%
Bank	146	2,472	35-230,000	76%
Building society	417	1,165	40-19,000	69%
Post office	128	2,022	9-45,000	43%
Betting shop	124	418	55-2,925	90%
Jeweller's shop	37	28,500	5-420,000	86%
Off-licence	33	500	25-4,893	85%
Other shop	47	371	30-27,000	89%
Filling station	16	300	45-4,120	75%
Other	46	950	5-116,000	87%

(*Source*: Metropolitan Police General Registry)

society as compared with 92% of attacks on branches of another equally well-known society. There was a similar, although less extreme, variation for banks: 64% of raids on the branches of one company were completed compared to 100% for another.

Scrutiny of the police records for each robbery in which the perpetrators left empty-handed showed that there was a variety of reasons why attacks were not completed. At some types of commercial premises, it was possible to identify several factors which were consistently associated with failure. As far as building societies were concerned, different defensive tactics seemed to produce different outcomes. For example at branches of one company, where 63% of attacks were completed, the unsuccessful robberies were almost always due to the swift activation of security screens which dropped down onto the counter. At another, which of all the major high street banks and building societies had by far the lowest rate of completed robberies (22%), raids were usually foiled when the cashiers, already behind secure screens, ran into a back office, thus leaving the counter area deserted, and the would-be offender standing on the other side of a security screen, unable to reach the money. In such incidents the robbers decamped empty-handed.

In the case of post offices, the target with the lowest overall rate of completed robberies (43%), offenders usually fled the scene when audible alarms were activated and staff ducked down behind the counters, where they were out of sight and protected from harm by secure screens. The low proportion of successful attacks on post offices may be a continuing effect of a major target-hardening initiative involving the upgrading of security screens and the installation of alarms which was embarked upon during the early 1980s in response to a worrying increase in the annual number of robberies[9].

Thus, there were several reasons why attacks failed, at least in the case of targets where there was no potential for immediate physical contact between victims and robbers. In such circumstances, it would appear that both staff behaviour (such as moving away from the vicinity of counters or ducking down below them), and crime prevention hardware (particularly security screens and audible alarms which can be activated by staff), may have important roles to play in the prevention of armed robbery.

The Type of Weapon as Described by Witnesses

According to witnesses 1,211 guns were used in the 1,134 robberies upon which this report is based. Only in cases where a firearm, or ammunition, had been recovered after the offence was it possible to establish whether the gun had been capable of firing live rounds. However, as more than 80% of guns were not recovered, this information was often unavailable. As far as could be ascertained from victim and witness statements and other information contained in police files, the types of firearm used in offences of robbery in the MPD in 1990 were as follows:

- 6% were *known* to be real guns (2.4% sawn-off shotguns and 3.6% handguns) because they were recovered afterwards by the police.

- 11% were *known* to be imitation guns because they were recovered afterwards by the police and found to be incapable of discharging any shot.

In the remaining 83% of cases, no weapon was recovered, and the guns used were categorised as follows:

- 12% were seen by witnesses and *believed* to be real shotguns. All had been 'sawn-off'.
- 55% were seen by witnesses and *believed* to be real handguns.
- 16% were *not seen* by witnesses but the robber's demeanour (for example, a protrusion from his pocket or a plastic bag), together with either a demand note (10%) or a verbal demand (6%) gave the victims the impression that he possessed a firearm.

The types of gun employed in robberies against different categories of target are shown in *Table 2*. It was virtually unheard of in attacks on security vans or jewellers' shops for robbers not to display something resembling a

TABLE 2

Type of Gun Used Against Different Targets According to Police Records
(Row percentages)

Target	Sawn-off shotgun (known or believed real)	Handgun (known or believed real)	Handgun (known imitation because recovered)	No gun seen (demand note only)	No gun seen (verbal demand only)	All
Security van	19	75	1	0	4	100
Bank	19	47	11	17	6	100
Building society	7	54	15	16	8	100
Post office	25	61	7	4	2	100
Betting shop	11	64	8	12	5	100
Jeweller's shop	33	60	5	0	2	100
Off-licence	9	60	29	0	3	100
Other shop	15	45	36	0	4	100
Filling station	19	62	12	0	6	100
Other	26	65	6	0	2	100

(*Source*: Metropolitan Police General Registry)

firearm. However, in around one-quarter of attacks on banks and building societies and one in six raids on betting shops, the threat took the form of a note or a verbal demand, and although witnesses did not report seeing anything which resembled a gun, robbers usually intimated the presence of a firearm by indicating a protrusion in a bag or under a coat. This differential pattern of gun use against the main categories of target is shown clearly in *Figure 1*.

Firearms were rarely discharged during robberies. Indeed they were fired in only 45 (4%) of the 1,134 incidents included in this sample, and in 90% of these cases they were fired without causing any physical injury. In one-third of robberies where shots were fired they were directed into the ground, in the air or towards the ceiling, usually at the beginning of an attack or when the robber perceived that his demands were not being met. On a small number of occasions shots were fired into the air as robbers vacated the premises. On 13 occasions shots were fired at the robbery victims. Fortunately, in many of these cases the victims were out of harm's way behind a security screen or in the cab of a cash-in-transit vehicle and the shots were fired into the reinforced glass.

Around two-thirds of all shots fired came from real guns, the remainder being blanks fired by imitation pistols and very occasionally pellets or darts shot from air weapons. Thus, guns which had lethal potential were fired in

FIGURE 1

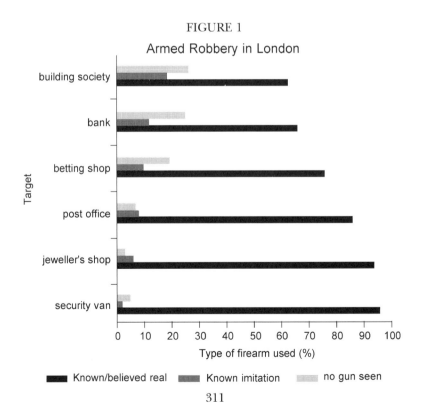

2.5% of the robberies studied. Shots were fired most often in attacks on security vans, but even for this category of target no shots were discharged in 90% of incidents.

In 7% of armed robberies (84 incidents) victims were physically injured. The likelihood of a victim being injured differed greatly according to the type of target attacked. Injuries were recorded in less than 2% of attacks on building societies, banks and betting shops. They were more frequent for attacks on security vans (16%), post offices (11%) and jewellers' shops (24%). As far as could be inferred from police files, the attacks which led to victims or bystanders being injured were commonly precipitated by attempts to intervene in order to prevent the robbery proceeding, or by a refusal to follow orders. In some cases violence was used to frighten and intimidate the victims so as to secure their compliance.

Most injuries were caused by using the firearm as a blunt instrument (28%), by punching or kicking (24%), by a different kind of weapon (18%) or by other means, for example cuts and bruises which resulted from being handcuffed or tied up during the commission of the offence (25%). In only 6% of the 84 robberies where a victim was injured – five incidents – were the injuries caused by gunfire.

Furthermore, in the five robberies where injuries resulted from the discharge of a firearm it was not always the case that shots were deliberately fired at victims or that the victim's life was in danger – the victim of a betting shop robbery was shot at close range with a blank-firing pistol and sustained burns to his shoulder; a shop owner was hit on the head with a dart from an air pistol; a jewellery shop employee was shot in the leg by a robber as he gave chase after an attempted robbery; the guard of a security van was injured when a robber fired at his leg with a shotgun; the victim of a street robbery received a head wound from a bullet discharged during a struggle with his attacker.

Thus, victims were injured in 7% of the serious armed robberies which we studied, and in 6% of these robberies the injuries were due to gunfire. In other words, less than 0.5% of serious armed robberies (1 in 200) resulted in injuries which were caused by the firearm being discharged[10].

One interesting aspect of the *modus operandi* of a minority of armed robbers was their use of written demands. Such demands were never made in robberies or attempted robberies of cash-in-transit vans or jewellers' shops and the highest proportionate use of demand notes was in raids on building societies. Notes were almost always handwritten (one or two were made from newspaper cuttings), and usually stated that the robber had a gun and was prepared to use it. They sometimes specified the amount of money required. For examples:

I've got a gun. Give me £200 or I'll shoot someone;
Money now or I start shooting;
This is a robbery I have a gun so don't try and be smart. Just hand over your cash. Just 50 and 20 pound notes. Have a merry Christmas;
If you value your life, hand over all the money;
Don't panic. Give me £4,000 or I shoot you in your head.

Demand notes were used much more frequently in cases where nothing resembling a gun had been seen by victims. Of the 184 incidents where demand notes were shown to robbery victims, it appeared from the police files that on 104 occasions (56%) nothing resembling a gun was ever displayed by the offender – in other words they relied on a subterfuge. Of course it is not possible to estimate from the police records in how many cases where no firearm was presented, the robber did in fact have a real gun which he decided not to produce.

The Robbers' Accounts

Because we could tell so little from police records about what proportion of the firearms used in robberies had been genuine and loaded, all of the 88 robbers interviewed for this project were questioned closely about the type of weapon they had used in the commission of their first armed robbery in 1990. In four cases the interviewee neither carried anything resembling a gun nor intimated to victims that he possessed a gun, the weapon being carried by an accomplice, and the interviewee's role being limited to acting as look-out or seizing the cash or goods. The following were the types of gun which the 84 'gun'-carrying robbers in our interview sample reported having used:

- 17% (14 persons) said that they had used a real pistol for the commission of the offence. All were loaded with live ammunition.
- 24% (20 persons) said that they had used a real sawn-off shotgun for the commission of the offence. Of these, 14 were loaded and six unloaded.
- 37% (31 persons) said that they had produced a weapon during the offence which bore a close physical resemblance to a real firearm but was in fact incapable of discharging live rounds. This category of imitation gun is called a 'replica' in this paper. On all but one occasion, where a toy shotgun was produced, replica handguns were used.
- 23% (19 persons) said that they had carried neither a real nor a replica firearm, but intimated from their demeanour, their verbal demands, or the contents of a demand note, that they possessed a gun. Examples of the devices used by interviewed robbers to simulate the shape of a gun – generally either in a pocket or a plastic bag – included a courgette, a tube of toothpaste and a candle. This category of imitation gun is called a 'simulated' firearm here, and the method employed is described as a 'subterfuge' or 'bluff'.

There was some variation in the type of gun used according to the category of target attacked. Security vans were never approached by robbers armed with anything other than at least one real and loaded gun. Yet, around half the robberies of post offices and banks involved robbers carrying replicas or simulating the possession of a firearm, as did the vast majority (84%) of attacks on building societies. The factors associated with weapon choice are discussed next.

Why Carry a Real Loaded Gun?

Those robbers who chose to use real guns did not do so simply because they were easily available. It became clear during our interviews that many of them believed a real firearm was an essential tool for the kind of target they planned to attack. They felt that in certain circumstances it might be necessary to fire shots, either to intimidate or to incapacitate, and therefore anything other than a genuine loaded weapon would not suffice. As some of them said:

If you fire the gun into the ceiling the money is handed over immediately.

I took a real gun in case I needed to use it.

To me it was like a tool of the trade – like a crowbar for a burglary.

Handguns and sawn-off shotguns were the preferred types of firearm because they could be easily concealed. It was interesting to note that some of those who chose sawn-off shotguns told us that they had done so specifically on account of their shocking visual appearance:

People know what a sawn-off is. If you use a pistol they might think it's a replica. If you use a sawn-off you don't have to use it if you see what I mean.

Shotguns are convincing. They look good. They put the fear of Christ into people.

As those who were in possession of real guns were capable of far greater harm than those carrying less potentially destructive weapons, it was important to discover whether they would have been prepared to use their guns to achieve their objective. Over half admitted that they had been willing to use some form of violence during the robbery if they had considered such action to be necessary, and almost all of these claimed that they would have been prepared to shoot anyone who had tried to get in their way. In other words, almost half of those robbers who carried real guns (or one in six of all the armed robbers we interviewed), stated that they were able, and willing, to shoot their victims if necessary. The threat they posed was real, and potentially fatal in its consequences:

You don't go out with a gun unless you're prepared to use it . . . Only a fool uses violence for violence's sake. Unfortunately, I'm in a violent trade. Outside, I'm a quiet man, a good neighbour. I'm not justifying it. There are different rules of engagement when I'm at 'work'. I'm never involved in violence outside a 'work' context. However, at 'work', I've always been very violent.

The determination of these offenders to commit robberies successfully and obtain large amounts of money – at almost any cost – is an important factor in explaining their weapon choice. Those who carried real firearms did so because they knew the stakes were high, and about half were prepared to shoot their guns if necessary, whether to frighten victims into compliance or to attempt to evade arrest. These offenders clearly participated in dangerous actions, putting at risk the lives of others and, indeed, themselves.

Why Carry a Replica?

Almost 90% of those who had used a replica firearm stated that if given a free choice between a replica and a real gun, they would still have opted for the replica. Indeed, three-quarters of those who used a replica firearm claimed that they could have obtained a real gun but decided not to. The usual reason why a real gun was not taken was because they felt that if they possessed one, then in certain circumstances they might fire it, and this was a risk which they were not prepared to take, as they did not want to shoot anyone. Others felt that a real gun was simply not necessary for the type of target which they wanted to attack:

I deliberately carried an imitation because I knew that if I had a real gun I would perhaps have to use it and the consequences would be catastrophic.

I chose to use an imitation so that in no circumstances could anyone be harmed.

I could have got a real shotgun but I thought that an imitation pistol was sufficient for a building society.

Thus, replicas clearly were not a weapon of second choice, taken because a real gun was unavailable, but had been deliberately selected because they were considered to be a satisfactory tool for the task. The gun was carried to intimidate rather than to cause harm, and the choice of gun reflected the limits on how far the robber was prepared to go to obtain money:

I'm only a small time thief – I'm not a gangster.

I didn't want to go into heavy stuff. Just something quick to get money.

Why Bluff?

Those robbers who carried no gun but relied on a subterfuge for the success of their attack, had also generally decided that a real firearm was not essential for the kind of robbery which they intended to commit. Almost three-quarters of bluffers said that they would have been able to obtain a real gun if they had wished to, but had decided against doing so either because 'it wasn't needed', or because they robbed on the 'spur of the moment', or because they felt that if they carried a real gun there was a chance that they would use it and this was an eventuality which they wished to avoid. In one case an interviewee had a real loaded pistol at his home but decided that simply to produce a demand note would be sufficient for the bank robbery which he carried out.

About half of our sample of bluffers claimed to have come up with the idea of carrying out a robbery in the minutes immediately before the offence took place. Another one-fifth had developed the idea from something they had read about or seen reported in the media:

You can learn a lot from Crimewatch. You see people's mistakes and it's exciting to watch. It gives people ideas.

Television gives you a good idea about what to do. I heard about someone who used a cucumber in a bag so I copied this method.

Given the spontaneity with which many of these offences occurred, it was not surprising to find that the level of planning was quite basic. Rarely did any of these offenders work out more than a simple escape route and sometimes they did not even do that, many fleeing from the scene of the crime on foot or catching a cab to take them to safety. Only a minority took the precaution of donning even a simple disguise. Bluffers committed rash, simple robberies that were often carried out to pay for some form of addiction which played

315

a momentous role in their lives. This may help to explain the nature of many of their offences, their impulsiveness, the rudimentary planning, the acceptance of comparatively small amounts of money as a satisfactory result – only 8% of them expected to obtain over £5,000 compared to 36% of replica users and 70% of real gun users – and, of course, the choice of 'weapon'. The haste with which they went ahead was expressed by many of them. For example, one robber said:

I felt there was no alternative. Time was running out. I had to do something desperate, quickly.

The most interesting facet of the robberies committed by those who simulated the presence of a firearm was the method they so often chose to make their demands – almost two-thirds handed their victim a note. Only one in ten of all other interviewed robbers adopted this method, and of these just one carried a real firearm. The relationship between the offender's use of a note and the operation of a subterfuge has a rather obvious explanation. Producing a note which stated that they had a gun was the only hope they had of making their position perfectly clear without having to show the weapon that they did not possess. Also, the use of a note may have been a reflection of the uncertainty that these offenders felt was attached to their 'bluff'. As one of them admitted:

I didn't expect it to work. I thought the cashier would laugh and I would have to leave with nothing.

Discussion

According to the analysis of police files, 73% of the guns used in robberies in the MPD in 1990 were *known* (6%) or *believed* (67%) to be real. In the remaining cases the gun was known to be an imitation (11%) or no gun had been presented (16%). In the light of our findings from interviews with convicted robbers it appeared that the proportion of real guns used – 41% – was just over half of the estimate based upon our study of police records. Furthermore, 30% of shotguns had not been loaded. Thus, the proportion of interviewees who carried guns capable of discharging lethal shot was 33%. Just under one-third of the 44 interviewed robbers who carried handguns, which must have appeared real to witnesses, possessed a genuine and potentially life-threatening firearm. The same was true for two-thirds of shotgun carriers.

It should be noted that the information obtained from robbers about the weapons they had used also differed markedly from the data published in the *Criminal Statistics for England and Wales 1990* (Home Office 1992) where it is shown in *Table 3.6* that in 57% of robberies in which a firearm had been used, the weapon was a pistol (without indicating whether it was real or not). According to the Home Office Research and Statistics Department pistols were even more popular in the MPD in 1990 where they were used in 68% of incidents[11]. However, this study revealed that only 17% of interviewed robbers had carried a genuine loaded pistol.

The Home Office also estimated that 7% of armed robberies in England

and Wales (and 4% in the MPD) in 1990 involved imitation firearms and a further 13% of cases (10% in the MPD) involved 'supposed' firearms. The category 'supposed', which refers to cases where a description of the gun used was not available, undoubtedly includes some imitation firearms, but must not be confused with the category of 'simulated' firearm as used here because some supposed guns are clearly real – 17% were discharged in 1990 and 27% in 1989. It is clear, therefore, that the official statistics greatly underestimate the number of imitation guns used in robbery, and must be interpreted with care.

Furthermore it was clearly the case that the decision not to carry a real loaded gun was not one forced upon robbers by the unavailability of genuine firearms. Indeed whether a robber carried a real firearm or not was due neither to chance nor availability, but to the robber's deliberate choice based upon their estimate of what degree of threat was needed to carry out the offence successfully. The option of obtaining a real gun was open to most offenders who carried an imitation or bluffed, but they explicitly chose not to carry one either because they felt it unnecessary or they feared the consequences of their actions were they to be placed in a situation where they had the capability of employing lethal force.

It is also important to note that, in all cases where robbers operated a subterfuge, and intimated to witnesses that they possessed a firearm, without in fact producing anything that resembled a gun, they claimed that they had been, in fact, unarmed. In every case where the robber had truly been armed the gun was displayed to victims. However, it is important to emphasise that the number of robbers in this study who operated a subterfuge was relatively small, and so any conclusions about the likelihood that a robber who does not display a gun will in reality be unarmed must remain tentative, if tantalising. Also, it would certainly not be advisable for robbery victims to refuse to comply with bluffers on the assumption that they will be unarmed, both because of the possible consequences for them of a concealed gun being produced, and on account of the finding presented in this paper that when injuries were caused it was often as a result of victim non-cooperation.

This paper has drawn attention to the inherent difficulties associated with the interpretation of statistics related to armed crime. Although the number of robberies believed to involve firearms has increased dramatically in recent years, it is important to note that in many cases real guns are not used in these offences. In contrast to the widespread notion that robbers are usually armed and dangerous, it would appear that the majority of robbers choose not to carry live firearms.

This is not to minimise the potential danger which armed robbers pose, or to suggest that victims (or the police) should respond to the threat of a firearm with scepticism about the weapon's authenticity. These results do, however, illustrate the wide range of behaviours and attitudes which characterise armed robbery, and demonstrate that robbers' motivations are more complex than is often assumed. In particular, it is worthy of note that while a proportion of robbers were prepared to use violence, and indeed lethal force, to achieve their objective, a majority deliberately set out to avoid causing physical harm to their victims.

To conclude therefore, it is hoped that a more thorough understanding of patterns of weapon use in robbery and the relationship between the characteristics of targets attacked and the choices of offenders – which this research goes some way towards providing – will help to inform the development of strategies for crime prevention and harm reduction.[12]

Notes

[1] When this paper was submitted for publication the most up-to-date *Criminal Statistics* related to 1993. More recent data show a fall in the number of recorded armed robberies from 5,918 in 1993 to 4,104 in 1994 and 3,963 in 1995.

[2] There is huge variation in the number of armed robberies recorded by different police forces in England and Wales. For example in 1993 the forces with the fewest recorded robberies involving firearms were Wiltshire (0), Dyfed-Powys (2), Gwent (5), Lincolnshire (6), South Wales (7) and Suffolk (10). After the Metropolitan Police District (2,488), the largest numbers were recorded for Greater Manchester (738), the West Midlands (434), West Yorkshire (288) and Merseyside (253).

[3] The Home Office category of 'supposed' firearms includes unknown weapon types. Such weapons may not have been seen and will not have been recovered.

[4] A de-activated weapon is one which has been rendered incapable of discharging any shot, bullet or other missile, and bears a stamp to this effect from either the London or Birmingham proof house. Such weapons cease to be firearms within the meaning of the Firearms Acts and can be sold without restriction.

[5] Defined by the Firearms Act 1968 (s. 57.1) as: '. . . a lethal barrelled weapon of any description from which any shot, bullet or other missile can be discharged . . .'

[6] Defined by the Firearms Act 1968 (s. 57.4) as: '. . . any thing which has the appearance of being a firearm . . . whether or not it is capable of discharging any shot, bullet or other missile . . .'

[7] According to the Home Office Research and Statistics Department there were 1,940 robberies involving firearms in the MPD in 1990. Files were available at the General Registry, and included in this study, for 84% of those incidents which were the preserve of the Flying Squad (that is, attacks on security vans, banks, building societies, post offices, betting shops, and jewellers' shops). However, only one in five attacks on other categories of target, which did not require the specialist attention of the Flying Squad, resulted in the production of a *specrim* and the opening of a file at the General Registry. Thus it is inevitable that this report is biased towards the more serious robberies against commercial targets for which dmore comprehensive information is available.

[8] Detailed accounts of the data collection from police records, how prisoners were selected for interview, the content of the interview schedule and the efforts made to ensure that any information collected in the interviews was both reliable and valid are contained in the final report to the Home Office (Morrison and O'Donnell 1994, ch. 1).

[9] The success of this initiative has been described by the Home Office (1986) and by Ekblom (1987).

[10] There was one killing of a victim in 1990 – a postmaster who refused to open his safe was shot in the groin and left to bleed to death, the three robbers departing without any money. This case however was not available for inclusion in our study as the murder enquiry was not handled by the Flying Squad.

[11] It is not possible to perform a direct comparison between what this study revealed about the frequency with which different types of firearm were used in robbery,

and the analyses of weapon type which are contained in the Home Office statistics. This is because the Home Office figures are based upon all robberies with firearms which are recorded by the police whereas this study focuses primarily upon the more serious armed robberies, mainly those dealt with by the Flying Squad, for which files were available at the General Registry.

¹² *Acknowledgements*: The research reported here was funded by the Home Office. While it was being carried out we were ably guided by Peter Southgate, Principal Research Officer at the Research and Planning Unit. At the Centre for Criminological Research the data entry was carried out swiftly and accurately by Sarah Frost. We are especially grateful to Roger Hood, Director of the Centre, whose support was unstinting throughout this study and whose insightful observations on successive drafts of this paper have been of invaluable assistance. Finally we would like to express our thanks to the armed robbers in 32 prisoners throughout England, who must remain anonymous, but without whose participation this research would not have been possible.

References

Archer, J. (1994) (Ed.) *Male Violence*, London: Routledge.

Austin, C. (1988) *The Prevention of Robbery at Building Society Branches* (Crime Prevention Unit Paper No. 14), London: Home Office.

Ekblom, P. (1987) *Preventing Robberies at Sub-Post Offices: An Evaluation of a Security Initiative* (Crime Prevention Unit Paper No. 9), London: Home Office.

Feeney, F. (1986) 'Robbers as decision makers', in: D. Cornish and R. Clarke (Eds.), *The Reasoning Criminal: Rational Choice Perspectives on Offending*, New York: Springer Verlag.

Gill, M. and Matthews, R. (1994) 'Robbers on robbery: offenders' perspectives', in : M. Gill (Ed.), *Crime at Work: Studies in Security and Crime Prevention*, Leicester: Perpetuity Press.

Greenwood, C. (1972) *Firearms Controls: A Study of Armed Crime and Firearms Control in England and Wales*, London: Routledge and Kegan Paul.

Haran, J. F. and Martin, J. M. (1984) 'The armed urban bank robber: a profile', *Federal Probation*, *48*, 47–73.

Harding, R. and Blake, A. (1989) *Weapon Choice by Violent Offenders in Western Australia: A Pilot Study* (Research Report No. 1), Nedlands: University of Western Australia: Crime Research Centre.

Health and Safety Executive (1993) *Draft Guidance on the Prevention of Violence to Staff in Banks and Building Societies*, London: HSE.

Hibberd, M. and Shapland, J. (1993) *Violent Crime in Small Shops*, London: The Police Foundation.

Home Office (1986) *Report of the Working Group on Commercial Robbery*, London: Home Office Standing Conference on Crime Prevention.

Home Office (1992) *Criminal Statistics England and Wales 1990*, London: HMSO.

Home Office (1994) *Criminal Statistics England and Wales 1993*, London: HMSO.

Kapardis, A. (1988) 'One hundred convicted armed robbers in Melbourne: myths and reality', in: D. Challinger (Ed.), *Armed Robbery*, Canberra: Australian Institute of Criminology.

Katz, J. (1988) *Seductions of Crime: Moral and Sensual Attractions in Doing Evil*, New York Basic Books.

Katz, J. (1991) 'The motivation of the persistent robber', in: M. Tonry (Ed.), *Crime and Justice: A Review of Research*, Chicago: University of Chicago Press.

Kleck, G. (1991) *Point Blank: Guns and Violence in America*, New York: Aldine de Gruyter.

Kopel, D. B. (1992) *Gun Control in Great Britain: Saving Lives or Constricting Liberty*, Chicago: University of Illinois Press.

Morrison, S. and O'Donnell, I. (1994) *Armed Robbery: A Study in London* (Occasional Paper No. 15), Oxford: Centre for Criminological Research.

Morrison, S. and O'Donnell, I. (1996) 'An analysis of the decision-making practices of armed robbers', in: R. Homel (Ed.), *The Politics and Practice of Situational Crime Prevention: Crime Prevention Studies*, vol. 5, New York: Criminal Justice Press.

Wright, J. D. and Rossi, P. H. (1986) *Armed and Considered Dangerous: A Study of Felons and Their Firearms*, New York: Aldine de Gruyter.

Date submitted: July 95
Date accepted: January 96

[14]

"Stick 'em up, buddy"
Robbery, lifestyle, and specialization within a cohort of parolees

Shawn L. Schwaner*

Department of Sociology, College of Arts and Sciences, University of Louisville, 110 Lutz Hall, Louisville, KY 40292, USA

Abstract

Clearly, criminal career research has successfully located chronic offenders within arrestee populations, prison populations, and parole populations through empirical research. Within the paradigm, some notable findings have demonstrated that there is specialization in violent crime, i.e., the likelihood of a second violent arrest, conviction, or incarceration is predicted by a previous like offense. Only a few researchers have examined whether there are specific forms of repeat violent offending, namely robbery. This research uses Wright and Decker's [Wright, R. T., & Decker, S. II. (1997). *Armed Robbers in Action*. Boston: Northeastern University Press.] *Armed Robbers in Action* to provide a theoretical framework that can explain and predict repeat incarceration periods for robbers within a cohort of parolees. Data used in this research examine a cohort of parolees released from the Department of Rehabilitation and Correction in Ohio. Logistic regression analysis showed that an initial robbery predicts a subsequent incarceration period for robbery after controlling for demographic and criminal history variables.

Introduction

One of the greatest threats to the integrity of parole is violent recidivism, including robbery. Empirical research has largely overlooked the examination of robbery recidivism for parolees, mostly because of a lack of theoretical grounding for such inquiries. Recently, research conducted by Wright and Decker (1997) on active robbers has shed some light on the contexts in which robbers select and engage in robbery, thus providing a contextual framework applicable to the understanding of consecutive robbery that leads to incarceration. This article uses a lifestyle theoretical model that is used to analyze and discuss robbery as a specialized criminal enterprise within a criminal career paradigm, and examines the conceptual efficiency of the "foreground factors in the etiology of armed robbery" (Jacobs & Wright, 1999) specialists.

This study follows a litany of longitudinal studies in which the criminal career literature identifies a chronic offender population within a birth cohort (Wolfgang et al., 1972). Commonly, this body of literature has shown that there is a small proportion of chronic offenders within various subpopulations, including street subcultures (Katz, 1988; Anderson, 1990), arrestee populations (Blumstein & Cohen, 1979; Van Dine et al., 1979; Martinez, 1997), prison populations (Greenwood, 1982), a parole cohort (Schwaner, 1998), and according to Conklin (1972), Gabor et al. (1987), and Wright and Decker (1997), within a robber population as well.

* Tel.: +1-502-852-6836; fax: +1-502-852-0099.

E-mail address: slschw01@ulkyvm.louisville.edu (S.L. Schwaner).

372 *S.L. Schwaner / Journal of Criminal Justice 28 (2000) 371–384*

In light of the importance of criminal career research and its linkage to public policy, specialization research has focused in a general sense on repeat violent criminal activity. Few studies have attempted to examine specific criminal repetition, such as robbery. The closest academicians have come to establishing specific repetition with the use of qualitative methodology to develop useful typologies of robbery (Conklin, 1972; MacDonald, 1975; Gabor et al., 1987). There is a paucity of studies that have used their qualitative findings to frame the understanding of quantitative data in any meaningful way, particularly for parole cohorts. As such, this research utilizes the lifestyle framework established in *Armed Robbers in Action* by Wright and Decker (1997) as applied to the analysis of robbery specialization within a cohort of parolees. The literature review presented here will cover three interrelated areas: (1) robbery and specialization in violent crime; (2) theoretical considerations of lifestyles, routine activity theory, identity and robbery; and (3) highlights from the findings of Wright and Decker (1997).

Robbery and violent specialization

In the wake of Wolfgang's Philadelphia Cohort Study, Blumstein, Cohen, & Farrington (1988) and other criminal career researchers have established the viability of career criminal research, though this view has been met with a great deal of controversy (see Hirschi & Gottfredson, 1988). Within the criminal career literature, specialization research was especially hard struck as it was regarded as too elusive for academic pursuit. As Kempf (1987, p. 399) stated in regard to criminal specialization research:

> there have been numerous investigations of the topic in the recent past, and the absence of support for such a relationship appears to be almost unanimous. It is not surprising, therefore, that the dismissal of specialization has become widely accepted among criminologists.

Consequently, specialization research has waned.

The primary specter haunting specialization research has been tied to three areas, including: (1) definitional issues, (2) criminal behavior between arrests, and (3) general vs. specific forms of criminal specialization. First, specialization research findings, in general, have been mixed due, in large part, to definitional variations. For instance, West and Farrington (1977) and Hamparian et al. (1978) defined specialization as exclusive violent offending by criminals, which made violent specialization an especially rare event. Walker, Hammond, & Stear (1967) defined specialization as any increased likelihood in a violent conviction given a previous violent conviction. Martinez (1997) examined repeat arrests for violence among a cohort of previously arrested violent offenders as evidence of specialization. Recently, Schwaner (1998) examined consecutive incarceration periods for a violent offense as evidence of specialization. As these examples demonstrate, definitional and operational variation of specialization proliferates within the literature.

Second, there is the problem of considering the likelihood that robbers commit various types of crime, which increases their likelihood of re-arrest, in general (Farrington, 1982). Gabor et al. (1987) demonstrated that robbers do, in fact, commit a wide array of crimes, but compared to other criminal offenders, they are much more likely to engage in the highest amount of robbery. It is apparent that, for some offenders, robbery provides the greatest opportunity for substantial rewards (Wright & Decker, 1997).

In spite of the limitations encumbered in the study of repeat violent offending, several studies have been held in high regard for their contribution to cohort research (see Wolfgang et al.'s, 1972 benchmark study *Delinquency in a Birth Cohort*, and Van Dine et al.'s, 1979 *Restraining the Wicked* stemming from the Dangerous Offender Project). Findings from the Dangerous Offender Project (Hamparian et al., 1978) conducted in Columbus, OH, examined the criminal histories of delinquents born between 1956 and 1960. The entire cohort consisted of 1138 youth who had been arrested for at least one violent crime. Of the 4499 offenses committed by this group, 20 percent consisted of violent crimes. In their examination of the extent to which youthful offenders were arrested for consecutive violent crime, these researchers found that the majority who were first arrested for assault, robbery, and sex offenses were most likely to be re-arrested for assault, robbery, and sex offenses, respectively. Germane to this study, they showed that of those whose second arrest was for robbery, 55.7 percent was arrested for robbery the first time. Interestingly, Hamparian et al. (1978, p. 79) noted that "the distribution, by no means, establishes a process of specialization." Using the definition of consecutive arrests by Martinez (1997), however, these figures were indicative of specialization, though the figures do not address between arrest behavior.

Hamparian et al. (1978) also examined the criminal velocity in which offenders repeated criminal behavior. When focusing only on violent crimes, and eliminating status offenses, public order offenses and property offenses, robbers were re-arrested quicker than any other group. Consistent with the findings of Petersilia and Turner (1986), and pertinent to this study, for those who were pushed

S.L. Schwaner / Journal of Criminal Justice 28 (2000) 371–384   373

further into the juvenile justice system, the quicker their criminal velocity between arrests became. For instance, robbers who were institutionalized were re-arrested nearly twice as quickly as those who went to jail or were under parole or probation, and nearly three times as fast as those who received less supervision. Clearly, the combination of robbery and penetration into the criminal justice system had an impact on the velocity in which robbers re-offended and were re-arrested.

A third issue regarding specialization research focuses on general and broadly defined violent behavior and specific forms of violent crime. For instance, Schwaner (1998) recently demonstrated that repeat violent offending within a parole cohort was a rare, but significant, occurrence. Consistent with other research (Ekland & Ekland-Olson 1991; Ekland-Olson et al., 1992) where those committed to prison for a violent crime recidivate, it is most likely that they do so for a new violent offense than for property, sex, drug, or other offenses. As suggested in past literature, this is not by chance. These findings, like Martinez's (1997) follow-up of the Dangerous Offender data, described broader patterns of violent activity, but did not focus on whether an initial incarceration for robbery preceded future robbery in any significant way.

With the resurgence in specialization research, which has addressed definitional considerations, the rarity of specialization in violent behavior, and practical considerations in addressing Kempfs' concerns, this research extends and builds upon the notions of specialization in crime by utilizing the findings of Wright and Decker (1997) (to be discussed shortly) pertaining to the relationship between criminal lifestyles and persistence in robbery. Although prior research on specialization has focused on "birth cohorts, cohorts of violent offenders, institutionalized offenders, gang members and students" (Kempf, 1987, p. 402), few have examined specialization of criminal behavior using data on a cohort of parolees. Schwaner (1998), however, utilized parole cohort data to demonstrate that violent commitment offending was a predictor of violent recidivism.

Pulling together findings on specialization and robbery, three key issues emerge. These issues include: (1) defining specialization, (2) criminal behavior between arrests, and (3) general patterns of specialization vs. specific forms of specialization. It may well be useful to add a fourth issue, which is the usage of sociological theory to ground empirical evidence. The present study focused on robbery specialization by examining recidivism patterns within a cohort of parolees by using a lifestyle theoretical framework.

Lifestyles, routine activities theory, identity, and robbery: theoretical considerations

In general, routine activities and lifestyle theory provide a sociological framework from which to understand patterns of victimization. The central theme of this framework is that a convergence occurs in time and space between a motivated offender, who identifies a suitable target, and a lack of capable guardianship (Cohen & Felson, 1979). Essentially, persons who engage in the riskiest behaviors are most likely to be the victims of crime, including robbery (Pettiway, 1982; Lasley, 1989; Mustaine & Tewksbury, 1998).

Quantitative research has shown that the risk of robbery victimization has been tied to several community structural factors. Roncek and Maier (1991) noted that robbery victimization occurred in places where there were more bars, taverns, and lounges in an area, particularly when there is a greater percentage of multiple unit housing, vacancy, residential population, social congestion, and crime in nearby areas. Kennedy and Forde (1990) added that young, unmarried men — who frequented bars and movies, spent more time out walking and were unemployed (Lasley, 1989) — were vulnerable to being robbed.

More importantly, a body of research has noted that those who have the highest risks of victimization share similar social and demographic characteristics as offenders (Singer, 1981, 1986; Fagan et al., 1987; Sampson & Lauritson, 1990; Baron & Hartnagel, 1998). In their study of "punks," Kennedy and Baron (1993) found that punks were both offenders against and victims of people who were socio-demographically similar. Sampson and Lauritson (1990) indicated that the critical demographic similarities included being young, black, male and urban. Within these parameters of victimization and offending, Jensen and Brownfield (1986) suggested that offense activity, such as robbery, was in and of itself a type of routine. Thus, authors using lifestyle theory have established some structural underpinnings in the understanding of the relationship between routine activities and robbery.

Qualitatively grounded research has established the process by which lifestyle, routine, and identity are tied to robbery by way of typology construction. Conklin (1972) chronicled a typology for robbery offenders that included the professional, the opportunist, the addict, the alcoholic. Gabor et al. (1987) offered four other categories of robbers including the chronic, professional, intensive, and occasional. Using Gabor et al.'s model, the chronic robber is most likely to have an identity and lifestyle tied into crime, drugs, and robbery. Consequently, the chronic robber, comprising 28 percent of their sample, engaged in a wide array of crimes, had an extensive criminal history, committed between twenty and twenty-five robberies a year during a career which, on average, spanned 7–8 years (p. 81). Following Gabor et al.'s assertions, the chronic robber is theoretically the type who is most likely to recidivate following an incarceration experience, while most other types of robbers would desist.

Within prison settings, several studies have identified criminal lifestyles, social systems, and identities of American prison inmates (Clemmer, 1958; Sykes, 1965; Irwin, 1970). Of those newly admitted to prison, Irwin and Austin (1994) identified several criminal lifestyles, including those "into crime," those with "crime episodes," those "around crime," and the "one shot criminal." Upon release from prison, Schwaner et al. (1998) noted that parole absconders could be identified as social isolates, drug fiends, villains, night life swingers, and family men and women. And McCleary (1992) noted that parole officers use a typology of parolees for pragmatic purposes. Hence, the connective tissue tying pre-incarceration and post-incarceration together is the salience of lifestyle and identity types through various situational contexts.

Schmid and Jones (1991), however, studying identity transformation in a maximum security prison, argued that there is a "suspended" identity among inmates. Prison acts as a social system that differs from the outside world. However, while identities may be suspended, Ebaugh (1988) suggested that former roles are never abandoned, but rather integrated into new identities. This former identity, Brown (1991) contends, facilitates the process of exiting from a deviant identity. This is particularly true for offenders who are socially isolated, family oriented (Schwaner et al., 1998), intensive, and occasional robbery offenders (Gabor et al., 1987). However, those addicted to street life (Anderson, 1990), were villains, drug fiends (Schwaner et al., 1998), and into crime (Irwin & Austin, 1994) had a greater chance of recidivism due to their lifestyle identity. Thus, the maintenance of identity transformation in post-incarceration depends a great deal on a parolee's return to, or diversion from, a street subculture tied to structural patterns of persistent inequality.

Additionally, Cornish and Clarke (1986) contend that lifestyles and routines provide the situational factors which shape, and are shaped by, choice. As offenders routinize their behavior and lifestyles via deeper penetration into a street subculture (Anderson, 1990; Baron & Hartnagel, 1998), many continue to develop a lengthy criminal career. Finally, specialization in robbery may, in fact, develop with age and as criminal careers become more established within this subculture (Bursik, 1980; Farrington, 1986).

Robbery, as an opportunistic crime, however, may be grounded within the opportunity structure of a street subculture, especially in metropolitan areas. Qualitative analysis of street subcultures has placed the impetus of robbery within expectations of toughness, strength, autonomy, fate, and smartness (Miller, 1958), honor, protection, and retribution (Baron & Hartnagel, 1998). In addition, the utility of using criminal behavior to support and maintain "heart" (Thomas, 1967), providing "an angle of moral superiority" (Katz, 1988), and providing control of the street (Anderson, 1990), has been identified as salient. Consequently, the preservation of respect and the pursuit of money structure are the behavioral contexts in which robbers operate. Theoretically, the suspended robber identity would re-emerge upon release from prison for those whose lifestyle and identity were most closely tied into a street subculture. This process is described in detail in *Armed Robbers in Action* by Wright and Decker (1997).

Wright and Decker's findings on robbery

Wright and Decker (1997) recently engaged in ethnographic work which focused on *Armed Robbers in Action*. Overwhelmingly, the eighty-six robbers studied in St. Louis were poor, young, African–American, and male. The majority (71 percent) had committed at least ten robberies in their lifetime while 36 percent committed over Forty-nine. Only 33 percent of the population had no previous arrests for robbery while 41 percent had been convicted for such a crime.

Wright and Decker (1997) argued that the majority of these robbers engaged in robbery to satisfy their manifest need for immediate cash. Grounded within a "street culture", robbers were in constant pursuit of money to maintain a lifestyle that centered around desperate partying — mostly related to drug usage, keeping up with appearances — maintaining social status within the street culture, and keeping things together — keeping up with bills and everyday subsistence obligations. The street culture provided a sense of identity that masked a sense of failure. As such, robbery tended to result from a social psychological process in which one could maintain a sense of independence and status in light of possessing nonsaleable job skills within a tight labor market. Thus, since robbery took less time, netted good money, and was always nearby, it paved the way for individual persistence in robbery.

In terms of specialization, it was noted that most of the robbers passed through other stages of more petty crime before committing robbery, indicating that robbery specialization tends to occur in the late teens and early twenties and that robbers engaged in a variety of criminal pursuits. Once they attained the robber status, however, one's embeddedness in a street culture — featuring a lack of employment opportunity and the constant need for immediate money — structures a situational context ripe for persistent robbery. Though robbers were inclined to commit whatever crime would net money, robbery was, by far, the most lucrative. Thus, robbery as a specialty was rooted within the overlap between structural limits to economic opportunity and social psychological needs to maintain identity and net cash. As such, specialization, which is often overlooked in quantitative exploration, is a dynamic rather than static process. For persisters, robbery is a crime of choice. For instance, Wright and Decker (1997, p. 44) cited that one "offender reported that he was doing stickups to 'reestablish' himself after serving a lengthy prison sentence for armed robbery." This suggested that upon release from prison, there is the possibility that an inmate incarcerated for robbery may return to robbery should the identity tied to the street culture resume. The study did not include any data on the rate of incarceration or recidivism for this group of robbers. Thus, it is hypothesized here that offenders originally incarcerated for a robbery conviction are more likely to return to prison for robbery as an outcome of the attempt to reestablish themselves.

In sum, Wright and Decker's findings establish a qualitative guideline for specialization. For offenders who escalate into robbery, the likelihood of specialization increases for those most closely tied into a street subculture. Specialization in robbery is grounded within a system of urban unemployment patterns coupled with individual identity formation within a street subculture. Theoretically, prison parolees who have a "suspended identity" (Schmid & Jones, 1991) will eventually revert back to familiar lifestyles in the face of thwarted opportunities and perceived blockades to success (Schwaner et al., 1998) upon release onto parole. Consequently, a robber who is paroled is eventually likely to engage in robbery again, pending opportunities for legitimate success upon release from prison. Within a parole cohort, robbery specialization would manifest as consecutive incarcerations for robbery.

Grounded in the theoretical dynamics of lifestyle and identity theory, and those findings espoused by Wright and Decker, three hypotheses guided this research.

Hypothesis 1: After controlling for demographic and criminal history variables, an original incarceration for robbery should predict reincarceration for another robbery offense.

Hypothesis 2: The predictors of robbery recidivism differ from the predictors of violent crime recidivism, in general.

Hypothesis 3: The predictors of robbery recidivism differ from the predictors of a return to prison for any crime.

The latter two hypotheses postulate that robbery is a recidivism offense that differs from other types of offenses as a consequence of lifestyle variability. Theoretically, such findings would suggest that specialization is grounded within social, lifestyle, and situational factors.

Data and methods

Data for this study were collected by the Department of Research at the Ohio Department of Rehabilitation and Correction. The population of study included 3,544 inmates released on parole in 1989.

In order to ensure consistency between the research of Wright and Decker (1997) and this current research, only parolees from Ohio's most urban counties were analyzed. These include those counties containing Cincinnati, Cleveland, Toledo, Columbus, Dayton, and Akron. Additionally, so few women were repeat robbery recidivists that they were excluded from the analysis. The final sample includes 2,263 parolees.

In Ohio in 1989, inmates were released as either parolee or by expiration of their determinate sentence. Non-violent property offenders and other less serious offenders with no prior history of violence were given determinate sentences. These inmates, by definition, did not receive parole and, consequently, were not used in this study. Parolees, however, were regarded by statute as serious felons. The majority had been incarcerated for either a current violent offense, a first or second degree property, drug, or sex offense, or had a past violent criminal record.

Parole board release decisions in Ohio are guided by parole guidelines similar to those used by the federal parole board (see Hoffman, 1994). The parole guidelines consist of nine salient criminal history factors, and these are used by the parole board in an effort to assess the risk a parolee poses for recidivism. These factors include: number of prior felony convictions, arrest within five years prior to current incarceration arrest, age at first arrest leading to felony conviction, problems with personal functioning as associated with alcohol (from this point on termed alcohol problems), problems with personal functioning as associated with drugs (from this point on termed drug problems), number of prior adult

376   S.L. Schwaner / Journal of Criminal Justice 28 (2000) 371–384

incarcerations, age of admission for current offense, number of prior parole/probation supervision periods, and number of prior parole/probation revocations. Each inmate is given a score for each salient factor. These scores are used as data for the current study. Other variables, such as age at release, time served, sex, and race, were also collected and utilized.

It should be noted that the salient factor scores, as well as other criminal history and demographic variables, act as the "foreground factors" discussed by Jacobs and Wright (1999). Hence, the Jacobs and Wright model (which utilizes the Wright and Decker data) examined street culture and conduct norms as independent factors explaining robbery, though they recognized that these were intervening variables in the larger criminal history process. The present study makes the assumption that the findings of Wright and Decker (1997) and Jacobs and Wright (1999) were reliable and valid in regard to this processual model. As such, the qualitative findings from the aforementioned authors and the quantitative analysis of the present study are complimentary in their analysis.

By pulling together information and findings from past research, this article defines robbery specialization as serving two consecutive incarceration periods for a robbery and uses logistic regression analysis to determine whether robbery re-offenders can be successfully distinguished from other inmates who are not robbery re-offenders. Using this definition, three steps are taken in assessing the nature of re-incarceration for a robbery offense. First, descriptive characteristics are provided in Table 1 for the total cohort, any recidivism offense (including technical parole violations), violent recidivism, and robbery recidivism. Secondly, logistic regression analysis results presented in Tables 2, 3, and 4 are used to assess which predictors are related to any recidivism, violent recidivism, in general, and specifically, robbery recidivism. Four models are presented in a hierarchical fashion. Model one provides the demographic variables; model two includes criminal history predictors; model three includes robbery; model four includes time served and age at release.

Unfortunately, there are two shortcomings of the present data. First, there are no direct measures for lifestyle, routine activities, or identity contained here, and second, there are no qualitative data to analyze the impact of street culture and conduct norms. However, it is the author's contention that the theory highlighted here places these shortcomings in a broader framework which promotes further research in the area of robbery specialization. In essence, this study, in conjunction with the Wright and Decker (1997) findings, lends itself to the marriage of qualitative and quantitative analysis.

Results

Table 1 shows that there is widespread general recidivism for this parole cohort. In a three-year follow-up period, 47.5 percent of the cohort was returned to prison. While the majority (see Schwaner, 1995) were returned to prison for technical violations, just over 20 percent was actually returned for a new criminal case. Within the cohort, only 8.5 percent was returned for a violent recidivism offense, and only 4.0 percent was returned for a robbery charge. Schwaner (1998) found that violent specialization within a parole cohort is a rare event, and, as expected, robbery is even less frequent. Robbers were returned to prison 51.5 percent of the time and had the greatest likelihood of returning to prison for a violent offense (11.3 percent) and most likely for robbery (5.5 percent) when compared to other variable categories.

Table 2 shows which predictors are related to general recidivism. Criminal history and race are consistently related to general recidivism. Other predictors related to general recidivism include number of prior felony arrests, two arrests within a five-year period, drug abuse issues, prior incarcerations, younger at current admission to prison, prior parole/probation supervisions and parole/probation revocations, and age at release from prison.

Age at first felony arrest, time served, alcohol abuse issues, and robbery are not predictive of general recidivism. The absence of robbery as a significant predictor of general recidivism suggests that robbers are not more likely to be returned to prison for technical violations or petty offenses when compared to the rest of the parolee population.

In Table 3, logistic regression models for return to prison for a violent recidivism crime are different than the predictors for any recidivism. Similar to Table 2, race, age at admission for current offense, prior probation/parole supervisions and prior probation/parole revocations are related to violent recidivism. All other variables lost their predictive power except for robbery and age at first arrest for a felony. The criminal history variables remain consistently significant in models 2, 3, and 4. Most notable, age at first felony arrest and robbery are significantly related to violent recidivism. Though not significant, the direction of influence of drugs and alcohol-related issues reverses as compared to Table 2.

These findings indicate that the predictors of recidivism vary by recidivism type. Prediction for general recidivism is broad, whereas violent recidivism is related to having had parole supervision and revocations as well as age factors including age at first felony arrest (onset) and being younger when admitted to prison. Most importantly, when compared to other offenders, robbers are significantly more

S.L. Schwaner / Journal of Criminal Justice 28 (2000) 371–384   377

Table 1
Distribution characteristics of cohort by recidivism type

Variable	Cohort		Any recidivism		Violent recidivism		Robbery recidivism	
	Frequency	Percent	Frequency	Percent	Frequency	Percent	Frequency	Percent
	2263	100	1076	47.5	193	8.5	90	4.0
Race								
White	818	36.1	347	42.4	53	6.5	25	3.1
Black	1445	63.9	729	50.4	140	9.7	65	4.5
Prior felony convictions								
None	437	19.3	120	27.5	20	4.6	7	1.6
One	446	19.7	174	39.0	41	9.2	19	4.3
Two or more	1380	61.0	7823	56.7	132	9.6	64	4.6
Arrest within 5 years								
No	319	14.1	779	24.1	16	5.0	7	1.6
Yes	1944	85.9	999	51.4	177	9.1	835	4.3
Age at first felony arrest								
Over 24	502	22.2	140	27.9	16	3.2	8	1.6
20–23	551	24.3	294	53.4	44	8.0	17	3.1
Less than 20	1210	53.5	642	53.1	133	11.0	65	5.4
Alcohol abuse issues								
No	945	41.8	433	45.8	91	9.6	45	4.8
Yes	1318	58.2	633	48.0	102	7.7	45	3.4
Drug abuse issues								
No	753	33.3	312	41.4	68	9.0	26	3.5
Yes	1510	66.7	7646	50.6	125	8.3	64	4.2
Prior incarcerations								
None	940	41.5	325	34.6	70	7.4	28	3.0
1–2	937	41.4	502	53.6	89	9.5	38	4.1
Three or more	386	17.1	249	64.5	34	8.8	24	6.2
Current admission age								
30 or more	812	35.9	327	40.3	43	5.3	24	3.0
Less than 30	1451	64.1	7498	51.6	150	10.3	66	4.5
Prior parole supervisions								
No	474	20.9	166	35.0	40	8.4	16	3.4
Yes	1789	79.1	910	50.9	153	8.6	74	4.1
Prior parole revocations								
No	806	35.6	257	31.9	52	6.5	24	3.0
Yes	1457	64.4	819	56.2	141	9.7	66	4.5
Time served in prison								
Less than 5 years	1466	64.8	680	46.4	113	7.7	54	3.7
5 or more years	797	35.2	396	49.7	80	10.0	36	4.5
Release age from prison								
30 or more	1332	58.9	588	44.1	95	7.1	48	3.6
Less than 30	931	41.1	488	52.4	98	10.5	42	4.5
Original offense type								
Robbery	764	33.8	404	52.9	92	12.0	46	6.0
Non-robbery	1499	66.2	672	44.8	101	6.7	44	2.9

Table 2
Logistic regression analysis of any recidivism

	Model one			Model two			Model three			Model four		
	β	S.E.	P level	β	S.E.	P level	β	S.E.	P level	β	S.E.	P level
Race	0.3235	0.0882	***	0.2986	0.0980	***	0.2928	0.0981	***	0.3287	0.0990	****
Prior felony arrests				0.1391	0.0406	****	0.1379	0.0407	****	0.1460	0.0409	****
Arrest within 5 years				0.1.573	0.0388	****	0.1554	0.0389	****	0.1531	0.0390	****
Age first felony arrest				0.0370	0.0336		0.0351	0.0337		0.0007	0.0351	
Alcohol abuse issues				0.0238	0.0237		0.0230	0.0237		0.0265	0.0239	
Drug abuse issues				0.0580	0.0243	**	0.0578	0.0280	**	0.0596	0.0245	**
Prior incarcerations				0.1823	0.0280	****	0.1826	0.0280	****	0.2038	0.0288	****
Age current admission				0.7277	0.1132	****	0.7036	0.1141	****	0.4902	0.1278	****
Prior parole supervision				-0.1393	0.0388	****	-0.1370	0.0388	****	-0.1210	0.0392	***
Prior parole revocation				0.1547	0.0310	****	0.1532	0.0310	****	0.1496	0.0311	****
Robbery commitment							0.1577	0.0963	****	0.1260	0.0987	
Age at release										-0.4795	0.1288	****
Time served										0.0918	0.1013	
Constant	-0.3055	0.0707	****	-2.4041	0.2021	****	-2.4258	0.2030	****	-2.0804	0.2237	****
-2 log likelihood	3118.197		****	2822.344		****	2819.663		****	2805.670		****
Model χ²	2263.00		****	309.393		****	312.075		****	326.067		****
Goodness of fit	2263.000		****	2258.716		****	2258.421		****	2264.257		****
df	2261			2252			2251			2249		
Correctly classified (%)	53.03			64.65			64.34			64.96		

** P level < 0.05.
*** P level < 0.01.
**** P level < 0.001.

Table 3
Logistic regression analysis of return to prison for any violent crime

	Model one			Model two			Model three			Model four		
	β	S.E.	P level	β	S.E.	P level	β	S.E.	P level	β	S.E.	P level
Race	0.4370	0.1676	***	0.4126	0.1757	**	0.3940	0.1758	**	0.3945	0.1766	**
Prior felony arrests				0.0722	0.0721		0.0649	0.0720		0.0658	0.0720	
Arrest within 5 years				0.0666	0.0730		0.0618	0.0727		0.0632	0.0729	
Age first felony arrest				0.1884	0.0648	***	0.1822	0.0650	***	0.1771	0.0671	***
Alcohol abuse issues				−0.0410	0.0399		−0.0439	0.0400		−0.0442	0.0401	
Drug abuse issues				−0.0314	0.0408		−0.0330	0.0409		−0.0323	0.0409	
Prior incarcerations				0.0255	0.0460		0.0301	0.0465		0.0313	0.0479	
Age current admission				0.6116	0.2037	***	0.5331	0.2066	***	0.5080	0.2257	**
Prior parole supervision				−0.1312	0.0654	**	−0.1248	0.0654	*	−0.1225	0.0658	*
Prior parole revocation				0.1132	0.0567	**	0.1104	0.0569	*	0.1081	0.0570	*
Robbery commitment							0.4748	0.1560	***	0.4552	0.1601	***
Age at release										−0.0446	0.2044	
Time served										0.0904	0.1671	
Constant	−2.6693	0.1420	****	−3.8697	0.3768	****	−3.9467	0.3798	****	−3.9293	0.4094	****
−2log likelihood	1312.123			1261.246			1252.098			1251.801		
Model χ^2	7.166			58.040		****	67.191		****	67.488		****
Goodness of fit	2262.756			2244.274		****	2257.867		****	2253.227		****
df	2261			2252			2251			2249		
Correctly classified (%)	91.47			91.47			91.47			91.47		

* P level < 0.1.
** P level < 0.05.
*** P level < 0.01.
**** P level < 0.001.

Table 4
Logistic regression analysis of return to prison for robbery

	Model one			Model two			Model three			Model four		
	β	S.E.	P level	β	S.E.	P level	β	S.E.	P level	β	S.E.	P level
Race	0.4014	0.2395	*	0.3159	0.2507		0.2905	0.2507		0.2038	0.2518	**
Prior felony arrests				0.0451	0.1078		0.0321	0.1074		0.0327	0.1075	
Arrest within 5 years				0.0764	0.1068		0.0757	0.1061		0.0745	0.1064	
Age first felony arrest				0.2164	0.0943	**	0.2099	0.0945	**	0.2081	0.0970	**
Alcohol abuse issues				-0.0731	0.0566		-0.0761	0.0569		-0.0757	0.0569	
Drug abuse issues				0.0475	0.0607		0.0472	0.0608		0.1373	0.0609	
Prior incarcerations				0.1262	0.0650	*	0.1351	0.0659	**	0.1373	0.0681	**
Age current admission				0.4663	0.2769	*	0.3584	0.2820		0.3442	0.3106	
Prior parole supervision				-0.1104	0.0969		-0.1024	0.0967		-0.1013	0.0974	
Prior parole revocation				0.0383	0.0800		0.0345	0.0800		0.0346	0.0803	
Robbery commitment							0.6495	0.2215	***	0.6548	22863	***
Age at release										-0.0306	0.2946	
Time served										-0.0242	0.2398	
Constant	-3.4569	0.2031	****	-4.8182	0.5571	****	-4.9671	0.5664	****	-4.9408	0.6053	****
-2log likelihood	753.851			727.083			718.559			718.531		
Model χ²	2.956		*	29.724		****	38.248		****	38.276		****
Goodness of fit	2262.927		****	2213.260		****	2237.141		****	2242.770		****
df	2261			2252			2251			2249		
Correctly classified (%)	96.0			96.0			96.0			96.0		

* P level < 0.1.
** P level < 0.05.
*** P level < 0.01.
**** P level < 0.001.

S.L. Schwaner / Journal of Criminal Justice 28 (2000) 371–384   381

likely to return to prison for a violent crime than other offenders, but not for general recidivism. This indicates that robbers may be more grounded in a lifestyle of violence. Tables 2 and 3 suggest that recidivism is bound by broader social and behavioral processes. The predictors of age of first felony conviction, age of commitment to prison, and race suggest that violent crime is strongly influenced by social factors and, theoretically, economic inequality (Blau & Blau, 1982; Wilson, 1987), in general.

Table 4 shows some interesting findings. First, race only predicts robbery recidivism in model one ($P < 0.1$). After adding in criminal history variables, the race effect disappears. This shows that race alone is not as related to robbery recidivism as a lengthy criminal past. Second, only robbery, age at first felony conviction, and number of prior incarcerations are related to repeat robbery incarceration periods. This suggests that robber specialists have a younger age of onset into crime and have had more penetration into the criminal justice system.

These findings support the previous criminal career literature in that the most violent offenders tend to be grounded in crime at a younger age. Consistent with Wright and Decker (1997), there is evidence here that robbers are significantly different than other criminal offenders. The only discrepancy in this research with Wright and Decker is the lack of predictive power of alcohol and drug-related issues on robbery specialization. This may be a reflection of measurement bias or sampling strategies employed in these two studies. After all, Wright and Decker (1997) interviewed nearly one hundred active robbers in inner city St. Louis compared to county level data used in this research. It would be interesting to design a study to attempt to bridge qualitative analysis with appropriate quantitative data to improve the overall discussion of robbery specialization within an urban male cohort of parolees.

It seems that specialization research must winnow through broad generalizations about repeat violent offending and examine specific subtypes. Not all violent offenders recidivate for the same crime, but a select group of robbers do. In spite of these findings, much work remains in understanding the nexus of robbery, identity and lifestyle, and economy.

Summary

For some time, criminal career research has played a major role in the development of criminology and criminal justice practice. Though debate continues in the area, it has become clear that there are a handful of violent repeat criminal offenders. Even though they are small in number, they account for a great deal of criminal behavior leading to arrest,

and create a great deal of fear within the general population. As such, the vitality of developing prediction and classification tools for repeat offending is important to criminal justice practitioners.

Specialization research has been plagued with definitional concerns, criminal behavior which never officially surfaces, and the lack of specificity in type of violent offense. However, there has been a recent resurgence in the specialization literature which suggests that there are indeed predictors of violent specialization (Guttridge et al., 1983; Brennan et al., 1989; Van Stelle et al., 1994; Martinez, 1997; Schwaner, 1998). This study has demonstrated that there may, in fact, be a specific brand of recidivism specialization that has been overlooked; i.e., not only does an instant robbery offense significantly predict a subsequent violent recidivism crime, it also predicts a subsequent incarceration period for robbery.

Theoretically, the further an individual is pushed into the criminal justice system, the quicker and more likely his/her subsequent recidivism offense is to occur. Since many inmates are released into a social environment in which a street culture proliferates, and structural opportunities for employment are low, the situational climate for recidivism is ripe. This is largely due to the fact that parolees generally suspend their identity while in prison (Schmid & Jones, 1991) only to return to that identity and lifestyle which is most salient upon release (Schwaner et al., 1998). Consequently, robbery begets robbery when access to money is tight and the lifestyle associated with the street culture is strong (Baron & Hartnagel, 1998).

Social and policy implications

This research suggests the need to establish a line of research that attempts to bridge the long, established gap between quantitative and qualitative methodology. Such tasks as quantitative prediction by parole boards are likely to produce a great number of false positives as parole guidelines do not adequately address qualitative concerns. New techniques that seek to utilize both methodologies have the brightest future.

Socially, it seems that post-release recidivism is hinged upon several structural factors related to the development of identity and lifestyle. Namely, when returning a parolee into an urban environment, which offers a viable opportunity structure (Cloward & Ohlin, 1960) for criminal indulgence, parolees must be linked into formal and informal community organizations that provide structure and alternative lifestyle choices. As Sampson and Lauritsen (1990) note, maturational reform best succeeds when the informal age gradient is most strongly in effect, i.e., parolees are bound into the community. The first step in such a process, particularly for robbers, and other parolees, is to address the need for money. Employment is critical in this domain. In other words, as suggested by Wright and Decker (1997, p. 131), "such a strategy will be effective only to the extent that it undermines the strong emotional attachment of the offenders to the street culture."

Even more, communities must be re-organized so as to address issues of residential segregation (Peterson & Krivo, 1993), concentration of disadvantage (Krivo et al., 1998), chronic unemployment (Glasgow, 1980; Blau & Blau, 1982; Wilson, 1987), and the continued de-industrialization of many urban communities. The process and structure of parole can assist parolees in this regard. However, for any such change to take place, however, it is of utmost importance that the criminal justice pendulum swing back toward a social work orientation from a predominantly law enforcement model (Culberston & Ellsworth, 1985). In other words, just as quantitative and qualitative methodologies need to be used in unison, parole needs to combine elements of both the social work and law enforcement models of parole to provide robbers, and other violent offenders, with viable lifestyle options upon release from prison.

On the other hand, Wright and Decker (1997) also suggested that employment opportunities alone may not be enough to overcome drug and alcohol-related issues, unreliability, and the inability to take orders. In addition, increasing the severity of the punishment would likely be ineffective as they are already severe for robbers. They also suggest that lengthier prison terms and incapacitation efforts could excite more criminal conduct among robbers upon release from prison. It seems as though a "just desserts" model could incapacitate robbers for a longer period of time and reduce individual activity during that period but not reduce violent robbery recidivism. Such implications create a true public policy quandary.

The solution seems to rest within resolute long-term policies and more intensive individual intervention; i.e., long-term structural changes, community reorganization, and intensive parole supervision for robbers may be necessary. A carefully developed plan of action, which increases parolee contact with formal organizations, develops life-training skills, and intensively addresses drug and alcohol concerns for individuals upon prison release, is needed.

Interestingly, these social and policy implications bring this research back to the starting point. In other words, the findings presented here and with the Wright and Decker (1997) data suggest more attempts to develop integrated theories and methodologies. It is apparent that these two orientations must be used in unison rather than as antagonistic positions. The bridging of such orientations, this author contends, could more adequately test the empirical questions which remain in this research, namely, "Is there a lifestyle that promotes specialization into a robber subculture, and if so, which criminal justice policies work best in circumventing such behavior?" These can be answered with more integrated research in this area.

Acknowledgments

The author would like to acknowledge several people for their helpfulness on the completion of this research. I would like to thank Mr. Steve Van Dine and the Bureau of Research at the Ohio Department of Rehabilitation and Correction for correcting and sharing these data. Additionally, I am thankful for the helpful comments of Dr. Simon Dinitz, Dr. Ruth Peterson, Dr. Richard Lundman, Dr. L. Allen Furr, Dr. Wayne usui, Dr. Patricia Gagne, Dr. Richard Tewksbury, and Dr. John Wieland.

References

Anderson, E. (1990). *Streetwise: Race, Class, and Change in an Urban Community.* Chicago: University of Chicago Press.

Baron, S. W., & Hartnagel, T. F. (1998). Street youth and criminal violence. *J Res Crime Delinquency 25*, 166–192.

Blau, J., & Blau, P. M. (1982). The cost of inequality: metropolitan structure and violent crime. *Am Sociol Rev 47*, 114–129.

Blumstein, A., & Cohen, J. (1979). Estimating individual crime rates from arrest records. *J Crim Law Criminol 70*, 561–585.

Blumstein, A., Cohen, J., & Farrington, D. P. (1988). Criminal career research: its value for criminology. *Criminology 26*, 1–35.

Brennan, P., Mednick, S., & John, R. (1989). Specialization in violence: evidence of a criminal subgroup. *Criminology 27*, 437–454.

Brown, J. D. (1991). The professional ex — an alternative for exiting the deviant career. *Sociol Q 32*, 219–230.

Bursik, R. (1980). The dynamics of specialization in juvenile offenses. *Soc Forces 58*, 851–864.

Clemmer, D. (1958). *The Prison Community.* New York: Rinehart.

Cloward, R., & Ohlin, L. E. (1960). *Delinquency and Opportunity: A Theory of Delinquent Gangs.* New York: Free Press.

Cohen, L. E., & Felson, M. (1979). Social change and crime rate trends: a routine activity approach. *Am Sociol Rev 44*, 588–608.

Conklin, J. E. (1972). *Robbery and the Criminal Justice System.* Philadelphia: J. B. Lippincott.

Cornish, R. V., & Clarke, R. V. (1986). *The Reasoning*

Criminal: Rational Choice Perspectives on Offending. New York: Springer-Verlag.

Culbertson, R. G., & Ellsworth, T. (1985). Treatment innovations in probation and parole. In L.F. Travis (Ed.), *Probation, Parole, and Community Corrections* (pp. 127–150). Prospect Heights, IL: Waveland Press.

Ebaugh, H. R. F. (1988). *Becoming an Ex: The Process of Role Exit.* Chicago: University of Chicago Press.

Ekland, W. R., & Ekland-Olson, S. (1991). The response of the criminal justice system to prison overcrowding: recidivism patterns among four successive parolee cohorts. *Law Soc Rev 3*, 601–620.

Ekland-Olson, S., Kelly, W. R., & Eisenberg, M. (1992). Crime and incarceration: some comparative findings from the 1980s. *Crime Delinquency 38*, 392–416.

Fagan, J., Piper, E., & Moore, M. (1987). Contributions of victimization to delinquency in inner cities. *J Crim Law Criminol 78*, 586–609.

Farrington, D. P. (1982). Longitudinal analysis of criminal violence. In M. E. Wolfgang & N. A. Weiner (Eds.), *Criminal Violence.* Beverly Hills: Sage Publications.

Farrington, D. P. (1986). Age and crime. In M. Tonry & N. Morris (Eds.), *Crime and Justice: An Annual Review of Research* (pp. 189–250, Vol. 7). Chicago: University of Chicago Press.

Gabor, T., Baril, M., Cusson, M., Elie, D., LeBlanc, M., & Normandeau, A. (1987). *Armed Robbery: Cops, Robbers, and Victims.* Springfield, IL: Charles C. Thomas Publishing.

Glasgow, D. G. (1980). *The Black Underclass: Poverty, Unemployment, and Entrapment of Ghetto Youth.* New York: Random House.

Gottfredson, M. R., & Hirschi, T. (1988). Science, public policy, and the career paradigm. *Criminology 26*, 37–56.

Greenwood, P. W. (1982). *Selective Incapacitation.* Santa Monica, CA: RAND.

Guttridge, P., Gabrielli, W. F., Mednick, S. A., & Dusen, K. V. (1983). Criminal violence in a birth cohort. In V. Dusen & V. Mednick (Eds.), *Prospective Studies of Crime and Delinquency* pp. 211–224. Boston: Kluwer-Nijhoff.

Hamparian, D., Schuster, R., Dinitz, S., & Conrad, J. P. (1978). *The Violent Few.* Lexington: D. C. Heath.

Hirschi, T., & Gottfredson, M. R. (1988). Science, public policy, and the career paradigm. *Criminology 26*, 37–56.

Hoffman, P. (1994). Twenty years of operational use of a risk prediction instrument: the United States parole commission's salient factor score. *J Crim Justice 22*, 477–494.

Irwin, J. (1970). *The Felon.* Englewood Cliffs, NJ: Prentice-Hall.

Irwin, J., & Austin, J. (1994). *It's About Time: America's Imprisonment Binge.* Belmont, CA: Wadsworth.

Jacobs, B. A., & Wright, R. (1999). Stick-up, street culture, and offender motivation. *Criminology 37*, 149–174.

Jensen, G. F., & Brownfield, D. (1986). Gender, lifestyles, and victimization: beyond routine activity. *Violence Victims 1*, 85–99.

Katz, J. (1988). *Seductions of Crime: Moral and Sensual Aspects of Doing Evil.* New York: Basic Books.

Kempf, K. L. (1987). Specialization and the criminal career. *Criminology 25*, 399–420.

Kennedy, L. W., & Baron, S. W. (1993). Routine activities and a subculture of violence: a study on the street. *J Res Crime Delinquency 30*, 88–112.

Kennedy, L. W., & Forde, D. R. (1990). Routine activities and crime: an analysis of victimization in Canada. *Criminology 28*, 137–152.

Krivo, L. J., Peterson, R. D., Rizzo, H., & Reynolds, J. R. (1998). Race, segregation, and the concentration of disadvantage: 1980–1990. *Soc Probl 45*, 61–80.

Lasley, J. R. (1989). Drinking routines/lifestyles and predatory victimization: a causal analysis. *Justice Q 6*, 529–542.

MacDonald, J. M. (1975). *Armed Robbery: Offenders and their Victims.* Springfield, IL: Charles C. Thomas Publishing.

Martinez Jr., R. (1997). Predictors of serious violent recidivism: results from a cohort study. *J Interpers Violence 12*, 216–228.

McCleary, R. M. (1992). *Dangerous Men: The Sociology of Parole.* New York: Harrow and Heston.

Miller, W. B. (1958). Lower class culture as a generating milieu of gang delinquency. *J Soc Issues 14*, 419–435.

Mustaine, E., & Tewksbury, R. (1998). Specifying the role of alcohol in predatory victimization. *Deviant Behav 19*, 173–200.

Petersilia, J., & Turner, S. (1986). *Prison versus Probation in California: Implications for Crime and Offender Recidivism.* Santa Monica, CA: RAND.

Peterson, R. D., & Krivo, L. J. (1993). Residential segregation and black urban homicide. *Soc Forces 71*, 1001–1026.

Pettiway, L. E. (1982). Mobility of robbery and burglary offenders: ghetto and nonghetto spaces. *Urban Aff Q 18*, 255–270.

Roncek, D. W., & Maier, P. A. (1991). Bars, blocks, and crimes revisited: linking the theory of routine activities to the empiricism of 'hot spots'. *Criminology 29*, 725–753.

Sampson, R. J., & Lauritsen, J. L. (1990). Deviant lifestyles, proximity to crime, and the offender–victim link in personal violence. *J Res Crime Delinquency 27*, 110–139.

Schmid, T. J., & Jones, R.S. (1991). Suspended identity: identity transformation in a maximum security prison. *Symb Interact 14*, 415–432.

Schwaner, S. L. (1995). A decade apart: parole process and outcome in the age of determinacy. Unpublished Dissertation. Columbus, OH: The Ohio State University.

Schwaner, S. L. (1998). Patterns of violent specialization: predictors of recidivism for a cohort of parolees. *Am J Crim Justice 23*, 1–18.

Schwaner, S. L., McGaughey, D., & Tewksbury, R. (1998). Situational constraints and absconding behavior: toward a typology of parole fugitives. *J Offender Rehabil 27*(1/2), 37–55.

Singer, S. (1981). Homogeneous victim–offender populations: a review of some research implications. *J Crim Law Criminol 72*, 779–788.

Singer, S. (1986). Victims of serious violence and their criminal behavior: subcultural theory and beyond. *Violence Victims 1*, 61–69.

Sykes, G. (1965). *A Society of Captives: A Study of a Maximum Security Prison.* New York: Athenaeum Books.

Thomas, P. (1967). *Down These Mean Streets.* New York: Vintage Books.

Van Dine, S., Conrad, J. P., & Dinitz, S. (1979). *Restraining the Wicked: The Dangerous Offender Project.* Lexington, MA: Lexington Books.

Van Stelle, K. R., Mauser, E., & Moberg, D. P. (1994). Recidivism to the criminal justice system of substance-abusing offenders diverted into treatment. *Crime Delinquency 2,* 175–196.

Walker, N., Hammond, W., & Stear, D. (1967). Repeated Violence. *Crim Law Rev* (August): 465–472.

West, D. J., & Farrington, D. P. (1977). *The Delinquent Way of Life.* New York: Crane Russek.

Wilson, W. J. (1987). *The Truly Disadvantaged.* Chicago: University of Chicago Press.

Wolfgang, M. E., Figlio, R. M., & Sellin, T. (1972). *Delinquency in a Birth Cohort.* Chicago: University of Chicago Press.

Wright, R. T., & Decker, S. H. (1997). *Armed Robbers in Action.* Boston: Northeastern University Press.

[15]

ROBBERY VIOLENCE*

PHILIP J. COOK**

I. INTRODUCTION

Robbery is both a property crime and a crime of violence. The definition of robbery delineates the relationship between these two dimensions: theft or attempted theft by force or the threat of violence. Victim losses from robbery-related theft are usually quite small; victim survey results indicate that only 15% of noncommercial robberies in 1983 resulted in a theft of more than $250.[1] The violence element of robbery makes it a serious crime. In all, approximately 30% of the victims of noncommercial robbery are injured, and about one-third of these injuries require treatment at a hospital.[2] More importantly, approximately 2000 robbery victims are murdered each year.[3]

Robbery is particularly fear-inspiring, as it usually involves an unprovoked surprise attack by strangers on an innocent victim. This fear has serious consequences. James Q. Wilson and Barbara Boland note that "[i]t is mostly fear of robbery that induces many citizens to stay home at night and to avoid the streets, thereby diminishing the sense of community and increasing the freedom with which crimes may be committed on the streets."[4]

This Article will provide a description of the patterns of robbery violence, including demographic characteristics of robbers and their victims as well as their relationship to each other, the type of weapon used, and the location of the crime. This description is

* This research was supported by a grant from the National Institute of Justice. Lois Mock was extremely helpful as both project monitor and critic throughout the life of the project. David Hintz supplied able assistance in computer programming.

** Professor of Public Policy Studies and Economics, Duke University. Ph.D., University of California, Berkeley, 1973; B.A., University of Michigan, 1968.

1 U.S. DEP'T. OF JUSTICE, BUREAU OF JUSTICE STATISTICS, CRIMINAL VICTIMIZATION IN THE UNITED STATES, 7 (1983).

2 Id.

3 U.S. DEP'T. OF JUSTICE, FED. BUREAU OF INVESTIGATION, CRIME IN THE UNITED STATES, 12 (1981-85).

4 Wilson & Boland, Crime, in THE URBAN PREDICAMENT 179, 183 (W. Gorham & N. Glazer eds. 1976).

drawn from data sets compiled by the Federal Bureau of Investigation and the Bureau of Justice Statistics. The statistics are national in scope and include thousands of observations on both robberies and robbery murders. The findings demonstrate that robbery homicides are more similar to other robberies than other homicides. The weapon type data provide an important exception to this generalization: although guns predominate in all types of homicide, they are relatively rare in nonfatal robberies.

This Article will develop evidence regarding the causal relationship between robbery and robbery murder. If robbery murder is an intrinsic by-product of robbery, then it follows that effective programs to reduce the robbery rate will also reduce the robbery murder rate. Alternatively, if robbery murders constitute an etiologically distinct group of events, then there will be no correlation between the rates of robbery and robbery murder, and, consequently, policies directed at one will have little effect on the other. The evidence strongly favors the "intrinsic by-product" characterization of robbery murder because variations in the robbery rate are closely linked to variations in the robbery murder rate. Finally, some types of robbery are much more likely to result in death than others. It is estimated that a reduction in gun robberies would save approximately five times as many lives as would a similar reduction in non-gun robberies.[5]

Part Two of this Article presents a description of robbery violence patterns. This description includes a multivariate analysis of nonfatal violence estimated from National Crime Survey (NCS) micro data files[6], as well as a three-way comparison between robbery, robbery murder, and other homicides. Part Three of this Article explores the relationship between the intertemporal changes in city-specific robbery rates and the corresponding robbery murder rates of 43 large American cities. Finally, this Article discusses the relevance of these findings to several policy questions, such as the appropriate sanctions for such crimes and methods of deterrence.

II.   PATTERNS OF ROBBERY VIOLENCE

Some robberies have much more serious consequences for the victims than others. Of the 1.5 million robbery attempts perpetrated each year,[7] the vast majority result in little or no loss of prop-

---

[5] *See infra* p.371.

[6] U.S. DEP'T. JUSTICE, BUREAU OF JUSTICE STATISTICS (1979).

[7] COOK, ROBBERY IN THE UNITED STATES: AN ANALYSIS OF RECENT TRENDS AND PATTERNS 3 (1983).

erty or physical injury. However, one in every 750 robbery victims is killed, and one in every forty is seriously injured.[8]

Developing a comprehensive description of robbery violence patterns is hampered by a lack of data. The Uniform Crime Reports data on robbery lack much detail. In particular, these reports do not contain information regarding the prevalence of injury to the robbery victims. The National Crime Survey (NCS) data include much more detail information about each of the robberies reported by survey respondents. These data also provides estimates of non-fatal injury patterns.[9] The NCS data, however, include no information about robberies committed against commercial targets, which constitute 20% of all robberies, and exclude information about robbery murders. This information is compiled by the FBI from Supplementary Homicide Reports submitted by state and local jurisdictions.[10]

The first description of robbery violence patterns presented below is compiled from NCS data and is, therefore, limited to non-fatal, non-commercial robberies. The second section utilizes Supplementary Homicide Reports data to characterize robbery murder and to compare it with robbery and other types of criminal homicide.

A. NON-FATAL INJURIES

Data for this description were taken from NCS files for the years 1973 to 1979 and include all cases reported to NCS interviewers which involved at least one male robber, age 18 or older.[11] Robberies committed by younger teenagers were excluded to avoid dilution of the sample by a large number of relatively trivial events such as extortion of lunch money from school children.

Table 1 reports the results of this multivariate probit analysis. The independent variables were selected from those available in the NCS records on the basis of previous findings and common sense. With one exception, these variables are binary, and they indicate the presence or absence of some characteristic, such as the presence of three or more robbers at the time of the incident or the fact that the victim was black. The only variable that is not binary is the median

---

8 *Id.* at 6. *See also* Cook, *Is Robbery Becoming More Violent? An Analysis of Robbery Murder Trends Since 1968*, 76 J. CRIM. L. & CRIMINOLOGY 480 (1983).

9 For an introduction to the NCS, see Sparks, *Surveys of Victimization—an Optimistic Assessment*, in CRIME AND JUSTICE: AN ANNUAL REVIEW OF RESEARCH 1 (M. Tonry & N. Morris eds. 1981).

10 *See* U.S. DEP'T. OF JUSTICE, FED. BUREAU OF INVESTIGATION, UNIFORM CRIME REPORTING HANDBOOK (1980).

11 This data set was provided to the author by Wesley Skogan, Professor of Political Science, Northwestern University.

income of the neighborhood in which the victim lives. This variable was drawn from 1970 census data and is measured in thousands of dollars. The estimated probability of violence in a robbery incident with specified characteristics can be calculated by summing the constant and the coefficient estimates associated with each of the applicable characteristics and converting the resulting Z-score to a probability by use of a table of the standard normal distribution.

Three definitions of "violence" are represented by the probit analysis reported in table 1. The most serious cases of violence result in victim hospitalization for treatment of his wounds. This type of violence is rare and occurs in only 2.6% of the cases included in the NCS sample.[12] The second definition of "violence" is "hospital treatment." This category comprises 10% of all cases and includes victims admitted to a hospital as well as victims treated in an emergency room and released. The third and broadest definition of "violence" is "victim attacked," which includes 51% of all cases.[13]

Each of the estimated coefficients in the last three columns of Table 1 represents a measure of the partial effect of the indicated characteristic of the robbery incident on the likelihood of violence, controlling for the influence of all the other characteristics listed. These estimated coefficients provide insight into the robbery process. Some of the patterns that emerge have been discussed in other literature.[14] Of considerable interest is the relationship between injury prevalence and weapon type. Although there is a direct link between weapon lethality and the likelihood of death in robbery, a number of studies have found that the likelihood of victim injury is related inversely to the lethality of the weapon.[15] This surprising pattern in victim injury can be attributed to the weapons-related difference in robbery technique. Non-armed robberies and robberies with clubs, known as "muggings" or "yokings", usually are initiated by an attack. Robberies with more lethal weapons, known as "hold-ups," usually are initiated with the threat and/or

---

[12] A recent study found that gunshot victims in assault and robbery cases were severely underrepresented in the NCS sample. *See* Cook, *The Case of the Missing Victims: Gunshot Woundings in the National Crime Survey*, 1 J. QUANT. CRIMINOLOGY 91 (1985).

[13] The phrase "victim attacked" is derived from a question in the National Crime Survey which reads: "Did person[s] hit you, knock you down, or actually attack you in any way?" The violence may be appropriately characterized as "victim attacked" if the victim responds affirmatively to this question.

[14] *See, e.g.*, J. CONKLIN, ROBBERY AND THE CRIMINAL JUSTICE SYSTEM (1972); Cook, *A Strategic Choice Analysis of Robbery*, in SAMPLE SURVEYS OF THE VICTIMS OF CRIME 173 (W. Skogan ed. 1976); Zimring & Zuehl, *Victim Injury and Death in Urban Robbery: A Chicago Study*, 15 J. LEGAL STUD. 1 (1986).

[15] *See* note 11 and accompanying text, Skogan, *Weapon Use in Robbery*, in VIOLENT CRIME: HISTORICAL AND CONTEMPORARY ISSUES (J. Inciardi & A. Pottieger eds. 1978).

TABLE 1

CORRELATES OF USE OF VIOLENCE IN NONCOMMERCIAL ROBBERY

Robber Characteristics	Relative Frequency (%)	PROBIT ANALYSIS OF COMPLETE SAMPLE ESTIMATED COEFFICIENTS		
		Victim Attacked	Hospital Treatment	Hospitalized Overnight
1. 3 or more robbers	22	.36**	.22**	.03
2. Black	55	−.01	.02	.01
3. Stranger to victim	74	−.09	−.27**	−.22*
4. Weapon type ("unarmed" category omitted)				
a. gun	22	−1.14**	−.14	.35**
b. knife	19	−.76**	.13	.30*
c. other	11	−.18**	.69**	.62**
d. unknown	11	−.45**	−.51**	−.01
Victim Characteristics				
5. 2 or more victims	8	−.27**	−.34**	−.29
6. Black	21	.05	.25**	.23*
7. Age ("12-17" category omitted)				
a. 18-24	33	.10	.26**	.42*
b. 25-54	40	.02	.30**	.36*
c. 55+	14	.17*	.55**	.87**
8. Male	67	−.17**	.09	.22*
9. Median income of neighborhood	—	−.018**	−.009	omitted
10. Location ("outdoor" category omitted)				
a. Home	14	.01	.05	−.21
b. Other indoor	16	−.11	−.07	−.15
11. Nighttime	63	.23**	.23**	.18
12. Constant		.59**	−1.68**	−2.75**
Sample Counts		1337/2608	260/2608	76/2875

* Coefficient exceeds standard error by factor of 1.65 - 1.96.
** Coefficient exceeds standard error by factor of 1.96 or more.
  Sample: All cases included in the National Crime Survey, 1973-1979, involving at least one male robber age 18 or more.

the display of the weapon. This choice of technique in both cases reflects the robber's objective of overcoming the victim's willingness to part with his or her valuables. The mere threat of injury is sufficient if made credible by the display of a gun or a knife.

If a robbery victim is attacked, the seriousness of injury is determined in part by the weapon employed in the attack. Thus, we expect to find greater weapon-related disparities in minor injury rates than in serious injury rates. In addition, as will be discussed below, the likelihood of *fatal* injury is highest in robberies involving the use of the most lethal weapons, reversing the weapons-related pattern for minor injury.

A second important correlate of robbery violence is the age of the victim. Older victims, age fifty-five or above, are more likely than others to be attacked, to seek hospital treatment, and to be hospitalized overnight. Data presented in Table 2 indicate that older victims are also much more likely to be killed in a robbery. This pattern may reflect the relative vulnerability of older victims rather than a systematic difference in the nature of the robbers' assaults.

Third, robberies by strangers appear less likely to cause serious injury than robberies by acquaintances. This finding may be the result of a survey reporting bias.[16] One may also speculate that robberies by acquaintances involve nonpecuniary motives conducive to violence such as a desire to avenge a drug rip-off.

Unfortunately, robbery murders cannot be incorporated into this data set. The analysis of robbery murder patterns presented in the next section, however, does include some of the same variables. These patterns are similar to those patterns for serious injuries discussed in Table 1.

B.   ROBBERY MURDER

The FBI's Uniform Crime Reports statistics for 1981 indicate that 22,516 criminal homicides were committed in that year.[17] Information on "circumstances/motives" was available for 20,053 of these homicides, of which 2,086 classified as "robbery-related."[18] This latter statistic is based on information submitted by local police departments known as Supplementary Homicide Reports (SHR). The SHR provide detailed information on each criminal homicide occurring in the department's jurisdiction. The SHR are the only routinely available source of information concerning a number of characteristics of robbery related homicides. These data are neither completely reliable nor accurate.[19]

The SHR circumstance codes include a "robbery" category to be used for murders that occur "in conjunction with" a robbery. Most homicide investigators determine whether the motive of the crime was robbery-based by means of circumstantial evidence, such as whether the victim's wallet is missing, the location of the killing,

---

[16] *See* Sparks, *supra* note 9 (respondents are less likely to report a crime committed against them by a relative or acquaintance than by a stranger, other things being equal).

[17] U.S. DEP'T. OF JUSTICE, FED. BUREAU OF INVESTIGATION, CRIME IN THE UNITED STATES, 1981 7 (1982).

[18] *Id.* at 12.

[19] Loftin, *The Validity of Robbery-Murder Classifications in Baltimore*, 1(3) VIOLENCE AND VICTIMS 191 (1986).

TABLE 2

PERCENT DISTRIBUTION OF CRIMINAL HOMICIDES AND ROBBERIES BY VICTIM AND OFFENDER CHARACTERISTICS - 1981

	ROBBERY	ROBBERY MURDER	NON FELONY HOMICIDE
Victim Sex			
Male	63	85	78
Female	37	15	22
Victim Race			
White	73	64	50
Black	25	33	48
Other	3	2	2
Victim Age			
Less than 20	27	6	12
20-34	40	34	49
35-49	15	21	24
Over 49	18	39	15
Offender Sex			
Male	92	92	82
Female	4	2	17
Both	4	6	1
(Unknown)	(0.9)	(36.3)	(7.7)
Offender Race			
White	34	39	48
Black	56	58	50
Other	5	1	2
Mixed	4	2	0
(Unknown)	(2.2)	(36.4)	(8.1)
Offender Age			
Less than 21	40	33	13
21 and over	46	56	85
Mixed	14	11	2
(Unknown)	(4.3)	(39.1)	(8.9)

Victim Race	White Off	Black Off	White Off	Black Off	White Off	Black Off
White	94	61	92	49	95	7
Black	6	39	7	51	4	93

Weapon Type	ROBBERY	ROBBERY MURDER	NON FELONY HOMICIDE
Gun	17	65	65
Knife or Other	28	25	25
Personal or Unknown	56	11	10
Relationship			
Relative	15	2	30
Acquaintance		26	58
Stranger	85	73	12
(Unknown)		(34.2)	(10.9)
N		2,091	11,599

Definitions: "Unknown" entries are percent of all cases for which information on the stated attribute was unknown. Other entries in each column sum to 100 percent.
"Non Felony Homicide" includes all homicides not classified as felony related, suspected to be felony related, or unknown circumstances.
"Robbery" includes noncommercial, nonfatal cases with victims aged 12 or more.

Sources: FBI Supplementary Homicide Reports, microfiles.
BJS *Criminal Victimization in the United States, 1981*

and the relationship, if any, between the victim and suspect. Cases that have some of the characteristics of robbery may be classified in the SHR system as "suspected felony type" or "unable to determine circumstances." Two recent studies evaluated homicide classification procedures in Chicago[20] and Baltimore.[21] Both studies concluded that while almost all cases officially recorded as robbery-related were correctly classified, a number of cases which were recorded in a different category were probably robbery-related.

Table 2 displays percentage distributions of robbery and robbery-murder cases over a number of dimensions, including the age, sex, and the role of the victim and the offender, the relationship, if any, between the victim and the offender, and the type of weapon used in the commission of the crime. By way of comparison, the distributions over the same dimensions are reported in the third column for "non-felony homicides," which are criminal homicides that did not occur in the context of a robbery or another felony. The first column of Table 2 presents the corresponding distributions of nonfatal robberies, calculated from published data in the 1981 National Crime Survey.[22] The NCS sample was drawn from a population that differs in certain respects from the population used for SHR data. The most important difference between NES and SHR data is that commercial robberies are not included in the NCS data. In the recent study of Chicago data, it was found that approximately 15% of the SHR's robbery-related murders occurred in the context of a commercial robbery.[23]

Although the data in Table 1 result from a multivariate analysis, the statistics in Table 2 are more primitive because each dimension is considered separately. Hence, there are possible problems in attribution introduced by collinearity among the dimensions. In any event, a comparison of distributions in columns 1 and 2 indicates that robbery murders differ from nonfatal robberies in ways similar to the differences reported in Table 1 between serious injury robberies and other robberies. In comparing robbery murder victims to robbery victims, a disproportionate number of robbery murder victims are over forty-nine years old (39% versus 18%), and are male (85% versus 63%). Robbery murder victims are more likely than robbery victims to be acquainted with or related to the perpetrator (26 % versus 15 %). This conclusion is supported by the sta-

---

20 Zimring & Zuehl, *supra* note 14.
21 Loftin, *supra* note 19.
22 U.S. DEP'T. OF JUSTICE, BUREAU OF JUSTICE STATISTICS, CRIMINAL VICTIMIZATION IN THE UNITED STATES (1981).
23 Zimring & Zuehl, *supra* note 14.

tistics on racial crossovers: for black offenders, robbery murder victims are more likely to be of the same race than are robbery victims (51% versus 39%).

The greatest difference between robbery murder and other types of robbery is the type of weapon used by the perpetrator. While 65% of all robbery murders are committed with a gun, guns are used in only 17% of all robberies. This result may be viewed as a logical extension of the weapons pattern shown in Table 1. Robbers using guns are relatively unlikely to attack their victims but are relatively likely to inflict serious injury; in other words, gun assaults are more serious than assaults with other weapons.

Comparison of robbery murders with other criminal homicide cases also yields interesting results. The third column of Table 2 reports the percentage distributions for "nonfelony homicides" in 1981. Nonfelony homicides include: all homicides not classified as felony-related, those homicides suspected to be felony-related, or homicides occurring in unknown circumstances. With respect to the demographic characteristics of the offender, robbery murders are much more similar to robberies than to other homicides. Robbers, regardless of whether they kill their victims, are more likely than nonfelony killers to be male, under twenty-one years of age, and nonwhite.

Generally speaking, there is a greater relational distance between victim and offender in robbery and robbery murder cases than in nonfelony homicides.[24] Figures in Table 2 reflect that in 85% of the robberies and 73% of the robbery murders, the victim and offender were strangers; however, only 12 % of nonfelony murder cases shared this characteristic. Other statistics give further evidence of this relational distance. With respect to race, only 7% of nonfelony homicides involve black offenders and white victims; the corresponding percentages for robbery murder and nonfatal robbery are 49% and 61% respectively. White offenders, on the other hand, almost always choose whites as victims for all three types of crime. Finally, there is a greater age disparity between victim and offender in robberies and robbery murders than in nonfelony homicides.

In the dimension of weapon type, robbery murder is identical to nonfelony homicide and much different from robbery. Sixty-five percent of both types of killing are committed with guns, while guns were used in only 17% of the robberies.

In considering these statistical comparisons, it is important to

---

24 *Id.*

keep in mind the imperfections of the data. The lack of data about commercial robberies bias the robbery statistics. For example, commercial robbery is more likely than non-commercial robbery to involve a gun.[25] Commercial robbery offenders tend to be older than non-commercial robbers.[26] Moreover, the robbery murder statistics may be distorted by the imprecision of police and FBI homicide classifications.[27] Finally, offender data for robbery murders and other homicides are incomplete because there are no suspects in some cases. These unknown offenders may have different characteristics than the typical known offenders. None of these problems, however, are severe enough to cast doubt on the basic pattern of findings. Furthermore, these data are the best available and have the virtue of being national in scope.

This description of robbery violence does not preempt the potential usefulness of intensive studies of single jurisdictions. In that context, there is a possibility of obtaining more data on the circumstances of the crime and the characteristics of offenders that are not readily observable, such as prior criminal record[28] and drug and alcohol involvement.[29]

In summary, the more interesting findings from the data in Table 2 are:

   * Robbery and robbery murder are both typically committed by offenders who do not know their victims. Nonfelony homicides, on the other hand, are only rarely committed by strangers.
   * Black offenders choose white victims in half of all robbery murders and in more than half of all robberies. In nonfelony homicides, however, such racial "crossover" is rare.
   * The age of robbery murder victims is considerably older than that of either robbery or nonfelony homicide victims. Furthermore, the percentage of robbery murder victims who are male is higher than the corresponding percentages of either robbery or nonfelony homicides.
   * The final significant difference between robbery and robbery murder is the distribution of weapons. Armed robbery is far more likely to result in death than is an un-armed robbery.

---

[25] *See* Cook, *Reducing Injury and Death Rates in Robbery*, 6 POLICY ANALYSIS 21, (1980).
[26] *Id.*

[27] *See* Loftin, *supra* note 19; Zimring and Zuehl, *supra* note 14, at 4.

[28] *See* P. COOK & D. NAGIN, DOES THE WEAPON MATTER? AN EVALUATION OF A WEAPONS-EMPHASIS POLICY IN THE PROSECUTION OF VIOLENT OFFENDERS (1979).

[29] *See* Goldstein, *Homicide Related to Drug Traffic*, 62 BULL. N.Y. ACAD. MED. 509 (1986); Zimring & Zuehl, *supra* note 14.

III. Murder as a By-product of Robbery

A. Alternative Scenarios

The statistical evidence presented in Part II suggests that homicides classified as "robbery related" have much in common with nonfatal robberies. However, criminal law and criminal justice system operating procedures view robbery murder as being much more analagous to other murders than to other robberies. The police investigation of a robbery murder will be conducted by detectives from the homicide division and will be accorded much higher priority than a robbery. The crime will be recorded as a murder and not as a robbery for uniform crime reporting purposes. In the event of an arrest and subsequent prosecution, the primary charge will be murder. Within the criminal justice system, the robbery component of robbery murder is only relevant as an aggravating circumstance that may influence the degree of murder charged and the priority assigned the case by the prosecutor. In any event, the criminal justice system channels robbery murders on the same track as other murders and channels nonfatal robbery cases on a quite different track. Nevertheless, the potential influence of the criminal justice system on the robbery murder rate is not limited to its success in solving robbery murder cases, because effective robbery-specific policies may reduce robbery murder. These policies include the deterrence of gun use in robbery,[30] the education of potential victims concerning the safest way to behave if robbed,[31] and the reduction of the overall volume of robbery by increasing the likelihood that robbers will be caught, convicted, and punished.[32] However, robbery-specific policies will only be effective in reducing robbery murders if murder is in some sense the direct and probabilistic consequence of robbery. If each robbery has an intrinsic and positive probability of resulting in the victim's death, then robbery-specific policies could reduce robbery murder. On the other hand, if robbery murders are etiologically distinct from nonfatal robberies, then policies directed at the latter will have little or no effect on the former. Thus, understanding the causal link between robbery and robbery murder is useful in the search for policies to make robbery a less lethal crime.[33]

---

[30] *See* Cook, *The Influence of Gun Availability on Violent Crime Patterns*, in Crime and Justice: An Annual Review of Research 4 (M. Tonry & N. Morris eds. 1983).

[31] *See* Cook, *The Relationship Between Victim Resistance and Injury in Noncommercial Robbery*, 15 J. Leg. Stud. 405 (1986).

[32] *See* Cook, *supra* note 7, at 25.

[33] This argument is developed further in Cook, *Reducing Injury and Death Rates in Robbery*, 6 Policy Analysis 21 (1980).

Possible connections between the robbery and the killing components of a robbery murder are illustrated by the following scenarios:

Scenario 1: Two gun-toting robbers enter a convenience store and order the clerk to lie on the floor. The clerk hesitates and then reaches under the counter. One of the robbers, afraid that the clerk is reaching for a gun, shoots and kills him.

Scenario 2: Three teenagers knock down an elderly woman and run off with her purse. In falling, she hits her head on the sidewalk and later dies from the concussion.

Scenario 3: Two hoodlums break into a room where a large heroin transaction is in progress, kill everyone there, and flee with the drugs and cash.

Scenario 4: Two acquaintances meet on the street and begin arguing about a ten dollar loan that one claims to have made to the other. The argument becomes violent. The "lender" stabs and kills the other. Then, as an afterthought, the lender takes the other's wallet as "compensation" for the loan.

The first two scenarios are meant to represent a class of robberies in which the robbers have the capability, but not the intent, to use lethal violence prior to initiating the robbery. The killing involved is, in effect, a probabilistic outcome of the underlying event. The number of such robbery murders will bear a close causal relationship to the number of such robberies that occur. In the last two scenarios, the murders would also most likely be classified by the police as "robbery related", but the relationship between the killing and the theft is quite different from the first two scenarios. In the third and fourth scenario, the assailants make a decision to use lethal violence that is unrelated to the immediate events of the robbery. A criminal justice system effort to deter robbery might, if successful, eliminate some of the robbery murders of the types illustrated by the first two scenarios. However, the other types of robbery are beyond the reach of a robbery-specific program.

Some robbery murders, therefore, are robberies that result in the victim's death as a result of a mistake, an escalation of violence induced by victim resistance, or some other factor inherent in the robbery process. In other robbery murders, the killing is a distinct event that occurs in conjunction with a robbery. Which sort of robbery murder predominates? Is robbery murder more closely related to robbery or to criminal homicide in its essential etiology? These are the questions that motivate the statistical inquiry which follows.

B.   INTERCITY DIFFERENCES IN ROBBERY AND MURDER RATES

If robbery murder is closely linked to robbery, then a close relationship between robbery rates and robbery murder rates, both over time and across jurisdictions, would be expected. As is apparent in the statistics in Table 2, there is indeed such a close relationship. The proper interpretation of this relationship requires a careful examination of the results.

1. Data

Available data permitted calculation of robbery rates, robbery murder rates, and criminal homicide rates by weapon type in each of forty-three large United States cities between 1976 and 1983. Robbery data were taken from the FBI's unpublished "Return A" files. Homicide rates were computed from the FBI's Supplementary Homicide Report files, which are also unpublished. Population-based rates for each city were averaged over the four years of "Period 1," 1976-79, and of "Period 2," 1980-83. Combining data over a four-year period in this fashion was necessary to provide meaningful robbery murder rates for the smaller cities in the sample, some of which had fewer than ten robbery murders in any one year.

2. Results

Table 2 indicates that the correlation between the robbery rate and the robbery murder rate is .81 for Period 1 and .80 for Period 2. Clearly, these two crime categories exhibit very similar geographic patterns, as would be expected if murder were a "by-product" of robbery. However, the fact that robbery murder is even more highly correlated with the overall homicide rate (net of robbery murders) calls this interpretation into question; this correlation is .83 in Period 1 and .87 in Period 2. Given this result, it appears that all three variables (robbery rate, robbery murder rate, overall homicide rate) are indicators of some underlying characteristic of these cities, which could be called "violence proneness." Cities with high robbery rates have high robbery murder rates and high rates of other types of homicide.

One method for sorting out the separate effects of somewhat collinear variables is a multivariate regression analysis. Table 3 presents the results of two sets of ordinary least squares regressions. In each case, the robbery murder rate per 100,000 is the dependent variable, computed for Period 1, for Period 2, and for the change between the two periods. The independent variables are computed for the corresponding periods.

From the results of Regression 2, it is apparent that the robbery rate and the net homicide rate make separate and distinguishable

TABLE 3
ROBBERY MURDERS PER 100,000, 43 CITIES ORDINARY LEAST SQUARES REGRESSION RESULTS

	ESTIMATED COEFFICIENTS (ESTIMATED STANDARD ERRORS)		
	Period 1 1976-79	Period 2 1980-83	Change Period 2 − Period 1
Regression 1			
Constant	−.406 (.368)	−.012 (.364)	−.294 (.140)
Robberies/1000	.498 (.057)	.363 (.043)	.305 (.058)
R^2	.65	.64	.41
Regression 2			
Constant	−1.136 (.293)	−.668 (.266)	−.259 (.146)
Robberies/1000	.284 (.054)	.176 (.040)	.256 (.081)
Net Homicides/100,000	.112 (.018)	.107 (.015)	.028 (.033)
R^2	.82	.83	.42

Note: "Net Homicides" means total criminal homicides minus robbery murders.

Sources: Robbery data: FBI's Return A file for individual cities. Homicide date: FBI's Supplementary Homicide Reports files.

contributions in explaining the cross-section structure of robbery murder rates. Interestingly, when the same regression is run on the data for the changes in rates between the two periods, reported in the last column, the coefficient on the net homicide rate is small and statistically insignificant. Thus, the rate of change in the robbery murder rate is closely linked to the robbery rate, but not the net homicide rate, of the forty-three cities. These results suggest that the intertemporal relationship between robbery and robbery murder is not a reflection of the city "violence proneness" factor, as measured by the homicide rate, but rather indicates a direct causal link between the robbery rate and the robbery murder rate.

B. THE IMPORTANCE OF WEAPON TYPE

While it is natural to evaluate the seriousness of robbery by viewing its consequences to the victim, i.e., degree of injury and financial loss, the legal distinction is actually based on the robber's choice of weapon. In particular, armed robbery is subject to more severe punishment than unarmed, "strong-arm" robbery. A number of states have recently delineated a further distinction between armed robbery and unarmed robbery.[34] A survey of 900 assistant prosecutors found that they perceived gun robbery as substantially more serious than robbery with a blunt object or with physical force.[35] One argument in favor of such weapons-based distinctions derives from the notion of "objective dangerousness": that the likelihood of serious injury or death in robbery is influenced *inter alia* by the type of weapon employed by the assailant. Hence, the seriousness of a robbery is associated with weapon type regardless of the outcome.[36] Gun robberies, therefore, are more dangerous than other armed robberies, and armed robberies are more dangerous than strong-arm robberies. If this hypothesis is correct, then effective policies to discourage the use of lethal weapons in robbery will reduce the fraction of robberies that result in serious injury or death.

In Part II, it was reported that a much higher fraction of robbery murders than robberies are committed with a gun. Table 4 presents the robbery murder/robbery ratios for each weapon category, using SHR data for large cities. The third row of this table demonstrates that the likelihood of death in a gun robbery (about 1

TABLE 4
ROBBERY MURDER—ROBBERY RATIOS FOR LARGE CITIES, BY
WEAPON TYPE, 1977

		GUN	KNIFE	OTHER	UNARMED
1.	Ratios calculated from Return A Robbery Count	0.70%	0.50%	0.19%	0.11%
2.	Robbery Reporting Rate	.590	.260	.231	.208
3.	Corrected Ratios	0.41%	0.13%	0.04%	0.02%

Notes:

    Row 1: Each entry is the ratio of robbery murders committed with the stated weapon type (SHR data) to the number of robberies reported to the police (Return A data) for cities over 250,000 population, 1977. Ratios are stated in percent form.

    Row 2: Each entry is the ratio of all U.S. robberies reported to the police. (*Crime in the United States, 1976*) to the number of robberies estimated from the National Crime Survey (*Criminal Victimization in the United States, 1976*), for the stated weapon type.

    Row 3: Each entry is the product of corresponding entries in Rows 1 and 2. The implicit assumption here is that the national robbery reporting rates in 1976 were the same as urban robbery reporting rates in 1977.

---

[34] E. JONES & M. RAY, HANDGUN CONTROL: LEGISLATIVE AND ENFORCEMENT STRATEGIES (U.S. Dept. Justice, 1981).

[35] Roth, *Prosecutor Perceptions of Crime Seriousness*, 69 J. CRIM. L. & CRIMINOLOGY 232, 241 (1978).

[36] F. Zimring, *The Medium Is the Message: Firearm Calibre as a Determinant of Death From Assault*, 1 J. LEG. STUD. 97 (1972).

in 250) is three times greater than the likelihood of death in knife robbery, which is, in turn, about three times greater than the corresponding likelihood of death in armed robbery involving other weapons. The likelihood of death in unarmed robbery, one in 5000, is the lowest.

In sum, the likelihood of death in robbery is linked to the lethality of the weapon, with "lethality" defined as the amount of effort and strength required to kill. One could hypothesize that the relatively high death rate in gun robbery is the direct consequence of the fact that a loaded gun provides the assailant with the means to kill quickly at a distance and without much skill, strength, or danger of a counterattack. A passing whim or even the accidental twitch of a trigger finger is sufficient. Thus, a gun is intrinsically more dangerous than other types of weapons.

Although this argument is certainly plausible, the ratios in Table 4 may exaggerate the differences due to weapon type. The robber's choice of weapon is correlated with other observable characteristics of the robbery such as the type of target and the age and number of robbers involved. The choice of weapon may also be associated with unobservable characteristics of the robbery, such as the assailant's intent. If the robber plans to kill the victim, then presumably he will try to equip himself with the most appropriate tool for that task. For most assailants, this tool would be some type of firearm.[37] Thus, armed robberies differ from other robberies; these differences, however, are not all based upon weapon type. Other dimensions of armed robbery may account for some part of the large differences in death rates shown in Table 4.

Strong evidence that gun robberies are nonetheless intrinsically more dangerous than other types of robberies is presented in Table 5. The equations estimated in this table are identical to those used in Table 3, except that the robbery rate is replaced with two variables: the gun robbery rate, and the nongun robbery rate. Looking at the results of change data in Regression 2, we see that a one unit increase in the gun robbery rate is associated with a 0.432 percentage point increase in the robbery murder rate. This percentage point increase represents approximately five times the effect of a one unit increase in the nongun robbery rate. As noted above, a change in the net homicide rate has little or no influence on the robbery murder rate.

Thus, the robbery murder rate is much more sensitive to

---

[37] A more thorough discussion of the interaction between intent and weapon type is presented in Cook, *supra* note 30.

TABLE 5
ROBBERY MURDERS PER 100,000, 43 CITIES ORDINARY LEAST SQUARES REGRESSION RESULTS

	ESTIMATED COEFFICIENTS (ESTIMATED STANDARD ERRORS)		
	Period 1 1976-79	Period 2 1980-83	Change Period 2 — Period 1
Regression 1			
Constant	−.524 (.275)	−.048 (.308)	−.175 (.159)
Gun Robberies/1000	1.043 (.103)	.884 (.130)	.479 (.128)
Non Gun Robberies/1000	.153 (.073)	.050 (.083)	.141 (.122)
R^2	.81	.75	.44
Regression 2			
Constant	−.928 (.287)	−.603 (.276)	−.132 (.165)
Gun Robberies/1000	.666 (.159)	.320 (.160)	.432 (.137)
Non Gun Robberies/1000	.173 (.067)	.123 (.069)	.081 (.137)
Net Homicides/100,000	.070 (.024)	.095 (.020)	.031 (.032)
R^2	.84	.84	.45

Note: "Net Homicides" means total criminal homicides minus robbery murders.

Sources: Robbery data: FBI's Return A file for individual cities. Homicide data: FBI's Supplementary Homicide Reports files.

changes in a city's gun robbery rate than to its nongun robbery rate. A reduction in the gun robbery rate yields a greater reduction in robbery murder than a corresponding reduction in nongun robbery. While this evidence is based on "natural" variations in crime data for forty-three cities, it is reasonable to infer that explicit policies which are successful in reducing gun use in robbery will also reduce the robbery murder rate.

C.   SUMMARY

Homicides classified as "robbery-related" may result from a number of different motivational patterns. In some cases, the victim is killed by accident in response to the victim's resistance or as a result of a momentary vicious impulse. In such cases, it is reasonable to view the killing as a by-product of the robbery. Effective policies to reduce the robbery rate would also be effective in reducing such robbery-related killings.

Not all robbery-related murders have this "Russian roulette" character. In some cases, the murder is a planned part of the robbery; in others, the assailant's primary motive is to kill the victim, and the robbery is a secondary concern. The volume of such cases will be less closely linked to the overall volume of robberies.

The evidence presented above strongly indicates the empirical importance of the first sort of robbery murder. In forty-three cities, the change in the robbery murder rate between two four-year periods was highly correlated with the contemporaneous change in the robbery rate. Although it is possible that some "third cause" accounts for this correlation, this appears unlikely. A contemporaneous change in the overall level of lethal violence in these cities can be ruled out as a "third cause." Such a change would be reflected in the net criminal homicide rate. However, when that variable was included in the regression on change data, it had essentially no effect on the results. Thus, robbery murder rate patterns suggest that killings were an intrinsic by-product of robbery. If this conclusion is valid, then policies affecting robbery rates will also affect robbery murder rates.

Different types of robberies are characterized by different probabilities of generating this "by-product." The age of the victim, the time of day, the victim-offender relationship, and other factors, may influence the likelihood that the robbery victim will be killed. One factor that is of special interest due to its importance in the criminal law is the type of weapon used by the robber. It is expected that gun robberies would be intrinsically dangerous due to the relative ease with which a gun robber can kill his victim. The percentage of gun robberies that result in murder is three times higher than the percentage of murders resulting from knife robberies.[38] This ratio is higher with respect to other weapon types. Regression results on the robbery murder rates for forty-three cities demonstrates that the use of a gun has a direct causal effect on the likelihood of the victim's death.[39] In these regressions, a change in the gun robbery rate is estimated to have a five times greater effect on the murder rate than would a similar change in the nongun robbery rate.[40]

IV. Concluding Thoughts on Policy

Violence and the possibility of injury make robbery a serious

---

[38] *See supra* 371, Table 4.
[39] *See supra* 373, Table 5.
[40] *See supra* 371.

crime. The criminal justice system can respond to this violence both directly and indirectly. The direct response is to punish robberies that result in serious injury or death more harshly and to give higher priority to the investigation and prosecution of such robberies than to those in which the victims are not injured. The indirect response is to give high priority to convicting and punishing robbers who commit relatively dangerous robberies, whether or not they injure their victims.

The criminal justice system obviously places a high priority on robbery murder cases. The felony murder rule and capital punishment statutes facilitate prosecution and the imposition of severe punishment for these cases. The threat of severe punishment resulting from this direct response to robbery violence may have some general deterrent value. Surprisingly, however, the high priority given to robbery killings does not necessarily carry over to serious injury cases. Some jurisdictions do not appear to distinguish between robbery defendants in injury cases and robbery defendants in otherwise similar cases in which the victim was not injured.[41]

The indirect criminal justice system response to robbery violence is reflected in the distinction between armed and unarmed robbery. This distinction plays an important role in prosecution and sentencing. A further distinction between gun robberies and other armed robberies appears justified by wide variations in the fatality rate among different weapon categories. More persuasive evidence of the objective dangerousness of gun robberies is found in the regression results of Part III, which demonstrate the close link between variations in the gun robbery rate and the robbery murder rate.

Gun robberies can be deterred by means other than more severe sentencing. For example, since gun robberies are concentrated on commercial targets, programs to discourage commercial robbery, such as installing automatic cameras[42] and instituting exact change policies,[43] are, in effect, anti-gun robbery programs. A quite different approach is to discourage the use of guns in robberies by reducing the general availability of guns or by instituting stringent

---

[41] *See* COOK & NAGIN, *supra* note 28; P. Rossi, E. Weber-Burdin & H. Chen, *Effects of Weapons Use on Felony Case Disposition: An Analysis of Evidence from the Los Angeles PROMIS System* (1981)(unpublished manuscript).

[42] D. WHITCOMB, SEATTLE—FOCUS ON ROBBERY—THE HIDDEN CAMERAS PROJECT (Law enforcement Assistance Administration—National Institute of Law Enforcement and Criminal Justice, 1979).

[43] Chaiken, Lawless & Stevenson, *The Impact of Police Activity on Subway Crime*, 3 J. URBAN ANALYSIS 173, 186-189 (1974).

enforcement of anti-carrying ordinances.[44] The evidence in Part III suggests that a reduction in the gun robbery rate achieved by these or other means will reduce the robbery murder rate.

Since criminal justice system resources are scarce, it is necessary to consider the likely consequences if increased priority for gun robbery cases comes at the cost of reduced priority to other types of robbery. There has been considerable speculation about the net social benefit of engineering a reduction in the fraction of armed robberies committed with guns, while leaving the overall armed robbery rate unchanged.[45] Based on the evidence in Parts II and III, it appears that robbery killings would decline, serious injuries would remain more or less constant, and minor injuries would increase.

The type of weapon used by the robber is not the only correlate of robbery violence. A number of others were identified in Part II, the most important of which is the age of the victim. The probabilities that a victim over age fifty will be attacked, injured, or killed during a robbery are much higher than for other age groups. The explanation for these results is not immediately obvious but deserves consideration in formulating criminal justice system policy.

Therefore, using the best and most extensive data available with national scope, some important patterns in robbery violence have been documented. Injury and death rates differ widely depending on the circumstances and the characteristics of the victims and offenders. However, robberies resulting in serious injury or death are not primarily the result of a distinct causal process. Rather, it appears that robbery violence is a probabilistic by-product of robbery encounters. Thus, it is logically possible to reduce the robbery murder rate indirectly by policies directed at nonfatal robbery. This indirect approach will be most effective in reducing deaths if it is directed at categories of robbery that are most dangerous, such as gun robberies.

---

[44] *See* Cook, *supra* note 30.
[45] *See* Cook, *supra* note 33, at 44-45; Skogan, *supra* note 15, at 72.

Part III
Gun Crime, Violence and Homicide

[16]

Weapon Use and Violent Crime

National Crime Victimization Survey, 1993-2001

By Craig Perkins
BJS Statistician

Highlights

Estimates from the National Crime Victimization Survey (NCVS) indicate that between 1993 and 2001 approximately 26% of the average annual 8.9 million violent victimizations were committed by offenders armed with a weapon. About 10% of the violent victimizations involved a firearm.

From 1993 through 2001 violent crime declined 54%; weapon violence went down 59%; and firearm violence, 63%.

Males, American Indians, and Hispanics, the young, and those with the lowest annual household income were more vulnerable to weapon violence in general and firearm violence in particular than their respective counterparts.

For the 9-year period beginning with 1993, 23% of white victims of violence and 36% of black victims were victims of violence involving an offender armed with a weapon. About 7% of white victims and 17% of black victims were involved in incidents in which an offender was armed with a gun.

Forty-five percent of all violence with a weapon involved victims between ages 25 and 49, and 38% involved victims between ages 15 and 24.

Blacks were about 9 times more likely than whites to be victims of gun-related homicides (25 per 100,000 blacks age 12 or older versus 3 per 100,000 whites.)

For nonfatal violent crimes, offenders were more likely to have a firearm than a knife or club. From 1993 to 2001 the rate of firearm violence fell 63%

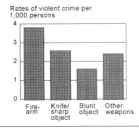

Rates of violent crime per 1,000 persons

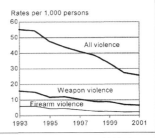

Rates per 1,000 persons

- Approximately half of all robberies, about a quarter of all assaults, and roughly a twelfth of all rapes/sexual assaults involved an armed assailant. About 90% of homicide victims were killed with a weapon.

- Firearm violence rates for blacks age 12 or older (8.4 per 1,000 blacks) were —
   40% higher than rates for Hispanics (6.0)

   200% higher than rates for whites (2.8 per 1,000).

- Blacks were about 9 times more likely than whites to be murdered with a firearm.

- On average black victims of firearm violence were 3 years younger than white victims — 29 versus 32.

- From 1993 through 2001 blacks accounted for 49% of homicide victims and 54% of victims of firearm homicide but 12% of the U.S. population.

- The likelihood of an injury was the same for victims facing armed and unarmed offenders (26%); serious injury was more likely from armed offenders (7% versus 2%).

- From 1993 through 2001 the number of murders declined 36% while the number of murders by firearms dropped 41%.

- From 1994 through 1999, the years for which data are available, about 7 in 10 murders at school involved some type of firearm, and approximately 1 in 2 murders at school involved a handgun.

While victimizations involving knives comprised 6% of all violent crimes resulting in an injury, these victimizations accounted for about 24% of all serious injuries experienced by crime victims.

Type of weapon	Violent crime		
	With/with-out injury	Serious injury	Minor injury
Total	100%	100%	100%
No weapon	66	37	72
Any weapon	26	57	23
Firearm	10	13	4
Knife/sharp object	6	24	4
Blunt object/other	10	20	14
Do not know*	8	6	5

Note: Data from cases for which injury information was available.
*Victim did not know whether the offender possessed a weapon.

The most common locales for armed violence and gun violence were the streets: those away from the victim's home (30% of violence with a weapon and 35% of gun violence) and those at or near the victim's home (27% of armed violence and 25% of gun violence).

Most violence involving a weapon and most firearm violence occurred while the victims were engaged in leisure activities away from home (27% and 27%) and commuting to work (23% and 25%, respectively).

Weapon use varied by type of crime. Offenders had weapons in about half of robberies, a fourth of assaults, and a twelfth of rapes/sexual assaults (table 1).

Weapons and violent crime

Between 1993 and 2001, about 26% (or an annual average of 2.3 million) of the estimated 8.9 million violent crimes in the United States were committed by offenders armed with guns, knives, or objects used as weapons. Firearm violence accounted for 10% of all violent crimes; about 6% were committed with a knife or other sharp object such as scissors, ice pick, or broken bottle; 4% with blunt objects such as a brick, bat, or bottle; and 5% were committed with unspecified/ "other" objects used as weapons.

Type of weapon	Average annual victimi-zations	Percent of —		
		All violent crime	All armed violence
Total	8,896,460	100%	
No weapon	5,863,750	66%	
Any weapon	2,304,340	26%	100%
Firearm	846,950	10	37
Handgun	737,370	8	32
Other gun	100,470	1	4
Type unknown	9,110	0	0
Knife/sharp object	569,990	6	25
Blunt object	356,340	4	16
Other	424,160	5	18
Unknown	106,890	1	5
Do not know*	728,370	8%	

Note: Detail may not add to total because of rounding.
*Victim did not know whether the offender possessed a weapon.

The National Crime Victimization Survey (NCVS)

The NCVS is the Nation's primary source of information on criminal victimization. Data are continuously obtained from a nationally representative sample of approximately 43,000 households comprising nearly 80,000 persons age 12 or older. Household members are asked about the frequency, characteristics, and consequences of victimization.

The survey enables the Bureau of Justice Statistics (BJS) to estimate the rate of victimization for rape, attempted rape, sexual assault, robbery, assault, theft, household burglary, and motor vehicle theft. The rates describe the vulnerability to crime by the population as a whole as well as by segments of the population such as women, the elderly, members of racial and ethnic groups, and city dwellers.

For the most current estimates of criminal victimization in the United States, see *Criminal Victimization 2001: Changes 2000-2001 with Trends 1993-2001* <www.ojp.usdoj.gov/bjs>.

Table 1. Weapon use, by type of violent crime, 1993-2001

Type of weapon	Homicide	Rape/sexual assault	Robbery	All assaults
Total	100%	100%	100%	100%
Any weapon	91	8	50	24
Firearm	70	3	27	8
Knife/sharp object	13	3	13	6
Blunt object	5	1*	5	4
Other	3	1	5	6
Do not know[a]	4	7	11	8
No weapon	4	85	39	69

Note: Detail may not add to total because of rounding.
*Based on 10 or fewer sample cases. See *Methodology*, page 11.
[a]Victim did not know whether the offender possessed a weapon.

Table 2. Violent crime, by type of weapon, 1993-2001

Violent crime	All crimes	No weapon	Any weapon	Firearm			Knife/ sharp object	Blunt object	Other weapon	Unspecified type of weapon	Do not know[a]
				All	Handgun	Other firearms					
Percent											
All nonlethal violence	100%	65.9%	25.9%	9.5%	8.3%	1.2%	6.4%	4.0%	4.8%	1.2%	8.2%
Rape/sexual assault	100	84.9	8.0	3.4	3.4	0.0*	2.8	0.7*	0.5*	0.6*	7.1
Robbery	100	39.2	49.7	26.8	25.1	1.7	12.8	4.7	3.7	1.7	11.1
All assaults	100	68.5	23.6	7.5	6.3	1.2	5.7	4.1	5.1	1.2	7.9
Rates[b]											
All nonlethal violence	40.3	26.6	10.4	3.8	3.3	0.5	2.6	1.6	1.9	0.5	3.3
Rape/sexual assault	1.7	1.4	0.1	0.1	0.1	0.0*	0.0	0.0*	0.0*	0.0*	0.1
Robbery	4.5	1.8	2.2	1.2	1.1	0.1	0.6	0.2	0.2	0.1	0.5
All assaults	34.2	23.4	8.1	2.6	2.2	0.4	2.0	1.4	1.7	0.4	2.7

Note: Detail may not add to total because of rounding.
*Based on 10 or fewer sample cases. See *Methodology*, page 11.
[a]Victim did not know whether the offender possessed a weapon.
[b]Rates per 1,000 persons age 12 or older.

Definitions of weapons

Firearms include handguns (pistols, revolvers, derringers) and shotguns, rifles, and other firearms (excluding BB and pellet guns and air rifles).

Sharp objects include knives and other sharp edged and/or pointed objects (scissors, ice picks, and axes).

Blunt objects include rocks, clubs, blackjacks, bats, and metal pipes.

Other weapons include ropes, chains, poison, martial arts weapons, BB guns, and objects that could not be classified.

Firearms

Between 1993 and 2001 victims were confronted by offenders armed with guns in about 27% of robberies, 8% of assaults, and 3% of all rapes/sexual assaults (table 2).

U.S. residents were victims of crimes committed with firearms at a annual average rate of 4 crimes per 1,000 persons age 12 or older. Of the average 847,000 violent victimizations committed with firearms, about 7 out of 8 were committed with handguns.

	Violent victimizations, 1993-2001		
Type of firearm	Average annual number	Percent	Rate per 1,000 age 12 or older
Total	846,940	100%	3.8
Handgun	737,360	87	3.3
Other	109,580	13	0.5

Knives and sharp objects

Annually during the 9-year period, about 570,000 violent victimizations were committed with a knife or other sharp object, accounting for 6% of all violent crimes. Thirteen percent of robberies, 6% of assaults, and 3% of rapes were committed with a knife or other sharp object.

From 1993 through 2001 crimes involving knives and sharp objects were committed at an average annual rate of 3 per 1,000 persons age 12 or older. In 85% of these victimizations, about 482,000 annually, the weapon was a knife. In the remainder, about 88,000 victimizations per year on average, the weapon was another type of sharp object.

	Average		Rate per
Type of sharp edged weapon	annual number	Percent	1,000 age 12 or older
Total	569,990	100%	2.6
Knife	481,870	85	2.2
Sharp object	88,120	15	0.4

Blunt objects

Armed with blunt objects such as bats, sticks, rocks, clubs, or blackjacks, offenders committed approximately 356,000 violent crimes as an annual average from 1993 through 2001.

Crimes by offenders armed with blunt objects were committed at an annual average rate of 2 per 1,000 persons age 12 or older.

Other weapons

Between 1993 and 2001 about 5% of all violent crimes were committed with weapons other than guns, knives, or blunt objects. Such weapons include ropes, chains, poison, martial arts weapons, BB guns (not considered to be firearms by the NCVS), and objects that could not be classified.

Weapon use and crime outcome

Weapon use varied by crime. Robberies, followed by all assaults, were more likely to involve an armed assailant while rape/sexual assault was the least likely.

Robbery

Armed robberies were more likely to be completed, resulting in loss of property, than unarmed robberies. Higher completion percentages occurred for robberies committed with firearms than for robberies with knives and other sharp objects or blunt objects/other weapons. Robberies committed with knives and unarmed robberies were completed at similar percentages.

	Robberies, 1993-2001		
Type of weapon	Total	Com-pleted	At-tempted
All robberies[a]	100%	66%	34%
No weapon	100	60	40
Any weapon	100	71	29
Firearm	100	79	21
Knife/sharp object	100	57	43
Blunt object/other[b]	100	67	33

[a]Includes victims who did not know whether the offender possessed a weapon.
[b]"Other" includes ropes, chains, poison, and unspecified objects used as weapons.

Assaults

All assaults in this report represent simple and aggravated assault examined together.

Simple assault is an attack *without a weapon* resulting in either no injury or minor injury.

Aggravated assault is an attack or attempted attack with a weapon, regardless of whether an injury occurred and attack without a weapon when serious injury results.

All assaults	100%
Aggravated assault	27
Involved a weapon	26
Did not involve a weapon	1
Simple assault	73

A discussion of minor and serious injury appears on page 6.

Rape/sexual assault

For the 9-year period beginning in 1993, the percentage of rapes/sexual assaults that was completed did not vary significantly depending on the offenders' possession of a weapon. About 71% of rapes/sexual assaults involving no weapon were completed; of such assaults with a weapon, 67% were completed.

	Rapes/sexual assaults, 1993-2001		
Type of weapon	Total	Com-pleted	At-tempted
All rapes/sexual assaults	100%	69%	31%
No weapon	100	71	29
Any weapon	100	67	33
Firearm	100	74	26

Note: "Completed" includes rapes and sexual assaults, and "attempted" includes attempted rape. There were too few sample cases for analysis by type of weapon.

Assault

The outcome for incidents of assault is measured by whether a victim sustained an injury as a result of the crime.

Overall, about 1 in 4 assault victims were injured during the incident. Victims of firearm violence were less likely than other victims to be injured. About 1 in 3 assault victims were injured when the offender possessed a blunt object or some unspecified type of weapon. About 1 in 4 victims were injured when the assailant had a knife.

Type of weapon	Assaults, 1993-2001		
	Total	Not injured	Injured
All assaults[a]	100%	76%	24%
No weapon	100	76	24
Any weapon	100	75	25
Firearm	100	87	13
Knife/sharp object	100	74	26
Blunt object/other[b]	100	66	34

[a]Includes victim who did not know whether the offender possessed a weapon.
[b]"Other" includes ropes, chains, poison, and unspecified objects used as weapons.

Table 3. Type of weapon, by gender of victims, 1993-2001

	Nonlethal violent victimization						
Gender of victim	All crime	No weapon	Any weapon	Firearm	Sharp object	Blunt object/ other[a]	Do not know[b]
Percent							
Male	100%	60.8%	30.5%	11.5%	7.4%	11.6%	8.8%
Female	100	72.5	20.0	7.0	5.1	7.9	7.5
	Violent victimizations per 1,000 persons age 12 or older						
Rate							
Male	46.9	28.5	14.3	5.4	3.5	5.4	4.1
Female	34.2	24.8	6.8	2.4	1.8	2.7	2.5

Note: Detail may not add to total because of rounding.
[a]"Other" includes ropes, chains, poison, and unspecified objects used as weapons.
[b]Victim did not know whether the offender possessed a weapon.

Victim characteristics

Males, blacks, Hispanics, and those between ages 15 and 24 were more vulnerable than their respective counterparts to violent crime committed by armed assailants.

Gender

Between 1993 and 2001, approximately 1 in 3 male victims of violent crime faced an armed offender. About 1 in 5 female victims of violent crime faced an armed assailant (table 3). Males were twice as likely as females to be confronted by an armed offender

Offender use of firearms

Of incidents involving offenders with firearms, victims —
• were shot (3%)
• were shot at but not hit (8%)
• were struck with a firearm (4%)
• were threatened with a firearm (72%)
• did not describe offender's use of firearms (13%).

(14 versus 7 per 1,000 persons respectively). This pattern was generally consistent across weapon types; for each type of weapon, the victimization rate for males was about twice that for females.

Race and ethnicity

For each type of weapon, victimization rates for whites were lower than those for blacks or Hispanics.[1] Blacks were victimized by offenders armed with guns at higher rates than Hispanics but at similar rates as American Indians. Blacks had similar victimization rates as Hispanics for crimes committed with knives or blunt objects/other weapons.

The rate of firearm violence for blacks was more than twice that for whites (8 versus 3 per 1,000) (table 4). The rate

[1]In this report race and ethnicity are analyzed together. *White, black, Asian/Pacific Islander,* and *American Indian* refer to non-Hispanic persons.

for Hispanics (6 per 1,000) was about twice that for whites.

No significant differences separated the rates at which whites and blacks were victimized by unarmed offenders.

The rate of armed violence for American Indians (25 per 1,000 American Indians) was —
• 43% higher than the rate for blacks (18 per 1,000 blacks)
• 78% higher than the rate for Hispanics (14 per 1,000 Hispanics)
• 184% higher than the rate for whites (9 per 1,000).

Age, weapons, and violence

For overall violence, persons age 12-14, 15-17, and 18-20 were victimized at similar rates, higher than those for persons age 21 or older (table 5). Vulnerability to victimization by an armed offender similarly varied by the age of victim. Younger persons, particularly those age 18-20, had higher rates of victimization by armed offenders.

The rate of firearm violence was also highest for persons age 18-20. Their rate (12 per 1,000 persons) was about 40% higher than the rate for persons ages 15 to 17 and 21 to 24.

Except for victims age 12-14, for whom firearm violence constituted about 3% of all violent crime, firearm violence accounted for between 9% and 13% of all violent crime for each age group.

Similarly, crimes committed with knives/sharp objects accounted for 6% to 8%, and crimes with other weapons, 9% to 11% of all violent crime for each age group examined.

Table 4. Race and ethnicity of victims of violent crime, by type of weapon, 1993-2001

	Nonlethal violent victimization						
Race/ethnicity of victim of violence	All	No weapon	Any weapon	Firearm	Sharp object	Blunt object/ other[a]	Do not know[b]
Percent							
White	100%	69.4%	22.7%	7.3%	5.7%	9.8%	7.9%
Black	100	54.2	36.1	17.2	8.4	10.5	9.7
American Indian	100	66.8	26.1	8.0	5.0	13.1	7.1
Asian	100	58.1	31.2	13.3	8.1	9.8	10.7
Hispanic	100	59.3	33.0	14.0	8.5	10.4	7.8
	Violent victimizations per 1,000 persons age 12 or older						
Rate							
White	39.2	27.2	8.9	2.8	2.2	3.8	3.1
Black	48.9	26.5	17.6	8.4	4.1	5.1	4.7
American Indian	97.2	65.0	25.3	7.7	4.9	12.7	6.9
Asian	20.7	12.0	6.5	2.7	1.7	2.0	2.2
Hispanic	42.9	25.4	14.2	6.0	3.7	4.5	3.3

[a]"Other" includes ropes, chains, poison, and unspecified objects used as weapons.
[b]Victim did not know whether the offender possessed a weapon.

For each age category, blacks and Hispanics had higher rates of violence than whites — involving a weapon and involving a firearm

All weapon violence
Age of victim

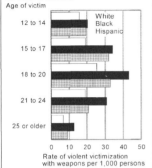

White
Black
Hispanic

12 to 14

15 to 17

18 to 20

21 to 24

25 or older

0 10 20 30 40 50
Rate of violent victimization
with weapons per 1,000 persons

All firearm violence
Age of victim

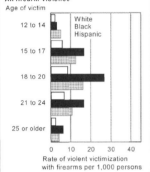

White
Black
Hispanic

12 to 14

15 to 17

18 to 20

21 to 24

25 or older

0 10 20 30 40
Rate of violent victimization
with firearms per 1,000 persons

Figures 1 and 2

Age of victim	Popu-lation	All weapons	Firearm
Total	100%	100%	100%
12 to 14	5	8	3
15 to 17	5	11	11
18 to 20	5	14	16
21 to 24	7	13	14
25 to 34	18	23	24
35 to 49	28	22	24
50 to 64	17	6	6
65 or older	15	2	2

Note: Detail may not add to totals because of rounding.

Forty-five percent of all armed violence involved victims between 25 and 49, and 38% was against victims age 15-24.

Table 5. Weapons used in violent crime, by age of victims, 1993-2001

Age of victim	All crime	No weapon	Any weapon	Firearm	Sharp object	Blunt object/other[a]	Do not know[b]
Percent							
12 to 14	100%	77.2%	17.9%	2.6%	6.3%	9.0%	4.9%
15 to 17	100	67.3	25.1	8.9	6.5	9.7	7.6
18 to 20	100	62.6	30.1	12.6	7.1	10.5	7.3
21 to 24	100	63.7	28.8	11.9	7.6	9.3	7.5
25 to 34	100	64.5	27.4	10.3	6.4	10.7	8.1
35 to 49	100	64.9	25.5	9.8	5.7	9.9	9.6
50 to 64	100	63.4	24.9	9.1	5.5	10.2	11.7
65 or older	100	54.4	30.4	13.1	6.1	11.2	15.2
Rates per 1,000 persons							
12 to 14	91.7	70.8	16.4	2.4	5.8	8.2	4.5
15 to 17	90.3	60.7	22.7	8.1	5.9	8.7	6.9
18 to 20	94.3	59.0	28.4	11.8	6.7	9.9	6.9
21 to 24	71.3	45.4	20.5	8.4	5.4	6.7	5.3
25 to 34	48.6	31.4	13.3	5.0	3.1	5.2	4.0
35 to 49	32.6	21.2	8.3	3.2	1.9	3.2	3.1
50 to 64	15.1	9.6	3.8	1.4	0.8	1.5	1.8
65 or older	4.5	2.4	1.4	0.6	0.3	0.5	0.7

[a]"Other" includes ropes, chains, poison, and unspecified objects used as weapons.
[b]Victim did not know whether the offender possessed a weapon.

Race, ethnicity, and age

When race and ethnicity are added to the considerations of age, some differences in victimization rates between age categories emerge for crimes committed with any weapon or with a firearm. Both for crimes committed with any weapon and for firearm violence specifically, differences between black and Hispanic victimization rates were greatest within the age category 18-20 (figures 1 and 2).

Whites and blacks, age 18-20, were more likely than whites and blacks of other ages to have been victims of weapon violence in general and firearm violence in particular.

Hispanics of ages 15-17 and 18-20 were more vulnerable than other Hispanics to violence involving a weapon and violence involving a firearm.

The rates of violent victimization, violent victimization involving a weapon, and violent victimization involving a firearm for persons age 18-20 were approximately 20 times those of persons age 65 or older.

For blacks, whites, and Hispanics, victims of violent crime were, on average, younger than the general population. For the general population

as well as for the victim population, the mean age of whites was greater than the mean age of blacks (table 6).

Overall among the victims, blacks were older than Hispanics, the youngest racial or ethnic group considered. This pattern of relative ages was true for victims of violence involving firearms.

Annual household income

Persons with annual household incomes of less than $7,500 experienced both armed violence and firearm violence at about 3 times the rates of persons with annual household incomes of $50,000 or more (23.1 versus 7.3 armed victimizations per 1,000 persons, and 8.4 versus 2.4 firearm victimizations, respectively) (table 7).

Table 6. Mean age of victim, by race/Hispanic origin and type of weapon, 1993-2001

Type of weapon	White	Black	Hispanic
All persons age 12 or older	43 yr	38 yr	34 yr
All victims of violent crime	29	27	26
All weapons	30	28	26
Firearms	32	29	26

At almost every level of household income, blacks were more vulnerable than whites and Hispanics to violence involving a weapon and involving a firearm

All weapon violence
Annual household income

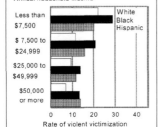

Rate of violent victimization
with weapons per 1,000 persons

All firearm violence
Annual household income

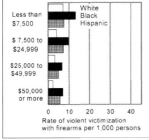

Rate of violent victimization
with firearms per 1,000 persons

Figures 3 and 4

Annual household income and race/ethnicity

Blacks at every income level were more vulnerable than whites to be victims of firearm violence. Whites and blacks with household incomes below $7,500 were more vulnerable to armed violence than their counterparts with higher incomes.

For violence by an offender with a weapon and for violence by an offender armed with a gun, blacks with household incomes of less than $50,000 were victimized at rates higher than those of Hispanics or whites with similar incomes.

Weapons and injuries

For 1993-2001 about a quarter of violent crimes overall resulted in an injury to the victim (table 8). Crimes committed with weapons and crimes committed without weapons were about equally likely to result in victim injury (26%). Crimes committed with weapons, however, were about 3.5 times as likely to result in serious injury as crimes committed by unarmed offenders (7% versus 2%, respectively).

Of all violence with a weapon, the crimes committed with blunt objects/ other weapons were the most often associated with victim injury (36%). Twenty-eight percent of the crimes

with knives/sharp objects and 15% of crimes with firearms involved injury.

Offenders armed with knives accounted for 6% of all violence but 24% of all serious injuries — having inflicted serious injury on about 1 in 8 of their victims. About 1 in 15 victims of offenders using a blunt object/other weapon and 1 in 22 victims of offenders with a firearm sustained serious injury.

	Violent crime		
Type of weapon	With/with-out injury[a]	Serious injury	Minor injury
Total	100%	100%	100%
No weapon	66	37	72
Any weapon	26	57	23
Firearm	10	13	4
Sharp object	6	24	4
Blunt object/other	10	20	14
Do not know[a]	8	6	5

[a]Victim did not know whether the offender possessed a weapon.

Because completed rape is considered an injury, victims of rape/sexual assault were more likely than robbery or assault victims to be injured, regardless of offender weapon use. For all weapon types, robbery victims were more likely than assault victims to sustain injury.

Definition of types of injuries

Serious injuries include gunshot or knife wounds, broken bones, loss of teeth, internal injuries, loss of consciousness, and undetermined injuries requiring 2 or more days of hospitalization.

Minor injuries include bruises, black eyes, cuts, scratches, swelling, chipped teeth, and undetermined injuries requiring less than 2 days of hospitalization.

Rape is sexual intercourse forced on the victim through physical or psychological coercion. Forced sexual intercourse means vaginal, anal, or oral penetration by the offender(s), including penetration by a foreign object. Victims can be male or female, and the rape can be heterosexual or homosexual. NCVS defines completed rape as a serious injury.

Rape without additional injuries, for the purposes of this report, were categorized as an injury but not as a serious or minor injury. Cases in which the victim suffered additional injuries were grouped according to the severity of those additional injuries.

Table 7. Annual household income, by type of weapon, 1993-2001

Annual household income of victims of violent crimes	All crime	No weapon	Type of weapon				Do not know[b]
			Any	Firearm	Sharp object	Blunt object/other[a]	
Percent							
Less than $7,500	100%	60.7%	31.0%	11.2%	8.8%	11.0%	8.3%
$7,500 to $24,999	100	63.7	28.3	11.1	6.7	10.5	7.9
$25,000 to $49,999	100	68.6	23.8	8.4	5.8	9.7	7.6
$50,000 or more	100	69.7	22.2	7.4	5.5	9.4	8.1
Rates[c]							
Less than $7,500	74.7	45.3	23.1	8.4	6.6	8.2	6.2
$7,500 to $24,999	47.5	30.3	13.5	5.3	3.2	5.0	3.8
$25,000 to $49,999	41.0	28.1	9.8	3.4	2.4	4.0	3.1
$50,000 or more	32.9	23.0	7.3	2.4	1.8	3.1	2.7

Note: Detail may not add to totals because of rounding.
[a]"Other" includes ropes, chains, poison, and unspecified objects used as weapons.
[b]Victim did not know if the offender possessed a weapon.
[c]Rates of victimization per 1,000 persons age 12 or older.

Robbery and injuries

About half of victims of robbery by offenders armed with blunt objects/other weapons sustained an injury during the crime.

About a third of victims of robbery by unarmed offenders (36%) and offenders armed with knives or sharp objects (31%) sustained injury during the victimization.

Offenders armed with any weapon other than a firearm inflicted a serious injury during about 1 in 7 robberies that they committed.

Type of weapon	All	Did assailant threaten before attacking you?		
		Yes	No	Unsure
Robbery[a]	100%	36%	63%	1%
No weapon	100	35	64	1
Any weapon	100	41	58	1
Firearm	100	48	50	1
Knife/ sharp object	100	42	57	0
Blunt object/ other[b]	100	33	67	1

Note: Detail may not add to totals because of rounding.
[a]Includes victims who did not know whether the offender possessed a weapon.
[b]"Other" includes ropes, chains, poison, and unspecified objects used as weapons.

Victims of robbery by offenders armed with blunt objects/other weapons were more likely than victims of robbery by offenders armed with a firearm to be attacked without a prior threat.

Assault

Victims were injured in a third of all assaults by offenders armed with blunt objects/other weapons. Less than a third of assaults by offenders armed with guns or knives resulted in injury (13% and 26%, respectively). Victims of offenders armed with a knife or sharp object were the most likely to sustain a serious injury; 12% of such offenses resulted in serious injury.

Rape/sexual assault

About half of all victims of rape/sexual assault committed by unarmed offenders were injured, compared to three-quarters of victims of such crimes by armed offenders.[2] Injuries sustained include completed rape. (See definitions of type of injuries on page 6.)

[2]The small number of sample cases of rape/sexual assault, the least frequent nonlethal violent crime, prevents further examination of injuries by type of weapon.

Time of incident	All crime	Any weapon	Firearms
Total	100%	100%	100%
Day	54	45	38
Night	46	55	62

Characteristics of the incident

Time of incident

Violent crimes at night were more likely than crimes occurring during the day to involve a weapon (30% versus 21%, respectively) or a firearm (12% versus 6%, respectively). Three of every five crimes committed by an offender with a firearm occurred at night.

Type of weapon	Percent of violent crime occurring during —	
	Day	Night
Total	100%	100%
No weapon	71	62
Any weapon	21	30
Firearm	6	12
Sharp object	6	7
Blunt object/other*	9	11
Do not know if weapon present	8	8

*"Other" includes ropes, chains, poison, and unspecified objects used as weapons.

About a third of violent crimes involving a weapon or a firearm occurred on the street away from the victim's home

*Such as open areas, playgrounds (other than at school), or public transportation.

Figures 5 and 6

Table 8. Injury from violent victimizations, by type of weapon, 1993-2001

Type of crime by type of weapon	All crime	No injury	Type of injuries			
			All	Serious	Minor	Rape[a]
Total[b]	100%	74.4%	25.6%	3.3%	21.0%	1.2%
No weapon	100	73.7	26.3	1.9	22.8	1.6
Any weapon	100	73.8	26.2	7.3	18.5	0.4
Firearm	100	85.0	15.0	4.6	9.8	0.6
Knife/sharp object	100	72.3	27.7	12.7	14.5	0.5
Blunt object/other[c]	100	64.0	36.0	6.5	29.3	0.1
Rape/sexual assault[b]	100%	46.8%	53.2%	2.9%	21.1%	29.3%
No weapon	100	48.4	51.6	1.7	19.9	30.0
Any weapon	100	24.8	75.2	10.1	35.0	30.1
Robbery[b]	100%	69.2%	30.8%	5.9%	24.9%	/
No weapon	100	64.3	35.7	3.1	32.6	/
Any weapon	100	72.8	27.2	8.5	18.7	/
Firearm	100	83.6	16.4	4.2	12.2	/
Knife/sharp object	100	69.1	30.9	13.5	17.4	/
Blunt object/other[c]	100	48.9	51.1	13.8	37.3	/
Assault[b]	100%	76.5%	23.5%	3.0%	20.5%	/
No weapon	100	76.0	24.0	1.8	22.3	/
Any weapon	100	74.9	25.1	7.0	18.2	/
Firearm	100	87.0	13.0	4.8	8.1	/
Knife/sharp object	100	74.5	25.5	12.3	13.2	/
Blunt object/other[c]	100	66.2	33.8	5.6	28.2	/

Note: Detail may not add to totals because of rounding.
/No sample cases.
[a]Includes rape without additional injuries. All the detail of weapon type for rape would have been based on 10 or fewer cases and are therefore not reported.
[b]Includes victims who did not know whether the offender possessed a weapon.
[c]"Other" includes ropes, chains, poison, and unspecified objects used as weapons.

Table 9. Type of weapon, by victim's activity at time of incident, 1993-2001

Victim's activity at time of the incident	All crime	No weapon	Any	Firearm	Sharp object	Blunt object/ other[a]	Do not know[b]
				Type of weapon			
							Percent of violent victimizations
Total	100%	100%	100%	100%	100%	100%	100%
Work	18.0	19.8	14.5	15.0	16.0	13.0	14.5
School	8.5	11.3	2.8	1.1	4.6	3.3	4.6
Home	22.5	23.8	20.5	18.4	23.2	20.7	17.9
Shopping	3.8	3.1	4.7	5.6	4.8	3.8	6.3
Leisure away from home	22.8	21.0	26.9	26.6	25.1	28.4	24.5
Traveling to or from work	16.9	13.6	22.9	25.4	18.6	23.2	25.0
Other	7.5	7.4	7.8	7.9	7.7	7.7	7.2

Note: Detail may not add to totals because of rounding.
[a]"Other" includes ropes, chains, poison, and unspecified objects used as weapons.
[b]Victim did not know whether the offender possessed a weapon.

Activity and location

Crime by armed offenders was most likely to occur while the victim was engaged in leisure activity away from home (27%) or traveling to or from work or school (23%) (table 9). Nearly 21% of victims of armed violence were involved in some activity at home at the time of the incident.

The most common location for crimes by armed offenders was on the street away from the victim's home (30%) (figure 5). About a quarter of all violence by armed offenders occurred at or near the victim's home.

About 6% of armed violence, and 2% of firearm violence occurred at a school or on school grounds (figure 6).

Victim-offender relationship

Crimes committed by intimates were less likely than crimes committed by strangers to involve a weapon. The offender was armed in a third of all violence by a stranger and in a sixth of all violence committed by an intimate.

Victims of crimes by strangers were also more likely than victims of crimes by intimates to be confronted by an offender with a firearm (14% versus 5%, respectively).

Type of weapon	Intimates	Known non-intimate	Stranger
		Victim-offender relationship	
Total	100%	100%	100%
No weapon	80	75	56
Any weapon	16	20	33
Firearm	5	5	14
Sharp object	4	6	7
Blunt object/ other[a]	7	9	11
Do not know[b]	4	5	11

Note: Detail may not add to totals because of rounding.
[a]Blunt objects as well as other objects such as ropes, chains, poison, and unspecified objects.
[b]Victim did not know whether the offender possessed a weapon.

Trends

Violent victimization rates declined from 1993 to 2001. Rates for crimes committed with firearms reflected a larger decrease than did the rates for overall violence and armed violence in general. Between 1993 and 2001 overall violence decreased 54%, armed violence fell 59%, and firearm violence declined 63%.

The rates of firearm violence for blacks and Hispanics fell relatively more than the rate for whites, 1993-2001. In 1993 blacks and Hispanics were victims of firearm violence at a rate of 13 firearm crimes per 1,000 persons, about 3 times the rate for whites. By 2001 the rate for blacks had fallen to about 4 per 1,000, roughly 2.5 times that for whites. In 2001 Hispanics experienced firearm violence at a rate per 1,000 similar to those for both blacks and whites.

From 1993 to 2001, rates of violence involving firearms declined among all age groups. The decline was greatest among the youngest victims: by 2001, persons age 12-14 had experienced a 97% decrease in the rate of firearm violence, and those age 15-17, a 77% decrease.

Homicide and weapons

Between 1993 and 2001 local law enforcement agencies reported 160,396 murders and nonnegligent manslaughters of persons age 12 or older to the FBI's Supplementary Homicide Reports. (The homicides that occurred in the events of September 11, 2001, were not included.) There was an annual average of 17,822 murders of persons age 12 or older (table 10). A weapon was used in 91% of these crimes. In 4% of the homicides, the offender used a means such as strangling, punching, and kicking. Information about the weapon used was unavailable in 5% of all homicides.

Seventy percent of homicide victims were killed with a firearm. Handguns were used in 56% of all homicides.

Table 10. Homicides of persons age 12 or older, by weapon type, 1993-2001

Type of weapon	Average annual number	Percent	Rates per 100,000 persons
	Homicide of persons age 12 or older		
Total	17,822	100%	8.1
Any weapon	16,207	90.9	7.3
Firearm	12,486	70.1	5.7
Handgun	10,058	56.4	4.6
Shotgun	771	4.3	0.3
Rifle	611	3.4	0.3
Other gun	44	0.2	0.0
Unknown type	1,002	5.6	0.5
Knife/ sharp object	2,406	13.5	1.1
Blunt object	823	4.6	0.4
Other weapon	492	2.8	0.2
No weapon[a]	767	4.3	0.3
Do not know[b]	847	4.8	0.4

Note: Detail may not add to subtotals because of rounding. The homicides that occurred in the events of September 11, 2001, were not included.
[a]Includes hands and feet.
[b]The police record did not contain information on the type of weapon used in the homicide.

From 1993 through 2001 nonfatal firearm violence declined for all races, for Hispanics, and for all age groups

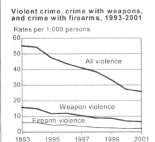

Violent crime, crime with weapons, and crime with firearms, 1993-2001

Rates per 1,000 persons

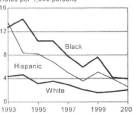

Firearm violence, by race and Hispanic origin of victims, 1993-2001

Rates per 1,000 persons

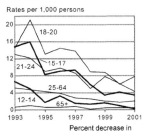

Firearm violence, by age of victim, 1993-2001

Rates per 1,000 persons

Type of victimization	Percent change in the rate per 1,000 persons age 12 or older, 1993-2001
All violence	-54%
Weapon violence	-59
Firearm violence	-63

Race/Hispanic origin of victim	Percent change in the rate of violence involving firearms per 1,000 persons age 12 or older, 1993-2001
Hispanic	-80%
Non-Hispanic black	-70
Non-Hispanic white	-54

Age of victim	Percent decrease in the rate of violence involving firearms per 1,000 persons age 12 or older, 1993-2001
12-14*	-97%
15-17	-77
18-20	-47
21-24	-67
25-64	-60
65 or older*	-29

*Estimates for some data years are based on 10 or fewer sample cases.

Figures 7,8, and 9

Gender

Male homicide victims were more likely than female victims to have been killed by a firearm. Eight in ten male homicide victims were killed with a firearm, compared to 6 in 10 female victims.

Type of weapon	Gender of homicide victim	
	Male	Female
Percent	100%	100%
Firearm	81	61
Knife/sharp object	13	22
Blunt object/other	6	17
Rates*		
Any weapon	12	3
Firearm	10	2
Knife/sharp object	2	1
Blunt object/other	1	1

Note: Detail may not add to totals because of rounding. The homicides that occurred in the events of September 11, 2001, were not included.
*Per 100,000 persons age 12 or older.

Knives or other sharp objects were the second most frequently used weapon in homicides of both males and females (13% and 22%, respectively). Males were 5 times more likely than females to be a victim of a homicide committed with a firearm (10 versus 2 per 100,000 persons, respectively),

and twice as likely to be murdered with a knife or other sharp object (2 versus 1 per 100,000, respectively).

Race

From 1993 to 2001, blacks were 12% of the U.S. population age 12 or older but 49% of all homicide victims and 54% of all victims of firearm homicide. Among homicide victims, blacks were more likely than whites to have been killed with a firearm. About 8 in 10 black homicide victims and 7 in 10 white homicide victims died from gunshot injuries.

Race of victim	Population	Homicides	
		All	Firearm
Total	100%	100%	100%
White	84	48	44
Black	12	49	54
Other	4	3	2

Note: Excludes homicides that had unknown race of victim or unknown means of homicide.

Blacks were about 7 times more likely than whites to be a homicide victim (30 versus 4 per 100,000 persons age 12 or older respectively), and approximately 9 times more likely to be a victim of a homicide committed with a firearm (25 versus 3 per 100,000 persons age 12 or older, respectively).

Type of weapon	Race of homicide victim	
	White	Black
Percent	100%	100%
Firearm	72	82
Knife/sharp object	17	12
Blunt object/other	11	5
Rates*		
Firearm	4	30
Knife/sharp object	3	25
Blunt object/other	1	2
	‡	2

Note: Detail may not add to totals because of rounding. The homicides that occurred in the events of September 11, 2001, were not included.
‡Less than 0.5.
*Rates per 100,000 persons age 12 or older.

Age

Persons age 18 to 24 were victims of homicide overall as well as firearm homicides at the highest rates (table 11). Those age 18 to 24 were 3.5 times as likely as persons age 12 to 17 and about 3 times as likely as those age 25 to 64 to be killed with a firearm.

There appears to be a relationship between the age of the victim and the type of homicide weapon. Victims of firearm murders were, on average, 6 years younger than victims of homicides committed with knives/other

Murders of children under age 12

Weapons in general and firearms specifically were less commonly used against murder victims under age 12 than against those age 12 or older.

From 1993 through 2001, about 2 in 5 murders of children under age 12 involved a weapon, and about 1 in 6 involved a firearm. Among victims age 12 or older, 91% of the

murders were committed with a weapon, and 70% were committed with a firearm.

In 1993 firearms accounted for 19% of murders of persons under age 12. This peak of 195 incidents preceded a decline; in 2001, 15% of all such murders (127 of the 824 total) involved a firearm.

	Murders of persons younger than age 12, 1993-2001		
Type of weapon	Average annual number	Percent	Rate per 100,000 persons under age 12
Total	881	100%	1.9
Any weapon	356	40.5	0.8
Firearm	141	16.0	0.3
Knife/sharp object	40	4.6	0.1
Blunt object	56	6.3	0.1
Other weapon	120	13.6	0.3
No weapon*	399	45.3	0.9
Missing data	126	14.3	0.3

Note: Detail may not add to total because of rounding.
*Includes hands/fists and feet.

Number of murders of children under age 12

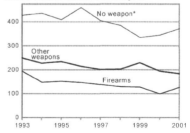

*Includes hands/fists and feet.

Table 11. Homicide, by the victim's age and the type of weapon, 1993-2001

	Homicides				
Type of weapon	12-17	18-20	21-24	25-64	65 or older
Percent	100%	100%	100%	100%	100%
Firearm	86	88	86	73	46
Knife/sharp object	9	9	10	17	26
Blunt object/ other	5	3	4	9	27
Rate*	5	18	18	7	2
Firearm	4	16	15	5	1
Knife/sharp object	‡	2	2	1	1
Blunt object/ other	‡	1	1	1	1

Note: Detail may not add to totals because of rounding. The nonnegligent homicides that occurred in the events of September 11, 2001, were not included.
‡Less than 0.5.
*Rates per 100,000 persons in each age category.

Table 12. Mean age of homicide victims age 12 or older, by race and type of weapon, 1993-2001

	General popu- lation age 12 or older	Mean age of homicide victims			
Race of victim		All homicides	Firearm	Sharp object	Blunt object/other
Overall	41 yr	33 yr	31 yr	37 yr	43 yr
White	42	36	33	38	44
Black	38	31	28	36	42

sharp objects (31 versus 37 years old, respectively), and 12 years younger than victims of homicides committed with blunt objects (age 43) (table 12).

Race and age

On average, black murder victims were 5 years younger than white victims (age 31 versus age 36, respectively). The same age difference existed for firearm murders (age 28 versus age 33, respectively). Black and white victims of murders committed with knives or blunt objects were, on average, closer in age.

Trends in homicides, 1993-2001

The number of homicides declined 36% between 1993 and 2001. Firearm-homicides decreased 41% during the

period. In 1993, 72% of homicides of persons age 12 or older were committed with firearms. In 2001, 66% were committed with firearms.

	Homicide of persons age 12 or older		Percent of homicides with a
Year	All	Firearms	firearm
Average number	17,822	12,486	70.1%
1993	23,179	16,697	72.0
1994	21,967	15,967	72.7
1995	20,350	14,383	70.7
1996	18,411	12,968	70.4
1997	17,007	12,027	70.7
1998	15,742	10,718	68.1
1999	14,462	9,895	68.4
2000	14,453	9,906	68.5
2001	14,826	9,814	66.2
Average rate*	8.1	5.7	
1993	11.0	7.9	
1994	10.3	7.5	
1995	9.4	6.7	
1996	8.4	5.9	
1997	7.7	5.5	
1998	7.1	4.8	
1999	6.4	4.4	
2000	6.4	4.4	
2001	6.4	4.3	

Percent change in number of homicides		
Annual average	-4.8%	-5.7%
Overall, 1993-2001	-36.0	-41.2

*Rates per 100,000 persons age 12 or older. The nonnegligent homicides that occurred in the events of September 11, 2001, were not included.

Weapons, juveniles, and school violence

Annually on average, 1993 to 2001, about 703,800 violent crimes against persons age 12-17 occurred at school or on school property. About 8% of these crimes were committed with a weapon; about 1% with a firearm.

Type of weapon	Violent school crime
All victims	100%
No weapon	88
Any weapon	8
Firearm	1
Sharp object	3
Blunt object/other[a]	4
Do not know[b]	4
Annual average	703,810

[a]"Other" includes ropes, chains, poison, and unspecified objects used as weapons.
[b]Victim did not know whether the offender possessed a weapon.

About a third of armed assaults in schools resulted in injury to the victim.

Type of weapon	All	Not injured	Injured
Total	100%	77%	23%
No weapon	100	77	23
Any weapon	100	67	33
Firearm	100	92	8*
Sharp object	100	68	32
Blunt object/other[a]	100	61	39

*10 or fewer cases.
[a]"Other" includes ropes, chains, poison, and unspecified objects used as weapons.

Between 1994 and 1999, the most recent year of available data, 172 homicides of both students and nonstudents took place at school or on school property in the United States.

Type of student and nonstudent fatalities	Violent deaths at school, 1994-99	
	Number	Percent
Total	220	100%
Homicide	172	78
Suicide	30	14
Homicide/suicide	11	5
Legal intervention	5	2
Unintentional	2	1

Of these, 69% were committed with a firearm. Eighteen percent were committed with a knife or other sharp object. Of the firearm homicides at school, three-quarters were committed with handguns.

Type of weapon	School homicides, 1994-99	
	Number	Percent
Total	172	100%
Firearm	119	69
Handgun	89	52
Rifle[a]	18	11
Unknown	12	7
Sharp object	31	18
Beating[b]	12	7
Strangulation	5	3
Other	5	3

Note: Detail may not add to totals because of rounding.
[a]Includes shotguns and other "long guns."
[b]Includes blunt objects.

Source for school homicide data: Anderson, M. and others. "School Associated Violent Deaths in the United States, 1994-99," *Journal of the American Medical Association*, Dec. 5, 2001, 286, 21, pp. 2695-2702.

Victim self-defense

Between 1993 and 2001, about 61% of all victims of violent crime reported taking a self-defensive measure during the incident.

Most used nonaggressive means, such as trying to escape, getting help, or attempting to scare off or warn the offender. About 13% of victims of violent crime tried to attack or threaten the offender. About 2% of victims of violent crime used a weapon to defend themselves; half of these, about 1% of violent crime victims, brandished a firearm.

All victims' responses to violent crime	100%
Offered no resistance	39.3
Took some action	60.5
Used physical force toward offender	13.0
Attacked/threatened offender without a weapon	10.8
Attacked/threatened offender with a gun	0.7
Attacked/threatened offender with other weapon	1.4
Resisted or captured offender	15.0
Scared or warned off offender	4.2
Persuaded or appeased offender	5.5
Escaped/hid/got away	9.8
Got help or gave alarm	3.9
Reacted to pain or emotion	0.3
Other	8.9
Method of resistance unknown	0.2

Note: Detail may not add to total because of rounding.

Methodology

Except for homicide data obtained from the FBI's Uniform Crime Reporting Program, this report presents data from the BJS National Crime Victimization Survey (NCVS). Between 1993 and 2001 the Census Bureau interviewed approximately 651,750 individuals age 12 or older in 336,295 households. For the NCVS data presented, response rates varied between 93% and 96% of eligible households, and between 89% and 92% of eligible individuals.

Violent acts covered in this report include murder, rape, sexual assault, robbery, and assault (aggravated and simple) against persons age 12 or older. Overall violent crime is a combination of each type of crime.

Hypothesis testing and the NCVS

Standard error computations

Comparisons of estimates discussed in this report were tested to determine if the differences were statistically significant. Differences described as *higher*, *lower*, or *different* passed a hypothesis test at the .05-level of statistical significance (95%-level of confidence). That is, the tested difference was greater than about twice the standard error of that difference. Comparisons of estimates statistically significant at the 0.10 level (90%-confidence level), have differences described as *somewhat*, *marginal*, or *slight*.

Caution is required when making comparisons of estimates not explicitly discussed in this report. What may appear to be a large difference in estimates may not test as statistically significant at the 95%- or even the 90% confidence level. Significance testing calculations were conducted at BJS using statistical programs developed specifically for the NCVS by the U.S. Census Bureau. These programs consider the complex NCVS sample design when calculating generalized variance estimates.

Estimates based on 10 or fewer sample cases have high relative standard errors so that care should be taken when comparing such estimates to other estimates. It is inadvisable to compare estimates when both are based on 10 or fewer sample cases. Asterisks mark estimates based on 10 or fewer sample cases in this report.

Comparisons of rates made in this report are based on the unrounded estimates.

Testing trends in weapons violence

Unless stated otherwise when a statement is made describing differences in estimates between years, it was tested for significance using a computer program designed specifically for the NCVS. These tests determine whether

an estimate in one year differs from that of another, regardless of intervening estimate variation.

Definitions of crimes:

Aggravated assault - Attack or attempted attack with a weapon, regardless of whether or not an injury occurred and attack without a weapon when serious injury results.

Rape - Forced sexual intercourse including both psychological coercion as well as physical force. Forced sexual intercourse means, vaginal, anal, or oral penetration by the offender(s). This category also includes incidents where the penetration is from a foreign object. Includes rapes of male and female victims and both heterosexual and homosexual rape. Attempted rape includes verbal threats of rape.

Robbery - Completed or attempted theft, directly from a person, of property or cash by force or threat of force, with or without a weapon, and with or without injury.

Sexual assault - A wide range of victimizations, separate from rape or attempted

rape. These crimes include attacks or attempted attacks generally involving unwanted sexual contact between victim and offender. Sexual assaults may or may not involve force and include such things as grabbing or fondling. Sexual assault also includes verbal threats.

Simple assault - Attack without a weapon resulting either in no injury, minor injury (for example, bruises, black eyes, cuts, scratches, or swelling) or in undetermined injury requiring less than 2 days of hospitalization. Also includes attempted assault without a weapon.

The Bureau of Justice Statistics is the statistical agency of the U.S. Department of Justice. Lawrence A. Greenfeld is director.

Craig A. Perkins, BJS Statistician, wrote this Special Report under the supervision of Michael R. Rand. Tim Hart and Cathy Maston verified the report. Tom Hester and Tina Dorsey produced and edited it.

September 2003, NCJ 194820

U.S. Department of Justice
Office of Justice Programs
Bureau of Justice Statistics

Washington, DC 20531

[17]

TO KILL OR NOT TO KILL?
LETHAL OUTCOMES IN
INJURIOUS ATTACKS*

RICHARD B. FELSON
STEVEN F. MESSNER
University at Albany, SUNY

This research explores the utility of the notion of lethal intent for understanding the outcomes of injurious attacks. We suggest that assailants sometimes kill rather than merely injure victims to avoid either retaliation or criminal prosecution. We hypothesize that, for these tactical reasons, offenders will be more likely to kill when they have no accomplices, when their victims are male or black, and when the victim can identify them. These hypotheses are tested with a merged data set containing information on homicides and nonlethal victimizations involving robbery, rape, and pure assault. The results of multiple logistic regression analyses are largely consistent with theoretical expectations.

Criminologists have adopted different perspectives with respect to the role of lethal intent in the etiology of homicide. At one end of the spectrum are those who question the prevalence of distinctive lethal intent and minimize its causal significance. For example, Block (1977:10) argues that "most killings are the outcome of either an aggravated assault or a robbery which somehow progressed beyond the degree of harm intended by the offender." While Block acknowledges that there are a "few well planned intentional homicides," he implies that these crimes typically evolve in an erratic and unintended way.

Zimring (1968, 1972) adopts a similar stance in his classic formulation of the thesis of "weapon instrumentality effects" to explain the association between lethal weapons and lethal outcomes in violent crimes. Zimring assumes that, in the vast majority of homicides, the offender does not possess an unambiguous or sustained intent to kill the victim. As a result, the death or survival of the victim of personal violence is largely a matter of chance, which depends in large measure on the lethality of the weapon used to inflict injury.[1] Fatalities would presumably be reduced if other

---

* We are grateful to Scott South and James Tedeschi for helpful comments on earlier drafts of this paper.
   1. The survivability of the victim and access to timely medical care also play a role (Block, 1977; Doerner and Speir, 1986). See Wright et al. (1983) for a critique of the weapon instrumentality thesis, and Cook (1991) for a more sympathetic evaluation.

520   FELSON AND MESSNER

weapons were substituted for firearms because these other weapons ordinarily require more vigorous and sustained effort for killing the victim (Cook, 1991:14).

This skepticism about the prevalence and importance of distinctive lethal intent has been accompanied by the view that homicide is for all practical purposes identical in its dynamics to other forms of criminal violence. Harries (1990:48), for example, argues that "the legal labels 'homicide' and 'assault' represent essentially similar behaviors differing principally in outcome rather than process." Accordingly, Harries concludes that "the typical homicide is most appropriately considered a fatal assault" (p. 60).

An alternative perspective allows for distinctive causal dynamics in homicidal crimes associated with the formation of lethal intent. According to this point of view, a substantial portion of homicide offenders really do intend to kill their victims and not merely to injure them. The death of a victim, therefore, is not an incidental outcome that reflects extraneous considerations but rather is an integral part of the incident that is likely to be systematically related to other features of that incident (see, for example, Kleck, 1991:153–222; Reidel, 1993:13–14).

In this research, we explore the potential utility of the notion of lethal intent for an understanding of the causal dynamics of homicides. We begin by discussing the decision-making process in criminal violence in general and consider theoretical reasons why offenders might be motivated to formulate distinctively lethal intent. Our primary focus is on tactical concerns, that is, features of the incident that would make it more or less advantageous for criminal assailants to kill rather than merely injure their victims. Drawing on this theoretical discussion, we propose specific hypotheses about the effects of type of crime, gender, race, number of offenders, type of weapon, and victim-offender relationship on the likelihood of a lethal outcome, given that an injurious attack has occurred. These hypotheses are then tested in multivariate analyses with a merged data set of homicides and nonlethal victimizations involving injury. For purposes of comparison, we also examine the effects of the same set of independent variables on the likelihood of serious injury versus minor injury and on the likelihood of lethal outcomes versus serious injury, omitting incidents resulting in minor injury.

THE DECISION-MAKING PROCESS AND MOTIVATIONS TO KILL

To understand the decision to kill a victim requires an understanding of the causal processes underlying interpersonal violence more generally. Our approach to violence is predicated on the premise that violent acts

TO KILL OR NOT TO KILL? 521

involve intentional action. (See Tedeschi and Felson, 1994, for a full exposition of this approach.) Intentions, moreover, encompass both expectations and values. Actors who intend harm expect harm to result from their actions, and they desire or value that harm.

While violent actions may sometimes appear to be purely impulsive and therefore lacking meaningful intent, we prefer to view these actions as the result of quick and sometimes careless decisions rather than involuntary behavior (Cornish and Clarke, 1986). The level of information processing may be limited in these encounters given the usually strong emotions and the constricted time frame requiring "split-second decisions." Strong emotions (e.g., anger and fear) may also increase risk taking since they tend to focus the person's attention on ongoing events rather than future consequences.

We further assume that people who engage in violent actions value either compliance or harm (Tedeschi and Felson, 1994). These outcomes are valued because they lead to more distal values, such as justice, a favorable self-image, money, or physical safety. Not all anticipated outcomes of violent encounters are valued, however. A robber usually values the victim's compliance and the financial reward but is indifferent to the victim's suffering. Harm to the victim is an outcome in many robberies, but it is usually not the offender's goal. It is thus important to recognize that most behaviors have multiple outcomes, only some of which are desired by the actor.

Our approach differs from earlier approaches that distinguish between instrumental and angry aggression (e.g., Buss, 1961). In angry aggression the organism values harm as an end in itself because of its innate response to frustration or aversive stimuli (Berkowitz, 1989; Dollard et al., 1939). We view harm as a means to some end and all aggression as instrumental or goal-oriented action.

Offenders also consider costs in making decisions about the use of violence. Two types of costs are likely to be critical: those imposed by third parties and those imposed by the target. Target-imposed costs are those that can be inflicted on the initiator of a coercive interaction by the target. A critical consideration in the assessment of target-imposed costs in hostile encounters is that of "coercive power." Coercive power refers to the capacity to force a change in behavior using threats of harm or actual harm (Tedeschi and Felson, 1994). Coercive power is affected by the skills and resources of the antagonists and their allies. Relative physical size and strength, the possession of weapons, and the support of allies—all affect the power equation.

The coercive power of actors in violent encounters can have contradictory effects on their behavior. On the one hand, coercive power encourages actors to use coercion because they anticipate that they will be successful and that their costs will be low (Fischer, 1969; Hornstein, 1965; Kipnis and Schmidt, 1983). Their actions are also more likely to be harmful precisely because of their superior resources. At the same time, however, actors with high levels of coercive power are not very vulnerable to retaliation. Their invulnerability may weaken their incentive to use extreme forms of coercion, especially coercion that effectively incapacitates the victim.

An additional consideration in the decision-making process underlying violence is the probable costs imposed by third parties. The fear of punishment from legal authorities and more informal punishment may deter the use of violence and/or limit the level of violence. Given such considerations, offenders will typically choose locations and situations in which capable guardians are absent (Cohen and Felson, 1979). In addition, offenders are likely to take actions during a violent crime to avoid criminal prosecution.

The discussion above considers factors relevant to the use of any form of coercion in antagonistic encounters. It is also possible to draw upon this general theoretical framework to identify reasons why an offender might prefer to kill rather than simply harm (i.e., injure) the victim.

First, the desire to kill the victim may reflect concerns for justice and identity. Offenders may feel so angry or aggrieved at the victim that they desire the ultimate penalty. From their point of view, the victim "deserves to die." The killing may reflect an attempt to demonstrate power, particularly when offenders feel they have been humiliated by the victim. Those theorists with a frustration-aggression approach might argue, in contrast, that the level of aggressive drive or negative effect reaches such a high level that the organism responds blindly in an extreme way.

Second, offenders may kill the victim for practical reasons. For example, drug dealers may kill competitors in order to acquire their territory. People may kill their spouses for insurance or inheritance, or to free themselves to become involved with someone else. Those involved in love triangles may kill their rivals in hopes of securing an exclusive relationship.

Third, offenders who kill their victims may be attempting to avoid target-imposed costs. Killing the victim prevents the victim from retaliating either immediately or at a later date. By permanently incapacitating the victim, offenders secure their own personal safety. They may, in other words, believe that it is "kill or be killed." Fear of retaliation is likely to be greater when the victim has a high level of coercive power relative to the offender. Support for the notion that offenders kill victims with coercive power in order to avoid retaliation comes from research by Felson and Steadman (1983) that compared homicide and serious assaults. They report that offenders are more likely to kill victims when the victims are

TO KILL OR NOT TO KILL? 523

armed. Presumably, one factor in offenders' decision to kill victims is to avoid being killed (or seriously harmed) themselves.

Finally, offenders may kill the victim to avoid costs from third parties. The victim is a potential witness whom offenders may kill in order to prevent identification and later criminal prosecution. An alternative scenario is that offenders may be deterred from killing the victim by the anticipation of a more severe sentence. Evidence suggests, however, that criminals pay more attention to certainty of punishment than severity (e.g., Tittle and Logan, 1973), and killing a victim decreases the certainty of punishment by eliminating the prospect of identification by the victim.[2]

To summarize, offenders in injurious attacks might intend to bring about the death of their victims for several reasons: to resolve intense grievances, demonstrate power, eliminate rivals, make money, forestall retaliation, and prevent identification and subsequent prosecution. The last two reasons are tactical ones. The offender's goal is to avoid costs, a goal which may be well served by a lethal outcome. This lethal intent may be premeditated, or it may develop during the course of violent interaction.

HYPOTHESES

In principle, our perspective on the formation of lethal intent could generate a wide variety of hypotheses about the determinants of fatal outcomes. Available data sets, however, contain only a restricted number of variables that can be included in testable hypotheses. These variables include the gender and race of offenders and victims, the number of participants, the relationship between offenders and victims, the type of crime (i.e., incidents involving elements of robbery, rape, or "pure" assaults), and the type of weapon (if any) employed.

Our main dependent variable is whether incidents involving injuries produce a lethal outcome. We assume that the effects of our independent variables on the likelihood of a lethal outcome are mediated by lethal intent, which is an unmeasured variable. We recognize that some offenders have lethal intent but are unsuccessful, while others lack lethal intent yet produce a lethal outcome. Nevertheless, it seems reasonable to assume that the presence of lethal intent increases the likelihood of a killing, even though the association between intent and actual outcome is not perfect.

Considerations of fear of retaliation allow us to predict effects for the demographic characteristics of victims and the presence of multiple

---

2. The reduced certainty of punishment associated with the elimination of the victim-as-witness is counterbalanced to some extent by the greater effort on the part of law enforcement officials to prosecute homicide cases in comparison with other assaults.

524   FELSON AND MESSNER

offenders. We hypothesize that an offender is likely to have greater fear of retaliation from a male victim than a female victim. In addition, a male victim is more likely than a female victim to take violent protective actions against the offender, according to data from the National Crime Victimization Survey (NCVS) (Bureau of Justice Statistics, 1992a:86). For tactical reasons, then, offenders should be more likely to kill male victims than female victims. It is possible that only female offenders are likely to fear male victims, which would imply that lethal outcomes would be more likely when the offender is female and the victim is male.

The race of the victim may also have an effect. To the extent that blacks are perceived as posing a greater threat of retaliation, greater fear of blacks would lead to more lethal outcomes for black victims. This fear could reflect either racial stereotypes or racial differences in the victim's behavior. The NCVS data suggest that black and white victims actually exhibit similar patterns of violent self-protective action (Bureau of Justice Statistics, 1992a:86), suggesting that stereotypes may play a greater role.

We also anticipate that single offenders will tend to be more fearful of retaliation than multiple offenders. Therefore, the presence of multiple offenders in an incident should reduce the likelihood that the victim will be killed.

As noted earlier, an additional tactical concern that might lead to the formation of lethal intent is identifiability. Strangers are less likely to be identifiable than nonstrangers, virtually by definition. We accordingly predict that, all other things being equal, victims are more likely to be killed by nonstrangers than by strangers.

Previous research clearly reveals that weapon type is an important determinant of lethal outcomes. We expect that the use of a gun or, to a lesser extent, a knife should increase the chances of a lethal outcome. These relationships can be attributed either to the greater lethality of guns and knives (the so-called weapon-instrumentality effect; see Cook, 1991) or the tendency of offenders with premeditated lethal intent to choose a more lethal weapon. Note that the predictions based on weapon instrumentality run counter to those that would be derived from considerations of retaliation alone. Armed offenders are likely to have less fear of retaliation from an injured victim than are unarmed offenders. Fear of retaliation should produce a negative effect of weapons on lethal outcomes, thereby offsetting part of the positive effect produced by motivational and weapon-instrumentality effects. Unfortunately, it is not possible to sort out these causal processes with the available data.

Our argument concerning the preference for harm provides a rationale for hypothesizing a relationship between type of crime and fatal outcomes. We predict that victims are more likely to be killed in a pure assault than in a robbery because offenders are more likely to have a lethal intent.

TO KILL OR NOT TO KILL? 525

Assault offenders are more likely to value harm—including the ultimate harm, death—while robbers are more likely to value compliance. From the point of view of frustration-aggression theorists, pure assault is more likely to involve angry aggression, while robbery is more likely to involve instrumental aggression. In most robberies, the offender should have no desire to harm or kill the victim except when such harm facilitates the primary goal of securing property. Consistent with this argument, Block (1977:31) found that 1% of robberies and 6% of aggravated assaults resulted in death to the victim. We are uncertain what to predict for rape. If rapists want compliance, they should behave more like robbers. If harm is their goal, they should behave more like assault offenders.

We can also examine statistical interactions between the use of lethal weapons and the type of crime. Given the assumption that offenders are more likely to value harm in pure assaults than in robbery, type of crime can be used as a proxy for the motivation to harm the victim. Evidence consistent with our predictions about type of crime would support this assumption, that is, evidence that pure assaults are more likely to have lethal outcomes than the other crime types.

Two competing hypotheses can be made, then. According to a *compensation hypothesis*, offenders who are determined to kill the victim will be likely to do so regardless of the type of weapon they use. If less lethal weapons require more effort, they will engage in more effort. Offenders who have lethal intent will select a gun, and if they have no gun, they will compensate; the weapon does not matter to the determined offender. For robbers, who are less likely to have lethal intent, the lethality of the weapon will be the determining factor of death. According to this reasoning, the effect of a lethal weapon should be weaker in pure assaults, where there is greater lethal intent, than in robberies. We cannot examine weapon effects on lethal outcomes in rape with these data because such outcomes are so rare.

An alternative possibility is that lethal weapons facilitate a lethal outcome for offenders who are motivated to harm the victim. According to the *weapon facilitator hypothesis*, offenders who value harm will produce more of it when they have lethal weapons. Offenders who desire to kill the victim will find it easier to do so with a more lethal weapon. According to this reasoning, the effect of a lethal weapon should be stronger in pure assaults than in robberies or rapes.

Finally, we include in our models the offenders' gender and race, even though it is unclear how these characteristics will affect the outcome. With respect to gender, opposing predictions can be derived. On the one hand, males tend to be more violent than females, physically bigger and stronger, and more skilled at violence. These considerations suggest that males will be more likely to kill their victims. On the other hand, male

526   FELSON AND MESSNER

offenders may be less vulnerable to retaliation than female offenders, so they have less incentive to kill the victim. We accordingly make no a priori prediction about the effect of the offender's gender. Similarly, there are no strong theoretical grounds for predicting distinctive effects of race of offender. While the evidence indicates a relationship between race and involvement in criminal violence in general (Harries, 1990), our focus is on the conditional probability of death given that an injury has been inflicted. The gender and race of the offender are nevertheless included in the analyses as control variables.

Suggestive support for some of our hypotheses can be found in previous research by Kleck (1991). Kleck examines the effects of several of the independent variables cited above on the probability of death for selected homicide and nonlethal incidents involving injury. He finds that the use of guns and knives and the presence of black victims increase the chances of lethal outcomes. A numerical advantage for offenders (more offenders than victims) decreases this probability (Kleck, 1991:213). These findings are consistent with our hypotheses.

Kleck's research, however, is limited in a critical respect: He examines only cases involving strangers. He does so out of concern for the known response bias associated with violence among intimates in victimization surveys (1991:177). An obvious limitation of Kleck's selection criterion is that it makes it impossible to assess the effects of offender-victim relationship on outcome. More important, such a procedure entails severe sample biasing with respect to homicide. A clear majority of homicides involve nonstrangers. To illustrate, stranger homicides made up only about 15% of homicides with a known relationship (8% of all homicides) in 1989.[3] Excluding nonstranger homicides thus results in the exclusion of the most common types of homicide. We accordingly examine homicide incidents involving both nonstrangers and strangers, although we recognize potential response and selection biases and anticipate their effects where possible. We also examine interactions between victim-offender relationship and other predictors to see if their effects differ for incidents involving strangers versus those involving nonstrangers.

SUPPLEMENTARY ANALYSES

Our interpretation of the determinants of lethal outcomes relies on

---

3. These data are based on the Federal Bureau of Investigation's (FBI's) *Supplementary Homicide Reports* (SHR). As Reidel (1993:19–51) explains, the SHR data source is likely to underestimate stranger homicides in comparison with local police sources. Nevertheless, the local police data also indicate that "stranger" homicides represent a distinct minority of homicides. Reidel (1993:50–51) reports an average estimate of stranger homicides across a sample of cities of about 25%.

inferences about the offender's decision to kill the victim, primarily for tactical reasons. An alternative possibility is that killing is simply an intense, aggressive response governed by the seriousness of the grievance or by irrational factors. To assess this possibility, we compare determinants of seriousness of injury for nonlethal incidents to the determinants of lethal outcomes. If killing reflects the tactical factors we have suggested, the effects of variables on *lethal* outcomes should differ in certain respects from those predicting a *serious but nonlethal* injury. On the other hand, if seriousness of injury and lethal outcomes have the very same determinants, other explanations, not involving the hypothesized tactical concerns, are indicated.

We also eliminate incidents involving mild injuries from some of our analyses. This strategy reflects a concern that sampling biases may affect the nonlethal assault sample. Such biases are likely to be weaker for the most serious assaults.

The hypotheses described above focus on the direct effects of predictors on lethal outcomes. It is also possible that weapon choice mediates the effects of other variables. As Kleck (1991) observes, offenders with lethal intent are more likely to select a lethal weapon. Offenders may also choose weapons for other tactical reasons. They may use guns when they are concerned about the victim retaliating. Thus, a robber's choice of weapon depends on the vulnerability of the target (Letkemann, 1973). Kleck (1991:157) found, in cross-tabular analyses, that homicide offenders are more likely to use guns when they are alone rather than in groups and when the victim is male rather than female. To examine the role of these factors in choice of weapon, we will look at determinants of gun use in addition to the determinants of lethal outcomes. We predict that, for tactical reasons, offenders who face males, or blacks, or who act alone will be more likely to use a gun.

DATA AND METHODS

Our data collection procedures are modeled on the innovative strategy devised by Kleck (1991; see also Kleck and McElrath, 1991). Kleck's research is unique "in combining nationally representative samples of both fatal and nonfatal violent incidents in a single analysis" (Kleck, 1991:174). The basic logic underlying this approach is straightforward: victimization data on nonlethal incidents are taken from the National Crime Victimization Survey and merged with the national data on "homicides known to the police" as recorded in the FBI's Supplementary Homicide Reports (SHR).

The NCVS provides estimates of victimizations from nationally representative samples of the U.S. population ages 12 and over. Respondents

528   FELSON AND MESSNER

are asked a series of screening questions to determine whether they experienced any criminal victimization during a six-month period prior to the month of the interview (Bureau of Justice Statistics, 1992b:v–vi). Those respondents who report victimizations are then asked for details about them. Among these details is the question of whether respondents suffered any injuries. If so, respondents are asked to describe the nature of the injuries and the type of medical care that they received (if any) to treat the injuries. We select for the analysis only those victimization incidents that resulted in some injury.[4] Because incidents with injury are relatively uncommon, and because the NCVS is based on sample data, we pool victimization incidents over a multiyear period, 1987–1991, to ensure sufficient numbers of cases for multivariate analyses. (At the time of data collection, only incidents for the first two quarters of 1991 were available for analysis.)

We further classify these nonlethal injuries on the basis of seriousness. As noted above, this allows us to compare the determinants of lethal outcomes with the determinants of serious, nonlethal injuries. It also permits an investigation of whether the factors predicting a lethal outcome, given any injury, are similar to those predicting a lethal outcome, given a serious injury. The criterion for identifying a "serious" nonlethal injury is the respondent's report that the injury required medical treatment.

Incidents involving lethal violence are taken from the SHR in 1989 (the mid-point of the 1987–1991 period). To maintain comparability with the types of violent encounters covered by the NCVS, we exclude homicides involving victims younger than 12 years of age and those classified as negligent manslaughters or justifiable homicides. Victimizations that occurred outside the United States are excluded for similar reasons (see Kleck, 1991:177).

The nonlethal incidents involving injury reported in the NCVS samples and the homicides in the SHR are then combined into a single data set and weighted. Weighting is performed to adjust the frequencies of lethal and nonlethal incidents to reflect the estimated proportions of the respective incidents for the nation at large. An estimate of the annual number of

---

4. Limiting the analysis to incidents involving injury raises the issue of sample selection bias. Following Heckman (1979) and Berk (1983), a common procedure for dealing with this problem is to estimate a "correction factor" reflecting the predicted probability of inclusion in the sample and entering this factor into the "substantive equations" (see Kleck, 1991:178). Research by Stolzenberg and Relles (1990) using Monte Carlo simulations has questioned the "mechanical" application of this procedure; the authors note that "the method can easily do more harm than good" (p. 408). In view of these methodological concerns, and given that our substantive interest lies in injurious incidents and not all assaultive incidents, we do not apply the Heckman–Berk corrections.

TO KILL OR NOT TO KILL?   529

nonlethal victimizations involving injury is obtained by computing the weighted total of such incidents in the NCVS data (using the NCVS weights) and dividing by 4.5 (reflecting 1987–1990 and the first two quarters of 1991). This figure is added to the number of homicides reported in the 1989 SHR to yield an estimate of the total annual number of injurious victimizations (after the exclusions noted), lethal and nonlethal. We assume that the number of homicides reported to the police is a reasonable indicator of the actual total, although some homicides obviously go unreported. Moreover, following Reidel (1993:30), we assume the SHR provides a reasonably complete recording of homicides known to local police agencies.

The results indicate that an estimated 1,654,376 injurious attacks of persons aged 12 and over occur annually, of which approximately 99% are nonlethal and 1%, lethal. Weights were constructed to yield a sample reflecting these relative frequencies of the different kinds of incidents. This weighted sample was "normed" so that the weighted "N" was identical to the actual number of incidents in the merged data set (see Frankel, 1983:46). We have also conducted analyses without weighting. The signs of the coefficients and levels of statistical significance in the unweighted analysis are similar to those reported below for the hypothesized predictors of lethal outcomes. Hence, our principal substantive conclusions are unaffected by the weighting procedure.

INDEPENDENT VARIABLES

One of the hypothesized predictors of a lethal outcome is type of crime. In the NCVS, respondents who report an unlawful physical attack are asked whether the incident involved additional criminal elements, such as completed or attempted theft (robbery), involuntary sexual contact (rape), or unlawful entry of a residence (burglary). We exclude burglaries from the analysis because there are so few and because their motivational dynamics are likely to be different from those of other incidents. For the other two crime types, we construct dummy variables to reflect whether a robbery or rape element was involved in the incident. Analogous procedures are applied to the homicide incidents using the variable for "circumstance."[5] The reference category for these dummy variables is "pure assault," that is, assaultive incidents with injury that do not contain elements of other felonious activity.

---

5. The "circumstance" variable in the SHR enumerates detailed categories for "felony type" and "other than felony type" homicides. The felony categories for "rape" and "robbery" are used to construct the respective dummy variables, while "burglary" and all other felony-type homicides are excluded for reasons explained in the text. The circumstance classification is based on the "first offender," which is assumed to reflect the principal circumstance surrounding the incident.

530   FELSON AND MESSNER

All of the other independent variables are also treated as dummy variables. Incidents with multiple offenders are scored 1, and single-offender incidents are scored 0. With respect to gender and race, the following scores are assigned: female = 0, male = 1; nonblack = 0, black = 1. The coding of these demographic characteristics is straightforward for incidents involving a single victim and a single offender and for incidents with multiple offenders/victims of the same gender or race. For incidents involving multiple victims and/or offenders of mixed gender, the gender variable is coded to reflect the presence of a male. Thus, for example, an incident involving both a male and a female victim is coded "male" on victim gender. The rationale here is to have the coding scheme reflect the presence of the attribute reflecting higher coercive power, and males are assumed to have higher coercive power due to greater physical strength and experience with violence. For race, the category representing power advantage is indeterminate. We accordingly exclude incidents involving multiple offenders or multiple victims of mixed race (which are relatively rare).

A similar logic is used in the coding of victim-offender relationship. In incidents with a single victim and a single offender, this variable is based on the relationship between those two parties and is coded as follows: nonstranger = 0; stranger = 1. For multiple offender/victim incidents, the most intimate relationship between any offender and any victim is coded. Finally, dummy variables are created representing the presence of the following weapons: gun, knife, blunt object, or other weapon. The reference category for these dummy variables is "no weapon."

STATISTICAL PROCEDURES

Four dependent variables are considered at various stages of the analysis: death vs. any injury; death vs. serious injury; serious (nonlethal) injury vs. nonserious injury; and the presence of a gun vs. no gun present. Given the dichotomous nature of these variables, we employ logistic regression to estimate the effects of the predictor variables (Hanushek and Jackson, 1977). The logistic regression coefficients indicate the change in the log odds of a given outcome for a dependent variable associated with switching from one category of the independent variable to the other. These coefficients can also be expressed in terms of an odds ratio (equal to e^b). To facilitate the interpretation of the odds ratio, we express it in terms of increased (rather than decreased) risk of an outcome, reversing the sign of the logistic regression coefficient when required. In evaluating the statistical significance of logistic regression coefficients, we use one-tailed tests when the direction of the relationship is predicted and two-tailed tests otherwise.

TO KILL OR NOT TO KILL? 531

DATA LIMITATIONS

Before turning to the results, it is important to acknowledge limitations associated with the data. A particularly problematic feature of the NCVS is underreporting bias, particularly for assault and rape (e.g., Murphy and Dodge, 1981). This implies that the level of nonlethal incidents will be underestimated relative to lethal incidents in the data set. We expect that this underreporting bias is less for the specific type of violent incidents under investigation—those involving injury—than it would be for incidents with no injury. The bias should be even weaker in the analyses limited to serious nonlethal injuries (those requiring medical treatment).

A particularly frustrating problem associated with the use of SHR data is that of extensive missing values (see Reidel, 1989). Information on the characteristics of offenders and features of the incident that presuppose information about offenders is likely to be missing. The most severe biases are likely to occur for the variable reflecting the relationship between victim and offender (stranger/nonstranger) because the biases of the NCVS and the SHR are compounded. Research has shown that incidents involving family members tend to be underreported in the NCVS (Turner, 1981). Consequently, the proportion of stranger incidents in the nonlethal data set is likely to be artificially high. In the SHR, on the other hand, stranger homicides are probably underestimated because of the greater difficulty in solving these kinds of cases and identifying an offender. The joint effect of such biases would be to create an artifactual relationship between victim-offender relationship and lethality of outcome—stranger incidents would appear to have a lower probability of death. Unfortunately, this artifactual relationship is in the same direction as our hypothesized relationship. Hence, any results involving the variable "stranger/nonstranger" must be interpreted cautiously.

There is no entirely satisfactory solution to the problem of missing data on homicide incidents.[6] We can nevertheless explore the potential implications of sample attrition by comparing the effects for those variables with little missing data, such as victim characteristics and weapon type, across two samples: (1) the maximum sample that can be used with a model limited to the predictors with little missing data and (2) the smaller

---

6. Kleck (1991:475–476) attempts to deal with this problem by creating "undetermined" dummy variables. This procedure involves coding all missing data as zero, and for each of the variables for which there are missing data, assigning a score of 1 to a corresponding "undetermined" variable for those cases with missing values. Including such variables in the equations then indicates whether the missing data pattern for a variable is systematically related to the dependent variable under examination. We have estimated our main models using such undetermined dummy variables. The effects of the independent variables in these analyses are highly similar to those reported below.

subsample that must be used to estimate the complete model. If the effects can be shown to be similar, we will have greater confidence that biased sampling is not seriously distorting our results.

RESULTS

A frequency distribution for the merged, weighted sample is presented in Table 1. Note that the distribution for the primary dependent variable—"incident outcome"—reflects the highly skewed proportions of the two kinds of incidents, as estimated for the U.S. population at large. Continuing down Table 1, the percentages for robbery and rape indicate that the presence of these criminal elements is relatively uncommon in comparison with the frequency of pure assaults, the omitted category for the offense dummy variables. Injurious incidents involving nonstrangers and single offenders are relatively more frequent than those involving strangers and multiple offenders. The proportions of incidents with female and male victims are roughly equivalent, whereas incidents with male offenders are much more common than those with female offenders. The majority of incidents involve nonblack victims and offenders. Finally, incidents with knives are the most common type of incident with a weapon, followed by blunt objects, "other" weapons, and guns, in descending order. The majority of incidents fall into the omitted weapon-type category of "no weapon."

Logistic regressions are presented in Table 2. In the first column of the table, we present equations that predict whether the victim is killed or injured. We hypothesize that victims are less likely to be killed in a robbery than in a pure assault because robbery offenders are less likely to value harm to the victim. This hypothesis is supported. The logistic regression coefficient for the robbery dummy variable is negative and statistically significant ($b = -1.32$). Expressed in terms of the odds of the increased risk of pure assaults versus the other offense categories, offenders are 3.74 times more likely to kill the victim in a pure assault than in a robbery. Incidents involving rape also entail a reduced likelihood of a lethal outcome ($b = -2.23$), although the effect is not statistically significant. Offenders are 9.3 times more likely to kill the victim in a pure assault than in a rape. The failure to achieve significance with such a strong effect may be due to the fact that there are relatively few rapes in the sample and the fact that lethal outcomes in rape are so rare.

We also hypothesize that offenders are more likely to kill the victim if the victim is male or black or if the offender is alone. In these instances, we assume the offender's fear of retaliation is greater. All three of these hypotheses are supported. Offenders are 4.4 times more likely to kill male victims than female victims ($b = 1.49$), and they are 2.5 times more likely

Table 1. Frequency Distribution ($N = 12,471$)

Variable	Percent
Incident Outcome	
Nonlethal injury	99.0
Death	1.0
Robbery	
No	80.1
Yes	19.9
Rape	
No	95.6
Yes	4.4
Victim-Offender Relationship	
Nonstranger	65.0
Stranger	35.0
Number of Offenders	
Single	75.4
Multiple	24.6
Victims' Sex	
Female	48.2
Male	51.8
Offenders' Sex	
Female	11.5
Male	88.5
Victims' Race	
Nonblack	83.6
Black	16.4
Offenders' Race	
Nonblack	69.8
Black	30.2
Presence of Gun	
No	93.7
Yes	6.3
Presence of Knife	
No	89.8
Yes	10.2
Presence of Blunt Object	
No	91.6
Yes	8.4
Presence of Other Weapons	
No	92.3
Yes	7.7

NOTES: Percentages are based on weighted counts. The weighted n is normed to reflect the actual sample size.

Table 2.   Logistic Regressions for Incident Outcomes and Gun Use

Independent Variable	Dependent Variables			
	Any Injury vs. Death	Injury with Medical Care vs. Death	Minor Injury vs. Injury with Medical Care	Gun vs. No Gun
Robbery	−1.32*	−1.26*	−.19	.36*
Rape	−2.23	−2.28	.29	.86*
Male Victims	1.49*	1.33*	−.04	.67*
Black Victims	.90*	.92*	.13	1.14*
Multiple Offenders	−1.51*	−1.21*	.03	.34*
Strangers	−1.02*	−1.11*	.24*	.09
Gun	3.71*	3.50*	.69*	—
Knife	1.48*	1.55*	.55*	—
Blunt Object	−.00	.36	.54*	—
Other Weapons	−2.31	−2.11	.49*	—
Male Offenders	−.16	−.19	.05	.47*
Black Offenders	.41	.19	.33*	−.08
Model χ^2	491.40*	424.25*	136.69*	351.02*
N	12,471	6,270	3,666	12,471

* $p \leq .01$.

to kill black victims than nonblack victims ($b = .90$). Single offenders are 4.5 times more likely to kill the victim than multiple offenders ($b = -1.51$).

The hypothesis that victims are more likely to be killed by offenders whom they can identify is also supported. Offenders who are nonstrangers to the victim are 2.8 times more likely to kill the victim than offenders who are strangers ($b = -1.02$). An alternative interpretation of this effect is that lethal outcomes are more likely between nonstrangers because their grievances are more intense. This argument implies that the stronger the relational tie between the offender and victim, the greater the likelihood a lethal outcome.

To examine this possible interpretation, we coded the relationship between offenders and victims in more detail. Dummy variables were created based on whether the offender was a family member, a friend, or an acquaintance. Strangers were treated as the omitted category. The results indicate that the risk of a lethal outcome is greatest for family members, which is consistent with the intensity of grievance hypothesis. However, the risk is lower for friends than for acquaintances, which runs counter to

TO KILL OR NOT TO KILL? 535

the notion that risk varies directly with relational tie. These findings suggest that the distinction between strangers and nonstrangers, and not simply relational distance, is the key factor affecting a lethal outcome.

As expected, guns are strongly associated with lethal outcomes. Offenders who use a gun are over 40 times more likely to kill the victim than offenders who do not use a weapon ($b = 3.71$). Offenders who use a knife are 4.4 times more likely to kill the victim than offenders who do not use a weapon ($b = 1.48$). The use of a blunt object or other weapons is not significantly related to lethal outcomes.

We advance no prediction in regard to the effects of the offenders' gender, and no significant effect is observed. We also examined whether there is a statistical interaction between the gender of the offender and victim by creating a product term and introducing it into the logistic regression equation. The product term does not have a significant effect on lethal outcome (results not shown). This finding runs counter to arguments suggesting that females have a special fear of males or that any outgroup prejudice plays a role in the degree of harm produced in intergender incidents.

We also derive no prediction about the effect of the offenders' race, and once again no significant effect is observed. To explore the possibility of statistical interactions between the race of the offender and victim, we created a race of victim, race of offender product term and included it in the analysis. This variable fails to exhibit a significant effect on lethal outcome (results not shown).

In the second column of Table 2 we present results from an equation predicting whether the victim is killed or seriously injured, omitting incidents involving minor injury. Approximately one half (49.6%) of the incidents involving injury were serious. The results are very similar to those observed in the first column. They show that the factors predicting a lethal outcome, given any injury, are similar to those predicting a lethal outcome, given a serious injury. These findings give us more confidence that our results are not seriously distorted by sampling biases in the NCVS due to selective reporting by respondents. It seems unlikely that respondents would fail to report to interviewers incidents resulting in serious injury.

Determinants of whether the victim suffered a serious or minor injury, omitting incidents with lethal outcomes, are presented in the third column of Table 2. Weighting is not used for this equation because there is no need to adjust for the disproportionate sampling of lethal and nonlethal incidents. The effects are weak, in contrast to the effects reported in the first two columns. The use of weapons does have an effect: Injuries are likely to be more severe when offenders use any type of weapon. Severe injury is also significantly more likely to occur when the offender is a stranger, when the offender is black, and when the incident involves pure

536   FELSON AND MESSNER

assault rather than robbery. However, these coefficients are small. In a
further analysis (not presented) we examined determinants of whether the
injured victim was hospitalized or not. The results were similar to the
results obtained when medical care is used as the criterion for determining
a serious injury. The general conclusion is that, with the exception of
weapons, the variables that predict lethal outcomes do not predict seriousness of injury in a similar manner. These findings support the idea that
lethal outcomes are qualitatively different from nonlethal outcomes
instead of the endpoint in a continuum representing the severity of injury.

In the case of weapons, the use of guns and knives is associated with
more serious outcomes in all equations, but their use is a better predictor
of death than serious injury. Blunt objects significantly increase the likelihood of severe (nonlethal) injury but do not affect lethal outcomes. The
ambiguous variable representing "other weapons" has opposite effects on
deaths versus serious nonlethal injuries, although the effect for lethal outcome is not significant.

The characteristics of offenders described above may also affect lethal
outcomes indirectly, through their effects on gun use. Determinants of
gun use are presented in the last column of Table 2. There are a number
of statistically significant effects, although most of them are weak. The
results show that guns are more likely to be used in rape and robbery than
in pure assault. Guns are also more likely to be used when confronting
male victims or black victims. These results suggest that a victim's gender
and race have indirect as well as direct effects on whether the victim is
killed, through weapon choice. Offenders are more likely to use guns
when confronting males and blacks, and this choice is strongly associated
with more lethal outcomes.

The analyses described above are based on a restricted sample due to
missing data on offender characteristics in the homicide data. In Table 3,
we compare the effects of weapons and victim characteristics, which have
little missing data, in the restricted sample and the maximum sample possible. All of the variables in this model have similar effects on lethal outcomes in both samples. These analyses give us greater confidence that
biased sampling is not seriously distorting our results.

Our final analyses involve an examination of statistical interactions
between type of crime and type of weapon. Unfortunately, our weighting
procedure makes it very difficult to attain statistical significance for these
interaction terms given the small numbers of incidents. After weighting,
there are only 13 robberies and 1 rape with a lethal outcome. Our strategy
is therefore to present results separately for robbery and pure assault
(omitting an analysis of rape) without examining the statistical significance
of the differences we observe. These results accordingly must be viewed as
more tentative.

TO KILL OR NOT TO KILL?   537

Table 3. Logistic Regressions for Predictors with Minimal
          Missing Data Across Samples

| | Dependent Variable: Any Injury vs. Death | |
Independent Variable	Maximum Sample	Sample with Information on Offender Characteristics
Male Victims	.96*	.85*
Black Victims	.95*	.94*
Gun	3.17*	3.15*
Knife	1.18*	1.23*
Blunt Object	−.23	−.27
Other Weapons	−2.38	−2.48
Model χ^2	444.75*	374.11*
N	14,508	12,471

* $p \leq .01$.

As noted above, two competing hypotheses about the effects of lethal weapons in pure assault and robbery seem plausible. According to the compensation hypothesis, the effect of lethal weapons should be weaker in pure assaults than in robberies, because pure assaults are more likely to involve lethal intent. If offenders are determined to kill the victim, they will do so regardless of the type of weapon they use. On the other hand, the weapon facilitator hypothesis predicts stronger effects of lethal weapons in pure assault. Offenders who desire to kill the victim will find it easier to do so with a more lethal weapon.

The results, presented in Table 4, are more consistent with the weapon facilitator effect. The use of guns and knives—the two more lethal weapons—is more strongly related to lethal outcomes in pure assaults than in robberies. The use of a blunt object appears to be more strongly associated with lethal outcomes in robberies, but the effect is statistically insignificant for both types of crime.

Fear of retaliation also appears to play a more important role in pure assault than in robbery. The effects of gender of victim, race of victim, and multiple offenders are strong and statistically significant in pure assault. In robbery, the effects are weaker and statistically insignificant. The effects of victim's race reverses in sign. The relationship between the offender and victim also has a stronger effect on outcomes in pure assault than in robbery. Victims who know the offender are much more likely to be killed in pure assaults.

Perhaps the interactions we observe in Table 4 reflect the effects of relationship and not type of crime. Assaults are much more likely to involve nonstrangers than robberies. To examine this possibility, we estimated

538   FELSON AND MESSNER

Table 4. Logistic Regressions Separately for Robbery and
          "Pure" Assaults

| | Dependent Variable: Any Injury vs. Death | |
Independent Variable	Robberies	"Pure" Assaults
Male Victims	.99	1.68*
Black Victims	−.14	1.21*
Multiple Offenders	−.83	−1.75*
Strangers	−.51	−1.24*
Gun	2.71*	3.92*
Knife	.60	1.63*
Blunt Object	1.05	−.24
Other Weapons	−2.31	−2.30
Male Offenders	.28	−.12
Black Offenders	.36	.29
Model χ^2	27.41*	467.59*
N	2,482	9,440

* $p \le .01$.

separate equations for assaults involving strangers and assaults involving nonstrangers. The results were quite similar, indicating that the effects we observe for assaults in Table 4 are not affected by the relationship between the offender and victim. We could not obtain meaningful results estimating separate equations for robberies involving strangers and nonstrangers because there were very few homicides available for analysis in the weighted subsamples (14 and 6, respectively). It is therefore possible that the effects of predictor variables might differ across relationship categories for robbery incidents but not for assaults, although we can think of no theoretical reason to expect such a three-way interaction.

SUMMARY AND DISCUSSION

Some homicide offenders kill their victim when they only want to injure them or when they have no clear intent to bring about death. Others have a specific desire to kill the victim. Their lethal intent may be premeditated, or it may develop during the crime, sometimes in response to the victim's behavior. Lethal intent is an extremely difficult concept to measure. However, the pattern of results reported above allows us to make reasonable inferences about the characteristics of violent encounters that are likely to be associated with lethal intent.

Lethal intent is more likely to be involved in pure assault than in robbery or rape, as indicated by the fact that lethal outcomes are more likely for this type of crime. For robbery and rape offenders, the victim's compliance is evidently more important, and harm to the victim is often incidental. Whether rapists value compliance in order to demonstrate power or to attain sexual gratification cannot be determined from these data (see Tedeschi and Felson, 1994).

The evidence supports the notion that tactical considerations are important in lethal intent. One plausible reason why offenders may desire to kill the victim is to avoid retaliation, either during the crime or at some later time. At least three findings are consistent with this explanation: (1) offenders are more likely to kill male victims than female victims; (2) offenders are more likely to kill black victims than nonblack victims; and (3) single offenders are more likely than multiple offenders to kill the victim. We recognize that fear of retaliation is not the only possible explanation for the effects of victims' gender and race and multiple offenders on lethal outcomes. However, fear of retaliation does provide a plausible and parsimonious account for the full set of findings.

Further, the range of plausible alternative explanations is significantly reduced when the findings for the determinants of the severity of non-lethal outcomes are also considered. For example, one alternative to the fear of retaliation explanation is that offenders are less likely to attack victims who have a power advantage in the first place unless their anger is particularly intense. Those offenders who do attack such victims, then, could be more likely to kill simply because of their extreme anger, without regard for the risks of retaliation. The evidence that the number of offenders and the gender and race of the victim do not affect the seriousness of the nonlethal injury casts doubt on this argument. If offenders with a power disadvantage have high levels of anger to begin with, they should have injured victims more severely.

The findings regarding determinants of severity of nonlethal outcomes are also relevant to the issue of victim precipitation. It is possible that victims who are male or black and victims facing single offenders in fact engage in more violence. Offenders may kill them in response. We cannot determine from the data to what extent the victim's behavior plays a mediating role in these effects. However, if violence by the victim results in more severe attacks by the offender, we should have found effects of the victim's gender or race, and of multiple offenders, on the severity of nonlethal injury, which we did not. Note that whether or not the victim actually engages in violence, the offender's decision to kill the victim to avoid personal harm is still a tactical one.

The finding of distinct patterns for lethal and nonlethal outcomes is also relevant to an alternative tactical interpretation of the race-of-victim effect. It may be that offenders are inhibited from killing white victims because they anticipate more certain and severe legal punishment.

Offenders may believe that agents of the criminal justice system devalue black victims and take such crimes less seriously. If offenders consider this factor during the crime, one would expect them to be reluctant to seriously injure white victims, but as noted, we find no significant effect of race of victim on the severity of a nonlethal injury.

There is an alternative explanation that could explain why the victim's race affects lethal outcomes but not severity of injury. Black victims may be more likely than whites to die from their wounds because they receive less timely or lower quality medical care (cf. Doerner and Speir, 1986). Blacks certainly have more restricted access to high-quality medical care in general. On the other hand, blacks are more likely to be victimized in inner-city neighborhoods, and the hospitals in these neighborhoods may actually provide better treatment to trauma patients because their staffs have more experience with these medical problems than staffs in hospitals with a more suburban or rural clientele.

Fear of retaliation is not the only tactical concern of offenders. Offenders may intentionally kill the victim in order to avoid prosecution. A lethal outcome may eliminate the only witness to the crime. Consistent with this reasoning, we find that offenders are more likely to kill the victim when he or she is someone who could identify them than when the victim is a stranger.

Alternative interpretations are also possible for the observed "stranger" effect. Perhaps offenders simply have more serious grievances with people they know, which is why they are more likely to kill. Two pieces of evidence argue against this interpretation, however. First, the likelihood of a lethal outcome is not linearly associated with the relational distance between offender and victim. Second, serious injury is more likely than mild injury when the offender is a stranger; if offenders have more serious grievances with people they know, they should injure them more, not less, severely.

Stranger effects could also be due to biased sampling. If homicides involving strangers are undersampled, because strangers are less likely to be known to the police, an artifactual negative relationship between lethal outcomes and the involvement of strangers could be produced. Undersampling of incidents involving people who know each other in the NCVS could also produce this relationship. However, this undersampling is less likely given that we only include incidents in which there are injuries, and given that we observe the same relationship when we omit incidents involving mild injuries. In addition, the artifactual explanation cannot explain why stranger effects are stronger for assault than robbery. In fact, it might predict stronger effects for robbery than assault. Robbery homicides are more likely to be undersampled than homicides involving pure

TO KILL OR NOT TO KILL? 541

assault because they are less likely to be solved.[7]

Consistent with previous research, we find that lethal outcomes are much more likely when offenders use guns. The use of knives is also associated with lethal outcomes, although the effect is much weaker. These weapons are more strongly associated with lethal outcomes in pure assaults than in robbery. This pattern suggests that the weapons facilitate a lethal outcome for offenders with lethal intent, given the assumption that assault offenders are more likely than robbery offenders to have lethal intent. These findings run counter to the notion that offenders who are determined to kill their victims compensate with greater effort if they do not have a lethal weapon.

Type of crime (robbery vs. assault) appears to condition the effects of sociodemographic characteristics and number of offenders. The effects of the victim's race and gender and the involvement of multiple offenders appear to be stronger in pure assault than in robbery. These results imply that coercive power and the fear of retaliation play a greater role in pure assault. This pattern seems counterintuitive if one assumes that assaults are more likely to involve strong emotions than robberies and that emotions override tactical concerns.

We can advance two possible explanations for the interactions among sociodemographic characteristics, number of offenders, and type of crime. First, tactical concerns may not be enough to motivate offenders to kill victims in robbery in the absence of a strong grievance. Assault offenders, who are angry and aggrieved, may already be motivated to severely harm the victim. The situation may be similar to laboratory experiments in which experimenters cannot get subjects to deliver shocks in response to their manipulations without provoking them as well (Tedeschi and Felson, 1994).

Second, robbery offenders are likely to choose victims who are vulnerable and have low coercive power (e.g., Letkemann, 1973). When they target men, blacks, or when they commit offenses alone, they are likely to target those who do not pose a threat in the first place. To the extent that they make these choices, gender, race, and number of offenders would not be predictive of retaliatory threat in robbery. In other words, tactical decisions preceding the robbery probably reduce the need for tactical decisions during the robbery. In pure assaults, on the other hand, offenders often have less choice regarding the victims. The violent incident may

---

7. If assaults are more likely than robberies to be witnessed by third parties, then the incentive for killing the victim-witness would be less. This would also lead to undersampling of robbery homicides, since the victim-witness is deceased. Both of these processes would produce a stronger relationship for robbery than assault, which is the opposite of the pattern observed.

involve victims who have attacked or provoked them. Situational factors such as the gender and race of the victim and the presence of allies would then have a greater effect on the extent to which assault offenders feel threatened and perceive a need to use lethal force.

Similar arguments might be used to explain the interaction between type of crime and victim-offender relationship. The tactical consideration of identifiability, reflected in nonstranger relationships, may be insufficient to motivate robbery offenders to kill their prey in the absence of the kind of grievances typically associated with assaultive incidents. Moreover, if robbery offenders tend to choose victims for tactical reasons in the first place, they will likely select people that they believe will not go to the police, whether the victims can identify them or not. Perhaps these victims are afraid of the offender or are engaged in illegal activity themselves and are fearful of legal repercussions.

With respect to our control variables, the effect of the victim's gender on lethal outcomes does not depend on the gender of the offender. Male victims are apparently perceived as a greater threat by both male and female offenders. In addition, there is no evidence in our data that intergender incidents are any different from intragender incidents in lethal outcomes.

Nor are the effects of the victim's race on lethal outcomes dependent on the race of the offender. Black victims are apparently perceived as more threatening to both black and nonblack offenders. It could be argued that offenders of both races devalue black victims and therefore feel less inhibited about taking their lives. However, the fact that black victims are no more likely than white victims to be seriously injured indicates that this type of devaluation is probably not a factor. In general, there is no evidence that interracial incidents are any different from intraracial incidents or that intergroup attitudes play a role in lethal outcomes.

The victim's gender and race also have indirect effects on whether the victim is killed, through weapon choice. Offenders are more likely to use guns when confronting males and blacks, and the use of guns is strongly associated with lethal outcomes. The effects of the victim's gender and race on gun use probably also reflect tactical concerns. Fear of retaliation from males and blacks apparently leads their adversaries to use lethal weapons and to formulate lethal intent.

In conclusion, lethal outcomes are sometimes intended and sometimes unintended. We have interpreted violent actions with lethal intent as instrumental or goal-oriented behavior. The decision to kill a victim reflects tactical concerns, as well as the desire to eliminate rivals, gain retribution, and attain favorable social identities. Of course, we cannot rule out the possibility that lethal intent is also affected by frustration or some other innate, nonrational process. Thus, some aggression theorists would

TO KILL OR NOT TO KILL?   543

argue that lethal intent also reflects angry aggression and that we have only focused on part of the problem (e.g., Berkowitz, 1989). Whether all violence is instrumental cannot be answered by this research. Nevertheless, our analyses indicate the utility of applying this perspective in the study of injurious attacks and of taking seriously the notion of lethal intent.

REFERENCES

Berk, Richard A.
  1983   An introduction to sample selection bias. American Sociological Review 48:386–398.

Berkowitz, Leonard
  1989   The frustration-aggression hypothesis: An examination and reformulation. Psychological Bulletin 106:59–73.

Block, Richard
  1977   Violent Crime. Lexington, Mass: Lexington Books. Bureau of Justice Statistics.
  1992a   Criminal Victimization in the United States, 1990. Washington, D.C.: U.S. Department of Justice.
  1992b   National Crime Surveys: National Sample, 1986–1991. (Near-term data; computer file.) Conducted by Bureau of the Census. 4th ICPSR e. Ann Arbor, Mich.: Inter-University Consortium for Political and Social Research.

Buss, Arnold H.
  1961   The Psychology of Aggression. New York: John Wiley & Sons.

Cohen, Lawrence E. and Marcus Felson
  1979   Social change and crime rate trends: A routine activity approach. American Sociological Review 44:588–608.

Cook, Phillip J.
  1991   The technology of personal violence. In Michael Tonry (ed.), Crime and Justice: A Review of Research. Vol. 14. Chicago: University of Chicago Press.

Cornish, Derek and Ronald Clarke (eds.)
  1986   The Reasoning Criminal: Rational Choice Perspectives on Offending. New York: Springer–Verlag.

Doerner, William G. and John C. Speir
  1986   Stitch and sew: The impact of medical resources upon criminally induced lethality. Criminology 24:319–330.

Dollard, John, Leonard W. Dobb, Neil E. Miller, O. Hobart Mowrer, and Robert R. Sears
  1939   Frustration and Aggression. New Haven: Yale University Press.

Felson, Richard B. and Henry J. Steadman
  1983   Situational factors in disputes leading to criminal violence. Criminology 21:59–74.

544   FELSON AND MESSNER

Fischer, Claude S.
    1969   The effect of threats in an incomplete information game. Sociometry
            32:301–314.

Frankel, Martin
    1983   Sampling theory. In Peter H. Rossi, James D. Wright, Andy B. Anderson
            (eds.), Handbook of Survey Research. New York: Academic Press.

Hanushek, Eric A. and John E. Jackson
    1977   Statistical Methods for Social Scientists. New York: Academic Press.

Harries, Keith D.
    1990   Serious Violence. Springfield, Ill.: Charles C Thomas.

Heckman, James J.
    1979   Sample Selection Bias as a Specification Error. Econometrica 45:153–161.

Hornstein, Harvey A.
    1965   The effects of different magnitudes of threat upon interpersonal bargain-
            ing. Journal of Experimental Social Psychology 1:282–293.

Kipnis, David and Stuart M. Schmidt
    1983   An influence perspective on bargaining in organizations. In Max
            Bazerman and Roy Lewicki (eds.), Negotiating in organizations. Beverly
            Hills, Calif.: Sage.

Kleck, Gary
    1991   Point Blank: Guns and Violence in America. New York: Aldine de
            Gruyter.

Kleck, Gary and Karen McElrath
    1991   The effects of weaponry on human violence. Social Forces 69:669–692.

Letkemann, Peter
    1973   Crime as Work. Englewood Cliffs, N.J.: Prentice–Hall.

Murphy, Linda R. and Richard W. Dodge
    1981   The Baltimore recall study. In Robert G. Lehnen and Wesley G. Skogan
            (eds.), The National Crime Survey: Working Papers. Vol. I: Current and
            Historical Perspectives. Washington, D.C.: U.S. Government Printing
            Office.

Reidel, Mark
    1989   Nationwide homicide data sets: An evaluation of UCR and NCHS data.
            In Doris L. MacKenzie, Phylis J. Baunach, and Roy R. Roberg (eds.),
            Measuring Crime: Large-Scale, Long-Range Efforts. Albany, N.Y.:
            SUNY Press.
    1993   Stranger Violence: A Theoretical Inquiry. New York: Garland Publish-
            ing, Inc.

Stolzenberg, Ross M. and Daniel A. Relles
    1990   Theory testing in a world of constrained research design: The significance
            of Heckman's censored sampling bias correction for nonexperimental
            research. Sociological Methods and Research 18:395–415.

Tedeschi, James T. and Richard B. Felson
    1994   Violence, Aggression, and Coercive Actions. Washington, D.C.: Ameri-
            can Psychological Association.

Tittle, Charles R. and Charles H. Logan
  1973   Sanctions and deviance: Evidence and remaining questions. Law &
          Society Review 7:371–392.

Turner, Anthony G.
  1981   The San Jose recall study. In Robert G. Lehnen and Wesley G. Skogan
          (eds.), The National Crime Survey: Working Papers. Vol. I: Current and
          Historical Perspectives. Washington, D.C.: U.S. Government Printing
          Office.

Wright, James D., Peter H. Rossi, and Kathleen Daly
  1983   Under the Gun: Weapons, Crime, and Violence in America. New York:
          Aldine de Gruyter.

Zimring, Franklin E.
  1968   Is gun control likely to reduce violent killing? University of Chicago Law
          Review 35:721–737.
  1972   The medium is the message: Firearm calibre as a determinant of death
          from assault. Journal of Legal Studies 1:97–124.

Richard Felson is Professor of Sociology at the University at Albany, State University of New York. In recent research he examines whether marital violence is similar to other forms of violence, and why chivalry sometimes fails to deter male violence against wives. He is the co-author (with James Tedeschi) of *Violence, Aggression and Coercive Actions* (APA Books, 1994).

Steven F. Messner is Professor of Sociology in the Department of Sociology, University at Albany, State University of New York. In addition to research on gender and violence, he is currently studying crime and delinquency in China. He is also engaged in research on the cultural and institutional determinants of serious crimes in market societies and is co-author (with Richard Rosenfeld) of *Crime and the American Dream* (Wadsworth).

[18]

Exploring the Drugs-Homicide Connection

SEAN P. VARANO
Northeastern University

JOHN D. MCCLUSKEY
University of Texas at San Antonio

JUSTIN W. PATCHIN
University of Wisconsin-Eau Claire

TIMOTHY S. BYNUM
Michigan State University

The relationship between drugs and homicide has been well documented for some period of time. Drugs can play many different roles in homicide events. Drug homicides are disaggregated into *peripheral drug homicides* and *drug-motivated homicides*. In the former, drugs were present at the scene or drugs were being used by the victim or offender but were not the central causal feature of the event. In the latter, the sale or use of drugs was the primary cause of the lethal interaction. Using multinomial logistic analysis, we analyze the extent to which individual, situational, and contextual factors discriminate between different drug-homicide events. We found variables indicative of risky lifestyles were significant predictors of the different types of drug homicides. More important, findings suggest the variables considered in the multivariate model had different effects on different measures of the dependent variable. Policy implications are discussed.

Keywords: drugs; homicide; violent crime; tripartite framework

Although research generally assumes a close relationship between drugs and violence, very little is known about the many different roles drugs can play in criminal events. *Drug related* as an event classification scheme is relatively common in homicide research, as well as other areas of inquiry, and is usually understood to be an important component in the causal processes of criminal events. Yet such classification schemes often suggest a simple, unidimensional construct. In reality, drug-related crimes are com-

370   Journal of Contemporary Criminal Justice / November 2004

plex events. The purpose of this research was first to disaggregate the concept of drug-related homicide by providing an event classification scheme that conceptualizes the diverse roles drugs play in drug-related events. A categorical coding scheme is presented that is similar to that proposed by Goldstein (1995) and later tested by Brownstein and colleagues (Brownstein & Goldstein, 1990; Brownstein, Baxi, Goldstein, & Ryan, 1992) that specifies three distinct types of homicide events. Included among these are (a) events that involved no evidence of illicit drugs associated with the homicide event, (b) those that involved the presence of drugs or drug use at the scene as well as events where either the victim and/or offender were buying or selling drugs (we term this *peripherally drug-related homicides*), and (c) events where the sale or use of drugs was the motivating feature of the homicide event. In some situations, there may be overlap between categories b and c; however, category c is distinct in that it includes features of motivation. The second purpose was to determine the relative importance of various situational and contextual characteristics of homicide events in understanding different types of drug-related events. Delineating these features will be an important step in filling in the gaps of knowledge about the assumed relationship between drugs and violence.

LITERATURE REVIEW

Connections between the use of drugs and crime are not new but have been exposed for much of history (Weil, 1995). The 1938 movie *Reefer Madness* was an iconic representation of the connection made in popular culture between drug use and undesirable behavior. More recent attention to the relationship is based, in part, on crime trends that indicate a simultaneous spike in violent crime and an emerging crack-cocaine market during the 1980s. Researchers noted a sharp increase in violent crime, especially murder and robbery, from approximately 1985 through the early 1990s. Common wisdom attributed the rising homicide rates to increases in arrests of young urban dwellers armed with firearms.

Crack cocaine made its way into urban communities in the United States in 1985. As an inexpensive alternative to powder cocaine that was available in

An earlier version of this paper was presented at the Annual Meeting of the American Society of Criminology in Denver, Colorado, November 18-22, 2003. We would like to thank Karen Ream, Jennifer Robinson, Jeb Booth, and two anonymous reviewers for their insightful comments on earlier drafts. All correspondence related to this article should be directed to Sean P. Varano, Northeastern University, College of Criminal Justice, 405 Churchill Hall, Boston, MA 02115: e-mail: s.varano@neu.edu single hits, the crack market flourished at an unprecedented rate (Blumstein, 1995). Early crack markets quickly grew into high volume industries as greater numbers of individuals made more frequent buys. Market growth forces created a need for large numbers of new sellers, a market demand that was filled largely by young Black men. In many ways, these new entrepreneurs were an ideal source of labor. Young urban Black men were excluded from the legitimate labor market at a rate much higher than their older, suburban, and nonminority counterparts. They were also more willing to work at cheaper rates because, as suggested by Blumstein (1995), "They may be less vulnerable to the punishments imposed by the adult criminal justice system" (p. 30). Younger individuals were also perceived to be more daring and less risk averse. In the end, younger individuals who were more likely to carry firearms and use violence became an integral part of the crack cocaine market (Blumstein, 1995; Blumstein & Rosenfeld, 1998).

The association between drugs and crime is evidenced through a variety of data sources. Official crime statistics indicate that the involvement of poor young minority men as victims and offenders of serious violent crime grew at an alarming rate during much of the late 1980s and into the 1990s. Murder arrest rates for 18-year-old individuals almost tripled between 1985 and 1992 from approximately 25 to 60 per 100,000 (Blumstein & Rosenfeld, 1998). During the same period, drug arrest rates for non-White urban youth also nearly tripled while rates for White youth decreased. Data from the Arrestee Drug Abuse Monitoring Program (ADAM) indicate that between 40% and 80% of adult male arrestees tested positive for cocaine use in 1998 (ADAM, 2000). MacCoun, Kilmer, and Reuter (2003) also reported that approximately 30% of state and federal inmates incarcerated for robbery or breaking and entering reported they committed the offense to acquire drugs. In one study of 500 incarcerated felons in Michigan, approximately one half reported they purchased and sold drugs nearly every day before their incarceration (Bynum, Huebner, & Hinduja, 2001). Thus, a large percentage of individuals involved in serious crime are heavily involved in the sale and use of drugs.

Many criminal justice officials strongly believed the sale or use of drugs was one of the primary factors behind violence in the 1980s and 1990s. Local government officials often report drugs near the top of the most important factors underlying homicide rates (Lattimore, Trudeau, Riley, Leiter, & Edwards, 1997, p. 72). The drugs-violence relationship is most often associated with crack cocaine; however, some officials report changing marijuana markets as emerging sources of violence. It is interesting to note these perceptions seem to be more driven by news accounts of national trends than analyses of local drug-use indicators.[1]

372   Journal of Contemporary Criminal Justice / November 2004

Involvement of Drug Circumstances in Homicide Events

Drugs play a prominent role in homicide events. Research indicates that more than one half of all homicides may involve drug circumstances (Brownstein et al., 1992). In an analysis of all homicide incidents that occurred in St. Louis between 1985 and 1989, Rosenfeld (1991) reported 26% were drug related. *Drug related* referred to instances where an event was identified as such in the police case file or where the victim, offender, or aspects of the homicide incident were identified as associated with the sale or use of narcotics.

Although a substantial percentage of homicide incidents in places such as St. Louis are considered drug related, the relative level of drug-related homicides appears to vary by city—a difference presumably linked to features of local drug markets. In a study of Latino homicide, Martinez (2002) reported steady and substantial decreases in drug-related homicide rates in Miami between the years 1985 and 1995 while Chicago's rate was static. In contrast, the rate of drug-related homicides among Latino victims in San Diego increased dramatically between 1985 and 1992 and then decreased just as dramatically from 1993 to 1995. Although there is no definitive explanation for these varying trends, they likely can be attributed, at least in part, to differences in market stability as observed in places such as New York City (see Fagan & Chin, 1989).

Other studies have confirmed the prevalence of drug circumstances in homicides across the nation. In a study of nearly 800 homicide cases in four different cities throughout the United States, Wellford and Cronin (1999) reported that approximately one fourth of all homicides were drug-related offenses. The drug-related category was substantially more common in open[2] cases (41%) compared to closed cases (23%) (pp. 11-13). Varano and Cancino's (2001) analysis of nearly 10,000 homicide events from Chicago between 1975 and 1995 indicated that approximately 8% were considered drug-motivated events. Although 8% represents a reasonably small proportion of events, the motivated classification represents only those cases where the "sale or use of illegal narcotics was the motivating factor for the lethal altercation" (Varano & Cancino, 2001, p. 13), a classification scheme that is much more restrictive than drug related.

Drug motivation or the presence of drugs not only are the prevalent characteristics of homicide events but also have implications for understanding certain features of homicide events. Wellford and Cronin (1999) reported certain features of drug involvement in homicide events significantly reduced the likelihood of clearance for such cases. It is most important to note that cases were 46% less likely to be cleared if the victim had a history of drug use, 46% less likely if the victim had a history of association with drug dealers and users, and 35% less likely if the victim was identified as a drug buyer or had a prior drug arrest (Wellford & Cronin, 1999, Tables 12 & 13). It seems, however, the importance of these characteristics was relevant only as they relate to victims, not offenders. For example, of those drug-related victim characteristics just mentioned only offender identified as drug buyer significantly reduced the odds of clearance (57% reduction).

Conceptual Links Between Drug Use and Violence

Goldstein (1995) proposed the notion of the *tripartite framework* for understanding the multiple causal roles drugs can play in violent behavior. Drugs and violence may be connected through psychopharmacological effects of the drugs, economic-compulsive behavior associated with the desire to get money to buy drugs, or systemic or normal violence associated with drug markets.

First, violence may be a result of psychopharmacological effects of drug use itself. Individuals using alcohol, stimulants, barbiturates, or related substances may experience a psychological episode that results in unusual or unpredictable behavior. This behavior could be the result of drug-induced erratic behavior that is commonly associated with drugs such as PCP, or a result of irritability associated with certain symptoms of withdrawal. A narrative description of a psychopharmacological event is provided by Brownstein and colleagues (1992):

> A 29-year-old woman and a 41-year-old man were living together for eight years in a common law marriage. They had two children together. He believed that she was seeing other men. In addition, she had a job and he did not; he felt belittled by the fact that he was out of work. So they often fought. During one fight, when he was high on alcohol and cocaine, he lost control. He grabbed a kitchen knife that she was holding and stabbed her repeatedly. She died of multiple stab wounds to the body (Case #100). (p. 34)

Second, economic-compulsive behavior denotes the type of violence associated with the desire to obtain sufficient monetary resources to procure drugs. In this case, the violence is perpetuated not by psychopharmacological impulses, but instead the compulsion to obtain money to purchase drugs. Approximately one third of state and federal inmates incarcerated for robbery or breaking and entering reported they committed the offense to acquire money to purchase drugs (MacCoun et al., 2003). Wright and Decker's (1997) ethnographic study of armed robbers clarifies this connection. In explaining the decision to conduct an armed robbery, one research participant reported:

> I like to mix and I like to get high. You can't get high broke. You really can't get high just standing there, you got to move. And in order to move, you got to have some money. . . . Got to have some money, want to get high (No. 14). (Wright & Decker, 1997, p. 35)

The final aspect of Goldstein's tripartite framework is systemic violence. In contrast to the former, systemic violence is the violent behavior associated with drug-related business interests. Drug markets are analogous to many other business environments where multiple competitors aggressively push their product while trying to exclude other local competitors. Similar to other legitimate industries, there are (to some degree) rules of the game that dictate proper business etiquette. These represent the rules that govern business transactions. A substantial amount of drug violence is associated with strict enforcement of drug market–related business rules. Fagan and Chin (1989) attributed much of New York's crack-related violence in the 1980s to systemic violence. Although conventional wisdom blamed the violent crack markets of the 1980s on drug-induced psychopathy, Fagan and Chin reported the increased levels of violence to problems associated with attempts to control unregulated drug markets. The crack epidemic discussed above occurred at a unique time when New York drug markets were not controlled by a central group of individuals. Instead, markets were highly decentralized and locally controlled. Large profit margins associated with unregulated markets resulted in high levels of violence as individuals fought for control of profits.

Classification Schemes for Drug-Related Homicides

Goldstein's (1995) taxonomy is arguably one of the most influential ideas in criminal-event classification schemes since Wolfgang's (1958) 11-point categorization of the victim-offender relationship more than 45 years ago. It represents one of the most widely accepted explanations for the drug-crime nexus to date.

Brownstein, Goldstein, and colleagues have applied the tripartite framework to two separate samples of homicides and have argued the scheme is useful for categorizing drug-homicide incidents. Approximately 40% ($n = 129$) of the homicides that occurred in New York State (excluding New York City) in 1984 were considered drug related. Of the drug-related offenses, nearly 60% were considered psychopharmacological events, 21% systemic violence events, and 3% economic compulsive events (Brownstein & Goldstein, 1990, p. 177). The relative proportion of the different types of drug homicides appears dependent on time and/or location. In another sample of homicide incidents that occurred in New York City between March and October 1988 ($n = 414$), the largest percentage of drug homicides were systemic violence events (74%), followed by psychopharmacological (14%), and economic compulsive events (4%) (Brownstein et al., 1992, p. 33).

Rosenfeld's (1991) analysis of St. Louis homicides also focused on drug-related events. Drug-related homicides (DRH) were deconstructed into drug-transactions, drug-role, and drug-use events. As aptly stated by Rosenfeld (1991), "Violent outcomes, including homicides, may result from the properties of drugs or from the properties of drug markets" (pp. 3-6). Events were classified as a drug transaction if they occurred during or in direct connection to the purchase or sale of drugs. Drug-role homicides involved victims or offenders in the role of seller, buyer, or both. They differ from the former in that they were not connected to a particular drug transaction but instead were connected to the drug market as a whole. Finally, the drug-use classification involves the use of drugs by the offender or victim on the same day as the incident. This scheme is strongly reminiscent of Goldstein's psychopharmacological, economic-compulsion, or systemic violence.

Factors Differentiating Drug Events

Evidence supports the perception that there are important substantive differences between various types of drug-related homicides. Rosenfeld (1991) reported drug-use events involved a greater number of personal weapons such as a knife (28%), while almost 90% of drug-transaction and drug-role events involved firearms (pp. 3-15). A larger percentage of drug-use events also involved victims and offenders who were closely connected with each other (e.g., 49%) compared to drug-transaction (12%) or drug-role homicides (13%). In terms of motives, a substantially higher percentage of drug-transaction and drug-role events were motivated by economic issues. For example, 33% of motives for drug-transaction events were coded as "bad deal," 21% as "bad debt," and 19% as "rip off." In strong contrast, almost 80% of drug-use events were motivated by drug-induced behavior (e.g., Goldstein's psychopharmacological violence).

Research findings also suggest drug and nondrug events can be differentiated based on victim and offender characteristics. In St. Louis, drug-related events involved a significantly larger proportion of younger victims and offenders between ages 22 and 27 years than non-drug-related events (Rosenfeld, 1991, pp. 3-12). In the latter incidents, victims and offenders tended to be older. Victims and offenders in drug-related homicides were also more likely to be African American, male, and involve a gun as the central weapon. Drug-related homicides involved a significantly larger percentage of victims and offenders classified as acquaintances compared to those with close personal relationships.

376 Journal of Contemporary Criminal Justice / November 2004

Situational differences among the various types of drug-involved events have been confirmed elsewhere. Brownstein and colleagues (1992) reported non-drug-related homicides were more likely to involve strangers (30% compared to 13% for drug-related events) and more likely to involve unknown victim-offender relationships (23% for non-drug-related compared to approximately 8% for drug-related events) (p. 35). The authors also reported that a greater percentage of drug-related offenses occurred in known drug locations, involved perpetrators and victims who were known drug users and traffickers, and involved perpetrators and victims with prior arrests for drug possession and sales (p. 37).

Goldstein's taxonomy provides a meaningful framework for understanding the drugs-homicide nexus. The tripartite framework has had a considerable impact on the understanding of the drugs-homicide association; however, with a few notable exceptions, the framework has gone largely untested. The purpose of the current research is to advance the discussion of the drugs-homicide nexus by proposing a classification scheme that is similar to that proposed by Goldstein. Employing multivariate data analysis, we also intend to determine victim and situational characteristics important to differentiating such events.

METHOD

Sample and Data

Data were collected on 175 homicides that occurred throughout the city of Detroit between January 1999 and December 2002. The sample includes the entire population of homicides from one of Detroit's 13 precincts ($n = 129$) and a subsequent random sample of citywide cases ($n = 46$) that occurred during the period identified above. The sampling frame was a list of all homicides recorded in the homicide book, a running log of incoming homicides maintained by the Homicide Section of the Detroit Police Department. The homicide book records vital information about all suspicious deaths that occur in the city including the date, time, and location of the incident. Also collected is the name of the victim, manner of death, and status field that tracks if the status of the death was later changed to natural or justifiable.

The larger set of cases was coded as part of a firearm-violence reduction program sponsored by the U.S. Attorneys Office. As part of the project, every nonjustified homicide that occurred in the target precinct during the 4-year period was coded by research staff. Project personnel were interested in understanding the factors underlying serious violent crime in this particular area of Detroit. To expand the representatives of the sample, the research staff also randomly selected and coded an additional 46 cases that occurred in other areas of Detroit during the same period.[3]

Homicides were coded using an instrument developed in previous research (see Wellford & Cronin, 1999). Many features of the incidents were coded including demographic characteristics and criminal histories of victims and offenders, and temporal and spatial characteristics of the event including date, time, and location. Data were also coded on various situational characteristics including gang involvement, apparent motive for the event, and level of drug involvement.

Dependent Variable

The dependent variable is a measure of drug relatedness gleaned from the official homicide case files in our sample. This included coding aspects of the homicide event such as whether drugs were present at the scene, if the victim or offender were buying or selling drugs at the time of the incident, or if the event were drug motivated such as a killing of a rival drug dealer. As presented in Table 1, we chose to create a three-category variable of cases where no relationship to drugs was found (50%); cases where evidence of drug use, sales, or purchase was found (31%); and cases where drugs provided a direct motivation for the homicide (19%). Table 1 also details the degree of overlap between groupings. As one might surmise, drug-motivated homicides also included proportionately more peripheral elements, as coded from the files and presented in Table 1. Narrative examples of each category, from the homicide files, are presented in the Appendix as illustrations. Below we contrast these levels of drug relatedness (nondrug related, peripherally drug related, and drug motivated) in a multivariate model.

The coding scheme for the dependent variable is similar to that proposed by Goldstein (1995) and later tested by Brownstein and colleagues (Brownstein et al., 1992; Brownstein & Goldstein, 1990) but also differs in important ways. In fact, the coding more closely resembles that proposed in Rosenfeld's (1991) comparison of drug-use and drug-transaction homicides with the added category of drug-motivated incidents. Most notably missing from the current operational definition of the dependent variable from that proposed by Goldstein is a category that reflects psychopharmacological classification. Although we support the proposition that the category is conceptually meaningful, actually determining if an event was caused by a drug-induced psychopathic episode was exceedingly difficult. In situations where violence erupts after the use of drugs, it is often impossible to determine if the violence was a cause of the drug use or merely incidental to its use. Referring to the homicide description provided by Brownstein and colleagues (1992)

TABLE 1

Categorical Measure of Drug Relatedness (N = 175)

	No Drug Presence (n = 88; 50%)		Peripheral Drug Presence (n = 54; 31%)		Drug Motivated (n = 33; 19%)		Proportion of All Homicides With Characteristic	
Subcategories of drug influences coded from homicide records								
No drug	88	(100%)	0	(0%)	0	(0%)	88	(51%)
Drugs or paraphernalia on scene[a]	0	(0%)	21	(39%)	23	(70%)	44	(25%)
Victim or offender possessing drugs[a]	0	(0%)	24	(44%)	24	(73%)	48	(27%)
Victim or offender consuming drugs[a]	0	(0%)	13	(24%)	12	(36%)	25	(14%)
Victim or offender selling drugs[a]	0	(0%)	38	(70%)	30	(91%)	68	(39%)
Sale or use was motivation for homicide	0	(0%)	0	(0%)	33	(100%)	33	(19%)
Category total	88	(50%)	54	(31%)	33	(19%)	175	(100%)

NOTE: Raw numbers reported, percentages of within-category cases in parentheses for subcategories.
a. Peripheral elements.

and detailed above, we argue it can be difficult to accurately make the determination that the violence was a result of drug use.

Independent Variables

The independent measures capture aspects of the location of the homicide, the characteristics of the victim, as well as suspect, and situational characteristics and are presented in Table 2. First, we measured whether the neighborhood within which the event occurred was an active drug market. The scout car area within which the homicide occurred was ranked on the level of reported drug offenses within its border during the year that the homicide was recorded. Detroit is divided into 133 scout car areas (approximately 1-square-mile geographic subdivisions). The homicide events included in the sample were geocoded using ARC VIEW 8.2 and placed in the corresponding scout car area. Homicide events that occurred in scout car areas that were in the highest quartile of narcotics reports were considered to be within drug markets. Using this operationalization, 17% of the homicides in our sample occurred in areas characterized as drug markets. It should be noted that during the 4-year period, 42 different areas were ranked in the top quartile; of those 42, however, one half were highly ranked in 3 or more of the years, indicating that they had characteristics suggestive of persistent drug markets.

With respect to victim characteristics, four variables were employed. Gender was measured with a dummy variable (1 = male), and 79% of the victims in our sample were males. Victim minority status was measured as a dummy variable (1 = minority), and 89% of the sample victims were minorities, with African Americans comprising the entire category. The minority category comprised entirely African Americans. A variable capturing youthful victims between the ages 14 and 25 years was also dummy coded, with 29% of the victims falling in that age range. With respect to these characteristics, we would expect youthful and male victims, in particular, to be significant predictors of drug motivation when contrasted with nondrug events. The fourth victim characteristic, lifestyle, reflects victims' prior involvement with drugs. Three indicators were coded from information in the homicide files that indicated (a) the victim had prior associations with known drug dealers, (b) the victim had prior evidence of drug abuse, and (c) the victim had an arrest history that included at least one drug arrest. Each indicator was dummy coded (1 = present, 0 = not present) and finally summed to create an index of prior drug involvement (ranging from 0 to 3). The mean level of the drug involvement index was .90 with 57% of the victims having no evidence of prior involvement with drugs. We would expect that level of involvement as measured by arrest, abuse, and association would be significant in making contrasts between drug and nondrug homicides.

TABLE 2
Descriptive Statistics

	Full Sample: 1999-2002 (N = 175)				Supplemental Homicide Reports: 1999-2002 (N = 1581)			
	M	SD	Minimum	Maximum	M	SD	Minimum	Maximum
Outcome variable								
Drug relatedness	1.09	1.21	.00	3.00				
Explanatory variables								
Location variables								
Occurred in drug market (1 = Yes)	.17	.30	.00	1.00				
Victim variables								
Male (1 = Yes)	.79	.41	.00	1.00	.84	.37	.00	1.00
Minority (1 = Yes)	.89	.31	.00	1.00	.88	.32	.00	1.00
Age 14-25 (1 = Yes)	.29	.46	.00	1.00	.31	.46	.00	1.00
Drug lifestyle	.90	1.17	.00	3.00				
Situational variables								
Gun homicide (1)	.86	.34	.00	1.00	.81	.39	.00	1.00
Victim-offender relationship[d]								
Family	.15	.36	.00	1.00	.04	.21	.00	1.00
Friend[b]	.14	.35	.00	1.00	.25	.44	.00	1.00
Other acquaintance[b]	.20	.40	.00	1.00				
Stranger[a]	.51	.50	.00	1.00	.09	.28	.00	1.00
Unknown[c]					.61	.49	.00	1.00

a. Reference category in multivariate models.
b. Friend and other acquaintance categories were grouped for SHR comparison. It was not possible to clearly denote between these categories based on how the SHR data were coded.
c. Unknown/Missing victim-offender relationship was estimated for sample data.
d. Means may sum less than 100 due to rounding.

Our final measures capture offender and situational characteristics that may aid in predicting the drug relatedness of homicides in this sample. First, victim-offender relationship was operationalized with a series of dummy variables. The variables include family, friends, other acquaintances, and stranger. For each indicator, the value *0* reflects the absence and *1* the presence of the characteristic. We expect that nondrug events are more likely to involve those with closer personal relationships such as family or friends, and those involving drugs to involve victims and offenders with greater social distance (other acquaintances and strangers).

Victim-offender relationship (VOR) was missing for 23 of the incidents or approximately 13% of the sample. Missing VOR information is a common problem in homicide research. Supplemental homicide report data indicate that, on average, VOR information is missing for approximately one third of all homicide incidents (Decker, 1993). Prior research has handled missing VOR data in a number of different ways, everything from listwise deletion strategies that exclude such cases, to a variety of substitution or imputation models (see Regoeczi & Riedel, 2003 for a comprehensive discussion on the various ways of handling missing VOR data). Pampel and Williams (2000) and Regoeczi and Riedel (2003) have argued it is important to develop imputation models that provide reasonable estimations of missing values. They argued missing VOR data is most likely not a random process and exclusion of such cases may distort research findings. We utilized a multinomial logistic regression imputation process (see Pampel & Williams, 2000 for a more in-depth discussion) that estimated the missing value based on victim age, victim gender, victim minority status, victim history of drug involvement, involvement of firearm, and if the event occurred in a high drug-crime area. The model estimates a predicted probability for each category (family, friend, other acquaintance, and stranger) of the dependent variable based on known cases and assigns the predicted value to the category with the highest probability.[4]

The modal category is stranger, with 51% of the cases falling in this category. We hypothesized that level of drug relatedness would be positively associated with greater relational distances between interactants. Finally, we measured whether the event included the use of a gun in the homicide with a dummy variable indicating the presence and use of a firearm. Consonant with the aforementioned research by Blumstein and Cork (1996), we suspected that gun usage is likely to be most strongly associated with drug-motivated homicides. As noted, all data were compiled and coded from the homicide case files in each of the 175 cases.

382 Journal of Contemporary Criminal Justice / November 2004

FINDINGS AND RESULTS

Because our dependent variable had three nominal categories we chose to analyze it using a multinomial logistic regression model available in SPSS 11.0. Multinomial logistic regression is a maximum likelihood technique similar to binary logistic regression except that it is used when the dependent variable has three or more unordered categories. The procedure estimates a series of binary regressions that compare each group to a baseline or reference group. In the current research, a regression equation was estimated for both drug-related categories of the dependent variable (peripheral drug involvement and drug-motivated homicides) and compares them to the reference category (nondrug homicides).

In Table 3 we present a multinomial regression model, which indicates the contrasts between nondrug events and peripheral and motivational drug involvement appear to be a matter of degree.[5] Drug market location, it is surprising to note, played no role in predicting whether a homicide had any relationship, peripherally or in terms of motivation, with drugs. With respect to the victim's characteristics, only youthful status was a significant predictor of drug-motivated homicide. Gender and minority status were not significant predictors. Nevertheless, the finding that youthful status was more than 4 times more likely to predict involvement in drug-motivated homicides comports with the arguments of Blumstein, Cohen, Cork, Engberg, and Tita (1999). With respect to victim characteristics, the index of drug involvement was significant in predicting peripheral and motivational aspects of homicides. Recalling that variable captured prior association with drug dealers, abuse, and arrest, a one-unit change increased the likelihood of peripheral involvement 5.5 times, when compared with non-drug-involved crimes. The odds ratio for the contrast between nondrug and drug-motivated crimes indicated that a one-unit increase in the index increased the likelihood of a drug motivated homicide by nearly 13 times. This comports with the lifestyle arguments proposed above; those involved, even on the periphery of the drug trade, are at risk for violence emanating from that illicit activity.

Two indicators of the offender's status and the situation, the VOR and gun use in the homicide transaction, yielded significant predictors of peripheral and drug-motivated homicides. The VOR dummy variable for family was positively related to peripheral drug involvement, and as one might expect, in a drug trade characterized by some degree of familiarity among interactants, the dummy variable representing friends was a significant predictor of drug-motivated events. It is possible, therefore, that a high level of lethal, nondrug, stranger violence, associated perhaps with robbery, may be responsible for this pair of unexpected relationships. Finally, events in which guns were used to commit homicides were associated with an increased likelihood of periph-

TABLE 3

Multinomial Logistic Regression Equations (N = 175)

	Peripheral Drug Involvement			Drug-Motivated Homicides			
	b	SE	EXP(b)	*b*	SE	EXP(b)	VIF
Constant	−4.28	1.07	−7.00	1.59			
Location variables							
Drug market (1 = yes)	−.42	.68	.66	−1.01	.91	.37	1.15
Victim variables							
Victim gender (1 = male)	.85	.63	2.35	−.11	.89	.89	1.21
Victim minority (1 = yes)	.55	.74	1.73	.59	1.11	1.81	1.07
Victim age 14 to							
25 years (1 = yes)	.14	.50	1.15	1.48*	.66	4.41	1.06
Drug lifestyle	1.71***	.31	5.52	2.56***	.39	12.95	1.14
Situational variables							
Gun homicide							
(1 = yes, 0 = no)	1.41*	.62	4.09	1.99*	.95	7.29	1.14
Victim-offender relationship							
(Reference = Stranger)							
Family	1.92**	.65	6.81	1.87	1.21	6.50	1.28
Friend	.89	.67	2.45	3.13***	.89	22.87	1.16
Other acquaintance	−.15	.67	.86	1.27	.83	3.57	1.14
Model χ^2	124.37***						
df	18						
Negelkerke R^2	.58						

NOTE: VIF = variance inflation factor.
$*p \leq .05.$ $**p \leq .01.$ $***p \leq .001.$

eral and drug-motivated homicides when contrasted with nondrug events. Consonant with research on drug violence, the odds of drug motivation in the homicide event were nearly double the odds of peripheral drug involvement. This relationship is also supportive of the drug-gun nexus discussed earlier.

The model summary statistics provide details of the goodness of fit for the data. The model chi-square value tests if knowledge of independent variables accurately predicts the value of the dependent variable more efficiently than chance alone. The model achieved statistical significance (χ^2 = 124.37, df = 18, $p < .001$). The Nagelkerke R^2 indicates that the independent variables explain a high degree of variation in the dependent measure.[6]

Overall, the model indicates that the location of homicide event and the demographic characteristics of the offender have little bearing on the type of drug involvement in the homicides in this sample. Rather victim's lifestyle, as measured by prior involvement in drugs, the offender's relationship with the victim, and the use of a firearm as a weapon all show associations with homicide events that were drug motivated and peripherally related to drugs.

384 Journal of Contemporary Criminal Justice / November 2004

The separation of models is important because peripheral involvement was less strongly contrasted with nondrug events than drug-motivated crimes by those three kinds of independent predictors. In addition, drug motivation but not peripheral drug involvement also generated a statistically significant contrast for youthful victims.

DISCUSSION AND CONCLUSION

Drugs play an important role in violent interactions. Although drug (or alcohol) use is neither a necessary nor sufficient cause of violent events, there is a close connection between the use of mood-altering substances and the increased likelihood of violence. The drugs-violence link is thought to exist along three separate causal paths: caused by psychopharmological effects of drug use itself, the desire to obtain money to obtain drugs, or systemic violence associated with the drug business itself (Goldstein, 1989).

In this article, we give special attention to drug homicides. In particular, we argue although drug homicides can be considered a homogeneous subset of violence to some degree, they are, in fact, not a universal class of phenomena. Based in part on prior work by Rosenfeld (1991), Goldstein (1995), and Brownstein and colleagues (Brownstein et al., 1992; Brownstein & Goldstein, 1990), we sought to further explore the drugs-homicide connection with a sample of homicide incidents from Detroit, Michigan.

The dependent variable was conceptualized as a multinomial variable that differentiated drug-related into categories based on the role drugs played. Approximately 50% of the homicides in the current sample ($N = 175$) involved no drug circumstances whatsoever. To some degree, this initial finding is surprising especially when one considers peripheral drug involvement to be an extremely loose definition of drug circumstances. One might reasonably expect a larger percentage of homicide incidents to involve drugs in a major metropolitan area with high levels of drug use and violence. However, such a finding does not necessarily refute the drugs-violence connection by any means. To the contrary, the relationship may very well exist at a macrolevel; meaning, general patterns of illegal drug use or abuse may coexist with higher levels of violence. Yet in this instance, the relationship does not appear at the micro-or incident level to the degree expected.

An unanticipated finding from this research is the negligible role drug markets seem to play in predicting different types of homicide events. Drug markets were expected to be strongly associated with all types of drug homicides, and especially drug-motivated killings. Contexts can influence the characteristics of homicide through one of several channels. First, the context affords potentially likeminded individuals who are predisposed to drug use and violence the opportunity to meet in time and space. The notion of a drug market itself suggests a location where individuals meet to agree on given business transactions. However, some have also noted a less direct effect of local context. Blumstein and colleagues (1999) noted a diffusion process where individuals who live in and frequent certain locations become aware that heavily armed individuals frequent a given area. However real or imaginary, this quasi-community characteristic develops a life of its own and subsequently encourages others to arm themselves with similar weaponry. In such a scenario a neighborhood could have a reputation as being frequented by heavily armed, violence-prone drug dealers. Likely aware of such a reputation, residents or other visitors may be more inclined to use violence in a preemptive manner.

The lack of a significant relationship is a bit perplexing. However, this finding can be interpreted as consistent with recent literature. The drugs-violence nexus is connected as much to the stability of drug markets as it is to the presence of a drug market itself (Fagan, Zimring, & Kim, 1998). Levels of systemic violence (see Goldstein, 1989) associated with drug markets has been found to be related to the stability of markets. In drug market terms, *stability* refers to a degree of central control of the drug distribution network that remains relatively unchallenged. Lower levels of violence would be associated with highly stable markets because interactants understand the rules of the game and fewer individuals are willing to exert violence to gain financial control of the local drug trade. Thus, violence is not seen as necessary to maintain control. It is interesting to note, similar arguments have also been advanced as it relates to drug-related gang violence (Curtis, 2003).

The only victim-level characteristic to reach the level of statistical significance was age. Contrary to the hypotheses, neither victim race nor gender was a significant discriminate as it related to drug-related homicide events. One possible explanation is due to the limited variation for these variables. African Americans comprise a substantial proportion of Detroit's residents (approximately 80%) but an even larger proportion of homicide victims (approximately 90%). Similarly, a large percentage of homicide victims are men (approximately 80%). These features hold true across different types of homicide events. However, age of victim is an important predictor, especially of drug-motivated homicides. This finding supports the notion that violent drug crimes are a youthful pursuit.

What remains unclear is the exact role age plays in different types of drug-homicide events. On one hand, the relationship between victim age and peripheral drug events suggests a lifestyle effect; that is, young people are more likely to be involved in a lifestyle of partying, using drugs, and spending time in dangerous places accompanied by dangerous people. One author was reminded of a ride-along where police encountered a 15-year-old male youth gambling on a street corner in Detroit with five 20+year-old men. All were gambling and smoking marijuana; however, the 15-year-old was also carrying $1,500 in cash in one of Detroit's most dangerous neighborhoods at 2:00 AM. Most alarming, the 15-year-old had only recently been released from the hospital after being shot in the neck in a similar situation 2 weeks earlier. This suggests a possible lifestyle effect where young males congregate, use drugs, and involve themselves in situations where violence is likely.

The relationship between victim age and drug-motivated homicide events can be interpreted as very different. Although the relationship also suggests a possible lifestyle effect, the substantive meaning applied would be quite different. In this scenario, youth could be an indicator of the business role in drug markets. For the small subset of homicide events that fit into the stereotypical drug-homicide conceptualization, the characteristics of victims conform to the observations by Blumstein and colleagues (1999).

Another key finding also supports the lifestyle effect thesis. Victim drug lifestyle is a summary index reflecting victim's association with known drug dealers and/or users, victim's prior history of drug dealing and/or use, and victim's history of a prior drug arrest. For the peripheral drug involvement and the drug-motivated models, prior drug involvement has the largest single effect. This supports other key findings, and the conclusion that it is not as much the neighborhood in which you live that increases odds of drug-related death but lifestyle choices as related to drug markets that increase risk.

It is also important to note the role firearms play in different drug-related homicides. Similar to several other independent variables, the presence of a firearm as the primary weapon of injury was predictive of peripheral and drug-motivated homicides. However, the odds associated with the drug-motivated homicides suggested the likelihood is increased nearly twice as much for drug-motivated events. Assuming drug-motivated homicides to be most similar to the popular idea of drug crime then this finding supports the argument that the use of firearms in drug transactions was partly responsible for the post-1980s rise in violent crime.

Finally, the data suggest important findings relative to the VOR. Homicide events involving friends were nearly 23 times more likely to be drug-motivated events compared to those involving strangers. This finding runs counter to what was hypothesized, namely, that events involving strangers would be more likely to involve drug circumstances. The nature of the VOR is an indicator of regularity and type of interaction between individuals. Relationships characterized by closer social distance (e.g., family and friends) often involve more frequent interactions. Williams and Flewelling (1988) argued close relations (e.g., family member, lover, and close friend) protect individuals from certain forms of instrumental violence (e.g., robbery) but, at the same time, expose individuals to greater risk for expressive forms of violence (e.g., violence stemming from jealousy, lovers' triangles, etc.). This finding does not hold up in the current research as it relates to drug-motivated events, presumably instrumental crimes. It is interesting to note, Decker (1996) and Varano and Cancino (2001) reported that drugs have diminished the protective features of VOR and exposed individuals to types and degrees of violence not previously thought to be common. We hypothesize that the diminished protective features of the friend VOR are linked to the nature of the drug culture and market in Detroit. It appears that individuals are more likely to enter into drug transactions with people whom they know reasonably well. Thus, the opportunity for drug-motivated events is reduced in the absence of stranger-to-stranger drug transactions.

FUTURE RESEARCH AND POLICY IMPLICATIONS

There is tremendous value in studying conceptually meaningful subtypes of homicide events. Williams and Flewelling (1988) persuasively argued that inconsistent findings in comparative homicide research are due, in large part, to the diverse nature of aggregate homicide data. Similar to Williams and Flewelling (1988), we support that researchers need to consider that homicide events are not universal types of lethal incidents. Instead, there are important differences between different subclasses of events. Although there is evidence researchers have heeded this recommendation, the drug-related typology remains rather vague. Findings supporting the conclusion that there are important differences between peripheral compared to drug-motivated homicides could have important implications for informing criminological theory and in structuring effective interventions.

Future research should also integrate offender-level data into such analyses. Because of problems of missing data where no offender is identified, offender-level attributes are excluded as explanatory variables. Approximately 30% of the cases used in the current research were open, that is, no offender was identified. Although features of the offender's behavior as reflected by witness statements and other evidence are included in the dependent variable, individual offender attributes are excluded as independent variables because of the missing data. Thus, substantially larger sample sizes are likely necessary in future research that seeks to further disentangle the role of illicit drugs in lethal events.

It is also certainly important for researchers to consider possible situational or contextual effects. It is important to note our research suggests little effect of location within a drug market. Yet the measure included in this research is not the best measure of drug markets. Future research should consider the presence of a drug market and the stability of the drug market. The latter measure is seemingly difficult to measure. Moreover, it is also important to simultaneously consider the effects not only of drug markets but also of gun mar-

388   Journal of Contemporary Criminal Justice / November 2004

kets. It is plausible to anticipate the availability of firearms could affect the type and levels of violence.

The implications for policy, we argue, fall along the drug and gun nexus. Sherman and Rogan (1995) found a link between gun seizures and a decline in lethal violence in Kansas City. Similarly, McGarrell, Chermak, Weiss, and Wilson (2001) found a negative association between aggressive police patrol focusing on suspicious or known offenders and violence in Indianapolis. Our findings, with respect to drug-motivated homicides and homicides where drugs played a peripheral role, indicate that perhaps drug involvement facilitates the confluence of guns, offenders, and victims that result in lethal outcomes. Recent gun-focused strategies, if targeted particularly at those likely to be involved in street-level drug markets and carrying guns, should depress the level of homicides that are peripherally drug related. Drug-motivated homicides might also be reduced in a similar fashion. Both inferences require an assumption that weapon substitution would not occur.

The data we examined here, when combined with the results of prior research, help to illustrate how gun seizures may operate in depressing homicide levels. The homicide transactions we observed in this sample were often the genesis of fleeting disputes, which, but for the presence of firearms, would likely have not had lethal outcomes. These events are most amenable to programs focused on reducing the numbers of guns on the street through supply-side seizures or by working on the demand side and making the cost for carrying weapons too great when compared with the risk of being on the street without one.

APPENDIX
Examples of Drug-Related Homicide Types

No-Drug Involvement Example

The victim opened the door to the dwelling, an armed robbery was occurring of the pizza delivery person. The perp fired one shot (handgun) through the door and into the chest of the victim. Victim died in emergency room. Perp escaped on foot. Perp lived next door to the address of the homicide and was charged with felony murder, armed robbery, and felony firearm. (Coded as nondrug because motive was robbery and no evidence of drugs found in homicide files.)

Peripheral Involvement Example

The victim, offender, and others gathered in offender's garage for a dogfight. Everyone was consuming alcohol and "having a good time." Offender and one of the other attendees got into an altercation that turned physical. Offender got up and went inside house, and the guy with whom he was fighting ran outside. Offender returned to garage and opened fire, striking victim. Somehow, the victim was transported by car (driven by another attendee?) to hospital, where he died. By most witness accounts, the offender was drunk and "got out of control." (Coded as peripheral because offender was selling drugs while at party.)

Drug-Motivated Example

Two perpetrators met with the victim to purchase 1 pound of marijuana. Victim's price was too high, so Perp 1 got angry and yelled at victim. Victim said, "Fuck you too!" and Perp 2 thought he was reaching for a gun. Perp 2 ran, pulled a gun, and fired at victim. Victim was hit once and then crashed his car. Victim died at scene from single gunshot wound. (Coded as drug motivated because the sale or use of drugs was the motivating factor in the event.)

NOTES

1. "Despite the fact that many of the communities in which interviews were conducted are Drug Abuse Warning Network (DAWN) and Drug Use Forecasting (DUF) sites, no respondents made mention of these data" (Lattimore et al., 1997, p. 75).

2. A case is closed when a likely offender has been identified; however this does not always mean the offender was arrested. For example, "exceptional clearances" are those where an offender has been identified but not arrested because he or she is dead, on the run, or otherwise not able to be arrested. Open cases generally refer to those instances where a likely offender has not been identified.

3. Oversampling homicide events from one precinct of Detroit raises concerns about the representativness of the sample. To account for any potential bias, several aspects of the sample were compared to known characteristics of the entire population of homicides that occurred in Detroit between 1999 and 2002 that were downloaded from the Inter-University Consortium for Political and Social Research (ICPSR) housed at the University of Michigan. The comparisons are made in the sections that follow.

4. The method described above is far from perfect but provides a reasonable estimate of missing values. Pampel and Williams (2000) suggested including additional independent variables, especially if the case involved a co-occurring felony crime (e.g., burglary, robbery); however, this information was not available in the current data set. Regoeczi and Riedel (2003) also included clearance status (open or closed) in their maximum likelihood method that increased the proportion of estimated stranger homicides. Clearance status was not included in our imputation model because the information was also not available. To determine the accuracy of our imputation model, we compared the predicted values with the actual VOR values for the known cases. To do this, we constructed a cross-tab of known with predicted values. The imputation predicted correct victim-offender relationship 74% of the time. The highest level of agreement was for the friend and stranger categories (86% accuracy), followed by family (72% accuracy) and other acquaintance (52% accuracy).

390 Journal of Contemporary Criminal Justice / November 2004

5. Before proceeding with the analyses, OLS regression diagnostic procedures were carried out to investigate the presence of multicollinearity. The variance inflation (VIF) statistics yielded no apparent problems with multicollinearity.

6. The Negelkerke R^2 is a modified version of the Cox and Snell pseudo R^2. The Cox and Snell can be difficult to interpret because it often cannot reach 1.0. Nagelkerke's R^2 divides Cox and Snell's R^2 by its maximum to achieve a measure that ranges from 0 to 1.

REFERENCES

Arrestee Drug Abuse Monitoring Program. (2000). *1999 annual report on drug use among adult and juvenile arrestees*. Washington, DC: National Institute of Justice.

Blumstein, A. (1995). Youth violence, guns, and the illicit-drug industry. *Journal of Criminal Law and Criminology, 86*(1), 10-36.

Blumstein, A., Cohen, J., Cork, D., Engberg, J., & Tita, G. (1999). *Diffusion effects in homicide*. Washington, DC: National Institute of Justice.

Blumstein, A., & Cork, D. (1996). Linking gun availability to youth gun violence. *Law and Contemporary Problems, 59*(1), 5-24.

Blumstein, A., & Rosenfeld, R. (1998). Explaining recent trends in U.S. homicide rates. *Journal of Criminal Law and Criminology, 88*(4), 1175-1216.

Brownstein, H. H., Baxi, H. R. S., Goldstein, P. J., & Ryan, P. J. (1992). Relationships of drugs, drug trafficking, and drug traffickers to homicide. *Journal of Crime and Justice, 15*(1), 25-44.

Brownstein, H. H., & Goldstein, P. J. (1990). A typology of drug-related homicides. In R. A. Weisheit (Ed.), *Drugs, crime, and the criminal justice system* (pp. 171-192). Highland Heights, KY: Academy of Criminal Justice Sciences.

Bynum, T. S., Huebner, B., & Hinduja, S. (2001). *Firearm use among Michigan's youthful offender population*. East Lansing: Michigan State University, School of Criminal Justice.

Curtis, R. (2003). The negligible role of gangs in drug distribution in New York City in the 1990s. In L. Kontos, D. Brotherton, & L. Barrios (Eds.), *Gangs and society* (pp. 41-61). New York: Columbia University Press.

Decker, S. H. (1993). Exploring victim-offender relationships in homicide: The role of individual and event characteristics. *Justice Quarterly, 10*(4), 585-612.

Decker, S. H. (1996). Deviant homicide: A new look at the role of motives and victim-offender relationships. *Journal of Research in Crime and Delinquency, 33*(4), 427-449.

Fagan, J., & Chin, K.-L. (1989). Initiation into crack and cocaine: A tale of two epidemics. *Contemporary Drug Problems, 16*(4), 579-617.

Fagan, J., Zimring, F. E., & Kim, J. (1998). Declining homicide in New York: A tale of two trends. *Journal of Criminal Law and Criminology, 88*(4), 1277-1323.

Goldstein, P. (1995). The drugs/violence nexus: A tripartite conceptual framework. In J. A. Inciardi & K. McElrath (Eds.), *The American drug scene* (pp. 255-264). Los Angeles: Roxbury.

Goldstein, P. J. (1989). Drugs and violent crime. In N. A. Weiner & M. E. Wolfgang (Eds.), *Pathways to criminal violence* (pp. 16-48). Newbury Park, CA: Sage.

Lattimore, P. K., Trudeau, J., Riley, K. J., Leiter, J., & Edwards, S. (1997). *Homicide in eight U.S. cities: Trends, context, and policy implications* (NCJ 167262). Washington, DC: National Institute of Justice.

MacCoun, R., Kilmer, B., & Reuter, P. (2003). Research on drugs-crime linkages: The next generation. In *Toward a drugs and crime research agenda for the 21st century* (pp. 65-96). Washington, DC: National Institute of Justice.

Martinez, R., Jr. (2002). *Latino homicide*. New York: Routledge.

McGarrell, E. F., Chermak, S., Weiss, A., & Wilson, J. (2001). Reducing firearms violence through directed police patrol. *Criminology and Public Policy, 1*(1), 119-148.

Pampel, F. C., & Williams, K. R. (2000). Intimacy and homicide: Compensating for missing data in the SHR. *Criminology, 38*(2), 661-680.

Regoeczi, W. C., & Riedel, M. (2003). The application of missing data estimation models to the problem of unknown victim/offender relationships in homicide cases. *Journal of Quantitative Criminology, 19*(2), 155-183.

Rosenfeld, R. (1991). *Anatomy of the drug-related homicide*. St. Louis: University of Missouri at St. Louis, St. Louis Metropolitan Police Department, City of St. Louis, Missouri Department of Health.

Sherman, L., & Rogan, D. P. (1995). Effects of gun seizures on gun violence: "Hot spots" patrol in Kansas City. *Justice Quarterly, 12*(4), 673-693.

Varano, S. P., & Cancino, J. M. (2001). An empirical analysis of deviant homicides in Chicago. *Homicide Studies, 5*(1), 5-29.

Weil, A. (1995). Why people take drugs. In J. A. Inciardi & K. McElrath (Eds.), *The American drug scene* (pp. 3-11). Los Angeles: Roxbury.

Wellford, C., & Cronin, J. (1999). *An analysis of variables affecting the clearance of homicides: A multistate study*. Washington, DC: Justice Research and Statistics Association.

Williams, K. B., & Flewelling, R. L. (1988). The social production of criminal homicide: A comparative study of disaggregated rates in American cities. *American Sociological Review, 53*(3), 421-431.

Wolfgang, M. E. (1958). *Patterns in criminal homicide*. Philadelphia: University of Pennsylvania Press.

Wright, R. T., & Decker, S. H. (1997). *Armed robbers in action: Stickups and street culture*. Boston: Northeastern University Press.

Sean P. Varano is an assistant professor in the College of Criminal Justice at Northeastern University. His research interests include juvenile justice policy, intervention programs for serious juvenile offenders, homicide characteristics, and aspects of technology in the criminal justice system. His recent publications involve exploring changing characteristics of homicide events and gang suppression strategies in Detroit, Michigan.

John D. McCluskey is an assistant professor in the Department of Criminal Justice at University of Texas at San Antonio. He is presently working on the team responsible for research and evalu-

ation of the Strategic Approaches to Community Safety Initiative (SACSI) in Detroit, Michigan. His recent publications involve examining police and citizen behaviors in the context of face-to-face encounters.

Justin W. Patchin is an assistant professor of criminal justice in the Department of Political Science at the University of Wisconsin-Eau Claire. His research areas focus on policy and program evaluation, juvenile delinquency prevention, and community-level factors associated with violence.

Timothy S. Bynum is a professor in the School of Criminal Justice at Michigan State University and the director of the Michigan Justice Statistics Center. His research centers on the evaluation of criminal justice policies and interventions. His recent work has involved studies of firearms violence, sex offenders, and community interventions with serious juvenile offenders.

[19]

Retaliatory Homicide: Concentrated Disadvantage and Neighborhood Culture

CHARIS E. KUBRIN, *George Washington University*

RONALD WEITZER, *George Washington University*

Much of the research on violent crime is situated within an exclusively structural or subcultural framework. Some recent work, however, argues that these unidimensional approaches are inherently limited and that more attention needs to be given to the intersection of structural and cultural determinants of violence. The present study takes up this challenge by examining both structural and cultural influences on one underexamined type of homicide: retaliatory killings. Using quantitative data to examine the socioeconomic correlates and ecological distribution of homicide in St. Louis, Missouri, and narrative accounts of homicide incidents, we find that a certain type of homicide (what we call "cultural retaliatory homicide") is more common in some neighborhoods than in others due to the combined effects of economic disadvantage, neighborhood cultural responses to disadvantage, and problematic policing. Problems confronting residents of these communities are often resolved informally—without calling the police—and neighborhood cultural codes support this type of problem-solving, even when the "solution" involves a retaliatory killing. The findings thus lend support to a more integrated structural-cultural perspective on violent crime in urban neighborhoods.

One of the greatest challenges facing researchers interested in the causes of violent crime is explaining high levels of black-on-black violence. Although an extensive body of research addresses racial patterns in violence, some argue that current conceptualizations of the race-violence linkage are unsatisfactory (Bruce, Roscigno, and McCall 1998; Heimer 1997; Sampson and Wilson 1995). One problem is that most of the literature takes either an exclusively structural or cultural approach, and neglects the intersection between the two. Some researchers, however, are beginning to address both structural and cultural dimensions of race and crime. The present study contributes to this effort by examining structural and cultural factors related to retaliatory homicides in neighborhoods in St. Louis.

Integrating Structural and Cultural Approaches to Violence

Much of the literature on homicide focuses on either structural or cultural explanations. In the classic subcultural perspective, lower-class communities generate a distinctive moral universe that glorifies and legitimates aggressive behavior, particularly among male juveniles. This "subculture of violence" becomes self-perpetuating in disadvantaged communities and, according to Marvin Wolfgang and Franco Ferracuti (1967), explains why these neighborhoods generate high homicide rates. Why such violent subcultures resonate in some groups

The authors thank Rob Baller, James Holstein, Ross Matsueda, George Tita, and anonymous reviewers for helpful comments on this paper. The data used in this research come from the St. Louis Homicide Project and were collected as part of research funded by grants from the National Institute of Justice, the National Science Foundation, and the National Consortium on Violence Research. We thank Richard Rosenfeld, Scott Decker, Carol Kohfeld, and John Sprague for providing us with the data. Direct correspondence to: Charis E. Kubrin, Department of Sociology, George Washington University, Phillips Hall 409, 801 22nd St. N.W., Washington, DC 20052. E-mail: charisk@gwu.edu.

but not others, and why they are more robust in some geographic areas than others, are questions not adequately addressed by this subcultural approach. Moreover, the structural forces shaping cultural phenomena are for the most part invisible in this perspective.

The obverse problem can be seen in structural approaches, which typically neglect normative and cultural influences on behavior. Conflict theory, for instance, focuses almost exclusively on the material conditions that contribute to higher rates of street crime among the poor and minority groups. Social disorganization theory is another case in point. Although the original formulation of the theory by Clifford Shaw and Henry McKay (1942) did examine cultural influences on behavior, subsequent versions of the theory focus almost entirely on socioeconomic and ecological factors and explicitly dismiss subcultural explanations of crime (Kornhauser 1978).

A growing number of scholars are beginning to recognize that these unidimensional approaches are unsatisfactory in that they fail to capture the intersection of structural and cultural factors. Robert Sampson and William Julius Wilson (1995) incorporate both factors in their discussion of crime and inequality in American cities. Their basic thesis is that macro-social patterns of residential inequality give rise to the social isolation and ecological concentration of the disadvantaged, which leads to cultural adaptations that undermine social organization, and hence the control of crime. Poverty, heterogeneity, institutional instability, and other structural features of disadvantaged urban communities are hypothesized to impede communication and obstruct the quest for common values, weakening these neighborhoods' capacity for social control and thus increasing crime. Similarly, drawing on Anthony Giddens' (1984) theory of structuration, which emphasizes the dual and reciprocal role of structural and cultural forces, Marino Bruce and associates (1998) argue that social structure (i.e., economic deprivation, dangerous living conditions) influences levels of violence within a community by interacting with normative pressures and social psychological processes.

A number of ethnographic studies support the idea that structurally disorganized communities are conducive to the emergence of subcultural value systems and attitudes that seem to legitimate, or at least provide a basis of tolerance for, crime. Ruth Horowitz's (1983) study of a poor Hispanic community in Chicago found a prevailing "code of honor" shaping young residents' values and behavior. The code mandates deferential treatment of others and aggressive sanctions against those who show disrespect. Similarly, Elijah Anderson's (1999) study of a disadvantaged Philadelphia neighborhood and Jeffrey Fagan and Deanna Wilkinson's (1998) study of two inner-city New York communities identified a "code of the streets," whose norms govern interpersonal encounters in public and "supply a rationale allowing those who are inclined to aggression to precipitate violent encounters in an approved way" (Anderson 1999:33). Residents of such communities develop an acute sensitivity to disrespect from others, and a "disputatiousness" or inclination to respond violently to even trivial slights (Luckenbill and Doyle 1989). When these violent reactions occur in public places, the perpetrator often wins admiration from bystanders who witness the incident (Cooney 1998). Like Shaw and McKay (1942:164–83), these scholars document intra-neighborhood variation in residents' attachment to local cultural codes: a segment of the community does not embrace the code of honor on the streets and instead holds conventional values supportive of legal norms. Still, the street culture is potent enough that anyone who ignores it does so at his or her peril. The street culture becomes the dominant normative order in these communities.

Although neighborhood cultural codes are likely to shape certain types of violent encounters such as retaliatory killings, studies of retaliatory homicide have largely ignored the neighborhood context. This literature shows that, in the typical encounter, one party issues a challenge to another because of some perceived affront, leading to a "character contest" in which one or both parties attempt to "save face" at the other's expense (cf. Felson and Steadman 1983; Katz 1988; Luckenbill 1977). The parties exchange increasingly belligerent accusations and threats, the encounter escalates, and ultimately, one person responds to the other's insults with a lethal assault. This literature examines homicide incidents solely at the situational level, yet others argue that retaliatory homicide is more pervasive among some classes or in some communities than in others (Anderson 1999; Black 1983; Markowitz and Felson 1998). Such homicides are more common in disadvantaged communities. These neighborhoods offer residents few avenues for gaining status and prestige, creating conditions conducive to the development of alternative normative codes, including ones that legitimate violence as a means of enhancing one's reputation (Anderson 1999; Fagan and Wilkinson 1998; Horowitz 1983). Respect and honor are especially prized among males who have few "personal accomplishments or cannot draw on valued social roles to protect their self-esteem when they are confronted by an insulting action" (Horowitz 1983:81). In Fagan and Wilkinson's (1998) study of young men (aged 16–24) in two inner-city New York neighborhoods, *all* of the 125 respondents cited the need to use violence to gain prestige and personal security. Concentrated socioeconomic deprivation in these communities reduces conventional opportunities for status attainment and generates alternative routes to winning prestige.

Disputes are often resolved informally and violently because residents of disadvantaged communities are dissatisfied with police protection. Over time, police practices may help to shape neighborhood residents' values and behavior (Jacob 1971), including the development of a street code that supports informal violent resolution of problems. The literature indicates that policing in poor neighborhoods may have this effect in two ways—through inadequate crime control and through abusive treatment of residents, both of which foster community alienation from the police.

Residents of disadvantaged minority neighborhoods frequently complain that they receive inadequate police protection, and that officers are often unresponsive to residents' calls and take a fairly tolerant approach to street deviance (Huang and Vaughn 1996; Kennedy 1997). Three-quarters of African Americans in Los Angeles, for instance, said there were not enough police in their neighborhoods, while only 1 percent said there were too many police in their neighborhoods (*Los Angeles Times* 1988). A study of 343 neighborhoods in Chicago found that residents of disadvantaged areas were significantly more likely than residents of middle-class communities to report that the officers working in their neighborhoods were not responsive to "local issues," performed poorly in preventing crime and in maintaining order on the streets, and responded poorly to crime victims (Sampson and Bartusch 1998), even after controlling for neighborhood violent crime rates and racial composition. Similarly, studies of Indianapolis, Rochester, Tampa–St. Petersburg, and St. Louis (Reisig and Parks 2000; Smith, Graham, and Adams 1991; Velez 2001) found that residents of extremely disadvantaged neighborhoods were more likely than residents of less disadvantaged neighborhoods to report dissatisfaction with the kind and quality of police services to their neighborhood.

Research on police practices lends supporting evidence to residents' complaints. One study found that police see residents of high-crime communities as "deserving victims," whose lifestyles invite victimization. In such neighborhoods, officers tend to normalize residents' victimization, which leads them to respond less vigorously to crime than in more affluent areas (Klinger 1997; see also Velez 2001). And a study of three cities (including St. Louis) found that police officers were much less likely to make arrests of blacks than of whites who were involved in interpersonal violence (Smith 1987). This study supports Donald Black's (1976) argument that the police are less likely to invoke the law when blacks are victimized, perhaps because officers normalize black-on-black violence. For their part, police complain that they often find it difficult in poor neighborhoods to get witnesses to crimes to provide information or testify in court because of their fear of retribution and/or lack of confidence in the police. Highly disadvantaged, high-crime neighborhoods thus suffer from something of a policing vacuum, which may, in turn, lead residents to take matters into their own hands to protect themselves and their honor: "Where enforcement of the law is inadequate, it becomes important to defend one's reputation . . . to establish that one is not to be trifled with" (Cohen and Nisbett 1994:551).

At the same time, the policing that does take place in these communities is often considered abusive. Unwarranted police stops, verbal and physical abuse, and racial bias toward residents of poor minority communities have a long history in the United States and continue to strain residents' relations with the police (Fagan and Davies 2000; Smith 1986; Weitzer 1999, 2000). Police misconduct in these neighborhoods thus drives a wedge between officers and residents, which only reinforces the salience of the street code's prescriptions for dealing with interpersonal problems. Police abuse of residents, coupled with underenforcement of the law and unresponsiveness to residents, constitute multiple sources of alienation from the authorities that, we argue, increase the likelihood of residents resolving disputes on their own and responding to victimization with retaliatory violence. The thinness of formal social control in socially distressed neighborhoods contributes to the development of cultural codes that legitimate informal tactics for resolving problems. In this context, at least some types of homicide may be related to residents' cynicism regarding the police as an appropriate or effective mechanism of social control. Horowitz (1983:82) notes that "disputes over honor must be settled personally, not through the legal system," and Anderson (1999:34) argues that the street code is "a cultural adaptation to a profound lack of faith in the police and the judicial system. . . . The code of the street thus emerges where the influence of the police ends." This does not mean that the policing vacuum is directly related to all types of retaliatory killings in these neighborhoods, since offended parties have no legal recourse when the affront is a simple matter of disrespect. But when the offense is a criminal act (an assault, shooting, theft), offended parties do have legal recourse but instead may decide to settle the score on their own, rather than calling the police. It is in these types of disputes that the policing vacuum is most evident.

Bruce and associates (1998:41) write that the "real challenge . . . is to identify mechanisms linking structural disadvantage to the perpetration of violence within the African American community." The present study takes up this challenge by providing a more systematic examination of the relationship between neighborhood disadvantage and retaliatory killings, utilizing both quantitative data and narrative accounts of homicides in St. Louis, Missouri. We argue that retaliatory homicide is more common in disadvantaged neighborhoods than in other types of neighborhoods because of a combination of structural disadvantage and neighborhood-cultural responses to deprivation and problematic policing. The article thus provides empirical support for the argument that structural and cultural factors jointly shape homicide at the neighborhood level.

The City and the Neighborhoods

Residential segregation of blacks and whites is pervasive in cities throughout the United States. According to the 1990 U.S. Census, the city of St. Louis is no exception: blacks (48 percent of the population) live primarily in the northern parts of the city, whites (50 percent) primarily in the southern parts, and there are few racially mixed neighborhoods. Similarly, urban poverty in American cities is concentrated among blacks. In St. Louis, the mean percentage of persons living below the poverty level in predominantly black tracts (tracts that are greater than 75 percent black) is nearly 38 percent, while the mean percentage in poverty in predominantly white tracts (tracts that are greater than 75 percent white) is only 11 percent. The average unemployment level in black tracts exceeds 9 percent, whereas it is less than 4 percent in white tracts; median family income in black neighborhoods is $16,927, far below that in white neighborhoods: $31,198. Moreover, black neighborhoods, on average, have a much higher percentage of households on public assistance (26 percent) than do white neighborhoods (6 percent).

Table 1 • *Descriptive Statistics on Retaliatory and Non-Retaliatory Homicides, 1985–1995*

Variable	Retaliatory Homicide		Non-Retaliatory Homicide	
	%	N	%	N
Alcohol-related homicide	34	335	38.5	1379
Drug-related homicide	42.9	336	34.4*	1388
Gang-related homicide	17.9	335	11.2*	1389
V/O relationship: family	5.4	313	19.8*	1253
V/O relationship: friends/acq.	78	313	55.5*	1253
V/O relationship: stranger	16.6	313	24.7*	1253
Black suspect	96.3	327	89.5*	1315
Male suspect	96	327	89.8*	1315
Juvenile suspect	12	326	13.4	1308
Victim injury: gunshot wound	86.9	337	70.9*	1396
Victim injury: stab/slash	5.3	337	15*	1396
Mean suspect age	24.5	326	27.1*	1308
Mean victim age	26.5	326	31.7*	1397

* Means across the groups are statistically significant at the .05 level based on t-tests.

In addition to economic disadvantage, black neighborhoods in St. Louis have higher levels of family disruption than white neighborhoods; the mean percentage of children 18 years and under living in a single parent household in black neighborhoods is nearly 53 percent, compared to only 23 percent in white neighborhoods. Finally, on average, white neighborhoods have more than twice the percentage of college graduates than black neighborhoods (nearly 10 percent versus 4 percent). In sum, it is clear that in St. Louis, the most disadvantaged neighborhoods are black neighborhoods.

Regarding homicide in St. Louis, descriptive statistics from the St. Louis Homicide Data Set on retaliatory and non-retaliatory killings from 1985–1995 show that retaliatory homicides differ from non-retaliatory homicides along a number of dimensions (Table 1). First, a greater percentage of retaliatory homicides are drug-related (43 percent versus 34 percent) and gang-related (18 percent versus 11 percent).[1] Second, victims of retaliatory homicides are more likely to be killed by gunshot (nearly 87 percent) than are victims of non-retaliatory homicides (71 percent). Third, while the average age of suspects in retaliatory and non-retaliatory homicides is similar (around 25 years old), the average victim age differs: retaliatory victims, on average, are younger (27 versus 32). Fourth, nearly all retaliatory offenders are male (96 percent versus 90 percent for non-retaliatory offenders) and African-American (96 percent versus 90 percent). Finally, whereas nearly 20 percent of non-retaliatory homicides occur between family members, only 5 percent of retaliatory homicides do. Most retaliatory homicides occur between friends or acquaintances (78 percent).

To begin to examine the relationship between disadvantage and retaliatory homicide, we compared neighborhoods of differing poverty levels in terms of the percentage of total homicides that were retaliatory in nature. We first employed the categorization of poverty used by Lauren Krivo and Ruth Peterson (1996; cf. Wilson 1987). Here, low poverty tracts are those

---

1. A case was coded 1 (presence) for drug- or alcohol-related homicide if there was any mention of drugs or alcohol being present. This could include bottles or drug paraphernalia found at the scene; evidence that the suspect, the victim, or both were intoxicated; or substantiated witness testimony that the victim, offender, or both had been drinking/using drugs immediately prior to the homicide. Likewise, a homicide was classified as gang-related if the homicide involved a suspect or victim identified in the police report as a gang member, but did not arise from gang activity per se (Rosenfeld, Bray, and Egley 1999).

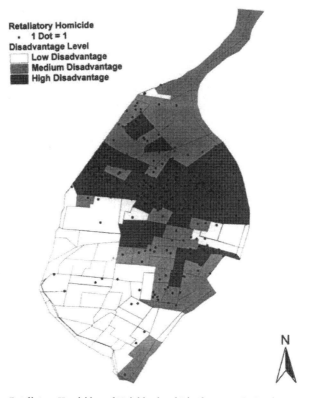

Figure 1 • *Retaliatory Homicide and Neighborhood Disadvantage, St. Louis*

that have mean poverty levels of less than 20 percent, high poverty tracts are those that have mean poverty levels between 20 and 39 percent, and extreme poverty tracts are those that have mean poverty levels greater than 39 percent. As expected, the percentage of total homicides that are retaliatory increases linearly with successive levels of disadvantage. In low poverty tracts (n = 46), 12.6 percent of all homicides were retaliatory; in high poverty tracts (n = 46) 14.2 percent of all homicides were retaliatory; and in extreme poverty tracts (n = 19), 19 percent of all homicides were retaliatory.

Our use of a more inclusive measure of disadvantage provides further support for these findings. We divided St. Louis census tracts into quartiles based upon the distribution of disadvantage levels (an index comprised of poverty, percent of children not living with both parents, median family income, percent unemployed, and percent black). Based on the distribution, we classified neighborhoods as having low, medium, high, and extreme levels of disadvantage. We found that, once again, as disadvantage levels rise, so does the percentage of homicides that are retaliatory. Going from low to medium to high to extreme levels of disadvantage produces corresponding increases in the percent of homicides that are retaliatory: 11.5 percent, 12.5 percent, 13.7 percent, and 17.9 percent, respectively. The greatest jump occurs when moving from high to extreme disadvantage.

These differences are illustrated in a map that plots the distributions of disadvantage and retaliatory homicide in St. Louis neighborhoods. As Figure 1 shows, retaliatory homicides are not randomly distributed across the city, but are clustered primarily in the north. While clustering also occurs for non-retaliatory killings, and the mapping of all homicides would look relatively similar to this Figure, the clustering is somewhat greater for retaliatory homicides. Seventy-five percent of all retaliatory homicides (n = 252) are located in just 34 census tracts (out of 114), whereas 75 percent of all non-retaliatory homicides (n = 1045) are located in 42 tracts. More importantly, Figure 1 suggests a strong relationship between retaliatory homicide levels and disadvantage. The darkest areas of the map—which indicate those neighborhoods with the highest disadvantage levels—have by far the greatest number of retaliatory homicides, while the least disadvantaged areas located in the southwestern section of the city have very few (only 10 percent of all retaliatory homicides from 1985–1995 occurred in low disadvantaged tracts). Thus, retaliatory homicides occur most often in areas that are economically and socially disadvantaged. These differences in disadvantage levels and homicide rates are consistent with findings from recent research (McNulty 2001; Parker and Pruitt 2000; Shihadeh and Steffensmeier 1994).

Methods

The study uses both quantitative and qualitative data to examine the disadvantage-retaliatory homicide relationship. The quantitative data address questions related to the socioeconomic correlates and ecological distribution of retaliatory homicide, and the qualitative data illustrate how neighborhood cultural codes manifest themselves in encounters leading to retaliatory killings, including culturally-specific interpretations of respect, disputatiousness, and legitimate violence.

The St. Louis Homicide Data Set

The sample of killings, taken from the St. Louis Homicide Data Set, contains information on 2,161 homicides that occurred in St. Louis between 1985–1995. These killings represent criminal homicides that were compiled from case files maintained by the St. Louis Metropolitan Police Department and supplemental files submitted by investigating officers. For each case, information about the suspect(s), victim(s), and event were recorded; the coding instrument includes over 80 items related to the homicide.

All information from police files was hand-coded by trained coders. In addition to coding relevant variables, the coders created a narrative of each homicide that provides an account of the event, describing what occurred, who was present, and other important information. The source of these narratives is police reports, which include a detailed description of the crime scene and physical evidence, information from suspects and witnesses, and other pertinent information. The narratives were not constructed with the code of the street or police practices in mind, but they nevertheless contain data that address these issues.[2]

Of the 2,161 homicides that occurred from 1985–1995, 1,731 (80 percent) have identified motives. As the motive is a central factor in this study, we exclude those cases without a motive.[3] Of those with an identified motive, 19.5 percent (n = 337) are retaliatory, while the

---

2. It should be noted that the narratives vary in length, with some providing much more detail than others on the events leading up to the retaliatory killing. Thus, some encounters likely contained elements of the code of the street or police practices that were not mentioned in the respective narratives.

3. To determine if motive-unknown and motive-known homicides are significantly different, we compared frequency distributions on a subset of homicide characteristics across the samples. With a few exceptions (drug- and alcohol-related homicides are underrepresented in motive-unknown cases), the means and distributions for all variables are

remaining 1,394 (80.5 percent) are non-retaliatory homicides. The classification of motive refers to the police-recorded motive. All retaliatory killings involve at least two time points: (1) an initial disputatious interaction, in which an affront to one party remained unanswered or unresolved, which prompted (2) a subsequent encounter during which the offended party exacted deadly retribution for the earlier offense. In all cases examined here, the St. Louis police were able to establish that the homicide was a response to an earlier altercation between the parties.

A potential limitation of police-recorded data concerns the accuracy, completeness, and consistency of the information. The St. Louis police department clears a high percentage of cases and thus has more complete records than cities with lower clearance rates (Decker 1996:431). In addition, a test of inter-coder reliability was carried out. An independent researcher read through the narratives and coded a random subset of the cases (roughly 10 percent). Agreement coefficient alphas were computed for the variables and the alphas indicate that the high agreement levels between the coders did not result from chance; all of the alphas are above .75.

Measures and Analytic Procedures

To examine whether neighborhood disadvantage is significantly associated with retaliatory homicide, we performed a regression analysis using 1990 Census data for the city of St. Louis. For comparison purposes, we also examine the relationship between these factors and non-retaliatory killings. The regression models adjust for spatial autocorrelation. The units examined are census tracts. Of St. Louis' 114 tracts, three were excluded from the analyses because they have populations of less than 200, compared to a tract average of 3,572. A sizable population allows one to construct reliable rates (Rosenfeld et al. 1999).

Nine variables were constructed from the 1990 Census to reflect neighborhood differences in poverty, race, employment, age composition, family structure, and residential stability. The list of independent variables encompasses the key correlates of neighborhood homicide rates found in the literature (Kubrin 2003; McNulty 2001; Miles-Doan 1998). They include: (1) *percent black*; (2) *median family income*; (3) *percent poverty*, defined as the percentage of persons living below the poverty level; (4) *percent young males*, defined as the percentage of males aged 14–24; (5) *percent residential mobility*, defined as the percentage of persons aged 5 and over who have changed residences in the last five years; (6) *percent children not living with both parents*, defined as the percentage of children 18 years of age and under not living with both parents; (7) *percent unemployed*, defined as the percentage of unemployed persons 16 years of age and over; (8) *percent divorced*, defined as the percentage of divorced persons 15 years of age and over; and (9) *population size*, defined as the total resident population.

Given the strong correlation between the independent variables, and consistent with a number of recent studies (Land, McCall, and Cohen 1990; Sampson and Bartusch 1998), we conducted factor analysis (a principal components analysis using the varimax rotation method). The analysis of these neighborhood items yielded two factors with eigenvalues above the conventional threshold of 1.00 that explain 80 percent of the cumulative variance. Consistent with existing research, the poverty-related variables are highly associated and load on the same factor. Thus, the first factor, labeled *Neighborhood Disadvantage*, exhibits high loadings for poverty (.94), percent children not living with both parents (.93), median family

---

similar. For example, in motive-unknown homicides, 91 percent of the offenders are black, 97 percent are male, and 8 percent are juveniles; likewise, in motive-known homicides, 91 percent of the suspects are black, 91 percent are male, and 13 percent are juveniles. Moreover, the distribution of victim/offender relationship is similar across the subsamples. Nearly 17 percent of both motive-unknown and motive-known homicides are between family members, 68 percent (motive-unknown) and 60 percent (motive-known) are between friends or acquaintances, and 15 percent (motive-unknown) and 23 percent (motive-known) are between strangers. These similarities suggest that excluding motive-unknown homicides from the analyses does not pose a serious problem.

income (.91), unemployment (.87), and percent black (.84). Recent research points to the need to examine multiple disadvantages facing the black population instead of single factors, such as poverty (Parker and Pruitt 2000:566; Ricketts and Sawhill 1988; Sampson and Wilson 1995),[4] and our measure captures these multiple disadvantages.

Percent residential mobility (.89) and percent divorced (.83) are the measures with appreciable loadings on the second factor, labeled *Neighborhood Instability.* The clear emergence of a residential instability factor is consistent with past research (Miles-Doan 1998; Sampson and Bartusch 1998). The two factor scores, neighborhood disadvantage and neighborhood instability, are used along with percent young male and population size to capture the various dimensions of community context.

An examination of the univariate distributions revealed skewness in the homicide rates (but not in the independent variables), a finding not too surprising given that urban spatial data such as these are frequently non-normal in their distribution. Homicide is a rare event and most neighborhoods in St. Louis have few homicides and even fewer retaliatory homicides, despite our pooling the data over a 10-year period. Moreover, when populations are small relative to offense rates, the discrete nature of the homicide counts cannot be ignored and traditional Ordinary Least Squares (OLS) analyses cannot be employed.

An alternative approach that resolves these problems is the Poisson-based regression model. Poisson regression has the advantage of being precisely tailored to the discrete, highly skewed distribution of the dependent variable. However, the basic Poisson regression model is appropriate only if the data are not overdispersed; applying the basic Poisson regression model to overdispersed data can produce underestimation of standard errors of the βs, which in turn leads to misleading significance tests. A solution is found in the negative binomial regression model, the best known and most widely available Poisson-based model that allows for over-dispersion (for a complete description, see Osgood 2000). In light of these issues, this study employs counts for retaliatory and non-retaliatory homicides as the dependent variables, and uses a negative binomial estimation procedure to determine the relationship between neighborhood disadvantage and retaliatory homicide.

Homicide is typically concentrated in certain areas of a city. Formally, this pattern is indicated by the concept of spatial autocorrelation, or the co-incidence of similarity in value with similarity in location (Anselin et al. 2000:14). When high (or low) values in a location are associated with high (or low) values at nearby locations, positive spatial autocorrelation or spatial clustering is indicated. In analyses using spatial data, estimates and inferences from regression analyses must adjust for spatial autocorrelation; ignoring spatial dependence in the model may lead to false indications of significance, biased parameter estimates, and misleading suggestions of fit (Messner et al. 2001:427).

Spatial dependence can be controlled for using either a spatial error or spatial lag model (Baller et al. 2001:566). The spatial error model evaluates the extent to which the clustering of homicide rates not explained by measured independent variables can be accounted for by the clustering of error terms; it captures the spatial influence of unmeasured independent variables. The spatial lag model incorporates the spatial influence of unmeasured independent variables but also stipulates an additional effect of neighbors' homicide rates (i.e., the lagged dependent variable). This model is more compatible with notions of diffusion processes because it implies an influence

---

4. Race is distinct from disadvantage; treating them as attributes of the same dimension confounds attempts to identify their distinct influences on homicide levels. Nevertheless, the finding that percent black loads heavily with the poverty-related variables makes sense ecologically (in St. Louis), since this reflects neighborhood segregation mechanisms that concentrate poor, African-Americans, and single-parent families with children (Wilson 1987). In such a segregated context, it is problematic to try to separate empirically the influence of percent black from the other components of the disadvantage scale, for there are in fact no predominantly white (>75 percent white) neighborhoods that map onto the distribution of extreme disadvantage that black neighborhoods experience. For example, when we divided St. Louis into thirds on poverty level, no predominantly white neighborhoods fell into the high-poverty category. This finding is consistent with the literature (Krivo and Peterson 2000; Sampson and Wilson 1995).

of neighbors' homicide rates that is not simply an artifact of measured or unmeasured independent variables. Rather, homicides in one place may actually increase the likelihood of homicide in nearby locales (Baller et al. 2001). We expect this to be the case with retaliatory homicides.

In the regression models, we estimate the effects of neighborhood characteristics on retaliatory and non-retaliatory homicide levels with adjustments for spatial dependence by incorporating a spatial lag model.[5] The first step in this procedure consists of the analysis of patterns of spatial autocorrelation in the homicide levels. A large number of spatial autocorrelation tests have been developed, the most common of which is Moran's I (Anselin et al. 2000). Moran's I is a cross-product coefficient similar to a Pearson correlation coefficient and is bounded by 1 and -1. Significant positive values for Moran's I indicate positive spatial autocorrelation or clustering, while negative values suggest clustering of dissimilar values. In the analysis presented here, we use the Spacestat software to carry out the Moran's I test for spatial autocorrelation.[6]

Assuming that spatial dependence is observed, we include a spatial lag model in the regression analyses. Kenneth Land and Glenn Deane (1992:228) assert that in spatial-effects models, the spatial diffusion or interaction processes are determined simultaneously with the dependent variable. This produces a nonzero correlation between the potential (spatial lag) variable and the error term, which violates the assumptions under which OLS produces unbiased (and therefore consistent) estimates of the regression coefficients. As a corrective method, they propose a two-stage least squares (2SLS) technique to derive consistent estimators in spatial-effects models with potential variables. Thus, following recent research (Morenoff and Sampson 1997:43), we apply Land and Deane's 2SLS technique, and in particular, the Anselin-Alternative method, to create measures of homicide potentials.[7] These variables capture the spatial dependence of retaliatory and non-retaliatory homicide levels in a given census tract on homicide levels in the surrounding area, and the significance of their coefficients provides a test for spatial autocorrelation.

Results

Neighborhood Correlates of Retaliatory Homicide

Means, standard deviations, and bivariate correlations for all variables are presented in Table 2. As shown, the mean number of retaliatory and non-retaliatory homicides from 1985–1995 are 3 and 12.56, respectively. Looking at neighborhood characteristics, in 1990, the average poverty level across neighborhoods was 25 percent, the average percentage of children not living with both parents was 40 percent, and the average percentage of persons unemployed was nearly 7 percent. Other characteristics of interest include the average percentage of persons

---

5. Although Robert Baller and associates (2001) distinguish between spatial error and spatial lag models, the procedures discussed in their study to determine the most appropriate model in a given study are available only for OLS-based regressions, and not for Poisson-based regressions (personal correspondence with Baller). At present, the methods are not sufficiently developed to run the different diagnostic tests in Spacestat that would determine which model is appropriate to deal with autocorrelation. In particular, the series of Lagrange Multiplier tests that perform this procedure are currently available only for OLS-based regressions. Thus, we chose to run the spatial lag model, which is sufficient as the error model is nested within the lag model (see Baller et al. 2001:566).

6. Moran's I was computed using a first power inverse distance weights matrix (row standardized) based on the distance between census tract centroids for all tracts excluding the one under consideration. Thus, greater weight is given to tracts that are closer than to those that are farther away. We then multiplied the spatial weights matrix by predicted values of each of the dependent variables. This potential indicates the influence of homicide in neighboring tracts, with the influence decaying as the distance between tracts increases (Land and Deane 1992:228).

7. In the first stage, we save the predicted values of the dependent variables from a regular regression. The predicted values are then multiplied by the spatial weights matrix. That product, as a variable, is used in the final regressions to control for spatial lag dependence.

Table 2 • Basic Statistics and Correlations

	1	2	3	4	5	6	7	8	9
1. Retal. hom. count	1.00								
2. Non-retal. hom. count	.78**	1.00							
3. Percent black	.69**	.78**	1.00						
4. Median family income	−.61**	−.65**	−.67**	1.00					
5. Percent poverty	.64**	.66**	.73**	−.84**	1.00				
6. Percent young males	.23*	.27**	.35**	−.30**	.32**	1.00			
7. Percent residential mobility	−.09	−.04	−.16	−.02	.08	.10	1.00		
8. Percent children not living with both parents	.61**	.69**	.74**	−.85**	.85**	.21*	.22*	1.00	
9. Percent unemployed	.65**	.68**	.72**	−.73**	.80**	.24*	−.04	.73**	1.00
10. Percent divorces									
11. Population size									
X	3.00	12.56	48.96	24.298	24.92	7.48	43.96	39.62	6.76
SD	3.58	11.31	40.87	9,238	15.42	3.49	12.04	17.09	3.74

*p < .05   **p < .01

Table 3 • *Regression Results for Neighborhood Characteristics on Retaliatory and Non-Retaliatory Homicides*[a]

Variable	Retaliatory Homicide	Non-Retaliatory Homicide
Neighborhood disadvantage	.766 (.106)***	.575 (.065)***
Neighborhood instability	−.034 (.092)	.074 (.048)
Percent young males	.018 (.021)	.014 (.012)
Population size	.0002 (.000)***	.0003 (.000)***
Spatial effects	.561 (.150)***	.184 (.025)***
Constant	−2.046 (.589)**	−1.338 (.378)***
Pseudo R^2	.24	.23
−2LL	−189.160	−304.648

[a] Entries are unstandardized coefficients followed by standard errors in parentheses. N = 111 census tracts.
* $p < .05$ ** $p < .01$ *** $p < .001$

divorced (9 percent), the average percentage of persons who have changed residences in the last five years (44 percent), and the average median family income ($24,298).

Turning to the relationship between these characteristics and homicide counts, we see that the correlations in Table 2 illustrate a significant positive association between disadvantage and retaliatory homicide. Each of the dimensions of economic disadvantage—percent poverty, percent unemployed, and median family income—is correlated with retaliatory homicide. Moreover, percent black, percent young males, and percent children not living with both parents are all significantly positively associated with retaliatory homicide. Retaliatory killings are negatively associated with percent divorced, suggesting that neighborhoods with higher levels of divorce have lower levels of retaliatory violence. Finally, neither residential mobility nor population size is associated with retaliatory homicide in St. Louis. To see if the strong association between disadvantage and retaliatory homicide holds when controlling for other factors, we turn to the regression results.

Neighborhood Structure and Retaliatory Homicide: Regression Results

Table 3 presents regression results on the relationship between neighborhood disadvantage and retaliatory homicide counts. In reviewing the results, we caution against making causal inferences, recognizing the possibility that retaliatory homicide levels may have reverse causal effects on some of the independent variables. If the true relationship between retaliatory homicide and indicators of neighborhood composition is reciprocal, then the analysis is affected by simultaneity bias because there is no control for the effect of homicide levels on the indicators of neighborhood disadvantage and instability and the other covariates. It is likely, however, that neighborhood characteristics have a stronger effect on homicide levels than the reverse. Nevertheless, we avoid causal interpretations of the results.[8]

---

8. A related issue has to do with the implications of the homicide data spanning a 10-year period with 5 years preceding the 1990 census data from which the structural covariates are derived. This situation could be problematic if it is the case that homicide levels from 1985–1990 influence changes in neighborhood characteristics (that are measured in 1990). A 1992 report by the Federal Reserve Bank of St. Louis (Community Affairs Office) on St. Louis demographics suggests that during this time period, St. Louis communities were relatively stable. The report states that "overall, the region (city of St. Louis) has been in a period of population stability" (p. 4). This suggests that including homicide data from 1985–1990 is not likely to be problematic. In addition, given the rarity of homicide, it is a common practice in studies to aggregate the data over a number of years (Messner and Golden 1992; Parker and Pruitt 2000). This is especially true when examining one type of homicide across census tracts, as is the case here.

First, as Table 3 shows, neighborhood disadvantage is significantly related to all kinds of homicide. For non-retaliatory killings, neighborhood disadvantage emerges as the strongest factor (β = .58; p < .001); a unit change in neighborhood disadvantage would increase the expected number of non-retaliatory homicides by 78 percent (percent change = 100*[exp(.575) − 1]), holding all else constant. Likewise, neighborhood disadvantage is significantly positively associated with retaliatory killings (β = .77; p < .001). The coefficient of .766 indicates that a unit change in neighborhood disadvantage would increase the expected number of retaliatory homicides by 115%. While neighborhood disadvantage is correlated with both types of killings, a closer look reveals that disadvantage has a stronger influence on retaliatory than non-retaliatory homicide (.77 versus .58; t = 1.54; p = .063).[9] This suggests that neighborhoods with higher levels of concentrated disadvantage are *especially* likely to experience greater numbers of retaliatory than non-retaliatory killings.

The results also indicate that spatial autocorrelation exists in the models. First, the Global Moran's I coefficients for both homicide types are greater than zero and significant at the p < .05 level. These results provide strong evidence of a significant spatial pattern. Second, the regression results indicate that spatial autocorrelation in the homicide distributions remains after accounting for neighborhood context: the coefficient for the autocorrelation term is significant in both equations. These results are consistent with a diffusion hypothesis. Finally, Pseudo R^2 statistics displayed at the bottom of Table 3 indicate that the regression model accounts for 24 percent and 23 percent of the variance in retaliatory and non-retaliatory homicides at the neighborhood level.

While these findings indicate that disadvantaged neighborhoods are more likely to experience retaliatory than non-retaliatory killings, the results tell us little about the nature or type of retaliatory violence that these communities experience. Anderson (1999), Horowitz (1983), and others claim that many killings in disadvantaged communities result from a prevailing code of honor and respect that shapes residents' values and behavior, and encourages the use of violence in response to others' challenges and disrespectful treatment. If these arguments are correct, we would expect to find that disadvantaged neighborhoods not only experience a greater number of retaliatory killings than non-disadvantaged neighborhoods, but that retaliatory killings in poor communities are more likely to reflect elements of the street culture.

To test this idea, we performed a content analysis of all retaliatory homicide narratives, classifying each case into one of three categories: (1) street code (n = 90), (2) likely street code (n = 213), and (3) not street code (n = 31) (in 3 cases narratives were missing). Cases were classified as "street code" and scored a 1 if they had strong evidence of (a) disrespect (e.g., insults and provocative gestures, refusal to show proper deference, character assassinations, challenges to masculinity, embarrassment in front of others, affronts against female significant others); (b) community or family support for retaliatory violence; and/or (c) actors' decisions to resolve problems through direct action and not involve the police. Retaliatory cases that were clearly unrelated to these factors were categorized as "not street code" and scored a 3 (e.g., a customer of a car repair shop killed the owner for cheating him; two mentally ill tenants killed their landlord because they were unhappy about their living quarters; a man killed his boss for firing him; a woman smothered her child to retaliate against the child's father, who had left the woman). In the majority of the remaining cases, the "likely street code" category (scored a 2), the narratives suggested elements of the code of the street but lacked sufficient detail to be definitively classified as street code killings.

For the analysis, we combined "street code" and "likely street code" cases into one category labeled, "cultural retaliatory homicides." The remaining cases have been labeled "situa-

---

9. The formula for the standard test for coefficient differences across equations is: t = $b_1 - b_2 / \sqrt{(SEb_1^2 + SEb_2^2)}$ (Paternoster et al., 1998). All coefficient comparisons are based on a one-tailed test. See also McNulty (2001:479).

Table 4 • *Regression Results for Neighborhood Characteristics on Cultural and Situational Retaliatory Homicides*[a]

Variable	Cultural Retaliatory Homicide	Situational Retaliatory Homicide
Neighborhood disadvantage	.857 (.115)***	.068 (.285)
Neighborhood instability	−.017 (.102)	.079 (.205)
Percent young males	.022 (.023)	.025 (.052)
Population size	.0002 (.000)**	.0002 (.000)
Spatial effects	.743 (.173)***	12.181 (18.834)
Constant	−2.725 (.649)***	−5.430 (4.980)
Pseudo R^2	.28	.03
−2LL	−172.195	−68.182

[a] Entries are unstandardized coefficients followed by standard errors in parentheses. N = 111 census tracts.
* p < .05   ** p < .01   *** p < .001

tional retaliatory homicides," which means that the killing appeared to be shaped by interpersonal circumstances unrelated to neighborhood values and norms (cf. Felson and Steadman 1983; Luckenbill 1977). To determine whether disadvantage is more strongly associated with cultural than situational retaliation, we performed regression analyses and compared the coefficients for neighborhood disadvantage across the two equations (see Table 4).

As expected, neighborhood disadvantage is strongly related to cultural retaliatory killings (β = .86; p < .001); a unit change in neighborhood disadvantage would increase the expected number of these homicides by 136 percent. On the other hand, neighborhood disadvantage is *not* significantly associated with situational retaliatory killings. More importantly, results from a standard test for coefficient differences across equations reveal that neighborhood disadvantage is more strongly associated with cultural than situational homicides (.86 versus .07; t = 2.57; p < .01). This finding was further confirmed when we compared street code killings (category 1 cases only, excluding "likely street code" cases) to situational retaliatory killings (t = 2.44; p < .01). These findings provide strong evidence that poor neighborhoods have greater numbers of cultural retaliatory killings, where honor and disrespect play a prominent role in the production of retaliatory violence.

In sum, both the descriptive statistics and the regression results indicate that disadvantaged neighborhoods experience a greater number of homicides that are retaliatory in nature, and that these retaliatory killings are more likely to reflect elements of the street culture. Retaliatory homicides differ markedly from non-retaliatory homicides on a number of dimensions (Table 1), and there is a strong bivariate correlation between disadvantage and retaliatory homicide (Figure 1 and Table 2). Neighborhood disadvantage is the factor most strongly associated with this type of murder (Table 3), and poor neighborhoods are more likely to experience cultural than situational retaliatory killings (Table 4).

Cultural Retaliatory Homicide: Accounts Illustrating the Street Culture

These findings establish a statistical relationship between neighborhood disadvantage and a particular type of retaliatory homicide that we call "cultural." To elaborate the connection between community structure and culture, we turn to a second data source: the homicide narratives. We use these data as a descriptive supplement to the regression analyses; they provide additional insights into the nature of retaliatory homicide and illustrate important patterns in accounts of retaliatory violence. The narrative descriptions demonstrate various components of culturally motivated homicides—features that distinguish these killings from situational retaliatory homicide.

All narratives quoted below involve instances of cultural retaliatory homicide. They are drawn from highly (61 percent) or extremely (39 percent) disadvantaged areas (based on Krivo and Peterson's [1996] categorization), and these neighborhoods are socio-economically similar to other disadvantaged neighborhoods in St. Louis (e.g., the mean percentage of persons in poverty in tracts comprising our sample narratives is 39 percent, compared to 35 percent for all highly/extremely disadvantaged tracts in St. Louis, and the mean percent unemployed is 10 percent and 9 percent, respectively).

As we suggested earlier in the article, there is an inclination among some residents of disadvantaged neighborhoods to resolve problems through lethal violence. Many of the actions that precipitate violent retribution may appear extremely minor to outsiders (e.g., being stared at, called a name, losing at a game, the theft of $10 or a car stereo, etc.), but these "trivial" catalysts must be understood in the context of neighborhood conditions that increase the chances of residents' disputatiousness. Based on what we know of the "code of the streets" in disadvantaged communities, it is expected that encounters that result in retaliatory homicide will be shaped by: challenges interpreted as disrespectful or damaging to oneself or to one's significant other or friends; some level of community tolerance for this informal social control; and reluctance to involve the police. Each of these motives or conditions is evidenced in the narrative accounts drawn from disadvantaged areas,[10] but are less apparent in the accounts drawn from affluent neighborhoods. Of the 34 retaliatory cases in affluent neighborhoods, in only one case did the motive clearly resemble elements of the street code of respect. In affluent neighborhoods, retaliatory killings were motivated by prior physical attacks (6 cases) or by miscellaneous conflicts (e.g., a feud over a car battery, nonpayment for services rendered, theft of money or property [4 cases], disputes over drugs [6 cases], child abuse victims killing their abusers [3 cases], tenants killing their landlords because they had been evicted [2 cases]). These homicides did not appear to be driven by considerations of personal honor, status, and respect. The following discussion of retaliatory killings in disadvantaged areas is organized around four conditions associated with the street code: retribution for disrespect, insults toward female significant others, a policing vacuum, and community and family support for retaliation.

Retribution for Disrespect

Disrespect comes in many flavors. In one case, a man who tried to buy powder cocaine on the street was rebuffed by the seller, who only had crack cocaine for sale. The victim went around the corner, bought crack, and returned to the seller and told him he was "not the only game in town." The seller had been trying to establish himself in the drug trade—"flexing muscle as a distributor" according to the narrative account—and the charge that he was "not the only game in town" was evidently interpreted as a challenge to his business acumen. The seller, along with two accomplices, killed the victim, and the accomplices were later shot in retaliation for the killing (Case 058). In the following case, the suspect was attacked by someone he had formerly thought was afraid of him and who also questioned his manhood, adding insult to injury and calling for retribution:

---

10. We did not quantify the narrative data in terms of its frequency by category because some cases fall into two or more categories, and because these data are intended solely as illustrative of the ways in which subculture can contribute to violence.

The suspect liked to bully the neighborhood youths and order them around. On the day in question, the victim had apparently had enough. When the suspect told the victim to go to the store for him, the victim refused. The suspect then called the victim a "punk." The victim punched the suspect once in the mouth and the suspect hit the ground. The victim told the suspect to get his nine [gun], calling the suspect a punk because the suspect needed a weapon to be tough. Friends of the suspect later told police that the suspect was "in shock" that the victim would hit him; the suspect said that he thought the victim was afraid of him. The suspect said he would "take care of business" and his friends knew he would shoot the victim, because the suspect was no fighter and would only settle things with a gun. As the victim was sitting in a car with friends, the suspect shot into the car, then fled the area. (Case 059)

When the victim physically resisted the suspect's bullying and challenged the suspect's manhood (claiming he could not dominate others without a weapon), the suspect felt compelled to "take care of business" and eliminate the challenger.

In one case, a police officer's routine act of writing a parking ticket was construed as disrespectful and deserving of the ultimate retribution:

The suspect drove at a high speed, hitting an officer who was writing a parking ticket. The victim was thrown into the air and landed on the hood of the suspect's car. The car carried the officer approximately fifty feet down the street and he rolled off the car. Suspect then walked to the victim, searched him, and kicked him repeatedly in the face. The suspect said, "He'll think twice before he gives me another ticket," and "That'll teach him to embarrass me in front of my grandchildren," and "You don't know how much hate I got in me." The suspect had gotten a parking ticket that day, but there was no evidence that this officer had written it. It appears that the suspect was so angry over the ticket, he simply went looking for a police officer. He told police he wasn't sorry and would do it again. (Case 534)

Particularly galling to the offender was the fact that he had been embarrassed in front of his grandchildren, even though the officer killed was not the culprit.

In several cases, a victim dares another to kill, a striking type of victim precipitation that is construed as both disrespectful and invitational (Katz 1988; Luckenbill 1977). In one case,

The suspect accused the victim of blocking his entrance to a doorway, called the victim a name, and ordered the victim out of his way. The victim and suspect then got into a fistfight. Victim and suspect exchanged threats before leaving. Later, the suspect drove up in a car and said something to the victim, who responded, "Go ahead and shoot me," which the suspect did. (Case 165)

Disrespect can be elevated from the personal level to the community level—i.e., acting in a way that shows disrespect toward the entire neighborhood. Community members sometimes take offense at this more diffuse kind of disrespect, and attempt to assert informal social control over those whose deviant behavior is deemed unacceptable. "Bullying" people in the neighborhood was a problem in the following case:

One of the suspects said he and his friends were tired of the victim's son bullying the neighborhood. He said it had "gotten out of hand." Victim's son tried to bully people into joining the Bloods [gang]. A source said the victim's son was responsible for a shooting several months prior in which an infant and five others were shot. On the night in question, according to one suspect, they decided to "take care of the problem." The suspects distributed guns and walked to the home of the victim's son. The victim was sitting on the front porch with her son and two others. The suspects took up positions in two gangways and opened fire. The son and one witness returned fire with 9mm pistols. The victim [the son's mother] was shot, and the suspects fled the scene. The victim's son said that "someone would pay" for his mother's death. (Case 042)

In another instance, the perpetrator presents himself as performing a community service by killing someone who had been victimizing the neighborhood:

He said to police, "That wasn't a college boy I shot! He was nothing but a junkie. He's been all over town trickin' and beatin' folks." Not only did the victim sell "burn bags" [in the neighborhood], but he also led people to believe that the drugs "came from the neighborhood" [apparently damaging the reputation of other drug dealers]. (Case 452)

Not only is disrespect a common *motive* for retaliatory killings, but the killing can *earn the perpetrator respect* from peers. This is a central feature of the street code in disadvantaged neighborhoods (Anderson 1999). An example follows:

The suspect was very tight with two brothers, whose sister had been killed in 1990, for which the victim had been arrested. Reportedly, the two brothers had put out a contract of $10,000 for the death of the victim. At the time of the shooting, the victim was walking across a parking lot when the suspect approached and began shooting. The victim fell, and the suspect then stood over him and continued firing at his face. The suspect then calmly walked to his grandmother's house near the scene. As police investigated, he went back outside and watched the police. *He and his friends congratulated one another and laughed.* No one in the crowd pointed him out to the police as the shooter. Reportedly, the victim was killed on this day because it was the birthday of one of the brothers [who was] seeking revenge for his sister. (Case 344, our emphasis)

Further evidence of the code of respect in disadvantaged neighborhoods can be found in accounts that make direct reference to local expectations and norms. Actors sometimes tell others that they fully expect their disrespectful behavior to be punished by persons whom they offend. For instance, after stealing a man's car stereo and selling it to a friend, the thief told the friend to keep quiet about it, because if the owner found out who had stolen it, he would kill the thief—which he subsequently did (Case 591). In many other accounts, actors appear to believe they have no choice but to retaliate for some affront, no matter how minor. Consider the "suspect [who] didn't like the way the other man looked at him and said, as a result, he would *have to* kill the man" (Case 313). Opting not to retaliate against someone who shows disrespect may suggest that the offended party is weak and available for future abuse by others in the neighborhood (Anderson 1999).

Insults Toward Female Significant Others

In "cultures of honor" generally, "Insults or attacks against female members of the family are considered especially heinous" (Cohen and Nisbett 1994:552). We found a similar pattern regarding disrespect toward female significant others. In several cases, one or both of the antagonists had some kind of involvement or problem with a female third party—a sister, girlfriend, mother, etc. In these cases, one party's treatment of a woman is interpreted by the other party as a sign of direct disrespect toward the woman and/or vicarious disrespect toward a man associated with the woman. The readiness with which such relatively minor affronts are defined as worthy of lethal violence is striking in the following accounts, illustrating how status conditions in disadvantaged neighborhoods seem to predispose males to respond violently to other males' offenses (Anderson 1999). In the course of a card game, the victim drank and increasingly used foul language:

He was asked to stop, and would apologize, but he would then curse again. The victim kept apologizing, but said he "couldn't help" cursing because he was drinking. Finally, the suspect's aunt said that the game was over and it was time for everyone to leave. The victim left and the suspect ran outside and shot him. Suspect apparently felt victim had insulted or failed to respect his aunt. (Case 406)

Some of the conflicts revolve around perceived challenges to a person's manhood, an asset highly valued in disadvantaged neighborhoods (Anderson 1999; Horowitz 1983). A case in point follows:

The victim had been at the lounge with friends and family celebrating his birthday. He had started a conversation with a woman at the bar, and her boyfriend (one of the suspects) became extremely angry, accusing the victim of "hitting on" the woman. After the argument, the boyfriend/suspect was heard saying that he would kill the victim, repeating this over and over. When the bar closed, there was a crowd out front, a car drove up and its passengers fired into the crowd. The victim ran and two men jumped out of the car and ran after him, shooting. They were the two men who had stood behind the boyfriend/suspect in the bar. (Case 450)

Two other instances of disrespect involving a woman follow:

Suspect 1 was talking to a woman acquaintance. She told police they were only friends. The victim, her ex-boyfriend, saw them talking and ordered the woman into the house. He told them that "the talking was over." Suspect 1 drove away, and later returned with suspect 2. When they saw the victim, suspect 1 asked him why he had "dissed" him. Suspect 2 then pointed a rifle out the window of the car and opened fire. (Case 089)

Witness 3 had been in a fast-food restaurant in the neighborhood and had seen the victim harass a woman whom witness 3 knew. The woman had been upset and couldn't get the victim to stop. Witness 3 went home and told witness 1 and the suspect what had happened. Witness 1 picked up a stick and the suspect picked up a shotgun. They found the victim on the street and confronted him, demanding to know why he had harassed the woman, who was seven months pregnant. Witness 1 swung the stick and the suspect shot the victim. (Case 800)

Retaliation can occur even when the woman in question tries to prevent it:

The victim and his ex-girlfriend had a three year-old daughter, and the woman was six months pregnant by suspect 2, who lived with her. The day before, the victim and the woman had argued about their child, and the victim told her he would "slap her silly," though he did not do so. The woman told suspect 2 about the incident. On the day in question, the suspects were in the parking lot when the victim approached, preparing to enter the building. The woman was watching from a window, and hollered at suspect 2, reminding him of what the victim had said to her the day before. Suspect 2 engaged the victim in conversation, and punched and kicked him. Suspect 1 then ran into the building and returned with a shotgun, which he handed to suspect 2. The woman claimed that she hollered out the window, telling suspect 2 not to shoot the victim, and that other people in the area did the same. But suspect 2 placed the gun to victim's head and fired. (Case 572)

Simply *threatening* a woman, to "slap her silly," provided grounds for murder, showing how little "provocation" is needed to justify the ultimate punishment.

The following example shows how a minor slight, a teasing remark about a female, can have deadly consequences where the street code reigns:

The victim was visiting friends when the suspect stopped by to pick up an ID card from a 19-year-old female who was an acquaintance of the victim. As the suspect was leaving, the victim told the girl that she was "picking 'em young these days." The suspect asked the victim who he was talking to and said "you better check yourself before you wreck yourself." Shortly after, when the victim left the apartment, the suspect shot him. (Case 335)

To suggest that the suspect was too young for the girl was evidently a sign of disrespect that could not go unpunished.

One subcultural feature of these communities is the acceptability of teenage girls having babies (Anderson 1999), but not everyone endorses this practice. In the following case, a critical comment about such a girl provided the backdrop for a violent attack, which may be seen as an attempt to defend the legitimacy of the prevailing code regarding youth pregnancy:

A friend of the victim's had made some remarks about the suspect's pregnant girlfriend, that "she is only 16 and already has two kids." This angered the suspect, who pulled a gun on the victim's friend. Later, the victim and his friend were standing near the housing project when the suspect and girlfriend walked by. The victim's friend then said to the suspect, "maybe you should have shot me when you had the chance," and he and the victim put their hands behind their backs, acting like they had weapons. The suspect said, "Man, what's your problem? I thought this thing was over with you." Suspect then chased the victim and friend, firing shots. (Case 447)

A Policing Vacuum

The street culture calls for the use of informal control or summary justice in response to others' "offensive" behavior, instead of calling the police. Earlier in the article we cited evidence of a policing vacuum in extremely disadvantaged St. Louis communities, whose residents tend to believe that police services to their neighborhoods are inadequate (Velez 2001). The narrative data suggest that residents often do not call for police intervention when they have been victimized by others. Instead, they take direct action and may even publicly broadcast their intention to take revenge, by putting "word on the street" that another person is about to be attacked or killed. In several cases, suspects let it be known that they were "out to get" the victim, demonstrating little concern about repercussions from the police.

As indicated earlier in the article, the policing vacuum does not apply to the initial stages of every conflict. When it comes to certain types of transgressions (such as theft of drugs, a stare that seems challenging, and other signs of disrespect), the offended party simply has no legal recourse. But when the precipitating acts are serious, criminal offenses (an aggravated assault, shooting, rape, etc.), the offended party might be expected to call the police. Despite the gravity of these crimes, however, it is noteworthy that suspects typically decided to settle the score on their own, without invoking the police. It is in these types of conflicts that the policing vacuum is most evident.

One theme running throughout the narratives is the unwillingness of witnesses to give information to the police. It was frequently the case that people known to have information about a crime refused to contact the police—for two reasons. First, some of the persons killed were seen by others as legitimate victims. In one case, not only did the suspect justify the murder to the police, but witnesses also condoned the killing:

> The suspect told police that no one "gave a shit" or "gave a fuck" about the victim, and told police that they were wasting their time. Witnesses said they weren't going to become involved. No one would "witness" against the suspect because the victim was no good. (Case 667)

Similarly, with regard to a victim who had been stealing cars for a year, "residents told police that neighbors would not mourn the victim and would not cooperate" with police because the killing was deserved (Case 716). Another man, who was killed because he had a habit of robbing drug dealers, "was not well-liked in the neighborhood, so no one wanted to cooperate with the investigation" (Case 898).

Fear of retribution is another reason why people avoid talking to the police. Residents of these neighborhoods have little or no confidence that the police are capable of protecting them if they provide information. During the investigation of one shooting, young men emphasized to police that "life in the projects was rough." One person didn't want to talk because "I have to live down there"; another told police, "you have no idea what it's like down there" (Case 570). Neighborhood conditions are such that talking to the police might compromise one's personal safety. One witness to a killing was "so afraid of the suspect that he would rather go to jail than cooperate in the prosecution" (Case 088). After one killing, residents believed that the suspect was watching the police station to see who was being questioned, which "terrified" witnesses (Case 344). As many as 50 bystanders witnessed this killing, but no one was willing to talk to the police. About 20 youths were nearby at the time of another killing, but all denied being present and refused to give their names to police (Case 688). That this may be a rational decision under the circumstances is demonstrated by instances when informants are subsequently attacked. Some of our narratives describe police "snitches" who were later killed for talking to the police. One victim, who had acted as a lookout during one of the suspect's previous killings, was now believed ready to testify against the suspect at another murder trial, and was killed before he could do so (Case 283). In another case, the police stopped a man whose car had been used in a crime, and took him to the police station for questioning. Three suspects, who ran a "dope house," thought that the victim had "snitched to police" about the dope house—though he had not, according to the narrative. After the police returned the man to the location where he had been picked up by officers, the suspects shot and killed him (Case 100).

Those who did contact the police sometimes insisted on doing so secretly. Several cases involve "confidential informants" and "secret witnesses." One person said he would talk to police, but only if he could enter the police station through a tunnel (not the front door where he might be observed by the suspect) or if the police staged a "mock arrest" as cover (Case 344).

Community and Family Support for Retaliation

Neighbors who have no relation to those involved in a dispute may not only tolerate but also actively support the use of retaliatory violence. Such support may come from third parties who observe the initial or subsequent (fatal) altercation (Cooney 1998; Luckenbill 1977) or more generally from a wider section of the community. The latter form of support seems implicit in the case where the victim had been acting in a way that aggravated the entire community, such as "bullying" the neighborhood (Case 042 above), or in the case of "a common thief and troublemaker, who wouldn't survive the summer because he 'fucks' with too many people," in the words of this victim's former friend (Case 461). In another case, a suspect who was visiting someone in the neighborhood was told that the victim had been trying to break into the suspect's car. A neighbor who did not know the suspect, upon hearing what had happened and knowing that the suspect was going to the victim's house to confront him, offered the suspect a sawed-off shotgun, which the suspect accepted and used (Case 298). As noted above, in several cases residents were quite vehement in saying that the person killed was a legitimate victim, so disliked in the neighborhood that his passing was regarded as good riddance, and for this reason they would not cooperate with the police (e.g., Cases 667, 716, and 898 above).

Familial support for retaliatory violence is also evident in our data. In several instances, the killer proudly tells family members about a planned or completed killing—suggesting that the killer expects approval. In other cases, family members actively encourage the killing. In one incident (Case 421), the suspect had shot at the victim earlier in the day because the victim had sold one of the suspect's guns. The victim then told his family that he would "have to kill" the suspect, but the suspect ambushed the victim and killed him. Apparently the victim had no compunction about telling his family that he would retaliate with a killing. In another case, after killing a man,

> the suspects ran back to suspect 2's house and told suspect 2's mother, cousins, and aunt. Suspect 1 claimed they "had" to do it because the victim had stolen articles from suspect 2. Suspect 2 told the mother of another friend about the homicide. He laughed, and told her she should have seen the expression on the victim's face when he was shot. (Case 239)

Note how the suspects readily informed relatives and others about the killing, suggesting that they believed others would agree that the victim's death was a proper sanction for their own material loss.

Another incident began with a violent argument between the victim and a suspect, who were former lovers:

> Suspect 1 called her husband (suspect 2) and said a man had broken into their home and was beating her. Suspect 2 arrived with his mother. Suspect 1 was waiting on the porch and told her husband, "go into the house and shoot that bastard." Suspect 2 did, and then turned over the victim with his foot and said, "He's not dead. Give me the gun." Suspect 2's mother said he shouldn't shoot the man any more. Emergency Medical Services arrived. The victim was conscious and told paramedics he wanted to prosecute the suspects. Suspect 2's mother said, "He's got his nerve. He wants to prosecute my son. [My son] should have killed him." She then started to take a gun from her purse, but a companion persuaded her to put it away. (Case 158)

Not only does the mother take offense at the victim's request to prosecute her son, she is also prepared to personally administer summary justice on his behalf. In other cases as well, a parent demonstrates by his or her behavior, or instructs a child about, the street code of retaliation. For example,

> During a party, the victim went upstairs and had sex with the suspect's 13-year-old sister. The girl's mother claimed that the girl was physically ill the next day and only after questioning did she learn of the rape. The mother told the girl's brother to shoot the victim and drove him to the location. (Case 688)

Familial support for violence is also indicated in cases where parents take revenge against persons who have offended one of their children. One father was so angered by an assault against his son that he told police he would retaliate:

> When the father [the suspect] was informed that his son was hit by the victim during an argument, he said to the police, "You mean his uncle [the victim] hit my son? I'll kill the motherfucker." He later hired another person to kill the victim. (Case 774)

Or consider the father of a 14-year-old boy who had been punched and knocked unconscious by another boy:

> While driving the [injured] boy to the hospital, the father (suspect) decided to find the person who had hit his son. He drove up to where the youngsters were playing basketball, got out of the car and said, "Which one is it?" Either the son pointed to the victim or the father thought that he did; the father grabbed the victim by his collar and shot him in the face. (Case 877)

This was a case of mistaken identity.

Several other incidents involved killings of persons who were not the real culprits. This is part of a larger pattern in which offended parties often seem to have a short fuse, to react violently without taking the time to verify that a particular person had indeed committed the "offense" in question. On occasion, offenders seem prepared to mete out vengeance indiscriminately:

> The victim's sons had just robbed the suspect's mother of drugs and money. According to a confidential informant, the victim's sons had gone to the suspect's mother's residence and were admitted because they said they wanted to buy crack. Once inside, they used a sawed-off shotgun to rob the woman of drugs and money. When the suspect returned home, his mother told him. He and his brother went to ___ location, *determined to shoot whoever opened the door* [fatally shooting the father of the robbers]. (Case 471, our emphasis)

The accounts presented here illustrate how retaliatory homicides in impoverished neighborhoods can be shaped by conditions and motives associated with the street code—conditions and motives that are largely absent in more affluent neighborhoods, where retaliatory violence occurs rarely and is driven by other motives.

Conclusion

Our findings underscore the importance of two dimensions of neighborhood context in understanding patterns of retaliatory homicide: structural disadvantage and subcultural support for violence. Retaliatory homicide, and cultural retaliatory homicide in particular, more so than other types of homicide, is unevenly distributed across St. Louis and concentrated in socioeconomically disadvantaged neighborhoods. Few retaliatory homicides occurred in more affluent neighborhoods.

To fully understand why retaliatory killings take place in disadvantaged neighborhoods, one needs to explore the neighborhoods' cultural and interpersonal dynamics. Drawing on earlier work, we expected that violent solutions to problems in disadvantaged communities would be an essential part of the local subculture—a means of defending one's honor and winning respect from residents. These cultural codes legitimate aggressive responses to individuals who show disrespect, "a rationale allowing those who are inclined to aggression to precipitate violent encounters in an approved way" (Anderson 1999:33). Residents have an acute sensitivity to signs of disrespect from others, which increases their inclination to respond violently to even minor insults.

Our narrative data support this cultural code perspective. In disadvantaged St. Louis communities, the cases illustrate the importance of retribution for disrespectful treatment experienced either personally or vicariously. Offensive behavior directed towards a woman who is associated with a man is often interpreted as an affront to *both* the woman and the man. We also found evidence of community and family support for retaliatory violence, which points to neighborhood subcultural influences on violent behavior in these communities. Far from being an isolated, individual affair, the narrative data show that retaliatory violence can be collectively tolerated, endorsed, and rewarded by other residents. The analysis also shows that the motives characterizing retaliatory homicides in disadvantaged areas differ from those in affluent communities. Only one of the 34 retaliatory killings in affluent areas bore any resemblance to the code of the street, where honor and social status figure so prominently.

Another condition conducive to retaliatory violence in poor communities is the neighborhood cultural response to problematic policing. Interpersonal violence may be seen as a way of resolving problems and asserting social control in neighborhoods where the agents of formal control are often "out of the loop" when it comes to crime and punishment. People settle scores on their own—because such action is subculturally supported, because they have little trust in the police, and because they fear for their own personal safety if they involve the police. One interesting dimension of this reliance on street justice is the possibility that violent retribution, and residents' fear of it, may serve as a form of social control—perhaps *preventing* some types of crime in the community (Black 1983; Parenti 2000). Supporting evidence of this "crime as social control" phenomenon is found in Anderson's (1999) and Mary Pattillo-McCoy's (1999) discussions of the role of drug dealers, gang members, and other street criminals in exerting social control over other community residents in either conventional or deviant ways. It is possible that retaliatory killings have similar social control effects in a community, and this possibility deserves further attention in future research. Similarly, more research is needed on the role of policing in disadvantaged communities, and how this may condition residents' informal social control practices.

References

Anderson, Elijah. 1999. *Code of the Street.* New York: W.W. Norton and Company.

Anselin, Luc, Jacqueline Cohen, David Cook, Wilpen Gorr, and George Tita. 2000. "Spatial Analyses of Crime." Pp. 213–62 in *Criminal Justice 2000,* vol. 4, *Measurement and Analysis of Crime and Justice,* edited by David Duffee. Washington, DC: National Institute of Justice.

Baller, Robert D., Luc Anselin, Steven F. Messner, Glenn Deane, and Darnell F. Hawkins. 2001. "Structural Covariates of U.S. County Homicide Rates: Incorporating Spatial Effects." *Criminology* 39:561–90.

Black, Donald. 1976. *The Behavior of Law.* New York: Academic Press.

———. 1983. "Crime as Social Control." *American Sociological Review* 48:34–45.

Bruce, Marino A., Vincent J. Roscigno, and Patricia L. McCall. 1998. "Structure, Context, and Agency in the Reproduction of Black-on-Black Violence." *Theoretical Criminology* 2:29–55.

Cohen, Dov and Richard E. Nisbett. 1994. "Self-Protection and the Culture of Honor: Explaining Southern Violence." *Personality and Social Psychology Bulletin* 20:551–67.

Cooney, Mark. 1998. "The Dark Side of Community: Moralistic Homicide and Strong Social Ties." *Sociological Focus* 31:135–53.

Decker, Scott H. 1996. "Deviant Homicide: A New Look at the Role of Motives and Victim-Offender Relationships." *Journal of Research in Crime and Delinquency* 33:427–49.

Fagan, Jeffrey and Garth Davies. 2000. "Street Stops and Broken Windows: Terry, Race, and Disorder in New York City." *Fordham Urban Law Journal* 28:457–504.

Fagan, Jeffrey and Deanna Wilkinson. 1998. "Guns, Youth Violence, and Social Identity in Inner Cities." *Crime and Justice* 24:105–88.

Felson, Richard B. and Henry J. Steadman. 1983. "Situational Factors in Disputes Leading to Criminal Violence." *Criminology* 21:59–74.

Giddens, Anthony. 1984. *The Constitution of Society.* Cambridge, U.K.: Cambridge University Press.

Heimer, Karen. 1997. "Socioeconomic Status, Subcultural Definitions, and Violent Delinquency." *Social Forces* 75:799–833.

Horowitz, Ruth. 1983. *Honor and the American Dream: Culture and Identity in a Chicano Community.* New Brunswick: Rutgers University Press.

Huang, W. S. Wilson and Michael Vaughn. 1996. "Support and Confidence: Public Attitudes toward the Police." Pp. 31–45 in *America's View of Crime and Justice: A National Opinion Survey,* edited by Timothy Flanagan and Dennis Longmire. Thousand Oaks, CA: Sage.

Jacob, Herbert. 1971. "Black and White Perceptions of Justice in the City." *Law and Society Review* 6:69–90.

Katz, Jack. 1988. *Seductions of Crime.* New York: Basic Books.

Kennedy, Randall. 1997. *Race, Crime and the Law.* New York: Vintage Books.

Klinger, David. 1997. "Negotiating Order in Police Work: An Ecological Theory of Police Response to Deviance." *Criminology* 35:277–306.

Kornhauser, Ruth. 1978. *Social Sources of Delinquency.* Chicago: University of Chicago Press.

Krivo, Lauren J. and Ruth Peterson. 1996. "Extremely Disadvantaged Neighborhoods and Urban Crime." *Social Forces* 75:619–50.

———. 2000. "The Structural Context of Homicide: Accounting for Racial Differences in Process." *American Sociological Review* 65:547–59.

Kubrin, Charis E. 2003. "Structural Covariates of Homicide Rates: Does Type of Homicide Matter?" *Journal of Research in Crime and Delinquency* 40:1–32.

Land, Kenneth and Glenn Deane. 1992. "On the Large-Sample Estimation of Regression Models with Spatial- or Network-Effects Terms: A Two-Stage Least Squares Approach." *Sociological Methodology* 22:221–48.

Land, Kenneth, Patricia L. McCall, and Lawrence E. Cohen. 1990. "Structural Covariates of Homicide Rates: Are There Any Invariances Across Time and Social Space." *American Journal of Sociology* 95:922–63.

Los Angeles Times. 1988. Poll number 148, March 20th, unpublished results.

Luckenbill, David. 1977. "Criminal Homicide as a Situated Transaction." *Social Problems* 25:176–86.

Luckenbill, David and Daniel P. Doyle. 1989. "Structural Position and Violence: Developing a Cultural Explanation." *Criminology* 27:419–35.

Markowitz, Fred E. and Richard B. Felson. 1998. "Social-Demographic Attitudes and Violence." *Criminology* 36:117–38.

McNulty, Thomas L. 2001. "Assessing the Race-Violence Relationship at the Macro Level: The Assumption of Racial Invariance and the Problem of Restricted Distributions." *Criminology* 39:467–87.

Messner, Steven F., Luc Anselin, Robert D. Baller, Darnell F. Hawkins, Glenn Deane, and Stuart E. Tolnay. 2001. "The Spatial Patterning of County Homicide Rates: An Application of Exploratory Spatial Data Analysis." *Journal of Quantitative Criminology* 15:423–50.

Messner, Steven F. and Reid M. Golden. 1992. "Racial Inequality and Racially Disaggregated Homicide Rates: An Assessment of Alternative Theoretical Explanations." *Criminology* 30:421–47.

Miles-Doan, Rebecca. 1998. "Violence Between Spouses and Intimates: Does Neighborhood Context Matter?" *Social Forces* 77:623–45.

Morenoff, Jeffrey D. and Robert J. Sampson. 1997. "Violent Crime and the Spatial Dynamics of Neighborhood Transition: Chicago, 1970–1990." *Social Forces* 76:31–64.

Osgood, Wayne D. 2000. "Poisson-Based Regression Analysis of Aggregate Crime Rates." *Journal of Quantitative Criminology* 16:21–43.

180   **KUBRIN/WEITZER**

Parker, Karen F. and Matthew V. Pruitt. 2000. "Poverty, Poverty Concentration, and Homicide." *Social Science Quarterly* 81:555–70.

Parenti, Christian. 2000. "Crime as Social Control." *Social Justice* 27:43–49.

Paternoster, Raymond, Robert Brame, Paul Mazerolle, and Alex Piquero. 1998. "Using the Correct Statistical Test for the Equality of Regression Coefficients." *Criminology* 36:859–66.

Pattillo-McCoy, Mary. 1999. *Black Picket Fences: Privilege and Peril Among the Black Middle Class.* Chicago: University of Chicago Press.

Reisig, Michael and Roger Parks. 2000. "Experience, Quality of Life, and Neighborhood Context." *Justice Quarterly* 17:607–29.

Ricketts, Erol R. and Isabel V. Sawhill. 1988. "Defining and Measuring the Underclass." *Journal of Policy Analysis and Management* 7:316–25.

Rosenfeld, Richard, Timothy M. Bray, and Arlen Egley. 1999. "Facilitating Violence: A Comparison of Gang-Motivated, Gang-Affiliated, and Non-Gang Youth Homicides." *Journal of Quantitative Criminology* 15:495–516.

Sampson, Robert J. and Dawn Jeglum Bartusch. 1998. "Legal Cynicism and (Subcultural?) Tolerance of Deviance: The Neighborhood Context of Racial Differences." *Law and Society Review* 32:777–804.

Sampson, Robert J. and William Julius Wilson. 1995. "Toward a Theory of Race, Crime and Urban Inequality." Pp. 37–54 in *Crime and Inequality,* edited by John Hagan and Ruth D. Peterson. Stanford, CA: Stanford University Press.

Shaw, Clifford R. and Henry D. McKay. 1942. *Juvenile Delinquency and Urban Areas.* Chicago: University of Chicago Press.

Shihadeh, Edward S. and Darrell J. Steffensmeier. 1994. "Economic Inequality, Family Disruption, and Urban Black Violence: Cities as Units of Stratification and Social Control." *Social Forces* 73:729–51.

Smith, Douglas. 1986. "The Neighborhood Context of Police Behavior." *Crime and Justice* 8:313–41.

———. 1987. "Police Response to Interpersonal Violence: Defining the Parameters of Legal Control." *Social Forces* 65:767–82.

Smith, Douglas, Nanette Graham, and Bonnie Adams. 1991. "Minorities and the Police: Attitudinal and Behavioral Questions." Pp. 22–35 in *Race and Criminal Justice,* edited by Michael Lynch and E. Britt Patterson. New York: Harrow and Heston.

Velez, Maria B. 2001. "The Role of Public Social Control in Urban Neighborhoods." *Criminology* 39:837–63.

Weitzer, Ronald. 1999. "Citizen's Perceptions of Police Misconduct: Race and Neighborhood Context." *Justice Quarterly* 16:819–46.

———. 2000. "Racialized Policing: Residents' Perceptions in Three Neighborhoods." *Law and Society Review* 34:129–55.

Wilson, William Julius. 1987. *The Truly Disadvantaged: The Inner City, the Underclass, and Public Policy.* Chicago: University of Chicago Press.

Wolfgang, Marvin and Franco Ferracuti. 1967. *The Subculture of Violence.* London: Tavistock.

[20]

SOCIAL CAPITAL, INCOME INEQUALITY, AND FIREARM VIOLENT CRIME

BRUCE P. KENNEDY,[1]* ICHIRO KAWACHI,[2] DEBORAH PROTHROW-STITH,[1] KIMBERLY LOCHNER[2] and VANITA GUPTA[1]

[1]Division of Public Health Practice, Harvard School of Public Health, 718 Huntington Avenue, Boston, MA 02115, U.S.A. and [2]Department of Health and Social Behavior, Harvard School of Public Health, 718 Huntington Avenue, Boston, MA 02115, U.S.A.

Abstract—Studies have shown that poverty and income are powerful predictors of homicide and violent crime. We hypothesized that the effect of the growing gap between the rich and poor is mediated through an undermining of social cohesion, or social capital, and that decreased social capital is in turn associated with increased firearm homicide and violent crime. Social capital was measured by the weighted responses to two items from the U.S. General Social Survey: the per capita density of membership in voluntary groups in each state; and the level of social trust, as gauged by the proportion of residents in each state who believed that "most people would take advantage of you if they got the chance". Age-standardized firearm homicide rates for the years 1987–1991 and firearm robbery and assault incidence rates for years 1991–1994 were obtained for each of the 50 U.S. states. Income inequality was strongly correlated with firearm violent crime (firearm homicide, $r = 0.76$) as well as the measures of social capital: per capita group membership ($r = -0.40$) and lack of social trust ($r = 0.73$). In turn, both social trust (firearm homicide, $r = 0.83$) and group membership (firearm homicide, $r = -0.49$) were associated with firearm violent crime. These relationships held when controlling for poverty and a proxy variable for access to firearms. The profound effects of income inequality and social capital, when controlling for other factors such as poverty and firearm availability, on firearm violent crime indicate that policies that address these broader, macro-social forces warrant serious consideration.

Key words—social stratification, poverty, social capital, inequality, homicide, crime, firearms

INTRODUCTION

"Take the people of Briançon. They allow the needy, the widows and orphans, to cut their hay three days earlier than the rest. When their homes are in ruins they repair them for nothing... In the past hundred years they have not had a single murder".

Victor Hugo, Les Misérables (1862)

Intentional injuries resulting from violence make a significant contribution to the mortality and morbidity of the U.S. population. Injuries caused by violent behavior are estimated to cost American society approximately $26 billion dollars a year (Rice *et al.*, 1989). Currently, homicide is the leading cause of death for young African–American males and females (15–34) and the second leading cause of death for all 10–19 year-olds with an increasing number attributable to firearms (Hammett *et al.*, 1992; Fingerhut *et al.*, 1992).

Much of the recent policy debate concerning ways to reduce intentional injuries due to violence has focused on restricting access to lethal means such as firearms. Recent studies suggest a strong association between gun availability and homicide

rates (Cook, 1991; McDowell *et al.*, 1992; Kellermann *et al.*, 1993). Furthermore, there has been an increase in adolescent self-reports of carrying firearms that may have contributed to the homicide problem, although whether the increase in weapon-carrying is due to increased access to weapons or some other factor remains unclear (Reiss and Roth, 1993).

Unfortunately, the debate about restricting access to firearms has focused attention on individual behaviors often to the exclusion of other important determinants of violent crime. The role that broader social factors, such as income inequality and poverty, play in determining the incidence of violent crime have been increasingly neglected in the current policy debate. Studies have shown that poverty and income inequality, whether at the city, state, or national level, are powerful predictors of homicide and violent crime (Blau and Blau, 1986; Krahn *et al.*, 1986; Land *et al.*, 1990; Hsieh and Pugh, 1993). Income inequality, or other indices of relative deprivation, are considered to be stronger predictors of homicide and violent crime than indices of absolute deprivation, such as poverty (Baily, 1984; Messner, 1989). Recently, Kennedy *et al.* (1996) found that the Robin Hood Index, a measure of income inequality, predicted state-level variations in homi-

*Author for correspondence.

cide rates. Even after adjusting for poverty, income inequality accounted for 52% of the between-state variance in homicide rates.

A number of theories have attempted to explain the observed relationship between income inequality and violent crime (Shaw and McKay, 1942; Blau and Blau, 1986; Wilson, 1987). Much of this work is built on an initial hypothesis by Shaw and McKay (1942) that inequality, and the concentration of poor economic conditions, lead to social disorganization through a breakdown of social cohesion and normlessness. It is hypothesized that communities lacking in social cohesion (social capital) are less effective in exerting informal means of social control through establishing and maintaining norms to reduce violence compared to communities with higher levels of social capital (Sampson and Wilson, 1995).

The present study was undertaken to examine two related hypotheses: (1) state-level variations in income inequality predict firearm homicide, assault, and robbery rates independent of poverty and firearm availability; (2) state-level variations in social capital predict firearm homicide, assault, and robbery rates independent of poverty and firearm availability; and (3) the effect of income inequality on violent crime is mediated by its effect on social capital.

DATA AND METHODS

Measurement of poverty and income inequality

Poverty and household income data for each state were obtained from the 1990 U.S. Census Summary Tape File STF 3A. The poverty variable represents the percentage of households in a state that were considered to be below the federal poverty index. The federal poverty index is a wage-income based measure that does not include income from other sources, such as public assistance programs. The index is updated annually to reflect cost of living changes in the Consumer Price Index. In 1990, this represented a household income of less than $13,359 for a household of four (U.S. Census, 1993). We also obtained median household income, per capita income, and the percentage of the population living in urban areas data for each state.

Data from the Census provides annual household income for 25 income intervals (0–$5,000 at the bottom and $150,000 or more at the top). To calculate income inequality, counts of the number of households falling into each of the 25 income intervals along with the total aggregate income were obtained for the state. The interval data was converted into income deciles using a program developed by Welniak (1988) at the U.S. Census Bureau for this purpose.

Our measure of income inequality, the Robin Hood Index (RHI), was estimated for each state from the income decile distribution (Atkinson and Micklewright, 1992), which represents the share of total household income in each decile (see Table 6 for an example derivation). The RHI is calculated by summing the excess shares of income for those deciles with shares that exceed 10%. In the case of Massachusetts, the RHI is 30.26% (Table 6). This represents the share of income that would have to be transferred from those above the mean to those below the mean to achieve an income distribution of perfect equality (Atkinson and Micklewright, 1992). Hence, the higher the value of the Index, the greater the degree of inequality in the distribution of incomes.

Measurement of social capital

Two core constructs of social capital, as presented by its principal theorists (Coleman, 1990; Putnam, 1993a,b, 1995), consist of levels of mutual trust among community members, and civic engagement. Civic engagement refers to the level of commitment of citizens to their communities and is reflected by their involvement in community affairs. Typically, this is measured by membership in civic-related and other associations and groups that bring members of a community together around shared interests. Following Putnam (1993a,b, 1995), we used weighted data from the general social survey (GSS), conducted by the National Opinion Research Center (Davis and Smith), to estimate state variations in group membership and levels of social trust. The GSS is a national survey that samples noninstitutionalized English-speaking persons 18 years or older living in the United States. The survey has been repeated 14 times over the last two decades, and has included a set of questions on social trust and organizational membership. In the present study, we averaged 5 years of cumulated data (1986–1990) from the GSS, representing 7,679 individual observations from 39 states.

Level of civic engagement was measured by the per capita number of groups and associations (e.g., church groups, labor unions, sport groups, professional or academic societies, school groups, political groups, and fraternal organizations) that residents belonged to in each state. The other component of social capital, trust in others, was assessed from responses to two GSS items that asked: "Do you think most people would try to take advantage of you if they got a chance, or would they try to be fair?" and "Generally speaking, would you say that most people can be trusted or that you can't be too careful in dealing with people?" For each state, we calculated the percentage of respondents who agreed with the first part of the above statements. Belief in the goodwill and benign intent of others facilitates collective action and mutual cooperation, and therefore adds to the stock of a community's social capital. Collective action, in turn, further reinforces community norms of reciprocity. In addition to the social trust items, we evaluated the response to another item on the GSS as a marker of social capital: "Would you say that most of the time people try to be helpful, or are they mostly looking out for themselves?"

The GSS was designed to provide a national and census region representative population sample, and as such, responses to the GSS are not necessarily representative of a state's population. To correct for this potential bias when disaggregating to the state level, we used post-stratification weights (as per Dr. Smith: personal communication) to adjust for the extent to which GSS respondents in a given state were over/under represented. To accomplish this, we developed post-stratification weights based on the distribution of age, race, and educational attainment of GSS respondents. The stratum-specific weights were calculated as follows:

$$w_{i,j,k,l} = P_{i,j,k,l}/p_{i,j,k,l}$$

where $w_{i,j,k,l}$ is the post-stratification weight for the GSS respondent residing in the i-th state, and being of j-th age-group, k-th race, and l-th level of educational attainment; $P_{i,j,k,l}$ is the proportion of individuals with these characteristics residing in the i-th state, obtained from the 1990 U.S. Census; and $p_{i,j,k,l}$ is the corresponding proportion of such respondents in the GSS.

These weights were then used to adjust the individual responses to the social capital items in the GSS, using the *weight* procedure in SAS. For example, in states where the GSS over-sampled younger, black, and less educated respondents, the levels of social trust were adjusted upwards. In all of the subsequent analyses, we used the weighted responses.

Firearm homicide and violent crime

Age-adjusted overall and race-specific homicide rates attributable to firearms (ICD 9th revision codes E965.0–E965.4) were obtained for each state from the Compressed Mortality Files compiled by the National Center for Health Statistics, Centers for Disease Control and Prevention (CDC). Data for years 1987–1991 were combined to provide more stable estimates of the firearm homicide rates. The firearm homicide rates were directly age-standardized to the U.S. population, and are expressed as the number of deaths per 100 000 population.

In addition to age-adjusted firearm homicide rates, firearm assault and firearm robbery incidence rates were calculated by combining data from the Federal Bureau of Investigation's Uniform Crime Reports (UCR) for the years 1991–1994 (these years were used instead of 1987–91 as the FBI only began collecting these data in 1991) (Federal Bureau of Investigation, 1991–1994). These rates are based on the number of *incidents* involving assaults or robberies with a firearm reported to

police, and subsequently to the FBI through the crime reporting program. Incidence data, while subject to various biases due to factors that influence reporting, is considered less susceptible to bias compared to arrest data (Reiss and Roth, 1993). The rates were calculated by summing the number of incidents for each state across the four years and dividing by the sum of the estimated total population for each state across the same four years. We used the state population data that is provided along with the incidence data in the UCR. Unlike the firearm homicide rates, these incidence rates could not be adjusted for age as this information was not available in the UCR. Nor could the data be disaggregated by race, so that rates represent crude overall firearm assault and robbery incidence rates.

Firearm availability

As state-specific measures of gun ownership are not available, we used the fraction of *successful* suicides completed with a firearm as a surrogate for gun availability. This measure is the best currently available and has been used in numerous studies as a proxy for firearm availability (Cook, 1978; Lester, 1989, 1991). Suicide data were also obtained from the Compressed Mortality Files by combining years 1987–1991 (ICD-9 codes E955.0–E955.4; E950–E959).

Data analysis

All analyses were conducted using Pearson's correlation and ordinary least squares (OLS) regression with variables in their nontransformed state. Due to problems of collinearity, the Robin Hood Index and social capital measures were not included in the same model. Instead, separate models were used to test for their effects on firearm violent crime. For each of these models we ran two separate regressions. In the first, we simply regressed each univariate predictor (group membership, social trust, RHI) on each of the measures of firearm violent crime (age-adjusted firearm homicide, firearm assault, firearm robbery). In the second set of regressions we examined the effects of each of the predictors adjusting for the effects of poverty and firearm availability (percentage of suicides completed with a firearm). To model the joint effects of income inequality (RHI) and social capital (as measured by social trust), we conducted a path analysis to decompose their relationship to the age-adjusted firearm homicide rate into direct and indirect effects (Pedhazur, 1973; Alwin and Hauser, 1975).

10

B. P. Kennedy *et al.*

RESULTS

Relationship between income inequality and firearm violent crime

There was substantial variation in the degree of income inequality among the states. The overall RHI for the U.S. was 30.22%. New Hampshire (RHI = 27.13%) had the least income inequality and Louisiana (RHI = 34.05%) the greatest (Fig. 1). In the univariate regression analyses, RHI was significantly related to both the age-adjusted overall homicide (adjusted $R^2 = 0.54$) and age-adjusted firearm homicide (adjusted $R^2 = 0.56$) rates

(Table 1). RHI was also significantly related to firearm assault (adjusted $R^2 = 0.36$) and robbery (adjusted $R^2 = 0.23$) rates, although these relationships were not as strong (Table 1). The association of RHI to all of the firearm violent crime variables remained highly statistically significant after adjusting for poverty and firearm availability in the multivariate regression analyses: a one unit change in the RHI, which is the equivalent to transferring a one percent share of total income from the wealthy to the less wealthy, was associated with a change in the age-adjusted firearm homicide rate of 1.55 per 100 000 (95% confidence interval [CI]: 1.12 to 1.99)

Fig. 1(a).

(Table 2). This association was stronger for whites (adjusted $R^2 = 0.55$, $p < 0.0001$) than for blacks (adjusted $R^2 = 0.20$, $p < 0.0006$) in the univariate regression. RHI continued to be a statistically significant predictor of age-adjusted firearm homicide rates after adjusting for poverty and firearm availability among both whites ($B = 0.69$; 95% CI: 0.45 to 0.92; $p < 0.0001$) and blacks ($B = 4.82$; 95% CI: 2.57 to 7.07; $p < 0.0001$).

To further determine the robustness of this relationship, we also examined the effects of RHI after adjusting for state variations in median household income, per capita income, and percentage of the population living in urban areas. None of these variables changed the association of the Robin Hood Index with firearm violent crime (data not shown).

Relationships among social capital variables and firearm violent crime

All of the social capital measures were highly correlated with each other and with the violent crime measures (Table 3). Higher levels of social mistrust were associated with higher levels of firearm violent crime, while higher per capita group membership was associated with lower levels of firearm violent

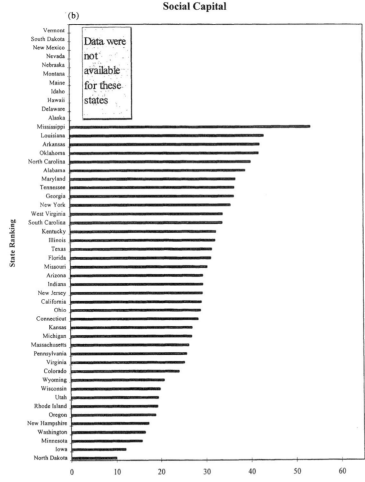

Fig. 1(b).

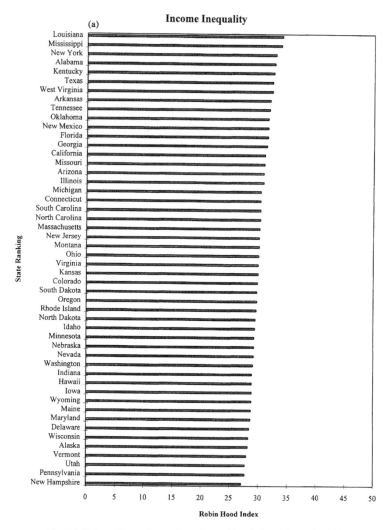

Fig. 1(c). State rankings on income inequality, social capital, and firearm homicide

crime. Social trust (percentage of people who agreed that "most people would try to take advantage of you if they got a chance") was more strongly associated with firearm homicide rates (adjusted $R^2 = 0.68$) than per capita group membership (adjusted $R^2 = 0.23$) (Table 4). These relationships remained statistically significant after adjusting for poverty and firearm availability (Table 5). A one unit change in social trust (percentage of people who agreed that "most people would try to take advantage of you if they got a chance") was associated with a change in the age-adjusted firearm

Table 1. Effects of income inequality on overall homicide and firearm homicide, assault, and robbery rates (50 states)

Violent crime rates	Years	B	S.e.	Adjusted R^2	$F_{1,48}$	$p<$
Overall homicide	1987–91	1.77	0.23	0.54	57.94	0.0001
Age-adjusted firearm homicide	1987–91	1.31	0.16	0.56	64.63	0.0001
Firearm assault	1991–94	28.56	5.30	0.36	28.08	0.0001
Firearm robbery	1991–94	23.75	6.04	0.23	15.47	0.0002

Social capital and firearm violent crime 13

Table 2. Effects of income inequality on overall homicide and firearm homicide, assault, and robbery rates, adjusted for poverty and firearm availability (50 states)

Violent crime rates	B	S.e.	$t, p <$	Adjusted R^2	$F_{3,46}$	$p <$
Age-adjusted homicide	2.04	0.33	6.11, 0.0001	0.56	21.80	0.0001
Age-adjusted firearm homicide	1.55	0.22	6.92, 0.0001	0.62	27.67	0.0001
Firearm assault	30.82	7.95	3.88, 0.0001	0.35	9.94	0.0001
Firearm robbery	40.22	8.45	4.76, 0.0001	0.30	8.08	0.0002

Table 3. Correlations among indicators of social capital, income inequality, and firearm violent crime (39 states)

		1	2	3	4	5	6	7	8	9
1	age-adjusted homicide									
2	age-adjusted firearm homicide	0.99*								
3	firearm assault	0.61*								
4	firearm robbery	0.57*	0.56*	0.53*						
5	firearm suicide	0.41*	0.48*	0.50*	0.45*					
6	income inequality	0.73*	0.76*	0.48*	0.31*	0.43*				
7	group membership	−0.51*	−0.49*	−0.34*	−0.33*	−0.05	−0.40*			
8	trust 1[a]	0.82*	0.83*	0.55*	0.52*	0.49*	0.73*	−0.54*		
9	trust 2[b]	0.72*	0.73*	0.34*	0.46*	0.44*	0.71*	−0.65*	0.79*	
10	helpfulness[c]	0.72*	0.75*	0.60*	0.54*	0.51*	0.71*	−0.54*	0.81*	0.78*

*$p < 0.05$.
[a]Percent responding: "most people would try to take advantage of you if they got the chance".
[b]Percent responding: "you can't be too careful in dealing with people".

Table 4. Effects of social capital on overall homicide and firearm homicide, assault, and robbery rates (39 states)

Violent crime rates	Years	B	S.e.	Adjusted R^2	$F_{1,37}$	$p <$
Social trust: Percentage of respondents who agreed that "most people would try to take advantage of you if they got a chance".						
Overall homicide	1987–91	0.41	0.05	0.66	75.42	0.0001
Age-adjusted		0.30	0.03	0.68	80.39	0.0001
firearm homicide	1987–91					
Firearm assault	1991–94	6.17	1.28	0.37	23.27	0.0001
Firearm robbery	1991–94	5.72	1.35	0.31	17.99	0.0001
Per capita group membership						
Overall homicide	1987–91	−5.06	1.37	0.25	13.67	0.0007
Age-adjusted		−3.49	1.03	0.23	11.59	0.002
firearm homicide	1987–91					
Firearm assault	1991–94	−65.39	29.89	0.09	4.79	0.035
Firearm robbery	1991–94	−72.10	29.75	0.11	5.87	0.02

homicide rate of 0.27 (95% CI: 0.24 to 0.36) per 100 000 which is equivalent to about a 5% change in the age-adjusted firearm homicide rate. For per capita group membership, a one unit change in group membership was associated with a change in age-adjusted firearm homicide rates of 3.00 (95% CI: 1.22 to 4.78) per 100 000. As with the RHI, the social trust variable explained more of the between-state variance in age-adjusted firearm homicide rates among whites (adjusted $R^2 = 0.53$, $p < 0.0001$)

than among blacks (adjusted $R^2 = 0.21$, $p < 0.002$). These effects persisted after adjusting for poverty and firearm availability: $B = 0.10$ (95% CI: 0.05 to 0.15; $p < 0.0001$) and $B = 0.63$ (95% CI: 0.23 to 1.04; $p < 0.003$) respectively. The results were similar for per capita group membership (data not shown).

We also examined the relationships of the other social trust item (percentage of respondents who agreed that "most people can be trusted") and the

Table 5. Effects of social capital on overall homicide and firearm homicide, assault, and robbery rates, adjusted for poverty and firearm availability (39 states)

Violent crime rates	B	S.e.	$t, p <$	Adjusted R^2	$F_{3,35}$	$p <$
Social trust: Percentage of respondents who agreed that "most people would try to take advantage of you if they got a chance".						
Age-adjusted homicide	0.38	0.05	6.79, 0.0001	0.67	26.65	0.0001
Age-adjusted firearm homicide	0.27	0.04	6.85, 0.0001	0.69	28.69	0.0001
Firearm assault	5.52	1.53	3.59, 0.0009	0.35	7.83	0.0004
Firearm robbery	7.37	1.51	4.85, 0.0001	0.37	8.59	0.0002
Per capita group membership						
Age-adjusted homicide	−4.39	1.21	−3.63, 0.0009	0.44	11.09	0.0001
Age-adjusted firearm homicide	−3.00	0.88	−3.39, 0.002	0.45	11.22	0.0001
Firearm assault	−54.68	28.87	−1.89, 0.066	0.19	4.03	0.014
Firearm robbery	−67.34	31.14	−2.16, 0.037	0.08	2.05	0.124

perceived helpfulness item (percentage of respondents who agreed that "most of the time people try to be helpful") to the firearm violent crime variables. The effects of both these variables on age-adjusted firearm homicide rates were essentially identical to the social trust variable discussed above: adjusted $R^2 = 0.54$ ($F_{1,37} = 42.95$, $p < 0.0001$) and adjusted $R^2 = 0.56$ ($F_{1,37} = 46.45$, $p < 0.0001$) respectively.

Relationships among inequality, social capital, and age-adjusted firearm homicide: Path analysis

State-level variations in income inequality (RHI) were strongly associated with lack of social trust: states with high inequality also had more respondents who agreed that "most people would try to take advantage of you if they got a chance" ($r = 0.73$, $p < 0.0001$). The other social capital measure, per capita group membership, was inversely related to the Robin Hood Index: states with low inequality had high per capita group membership ($r = -0.40$, $p < 0.003$).

The path analysis indicated that the effect of income inequality (as measured by the Robin Hood Index) on age-adjusted firearm homicide is mediated in part by social capital (as measured by level of social trust). According to our model, income inequality exerts a large indirect effect on age-adjusted firearm homicide through the social capital variable (Fig. 2). In Fig. 2, as income inequality increases so does the level of social mistrust which is in turn associated with increased age-adjusted firearm homicide rates.

DISCUSSION

The dominant current in the violence literature has sought to identify the individual factors that

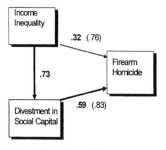

Fig. 2. Path coefficients for the effects of income inequality and social capital on age-adjusted firearm homicide rates (39 states). Note: zero-order correlations are in parentheses, path coefficients are bold. Inequality is measured by the Robin Hood Index and social capital is measured by the percentage of respondents who agree that "most people would try to take advantage of you if they got a chance"

distinguish violent offenders from nonoffenders, whereas the purpose of the present study was to ask what societal characteristics — including income inequality, poverty, and social capital — predict differential rates of homicide and violent crime. More than half a century ago, Shaw and McKay (1942) argued in their classic work, *Juvenile Delinquency and Urban Areas*, that crime could be linked to broad social forces such as socioeconomic deprivation. Shaw and McKay demonstrated that in socioeconomically depressed areas in 21 U.S. cities, high rates of crime persisted over several decades despite changes in the racial and ethnic composition of the communities. The authors thereby rejected individualistic explanations of crime and focused instead on the processes by which criminal patterns of behavior were apparently transmitted across generations in areas of social disorganization and weak social controls.

Following the path breaking work of Shaw and McKay (1942), a number of studies throughout the 1970s and 1980s have investigated the relationships of poverty and income inequality to violent crime, using cross-sectional, aggregate data at the national or subnational level (e.g., states, census tracts, cities, and standard metropolitan statistical areas [SMSAs]). Hsieh and Pugh (1993) have provided a meta-analysis of the 34 aggregate data studies that had been published on poverty, income inequality, and violent crime. Despite differences in methodology, the vast majority of studies agree that violent crime is related to poverty (pooled $r = 0.44$), as well as to income inequality (pooled $r = 0.44$). Interestingly, the effects of poverty were more homogeneous across the studies using lower levels of aggregation (e.g., cities). The converse was true for income inequality, which yielded more homogeneous effect sizes across studies using state and national levels of aggregation. This may be accounted for by the differences in how the two variables effect violent crime rates: income inequality, as a measure of *relative* deprivation, captures the effect of the individual's relationship to the larger society, whereas poverty, as a measure of *absolute* deprivation, captures the effect of resource deprivation on individuals. This is consistent with Richard Wilkinson's view that at lower levels of aggregation individual, or absolute income will matter more to health than income inequality — it is only within larger geographic areas that the social heterogeneity which is necessary for the effect of income inequality to occur that one finds a relationship between income inequality and health. As Wilkinson (1996) points out, it is not the inequality within Harlem that matters to its residents health, but rather the fact that so many are poor relative to the rest of the U.S..

Thus, there is growing consensus that societal-level variables such as material deprivation may be a cause of crime. However, much less empirical

Table 6. Data on derivation of Robin Hood Index (example: Massachusetts)

Decile of households	Percent of total income
1	1.08
2	2.48
3	4.13
4	5.74
5	7.33
6	8.97
7	10.83
8	13.09
9	16.41
10	29.93

work has been carried out to elucidate the pathways and mechanisms involved. According to one view, homicides and other violent crimes are explained as an individual's reaction to resource deprivation, subsequent personal frustration, and diffuse hostility directed against targets of opportunity (Messner, 1983; Crutchfield, 1989; Arthur, 1991). Another view is that residential segregation and the concentration of deprived groups in urban slums have given rise to subcultures that value toughness, excitement, and fatalism, and these subcultural values supposedly bring young people in conflict with the law (Blau and Blau, 1982). Our aim in the present study was to test yet a third hypothesis: that a pronounced and highly visible gap in the *distribution* of income (as distinct from the absolute standard of living) may give rise to social disorganization and low social cohesion, as indexed by the level of mutual distrust among members of society, as well as their propensity to associate with each other. In turn, we hypothesized that lack of social cohesion (or "social capital") would predict aggregate rates of homicide and violent crime.

Our findings suggest that income inequality is powerfully related to the incidence of homicide and violent crimes via the depletion of social capital. These findings hold even when controlling for poverty and access to firearms. A variety of sociological and criminological evidence supports these claims. In a pooled analysis of 20 years (1975–1994) of data from the General Social Surveys, involving over 29 000 respondents, Brehm and Rahn (1997) found that rising income inequality was a significant predictor of declining trust in others. In turn, a decline in social trust was predictive of diminished levels of group membership. According to the work of Wilson (1987, 1991), Anderson (1990) and others, a critical factor responsible for the high incidence of delinquency and crime in urban settings has been the loss of social buffers that normally exist in middle class neighborhoods. Such buffers consist of formal and informal networks of organizations (church groups, business groups, neighborhood associations), as well as the presence of social norms concerning work and education. These buf-

fers have become depleted in inner-city areas as a result of the increasing residential segregation of the poor. Conversely, a youth living in a neighborhood that includes a mixture of working and professional families "may observe increasing joblessness and idleness but he will also witness many individuals going to and from work... he may be cognizant of an increase in crime, but he can recognize that many residents in his neighborhood are not involved in criminal activity", (Wilson, 1987, p. 56).

While the work of Wilson (1987, 1991) and others refers to the situation of inner-city African–Americans, our data suggest that the relationships of income inequality and social capital to firearm violent crime holds equally for whites as well. Furthermore, these effects remain stable when controlling for poverty and the percentage of the population living in urban areas suggesting that income inequality, through its erosion of social capital, may have a broader social impact that extends beyond specific groups in high-risk urban settings. While our data are based upon analysis of aggregate data, the "ecological fallacy" — inferring individual relations based on grouped data — is not an issue here, since we have not made any cross-level inferences (Susser, 1994a,b). Our analyses have used purely ecologic variables (social capital, income inequality, prevalence of poverty) to predict purely ecological outcomes (population rates of firearm homicide and violent crime) and as such, do not provide the means for making predictions about individual behavior, yet can provide powerful indicators of macrosocial determinants of violent behavior (Schwartz, 1994; Susser, 1994a,b).

CONCLUSION

In his review of poverty and inequality and their relationship to crime, Braithwaite (1979) concluded that programs that simply targeted groups living in poverty would not have a significant impact on the overall crime rates in society. In contrast, he argued "that gross economic measures to reduce the gap between the rich and the poor and the rest of the population" (pp. 231) are necessary if a significant reduction in crime is to be expected.

This view runs against the conventional violence prevention wisdom which usually *only* targets high risk individuals and groups rather than attempting to shift the underlying societal forces that give rise to a high incidence of violence in the population. This is not to say that the effects of poverty on violent crime are negligible (firearm homicide, $r = 0.49$), and we would certainly not argue against policies to reduce the burden on families living in impoverished settings. Nor would we argue that policies that restrict access to firearms be neglected as one of the means to reduce violent deaths. The proxy for access to firearms was highly correlated with firearm homicide ($r = 0.44$) indicating that it is also a powerful determinant of firearm homicide as has been shown in other studies rates (Cook, 1991; McDowell *et al.*, 1992; Kellermann *et al.*, 1993). However, the profound effects of income inequality and social capital on firearm violent crime when controlling for both of these factors, indicate that policies and interventions that address these broader, macro-social forces warrant serious consideration.

Acknowledgements—Kawachi and Kennedy are recipients of the Robert Wood Johnson Foundation Investigator Awards in Health Policy Research.

REFERENCES

Alwin, D. F. and Hauser, R. M. (1975) The decomposition of effects in path analysis. *American Sociological Review* **40**, 37–47.

Anderson, E. (1990) *Street Wise*. University of Chicago Press, Chicago, IL.

Arthur, J. A. (1991) Socioeconomic predictors of crime in rural Georgia. *Criminal Justice Review* **16**, 29–41.

Atkinson, A. B., Micklewright, J. (1992) *Economic transformation in Eastern Europe and the distribution of income.* Cambridge University Press.

Baily, W. C. (1984) Poverty, inequality, and city homicide rates: Some not so unexpected findings. *Criminology* **22**, 531–550.

Blau, J. R. and Blau, P. M. (1982) The cost of inequality. Metropolitan structure and violent crime. *American Sociological Review* **47**, 114–129.

Blau, J. R. and Blau, P. M. (1986) The cost of inequality: Metropolitan structure and criminal violence. *Sociological Quarterly* **27**, 15–26.

Brehm, J. and Rahn, W. (1997) Individual-level evidence for the causes and consequences of social capital. *American Journal of Political Science* **41**, 999–1023.

Braithwaite, J. (1979) *Inequality, Crime and Public Policy.* Routledge and K. Paul, Boston.

Coleman, J. S. (1990) *The Foundations of Social Theory.* Harvard University Press, Cambridge, MA, pp. 300–321.

Cook, P. J. (1978) The effect of gun availability on robbery and robbery murder: A cross-section study of fifty cities. *Policy Studies Review Annual* **2**, 743–781.

Cook, P. J. (1991) The technology of personal violence: A review of the evidence concerning the importance of gun availability and use in violent crime, self defense, and suicide. *Crime and Justice: A Review of Research*, ed. M. Tonry, 14, pp. 1–71. University of Chicago Press, Chicago, IL.

Crutchfield, R. D. (1989) Labor stratification and violent crime. *Social Forces* **68**, 489–512.

Davis, J. A., Smith, T. W. *General Social Survey Cumulative File.* University of Michigan, Interuniversity Consortium and Social Research, Ann Arbor, MI.

Federal Bureau of Investigation (1991–1994) *Uniform Crime Reports.*

Fingerhut, L. A., Ingram, D. D. and Feldman, J. J. (1992) Firearm and nonfirearm homicide among persons 15 through 19 years of age. *JAMA* **267**, 3048–3053.

Hammett, M., Powell, K. E., O'Carroll, P. W. and Clanton, S. T. (1992) Homicide surveillance – United States, 1979–1988. *Morbidity and Mortality Weekly Report* **41**, 1–33.

Hsieh, C. C. and Pugh, M. D. (1993) Poverty, income inequality, and violent crime: A meta-analysis of recent aggregate data studies. *Criminal Justice Review* **18**, 182–202.

Kellermann, A. L., Rivera, F. P. and Rushforth, N. B. *et al.* (1993) Gun ownership as a risk factor for homicide in the home. *New England Journal of Medicine* **329**, 1084–1091.

Kennedy, B. P., Kawachi, I. and Prothrow-Stith, D. (1996) Income distribution and mortality: Test of the Robin Hood Index in the United States. *British Medical Journal* **312**, 1004–1007.

Krahn, H., Hartnagel, T. F. and Gartrell, J. W. (1986) Income inequality and homicide rates: Cross-national data and criminological theories. *Criminology* **24**, 269–295.

Land, K., McCall, P. and Cohen, L. (1990) Structural covariates of homicide rates: Are there any invariances across time and space? *American Journal of Sociology* **95**, 922–963.

Lester, D. (1989) Gun ownership and suicide in the United States. *Psychological Medicine* **19**, 519–521.

Lester, D. (1991) Crime as opportunity: A test of the hypothesis with European homicide rates. *British Journal of Criminology* **31**(2), 186–188.

McDowell, D., Loftin, C. and Wiersema, B. (1992) A comparative study of the preventive effects of mandatory sentencing laws for handgun crimes. *Journal of Criminal Law and Criminology* **83**, 378–394.

Messner, S. F. (1983) Regional differences in the economic correlates of the urban homicide rate. Some evidence on the importance of cultural context. *Criminology* **21**, 477–488.

Messner, S. F. (1989) Economic discrimination and societal homicide rates: Further evidence on the cost of inequality. *American Sociological Review* **54**, 597–611.

Pedhazur, E. J. (1973) *Multiple Regression in Behavioral Research.* Holt, Rinehart and Winston, New York.

Putnam, R. D. (1993a) The prosperous community. Social capital and economic growth. *The American Prospect* Spring, 35–42.

Putnam, R. D. (1993b) *Making Democracy Work.* Princeton University Press, Princeton, NJ.

Putnam, R. D. (1995) Bowling alone. America's declining social capital. *Journal of Democracy* **6**, 65–78.

Reiss, A. J., Roth, J. A., eds. (1993) National Research Council. *Understanding and Preventing Violence.* National Academy Press, Washington, DC.

Rice, D. P., MacKenzie, E. J. and Associates (1989) *Cost of Injury in the United States: A Report to Congress.* Intitute for Health and Aging, USC and Injury Prevention Center, The Johns Hopkins University, San Francisco, CA.

Sampson, R. J., Wilson, W. J. (1995) Toward a theory of race, crime, and urban inequality. In *Crime and Inequality*, eds. J. Hagan and R. D. Peterson. Stanford University Press, Stanford, CA.

Schwartz, S. (1994) The fallacy of the ecologic fallacy: The potential misuse of a concept and the consequences. *Am. J. Public Health* **84**, 819–824.

Shaw, C., McKay, H. (1942) *Juvenile Delinquency and Urban Areas.* University of Chicago Press, Chicago.

Susser, M. (1994a) The logic in ecological: II. The logic of design. *Am. J. Public Health* **84**, 830–835.

Susser, M. (1994b) The logic in ecological: I. The logic of analysis. *Am. J. Public Health* **84**, 825–829.

U.S. Bureau of Census (1993) Income and Poverty (CD-ROM).

Welniak, E. (1988) Unpublished software. U.S. Census Bureau.

Wilkinson, R. G. (1996) Income inequality and social cohesion. *American Journal of Public Health* **87**, 104–106.

Wilson, W. J. (1987) *The Truly Disadvantaged: The Inner City, the Underclass, and Public Policy.* University of Chicago Press, Chicago, IL.

Wilson, W. J. (1991) Studying inner-city social dislocations: The challenge of public agenda research. *American Sociological Review* **56**, 1–14.

APPENDIX

Table 6 shows the shares of income earned by each decile of household in Massachusetts in 1990. For example, the bottom 10% of households accounted for 1.08% of the total income in that state. If income were distributed perfectly equally, then each decile of household would account for exactly 10% of the share of total income. In the example of Massachusetts, households at or above the 70th percentile earned more than their "fair share" of total income.

The Robin Hood Index (RHI) is calculated by summing the excesses above the fair share of total income (i.e., > 10%) earned by each decile of households. In the case of Massachusetts,

$$RHI = (10.83 - 10.0) + (13.09 - 10.0)$$
$$+ (16.41 - 10.0) + (29.93 - 10.0)$$
$$= 0.83 + 3.09 + 6.41 + 19.93 = 30.26\%.$$

The Index is equivalent to the approximate proportion of aggregate income that must be redistributed from households above the mean, and transferred to those below the mean in order to achieve perfect equality in the distribution of household incomes.

[21]

National Case-Control Study of Homicide Offending and Gun Ownership*

GARY KLECK, *The Florida State University*

MICHAEL HOGAN, *University of Northern Colorado*

Does gun ownership increase the likelihood that a person will commit a homicide? Findings from a recent case-control study (Kellermann et al. 1993) were interpreted as indicating that persons who lived in households with guns were 2.7 times as likely to become homicide victims as persons in households without guns. Problems with that study are identified, and a different approach is described. Survey data on a nationally representative sample of persons in prison for criminal homicide were compared with data on a nationally representative sample of the general population, in the first national case-control study of homicide. A logistic regression analysis was performed on the data, with the dependent variable measuring whether the subject was a killer, and the key independent variable being whether the person owned a gun. Control variables included age, sex, race, Hispanic ethnicity, income, education, marital status, region, veteran status, and whether the subject had children. Results indicated that gun ownership had a weak (odds ratio = 1.36) and unstable relationship with homicidal behavior, which was at least partly spurious. The promise and pitfalls of case-control research are discussed.

The impact of gun availability and use on violence is the subject of intense debate among scholars, policymakers, and the general public. In 1993, about 39,600 people died of gunshot wounds, 19,000 of them in homicides, and offenders armed with guns committed about one million violent crimes. There are over 230 million guns in private hands, about half of U.S. households have at least one gun, and perhaps 2.5 million times a year a crime victim uses a gun for self-protection (Kleck 1997a; Kleck and Gertz 1995). Although both offenders and victims use guns in a large number of violent crimes, it is in dispute just how, or whether, guns influence the frequency and outcomes of violent crimes.

One of the most highly publicized studies of the guns-violence link in recent years was a case-control study of homicide victimization by Arthur Kellermann and his colleagues (1993) published in the prestigious *New England Journal of Medicine*. This frequently cited study concluded that gun possession increased the risk of homicide victimization by a factor of 2.8. This paper is designed to assess the credibility of this conclusion and to offer an improved estimate of the impact of gun ownership on homicidal violence.

Theory and Weapon Effects on Violence

Mainstream social science and criminological theory aims at explaining only certain aspects of crime-related phenomena, focusing heavily on why some individuals are more likely to engage in criminal, delinquent, or deviant behavior than others (e.g., see reviews in Akers 1994; Vold, Bernard and Snipes 1998). It has traditionally had little to say about what

* An earlier version of this paper was presented on November 21, 1996, at the annual meetings of the American Society of Criminology in Chicago, Illinois. The authors would like to thank one of the anonymous referees for her/his helpful suggestions. Direct correspondence to: Gary Kleck, School of Criminology and Criminal Justice, The Florida State University, Tallahassee, Florida 32306-2170. E-Mail: gkleck@mailer.fsu.edu

might affect the outcomes of individual criminal incidents, and thus why some encounters between criminals and their victims have very serious consequences for victims while other encounters do not.

For example, it would seem to be an important scientific goal, as well as an issue relevant to public policy, to discover why some victims of violence die, while others suffer nonfatal injuries, others are attacked but not injured, and still others are threatened but not actually attacked. But because mainstream theories of criminal behavior and deviance rarely address themselves to this sort of incident-oriented question, the task of trying to answer such questions has mostly fallen to empirical researchers who develop new theory on a fairly ad hoc basis to explain and organize their empirical findings.

More specifically relevant to the present paper, one would like theory to address the general question: "Why and how would gun ownership affect the likelihood of a person taking the life of another human being?" Part of the problem of answering this question has been that some people think the answer is already self-evident: guns are more lethal than other weapons that could be substituted for them. The following discussion (adapted from Kleck 1997a) is intended to provide a somewhat broader consideration of the potential effects of weaponry on interpersonal violence.

Guns and Power

The power that weaponry confers has been conventionally treated as exclusively violence-enhancing—it is commonly assumed that the use and possession of weapons serve only to increase the likelihood of the victim's injury and death (e.g., Zimring 1968, 1972). This is an unduly restrictive view of weaponry's significance. A broader perspective starts by recognizing weapons as sources of power, used instrumentally to achieve goals by inducing compliance with the user's demands. The ultimate goal behind an act of violence is not necessarily the victim's death or injury, but rather may be the acquisition of money, sexual gratification, respect, attention, or the humiliation and domination of the victim. Power can be, and usually is, wielded so as to obtain these things without inflicting injury. Threats, implied or overt, usually suffice and are often preferred to physical attack. Inflicting injury may even be an indication that the preferred mode of exercising power failed.

Weapon Effects on the Likelihood of Attacking an Adversary

It has long been argued that firearms give some people the courage to attempt aggressive acts that they would otherwise be afraid to attempt. In particular, a weapon may be especially important in facilitating attacks by weaker aggressors against stronger victims. Further, unlike other common personal weapons, guns permit effective attack from a great distance, although few assaults occur at ranges longer than the length of the average living room (Kellermann et al. 1996:1441).

Nevertheless, for some attackers, maintaining a distance of just a few feet or even inches from their victim may be essential to carrying out an attack. It has been hypothesized that guns may facilitate attack by persons too timid or squeamish to come into physical contact with their victims or to use messier methods to injure them (Wolfgang 1958:79). Some prospective attackers may be psychologically incapable of doing something as distasteful and ugly as plunging a knife into another person's chest cavity or bashing a victim's skull with a blunt instrument, yet capable of shooting their victims. Guns provide a more impersonal, emotionally remote, and even antiseptic way of attacking others, and could allow some attackers to bypass their inhibitions against close contact with their victims.

Possession of guns may also create a "triggering" effect on the likelihood that the weapon possessor attacks an adversary. Experimental psychologists Berkowitz and LePage (1967) proposed the "weapons effect" hypothesis, which stated that the sight of a weapon could trigger aggression from angered persons, due to the learned association between weapons and aggressive behavior.

On the other hand, weapon possession may also have aggression-inhibiting effects. In an early study of victim survey data from eight cities, Hindelang (1976:263) concluded that "when a gun is involved in a victimization, both the victim and the offender appear to be more restrained and interested in avoiding an attack with the weapon." At least twenty studies have consistently confirmed that criminal aggressors armed with guns are *less* likely to attack and injure (rather than merely threaten) their victims than aggressors without guns (reviewed in Kleck 1997a:225–226).

Thus, not only does the victim's defensive use of a gun inhibit aggressor attacks (Kleck 1997a:171–174), but even the aggressor's possession of a gun may inhibit their own aggression, as well as that of the victim. In many assaults, the aggressor not only lacks an intent to kill, but specifically wants to avoid killing the victim. Instead, they may want only to frighten or to hurt without killing. Possession of a lethal weapon gives such an assaulter more killing power than she/he needs or wants, and to attack would risk inflicting more harm than the assaulter wanted. The possession of deadly weapons raises the stakes into what may seem to be an all-or-nothing situation—kill or do not attack at all. Given that the intentions of assaulters, as a group, cluster predominantly at the less deadly end of the continuum, one common effect of aggressor possession of guns and other deadly weapons could therefore be inhibition of attack behavior.

There is another possible explanation for the lower injury rates in incidents where offenders are armed with guns. A deadly weapon empowers its possessor to terrify, coerce compliance with demands, deter another's aggression, nonfatally injure, or kill, and power increases the likelihood its user will get what he/she wants, whatever that may be. If most assaulters do not want to kill, then a lethal weapon enables its user to achieve the other goals. In robberies, the offender's use of a gun ensures compliance with the demands for money and deters the victim from resisting by convincing the victim that the robber has the capacity to inflict death or serious injury (Luckenbill 1982). Without a gun, it would often be impossible for the robber to achieve this without actually attacking the victim. Threat with a gun can thereby serve as a substitute for actual attack, rather than its vehicle, and possession of a gun can make a physical attack unnecessary.

This pattern need not be limited to acquisitive crime such as robbery. Aggressors in ordinary anger-instigated assaults have their own peculiar goals whose attainment can, if they have a weapon, be achieved without attacking. Those who want to frighten, humiliate, or dominate their victims can do so by merely pointing a gun, without firing it. On the other hand, without a gun, nothing short of attack may suffice. The same qualities of weapons that make them dangerous if used to attack can preclude the need to actually do so.

A combatant may also regain a favorable situational identity by using a weapon to control others and compel their unwilling obedience. They can demonstrate to their victim, to themselves, and to any bystanders that they cannot be pushed around, and that they must be granted respect, or at least fear. The weapon can place its possessor into a superordinate position in situations in which this might otherwise be impossible to achieve without an actual attack.

One combatant's use of a lethal weapon may also give the opponent a socially acceptable excuse for not retaliating for an insult or other challenge to her/his self-image: "only a fool attacks someone with a gun." The failure to retaliate, which might otherwise be regarded by witnesses as evidence of cowardice, is instead viewed as mere prudence in the face of greatly unequal power. The extreme imbalance of power can thus prevent an escalation to physical violence by exacting from the weaker opponent some gesture of deference or an exit from the scene.

Weapon Effects on the Likelihood of Injury

If an attack does occur, it may or may not result in injury. The attributes of weapons that can facilitate attack may also reduce the attack completion rate by encouraging attacks at a longer range, against more formidable opponents or under more difficult conditions. It is possible to shoot a victim from a great distance, but the rate at which this is achieved is likely to be far lower than the rate at which thrown punches land. Concerning the more common close-range gun attacks, those unfamiliar with firearms marksmanship might assume that shooters are virtually certain to hit their target. This assumption is not born out by the real-life experiences of persons shooting under conditions of emotional stress.

Weapon Effects on the Likelihood of the Victim's Death

Probably less than 15 percent of gunshot woundings known to police result in death (Cook 1985). Assuming that only half of nonfatal woundings (but all fatal woundings) are reported or known to police, the true fatality rate would be somewhere under 8 percent (based on a doubling of nonfatal woundings). Nevertheless, gunshot wounds are more likely to result in death than those inflicted by a knife, the weapon generally assumed to be the next most lethal, among those that could be used in the same circumstances as guns.

Only some of the difference in death rates of attacks with different weapons is attributable to the technical properties of the weapons themselves. Part of the difference may be due to the greater "lethality" of the users of the more deadly weapons. When a gun is used in an attack, it is almost always the result of a choice, however hastily made, among weapon alternatives. It is a rare gun homicide that occurs where a knife or blunt instrument is not also available, and all gun killers also have hands and feet with which they could have attacked the victim.

Those with more lethal intentions, a greater willingness to hurt others, or a stronger instigation to aggress will tend to choose more serious weaponry, regardless of how vague their intentions are, or how impulsively, quickly, and even unconsciously these might be arrived at. Thus, weapon lethality and attacker lethality should be closely associated, and their effects can easily be confused with one another (Cook 1982:247–248). If the wounding fatality rate of guns is four times higher than that of knives when the attackers are not matched regarding their lethality, then this ratio would necessarily be less than 4–1, though probably higher than 1–1, if one could control for the greater lethality of attackers choosing guns.

Finally, it is possible that possession and defensive use of guns by prospective *victims* influence the likelihood of an attack occurring and thus the likelihood that fatal or nonfatal injury could occur. Some prospective attackers could be deterred from attempting an attack by the specific knowledge that a prospective target is armed or by the knowledge that many victims in general are armed or could be armed. Further, a victim's actual use of a gun could deter an attack or cause the aggressor to cut off the attack before inflicting serious or fatal injury (Kleck 1988; 1997a:171–174).

Previous Research

The effort to assess the effects of guns on violence has involved an extremely diverse array of methodological strategies that can be broadly divided into macro-level and micro-level categories (see Cook 1991; Kleck 1995; 1997a for reviews).

Macro-level Research

Some scholars have used macro-level approaches, examining gun ownership levels and violence rates as they covary across areas or over time (summarized in Table 1). Most of this

Table 1 • *Macro-Level Studies of the Impact of Gun Levels on Violent Crime Rates*[a]

Study	Sample	Modeled 2-way Relat.?	Measure of Gun Level[b]	Crime Rates[c]	Results[d]
Brearley (1932)	42 states	No	PGH	THR	Yes
Krug (1968)	50 states	No	HLR	ICR	No
Newton & Zimring (1969)	4 years, Detroit	No	NPP	THR,TRR, AAR,GHR	Yes
Seitz (1972)	50 states	No	GHR,FGA,AAR	THR	Yes
Murray (1975)	50 states	No	SGR,SHR	GHR,AAR,TRR	No
Fisher (1976)	9 years, Detroit	No	NPP,GRR,PGH	THR	Yes
Phillips et al. (1976)	18 years, U.S.	No	PROD	THR	Yes
Brill (1977)	11 cities	No	PGC	ICR	No
				THR	Yes
				TRR	No
Kleck (1979)	27 years, U.S.	Yes	PROD	THR	Yes
Cook (1979)	50 cities	No	PGH,PGS	TRR	No
				RMR	Yes
Kleck (1984)	32 years, U.S.	Yes	PROD	THR	No
		No		TRR	Yes
Magaddino & Medoff (1984)	31 years, U.S.	Yes[e]	PROD	THR	No
Lester (1985)	37 cities	No	PCS	VCR	No
Bordua (1986)	102 counties, 9 regions	No[f]	GLR,SIR	HAR,THR, GHR	No
McDowall (1986)	48 cities, 2 years[g]	Yes	PGH,PGS	TRR	No
Lester (1988)	9 regions	No	SGR	THR	Yes
McDowall (1991)	36 years, Detroit	Yes	PGS,PGR	THR	Yes
Killias (1993)	16 nations	No	SGR	THR,GHR	Yes
Kleck & Patterson (1993)	170 cities	Yes	[h]	THR,GHR, TRR,GHR, AAR,GAR	No

Notes:

[a] Table covers only studies and findings where the dependent variable was a crime rate, as opposed to the fraction of crimes committed with guns.

[b] Measures of Gun Level: FGA = Fatal gun accident rate; GLR = Gun owners license rate; GMR = Gun magazine subscription rates; GRR = Gun registrations rate; HLR = Hunting license rate; NPP = Number of handgun purchase permits; PGA = % aggravated assaults committed with guns; PGC = % homicides, aggravated assaults and robberies (combined together) committed with guns; PCS = same as PGC, but with suicides lumped in as well; PGH = % homicides committed with guns; PGR = % robberies committed with guns; PGS = % suicides committed with guns; PROD = Guns produced minus exports plus imports, U.S.; SGR = Survey measure, % households with gun(s); SHR = Survey measure, % households with handgun(s); SIR = Survey measure, % individuals with gun(s).

[c] Crime Rates: AAR = Aggravated assault rate; GAR = Gun aggravated assault rate; GHR = Gun homicide rate; HAR = Homicide, assault and robbery index factor score; ICR = Index crime rate; RMR = Robbery murder rate; THR = Total homicide rate; TRR = Total robbery rate; VCR = Violent crime rate.

[d] Yes = Study found significant positive association between gun levels and violence; No = Study did not find such a link.

[e] Authors modeled two-way relationship, finding no effect of guns (see column 2 of their Table 9-5), and also reported an effect of guns in a less appropriate model where this was not done (see Column 1 of their Table 9-5).

[f] A few gun-violence associations were positive and significant, but almost all involved female gun ownership or male long gun ownership. Bordua interpreted the pattern to indicate the effect of violence on gun ownership.

[g] Panel design, two waves.

[h] 5-item factor composed of PGS, PGH, PGR, PGA, and the percent of dollar value of stolen property due to stolen guns.

research is technically weak, using (1) small samples, with correspondingly unstable findings, (2) unvalidated and often invalid measures of gun availability, and (3) few or no controls for other violence-related factors whose effects could be confounded with those of gun availability.

More important still, most of these studies do not distinguish (1) the positive effects of violence rates on gun acquisition for defensive reasons from (2) the positive effects of gun availability on violence rates. A number of individual-level studies indicate that acquisition of handguns and other weapons for protection is directly or indirectly increased by residence in a high crime area (Kleck 1997b; Lizotte, Bordua and White 1981; Smith and Uchida 1988), and macro-level studies support the hypothesis that higher violence rates increase gun levels (Kleck 1979, 1984; Magaddino and Medoff 1984; McDowall 1986; Kleck and Patterson 1993). Almost all of the studies that did take account of this possible two-way relationship and that used validated measures of gun availability have found that while violence rates affect gun levels, levels of gun or handgun ownership have no net impact on violence rates, including homicide rates (Table 1; Kleck 1997a).

Individual-Level Research

At the individual level of analysis, psychologists have conducted experimental studies of the effects of weapons on artificial forms of "aggression" in the form of mild electric shocks and other noxious stimuli. The relevance of these studies to serious real-world violence is questionable, and the results are evenly divided between those finding aggression-instigating effects and those not. Most of the more realistic studies, however, fail to find any aggression-increasing effects (Kleck 1991:158–161, 205–206; Toch and Lizotte 1991).

Other scholars have studied individual incidents of violence, such as robbery or assault incidents, comparing those committed by gun-armed offenders with those committed by offenders without guns (e.g., Kleck and DeLone 1993; Kleck and McElrath 1991; Kleck and Sayles 1990; Zimring 1968, 1972). Over twenty such studies have consistently found that possession of guns by aggressors reduces the likelihood they will attack and injure their victims (instead using guns only to threaten), but increases the likelihood that any injury inflicted will be fatal (Kleck 1997a).

Other research on the effects of guns in the hands of victims and prospective victims consistently indicates that victims who use guns for self-protection are less likely to be injured or to lose their property than otherwise similar victims who either do not resist at all or resist without a gun (e.g., Cook 1991; Kleck 1988; Kleck and DeLone 1993; see others reviewed in Kleck 1997a:225–226). There is scholarly debate about how often guns are used for protective purposes; while some scholars stress the low estimates implied by the National Crime Victimization Surveys (NCVS [e.g., McDowall 1995]), at least fifteen surveys indicate far larger numbers of uses, ranging from 700,000 up to 3.5 million or more. As yet, no other survey has even approximately confirmed the low NCVS-derived estimates (Kleck 1997a:149–159, 187–189; Kleck and Gertz 1995).

Case-Control Research on Homicidal Behavior

Recently an old methodology has been newly applied to the issue of how gun possession might influence the incidence of homicide. Kellermann and his colleagues (1993) applied case-control methods comparing homicide victims with matched control subjects, to see whether gun ownership was more common in the victims' households than in those of the matched controls.

A case-control study is a retrospective comparison of (1) individuals possessing a given trait (the "cases"), often a relatively rare one (e.g., delinquency, violent behavior, or lung cancer) with (2) individuals lacking the trait (the "controls"). The purpose is to explore possible causes of the trait by comparing persons possessing the trait with those lacking the trait. The case-control design also commonly involves the rare trait being oversampled through the use of archival records or lists of known cases, which helps insure that the investigator has enough rare cases to compare with the more numerous persons lacking the trait (Goodman et al. 1988; Schlesselman 1982).

"Case-control study" is a fairly recent term for a research design that has been around for decades. By the 1920's, sociologists studying the causes of delinquent behavior were comparing caught delinquents, typically the inmates of juvenile institutions, with samples of the general adolescent population, typically students. These sociologists sometimes matched cases and controls with respect to possibly confounding factors (Lilienfeld and Lilienfeld 1979:10). In 1926, epidemiologists, possibly influenced by sociologists, also began to match cases and controls on confounding variables in studying diseases, a development that Schlesselman (1982:25) identified as the start of modern case-control research, though matching is not a defining element of the case-control design.

Arthur Kellermann and his colleagues (1993) applied this design to homicide victimization, looking for a link with household gun ownership. They obtained lists of persons killed in or near their homes in three urban counties and then located persons of the same sex, race, and approximate age living in the same neighborhood. After interviewing survivors of the homicide victims and the matched controls (or their proxies), they found that gun ownership was 2.7 times more common in the homicide victims' households, controlling for five other risk factors (1089). They concluded that guns kept in the home "pose a substantial threat to members of the household" and that therefore "people should be strongly discouraged from keeping guns in their homes" (1090). The conclusions were phrased in unambiguously causal terms and were not in any way qualified regarding subsets of the population to which they might apply.

This was an oddly indirect approach to the guns-homicide link since it has usually been assumed that if such a link existed it would be due to a given person's risk of homicide being raised by guns belonging to other people, mostly outside the person's household (only 7.2% of homicide victims in the U.S. in the years 1976–1992 were killed with guns by a family member, a roommate, or lover—analysis of Supplementary Homicide Reports—see Fox 1994). The narrow focus on gun ownership in the prospective victim's household made it impossible to detect the far more prevalent risks from sources outside the person's household, including risks from guns.

The association found by Kellermann et al. (odds ratio = 2.7) was repeatedly described by the authors as a strong one, but they did not cite any criterion justifying this assessment. As a rough rule of thumb, epidemiologists using case-control methods to study cancer give little weight to a risk factor discovered in a single study unless it carries a risk ratio of at least three (Taubes 1995:165; see also Lilienfeld and Stolley 1994). The Kellermann association did not even meet this minimal standard for being taken seriously, never mind any standard defining a strong association.

The association was in fact so weak that merely correcting for the modest amount of measurement error that Kellermann's own research had documented could be enough to eliminate the association altogether, if control subjects denied gun ownership at a higher rate than case subjects. Kellermann carried out a small-scale local check on the validity of responses to survey questions on gun ownership using lists of registered gun owners, a group who, by definition, had already shown themselves willing to let strangers (the legal authorities) know that they owned guns. Results indicated that even among this presumably candid group of gun owners, 11.4 percent of the known owners denied having a gun in the household, some claiming that they used to own guns but no longer did so, even though all of the sample members had registered handguns just 30–90 days earlier, while one even denied ever owning a gun (Kellermann et al. 1990). In a similar study, Rafferty and her colleagues (1995) found that 10.3 percent of hunting license holders and 12.7 percent of handgun registrants denied household gun ownership in interviews. Thus, 11 percent would seem to be a conservative estimate of the level of false denial of gun ownership to be found among gun owners. Among the residents of the high-crime areas from which the case-control samples were drawn, the denial level would almost certainly be higher. (For additional evidence of under-reporting of gun ownership, see Kleck 1991:455–460.)

Kleck (1997a:245, 260) demonstrated that underreporting by as little as 7.7 percent over-all could render the Kellermann association nonsignificant, if there were more underreporting among controls than among cases. This would be an example of "recall bias resulting from dif-ferential recollection of past events for cases and controls," which one group of epidemiolo-gists has identified as one of the three biggest threats to validity in case-control studies (Austin et al. 1994:75).

There was also a problem of generalizability. Few would dispute that there are some high-risk subsets of the population where gun possession might raise the risks of homicide. Kellermann et al. (1993), however, stated their conclusions without qualifying them with respect to subsets of the population to which they might apply. However, their sample (both cases and controls), was almost entirely urban, 63 percent male, 62 percent black, probably largely poor, and (given the typical geographical concentration of homicide locations) drawn almost exclusively from high crime areas of the three urban counties studied (1087). Instead of comparing homicide cases with a set of controls representative of the entire non-victim populations of the three counties, the authors chose to obtain a set of controls matched to the cases by area of residence, sex, race, and approximate age. This eliminated any formal basis for generalizing the results to any larger population. Thus, the authors could not even generalize their claims about the risk-elevating effects of household gun ownership to the three counties from which their cases were drawn, never mind the entire U.S. population.

Another case-control study following along the same lines has been conducted (Cum-mings et al. 1997), but with even fewer controls for likely confounders. The most interesting finding of this study was that while homicide victimization in general was positively associ-ated with gun ownership, the association was just as high for nongun homicide as for gun homicide. Since gun ownership should affect homicide risks, if at all, by elevating the risk of *gun* homicide (Kellermann et al. 1993), this combination of results supports the view that the homicide-guns association was spurious, due to uncontrolled confounding factors that elevate the risk of homicide victimization in general.

In sum, researchers have approached the gun-violence linkage in various ways, all of them subject to limitations. Case-control research offers another useful strategy for gaining some insight, as long as its limitations are recognized. This paper addresses its promise and its pitfalls.

A National Case-Control Study of Homicide Offending

Rather than studying homicide victimization, as Kellermann et al. (1993) did, we directly studied homicide *offending*, contrasting killers and nonkillers. The present study also improves on the Kellermann et al. study by using large (unweighted n = 13,168, versus n = 420 matched pairs) and nationally representative samples of the incarcerated homicide offender population and the general adult (nonkiller) population, allowing generalizations to legiti-mately be made to the U.S. adult population, and providing more stable estimates and greater statistical power to discover a guns-homicide association, as well as less vulnerability to a small number of measurement errors. Further, it encompasses all kinds of intentional criminal homicides, not just those committed in or near the victim's home, allowing us to assess the impact of gun ownership on homicidal behavior regardless of where killings might occur or where a homicide-linked gun is normally kept.

Sample

Our sample links two originally separate samples: (1) inmates in state prisons interviewed in the U.S. Census Bureau's Survey of State Prison Inmates (SSPI) in the Summer of 1991 (U.S. Department of Justice 1993a; 1993b) who had committed a homicide as an adult between 1980 and 1991 (the "cases"), and (2) a general sample of U.S. adults (age 18 or older) interviewed in the General Social Surveys (GSS) in the 1982, 1984, 1985, and 1988–1991 surveys (the "controls" [Davis and Smith 1994]). The response rate in the SSPI was 93.7 percent (U.S. Department of Justice 1993b:29) and in the GSS for the years used in this study it was 77.2 percent (Davis and Smith 1994:793–794). In the inmate sample, only those who had committed an intentional criminal homicide when age 18 or older were included, to match the age range covered by the General Social Surveys. Thus, the SSPI sample is a nationally representative sample of persons serving sentences in state prisons in 1991 for committing intentional criminal homicides while adults between 1980 and 1991, and the GSS sample is a nationally representative sample of the adult household population of the continental U.S., of whom we can be confident that over 99 percent had *not* committed homicides. By combining the two samples, we have a nationally representative sample of U.S. adults, of whom a disproportionately large share (8%) are killers— 1,095 killers and 12,074 nonkiller members of the general adult population (unweighted frequencies).

Are imprisoned killers representative of all killers? In 1992, an estimated 23,760 murders and nonnegligent manslaughters were committed in the U.S., resulting in about 12,548 felony convictions, of which about 93 percent, or 11,785, resulted in a prison sentence (U.S. Bureau of Justice Statistics 1996:324, 497, 499). Thus, assuming only one person in each homicide incident actually inflicted a fatal injury, about 50 percent (11,785 of 23,760) of killers are sent to prison. We do not know how representative imprisoned killers are of all killers, mainly because we know little about the killers responsible for the one-third of homicides that are not cleared by an arrest.

The two datasets were combined by identifying all variables possibly related to homicide or gun ownership that appeared in both datasets, creating names and category coding schemes for these variables that were identical across datasets, and then merging the two sets of cases.[1]

The central research question we sought to address was: Does gun ownership increase the likelihood that a person will commit a criminal homicide? The primary dependent variable was a dichotomous one, whether the person had committed an intentional criminal homicide, and the independent variable of central interest was whether the subject personally owned a gun. For GSS respondents (Rs), the gun ownership question referred to the time the person was interviewed, while for SSPI Rs, it referred to the month before they were arrested for the killing that resulted in imprisonment.

Personal gun ownership does not completely encompass all access to guns, since some who do not personally own a gun, nevertheless, have access to guns belonging to others, either in their own household or elsewhere. The SSPI did not have a measure of household gun ownership. The logic of this research, however, depends only on the reasonable assumption that those who personally own a gun are more likely to have access to a gun than those

---

1. The prisoner cases were weighted by the SSPI "Final Weight" that weights them up to the entire U.S. population of inmates of state prisons in the summer of 1991, while the GSS cases were weighted by the OVERSAMP variable, which adjusts for oversampling of blacks in the 1982 GSS, and ADULTS, which adjusts for the lower probabilities of selection for individual adults living in households with more adults (Davis and Smith 1994:788–791). For all SSPI cases, OVERSAMP and ADULTS were set to one, while for all GSS cases, Final Weight was set to one. The weight for each case in the combined sample was the product of all three weights, divided by the combined weight's mean value in the combined sample. The last step insured that the weighted sample size was the same as the unweighted size, so significance tests would not be distorted.

who do not personally own a gun. In short, this gun ownership measure is a valid though imperfect indicator of a given individual's access to a gun.

Multivariate models of homicide behavior were estimated using logistic regression, the method recommended for use in analyzing case-control data (Loftin and McDowall 1988). The estimates were computed using SPSS for Windows Version 6.13 software (Norusis/SPSS 1994).

It was not possible to separately analyze risks of committing gun homicides and nongun homicides, due to inconsistencies in prisoner responses to questions in the SSPI concerning details about the killings that got them sent to prison. Apparently, inmates misunderstood some questions, or interviewers may have failed to follow skip patterns correctly. Because matching would preclude using samples representative of larger populations, it was not desirable to match cases and controls. Instead of matching on sex, race, and approximate age as Kellermann et al. (1993) did, we statistically controlled for sex, race, and exact age, along with Hispanic ethnicity, personal income, marital status, education, whether the subject resided in the South, had any children under 18, or was a military veteran.

Results

Table 2 shows the variables used in this analysis and also provides a rough picture of the bivariate associations between killing and the independent variables. Killers are slightly more likely to own guns than other adults. They are also more likely to be male, black, or Hispanic, more likely to live in the South, and more likely to be a military veteran. Killers are also younger than the rest of U.S. adults, less educated, and less likely to be married or have children. Surprisingly, killers average only slightly less income than other U.S. adults.

Table 2 • *Variables Used in the Analysis*[a]

		Killers		Nonkillers	
Variable	*Description*	*Mean*	*S.D.*	*Mean*	*S.D.*
KILLER	Subject is incarcerated for intentional criminal homicide	1.00	0.00	0.00	0.00
GUNOWNER	Subject personally owns a gun	1.41	0.33	1.28	0.45
MALE	Subject is male	1.93	0.25	1.45	0.50
BLACK	Subject is African American	1.44	0.50	1.11	0.31
HISPANIC	Subject is Hispanic	1.14	0.34	1.05	0.21
AGE	Exact age of subject in years	29.36	10.24	43.91	17.44
INCOME	Midpoint of personal income category, $1,000s	16.45	16.77	16.64	17.07
MARRIED	Subject is married	1.17	0.38	1.63	0.48
EDUCATION	Highest grade completed	10.29	2.67	12.37	3.01
SOUTH	Subject resides in South	1.43	0.49	1.34	0.47
KIDS	Subject has children <18 years	1.62	0.49	1.72	0.45
VETERAN	Subject is veteran of military	1.24	0.43	1.17	0.38

Notes:

[a] For imprisoned killers, the variables describe the person at the time of their arrest on the homicide charge. For general population survey respondents, the variables describe the person at the time of interview. Means and standard deviations (S.D.) pertain to the set of cases used to estimate most of the models, i.e. those with nonmissing values on all of the listed variables. KILLER was coded 0/1 and all other binary variables were coded 1/2.

Multivariate Results—Main Effects

Table 3 shows the estimated logistic regression coefficients, and their antilogs, for multi-variate models of homicide behavior. The antilogs can be interpreted as odds ratios, showing the change in the odds of a person committing a homicide associated with a one-unit increase in the associated independent variable. For example, the odds ratio for MALE indicates that the odds of a male killing are 8.54 times higher than the odds for a female, controlling for the other variables in the equation, while the MARRIED odds ratio indicates that the odds of a married person killing are only 15 percent as high as the odds of an unmarried person doing so. The unweighted sample sizes are shown, indicating that sample sizes were large enough

Table 3 • Homicide Model Estimates[a]

Panel A • Main Effect of Personal Gun Ownership on Killing

Independent Variable	b (se)	Antilog of b
GUNOWNER	0.305 (.083)	1.36[b]
MALE	2.145 (.094)	8.54
BLACK	1.646 (.096)	5.19
HISPANIC	0.786 (.139)	2.19
AGE	−0.078 (.003)	0.93
INCOME	0.026 (.002)	1.03
MARRIED	−1.922 (.083)	0.15
EDUCATION	−0.329 (.015)	0.72
SOUTH	0.317 (.080)	1.37
KIDS	0.361 (.084)	1.43
VETERAN	1.003 (.100)	2.73
Constant	0.667	

Unweighted n = 7372   Model χ^2 = 5333.955   −2 log likelihood = 4881.575

Panel B • Interactions: Gun Effects within Subsamples[c]

Subsample	n	Antilog of GUNOWNER Coefficient
Full sample	7372	1.36
Males	3427	1.21 (p = .03)
Females	3945	2.54
Blacks	1378	2.02
Nonblacks	5994	1.22 (p = .03)
Age 18–30	2140	1.37
Age >30	5232	1.37
Income <$10k	4090	1.38 (p = .02)
Income >$10k	3282	1.46
Southern	2660	1.51
NonSouthern	4712	1.25 (p = .04)

Notes:
[a] All coefficients were significant at the .01 level except where indicated. b = logistic regression coefficient, (se) = standard error of coefficient.
[b] Because VET was missing for 40% of the full sample, the model was reestimated with it omitted. The GUNOWNER odds ratio became 1.41, based on 12,393 unweighted cases with valid data.
[c] For the Panel B estimates, the full model shown in Panel A was estimated, minus whatever variable was used to subdivide the sample. For simplicity's sake, however, only the antilogs of the coefficients for GUNOWNER are shown.

that even weak associations were likely to be statistically significant. Various measures of model goodness of fit are also shown (Aldrich and Nelson 1984:57).

The estimates in Panel A of Table 3 indicate that the odds of a person with a gun killing are about 1.36 times as high as the odds among persons without a gun, controlling for the other ten variables included in the model. This is only one-fifth as large an association as Kellermann et al. (1993) found with respect to homicide victimization (recalling that 1 represents no association, (2.7–1.0)/(1.36–1.00) = 4.7). Odds ratios smaller than 1.5 are regarded as "weak" in epidemiological case-control studies (Austin et al. 1994:66).

The association estimates are also sensitive to model specification. The antilog of the gunowner coefficient declines to 1.15 (not significant at the .05 level) when age is omitted, while increasing to 1.41 when veteran status is omitted. The point is not that the model is superior when either of these variables is omitted; rather, this variation merely illustrates the degree to which estimates of the guns-homicide association can be sensitive to the omission of even a single relevant control variable, something that could also be true with respect to variables we have not measured.

Multivariate Results—Interactions

Panel B of Table 3 shows the estimated gun effects within subsets of the sample, illustrating how the apparent effects vary across different subpopulations. Consistent with theory on the facilitating or "equalizer" effects of weaponry on violence (Kleck 1991:156–158; Kleck and McElrath 1991), gun ownership appears to have substantially more impact on homicidal behavior among women than men. Gun possession gives a smaller person of less physical strength the ability to inflict lethal violence on others, even larger, stronger victims, while a weapon is more likely to be redundant among male aggressors.

Guns also appear to contribute more to homicide among blacks than among whites, even controlling for likely correlates of race such as income, education, and residence in the South. Given these interaction results, it is possible that the Kellermann results did reflect a real gun effect, but one that was peculiar to the setting of their research and the composition of their sample, which was 62 percent black. On the other hand, there is virtually no difference in apparent effects for lower versus higher income persons, or younger versus older persons, and only slightly more apparent effect among Southerners than non-Southerners.

Caveats and Discussion

Uncontrolled Confounding Factors

The association between gun ownership and homicide victimization that Kellermann and his colleagues (1993) discovered, and the much weaker association between gun ownership and homicide offending found here, are at least partially spurious, attributable to uncontrolled antecedent confounding factors. Many factors known to increase the risk of homicide victimization should also increase the likelihood that persons exposed to those factors would acquire a gun for self-protection. In general, associating with dangerous persons or engaging in dangerous activities obviously raise the risks one will become a victim of violence, but these dangers are also likely to encourage some people to adapt to them by acquiring a gun for self-defense. Among the more important likely confounding factors that neither we nor Kellermann et al. controlled for are membership in a street gang and drug dealing. Callahan and Rivara (1992:3041) found that among Seattle high school students, the odds of handgun ownership were 12 times higher among youth who sold illicit drugs, and 26 times higher among gang members, than among youth without these traits. Sheley (1994:373) studied inmates in six juvenile institutions and found the odds of gun ownership to be five times higher among those who sold illicit drugs than among those who did not. Likewise, Sheley and Wright's (1995:85) surveys of high school students in five big cities found the odds of gun ownership to be seven times higher among those who sold drugs, and three times higher among gang members, than among juveniles without those attributes (these figures are all crude odds ratios). (See also Bjerregaard and Lizotte 1995; Decker and Pennell 1995; Fagan 1990; Lizotte et al. 1994; and Lizotte et al. 1997 for similar findings). The omission of even one confounding factor with effects as large as these would be sufficient to completely account for odds ratios of 1.36 or even 2.7 (Schlesselman 1982:56).

Differential Measurement Error in Case Control Studies

Estimates of the impact of gun ownership can also be distorted by differential misreporting of ownership ("exposure" to the risk factor) across the killer and nonkiller groups (the "cases" and the "controls"). There is almost certainly underreporting of gun ownership in all surveys (Kellermann et al. 1990; Kleck 1991:455–460; Rafferty et al. 1995), including the SSPI and GSS. If the degree of underreporting were the same among imprisoned killers and free adults, this would have no impact on the gun effect estimates. If underreporting was higher among free adults, i.e., among nonkillers, this would result in an overestimate of gun effects, while greater underreporting among killers would result in an underestimate of gun effects.

Since most of the imprisoned killers committed their offenses with guns, presumably using their own guns, denying gun ownership (at the time of their arrest) in prison interviews would generally be futile. In contrast, members of the free adult population have both reasons to conceal gun ownership and a sound basis for thinking they could do so undetected.

On the other hand, although some evidence indicates that prisoners provide generally valid answers in surveys (Marquis 1981; Wright, Rossi and Daly 1983:32–38) and that general population adults frequently conceal gun ownership (Kellermann et al. 1990; Kleck 1991:455–460; Kleck 1997a:64–68, 100; Rafferty et al. 1995), one might nevertheless speculate that prisoners are simply generally more dishonest in their responses than members of the general public, and that this applies specifically to their reporting of gun ownership.

It should be stressed, however, that this is all nothing more than speculation and cannot be legitimately used to discount the empirical findings. Underreporting has, so far, only been documented in the nonincarcerated population. For example, Kleck (1997a:66–67) reported that reporting of household gun ownership in numerous national surveys has been consistently lower among married women respondents than among married men, even though household ownership levels should have been essentially identical in the two groups. At this point there is no empirical foundation for believing that response errors on the gun ownership questions have contributed to a net bias in estimates of the gun effect.

Possible Sample Bias Effects

There is, however, empirical evidence that sampling biases in the prisoner subsample related to gun ownership bias estimates of the gun effect. The SSPI sample includes only those killers who were convicted and sentenced to prison, thereby excluding those never arrested, and those arrested but not sentenced to prison. If the kinds of killers who are arrested and sentenced to prison have different rates of gun ownership from all killers, it could bias results. In separate analyses, we examined the possibility that killers who used guns were less likely to be arrested, perhaps because gun homicides are more likely to be premeditated or to involve victims who are strangers to the killer. Looking at FBI Supplementary Homicide Reports (SHR) data covering U.S. homicides from 1976 to 1992 (Fox 1994), we assumed that for any homicide where the offender's sex was unknown, the crime had not resulted in the killer's arrest, but that all other killings were cleared by an arrest. We found that an offender was apparently arrested in 72.8 percent of murders and nonnegligent manslaughters with a gun, and in a virtually identical 72.9 percent of those without a gun. In another large body of data, concerning a more local sample, but with an explicit measure of clearance by arrest, we looked at Chicago homicides committed between 1965 and 1990 (Block, Block and Illinois Criminal Justice Information Authority 1994). These data indicated that 74 percent of gun homicides were cleared by arrest, compared to 78 percent of nongun homicides. Thus, there is little difference in gun use between solved and unsolved killings, and no reason to expect arrest patterns to bias a prisoner sample with respect to gun ownership. On the other hand, Cook and Nagin (1979:48–52) found that among those arrested, murderers who used a gun or other weapon are more likely to be convicted. And among criminals who are convicted, use of a gun in a crime is also associated with more severe sentences (Cook and Nagin 1979; Loftin, Heumann and McDowall 1983; Wright, Rossi and Daly 1983:300–307). Indeed, 49 of the 50 states have sentence enhancement laws specifically providing for more severe punishment of felonies committed with a gun (Marvell and Moody 1995:259), most of them mandating a longer prison term. Thus, Cook and Nagin (1979:51) found that among murderers who were convicted, (1) 87 percent of those who used a gun were given an incarceration sentence, compared to 83 percent of those who used other weapons and 65 percent of those who were unarmed, and (2) the average minimum sentence was 83 months for gun killers, but only 34 months for those who used other weapons and 56 months for those who were unarmed. Loftin, Heumann, and McDowall (1983) found no impact of murderer gun use on conviction or imposition of incarceration, but did find that it increased sentence length. Similarly, Wright and his colleagues (1983:304) found that while gun use only mildly increased the likelihood of conviction, gun offenders were 74 percent more likely to receive a prison sentence than those who did not use weapons. On the other hand, Lizotte and Zatz (1986) found an effect of gun use on prison sentence length only for defendants with the most serious prior records.

Since gun use increases the probability of conviction or an incarceration sentence, and may increase the length of sentence, the likelihood that gun killers would be included in a prison sample is also increased. To the extent that those who kill with a gun are also more likely to own a gun, this sample bias will contribute to an overstatement of the gun ownership rate among killers, and thus an overstatement of the estimated gun effect on killing. In sum, sample biases contribute to an overstatement of the gun effect, while there is no empirical foundation for any judgment about different rates of errors on the gun ownership question.

Taking account of the sample bias, and the omission from the model of factors with empirically established positive effects on both gun ownership and homicidal behavior, it is likely that the estimated effect of gun ownership on killing is overstated in this study. The only way it is likely to be understated is if imprisoned killers underreport their preincarceration gun ownership to so much greater an extent than the free population that the effects of both bias in the prisoner sample and the failure to control confounding factors are reversed.

Conclusions

Taken at face value, the present results indicate that gun ownership may have a weak effect on homicidal behavior in the population in general, though the effects may be stronger among women and blacks. The failure to control confounding factors that are known to positively affect both violent behavior and gun acquisition, however, is probably at least partly responsible for the positive guns-homicide association. Therefore, an association this weak could be entirely spurious. Future case-control research needs to measure and control for more potentially confounding variables, for example, gang membership and involvement in drug dealing, and to explicitly test for the possibility of differing levels of underreporting of gun ownership among cases and controls.

The present results directly address the effect of gun ownership among potential aggressors on whether those gun owners will kill. Given the strong evidence, reviewed earlier, that defensive gun use by crime victims is both common and effective in preventing injury, gun ownership by prospective homicide *victims* should be even less likely to exert a strong positive effect on homicide victimization than gun ownership by prospective offenders. In this light, the positive association between household gun ownership and homicide victimization obtained in the Kellermann (1993) study—weak yet five times as large as the association obtained herein—is most likely to be largely or entirely spurious, reflecting the common effects of risk factors such as drug dealing and gang membership on homicide victimization and on the acquisition of guns for self-protection.

Leaving the results related to gun effects, this research could serve as a model for analyzing other offenses besides homicides, allowing systematic individual-level comparisons of offenders and nonoffenders involved in other serious crimes such as rape, robbery, burglary, and drug dealing, using samples of adult offenders and nonoffenders with more claim to national representativeness than any other samples known to us. Individual-level multivariate comparisons of known offenders with nonoffenders could serve as a useful supplement to self-report surveys, with their attendant validity and sampling problems, in testing hypotheses concerning the etiology of criminal behavior.[2]

References

Akers, Ronald L.
　　1994　Criminological Theories. Los Angeles, Calif.: Roxbury.
Aldrich, John H., and Forrest D. Nelson
　　1984　Linear Probability, Logit, and Probit Models. Beverly Hills, Calif.: Sage.
Austin, Harland, Holly A. Hill, W. Dana Flanders, and Raymond S. Greenberg
　　1994　"Limitations in the application of case-control methodology." Epidemiologic Reviews
　　　　16:65–76.
Bjerregard, Beth, and Alan J. Lizotte
　　1994　"Gun ownership and gang membership." Journal of Criminal Law and Criminology 86:37–
　　　　58.
Block, Carolyn R., Richard L. Block, and the Illinois Criminal Justice Information Authority
　　1994　Homicides in Chicago, 1965–1990 [computer file]. ICPSR version. Chicago, Ill.: Illinois
　　　　Criminal Justice Information Authority [producer]. Ann Arbor, Mich.: Inter-university
　　　　Consortium for Political and Social Research [distributor].
Bordua, David J.
　　1986　"Firearms ownership and violent crime." In The Social Ecology of Crime, eds. James M.
　　　　Byrne and Robert J. Sampson, 156–188. New York: Springer-Verlag.
Brearley, H. C.
　　1932　Homicide in the United States. Chapel Hill, N.C.: University of North Carolina Press.

2. Some ancillary findings are also worth noting. Students of the Southern subculture of violence thesis have commonly studied either (1) violence rates of macro-level units, such as states, across regions, while calling for more research at the individual level of analysis, or (2) survey data on individuals that measured cultural traits, but that did not allow a link to be tested between those traits and serious violent behavior (Ellison 1991). Our results supplement these approaches by linking individuals' region to homicidal behavior. They indicate that Southerners are more likely to kill, controlling for age, sex, race, income, and many other correlates of violent behavior. This is, to our knowledge, the first research to establish that multivariate association using individual-level data and a nationally representative sample.

Likewise, those interested in the "violent veteran" thesis (Archer and Gartner 1976) might be interested to note that our findings indicate that the odds of a military veteran committing a criminal homicide appear to be about 2.7 times as high as the odds for nonveterans. The reason for these associations deserve further exploration.

290   KLECK & HOGAN

Brill, Steven
   1977   Firearm Abuse: A Research and Policy Report. Washington, D.C.: Police Foundation.
Callahan, Charles M., and Frederick P. Rivara
   1992   "Urban high school youth and handguns." Journal of the American Medical Association
           267:3038–3042.
Cook, Philip J.
   1979   "The effect of gun availability on robbery and robbery murder." In Policy Studies Review
           Annual, eds. Robert Haveman and B. Bruce Zellner, 743–781. Beverly Hills, Calif.: Sage.
   1982   "The role of firearms in violent crime." In Criminal Violence, eds. Marvin E. Wolfgang and
           Neil Alan Weiner. Beverly Hills, Calif.: Sage.
   1985   "The case of the missing victims: Gunshot woundings in the National Crime Survey."
           Journal of Quantitative Criminology 1:91–102.
   1991   "The technology of personal violence." In Crime and Justice, vol. 14, ed., Michael Tonry.
           Chicago, Ill.: University of Chicago Press.
Cook, Philip J., and Daniel Nagin
   1979   Does the Weapon Matter? Washington, D.C.: INSLAW.
Cummings, Peter, Thomas D. Koepsell, David C. Grossman, James Savarino, and Robert S. Thompson
   1997   "The association between purchase of a handgun and homicide or suicide." American
           Journal of Public Health 87:974–978.
Davis, James Allan, and Tom W. Smith
   1994   General Social Surveys, 1972–1994. [machine-readable data file]. Principal Investigator,
           James A. Davis; Director and Co-Principal Investigator, Tom W. Smith. NORC ed. Chicago:
           National Opinion Research Center, producer; Storrs, Conn.: The Roper Center for Public
           Opinion Research, University of Connecticut, distributor. 1 data file (32,380 logical records)
           and 1 codebook.
Decker, Scott, and Susan Pennell
   1995   "Arrestees and guns: Monitoring the illegal firearms market." National Institute of Justice
           Research Preview. Washington, D.C.: National Institute of Justice.
Ellison, Christopher G.
   1991   "An eye for an eye? A note on the Southern subculture of violence thesis." Social Forces
           69:1223–1239.
Fagan, Jeffrey
   1990   "Social processes of delinquency and drug use among urban gangs." In Gangs in America,
           ed. C. Ronald Huff, 183–219. Newbury Park, Calif.: Sage.
Fisher, Joseph C.
   1976   "Homicide in Detroit: The role of firearms." Criminology 14:387–400.
Fox, James Alan
   1994   Uniform Crime Reports [United States]: Supplementary Homicide Reports, 1976–1992
           [computer file]. ICPSR version. Boston, Mass.: Northeastern University, College of Criminal
           Justice [producer]. Ann Arbor, Mich.: Inter-university Consortium for Political and Social
           Research [distributor].
Goodman, Richard A., James A. Mercy, Peter M. Layde, and Stephen B. Thacker
   1988   "Case-control studies: Design issues for criminological applications." Journal of
           Quantitative Criminology 4:71–84.
Kellermann, Arthur L., Frederick P. Rivara, Joyce Banton, Donald Reay, and Corine L. Fligner
   1990   "Validating survey responses to questions about gunownership among owners of registered
           handguns." American Journal of Epidemiology 131:1080–1084.
Kellermann, Arthur L., Frederick P. Rivara, Roberta K. Lee, Joyce G. Banton, Peter Cummings,
Bela B. Hackman, and Grant Somes
   1996   "Injuries due to firearms in three cities." New England Journal of Medicine 335:1438–
           1444.
Kellermann, Arthur L., Frederick P. Rivara, Norman B. Rushforth, Joyce G. Banton, Donald T. Reay,
Jerry T. Francisco, Ana B. Locci, Janice Prodzinski, Bela B. Hackman, and Grant Somes
   1993   "Gun ownership as a risk factor for homicide in the home." New England Journal of
           Medicine 329:1084–1091.

Killias, Martin
  1993 "Gun ownership, suicide, and homicide: An international perspective." In Understanding Crime: Experiences of Crime and Crime Control, eds. Anna del Frate, Uglijesa Zvekic and Jan J. M. van Dijk, 289-303. Rome, Italy: UNICRI.
Kleck, Gary
  1979 "Capital punishment, gun ownership, and homicide." American Journal of Sociology 84:882–910.
  1984 "The relationship between gun ownership levels and rates of violence in the United States." In Firearms and Violence: Issues of Public Policy, ed. Don B. Kates, Jr., 99–135. Cambridge, Mass.: Ballinger.
  1988 "Crime control through the private use of armed force." Social Problems 35:1–21.
  1991 Point Blank: Guns and Violence in America. New York: Aldine de Gruyter.
  1995 "Guns and violence: An interpretive review of the field." Social Pathology 1:12–47.
  1997a Targeting Guns: Firearms and Their Control. New York: Aldine de Gruyter.
  1997b "Crime, collective security, and gun ownership." Unpublished paper. School of Criminology and Criminal Justice, Florida State University.
Kleck, Gary, and Miriam DeLone
  1993 "Victim resistance and offender weapon effects in robbery." Journal of Quantitative Criminology 9:55–82.
Kleck, Gary, and Marc Gertz
  1995 "Armed resistance to crime: The prevalence and nature of self-defense with a gun." Journal of Criminal Law and Criminology 86:143–186.
Kleck, Gary, and Karen McElrath
  1990 "The impact of weaponry on human violence." Social Forces 69:669–692.
Kleck, Gary, and E. Britt Patterson
  1993 "The impact of gun control and gun ownership levels on violence rates." Journal of Quantitative Criminology 9:249–287.
Kleck, Gary, and Susan Sayles
  1990 "Rape and resistance." Social Problems 37:149–162.
Krug, Alan S.
  1968 "The relationship between firearms ownership and crime rates: A statistical analysis." The Congressional Record (January 30):H570-2.
Lester, David
  1985 "The use of firearms in violent crime." Crime and Justice 8:115–120.
  1988 "Firearm availability and the incidence of suicide and homicide." Acta Psychiatrica Belgium 88:387–393.
Lilienfeld, Abraham M., and David E. Lilienfeld
  1979 "A century of case-control studies: Progress?" Journal of Chronic Diseases 32:5–13.
Lilienfeld, David E., and Paul D. Stolley
  1994 Foundations of Epidemiology. 3d rev. ed. New York: Oxford University Press.
Lizotte, Alan, Gregory Howard, Marvin D. Krohn, and Terence P. Thornberry
  1997 "Patterns of illegal gun carrying among young urban males." Valparaiso University Law Review 31:375–393.
Lizotte, Alan, James M. Tesoriero, Terence P. Thornberry, and Marvin D. Krohn
  1994 "Patterns of adolescent firearms ownership and use." Justice Quarterly 11:51–73.
Lizotte, Alan, and Margaret Zatz
  1986 "The use and abuse of sentence enhancement for firearms offenses in California." Law and Contemporary Problems 49:199–221.
Lizotte, Alan J., David J. Bordua, and Carolyn S. White
  1981 "Firearms ownership for sport and protection." American Sociological Review 46:499–503.
Loftin, Colin, Milton Heumann, and David McDowall
  1983 "Mandatory sentencing and firearms violence: Evaluating an alternative to gun control." Law and Society Review 17:287–318.
Loftin, Colin, and David McDowall
  1988 "The analysis of case-control studies in criminology." Journal of Quantitative Criminology 4:85–98.

292   KLECK & HOGAN

Magaddino, Joseph P., and Marshall H. Medoff
1984   "An empirical analysis of federal and state firearm control laws." In Firearms and
        Violence: Issues of Public Policy, ed. Don B. Kates, Jr., 225–258. Cambridge, Mass.:
        Ballinger.
Marquis, Kent H.
1981   Quality of Prisoner Self Reports. Santa Monica, Calif.: RAND Corporation.
Marvell, Thomas B., and Carlisle E. Moody
1995   "The impact of enhanced prison terms for felonies committed with guns." Criminology
        33:247–281.
McDowall, David
1986   "Gun availability and robbery rates: A panel study of large U.S. cities, 1974–1978" Law and
        Policy 8:135–148.
1991   "Firearm availability and homicide rates in Detroit, 1951–1986." Social Forces 69:1085–
        1099.
1995   "Firearms and self-defense." Annals 539:130–140.
Murray, Douglas R.
1975   "Handguns, gun control laws and firearm violence." Social Problems 23:81–92.
Newton, George D., and Franklin Zimring
1969   Firearms and Violence in American Life. A Staff Report to the National Commission on
        the Causes and Prevention of Violence. Washington, D.C.: U.S. Government Printing
        Office.
Norusis, Marija J., SPSS Inc.
1994   SPSS Advanced Statistics 6.1. Chicago, Ill.: SPSS Inc.
Phillips, Llad, Harold L. Votey, and John Howell
1976   "Handguns and homicide." Journal of Legal Studies 5:463–478.
Rafferty, Ann P., John C. Thrush, Patricia K. Smith, and Harry B. McGee
1995   "Validity of a household gun question in a telephone survey." Public Health Reports
        110:282–288.
Schlesselman, James J.
1982   Case-Control Studies. New York: Oxford University Press.
Seitz, Stephen T.
1972   "Firearms, homicides, and gun control effectiveness." Law and Society Review 6:595–
        614.
Sheley, Joseph F.
1994   "Drug activity and firearms possession and use by juveniles." Journal of Drug Issues
        24:363–382.
Sheley, Joseph F., and James D. Wright
1995   In the Line of Fire: Youth, Guns, and Violence in Urban America. Hawthorne, N.Y.:
        Aldine de Gruyter.
Smith, Douglas A., and Craig D. Uchida
1988   "The social organization of self-help." American Sociological Review 53:94–102.
Taubes, Gary
1995   "Epidemiology faces its limits." Science 269:164–169.
Toch, Hans, and Alan J. Lizotte
1991   "Research and policy: The case of gun control." In Psychology and Social Policy, eds.
        Peter Suedfeld and Philip E. Tetlock, 223–240. New York: Hemisphere.
U.S. Bureau of Justice Statistics
1996   Sourcebook of Criminal Justice Statistics 1995. Washington, D.C.: U.S. Government
        Printing Office.
U.S. Department of Justice
1993a   Survey of Inmates of State Correctional Facilities, 1991: United States. Computer file.
        Conducted by U.S. Department of Commerce, Bureau of the Census. ICPSR ed. Ann
        Arbor, MI: Inter-university Consortium for Political and Social Research, producer and
        distributor.
U.S. Department of Justice
1993b   Survey of State Prison Inmates, 1991. Bureau of Justice Statistics. NCJ-136949.
        Washington, D.C.: U.S. Government Printing Office.

U.S. Federal Bureau of Investigation
  1995   Uniform Crime Reports for the United States—1994. Washington, D.C.: U.S. Government
          Printing Office.
Vold, George B., Thomas J. Bernard, and Jeffrey B. Snipes
  1998   Theoretical Criminology. 4th ed. New York: Oxford University Press.
Wright, James D., Peter H. Rossi, and Kathleen Daly
  1983   Under the Gun: Weapons, Crime and Violence in America. New York: Aldine de Gruyter.
Zimring, Franklin E.
  1968   "Is gun control likely to reduce violent killings?" University of Chicago Law Review
          35:721–737.
  1972   "The medium is the message: Firearm caliber as a determinant of death from assault."
          Journal of Legal Studies 1:97–123.

[22]

The prevalence and nature of violent offending by females

Barbara A. Koons-Witt[a],*, Pamela J. Schram[b]

[a]*Department of Criminology and Criminal Justice, University of South Carolina, Columbia, SC 29208, USA*
[b]*Department of Criminal Justice, California State University, San Bernardino, CA 92407, USA*

Abstract

The purpose of the current study was to examine the nature and prevalence of violent offending by females. Using National Incident-Based Reporting System (NIBRS) data from 1998, this study examined the relationship between cooffending and type of offense as well as the type of weapon(s) used during violent incidents and the race of the perpetrators. The findings suggest that females are more likely to be involved in aggravated assaults compared with robberies and murder or nonnegligent manslaughter. This is particularly true for females who commit their violent crimes alone. When females coffend with other females or males, however, they are more likely to commit robberies. Overall females are more likely to be involved in violent incidents where either personal weapons or knives are used. When females coffend with males, however, more likely to be involved in incidents with guns. Finally, the current study found that Black females were more likely to commit violent offenses with other females, whereas White females were more likely to commit violent offenses with males.

Introduction

Female offenders have garnered a growing amount of attention in the criminological literature during the last thirty years. Beginning in the 1970s, scholars such as Adler (1975), Simon (1975), and Smart (1976) introduced a new perspective of female offenders and the fact that much of what was known about those who violated the law was the result of research involving exclusively male populations. These early works set the stage for the abundance of scholarship that would follow and enhance the understanding of the female offender (also victims and workers). The common neglect of violent female offenders is likely the result of

* Corresponding author. Tel.: +1-803-777-0107; fax: +1-803-777-9600.
E-mail address: bakoons@gwm.sc.edu (B.A. Koons-Witt).

several factors, most of which are grounded in gender stereotypes. For example, Goetting (1988) suggests that the inattention to violent female offenders is related to the fact that "traditional female role expectations accommodate the woman as a victim but not as a perpetrator of violence" (p. 3). In committing crime, females violate their gender role expectations. As a result, they have not generated the same responses from scholars, practitioners, and the public as females who have been victimized. This false dichotomy of females as either offenders or victims masks much of what is understood about female criminality. Only recently has this dichotomy been challenged by the "blurring" of these boundaries from those doing research in these respective scholarly areas (Gilfus, 1992; Sanchez, 2001).

These same sexist stereotypes are evident in the early writings of scholars who sought to explain female criminality. More specifically, early scholars such as Lombroso, Thomas, Freud, and Pollak often characterized female offenders as masculine in their orientation and appearance. Masculinity versus femininity and good versus bad images, as defined by appropriate sex roles, shaped much of the early etiology of female criminality (Klein, 1995; Pollock, 1999). Violent female offenders were often portrayed as "monsters" and considered to be much more serious offenders and an affront to the stability of society than their violent male counterparts (Pollock, 1999).

Both Adler (1975) and Simon (1975) maintained that the changing organization of gender in society and varying gender roles would result in an increase in crimes by females. According to Adler, these changes would result in women exhibiting masculine-like behaviors including their involvement in committing violent crimes. This perspective suggests that a gender convergence of crime rates should occur over time and the gap between males' and females' offending would decrease so their patterns would become more similar (Belknap, 2001). Analyses of Uniform Crime Reports (UCR) and National Crime Victimization Surveys (NCVS) failed to provide support for the emancipation or liberation perspective (Belknap, 2001; Kruttschnitt, 2001; Steffensmeier, 2001). Despite several increases and decreases in violent crime rates between the 1960s and the 1990s, violent offending by females has remained, for the most part stable, thereby resulting in an even wider gap between males' and females' violent offending (Kruttschnitt, 2001; Pollock, 1999).[1] Violent female offenders continue to be an anomaly; they commit a very small proportion of all violent crimes.

The profile of the typical female offender reveals her marginalized status: a young, nonviolent offender who is uneducated, a single mother, lacks useful job skills necessary for being the primary caretaker, and a person of color. What is known about female offenders is primarily the result of research examining the typical female offender. The violent female offender is less prominent within the criminal justice system; however, research involving this offender population is necessary and important to understand how gender is linked to the commission of serious crimes. What explains the differences in women who are nonviolent offenders as compared with those who are involved in serious lawbreaking? How does gender influence violent crimes in comparison with nonviolent crimes? Recent work concerning violent female offenders has contributed to the literature in this area by focusing on the situation and context of violent incidents, including explorations of cooffending and crime roles, use of weapons, and differences among women based on race.

Nature and context of violent offending by females

Scholars generally recognize that the gap in offending patterns between males and females is largest for violent offenses (Pollock, 1999; Kruttschnitt, 2001; Steffensmeier & Broidy, 2001). Despite this significant gap, scholars have a limited understanding and explanation of these offense patterns. The current study examined the relationship between gender, race, cooffending, use of weapons, and type of offense. Specifically, this study analyzed whether gender and race influenced cooffending, the type of weapon used (if any), and the type of offense committed. A particular emphasis was placed on how these factors affected the commission of violent crimes such as murder/negligent manslaughter, robbery, and aggravated assault.

Prior review of the research on trends and patterns of violent offending indicated that men committed the vast majority of homicides. Men kill their current and former wives and girlfriends more often than women kill their current or former husbands or boyfriends. A larger percent of female-perpetrated homicides compared with male-perpetrated homicides involved intimate partners (Belknap, 2001, p. 115; Kruttschnitt, 2001). In 1998, the victims of female-perpetrated homicides included acquaintance (31.9 percent) followed by spouse (28.3 percent), boyfriend/girlfriend (14.0 percent), and child/stepchild (10.4 percent); the victims of male-perpetrated homicides included acquaintance (54.6 percent), stranger (25.1 percent), other family (6.9 percent), and spouse (6.8 percent) (Greenfeld & Snell,1999, p. 4).

Steffensmeier and Allan's (1998, p. 10) examination of UCR arrest profiles revealed that there was a decline in female arrests for murder (from 17 percent in 1960 to 9 percent in 1995). They argued that the decline may have been due to two main factors: (1) large increases in male arrests for felony murders associated with the drug trade and the increased availability of guns and (2) stable or declining rates of murders committed by women because of the increasing availability of domestic abuse shelters and abuse protection statutes—both of which protect women from abusive males and diminish the opportunity context for victim-precipitated mate slayings involving females as the homicide offender. To gain a better understanding of the general nature and context of violent offending by women, research must explore the importance and relevance of cooffending and crime roles.

Cooffending and crime roles

Some prior research on violent female criminality centered around understanding the likelihood of

B.A. Koons-Witt, P.J. Schram / Journal of Criminal Justice 31 (2003) 361–371   363

women committing crime alone or with other females or males and their role within these criminal work groups. Between 1993 and 1997, victims of violence attributed the crimes they experienced to approximately 2.1 million female offenders and about 13.1 million male offenders. Of the violent female offenders, 53 percent committed the offense alone, 40 percent committed the offense with at least one other female offender, and approximately 8 percent committed their offense with at least one male offender. Of the male offenders, 47 percent acted alone, 51 percent committed the offense with other male offenders, and another 1 percent committed the offense with at least one female offender (Greenfeld & Snell, 1999, p. 2). This research suggested that female offenders were more likely to commit violent crimes by themselves, without the assistance of other male or female offenders. The general belief was that when women committed crimes with men, they did so with either their boyfriends or husbands or their friends and acquaintances (Alarid, Marquart, Burton, Cullen, & Cuvelier, 1996; Ward, Jackson, & Ward, 1979). Pettiway's (1987) research on women drug users in New York City and Miami supported the notion that when women offended alongside males, it was very likely they had done so with their intimates. Pettiway notes,

> Being married or living with a boyfriend or husband is clearly one of the more important elements in establishing the probability of crime group participation. This measure of domesticity contributes to the likelihood for boyfriend and husband crime groups but reduces the likelihood for mixed-sex crime groups.[2] It is reasonable to assume that women who live with men in intimate arrangements do not find it necessary to enter crime groups with people outside of these primary relationships. (p. 761)

Pettiway (1987) found that women who participated in what would be perceived as "masculine-type" crimes or those of a predatory nature were more likely to occur when women were offending with their intimates (i.e., boyfriend or spouse). On the other hand, he found that women were much more likely to join other women in committing vice crimes.

Prior research involving gender and cooffending appeared to be more developed within the context of the illegal drug trade (Baskin & Sommers, 1993; Pettiway, 1987; Sommers & Baskin, 1997; Steffensmeier, 1983). This, coupled with the fact that there tended to be a strong relationship between use of drugs and involvement with other forms of serious crimes such as robbery, made this a fruitful area for examining the use of violence and the role of women in illegal drug networks (Sommers & Baskin, 1997). Some researchers believed that women's roles within deviant networks, including the illegal drug trade, changed over time and that women assumed more assertive, leadership roles within these deviant networks (Alarid et al., 1996; Bunch, Foley, & Urbina, 1983; Decker, Wright, Redfern, & Smith, 1993; Sommers & Baskin, 1993). Maher and Daly's (1996) work suggested the opposite. They found that women continued to work in marginalized areas of the drug world, either as "coppers" (i.e., buyers for White males who were outsiders) or temporary street-level sellers, and were unlikely to be in positions of power within the organizational hierarchy.

Alarid et al. (1996) attempted to determine the extent to which women served as either leaders or followers during serious offenses (e.g., drug offenses, burglary, and robbery). Results showed that 80 percent of the women in their study were involved with cooffenders when committing drug offenses, robbery, larceny, and burglary. Alarid et al. concluded that "nontraditional criminal behaviors were more likely to be committed with male accomplices who provided women with the opening into deviant networks" (p. 450). When women acted as "sole perpetrators," they did so when committing traditional female offenses such as forgery and theft but also when committing the nontraditional offenses of DWI and assault. This research also uncovered an interesting relationship between race, gender, deviant networks, and crime roles. Alarid et al. found that African American women committed offenses with other women, while Anglo or Hispanic women were more likely to team with men. The work of Alarid et al. seemed to suggest that the race of the woman and the type of offense were important influences when understanding the inner workings of deviant networks and the crime roles women assumed within them.

Sommers and Baskin (1993) interviewed sixty-five women who were arrested and/or incarcerated for violent street crime. They noted that most literature on female offenders argued that women usually assumed the status of secondary actors in a criminal event. Their research revealed, however, that 63 percent of the robberies were committed with accomplices and 60 percent of these involved female cooffenders. The remaining 37 percent were committed alone. Sommers and Baskin found,

> [f]rom early on in their criminal careers, women in the robbery sample reported that they acted out in self-determination and not in concert with or for boyfriends. Although the women sometimes were involved in criminal activities that involved men or activities that at times were controlled by men, they did so most often as equal partners. (p.147)

In reference to assaults, many of the respondents reported that these acts were often impulsive and unorganized with many in the state of intoxication and the use of dangerous weapons. Approximately 14 percent of these assaults were related to drug dealing. The interactions between the victim and the offender, and sometimes the interaction (i.e., verbal) of a third party, played an essential role in many of these assaultive incidents.

In conclusion, research on coffending and crime roles provided mixed results as to whether women were more likely today to be committing violent crimes by themselves, with other women, or with men. It was also unclear whether women were assuming new, more powerful roles when committing violent crimes with members of the opposite sex. Further research is needed to understand whether these arrangements and roles vary by offense type and by the race of the offender or offending group. Information on the use of weapons during the commission of violent crimes is also important to understanding the context and nature of such offenses.

Weapons use

Prior literature that considered the use of weapons by violent female offenders was scant. The little research that did exist appeared to suggest that the use of weapons by women was conditioned by coffending, characteristics of the targeted victim, and offense type. For example, Miller's (1998) ethnographic study of gender and street robberies found that women usually committed street robberies with other women. When women attacked other women, they typically did so without a weapon, but on some occasions used a knife. Both the choice of the victim and whether or not to use a weapon were based on the perception by female perpetrators that female victims were less likely to resist and physically overtake them. Miller (p. 61) reports, "both male and female robbers hold the view that females are easy to rob, because they are less likely to be armed and because they are perceived as weak and easily intimidated." When female targets did behave unexpectedly and resisted or fought back, female street robbers responded aggressively by physically attacking the victim(s) by hitting, punching, or stabbing them (Miller, 1998). When women victimized males, they tended to use this same perceived vulnerability as a member of the weaker sex to commit the crime. Additionally, they avoided the use of physical contact when the victim was male but instead used guns to commit the crime. When women committed street robberies with male accomplices, they were also more likely to carry a gun and the victim was typically male (Miller, 1998).

Pettiway's (1987) work on crime partnerships by female drug users found that females who committed their crimes with other women were not likely to carry or use weapons during their offenses. Pettiway states, "it is not surprising that this factor [weapons] shows a negative effect for female crime groups since most of the females in this sample do not commit offenses that either require weapons or involve the risks associated with most male-type crimes" (p. 762). Carrying and using guns during crimes committed by female drug users was associated with the likelihood of becoming a member of crime groups.

It has been generally thought that when women commit violent offenses they would commit the crime in a way that compensates for their slighter physical stature. For example, they would use a weapon that could offset a physical difference between them and a male victim or they would commit the crime when the victim was in a vulnerable state because of alcohol or sleep (Jurik & Winn, 1990). Jurik and Winn (1990) examined individuals who were charged with nonnegligent manslaughter or homicide and subsequently convicted in Maricopa County, Arizona between 1979 and 1984. Their research revealed that women who coffended with males were less likely to introduce a weapon into the crime (33 versus 80 percent) compared with their male counterparts. While previous research suggested that women used weapons such as kitchen knives, this study suggested that women were more inclined to use guns. The researchers discovered that the proportion of both males and females using guns were quite similar. This finding of gun use was related to the other key findings. Jurik and Winn found that women were more likely to kill their victims during a domestic altercation and were surprisingly found to kill a substantially lower proportion of victims who were impaired at the time of the offense.

In conclusion, it appears that the women may be using weapons differently now than they have in the past. Previously, it was thought that women were less inclined to use weapons, or when they did, their weapon of choice was a knife. Other research indicated that women might be more inclined to use guns, particularly in the case of crimes involving homicides. More research is needed to understand when and how women use weapons during a variety of crimes and in a variety of contexts.

Racial differences among women

Previous literature on female criminality suggested that race was an important consideration when developing theory and explaining female criminality (Hill & Crawford, 1990; Simpson,

B.A. Koons-Witt, P.J. Schram / Journal of Criminal Justice 31 (2003) 361–371 365

1991). Research demonstrated that Black female offenders compared with White female offenders were more inclined to commit violent offenses, such as homicides and aggravated assaults (Ageton, 1983; Cernkovich & Giordano, 1979; Laub & McDermott, 1985; Simpson, 1991), and some researchers argued that race might be a better predictor of violent offending than gender (Kruttschnitt, 2001). Black women more often committed violent crimes than White women, and their rates of offending tended to be closer to those of White males as compared with White females. In looking at the intersection of race and gender with regards to violence in other countries, Kruttschnitt (2001) concluded, "It seems likely that Black women's elevated risk of involvement in homicides is directly related to their and their partners' unique, and relatively disadvantageous, position in the U.S. economy and culture" (p. 81).

Hill and Crawford (1990) examined the possibility of varying theoretical perspectives for explaining the criminality of White and Black women. Their results indicated that overall there was no difference in prevalence of crime between Black and White women. When drug crimes were removed from the analysis, however, the authors found that Black women were significantly more likely to be involved in crimes (e.g., major property, minor property, assault, and hustling). Hill and Crawford observed that the criminality of White females was most likely related to sociopsychological factors such as sex role orientation and level of self-esteem, while the criminality of Black females was most likely related to structural and deprivation factors like educational strain and residing in an urban versus rural area. The authors suggested that explanations of differential criminality between White and Black females "may be tied to different experiences and/or to different ways of responding to similar experiences" (p. 622).

In conclusion, much of the literature on women offenders focused on typical female offenders by examining their nonviolent offenses and relating them to their life circumstances. Despite the trend that women had not become more violent in their offending pattern, this study explored the prevalence and context of violent lawbreaking by females. Three research questions were addressed in the current analysis of crime incidents: (1) What is the nature and prevalence of violent offending for females in relation to drug and property offending? (2) How are offending patterns related to whether or not women are cooffenders and use weapons? and (3) How does race influence the nature of violent offending by females?

Data and methodology

National Incident-Based Reporting System (NIBRS) data

During the 1980s, efforts were made to replace the UCR with the NIBRS. Since this replacement entailed major changes, however, law enforcement agencies made gradual steps to move to this new system (Maxfield & Babbie, 2001). The essential difference between the UCR and the NIBRS is that the UCR measures the overall number of incidents for an index crime and the NIBRS measures the overall number of incidents as well as the occurrence of each type of crime. NIBRS data provide more detailed information pertaining to the offense or what is referred to as "segments." These segments include administrative, victim, offense, and offender (Rantala & Edwards, 2000).

Data from the 1998 NIBRS[3] were used in order to examine the nature and prevalence of violent offending by women. NIBRS data were organized according to crime incident and permitted researchers to consider different characteristics of incidents including, offenses, victims, offenders, and arrestees. The 1998 NIBRS data were obtained from the Inter-University Consortium for Political and Social Research (ICPSR) at the University of Michigan. For the current study, the "Offender" segment level and the "Offense" segment level from the overall NIBRS data collection (ICPSR 3031) were used. Each segment was worked with separately to isolate the cases of interest before merging both data files.

Offender segment data

The offender segment provided information about any offenders involved in the crime incident. More specifically, NIBRS data contained information on the race, age, and sex of offenders. Specific crime incidents based on offender and offense information were identified and isolated. The main purpose of this study was to examine the offending patterns of women. Therefore, only those incidents that were reported to have involved women were included in the study.[4] This procedure resulted in an initial sample size of 210,016 crime incidents from fifteen states.[5] Another objective of the study was to determine whether or not cooffending was connected to certain types of offenses. Crime incidents were categorized into one of three "offender groups": (1) single female, (2) multiple females, and (3) mixed gender.

Offense segment data

The offense segment provided information on all offenses connected to the crime incident (up to ten). This segment detailed information about the incident date, UCR offense codes, whether or not the incident was completed, location of the incident, method of entry, and type of weapon(s) used during the incident. NIBRS comprised data for crime incidents involving twenty-two offense categories grouped together from forty-six distinct crimes. Several violent, property, and drug offenses were selected and included in the analyses and the remaining offenses were dropped (see Appendix A for a list of the offenses). A series of dummy variables were created to reflect that the incident involved each type of offense. Once the offenses and offenders were identified and selected, both data files were merged with each other using a unique incident number.

Findings

To explore the relationship between type of offense and type of offender group, a series of cross-tabulations were computed. First, a cross-tabulation was computed for each offender group and each offense category. Next, a cross-tabulation was computed for the type of offender group and the type of violent offense and then the type of weapon used during the course of the incident. Finally, the study examined the relationship between race and offender groups by computing a cross-tabulation for the type of offender group and the racial composition of the offending group.

Offender groups and offense categories

The first step of the analysis consisted of exploring the link between each offender group and the offense categories. Since the NIBRS data were organized so that the incident was the unit of analysis, there existed the possibility that incidents might contain more than one type of offense. For example, an incident could involve both a drug offense and a property offense. When incidents consisting of multiple offense categories were analyzed, it was determined that approximately 17 percent of the incidents had multiple offenses that crossed different offense categories.[6] For the purposes of the present study, those incidents containing more than one offense category were excluded from the current analysis in order to examine the associations between the variables of interest.[7]

The study first considered the relationship between offender group and offense categories. Tests for a

measure of association between both variables indicated that there was a significant relationship (Goodman and Kruskal's $\tau = 0.003$, $P < .001$) between whether females offended by themselves, with other females, or with males and the type of offense committed. The results for the first contingency table are presented in Table 1 and reflect the percentage of incidents for each offender group (i.e., single female, multiple female, and mixed gender) that pertain to the specific offense category. Overall, when involved in lawbreaking, women tended to commit their crimes by themselves. Just over half of all incidents in this study were committed by females who were acting alone (52.4 percent or $n = 68,692$), and almost 40 percent ($n = 51,552$) of all incidents were committed by both male(s) and female(s) perpetrators. For single female offender incidents, the largest number of incidents consisted of property offenses (79.2 percent or $n = 54,401$) followed by drug offenses (11.9 percent or $n = 8,195$) and violent offenses (8.9 percent or $n = 6,096$). In the case of multiple female offender incidents, the largest number of incidents consisted of property offenses (86 percent or $n = 9,333$) followed by drug offenses (7.4 percent or $n = 798$) and violent offenses (6.6 percent or $n = 719$). The results suggested a similar pattern among the mixed-gender incidents. Property offenses accounted for the largest number of incidents (81 percent or $n = 41,768$) followed by drug offenses (13.5 percent or $n = 6,975$) and violent offenses (5.4 percent or $n = 2,809$). The prevalence of incidents for each offense category followed a similar pattern for each of the offender groups.

Offender groups and violent offenses

Next, the study considered the relationship between offender group and different violent offenses including murder/nonnegligent manslaughter, rob-

Table 1
Prevalence and percentage of incidents involving offense category for each offender group ($N = 131,094$)

Offense category	Total f (%)	Group 1 (Single female) f (%)	Group 2 (Multiple females) f (%)	Group 3 (Mixed gender) f (%)
Property	105,502 (80.5)	54,401 (79.2)	9,333 (86)	41,768 (81)
Drug	15,968 (12.2)	8,195 (11.9)	798 (7.4)	6,975 (13.5)
Violent	9,624 (7.3)	6,096 (8.9)	719 (6.6)	2,809 (5.4)
Total	131,094	68,692	10,850	51,552

Table 2
Prevalence and percentage of incidents involving a violent offense for each offender group ($N = 23,383$)

Violent offense	Total f (%)	Group 1 (Single female) f (%)	Group 2 (Multiple females) f (%)	Group 3 (Mixed gender) f (%)
Murder/ nonnegligent manslaughter	232 (1)	55 (.8)	5 (.4)	172 (1.1)
Robbery	3,656 (15.6)	570 (8)	177 (14.4)	2,909 (19.4)
Aggravated assault	19,495 (83.4)	6,530 (91.3)	1,049 (85.2)	11,916 (79.5)
Total	23,383	7,155	1,231	14,997

bery, and aggravated assault. As noted previously, violent incidents might involve more than one offense (e.g., aggravated assault and robbery). For incidents where more than one incident was identified, the most serious offense was the one used in the analysis. For example, if a particular incident involved both a robbery and an aggravated assault, then only the robbery would be identified and included in the analysis of association between offender group and offense type. Results from an analysis of the measure of association between these two variables indicated a significant relationship between the type of offender group and the type of violent offense (Goodman and Kruskal's $\tau = 0.020$, $P < .001$).

Table 2 presents a summary of the numbers and percentages of these offenses for each offender group. When violent offenses were considered as a whole, the results suggested that women were much more likely to commit these crimes when cooffending with males (64.1 percent or $n = 14,997$) rather than with other females (5.3 percent or $n = 1,231$) or as sole perpetrators (30.6 percent or $n = 7,155$). Violent offenses committed by single females overwhelmingly involved aggravated assaults (91.3 percent or $n = 6,530$) followed to a lesser extent by robbery (8 percent or $n = 570$) and murder or nonnegligent manslaughter (0.8 percent or $n = 55$). Although there were changes in distribution, a similar pattern of offending existed for the other offender groups as well. For multiple female incidents, aggravated assaults were the most frequently cited violent offense (85.2 percent or $n = 1,049$) followed by robbery (14.4 percent or $n = 177$) and murder/nonnegligent manslaughter (0.4 percent or $n = 5$). Similarly, for incidents involving both male and female perpetrators, aggravated assaults were most prevalent (79.5 percent or $n = 11,916$), while robbery (19.4 percent or $n = 2,909$) was the second most cited violent offense

followed by murder or nonnegligent manslaughter (1.1 percent or $n = 172$).

The findings for each of the offender groups indicated that the largest number of incidents (and proportion) involved aggravated assaults followed by robberies and murder/nonnegligent manslaughter. It did appear, however, that females were more likely to commit aggravated assaults by themselves, whereas they were more likely to commit robberies with others including males. To understand more fully the nature of these violent offenses and possible group differences, additional analysis was completed involving the use of weapons.

Offender groups and use of weapons

The study also considered the relationship between the type of offender group and the use of weapons during violent incidents. Table 3 provides descriptive information for each offender group and whether or not a gun[8] was used during a violent incident or a knife/cutting instrument, a blunt object such as a club

Table 3
Offender group by type of weapon used during the violent incident ($N = 23,383$)

Use of weapons	Total f (%)	Group 1 (Single female) ($n = 7,155$) f (%)	Group 2 (Multiple females) ($n = 1,231$) f (%)	Group 3 (Mixed gender) ($n = 14,997$) f (%)
Gun				
No	17,920 (76.6)	6,148 (85.9)	1,050 (85.3)	10,722 (71.5)**
Yes	5,463 (23.4)	1,007 (14.1)	181 (14.7)	4,275 (28.5)
Knife/cutting instrument				
No	16,199 (69.3)	4,834 (67.6)	864 (70.2)	10,501 (70)*
Yes	7,184 (30.7)	2,321 (32.4)	367 (29.8)	4,496 (30)
Blunt object				
No	17,497 (74.8)	5,630 (78.7)	938 (76.2)	10,929 (72.9)**
Yes	5,886 (25.2)	1,525 (21.3)	293 (23.8)	4,068 (27.1)
Personal weapons				
No	13,658 (58.4)	4,828 (67.5)	693 (56.3)	8,137 (54.3)**
Yes	9,725 (41.6)	2,327 (32.5)	538 (43.7)	6,860 (45.7)

* $P < .05$.
** $P < .001$.

or hammer, or personal weapons such as one's hands, feet, or teeth. An analysis of association was performed between the offender group and the type of weapon(s) used during the incident. Each type of weapon was coded as yes or no, with yes indicating that at least one gun, for example, was involved in a particular violent incident. A significant association was found between the type of offender group and whether or not the incident involved any guns (Goodman and Kruskal's $\tau = 0.026$, $P < .001$), knives or cutting instruments (Goodman and Kruskal's $\tau = 0.001$, $P < .05$), blunt instruments (Goodman and Kruskal's $\tau = 0.004$, $P < .001$), and personal weapons (Goodman and Kruskal's $\tau = 0.018$, $P < .001$).

When use of weapons were considered more generally, the results indicated that violent incidents involving female perpetrators were more likely to involve personal weapons such as the use of hands, feet, or teeth (41.6 percent or $n = 9,725$) followed by knives or cutting instruments (30.7 percent or $n = 7,184$). Violent crimes committed by females were less likely to involve weapons such as blunt objects (25.2 percent or $n = 5,886$) or guns (23.4 percent or $n = 5,463$). When specific offender groups were considered, the findings suggested that females who committed their violent crimes alone more frequently used either personal weapons (32.5 percent or $n = 2,327$) or knives (32.4 percent or $n = 2,321$) followed by blunt objects (21.3 percent or $n = 1,525$) and guns (14.1 percent or $n = 1,007$). Multiple female offenders committing violent offenses were more likely to use personal weapons such as their hands, feet, or teeth (43.7 percent $n = 538$) followed by knives or other cutting instruments (29.8 percent or $n = 367$) and blunt objects (23.8 percent or $n = 293$). Like females who violated the laws by themselves, females who committed violent crimes with other females were not as likely to use a gun (14.7 percent or $n = 181$).

For females who committed violent offenses with males, the results seemed to suggest a different pattern of weapons usage. The results indicated that personal weapons (45.7 percent or $n = 6,860$) were the most frequently used weapon by this offender group followed by knives or other cutting instruments (30 percent or $n = 4,496$), guns (28.5 percent or $n = 4,275$), and blunt objects (27.1 percent or $n = 4,068$). Although the mixed-gender offender group was less likely to use a gun during the course of their violent crimes when compared with other weapons used by this particular group, offender groups consisting of both males and females were more likely to use guns compared with females who acted alone or with other females (28.5 versus 14.7 and 14.1 percent). Thus, it appeared that violent incidents that involved both male and female perpe-

Table 4
Racial composition of perpetrator(s) by offending group for violent offenses ($N = 14,433$)

Racial composition per group	Total f (%)	Group 1 (Single female) ($n = 6,848$) f (%)	Group 2 (Multiple females) ($n = 960$) f (%)	Group 3 (Mixed gender) ($n = 6,625$) f (%)
All Black offenders	5,333 (37)	3,233 (47.2)	497 (51.8)	1,603 (24.6)
All White offenders	9,100 (63)	3,615 (52.8)	463 (48.2)	5,022 (75.8)

trators were more likely to have at least one gun present during the crime when compared with violent incidents involving just one female or multiple females.

Racial composition and offender groups

The current study was also interested in examining the relationship between the race of the perpetrators and the type of offender group. A test of the measure of association between racial composition of the offenders involved in the violent incident was compared with the type of offender group based on sex. For the purposes of this particular analysis and for the ease of interpretation, only those incidents containing either all White offenders or all Black offenders were considered. Incidents involving both White and Black perpetrators were excluded since observations could not be obtained for incidents involving only single female perpetrators.[9] Table 4 presents cross-tabulation results between the racial composition of perpetrators for each incident and cooffending.

Results from the analysis indicated that there was a significant relationship between the racial composition of the offending group and whether females offended alone, with other females, or with males (Goodman and Kruskal's $\tau = 0.060$, $P < .001$). White females were more likely to commit violent crimes by themselves (52.8 percent or $n = 3,615$) when compared with Black females (47.2 percent or $n = 3,233$), whereas Black females were more likely to commit violent offenses with other Black females (51.8 percent or $n = 497$). Finally, White females were much more likely to commit violent offenses with males (75.8 percent or $n = 5,022$) than were Black females (24.6 percent or $n = 1,603$).

Discussion

Violent female offenders had been the focus of an increasing amount of scholarship over the last decade. This was due in part to the belief of some that the violent female offenders represented an emerging offender group. While it was true that arrests of women for violent crimes increased during the 1990s, violent offenses for women still represented a small share of their overall offenses. Furthermore, the largest gender gap for offenses occurred with violent crimes because women commit violent crimes much less often when compared with men (Pollock, 1999). Despite the fact that there was little or no evidence to support such an argument, research involving female violent offenders was important in furthering the understanding of why some females became involved in violent offending.

The purpose of this study was to examine the nature and prevalence of violent offending for females in relation to other types of offenses, such as property and drug. The present study also explored the relationship between cooffending and violent offending and uses of weapons. Finally, this study considered the importance of race when looking at the nature of violent offending by females. Each of these issues was addressed using one of the more comprehensive official data sets available for analysis.

Results from the current study suggest that consistent with prior literature, females are more likely to commit property crimes compared with drug crimes and violent crimes. The results presented in Table 1 seem to suggest that females are more likely to commit violent offenses by themselves. These results are probably the result of the high number of aggravated assaults committed by single female perpetrators; however, these findings should be interpreted with a certain amount of caution because of the incidents that were excluded from this part of the analysis. Many of the excluded incidents (those incidents involving multiple offense categories) involved both male and female perpetrators, and most of these incidents involved drug and violent offenses. This suggests that females actually had a much higher involvement in drug and violent offenses when they were cooffending with males.

These observations were consistent with the works of Pettiway (1987) and Alarid et al. (1996) who found that women were more likely to commit "masculine-type" crimes or nontraditional crimes with their intimates (male accomplices), but differed from the research of Greenfeld and Snell (1999). They found that the majority of women in their research acted alone when committing violent offenses. In this study, it appeared that women had not necessarily become more active in committing violent crimes, but seemed to be more involved in these types of offenses when cooffending with males.

When only violent incidents were considered, females were more likely to be involved in aggravated assaults compared with robberies and murder or nonnegligent manslaughter. This was particularly true for females who committed their violent crimes alone. When females cooffended with other females or males, however, they seemed to be more likely to commit robberies. This finding partially supported Miller's (1998) ethnographic study that found that women usually committed robberies with other women. The findings in the current study also supported the work of Alarid et al. (1996) who looked at differences between Black and White women. As in the case of Alarid et al.'s research, the current study found that Black women were more likely to commit violent offenses with other women, whereas White women were more likely to commit violent offenses with males.

Some prior research questioned whether women were more likely to use guns to commit their offenses. Jurik and Winn's (1990) study, for example, found that women were more inclined to use guns compared with knives when committing murder or nonnegligent manslaughter and that males and females were equally likely to use guns during these violent incidents. The findings from the current study indicated that females overall were more likely to use either personal weapons (e.g., hands, feet, or teeth) or knives/cutting instruments when involved in violent crimes; however, women were more likely to use guns when they were committing violent crimes with males.

The current study had several limitations that were important to note. The first limitation pertained to the generalizability of the findings. The 1998 NIBRS data contained information on crimes for only fifteen states and the findings from this research might not be necessarily generalizable to other states that were not included in the data set. Another limitation of the current study involved the examination of whether females committed their crimes alone, with other females, or with males. Researchers were unable to specifically determine the role of women offenders within mixed-gender crime groups. Despite these research limitations and the scant amount of literature on violent women offenders, this study revealed some findings that were informative. This study also provoked questions for further inquiry, including exploring the relation between the victim and the perpetrator.

Acknowledgements

An earlier version of this article was presented in 2001 at the American Society of Criminology Annual Meeting in Atlanta, Georgia.

370   *B.A. Koons-Witt, P.J. Schram / Journal of Criminal Justice 31 (2003) 361–371*

Appendix A. Categories and types of offenses

Property offenses:
Arson
Burglary/breaking and entering
Shoplifting
Theft from building
Theft from motor vehicle
Theft of motor vehicle parts
All other larceny
Motor vehicle theft
Counterfeiting/forgery
False pretenses/swindle
Credit card/automatic teller fraud
Welfare fraud
Embezzlement
Stolen property offenses
Destruction/damage/vandalism

Drug offenses:
Drug/narcotics violations
Drug equipment violations

Violent offenses:
Murder/nonnegligent manslaughter
Robbery
Aggravated assault

Notes

1. Many scholars maintain that there has been a change for women offenders and that the legal system is much more likely to incarcerate women instead of imposing alternative sanctions (Bloom, Chesney-Lind, & Owen, 1994; Chesney-Lind, 1997; Kruttschnitt, 2001; Nagel & Hagan, 1992). For instance, while arrest rates for women increased 29 percent between 1986 and 1990, during that same time period, incarceration figures increased for women by 73 percent in jails and 77 percent in prisons for women (Chesney-Lind & Pollock, 1995).

2. Mixed-sex crime groups exclude partnerships between women and their boyfriends or husbands.

3. U.S. Department of Justice, Federal Bureau of Investigation. National Incident-Based Reporting System, 1998 [Computer file]. Compiled by the U.S. Department of Justice, Federal Bureau of Investigation. ICPSR ed. Ann Arbor, MI: Inter-University Consortium for Political and Social Research [producer and distributor], 2000.

4. The analysis followed a complicated process in identifying the incidents involving women. First, the gender of each offender was recoded accordingly to "1" for females and "0" for males. Next, the gender variable was aggregated by summing its values according to each incident number. This created a gender score, which ranged "from 0 to 18." For example, if an incident involved two male offenders, then the aggregate score would have been "0," and if an incident involved one male and two females, then the aggregate score would have been "2." Based on the gender score, it could determine those incidents involving only

male offenders (score of "0") and those incidents involving at least one female (score of "1" or higher). Lastly, those cases involving only males were filtered out, leaving those incidents involving females.

5. The 1998 NIBRS data collection contained crime incidents from fifteen states including Colorado, Idaho, Iowa, Kentucky, Massachusetts, Michigan, Nebraska, North Dakota, Ohio, South Carolina, Tennessee, Texas, Utah, Vermont, and Virginia.

6. Approximately 11.1 percent ($n = 21,378$) of incidents had offenses from two of the three categories and 2.5 percent ($n = 4,816$) of incidents had offenses from each of the three categories.

7. Excluding incidents involving different types of offenses (17 percent) from the current analysis impacted the number of incidents for each offender group, particularly the mixed-gender group. For example, removing these incidents reduced the number of incidents for the mixed-gender group by 31 percent (from 74,492 to 51,552 incidents) compared with a reduction of 9 percent for the multiple female group (from 11,921 to 10,850 incidents) and 3 percent for the single female group (from 70,875 to 68,692 incidents). Specific offense categories involving mixed-gender incidents were also affected. The number of incidents involving violent crimes decreased by approximately 81 percent (from 14,997 to 2,809 incidents) and the number of incidents involving drug offenses decreased 69 percent (from 22,743 to 6,975 incidents). Thus, it appeared that incidents involving both males and females were more likely to involve multiple types of offenses (e.g., drug offense and violent offense).

8. The gun category includes automatic firearms and handguns, rifles, shotguns, and other types of guns.

9. Approximately 31 percent of the incidents involved a mixed-race offender group. These were excluded since cells for incidents involving single female offenders would be empty and would influence further analyses. A large amount of the mixed-race offender incidents were comprised of both Black and White perpetrators ($n = 6,588$). Ninety-eight percent ($n = 6,455$) of the incidents involving both Black and White offenders were mixed gender as well, whereas only 2 percent ($n = 133$) of incidents for the mixed-race offender group consisted of multiple female offenders.

References

Adler, F. (1975). *Sisters in crime: The rise of the new female criminal*. New York: McGraw-Hill.

Ageton, S. S. (1983). The dynamics of female delinquency, 1976–1980. *Criminology, 21*, 555–584.

Alarid, L. F., Marquart, J. W., Burton, V. S., Cullen, F. T., & Cuvelier, S. J. (1996). Women's roles in serious offenses: A study of adult felons. *Justice Quarterly, 13*, 431–454.

Baskin, D. R., & Sommers, I. (1993). Females' initiation into violent street crime. *Justice Quarterly, 10*, 559–583.

Belknap, J. (2001). *The invisible woman: Gender, crime and justice* (2nd ed.). Belmont, CA: Wadsworth.

Bloom, B., Chesney-Lind, M., & Owen, B. (1994). *Women in California prisons: Hidden victims of the war on*

B.A. Koons-Witt, P.J. Schram / Journal of Criminal Justice 31 (2003) 361–371   371

drugs. San Francisco: Center on Juvenile and Criminal Justice.

Bunch, B. J., Foley, L. A., & Urbina, S. P. (1983). The psychology of violent female offenders: A sex-role perspective. *Prison Journal, 63,* 66–79.

Cernkovich, S. A., & Giordano, P. C. (1979). A comparative analysis of male and female delinquency. *Sociological Quarterly, 20,* 131–145.

Chesney-Lind, M. (1997). *The female offender: Girls, women and crime.* Thousand Oaks, CA: Sage Publications.

Chesney-Lind, M., & Pollock, J. M. (1995). Women's prisons: Equality with a vengeance. In A. V. Merlo & J. M. Pollock (Eds.), *Women, law, social control* (pp. 155–175). Boston: Allyn and Bacon.

Decker, S., Wright, R., Redfern, A., & Smith, D. (1993). A woman's place is in the home: Females and residential burglary. *Justice Quarterly, 10,* 143–162.

Gilfus, M. (1992). From victims to survivors to offenders: Women's routes to entry and immersion into street crime. *Women and Criminal Justice, 4,* 63–89.

Goetting, A. (1988). Patterns of homicide among women. *Journal of Interpersonal Violence, 3,* 3–20.

Greenfeld, L. A., & Snell, T. L. (1999). *Women offenders.* Washington, DC: U.S. Department of Justice, Office of Justice Programs, Bureau of Justice Statistics.

Hill, G. D., & Crawford, E. M. (1990). Women, race, and crime. *Criminology, 28,* 601–623.

Jurik, N. C., & Winn, R. (1990). Gender and homicide: A comparison of men and women who kill. *Violence and Victims, 5,* 227–242.

Klein, D. (1995). The etiology of female crime: A review of the literature. In B. R. Price & N. J. Sokoloff (Eds.), *The criminal justice system and women: Offenders, victims, and workers* (pp. 30–53). New York: McGraw-Hill.

Kruttschnitt, C. (2001). Gender and violence. In C. M. Renzetti & L. Goodstein (Eds.), *Women, crime, and criminal justice* (pp. 77–92). Los Angeles: Roxbury Publishing.

Laub, J. H., & McDermott, M. J. (1985). An analysis of crime by young Black women. *Criminology, 23,* 81–98.

Maher, L., & Daly, K. (1996). Women in the street-level drug economy: Continuity or change? *Criminology, 34*(4), 465–491.

Maxfield, M. G., & Babbie, E. (2001). *Research methods for criminal justice and criminology* (3rd ed.). Belmont, CA: Wadsworth.

Miller, J. (1998). Up it up: Gender and the accomplishment of street robbery. *Criminology, 36,* 37–66.

Nagel, I. H., & Hagan, J. (1992). Gender and crime: Offense patterns and criminal court sanctions. In N. Morris &

M. Tonry (Eds.), *Crime and justice* (Vol. 4, pp. 91–144). Chicago: University of Chicago Press.

Pettiway, L. E. (1987). Participation in crime partnerships by female drug users: The effects of domestic arrangements, drug use, and criminal involvement. *Criminology, 25,* 741–766.

Pollock, J. M. (1999). *Criminal women.* Cincinnati, OH: Anderson Publishing.

Rantala, R. R., & Edwards, T. J. (2000). *Effects of NIBRS on crime statistics* [Special Report]. Washington, DC: U.S. Department of Justice.

Sanchez, L. (2001). Gender troubles: The entanglement of agency, violence, and law in the lives of women in prostitution. In C. M. Renzetti & L. Goodstein (Eds.), *Women, crime, and criminal justice* (pp. 60–76). Los Angeles: Roxbury Publishing.

Simon, R. J. (1975). *Women and crime.* Lexington, MA: D.C. Heath.

Simpson, S. S. (1991). Caste, class, and violent crime: Explaining differences in female offending. *Criminology, 29,* 115–135.

Smart, C. (1976). *Women, crime, and criminology: A feminist critique.* Boston: Routledge and K. Paul.

Sommers, I., & Baskin, D. R. (1993). The situational context of violent female offending. *Journal of Research in Crime and Delinquency, 30*(2), 136–162.

Sommers, I., & Baskin, D. R. (1997). Situational or generalized violence in drug dealing networks. *Journal of Drug Issues, 27,* 833–849.

Steffensmeier, D. (1983). Organization properties and sex-segregation in the underworld: Building a sociological theory of sex differences in crime. *Social Forces, 61,* 1010–1032.

Steffensmeier, D. (2001). Female crime trends, 1960–1995. In C. M. Renzetti & L. Goodstein (Eds.), *Women, crime, and criminal justice* (pp. 191–211). Los Angeles: Roxbury Publishing.

Steffensmeier, D., & Allan, E. (1998). The nature of female offending: Patterns and explanation. In R. T. Zaplin (Ed.), *Female offenders: Critical perspectives and effective interventions* (pp. 5–29). Gaithersburg, MD: Aspen Publications.

Steffensmeier, D., & Broidy, L. (2001). Explaining female offending. In C. M. Renzetti & L. Goodstein (Eds.), *Women, crime, and criminal justice* (pp. 111–132). Los Angeles: Roxbury Publishing.

Ward, D. A., Jackson, J., & Ward, R. E. (1979). Crimes of violence by women. In F. Adler & R. J. Simon (Eds.), *Criminology of deviant women* (pp. 116–117). Boston: Houghton Mifflin.

[23]

INVESTIGATING THE CONNECTIONS BETWEEN RACE, ILLICIT DRUG MARKETS, AND LETHAL VIOLENCE, 1984-1997

GRAHAM C. OUSEY

MATTHEW R. LEE

Many scholars have speculated that the dramatic rise of homicide rates in the late 1980s and their subsequent decline in the 1990s was driven by the expansion and contraction of illegal drug markets and/or law enforcement attempts to regulate these markets. However, the empirical evidence to this end is limited in important ways. This analysis extends prior research and provides evidence of the following: (1) Change in drug market indicators are positively associated with change in both Black and White homicide rates in large U.S. cities between 1984 and 1997. (2) This relationship is substantially stronger for Blacks than for Whites. (3) The socioeconomic moderators of the drug-market/violence link vary by race, with racial inequality being especially important for Blacks and resource deprivation being especially important for Whites. The main implications of the analysis are that the drug-market/ lethal violence connection is much more complex than previously thought, and that simplistic theoretical accounts of the drug market-violence nexus need additional development.

Keywords: drug markets; homicide; crime trends

Marked fluctuations in homicide rates have drawn a great deal of interest from social scientists (e.g., see Blumstein and Wallman 2000) in recent years. In the mid-1990s, much of the scholarly attention focused on the wave of youth violence that began a decade earlier. More recently, focus has shifted to the unprecedented drop in rates of lethal violence of the past several years. Speculation and empirical research (Blumstein and Wallman 2000; Blumstein and Rosenfeld 1998; LaFree 1998) on these trends have pointed to a number of possible explanations, with the most prominent of these stressing the impact of illicit drug markets on the recent rise and fall of homicide

An earlier version of this article was presented at the 2002 annual meeting of the Southern Sociological Society, Baltimore, MD. Direct all correspondence to Graham C. Ousey, Department of Sociology and Criminal Justice, 322 Smith Hall, University of Delaware, Newark, DE 19716 (e-mail: gousey@udel.edu).

rates (e.g., see Beckett and Sasson 2000; Blumstein 1995; Fox and Levin 2001).

In spite of the great interest generated by recent shifts in homicide rates, the criminological literature actually contains very few studies that empirically test potential explanations of these trends (but see Ousey and Lee, 2002). Although a large body of research has examined the connection between individual violent offending and drug *use* (e.g., see Fagan 1990), the aggregate-level relationship between drug *markets* and violence has received much less attention. Furthermore, the few prior studies that have investigated this issue are limited in important ways. For example, some of the widely cited drug market-violence studies (e.g., Goldstein et al. 1989, 1997) are descriptive profiles of a single locality that cannot be generalized to other places. In addition, several of the multi-city, multivariate analyses of the drug market/violence nexus feature cross-sectional designs (e.g., Baumer 1994; Ousey and Augustine 2001) that do not directly address the connection between *change* in illicit drug markets and *change* in homicide rates. Finally, recent studies that do explore the impact of drug markets on temporal change in homicide rates are not race-specific (Baumer et al. 1998; Ousey and Lee 2002). This is an especially important limitation because as we delineate below, several contemporary theoretical frameworks imply that the drug market/violence relationship may vary by racial group.

In light of these limitations, the present study extends prior research on the illicit drug market-violence relationship in key ways. Following the lead of Ousey and Lee (2002), we first examine whether within-city change in illicit drug markets is associated with change in homicide rates. However, rather than simply assuming racial invariance in the drug market-violence relationship, we extend that earlier work by outlining and testing a conceptual framework that predicts race differences in the impact of illicit drug markets (and their enforcement–see discussion below) on homicide rates. In addition, we examine whether the race-specific relationship between drug markets and homicide varies as a function of the social-structural conditions faced by Blacks and Whites in a sample of large U.S. cities.

CONCEPTUAL FRAMEWORK

Illicit Drug Markets and Homicide: Prominent Perspectives

Scholarly concern over the impact on criminal behavior of drug use, abuse, and addiction is evident in research going back several decades (Monteforte and Spitz 1975; White and Gorman 2000; Zahn and Bencivengo 1974). However, in recent years, interest in the drug-crime link has increasingly turned to the effect of illicit drug *markets* on rates of criminality, especially lethal violence. Indeed, the belief that markets for illegal drugs generate criminal violence is a common theme in the writings of drug legalization proponents (e.g., Hamowy 1987; Nadelmann 1989), popular journalists (Martz 1989), and crime scholars (e.g., Baumer et al. 1998; Blumstein 1995).

Systemic Violence

Most research on the connection between illegal drug markets and violence is theoretically anchored in Goldstein's (1985) systemic violence model. In contrast to research connecting drug-related violence to the mind-altering effects of drug use, the systemic violence model attributes drug-related violence to the basic structure of illegal commodity markets. According to Goldstein (1985), "[Systemic] violence arises from the exigencies of working or doing business in an illicit market—a context in which the monetary stakes can be enormous but where the economic actors have no recourse to the legal system to resolve disputes" (p. 116).

The underlying logic of the systemic model follows from Donald Black's (1976, 1983) theories of law and self-help. According to Black, violence (or "self-help") is simply one of many forms of conflict management used in a given society or social group. However, rather than being randomly distributed across social space, violence is most likely to occur among those whose social position puts the law effectively out of reach. For example, Black suggests that because of their low vertical social status, economically deprived groups are likely to have very limited access to the state's system of dispute resolution (i.e., the law). Therefore, they are more likely to utilize informal, aggressive tactics to resolve their grievances. Similarly, because drug market participants are exchanging illegal goods, the law is effectively unavailable as a tool of dispute resolution (see Cooney 1997). Consequently, those involved in the drug market are particularly likely to use violent means of self-help to redress drug-market-related grievances. Well-known illustrations of systemic violence include drug dealer battles over territory, disagreements over drug prices or payments, punishment or discipline for the theft of drugs, or retaliation for passing off an impure product.

The systemic violence model is rooted in basic scholarship on sociological markets (see Collins 1994) and is the most general of the drug market-violence models in the literature. Although intuitively accessible and useful as an orienting framework, it is limited in (at least) two ways. First, it offers no reason to expect variation in the drug market-violence relationship across demographic groups. Second, it does not account for contingencies that may further enhance the lethality of illegal markets, such as the preexistence of violence-conducive social conditions. In contrast, several recent accounts of the drug market/violence nexus suggest modifications to Goldstein's model that enhance its flexibility and thereby address these limitations. In the sections that follow, we discuss these accounts in turn.

Community Disorganization

Building directly upon the systemic violence model, the "community disorganization" perspective of Blumstein (1995) suggests that the rising rates of homicide in the late 1980s were largely a result of the dramatic explosion in demand for crack-cocaine, which was introduced to many major cities in the mid- to late-1980s. According to Blumstein, crack-cocaine's low price, short-lived effects, and addictive properties resulted in a rapidly growing segment of low-income drug buyers who frequently purchased small amounts of the drug. As a consequence of this pattern of drug-buying, drug market activity (i.e., the number of drug market transactions) rose dramatically.

Accompanying the increase in market activity, the expansion of the crack trade brought with it an elevation in risk for drug market participants. Primarily, this occurred because crack sales tended to take place in unprotected open-air street markets. Thus, dealers carrying loads of cash and drugs were vulnerable to assault and robbery. In addition, the public nature of many crack markets meant that dealers often competed for market share in the same geographic space, which elevated the potential that conflicts would arise between them. Because of the illegality of their activities, the police and legal system were not available to protect them against motivated offenders or to resolve their market-related conflicts. Consequently, firearms became a primary mechanism for protection and dispute resolution, thereby heightening the probability that drug dealer conflicts would become lethal (see Lizotte et al. 2000).

Although the elevated danger of the crack business alone may have contributed much to the increasing rates of lethal violence during the second-half of the 1980s, Blumstein (1995) argues that this trend was exacerbated by drug-market-linked factors seeping into surrounding communities. Specifically, he contends that as firearms and pro-violence norms became ubiquitous among drug market participants, other community residents began to adopt them as well. This seems quite plausible, particularly in cases in which drug dealers were socially integrated into communities in which their products were peddled (see Pattillo 1998).[1]

In addition to the preceding modifications of the systemic violence model, Blumstein's (1995) work also implies that the connection between illicit drug markets and rates of lethal violence is stronger for Blacks than Whites. To a large degree, this expected racial difference follows from the fact that dangerous open-air *crack* cocaine market transactions were more likely in impoverished predominantly African American communities, whereas more private and protected settings were more typical of the *powder* cocaine (a more expensive form of the drug) transactions common in predominantly White communities. Thus, given the public and potentially hostile context of the drug trade in predominantly Black ghetto communities, it seems reasonable that the link between drug-market activity and homicide would be enhanced among Blacks.

Code of the Streets

Developing cultural themes that resemble, but go beyond those evident in Blumstein's work, Anderson (1999) also delineates a connection between drug-market activities and criminal violence in inner-city, predominantly Black communities. However, in contrast to the above models, Anderson's race-specific view of the illicit drug market-violence relationship is framed within the context of dramatic social and economic changes affecting the urban landscape in the United States over the past few decades. Specifically, Anderson contends that deindustrialization, the globalization of the economy, and recent changes in welfare policy have created especially bleak economic and labor market prospects in inner-city Black communities. In response, many Blacks have adopted alternative economic and cultural frameworks, including underground or illicit economic activities (see also Beckett and Sasson 2000; Hagan 1994). Indeed, according to Anderson's (1999) view, the illicit drug economy has essentially risen to fill the void left by the exodus of blue-collar manufacturing jobs, which once provided the economic sustenance for residents of inner-city areas.

Related to the growth and normalization of the illicit drug economy is a "code of the street" (Anderson 1999). This refers to a cultural framework that inverts many of the norms and values observed among those in the middle-class mainstream, especially as they relate to the use of violence and the resolution of interpersonal disputes. Inner-city ghetto residents that internalize the code are likely to become extremely alienated from conventional society and to reject the legitimacy of the system that has effectively ostracized them. As a consequence, in areas where the "code of the street" is more evident, there is a heightened probability that violent means of protection and dispute resolution will be employed.

To reiterate, Anderson (1999) views the proliferation of the illicit drug economy and the emergence of the code of the street as related adaptations to the extreme economic disadvantage and cultural alienation that many Blacks have endured as a result of deindustrialization. However, because the implications of deindustrialization may have been less severe for White

Americans, it is less likely that these same economic and cultural adaptations would be evident among them. If this logic is correct, it follows that the code of the streets should enhance the connection between the drug trade and violence in predominantly Black, but not predominantly White, communities.[2]

Intensity of Drug Law Enforcement

A fourth conceptual framework suggesting a link between illegal drug markets and lethal violence focuses on the impact of drug law enforcement (see MacCoun, Kilmer, and Reuter 2003; MacCoun and Reuter 2001), rather than on drug market activity itself. According to this view, the vigorous enforcement of drug laws increases drug-related violence by affecting the potential payoff and degree of competition in the drug market. In particular, interdiction and drug law enforcement efforts may tighten the drug market and put an upward pressure on the price of drugs (MacCoun and Reuter 2001). Moreover, as law enforcement arrests remove dealers from the market, established market shares and turf arrangements are disrupted and competition for territory begins anew. Thus, by potentially raising prices and reinvigorating the competition for territory and associated dollars, drug-control efforts may actually work to drive up, rather than reduce, rates of lethal violence.

However, if the above scenario is valid, there is good reason to believe that it is more likely to be characteristic of the drug markets in predominantly Black rather than predominantly White communities. As Tonry (1995) and others (e.g., Beckett and Sasson 2000; Jonas 1999) have pointed out, recent drug laws as well as drug law enforcement practices are effectively racially biased. For example, although Blacks comprise roughly 7 percent of past month illegal drug users (Substance Abuse and Mental Health Services Administration [SAMHSA] 2001), more than one in three drug arrestees is Black (Maguire and Pastore 2002). Moreover, the mandatory minimum sentence for possession of five grams of crack, the form of cocaine commonly associated with low-income predominantly Black inner-city communities, is the same as the mandatory minimum sentence for 500 grams of powder cocaine, which is more commonly associated with middle-class Whites (Beckett and Sasson 2000). Given these disparities, it follows that the negative consequences of intense drug law enforcement described above vary by race, with Blacks likely bearing the brunt of the impact.[3]

Contingent Causation Model

A final model suggesting a link between illicit drug markets and homicide rates is the contingent causation model posited by Zimring and Hawkins

(1997). In their work, Zimring and Hawkins question whether the illicit drug market-homicide association is unconditional as Goldstein's systemic violence model suggests. Indeed, they note that there is little evidence of a link between drug markets and violence in European countries, despite fairly compelling support from research based in the United States. Given this conflicting evidence, Zimring and Hawkins contend that the drug market-violence relationship exists in some contexts, but not in others. Specifically, they argue that drug markets are most likely to produce violence when preexisting social conditions are conducive to violence.

Unfortunately, Zimring and Hawkins (1997) do not clearly identify the preexisting social conditions that are conducive to violence. However, in a recent test of the contingent causation thesis, Ousey and Lee (2002) report that the illicit drug market-homicide relationship varies with the level of socioeconomic disadvantage in U.S. cities. Specifically, in cities with above average levels of socioeconomic disadvantage, an increase in illicit drug markets corresponds with rising homicide rates. On the other hand, in cities with below average levels of socioeconomic disadvantage the illicit drug market-homicide relationship becomes nil, or in extreme instances, becomes negative (i.e., higher drug market activity is associated with lower homicide rates).

Although race group differences in the drug market-homicide nexus are not explicitly discussed by Zimring and Hawkins (1997), or modeled in Ousey and Lee's (2002) recent study, we believe that the contingent causation model anticipates them. Indeed, considering the United States' history of racial discrimination, current differences in the average socioeconomic contexts of Black and White communities, and the social context-drug market interaction effect reported by Ousey and Lee (2002), it seems reasonable to surmise that Blacks endure social and economic conditions that are more conducive to violence than Whites. Consequently, it follows that the illicit drug market-homicide association will be stronger among Blacks than Whites.[4] Furthermore, because prior studies suggest that the social conditions conducive to high rates of violence vary by racial group (see Harer and Steffensmeier 1992; LaFree and Drass 1996; Messner and Golden 1992; Ousey 1999; Ousey and Augustine 2001; Parker and McCall 1999), there is good reason to suspect that there are racial group differences in the social and economic factors that moderate the drug market-homicide relationship.

Assessment of the Research Literature

To date, the body of research on the illicit drug market-violence relationship generally supports the expected positive association between these two factors (e.g., Baumer et al. 1998; Blumstein 1995; Cork 1999; Goldstein et al.

1997; Ousey 2000a, 2000b; Ousey and Augustine 2001; Ousey and Lee 2002; Riley 1998). Yet, comprehension of this relationship remains rather rudimentary because the extant literature is limited in several important respects. First, most of the prior studies are either descriptive profiles of a single locality (e.g., Goldstein et al. 1997) or are cross-sectional analyses of the drug market-homicide link across multiple localities. Such research designs lack generalizability and/or offer limited evidence on the impact of change in illicit drug markets on change in homicide rates. Second, the majority of extant research—including recent longitudinal studies of the drug market–homicide relationship—is not race-specific (e.g., see Baumer et al. 1998; Cohen et al. 1998; Goldstein et al. 1997; Ousey and Lee 2002; Riley 1998). This is a serious shortcoming because as the above discussion indicates, many accounts of the drug market–violence nexus imply that the magnitude of this association may vary by race. Finally, prior theory and research implies that violence conducive social conditions may differ somewhat for Blacks and Whites. To the extent that is true, there may be important racial group differences in the structural factors that condition the drug market–homicide relationship. However, previous empirical studies (e.g., Ousey and Lee 2002) have not fully investigated these possibilities.

Given the above limitations, there remain important gaps in the literature on the link between drug markets and homicide. In response, we pursue several objectives in the current study. First, we examine whether within-city *change* in illicit drug markets is associated with within city *change* in Black and White homicide rates during the 1984-1997 period. Second, we explore whether the magnitude of this within-city, longitudinal relationship varies by racial group. Third, we investigate whether the conditions affecting the lethality of illicit drug markets for Blacks differ from those that affect the lethality of the market for Whites. To guide our pursuit of these objectives, we posit several research hypotheses, which are presented below.

SUMMARY OF HYPOTHESES

Hypothesis 1: According to the systemic violence model of Goldstein (1985), the illegality of the drug trade leads to the use of informal and violent means of "self-help" (see Black 1983) social control—much of which is lethal—because official law enforcement agents cannot be called upon to resolve disputes. Following this argument, we posit that *within-city change in illicit drug markets is positively associated with within-city change in homicide rates for both Blacks and Whites during the 1984-1997 period*.

Hypothesis 2: Although the specific explanatory mechanisms differ among them, several pieces of scholarship that are delineated above (see

Anderson 1999; Blumstein 1995; Tonry 1995; Zimring and Hawkins 1997) suggest that *the within-city association between illicit drug markets and homicide will be stronger for Blacks than for Whites.*

Hypotheses 3 and 4: Zimring and Hawkins (1997) contend that illicit drug markets are more lethal in areas where preexisting social conditions are conducive to lethal violence. However, prior research suggests that the degree to which structural conditions are conducive to violence varies across racial groups (Harer and Steffensmeier 1992; LaFree and Drass 1996; Parker and McCall 1999; Ousey 1999). Following this literature, we surmise one general and one race-specific hypothesis regarding the moderating impact of preexisting social conditions on the illicit drug market–homicide relationship. First, because prior research generally indicates that levels of socioeconomic disadvantage are associated with Black and White rates of lethal violence, we postulate that *the within-city drug market-homicide association (among both Blacks and Whites), will be stronger in cities with greater levels of resource deprivation.*

Second, because theory and empirical research suggest that race-based socioeconomic inequality may be linked to higher rates of homicide offending among Blacks but not among Whites (cf. Messner and Golden 1992; Ousey and Augustine 2001; Parker and McCall 1999), we posit that *the expected positive relationship between illicit drug markets and homicide among Blacks will be stronger in cities with greater levels of racial inequality.* No interaction effect between racial inequality and illicit drug markets is expected for Whites.

DATA AND METHOD

The units of analysis for this study are 1,708 "city-years" (i.e., 122 cities × 14 years). The cities included in our analysis meet the following criteria: (1) a minimum total population of 100,000 persons; no fewer than 1,000 Black and White residents; and sufficient data on key variables for the 1984 to 1997 period to permit estimation of our models.[5] Data employed in our research are extracted from three sources, all made available by the Inter-University Consortium for Political and Social Research (ICPSR).[6] Homicide offending data for the years 1984 to 1997 are taken from the Supplementary Homicide Report data file compiled by Fox (2000). Data on illicit drug market activity for the same time period were taken from a Uniform Crime Report data set compiled by Chilton and Weber (1999).[7] Social, economic and demographic characteristics of the cities were drawn from the 1980 Summary Tape File 3C from the U.S. Census Bureau.

DEPENDENT VARIABLES

The dependent variables in the analysis are race-specific homicide offending rates per 100,000 persons, calculated for each city in each of the years between 1984 and 1997. Because offender race is unknown in a considerable share of cases in the Supplementary Homicide Report (about one third of the homicide incidents in our sample of cities), we follow common practice and use imputed offender race characteristics for those cases with missing information. The imputation procedure used in the Supplementary Homicide Report data file compiled by Fox (2000) uses the nonmissing information for homicide cases (most notably the victim profile, which is fairly complete) to impute missing values on the offender profile (see also Pampel and Williams 2000, and Williams and Flewelling 1987 for similar imputation procedures). In addition, because there is a slight degree of underreporting of homicide incidents in the Supplementary Homicide Report data file, homicide counts were weighted to match the annual homicide totals reported in the Uniform Crime Report for each city.[8] Race-specific population figures used as the denominator in the homicide rate calculations were estimated via Uniform Crime Report and U.S. Census data.[9]

PRIMARY INDEPENDENT VARIABLES

Based on the preceding discussion of our conceptual framework, the key predictor variable is a race-specific measure of drug-market activity, the *sale of cocaine/opiate arrest rate* for Blacks and Whites. This is operationalized as the yearly (measured each year in the 1984-1997 period) city arrest rate for the *sale or manufacture* of cocaine, opiates or derivatives per 1,000 persons.[10] Admittedly, this is an imperfect drug market measure for at least two reasons. First, the Uniform Crime Report from which this measure is constructed does not allow us to separate out arrests for crack cocaine, powder cocaine, opium, and opium derivatives. Consequently, the drug market arrest rate for two cities (or for the same city at two different time points) may appear equal when in fact there are noteworthy differences in the types of drugs being trafficked. Second, critics have long noted that arrest rates confound criminal activity with political objectives and the responsiveness of law enforcement agencies; and this may be especially true for drug distribution arrests during a period corresponding with the initiation of the "War on Drugs" policies of the Reagan-Bush administration. As a result, variation in arrest rates across time may indicate changes in the extent to which law enforcement agencies target drug offenders rather than changes in actual levels of drug offending.

In spite of these very real limitations, recent evidence indicates that city-level drug arrest data have reasonable validity as indicators of drug offending (Baumer et al. 1998; Ousey and Lee 2002; Rosenfeld and Decker 1999). Indeed, prior studies suggest that city-level cocaine and opiate distribution arrest rates correlate highly with other indicators of drug activity in a small sample of major cities (Baumer et al. 1998; Rosenfeld and Decker 1999). Moreover, Ousey and Lee (2002) report that within-city, temporal variation in mean homicide rates is significantly associated with three different operationalizations of drug-market activity: (1) the rate of cocaine/opiate *sale or manufacture* arrests; (2) the rate of cocaine/opiate *possession* arrests; and (3) the percentage of arrestees in a city that test positive for the use of cocaine. On the basis of the evidence compiled in these studies, it seems apparent that city-level drug arrest data have considerable utility for exploring the issues that motivate this study.

Nevertheless, it remains unclear how much of the observed change in drug distribution arrests (and therefore, how much of their impact on change in homicide rates) is due to fluctuation in drug market *activity* and how much is due to change in drug market *enforcement*. On one hand, unpacking these separate dynamics is beyond the objectives of the current study. Indeed, for our purposes, what seems most crucial is that both the systemic-violence-related models and the differential enforcement model lead to the same prediction regarding our key predictor variable: rising drug-market arrests should positively correlate with rising rates of lethal violence. On the other hand, however, the theoretical and policy implications that may be drawn from our analyses hinge to some degree on whether the "drug market effect" derives from the inner-workings of the drug trade itself or from vigorous enforcement of drug laws on the part of the police. From the standpoint of the systemic-violence model, a positive drug market arrest–homicide association would be interpreted as evidence that informal, violent self-help social control is operative due to the unavailability of the law (i.e., too little law leads to violence). In contrast, from the perspective of the differential law enforcement model, this correlation may be viewed as an indication that the zealous pursuit and arrest of drug offenders works to disrupt whatever stability and social control the market may develop when left alone (i.e., too much law leads to violence).

Adjudicating between these possibilities with available data is difficult, at best. However, given the theoretical importance of this issue, we take an *initial* step in that direction. Specifically, we augment our primary analyses of the drug market-violence association by estimating additional models that include (separately and in combination with the aforementioned drug distribution arrest measure) an alternative drug market measure, the percentage of arrests in which the arrestee tests positive for cocaine (*percentage positive for cocaine*). This variable is computed with data from the Arrestee Drug Abuse Monitoring (ADAM) program, which collects survey data and urine specimens (for purposes of drug testing) from a sample of arrested individuals.

Given that this measure is based upon data from a nonprobability sample of arrestees, it can be argued that it, like drug arrests, is more reflective of police behavior than of drug use or drug-market activity. However, we note that the data collection procedures of the ADAM program are such that the selection of subjects charged with nondrug felony and nondrug misdemeanor offenses are given priority over subjects charged with drug offenses. Indeed, although some respondents in the ADAM data are booked on drug charges, it is typical that more than 80% of the respondents in a given city-year are charged primarily with nondrug crimes. Consequently, in comparison to the previously discussed sale of cocaine/opiate arrest rate, this measure is more likely to reflect change in drug-market activity rather than change in drug market enforcement. Nevertheless, because within-city temporal change in this variable may still be partially due to year-to-year fluctuation in the share of the ADAM sample arrested for drug offenses, we include a control for the percentage of the ADAM respondents arrested for drug offenses (*percentage ADAM drug charges*) in our supplemental models.[11]

CONTROLLING FOR TIME TRENDS

To the extent that the preceding measures of illicit drug markets and homicide rates follow similar temporal trends during the period of interest, it is possible that any observed relationship between them is spurious. In other words, the correlation among these variables may be a product of their common correlation with an unmeasured factor that varies systematically over time (for a discussion of spurious time-series correlations, see Gujarati 2002). To account for this possibility, and to model temporal trends in homicide rates, we include controls for time in our models. In particular, we model both the rise and subsequent fall of homicide rates in the 1984 to 1997 period by including both a linear (*Time*) and a quadratic (*Time-squared*) time trend variable in our analyses.[12]

DRUG MARKET–HOMICIDE MODERATORS: MEASURES OF PREEXISTING SOCIAL CONDITIONS

According to Zimring and Hawkins' (1997) model, the drug market–homicide relationship is moderated by social context. In particular, its magnitude is predicted to be stronger when violence conducive social conditions already exist in areas where illicit drug markets develop. In a preceding discussion, we proposed specific hypotheses about the impact on the drug market–homicide relationship of two socioeconomic characteristics that are especially prominent predictors in the race-disaggregated homicide literature: resource deprivation and racial socioeconomic inequality. *Resource deprivation* is measured as an index reflecting multiple dimensions of social and economic disadvantage. It is computed by averaging the standardized scores of the poverty rate, unemployment rate, percentage of families that are female-headed families, the percentage of persons age 25 or older with less than high school education and the gini coefficient of family income inequality. Each of these items is race-specific. As noted above, empirical research strongly suggests that communities with higher levels of resource deprivation experience more violence than those with lower levels of resource deprivation. *Racial socioeconomic inequality* is a three-item index reflecting Black/White inequality in income, educational attainment, and employment. Specifically, we take the average of the standardized scores of the ratio of White-to-Black mean family income, the ratio of Black-to-White unemployment, and the ratio of the percentage of Blacks with less than high school education to the percentage of Whites with less than high school education. Higher scores on this variable reflect greater Black disadvantage/White advantage. Prior research indicates that higher levels of racial inequality may be associated with homicide rates, especially among Blacks (Parker and McCall 1999).

In addition to these two key socioeconomic factors, prior macro-level homicide research identifies several other factors that may be considered violence conducive social conditions that could moderate the illicit drug market–homicide relationship. These include population size (measured in units of 10,000 persons), the percentage of the city population that is Black, and indicator variables for the west and south regions. Although the formulation of specific hypotheses regarding the interaction between these variables and illicit drug markets is not emphasized in this analysis, it is sensible to at least account for their potential influence on both the race-specific homicide rate and estimates of the interactive relationship between illicit drug markets and resource deprivation/racial inequality. Thus, as described below, all of these variables are included in preliminary specifications of the two-level hierarchical models that we estimate. Final models retain those variables that exhibit significant effects in one or more preliminary model specifications.

METHOD OF ANALYSIS

To test the hypotheses posited above, we utilize two primary estimation strategies. First, we examine hypotheses one and two via a "fixed-effects" seemingly unrelated regression model. Specifically, we restrict our initial models to the within-city relationship between illicit drug markets and homicide rates (while controlling for temporal trends) by centering these variables around their group-level means (for similar approaches, see Horney, Osgood, and Marshall 1995; Osgood et al. 1996). Then, to account for the fact that the separate observations for Blacks and Whites are drawn from the same city-year units (and therefore are not independent observations), we utilize the seemingly unrelated regression model (for details on SUR, see Greene 2000). This strategy allows for nonindependence of the error terms between the Black and White equations and also permits the error variances for the two groups to be unequal. In addition, it facilitates the calculation of across equation F-tests to test whether there are significant racial group differences in the effects of the drug market on homicide rates.

To examine our third and fourth hypotheses, which pertain to the impact of between-city differences in preexisting social-structural conditions on the within-city, temporal relationship between drug markets and homicide, we employ a second estimation strategy, commonly known as hierarchical linear modeling (see Raudenbush and Bryk 2001).[13] Specifically, we estimate a two-level hierarchical model in which repeated measurements on homicide rates and illicit drug markets (the level-1 units) are nested within cities (the level-2 units).[14] In general, when data have this nested structure, observations are not independent—those from the same group (e.g., repeated time-series observations from the same city) tend to be more alike than observations from different groups (e.g., observations from different cities)—which violates one of the key assumptions of ordinary regression models. Consequently, with no adjustment for clustering, ordinary regression will produce standard errors and *t*-test statistics that are biased. Therefore, methods like hierarchical linear models that are designed to account for clustered data are generally preferred.

RESULTS

Fixed-Effects Models for Full Sample

Following the logic of the systemic violence model, our first hypothesis pertains to the general relationship between illicit drug markets and homicide rates. Specifically, we examine whether the change in the (log) sale of cocaine/opiates rate is positively associated with change in homicide rates, for both Blacks and Whites. In the first panel of Table 1, we present coefficients from the seemingly unrelated regression models predicting within-city variation in Black and White homicide rates, respectively.[15]

Beginning with the equation for Blacks, the results of our analysis indicate that there is indeed a positive and statistically significant relationship between the logged black cocaine/opiates distribution arrest rate and the Black homicide offending rate. Likewise, we find a statistically significant ($p < .10$) relationship between the logged measure of drug market activity for Whites and the White homicide rate. Thus, the overall pattern of findings in the first panel of Table 1 are supportive of our first hypothesis and the basic predictions of Goldstein's systemic violence model (as well as related models discussed above). Indeed, after controlling for linear and quadratic trends in homicide, cities with increasing rates of drug market arrests also tend to exhibit rising rates of homicide during the 1984 to 1997 period.[16]

In spite of the similarity in the direction of the drug market-homicide association for the two racial groups, there are noteworthy differences in the magnitude of this relationship in the models for Blacks and Whites. Indeed, a unit increase in the logarithm of the drug market variable corresponds with an increase of 3.56 homicide offenses per 100,000 for Blacks; but only 0.38 additional homicides per 100,000 for Whites. Thus, the lethal violence impact for a similar relative change in drug market activity is considerably larger for Blacks than Whites. Moreover, this Black-White difference is statistically significant (as denoted by the superscript letter "c" in Table 1). Thus, the pattern of racial variation in the drug market-homicide relationship is consistent with our second hypothesis as well as the multiple conceptual arguments suggesting racial group variation in the impact of drug market activity and enforcement on homicide rates (e.g., Anderson 1999; Blumstein 1995; MacCoun et al. 2003; Zimring and Hawkins 1997). However, the existence of this race difference is not predicted by the more general systemic violence model of Goldstein (1985).

Fixed-Effects Models for ADAM Sample

In panels 2 through 4 of Table 1, we supplement our "full sample" results presented above by estimating additional SUR models using the city-year units derived from the Arrestee Drug Abuse Monitoring (ADAM) sample and the ADAM-based drug market measure. Focusing first on panel 2, we begin these supplemental analyses by first replicating the models of panel 1 using the smaller sample of city-year units. Consistent with the earlier results, we find that the log sale of cocaine/opiates arrest rate variable has a

TABLE 1: SUR Fixed-Effects Models Predicting Black and White Homicide Offending Rates

| | Full Sample[a] | | Using Only ADAM Cities[b] | | | | | |
| | Panel 1 | | Panel 2 | | Panel 3 | | Panel 4 | |
Predictor Variable	Black	White	Black	White	Black	White	Black	White
Log sale of cocaine/opiates arrest rate	3.56*	.38[c]	15.34*	2.11*[c]	—	—	14.04*	2.32*[c]
Percentage positive for cocaine	—	—	—	—	.76*	-.06[c]	.41**	-.05[c]
Percent ADAM drug charges	—	—	—	—	-0.53	-.07	-.75*	-.09[c]
Time	.98*	.04[c]	-.46	-.25*	1.42**	-.15[c]	.31	-.20**
Time-squared	-.19*	-.02*[c]	-.70*	-.11*[c]	-.83*	-.14*[c]	-.71*	-.11*[c]
Intercept	2.68	.28	6.24	1.01	6.95	1.23	6.21	.95
Equation system statistics								
Cross equation correlation	.16		.36		.34		.37	
System sample size (n)	3,216		328		328		328	

a. Includes years from 1984 to 1997; time variable centered around 1990.
b. Includes years from 1987 to 1997; time variable centered around 1992.
c. Coefficient significantly different than corresponding estimate in the model for Blacks.
*p < .05. **p < .10.

significant, positive relationship with both the Black and White homicide rate. In addition, as before, the results in panel 2 indicate that this drug market–homicide association is significantly stronger in the model for Blacks. A noteworthy difference between the first two panels is that the effect sizes are substantially larger in panel 2. This is not unexpected, and may reflect the fact that the ADAM sample contains particularly large cities (e.g., New York, Los Angeles, Washington, D.C.) where drug market activity, homicide, and the social conditions that amplify the relationship between drug markets and violence (e.g., resource deprivation, racial inequality) may be particularly prevalent.

In the next panel, we present results from the SUR models in which we substitute the alternative drug market indicator, the percentage testing positive for cocaine, for the drug distribution arrest rate variable used in the prior models. In addition, for reasons outlined earlier, we also include a control for changes in the extent to which the ADAM sample is comprised of offenders arrested on drug charges. Following the results from our earlier models, we again find that for Blacks, within-city change in the drug market measure has a significant positive association with within-city change in the Black homicide offending rate. Specifically, a one percentage point increase in arrestees that test positive for cocaine corresponds with a .76 unit increase in the Black homicide rate. As suggested by the earlier models, this positive association is significantly different from that observed in the model for Whites. Despite these similarities, the results of panel 3 differ from prior models in an important way: the effect of the drug market measure for Whites is not significantly different from zero. Specifically, change in the percentage of White arrestees that test positive for cocaine is not related to change in White homicide rates. Thus, although the findings in panel 3 support recent frameworks that suggest race differences in the drug market-homicide relationship, support for the basic drug market–violence relationship is contingent upon the race group studied. Moreover, although clearly not definitive, these results hint that for Blacks, the drug market effect on violence may derive from both internal (behaviors of drug users and other market participants) and external (vigorous pursuit of drug offenders on the part of law enforcement) dynamics, whereas for Whites, this effect emerges more from the latter than the former.

As a more direct attempt at disentangling the violence-generating effects of drug-market enforcement from other aspects of drug-market activity (e.g., drug use and drug dealing), we estimate another set of SUR equations that include both the (log) sale of cocaine/opiates arrest rate and the percentage of arrestees that test positive for cocaine. Results of these models are shown in panel 4. Generally consistent with the results in panels 1 through 3, the results suggest that within-city change in both drug-market measures have a

significant positive relationship with change in Black homicide rates during
the 1987 to 1997 period. However, it should be noted that the effect of the
ADAM-based percentage positive for cocaine is substantially weaker than it
was in panel 3. In contrast to the results for Blacks, the model for Whites indicates that only the change in the drug arrest rate measure is significantly associated with change in White homicide rates. With regard to race differences,
the results in panel 4 follow earlier models in that the effects of both drug
market variables are significantly different for Blacks and Whites.

In summary, the results presented in Table 1 provide basic support for our
first hypothesis and Goldstein's systemic violence framework. In 8 of 10
instances, we find that within-city change in the drug market indicator is significantly and positively associated with within-city change in homicide
rates. However, more consistent with our second hypothesis and recent conceptual extensions of the systemic violence framework, our analyses suggest
the existence of significant racial group differences in the drug market-
violence relationship. For Blacks, we find that (regardless of how "drug market" is operationalized) within-city variation in the drug market is significantly and positively associated with within-city variation in homicide rates.
For *Whites*, however, the expected significant positive relationship is
observed only when the drug market is measured by the drug distribution
arrest variable. In contrast, the ADAM-based measure of arrestee drug use
has only a negligible and nonsignificant association with within-city change
in the White homicide rate. Moreover, consistent with hypothesis 2, we find
that in all equations estimated, there is a statistically significant race group
difference in the magnitude of the drug market–homicide relationship. Specifically, we find that this relationship is significantly stronger for Blacks
than Whites. Finally, the findings presented in Table 1 yield rather consistent
support for the differential enforcement model. Indeed, in all relevant models, the effect of drug distribution arrests (i.e., drug law enforcement) is
statistically significant and in the expected direction.

The Conditional Effects of Drug Markets on
Black and White Homicide Rates

Drawing on Zimring and Hawkins' (1997) contingent causation model,
our final research hypotheses state the expectation that the effect of drug markets on homicide is conditioned by preexisting social and economic conditions. Specifically, for both Blacks and Whites, it is argued that the lethality
of the drug market is dependent on the degree of socioeconomic deprivation
that exists within each group. In addition, we predicted that the relationship
between drug market activity and murder rates among Blacks would be
stronger in cities in which Black-to-White socioeconomic inequality is

TABLE 2: Random Coefficient Regression Model for Black and White Homicide Offending Rates, 1984-1997

Fixed Effects	Black Homicide	White Homicide
Mean homicide rate		
Baseline intercept	53.55*	8.64*
Resource deprivation	12.00*	2.91*
Racial inequality	3.47	—
Population size	—[a]	.02*
Percentage Black	—	−.05*
South	—	3.40*
West	18.02*	4.76*
City-mean, (log) sale cocaine/opiates rate	.35	1.58*
Sale cocaine/opiates rate (log)		
Baseline slope	2.48*	0.14
Resource deprivation	—	.95*
Racial inequality	3.38*	—
Population size	—	—
Percentage Black	—	−.03*
South	−3.80*	—
West	—	1.15*
Time	.89*	.02
Time-squared	−.32*	−.01**

Random Effect	Variance Component	Variance Component
Mean homicide offending rate	250.61*	19.91*
Sale of cocaine/opiates rate	46.51*	2.33*
Level-1 residual variance	837.44*	16.04*
n	1,608	1,608

NOTE: Assumption of homogeneous level-1 variance is relaxed.
a. Effect not significant in preliminary submodels and excluded from final model estimation.
*$p < .05$. **$p < .10$.

greater. To address these hypotheses, we estimate a couple of two-level hierarchical linear models in which the intercepts and the drug market slope coefficients are predicted by several of the "preexisting social conditions" (resource deprivation, racial inequality, population size, percentage Black, south, west) described earlier.[17] The final specification of these models, which are reported in Table 2, only contains predictors that had significant effects on the outcome in preliminary analyses.[18]

Focusing first on results for the level-1 intercept coefficient (displayed under the heading "mean homicide rate"), we find that the average homicide rate among Blacks varies as a function of several structural factors. Consistent with prior aggregate-level research on homicide, the Black homicide rate tends to be significantly higher in cities with greater resource deprivation and in cities located in the western region of the nation.[19] Similarly, White homicide rates have a positive association with resource deprivation and location in the west region. However, in addition, White homicide rates also are elevated in cities with a larger population, a lower percentage of the population that is African American, a higher mean drug distribution arrest rate and in cities located in south region.[20]

Turning now to the results of primary interest (presented under the heading "sale cocaine/opiates rate") in Table 2, we examine the impact of between-city variation in preexisting structural conditions on the drug market-homicide slope coefficient. Consistent with prior results, the equation for Blacks suggests that the baseline slope for the log sale of cocaine/ opiates arrest rate is positive and statistically significant. This baseline slope suggests that when racial inequality is set at the sample mean, a unit change in the logged drug arrest variable corresponds with a 2.48 unit increase in the Black homicide rate.[21] However, the effect of change in the drug market variable on change in homicide is conditional. Specifically, the drug market-homicide slope for Blacks is significantly weaker in southern cities, but significantly stronger in cities with higher levels of Black-White inequality. Thus, hypothesis 4, which predicts a moderating impact of racial inequality on the drug market-homicide link among Blacks is supported by the results in the first model of Table 2. In contrast, the hypothesized interaction between resource deprivation and the sale of cocaine/opiates rate (hypothesis 3) is not supported. The level of Black resource deprivation does not significantly affect the magnitude of the slope coefficient for the drug-market variable.

Contrary to the results for Blacks, the baseline slope in the equation for Whites is not statistically significant. In this case, the baseline reflects the effect of a unit change in the logged white drug market variable on the White homicide rate in cities with average levels of resource deprivation and percentage Black (i.e., with these variables set at their sample mean). Although this baseline slope is not significant, it varies across cities as a function of several structural covariates. First, consistent with hypothesis 3, a unit increase in resource deprivation results in a significant increase of .95 in the drug market slope for Whites. In addition, a unit decrease in the percentage Black increases the slope by .03. Finally, the drug market-homicide association among Whites is found to be significantly stronger in cities located in the west region of the country.

Overall, the results in Table 2 offer considerable support for Zimring and Hawkins' contingent causation model.[22] As their work suggests, the lethality of the illicit drug market is conditioned by a number of preexisting structural conditions. However, as we anticipated, the violence-conducive social conditions are not uniform for Blacks and Whites. Indeed, partially consistent with our third hypothesis, we find that resource deprivation conditions the impact of illicit drug markets on homicide rates for Whites only. On the other hand, following our fourth hypothesis, the drug market-homicide association among Blacks is magnified in cities in which the socioeconomic discrepancy between Blacks and Whites is more pronounced. In addition, the drug market-homicide relationship among Blacks is attenuated in the south, although among Whites the relationship is enhanced among cities in the west and in cities with a smaller percentage of the population that is African American.

SUMMARY, DISCUSSION, AND CONCLUSION

Recent trends in lethal violence have drawn great interest from scholars. In response, a number of possible explanations for these trends have been proffered. Perhaps because it presents a plausible reason for both the upsurge and downturn of homicide rates in the past two decades, the explanation focusing on the proliferation and contraction of crack-cocaine markets has received the greatest attention. Although evidence from recent research linking drug markets to rates of murder has provided a basic empirical foundation for this argument, limitations in prior studies make the evidence incomplete. In this study, we identified and addressed several shortcomings of previous work in an attempt to advance knowledge of the nexus between drug markets and violence. Most notably, we extended earlier studies in the following ways. First, using annual data from 122 cities for the 1984 to 1997 period, we examined the race-specific, within-city relationship between a measure of illicit drug markets and homicide rates. Second, drawing upon various sociological frameworks, we developed and tested hypotheses suggesting that the magnitude of the drug market-homicide association varies for Blacks and Whites. In addition, we augmented our investigation of these issues by using alternative measures of illicit drug markets and by initiating efforts to determine whether the effects of drug markets on violence are due to drug law enforcement or to other processes that are endogenous to the market. Finally, we explored the extent to which various social-structural factors moderate the race-specific relationships between illicit drug markets and rates of lethal violence.

As expected, our analysis revealed that change in arrest rates for cocaine and opiate distribution correspond positively with change in both Black and White homicide rates over time within cities. However, consistent with recent work suggesting modifications to Goldstein's basic systemic-violence model, we found that the magnitude of the illicit drug market–homicide association is not racially invariant. In fact, using two different operationalizations of drug markets, our results indicated that the impact on homicide rates of within-city change in the drug market is significantly stronger among Blacks than among Whites. Moreover, we found race differences in the extent to which conclusions about the drug-market effect on violence were robust across different drug-market measures. For Blacks, both drug use and drug enforcement–based measures exhibited a significant positive relationship with homicide rates; for Whites, the expected relationship only appeared when the latter measure was employed.

In addition, following the logic of Zimring and Hawkins' (1997) contingent causation model, the results of our race-specific hierarchical linear models indicate the drug market–lethal violence connection varies as a function of "preexisting social conditions" for both race groups. Yet, the social conditions moderating the drug market-homicide slope differ by racial group. For Blacks, the key moderators are racial inequality and location in the southern region; for Whites, the important factors are resource deprivation, percentage Black, and western location. It should be noted, however, that these interaction effects only appeared in models using our full sample of city-year units. In contrast to the results of Ousey and Lee (2002), we found no significant interaction effects in models computed on the ADAM-based sample of city-year units. We suspect that our inability to find interactions in this "reduced sample" is partly due to a small number of level-2 units and to the division of the total ADAM-sample variation on the relevant variables into separate Black and White components (resulting in compressed variation on the predictors).

Overall, the findings are largely consistent with our expectations, but a main deviation is that resource deprivation is not found to be a factor that conditions the drug market–homicide slope for Blacks. Although a good deal of cross-sectional research indicates that urban Black violence is correlated with resource deprivation (a result we also get—see the intercept equation results in Table 2), it may be the case that high levels of disadvantage have become so endemic to many Black communities in the inner-city that modest fluctuations are not enough to alter the social context of drug markets in ways that raise their likelihood of producing violence. In contrast, elevations in racial inequality may be more telling because high-levels of (White) wealth may exist in close purview of minority-operated drug markets, which may increase the real or perceived payoffs of dealing drugs. If so, the intensity of competition among drug dealers may escalate and thereby increase conflict.

From a theoretical standpoint, we believe a couple of key implications follow from our analyses. First, our findings, like those reported in Ousey and Lee (2002), highlight the need for flexibility and contingencies in models that follow from Goldstein's systemic violence framework. Although parsimony and simplicity are certainly desirable properties for theory, reality is virtually always more complex than our theories dictate. Thus, although the systemic violence framework provides the shoulders upon which subsequent drug market–violence theory can perch, our results suggest that Zimring and Hawkins' (1997) contention regarding the lack of universality in the drug market–violence is appropriate. Consequently, we believe that with Zimring and Hawkins' contingent causation model as a foundation, theory, and research should seek to delineate the structural, cultural, and situational characteristics that make drug markets violent as well as those conditions that prevent this unfavorable consequence from emerging.

A second implication of our findings pertains to the"causal" dynamics by which drug markets affect violence. Although data and measurement limitations make our findings preliminary and somewhat ambiguous in this regard, our models at least suggest that both intrinsic (e.g., nature of drug demand; composition/characteristics/social location of market participants) and extrinsic (e.g., drug policy; law enforcement behavior) market-linked factors may contribute to the violent nature of (some) drug markets. However, the evidence also seems to suggest that the law enforcement response to the illicit drug trade is an especially critical, and perhaps more pervasive, factor in amplifying the violence of drug markets. Consequently, it seems to follow that theoretical development on the role of drug markets in the generation of violent crime must emphasize not just the dynamics of informal "self-help" social control that takes place among drug-market participants, but also the formal, state-sponsored mechanisms of social control.

From our perspective, an intriguing aspect of the above implication is that informal and formal social control mechanisms are generally found to be inversely related. Thus, it follows that if law enforcement is zealously enforcing laws against drug trafficking and/or drug use (i.e., there is a high level of formal social control), we would reasonably expect lower levels of informal social control. Assuming this informal social control is the self-help type that Black (1983) describes, we would therefore also expect a drop in rates of violence (because fewer drug-market participants would be handling their grievances via violent self-help methods). Of course, this is generally opposite of what our research findings indicate. One possible interpretation of this apparent paradox is that informal social control actually exists in two, inversely related forms: group-based and individual-based. In the case of the former, the image is of a network of social relations held together by a common value or instrumental objective that closely regulates behavior. Although a drug market that exhibits this form of informal social control may give rise to an occasional instance of violence; it tends to be highly measured and may have great symbolic purposes within an associational network (e.g., the prototypical punishment of a transgression within a mob family done to show others that such behavior will not be tolerated). In contrast, in the latter

case, individual market participants pursue their own self-interest with relatively little sense of connection or allegiance to a broader organization or set
of shared values. Consequently, in this context, violence is more unpredictable and may have less symbolic value.[23]

If this dual-conception of informal social control is valid, it would appear
that as Zimring and Hawkins (1997) argue, and as our results indicate, drug
markets are not necessarily violent. Although the illegality of the commodities and services exchanged in drug markets inherently entails some heightened vulnerability to violence, the added risk is likely to be minimal as long
as group-based informal social control is strong (i.e., when the drug distribution network is stable, highly structured and socially integrated in the community). In contrast, when group-based informal social control is weak and
individual-based, self-help social control is strong, the risk of drug market–
related violence is likely to be high. Therefore, an important question is when
and under what circumstances is this latter situation likely to occur? Based on
our work as well as our reading of the literature, we would argue that drug
market–related violence will be high in the early emergent stages of the life-
history of a drug market (e.g., see Cork 1999) and/or when the stability that
accompanies a maturing market is disrupted by some external force (e.g.,
when arrest of drug offenders disrupts "group-based" informal social control
in a community (see related discussion in Rose and Clear 1998).[24] However, a
full consideration of this question remains an important task for future
research.

In addition to the above question, there are a number of other avenues that
future studies should pursue. For instance, a main theme tying the various
perspectives we discussed is the interplay of culture and structure. This follows on important recent work that argues that harsh structural conditions
found in many urban areas promote cultural adjustments that eventually generate high levels of violence (Sampson and Wilson 1995). Yet, a problem
with much macro-level sociological research (including the current work) is
the difficulty encountered in trying to disentangle the effects of structure and
culture. Recent advances in the collection and analysis of multi-level data
such as that found in the Project on Human Development in Chicago Neighborhoods (e.g., Earls 1999) are well-suited to this task. In our view, research
on the links between drug markets and crime would benefit immeasurably
from efforts such as these that would allow the direct estimation of cultural
effects on drug market–related violence.

Future studies would also benefit from more precise measures of the different aspects of drug-market activity. As noted, the main measures of drug
markets employed in this study do not allow researchers to partition drug
activity into more precise categories such as crack cocaine, powder cocaine,
heroine, and so on. Although evidence suggests a high degree of

comparability across sources of data on drug activity, racial groups differ in the extent to which they are involved in the marketing and selling of particular types of drugs. In addition, different drug "epidemics" have hit different cities at different points in time. These variations by demographic group and space/time may be particularly important and further condition links between illicit markets and violence. Thus, to advance knowledge, it is critical that improved data collection efforts (e.g., recent expansions and advances in the Arrestee Drug Abuse Monitoring program) continue and be given all possible resources and support.

Finally, the fact that the socioeconomic violence–conducive social conditions were different for Blacks and for Whites also begs an additional question: Namely, do differences in pre-existing structural conditions explain the racial group differences we observed in the drug market–violence relationship? This is clearly an empirical question that can be addressed in a relatively straightforward manner with existing data, and we encourage researchers to attempt to add this important piece to the drug market–violence research literature.

NOTES

1. Blumstein's (1995) argument regarding drug markets, the proliferation of guns and normative diffusion pertains specifically to crack cocaine markets and the period spanning the mid-1980s through the early- to mid-1990s. Thus, his model is less generic than Goldstein's (1985) perspective and it is unclear whether he would expect similar processes to take place in all instances in which illicit drug markets develop and proliferate. Testing hypotheses regarding "general vs. specific" drug-market effects are beyond the objectives of this analysis but represent an important avenue for future studies.

2. For the purposes of the current study, we draw upon Anderson's (1999) work primarily to outline one possible rationale for expecting race differences in the drug market–homicide relationship. In addition, we believe his work helps to support the expectation that socioeconomic context moderates this relationship; an argument we make more explicit in our later discussion of Zimring and Hawkins' (1997) contingent causation model. It is important to note that Anderson's (1999) ideas would support a number of additional research hypotheses, including predictions regarding how change in industrial structure over the past several decades has affected the magnitude of the drug market–violence relationship as well as the timing of recent upward and downward trajectories of homicide rates. An exploration of these hypotheses is beyond the purview of the current research, but these are areas that deserve attention in subsequent research.

3. Although the above framework is the most widely recognized manner in which drug enforcement policies and procedures may result in race differences in the drug arrest–homicide relationship, another possibility exists. As Ousey and Augustine (2001) note, racially biased drug arrest practices may result in a drug arrest measure for blacks that contains many low-level, nonviolent drug offenders, which should dampen the relationship between drug arrest rates and homicide rates for this racial group (and thereby minimize race differences). However, because racial bias in arrest practices are likely to differ more across cities than within the same city over time, we would expect that this dampening effect would be particularly evident in the cross-

sectional relationship between drug-market arrests and homicide for Blacks. In contrast, if this racial arrest bias were relatively constant within a given city across time, temporal change in the arrest rate should largely reflect the pattern of change in drug-market activity. Thus, the within-city, longitudinal relationship between drug-market activity and lethal violence may remain evident despite the disproportionate arrest of Black drug offenders.

4. If all social, cultural, and economic conditions that vary between Blacks and Whites could be controlled, we would likely expect that race would no longer remain a factor that conditions the drug market–homicide relationship. However, many race-varying factors are extremely difficult to measure with available data (e.g., Anderson's [1999] cultural "code of the street"); therefore, as a proxy for these unmeasured factors, "race" can be viewed as a relevant moderator of the drug market–violence association.

5. We use 1980 data to characterize cities prior to the introduction of illicit markets for crack cocaine (following Zimring and Hawkins [1997] notion of "preexisting social conditions"). Therefore, these minimum population criteria are based on 1980 population figures. In addition, to ensure that our analyses reasonably and reliably capture the period of increase and decrease in drug markets and homicide rates in our sample of cities, we exclude cities with fewer than 10 years of data on key variables used in our within-city models.

6. The original collectors of these data and Inter-University Consortium for Political and Social Research (ICPSR) bear no responsibility for the findings reported in this analysis. Any errors in description, analysis or interpretation belong to the authors alone.

7. Because not all cities report data every month in a given year, yearly totals for a given offense category may reflect a full 12 months of information in some years and less than 12 months in other years. Therefore, Uniform Crime Reporting (UCR) data files, including the one compiled by Chilton and Weber (1999), contain a variable that indicates the number of months of data that were reported for a particular jurisdiction in a given year. By not utilizing this piece of information, there is a potential for yearly fluctuations in crime or arrest totals to reflect year-to-year inconsistency in monthly reporting of data. However, in the sample of cities that we analyze, there is a great deal of consistency in the monthly reporting of data. For instance, on average, the cities in our sample reported 11.9 months of data each year. Moreover, data were reported for 99 percent of all possible city-months. Consequently, numerical estimates are extremely similar and substantive results are identical when we analyzed data that are weighted to adjust for underreporting or data that are unweighted. Results presented below in Tables 1 and 2 use the unweighted data. Results from analyses of the weighted data are available from the first author.

8. We also estimated our models using race-specific homicide rates that used no offender race imputation and/or weighting. Coefficients from these models were generally slightly smaller than those reported below. However, the direction of relationships, statistical significance, and substantive conclusions from these models are very similar to those reported. These supplemental results are available from the first author on request.

9. Population figures were estimated via a three-step procedure. First, changes in the total, Black, and White populations of the 122 cities for the 1980 to 1990 period and the 1990 to 2000 period were calculated on the basis of decennial Census data. Second, these change figures were divided into equal intervals (reflecting the years in the decade) and added onto the total, Black, and White base population figures reported in the 1980 and 1990 Census to arrive at population estimates for each city-year. Third, the proportion Black and White for each city-year (calculated on the basis of the preceding population estimates) was multiplied by the total population figure reported in the Supplementary Homicide Report (to adjust for nonreporting precincts) for each city-year.

10. Preliminary diagnostic analyses showed evidence of a curvilinear relationship between drug-market arrests and homicide. Therefore, this variable is transformed to its natural logarithm.

378 JOURNAL OF RESEARCH IN CRIME AND DELINQUENCY

11. Primarily due to the limited number of sites and the later starting point (i.e., 1987 vs. 1984) in the ADAM data series, our supplemental analyses using these data are limited to 164 city-year units.

12. In models that use the "full" sample and the sale of cocaine/opiates arrest-rate measure, the linear time trend variable is centered around the year 1990, the approximate midpoint in our period of interest. Thus, the variable ranges from –6 (for the year 1984) to 7 (for the year 1997). In the supplemental models that use the smaller sample and ADAM data to measure drug markets, the linear time trend is centered around 1992 and the variable ranges from –5 (1987) to 5 (1997). Centering serves two purposes. First, it reduces collinearity between the linear and quadratic time trend variables, which helps to stabilize the estimation methods. Second, by centering around the approximate midpoint of the time-series, the linear time trend coefficient can be viewed as the "average rate of growth" during the time-period studied (see Raudenbush and Bryk 2002:181-82).

13. The SUR models are estimated with PROC SYSLIN in the SAS software package. The 2-level hierarchical models are estimated with PROC MIXED in SAS and with the HLM5 software.

14. Estimation of these hierarchical models is a two-step process. In the first step, a within-city regression equation for each city (and race group) is estimated: $Homicide_{it} = \beta_{0i} + \beta_{1i}$ (Drug $Market_{it}$) + β_{2i} (Time) + β_{3i} (Time^2) + r_{it}, where $Homicide_{it}$ is the (racial group-specific) homicide rate for city i at time t; β_{0i} is the mean homicide rate in city i in 1990 when the drug-market variable is set at their means for city i; β_{1i} is the slope coefficient for the drug-market variable (Drug $Market_{it}$) for city i; β_{2i} is the homicide growth rate in 1990 for city i; and β_{3i} is the rate of curvature in the homicide growth rate (i.e., the acceleration/deceleration parameter) in city i. Next, the level-1 intercept, β_{0i}, and the slope coefficient for the drug-market variable, β_{1i}, are specified as a function of a city's preexisting structural conditions: $\beta_{0i} = \pi 00 + \pi 01$ (Resource Deprivation$_i$) + π_{02} (Racial Inequality$_i$) + π_{03} (Population Size$_i$) + π_{04} (Percentage Black$_i$) + π_{05} (South$_i$) + π_{06} (West$_i$) + π_{07} (Mean Drug Market$_i$) + u_{0i}

$$\beta_{1i} = \pi_{10} + \pi_{11} \text{ (Resource Deprivation}_i) + \pi_{12} \text{ (Racial Inequality}_i)$$
$$+ \pi_{13} \text{ (Population Size}_i) + \pi_{14} \text{ (Percentage Black}_i) + \pi_{15} \text{ (South}_i)$$
$$+ \pi_{16} \text{ (West}_i) + \pi_{17} \text{ (Mean Drug Market}_i) + u_{1i}$$

$$\beta_{2i} = \pi_{20}$$

$$\beta_{3i} = \pi_{30}$$

where π_{00} is the average intercept (mean homicide rate) in 1990 (1992 for analyses based on ADAM sample) across the sample of cities when the level-2 predictors are set at their grand mean; π_{01} through π_{07} are the effects of the preexisting structural condition variables on the intercept for a given city; π_{10} is the average slope for the drug-market variable across cities when the level-2 predictors are fixed at their grand mean; π_{11} through π_{17} are coefficients for the "cross-level" interaction terms between the drug-market variable and the measures of preexisting structural conditions; π_{20} and π_{30} are the slopes for the linear and quadratic measures of time and u_{0i} and u_{1i}, are the residuals or unexplained between-city variation in the intercept and drug-market slope coefficients, respectively.

15. Some of the literature, especially the work of Blumstein (1995), suggests that the presence of guns play a role in the drug market–violence nexus. To account for this possibility, we supplemented the results presented below by estimating models that also included an indicator of gun presence—the percentage of homicide incidents that are gun-related that has been employed in prior work (e.g., see Blumstein 1995; Ousey and Lee 2002). When included in our supplemental models, this variable had a significant positive relationship with Black, but not White,

homicide rates. However, its inclusion had virtually no impact on the relationship between the drug-market measure and homicide that is described below. Results from these models are available from the author(s).

16. Although the time-trend variables are not our substantive interest in this article, they are interpreted as follows: (1) the linear time trend variable reflects the "instantaneous" rate of change (i.e., growth rate) in the homicide rate at the approximate midpoint of the time-series (the year around which this variable is centered); (2) the quadratic time trend variable reflects the rate of "acceleration" or "deceleration" in the homicide growth rate. For example, in the first model of panel 1, the linear time trend variable indicates that in 1990, the Black homicide rate is increasing by .98 per year. However, the quadratic time trend suggests that positive growth rate is decelerating or shrinking by –.19 per year.

17. For those unfamiliar with hierarchical linear models but familiar with the usual methods of regression analysis, this particular model is similar to a regression model that specifies a dependent variable that varies across time and space (e.g., homicide rates across a 10-year time span for a sample of 20 cities) as a function of both time-varying (e.g., yearly fluctuations in drug-market activity) and time-invariant (e.g., the poverty rate at a fixed point in time; geographic region) independent variables and also includes interaction effects between the time-varying and time-invariant predictors (e.g., the cross-product of yearly drug-market activity and a "south" region dummy variable).

18. However, we make one exception to this general rule. Despite having a nonsignificant effect on the intercept in the equation for Blacks—thereby justifying its exclusion from the model—we retain, in the model, the city mean of the sale of cocaine/opiates rate for Blacks. This procedure is followed so that between-city differences in the average level of the cocaine/opiates arrest rate are controlled in the equations that estimate effects of the structural conditions of primary interest (e.g., resource deprivation, racial inequality). Because these structural conditions likely co-vary with drug-market activity and/or arrest rates, we opt to control for this covariance by including the city-mean of the drug-market variable in the 2-level HLM equation.

19. In this case, the coefficient for the west dummy variable reflects a comparison of the average west Black homicide rate for the 1984 to 1997 period to the 1990 Black homicide rate for the non-West regions (recall that our time variable is centered around the year 1990). Although recent evidence suggests that Black homicide rates in the Western region tend to be on par with those in the South and above those in the Northeast and Midwest (e.g., see Parker and Pruitt 2000), the observed difference in our models is magnified because there exists a substantial regional difference in resource deprivation in 1980 for our sample of cities. When this regional difference in deprivation is controlled in our models, the baseline gap in homicide rates between the West and non-West grows considerably larger.

20. The coefficient for the drug-distribution rate reflects the "between-city" (i.e., cross-sectional) effect on the homicide rate for each race-group. Thus, in keeping with the findings of prior work (e.g., Ousey and Augustine 2001), our results suggest that drug-arrest rates and homicide rates have a cross-sectional relationship for Whites but not for Blacks. One possible explanation of this result centers on differences in the racial bias of drug law enforcement across cities. Details of this argument are sketched in note 3.

21. These results essentially reflect the interaction effects between the logged sale of cocaine/opiates rate and two "preexisting structural conditions," racial inequality and geographic region. Thus, as is often the convention in reports of regression analyses, the baseline slope can be thought of as the "main effect" of the drug-market variable. Because we have centered both racial inequality and the South-region dummy variable around their "grand mean" (i.e., mean of the full sample of city-year units), the baseline drug-market slope can be interpreted as the effect of the drug-market variable when averaged across regions and when racial inequality is at its sample mean.

22. We also estimated two-level models using only the ADAM city-year units and the alternative drug-market measure. With regard to the baseline effects of the drug-market variables, these results are consistent with those reported in Table 1. However, we suspect that due in part to the small number of level-2 units in these analyses ($n = 18$), no statistically significant interaction effects were found between the "preexisting social conditions" and either of the drug-market variables. These results are available upon request.

23. In this case, the violent action is likely to be directed at a particular person with whom one has a grievance and simply may be behavior designed to achieve an instrumental end in a given situational context. Yet, we also recognize that it is possible that those who use this type of self-help may be attempting to send a message that they are not to be messed with. However, we would argue that because the actor is operating outside of a clear organizational framework, the transmission of that message is likely to be less effective than it would be if the actor was integrated into a broader social network.

24. If so, it would seem that the decline in lethal violence rates of the past decade would be attributable either to non-drug-market linked factors or to other changes in drug markets (e.g., changing norms toward violence, aging of drug-market participants, decline of open-air markets, etc.) that have caused them to become more stable despite the continuation of the War on Drugs.

REFERENCES

Anderson, Elijah. 1999. *Code of the Street: Decency, Violence and the Moral Life of the Inner City.* New York: W.W. Norton.

Baumer, Eric. 1994. "Poverty, Crack and Crime: A Cross-City Analysis." *Journal of Research in Crime and Delinquency* 31:311-27.

Baumer, Eric, Janet L. Lauritsen, Richard Rosenfeld, and Richard Wright. 1998. "The Influence of Crack Cocaine on Robbery, Burglary, and Homicide Rates: A Cross-City, Longitudinal Analysis." *Journal of Research in Crime and Delinquency* 35:316-40.

Beckett, Katherine and Theodore Sasson. 2000. *The Politics of Injustice.* Thousand Oaks, CA: Pine Forge Press.

Black, Donald. 1976. *The Behavior of Law.* San Diego, CA: Academic Press.

———. 1983. "Crime as Social Control." *American Sociological Review* 48:34-45.

Blumstein, Alfred. 1995. "Youth Violence, Guns and the Illicit-Drug Industry." *Journal of Criminal Law and Criminology* 86:10-36.

Blumstein, Alfred and Richard Rosenfeld. 1998. "Explaining Recent Trends in U.S. Homicide Rates." *Journal of Criminal Law and Criminology* 88:1175-1216.

Blumstein, Alfred and Joel Wallman. 2000. *The Crime Drop in America.* New York: Cambridge University Press.

Chilton, Roland and Dee Weber. 1999. *Uniform Crime Reporting Program* [United States]: *Arrests by Age, Sex, and Race for Police Agencies in Metropolitan Statistical Areas, 1960-1995* [Computer File]. ICPSR version. Amherst, MA: University of Massachusetts [producer], 1998. Ann Arbor, MI: Inter-University Consortium for Political and Social Research [distributor].

Cohen, Jacqueline, Daniel Cork, John Engberg, and George Tita. 1998. "The Role of Drug Markets and Gangs in Local Homicide Rates." *Homicide Studies* 2:241-61.

Collins, Randall. 1994. *Four Sociological Traditions.* New York: Oxford University Press.

Cooney, Mark. 1997. "The Decline of Elite Homicide." *Criminology* 35:381-407.

Cork, Daniel. 1999. "Examining Space-Time Interaction in City-Level Homicide Data: Crack Markets and the Diffusion of Guns Among Youth." *Journal of Quantitative Criminology* 15:379-406.

Earls, Felton. 1999. *Project on Human Development in Chicago Neighborhoods: Community Survey, 1994-1995* [Computer file]. ICPSR version. Boston, MA: Harvard Medical School [producer], 1997. Ann Arbor, MI: Inter-university Consortium for Political and Social Research [distributor], 1999.

Fagan, Jeffrey. 1990. "Intoxication and Aggression." Pp. 241-320 in *Crime and Justice, Volume 13: Drugs and Crime*, edited by Michael Tonry and James Q. Wilson. Chicago, University of Chicago Press.

Fox, James Alan. 2000. *Uniform Crime Reports* [United States]: *Supplementary Homicide Reports, 1976-1997* [Computer File]. ICPSR version. Boston, MA: Northeastern University, College of Criminal Justice [producer], 1997. Ann Arbor, MI: Inter-university Consortium for Political and Social Research [distributor].

Fox, James Alan and Jack Levin. 2001. *The Will to Kill: Making Sense of Senseless Murder.* Needham Heights, MA: Allyn and Bacon.

Goldstein, Paul J. 1985. "The Drugs/Violence Nexus: A Tripartite Conceptual Framework." *Journal of Drug Issues* 14:493-506.

Goldstein, Paul J., Henry H. Brownstein, Patrick J. Ryan, and Patricia A. Bellucci. 1989. "Crack and Homicide in New York City, 1988: A Conceptually Based Event Analysis." *Contemporary Drug Problems* 16:651-87.

————. 1997. "Crack and Homicide in New York City: A Case Study in the Epidemiology of Violence." Pp. 113-30 in *Crack in America: Demon Drugs and Social Justice*, edited by Craig Reinarman and Harry G. Levine. Berkeley: University of California Press.

Greene, William H. 2000. *Econometric Analysis*, 4th ed. Englewood Cliffs, NJ: Prentice-Hall.

Gujarati, Damodar N. 2002. *Basic Econometrics*, 4th ed. New York: McGraw-Hill.

Hagan, John. 1994. *Crime and Disrepute.* Thousand Oaks, CA: Pine Forge Press.

Hamowy, Ronald. 1987. *Dealing with Drugs: Consequences of Government Control.* Lexington, MA: Heath.

Harer, Miles D. and Darrell Steffensmeier. 1992. "The Different Effects of Economic Inequality on Black and White Rates of Violence." *Social Forces* 70:1035-54.

Horney, Julie, D. Wayne Osgood, and Ineke Haen Marshall. 1995. "Criminal Careers in the Short-Term: Intra-Individual Variability in Crime and Its Relation to Local Life Circumstances." *American Sociological Review* 60:655-73.

Jonas, Steven. 1999. "Why the Drug War Will Never End." Pp. 125-150 in *The Drug Legalization Debate*, edited by James A. Inciardi. Thousand Oaks, CA: Sage.

LaFree, Gary. 1998. *Losing Legitimacy.* Boulder, CO: Westview.

LaFree, Gary and Kriss A. Drass. 1996. "The Effect of Changes in Intraracial Income Inequality and Educational Attainment on Changes in Arrest Rates for African Americans and Whites, 1957 to 1990." *American Sociological Review* 61:614-34.

Lizotte, Alan J., Marvin D. Krohn, James C. Howell, Kimberly Tobin, and Gregory J. Howard. 2000. "Factors Influencing Gun Carrying Among Young Urban Males Over the Adolescent-Young Adult Life Course." *Criminology* 38:811-34.

MacCoun, Robert J., Beau Kilmer, and Peter Reuter. 2003. "Research on Drugs-Crime Linkages: The Next Generation." *Toward a Drugs and Crime Research Agenda for the 21st Century.* Retrieved September 2003 from: http://www.ojp.usdoj.gov/nij/drugscrime/194616.htm

MacCoun, Robert J. and Peter Reuter. 2001. *Drug War Heresies: Learning from other Vices, Times, and Places.* New York: Cambridge University Press.

Maguire, Kathleen and Ann L. Pastore, eds. 2002. *Sourcebook of Criminal Justice Statistics.* Retrieved August 13, 2003 from: http://www.albany.edu/sourcebook

Martz, Larry. 1989. "A Tide of Drug Killings: The Crack Plague Spurs More Inner-city Murders. *Newsweek* 113 (3): 44.

Messner, Steven F. and Reid M. Golden. 1992. "Racial Inequality and Racially Disaggregated Homicide Rates: An Assessment of Alternative Theoretical Explanations." *Criminology* 30:421-47.

Monteforte, J. R. and W. U. Spitz. 1975. "Narcotic Abuse Among Homicides in Detroit." *Journal of Forensic Sciences* 20:186-90.

Nadelmann, Ethan A. 1989. "Drug Prohibition in the United States: Costs, Consequences, and Alternatives." *Science* 247:939-47.

Osgood, D. Wayne, Janet K. Wilson, Patrick O'Malley, Jerald G. Bachman, and Lloyd D. Johnston. 1996. "Routine Activities and Individual Behavior." *American Sociological Review* 61:635-55.

Ousey, Graham C. 1999. "Homicide, Structural Factors and the Racial Invariance Assumption." *Criminology* 37:405-26.

———. 2000a. "Deindustrialization, Female-Headed Families and Black and White Juvenile Homicide Rates, 1970-1990." *Sociological Inquiry* 70:391-419.

———. 2000b. "Explaining Regional and Urban Variation in Crime: A Review of Research." Pp. 261-308 in *Criminal Justice 2000, Volume 1, The Nature of Crime: Continuity and Change*, edited by Gary LaFree. Washington, DC: National Institute of Justice.

Ousey, Graham C. and Michelle Campbell Augustine. 2001. "Young Guns: Examining Alternative Explanations of Juvenile Firearm Homicide Rates." *Criminology* 39:933-68.

Ousey, Graham C. and Matthew R. Lee. 2002. "Examining the Conditional Nature of the Illicit Drug Market-Homicide Relationship: A Partial Test of the Theory of Contingent Causation." *Criminology* 40:73-102.

Pampel, Fred and Kirk R. Williams. 2000. "Intimacy and Homicide: Compensating for Missing Data in the SHR." *Criminology* 38:661-80.

Parker, Karen F. and Patricia L. McCall. 1999. "Structural Conditions and Racial Homicide Patterns: A Look at the Multiple Disadvantages in Urban Areas." *Criminology* 37:447-77.

Parker, Karen F. and Matthew V. Pruitt. 2000. "How the West Was One: Explaining the Similarities in Race-Specific Homicide Rates in the West and South." *Social Forces* 78:1483-1508.

Pattillo, Mary E. 1998. "Sweet Mothers and Gangbangers: Managing Crime in a Black Middle-Class Neighborhood." *Social Forces* 76:747-74.

Raudenbush, Stephen W. and Anthony S. Bryk. 2002. *Hierarchical Linear Models: Applications and Data Analysis Methods.* Thousand Oaks, CA: Sage.

Riley, K. Jack. 1998. "Homicide and Drugs." *Homicide Studies* 2:176-205.

Rose, Dina R. and Todd R. Clear. 1998. "Incarceration, Social Capital, and Crime: Implications for Social Disorganization Theory." *Criminology* 36:441-70.

Rosenfeld, Richard, and Scott H. Decker. 1999. "Are Arrest Statistics a Valid Measure of Illicit Drug Use? The Relationship Between Criminal Justice and Public Health Indicators of Cocaine, Heroin, and Marijuana Use." *Justice Quarterly* 16:685-99.

Sampson, Robert J. and William Julius Wilson. 1995. "Toward a Theory of Race, Crime and Urban Inequality." Pp. 37-54 in *Crime and Inequality*, edited by John Hagan and Ruth D. Peterson, Stanford, CA: Stanford University Press.

Substance Abuse and Mental Health Services Administration. 2001. *Summary of Findings from the 2000 National Household Survey on Drug Abuse.* Office of Applied Studies, NHSDA Series H-13, DHHS Publication No. (SMA) 01-3549. Rockville, MD.

Tonry, Michael. 1995. *Malign Neglect: Race, Crime and Punishment in America.* Oxford: Oxford University Press.

White, Helene Raskin and D. M. Gorman. 2000. "Dynamics of the Drug-Crime Relationship."
    Pp. 151-218 in *Criminal Justice 2000, Volume 1, The Nature of Crime: Continuity and
    Change*. Washington, DC: National Institute of Justice.
Williams, Kirk R. and Robert L. Flewelling. 1987. "Family, Acquaintance, and Stranger Homi-
    cide: Alternative Procedures for Rate Calculations." *Criminology* 25:543-60.
Zahn, Margaret A. and M. Bencivengo. 1974. "Violent Death: A Comparison Between Drug
    Users and Nondrug Users. *Addictive Diseases* 1:283-96.
Zimring, Franklin and Gordon Hawkins. 1997. *Crime Is Not the Problem: Lethal Violence in
    America*. New York: Oxford University Press.

*Graham C. Ousey is on the faculty of the Department of Sociology and Criminal Justice
at the University of Delaware. His current research focuses on: 1) contingencies in the
drug market-violence nexus and 2) how short-term changes in the structure and character of peer friendship networks affect levels of substance use and violence. His prior research has been published in a variety of professional outlets including* Criminology, Social Forces, The Sociological Quarterly *and* Rural Sociology.

*Matthew R. Lee is an associate professor in the Department of Sociology at Louisiana
State University. His previous research has appeared in* Criminology, Social Forces,
and Rural Sociology.

[24]

Deadly Demographics: Population Characteristics and Forecasting Homicide Trends

James Alan Fox
Alex R. Piquero

Violence research has identified demographic subgroups—distinguished by age, race and gender—having widely varying rates of offending. According to the demographic hypothesis used in criminology, as these segments grow or contract in proportionate size, the aggregate offending rate tends to rise or fall as a result. In this article, we use data from the Supplementary Homicide Reports from 1976 through 1999 to assess the extent to which demographic change can account for the massive drop in homicide rates that occurred during the 1990s, and then attempt to develop a demographically based forecast of future trends in murder.

Keywords: homicide; forecasting; demographics; population characteristics

Studying rates of crime has been a major focus of criminological research (Blumstein & Rosenfeld, 1999; Cook & Laub, 1998; Steffensmeier & Harer, 1999). In particular, the study of homicide has held a long-standing interest among academics, policy makers, and concerned citizens and has especially been the case in the United States where homicide rates far exceed those in other industrialized nations (Lane, 1999; Reiss & Roth, 1993). Interestingly, crime and homicide rates sloped downward in the 1990s. Although a number of factors may account for this encouraging trend, one potentially important contributor is demographic change—shifts in the age/race/gender mix of the population.

An interest in demographics has led to the demographic-change hypothesis. Under this notion, the general population is thought to consist of different demographic segments, some of which have a propensity to commit crimes (and homicides in particular) at relatively high rates. In periods when such

JAMES ALAN FOX: College of Criminal Justice, Northeastern University. ALEX R. PIQUERO: Center for Studies in Criminology & Law, University of Florida.

We would like to thank the reviewers for their helpful suggestions. This article revises the material originally presented in Fox (2000).

crime-prone segments are a growing percentage of the overall population (assuming all other things are equal), the aggregate offense rate will increase. Similarly (assuming all other things are equal), the aggregate rate will decrease during eras when crime-prone segments are a declining percentage of the total population.

The demographic-change hypothesis has frequently been used to explain fluctuations in crime rates. Research has illustrated that much of the increase in crime over the past 3 decades has been due, in part, to shifts in the demographic composition of the population (Blumstein & Nagin, 1975; Chilton, 1986, 1987, 1991; Chilton & Spielberger, 1971; Cohen & Land, 1987; Farrington & Langan, 1992; Ferdinand, 1970; Fox, 1978; Laub, 1983; Lee, 1984; President's Commission on Law Enforcement and the Administration of Justice, 1967; Sagi & Wellford, 1968; Steffensmeier & Harer, 1991; Wellford, 1973). For example, these studies demonstrated how the large number of children born in the post–World War II baby boom (which began in 1946 and lasted until 1964) were moving into the high crime-prone ages (14 to 24 years old) during the 1960s and 1970s, thus contributing to a sharp rise in crime. However, what do demographic changes tell us about the recent crime drop in America?

THE 1990s CRIME DROP

Within the United States, the 1990s may long be remembered as the decade when the crime rate crashed. Beginning in 1991, following 6 tumultuous years of soaring crime levels—particularly among the nation's youth— the rate of serious crime started a sharp and prolonged nosedive, engendering a more optimistic outlook concerning the effectiveness of crime prevention and crime control strategies. By the close of the 1990s, the nation had welcomed 8 straight years of declining crime rates, including a rate of homicide as low as that at any point since the mid-1960s.

The theories for why crime has dropped so precipitously during the past decade are numerous and varied (Blumstein & Wallman, 2000). Some observers attribute the decline to successful criminal justice initiatives, specifically, expanding police ranks with a commitment to community policing strategies, growing prison populations, and incapacitating increasing numbers of felons for longer periods of time (Spelman, 2000). Other criminologists point instead to changes in street drug markets, especially the diminished demand for crack cocaine (Johnson, Golub, & Dunlap, 2000). Other analysts cite the improved economy, whether it is reflected in reduced rates of joblessness or in the enhanced abilities of municipalities to afford crime control programs (Grogger, 2000). Still other observers praise grassroots efforts encouraging communities to organize and invest in their youth enrichment programs (Levin, 1999).

A further proposition for explaining at least part of the recent decline in crime is the changing demographic makeup of the U.S. population. As discussed earlier, the demographic argument suggests that the crime rate should vary according to the age/race/gender composition of the population—to increase when high-rate groups are expanding proportionately and conversely to fall when these groups are diminishing in their share of the population.

Although it is hard to question the validity of this argument, there certainly is much debate concerning its importance relative to other factors, such as higher incarceration rates or shifting drug markets (Zimring, 1998). Moreover, in contrast to year-to-year changes in crime rates that sometimes reach or exceed 10%, demographic change moves rather slowly. Actually, the most notable demographic correlate of offending rates— the sex ratio—is a virtual constant in terms of population composition and therefore cannot account for any of the trend. Age and race composition do change, of course—the former in a generational cycle and the latter more secularly—yet these shifts are surely gradual compared to the sharp rises and falls in crime trends of the past few decades. On the other hand, although the operation of demographics may be relatively modest (compared with, say, prison populations that have doubled in a decade), they are quite predictable.

Given this predictability, it is quite reasonable to attempt to provide a glimpse into the future, or what social scientists refer to as forecasting. At its most basic level, forecasting refers to the process used to predict the unknown, and when it comes to research on issues related to crime (including prison projections and criminal behavior), the use of forecasting has been useful, especially to policy makers, as they plan for the future (Office of Program Policy Analysis and Government Accountability, 1996).

CURRENT FOCUS

In response to recently declining crime rates, although many Americans remained incredulous—basing their perceptions and opinions more on graphic media reports of ghastly crimes than on statistical graphics trending downward—others wondered how low the crime rate would go. One of the purposes of this article is to examine this very question. Have we reached or are we soon to reach a low point—a criminological "limbo stick" below which the offense rate cannot reasonably be expected to dip—or can we anticipate more good news on the crime front well into the new millennium? More generally, our purpose is to examine the operation of one key correlate of crime trends—demographics—and how it can be used to forecast future crime trends, with a particular focus on homicide. Although offense types are also important in assessing the nation's well-being, homicide, more than any other offense type, drives public opinion and, therefore, policy responses.

Restricting the analysis to homicide has important methodological advantages. Unlike other offense categories, the murder count is not plagued by the so-called dark figure of crime: the problem of undercounting of nonreported offenses. Virtually all homicides come to the attention of the police. In many respects, therefore, the murder rate is a more reliable indicator of crime trends generally unaffected by victim reporting tendencies or local law enforcement recording practices.[1]

METHOD

Data

There are two primary sources for detailed data on homicides: the Vital Statistics Program of the National Center for Health Statistics and the Supplemental Homicide Reports data compiled by the FBI from law enforcement agencies. The former data includes individual records on all of the known homicides each year compiled from medical examiners' reports; however, these data are limited because they lack information on the circumstances of the homicides and characteristics of the perpetrators (Cook & Laub, 1998), a feature that is the primary focus of the current investigation.[2]

Given our focus on demographic characteristics, herein we use the FBI's Supplementary Homicide Reports (SHR). Unlike the other offenses contained in the FBI's Uniform Crime Reports (UCR), data from the SHR are available in incident form with detail on location, victim, and offender characteristics. The SHR is an incident-based reporting mechanism that includes information on victim and offender age, race, and gender; victim/offender relationship; weapon and circumstances; and month, year, and reporting jurisdiction for the overwhelming majority of homicides known to the police. Although the level of compliance by local agencies varies from year to year, on average more than 92% of homicides in America are reflected in these data.

The SHR data are not, however, without their limitations (Cook & Laub, 1998; Fox, 1997; Pampel & Williams, 2000). Although national coverage is quite high, missing reports can be corrected using weights to match national and state estimates prepared by the FBI.[3] The most significant problem in using SHR data to analyze offender characteristics, however, is the sizable and growing number of unsolved homicides contained in the data file. To the extent that the missing offender data is associated with certain offender characteristics, ignoring unsolved homicides would seriously underestimate rates of offending by particular subgroups of the population, distort trends over time among these same subgroups, and bias observed patterns of offending.

To adjust for unsolved homicides, a method for offender imputation has been devised, using available information about the victims murdered in solved and unsolved homicides (Fox, 1997). Through this imputation algorithm, the demographic characteristics of unidentified offenders are inferred based on similar homicide cases—similar in terms of the victim profile and state and year of the offense—that had been solved. In other words, offender profiles for unsolved crimes are estimated based on the offender profiles in solved cases matched on victim age, gender, and race as well as year and state.

The imputation algorithm uses a weighting approach to allow solved cases to serve as proxies for unsolved ones. Unsolved cases are assigned 0 weights, whereas solved cases are weighted inversely proportional to the percentage of matched cases that are solved and thus receive weights of at least 1. In terms of numerical value, 30.7% of the cases are unsolved and have 0 weights, 61.9% of the cases have weights of at least 1 but less than 2, another 6.0% have weights less than 3, an additional 1.0% have weights less than 4, and only about 0.4% have weights over 4. As evidence that this weighting process does not distort the results, homicide trends with and without weighting tend to be similar (in overall pattern, although not level) (see also Pampel & Williams, 2000).[4]

RESULTS

Figure 1 displays the rate of murder for the United States across the second half of the 20th century. The trend line exhibits large fluctuations over the five decades that beg for explanation. One potential hypothesis (among many others) for the cyclical pattern involves expansions and contractions in the population percentage of young people.

Figure 2 superimposes the percentage of the population ages 18 to 24 (long considered the age group most prone to committing violent crimes, including homicide). For years, these two variables closely tracked one another, consistent with the demographic argument stated earlier. The homicide rate rose sharply from the mid-1960s to the late 1970s just as the baby-

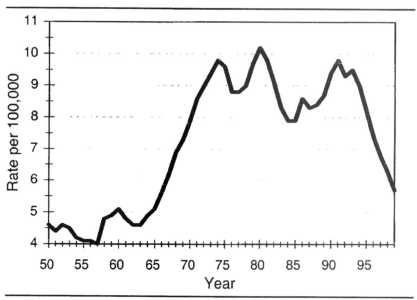

Figure 1:   U.S. Homicide Rate, 1950-1999

boom generation reached late adolescence and early adulthood, pushing this youthful, high-risk population into record territories. During the early 1980s—as some criminologists predicted (see Fox, 1978)—the homicide rate began to slip just as the baby-boom cohort was maturing into adulthood (taking on jobs, families, and other responsibilities), and the crime-prone age group started to shrink in proportionate size.[5] In fact, the homicide rate dropped by about one fourth during the first half of the 1980s.

In the mid-1980s, however, the two trend lines suddenly and sharply diverged as the demographic dividends produced by a declining young adult population vanished prematurely. This was sudden and unanticipated, occurring despite the countervailing forces of demographics. By the late 1980s, the homicide rate was once again headed upward even though the percentage of the population ages 18 to 24 continued heading downward.

The unexpected explosion in the murder rate surprised many and even prompted the Congress to convene hearings into America's latest epidemic (Biden, 1990). Many researchers have cited the sudden emergence of the crack cocaine market that seduced large numbers of youngsters (including minors) into the volatile and violent drug trade (Baumer, Lauritsen, Rosenfeld, & Wright, 1998; Blumstein, 1995). Moreover, the spread of guns

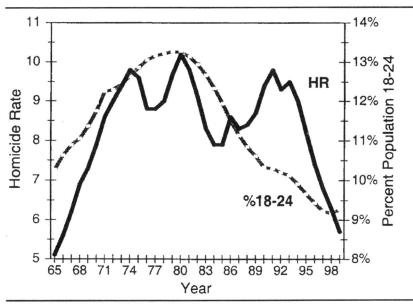

Figure 2:   Homicide Rate and Percentage of Population Ages 18 to 24

(Cork, 1999) and street gangs (Maxson, 1999) produced a new wave of youth violence unrelated to demographic change.

As shown in Figure 3, the rate of murder committed by adolescents changed abruptly in the mid-1980s (as did that for young adults).[6] The heavy involvement of teens in murder statistics was particularly startling. Youngsters ages 14 and 15 were traditionally known for petty crimes, not murder (Blumstein, Cohen, Roth, & Visher, 1986). However, the spread of crack, gangs, and guns appeared to have changed conventional wisdom (Blumstein & Rosenfeld, 1999). In the aggregate, teenagers began to behave less like their parents' generation and more like their siblings. In effect, even though the usual crime-prone age group was shrinking in numbers, the minimum age for membership dropped from 18 to 14 as teenagers more than took up the slack in the high-risk group.

The decline in youth homicide rates since their 1993 peak represents a reversal of the very conditions that drove the rates upward. The 1968 through 1972 birth cohorts were young and thrill-seeking enough during the mid-1980s to have been affected by the early introduction of crack in major urban centers, yet not old enough to know better. To account for this turn of events, Butterfield (1997) claimed that younger birth cohorts were scared off by the negative consequences that drug and gang involvement had had on their predecessors, whereas Blumstein and Rosenfeld (1999) postulated that crack

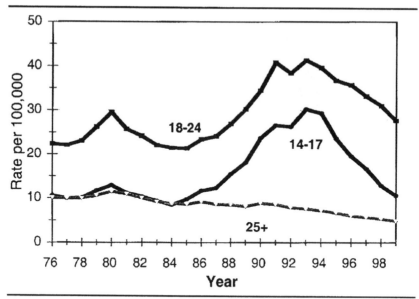

Figure 3: Homicide Offending Rate by Age, 1976-1999

markets started to decline during the 1990s, and as a consequence, so did rates of violence, including murder.

The role of demographics extends beyond age differences. Figure 4 shows similar age breakdowns for gender-race combinations. Trends in offending rates by age are remarkably similar between Blacks and Whites, although at dramatically different scales. Among White and Black males, offending rates rose and then dropped for younger age groups but declined steadily for adults ages 25 and older. By contrast, rates among women and girls showed no discernable trends upward or downward. Still, the rise and fall in youthful offending has been particularly pronounced among Black males. This is the very group that was most affected by the spread of guns, crack, and gangs in urban centers (Blumstein & Rosenfeld, 1999), and thus had the greatest room for improvement during the 1990s crime decline.

Although the age/race/gender-specific trends show distinct changes over time, these cannot be attributed to demographics. Increases and decreases in the proclivity of teens and young adults to commit homicide is not a function of the number of such youth (Cook & Laub, 1998). Rather, demographic change represents shifting levels of membership among the demographic subgroups: population segments moving from younger and higher risk to older and lower risk age groups (Fox, 2000).

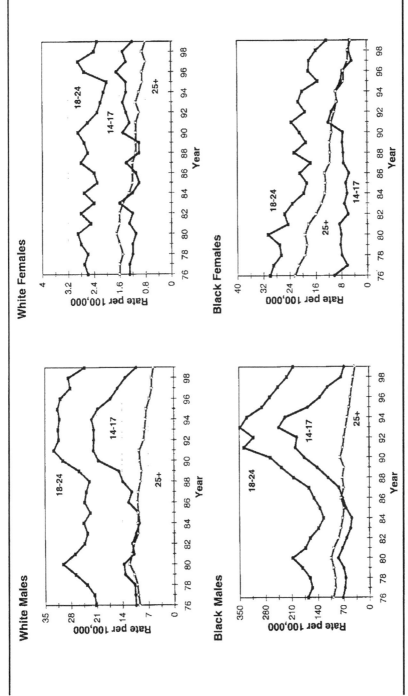

Figure 4:   Homicide Offending Rates by Age, Race, and Gender

347

TABLE 1:   1990s Crime Drop Due to Demographic Change

	Offending Rate per 100,000	Change in Offending Rate	Offending Rate Predicted From Demographics	Change Predicted From Demographics	Percentage Change From Demographics
1991	11.21		11.21		
1992	10.41	−0.80	11.13	−0.07	9.33
1993	10.72	−0.49	11.13	−0.08	16.19
1994	10.18	−1.03	11.05	−0.16	15.69
1995	9.21	−2.00	10.99	−0.22	11.10
1996	8.45	−2.76	10.92	−0.29	10.50
1997	7.70	−3.51	10.86	−0.35	9.88
1998	7.12	−4.09	10.81	−0.40	9.69
1999	6.38	−4.83	10.79	−0.42	8.61

Table 1 examines the extent to which the 1990s decline in murder can be linked to demographics. Using 1991 age/race/gender-specific offending rates as a baseline, demographically disaggregated offender counts have been predicted for each year through 1999 to re-create the aggregate offending rate per 100,000 population that would have resulted from demographic change alone. In other words, the age/race/gender-specific offending rates for 1991 were applied forward to later population segments in order to reconstruct a predicted homicide-offending rate based purely on demographic change.

Had we asked the question about the role of demographics following the 1993 or 1994 crime rates—just before the sharp downturn in youth offending—the contribution of demographics would have appeared to be slightly more than 15%. With the plunge in youth homicide since 1993, the contribution of demographics would, however, appear to have diminished to just under 10%. Specifically, had only demographics changed, the homicide rate would have dropped from 11.21 offenders per 100,000 in 1991, to 10.79 per 100,000 in 1999—not quite 10% of the actual drop (which was down to 6.38 per 100,000). Thus, demographics played a modest role in the 1990s crime rate decline.[7]

Despite this less-than-impressive result, the value on tracking demographic change lies in the fact that it is highly predictable, well into the future.[8] No one can say, for example, just how many police officers will be patrolling the streets of America in 2005, nor can anyone determine with certainty how many new prison beds will be available 5 years from now. By contrast, it is more easily determined how many 15-year-olds there will be in the year 2005: just about the same number of 10-year-olds in the year 2000 population.[9]

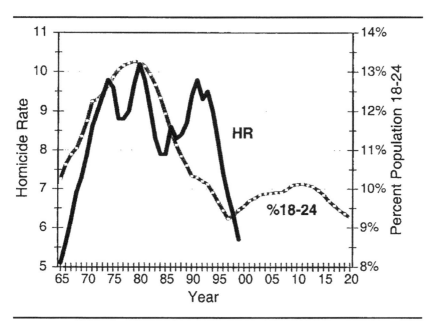

Figure 5:   Homicide and Projected Percentage of 18- to 24-Year-Olds

Over the next few years, the nation will experience an expansion of the youth population—the so-called baby-boomerang effect, representing the elevated numbers of second-generation baby boomers (e.g., offspring of the original baby-boom cohort) maturing into their higher crime-prone years. Public school enrollments have set new records 5 years running, and this will eventually translate into increased numbers of adolescents and then young adults (Fox, 2000).

Figure 5 extends the population trend shown earlier in Figure 2 out to the year 2020. The highest rate-age segment, 18- to 24-year-olds, has reached a trough and is beginning to climb once again in proportionate size. What effects this may have on the homicide rate remains to be seen. Whether this new and expanded population is any more or less violent than its predecessors depends on many unmeasurable and unpredictable factors.

Despite these caveats, the expected demographic turnaround prompted several observers incautiously to predict a future wave of youth violence (Bennett, DiIulio, & Walters, 1996; DiIulio, 1995; Fox, 1995, 1996a, 1996b). In reaction to these bleak and worrisome projections, critics questioned the size and significance of the expected demographic shift (Austin & Cohen, 1996). Murphy (1996), for example, argued,

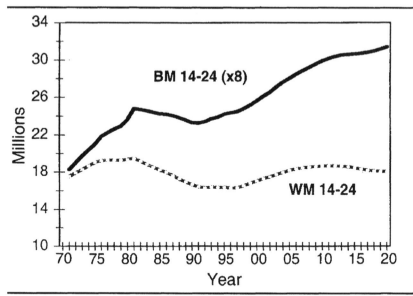

Figure 6: Projected Population of Young Men by Race

The male "at risk" population is expected to increase over the next decade, and this trend has led some to conclude that we need to brace ourselves for a new crime wave of juvenile violent crime that may well negate recent declines in violent crime rates. *However, a closer look at population projections shows that while the numbers of youth age 15-24 will increase, this increase will not exceed that for the 1980s.* (p. 4)

In an overall sense, Murphy and other critics are quite correct. Clearly, the projected increased in the proportion of 18- to 24-year-olds is quite modest compared to levels reached during the 1970s. What Murphy and others perhaps overlook is that the race-specific age curves, although similar, also differ in rather important ways.

Figure 6 displays population projections separately for White and Black young men ages 14 to 24 (with the Black population counts magnified by a factor of 8 to aid in making race comparisons). Although the overall pattern—downturn during the 1980s, a trough at or near 1990, and an increase thereafter—holds for both races, the slopes for the Black populations are noticeably steeper. The projected rise in the White youth population is indeed modest (as White female baby boomers had fewer children than their mothers did and tended also to delay childbirth in [the likely] pursuit of career goals), and the numbers are expected to plateau around the year 2010 at a level below that of the late 1970s. For Black youth, however, the population has already exceeded that of the late 1970s and will continue to rise sharply

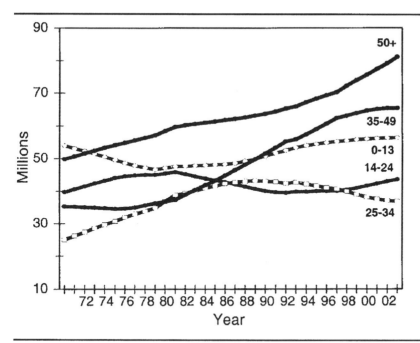

Figure 7: Projected Demographic Trends by Age Group

for decades to come. Given the higher rates of violence perpetrated by Black youth as compared with their White counterparts, the disproportionate increase in the number of Black teens and young adults could have a significant effect on the volume of youth violence in the years ahead. Moreover, the fact that many of these youngsters are born to teenage, unmarried women is also cause for concern (Blumstein, 1993).

Although the growth in youth population—especially among Blacks—is impressive, a different and brighter perspective comes from placing this in the context of other age groups. Figure 7 shows that the greatest growth is expected in the senior population. The baby boomers would hardly be considered babies anymore. In fact, by 2005, the population age 50 and older will increase to almost 90 million, representing an unprecedented 30% of the total population. Whatever boost in offending is created by an expanding youth population is likely to be negated by the even larger growth in seniors, the least violent group.[10]

To examine this prospect more fully, we generated a projection of the number of homicide offenders by age category, with certain assumptions concerning future age/race/gender-specific rates of offending. In particular, we assumed that offending rates for age groups under 25 years old remain

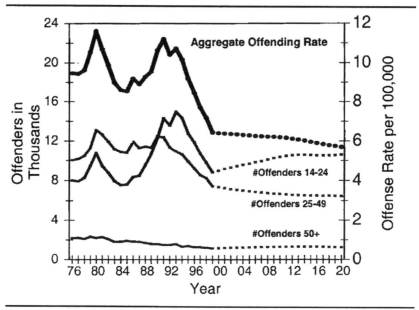

Figure 8:   Projected Homicide Offending Rate

unchanged from their current levels, whereas rates for older groups decline
(as they have for nearly 2 decades) at small and progressive rates (1% per year
for 25- to 49-year-olds and 2% per year for the 50+ age group). As shown in
Figure 8, the volume of youth homicide (offenders ages 14 to 24) is expected
to rebound because of population expansion within this age group. By contrast, the unprecedented growth in the older population (those ages 50 and
older) would not have any major effect on the overall volume of homicide.[11]

It is important not to be misled by aggregates. As shown also in Figure 8,
despite the projected youth offender counts, the aggregate rate of offending
(that by nature of population composition is heavily weighted toward older
age groups) is expected to move downward still. However, even if this
expected outcome eventuates and the UCR indicates further declines in violent crime, we must look closely within the overall figures to identify particular trends in youth violence. Thus, much like the recent research on criminal
careers (Nagin & Land, 1993), our analysis shows the importance of dissect-
ing aggregate trends to understand better potentially important subgroup
differences.

Before we conclude, it is important to point out that, as with all forecasting
exercises, certain assumptions must be made. It is instructive at this point,
then, to investigate the effect of modest departures from the assumptions
made in the analysis.

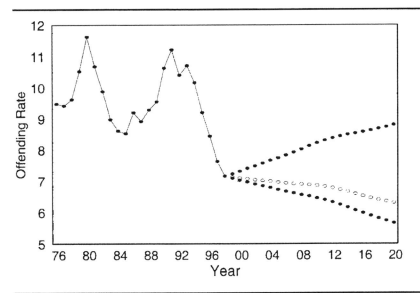

Figure 9: Alternative Homicide Offending Rate Forecasts
NOTE: The overall projected homicide-offending rate assumes annual age-specific offending rate changes of 0% for the under 25 group, −1% for the 25 to 49 group, and −2% for the 50+ group. The upper bound assumes a +1% annual change in offending rates for all age groups. The lower bound assumes a −1% change in offending rates for all age groups.

Figure 9 shows an analysis of how sensitive the forecast is to alternative assumptions about future changes in offending rates. The upper bound is based on an across-the-board increase of 1% per year in age/race/gender-specific offending rates. The lower bound is based on an across-the-board annual decrease of 1%. The middle series, drawn from Figure 7, assumes no change for those younger than age 25, a 1% decline per year for ages 25 to 49, and a 2% per year decline in the rate for those age 50 and older. As can be seen, under a 1% increase per year in the age/race/gender-specific offending rates, the offending rate increases dramatically over time, whereas the 1% decrease tracks the no-change line pretty well, although it still evidences a lower offending rate. In sum, this additional exercise indicates what can be expected to happen to the forecast when the key input quantities change.

DISCUSSION

The objective of this article was a modest one. First, we set out to highlight the importance of studying the role that demographics play in relation to crime trends in general, and homicide trends in particular. Second, we provided some information on how changes in demographic characteristics, namely age/race/gender, relate to changes in homicide rates. Third, we presented some estimates of the changing demographics of the U.S. population, as well as a preliminary forecast of homicide-offending rates through the first part of the 21st century.

Our analysis yielded three key conclusions. First, although several other factors, such as new-policing tactics and employment gains, may also be credited with reducing crime in the 1990s, our analysis indicates that about 10% of the 1990s decline in crime was due to demographics. Second, it appears that the age-specific downturns have plateaued, indicating that the crime drop may soon be over. Third, although the homicide rate may continue to decline—and decline more so for some groups but not others—there is a youth crime issue that is hidden in the overall aggregate trend. Although the aggregate homicide rate may appear to be on a decline, at the same time, the homicide rate for specific groups may exhibit an upswing, especially among those ages 14 to 24. In sum, although demographics are not the sole nor perhaps strongest predictor of crime rates in general (or the homicide rate in particular), they do present an important contributor. Clearly, other factors occurring during the same time period as these kinds of demographic changes present important contributors to homicide rates.

Several important directions for future research remain. First, and although not the focus of the current effort, we believe that attention should also be paid to etiological factors in the production of homicide. Although some research has been generated in this regard (Parker & McCall, 1999), much more work remains. For example, although evidence suggests that young, inner-city Black males are disproportionately offenders and victims of homicide, a complete understanding as to why this is the case remains elusive. We believe that one useful starting point is the fact that Whites and Blacks live in very different neighborhood contexts. Sampson and Wilson (1995) showed that in "not one city over 100,000 in the United States do blacks live in ecological equality with whites when it comes to [the] basic features of economic and family organization" (p. 42). The worst contexts in which Whites reside are considerably better than the average context of Black communities (Sampson, 1987). It is likely the case that these different ecological niches foster different cultures and methods of survival (Massey, 1995). A second point of future research for the study of homicide in general, and forecasting in particular, concerns the role of the Hispanic population. Given that persons of Hispanic groups are the fastest growing demographic group in the United States, the integration of Hispanics into the study of homicide appears especially relevant. Third, although not discussed in this article, a variety of forecasting extensions related to homicide would be help-ful and illuminating. For example, a forecast of homicide trends in high-homicide cities—New Orleans, Detroit, Chicago, and Washington, D.C.—would provide some useful information for city planners and public officials as they begin to think about the resources necessary for future prevention tac-tics in an effort to plan for saving lives now, rather than waiting until it's too late. Similarly, examination of future trends in homicide subtypes—gun homicides and homicides among intimate partners, for example—may help lawmakers and law enforcers fashion appropriate prevention strategies for the future. In sum, we hope that forecasting exercises, such as the one pre-sented herein, serve a useful purpose for scholars, policy makers, and citizens as they think about the future of homicide in the United States.

NOTES

1. A reviewer correctly pointed out some potential sources of disadvantage when using homicide data. For example, given that murder is normally a crime committed by someone against someone known to him or her and that autopsies are performed for only a few deaths, and then only if conditions are suspicious or unknown (and further that some rural areas do not have facilities for autopsies), it is possible that many times as many murders occur as are reported, and only the passionate, careless, and/or foolish offenders leave a trail of evidence. These factors can explain why, in some cases, a woman who has killed four or five husbands or children—one at a time over a period of years—only comes under suspicion after the coincidences mount and ear-lier natural-causes deaths are finally investigated. In sum, the reviewer is correct in noting that although many homicides do come to the attention of criminal justice officials, there are some murders that do not get reported, or even discovered.

2. Still, it is important to recognize that the Vital Statistics database contains more homi-cides per year than do the Supplementary Homicide Reports (SHR) (see Cook & Laub, 1998).

3. To adjust for nonreporting by certain law enforcement agencies (that results in an average SHR undercount of about 8%), the SHR records in this study were weighted so that victim counts matched the FBI estimates published annually in *Crime in the United States*.

4. To be sure, the imputation strategy used here makes the strong and clearly debatable assumption that solved and unsolved homicides of similar victim profiles have comparable offender characteristics. Admittedly, the characteristics of offenders who evade detection may differ from those who are identified by police. Still, we feel that using offender estimates based on imputed data is far superior to relying on official measures of offending rates, such as *known offenders per 100,000* or *rates of arrest*, which ignore missing data altogether. Cloning known offender distributions for unknown offenders is preferable to pretending they do not exist. Future research should continue to work through the kinds of issues that plague this line of research, as well as to continue to develop different imputation strategies to sort between the strengths and weaknesses of such approaches.

5. Maturing baby boomers may not have necessarily desisted from committing crimes alto-gether; rather, many may have shifted from high-risk street offending to low-risk (and high-profit) forms of offending once these opportunities became more available to them. This type of offense switching from more- to less-detectable crimes has been recognized by several criminol-

ogists (Spelman, 1994). Moreover, many baby boomers may not have been detected such that, with officially based records, they appear to have desisted, although self-report data may indicate otherwise (see Nagin, Farrington, & Moffitt, 1995).

6. Note that homicide offending rates (offenders per 100,000) are typically larger than the more customary homicide victimization rates (victims per 100,000) because multiple-offender incidents outnumber multiple-victim crimes (see Fox, 2000).

7. The debate over those factors responsible for producing the drop in crime has sometimes become overly polarized. For example, a *New York Times* story regarding then New York City Police Commissioner William Bratton reported,

> Perhaps the most popular theory, and the one most disdained by Mr. Bratton, argues that the crime rate is determined by the number of youths in society at any given time. At a news conference . . . Mr. Bratton disparaged the major proponent of demographic criminology, James Alan Fox of Northeastern University, as well as the journalists who go to him for his opinions. (Krauss, 1995, p. 1)

The demographic hypothesis suggests, however, that population composition is but one explanation for changes in crime rates, not the only (or even the most important) explanation.

8. An earlier forecasting effort using a simultaneous equation econometric model, which successfully predicted 1980s' crime trends, was largely based on demographic composition as exogenous input (see Fox, 1978).

9. To be sure, our projection of demographic-based population estimates is somewhat simplistic. In particular, it does not take into consideration immigration-related changes to population demographics. It is likely the case that a significant percentage of the 15-year-olds in 5 years will come from foreign lands and will be a dual product of their native acculturation blended with their Americanization.

10. The significant role that the senior population expansion is likely to have on the aggregate homicide rate may, at first, appear paradoxical. It is true, of course, that seniors have always had a low rate of offending. Moreover, even if this rate were to change dramatically, the effect on the homicide count would be quite small (even after a large percentage increase, a low rate is still a low rate). The upcoming growth in the number of older Americans will, however, drive the overall homicide rate downward because this will affect more on the crime rate denominator than its numerator. The increasing proportionate size of the population segment with the lowest proclivity toward violent offending could dramatically lower the overall rate, even if other subgroups (e.g., teens and young adults) increase in their level of offending.

11. Projections were made separately for combinations of age, race, and gender, and the resulting estimated offender counts were then aggregated across these subgroups.

REFERENCES

Austin, J., & Cohen, R. L. (1996, March 1). *Why are crime rates declining: An NCCD briefing report.* San Francisco: National Council on Crime and Delinquency.

Baumer, E., Lauritsen, J. L., Rosenfeld, R., & Wright, R. (1998). The influence of crack cocaine on robbery, burglary, and homicide rates: A cross-city, longitudinal analysis. *Journal of Research in Crime & Delinquency, 35,* 316-340.

Bennett, W. J., DiIulio, J. J., & Walters, J. P. (1996). *Body count: Moral poverty and how to win America's war against crime and drugs.* New York: Simon & Schuster.

Biden, J. (1990, July 31). Senate Judiciary Committee hearings on homicide trends in the United States. *Congressional Record*. Washington, DC: Government Printing Office.

Blumstein, A. (1993). Making rationality relevant: The American Society of Criminology 1992 presidential address. *Criminology, 31*, 1-16.

Blumstein, A. (1995). Youth violence, guns, and the illicit-drug industry. *Journal of Criminal Law & Criminology, 86,* 10-36.

Blumstein, A., Cohen, J., Roth, J. A., & Visher, C. A. (1986). *Criminal careers and "career criminals." Washington, DC: National Academy Press.*

Blumstein, A., & Nagin, D. S. (1975). Analysis of arrest rates for trends in criminality. *Socio-Economic Planning Sciences, 9*, 221-227.

Blumstein, A., & Rosenfeld, R. (1999). Trends in rates of violence in the U.S.A. *Studies on Crime & Crime Prevention, 8*, 139-168.

Blumstein, A., & Wallman, J. (Eds.). (2000). *The crime drop in America.* New York: Cambridge University Press.

Butterfield, F. (1997, June 8). Scared straight: The wisdom of children who have known too much. *The New York Times*, sec. 4, p. 1.

Chilton, R. (1986). Age, sex, race, and arrest trends for 12 of the nation's largest central cities. In J. M. Byrne & R. J. Sampson (Eds.), *The social ecology of crime* (pp. 102-115). New York: Springer-Verlag.

Chilton, R. (1987). Twenty years of homicide and robbery in Chicago: The impact of the city's changing racial and age composition, *Journal of Quantitative Criminology, 3*, 195-214.

Chilton, R. (1991). Urban crime trends and criminological theory. *Criminal Justice Research Bulletin.* Huntsville, TX: Sam Houston State University.

Chilton, R., & Spielberger, A. (1971). Is delinquency increasing? Age structure and the crime rate. *Social Forces, 49*, 487-493.

Cohen, L. E., & Land, K. C. (1987). Age structure and crime: Symmetry versus asymmetry and the projection of crime rates through the 1990s. *American Sociological Review, 52*, 170-183.

Cook, P., & Laub, J. H. (1998). The unprecedented epidemic in youth violence. In M. Tonry & M. Moore (Eds.), *Youth violence, crime and justice: An annual review of research* (pp. 27-64). Chicago: University of Chicago Press.

Cork, D. (1999). Examining space-time interaction in city-level homicide data: Crack markets and the diffusion of guns among youth. *Journal of Quantitative Criminology, 15,* 379-406.

DiIulio, J. (1995, November 27). The coming of the super-predators. *Weekly Standard*, p. 23.

Farrington, D. P., & Langan, P. (1992). Changes in crime and punishment in England and America in the 1980s. *Justice Quarterly, 9*, 5-46.

Federal Bureau of Investigation. (n.d., published annually). *Crime in the United States.* Washington, DC: Government Printing Office.

Ferdinand, T. N. (1970). Demographic shifts and criminality: An inquiry. *British Journal of Criminology, 10*, 169-175.

Fox, J. A. (1978, February 18). *Forecasting crime data: An econometric analysis.* Lexington, MA: Lexington Books.

Fox, J. A. (1995, February 18). *Homicide offending patterns, 1976-1993.* Paper presented at the annual meeting of the American Academy for the Advancement of Science. Atlanta, GA.

Fox, J. A. (1996a). *Trends in juvenile violence: A report to the United States Attorney General on current and future rates of juvenile offending.* Washington, DC: U.S. Department of Justice, Bureau of Justice Statistics.

Fox, J. A. (1996b, September). The calm before the juvenile crime storm. *Population Today*, pp. 4-5.

Fox, J. A. (1997). *Trends in juvenile homicide, 1976-1996: An update of the March 1996 report to the U.S. Attorney General on current and future rates of juvenile violence.* Washington, DC: U.S. Department of Justice, Bureau of Justice Statistics.

Fox, J. A. (2000). Demographics and U.S. homicide. In A. Blumstein & J. Wallman (Eds.), *The crime drop in America* (pp. 288-318). New York: Cambridge University Press.

Grogger, J. (2000). An economic model of recent trends in violence. In A. Blumstein & J. Wallman (Eds.), *The crime drop in America* (pp. 266-287). New York: Cambridge University Press.

Johnson, B., Golub, A., & Dunlap, E. (2000). The rise and decline of hard drugs, drug markets, and violence in inner-city New York. In A. Blumstein & J. Wallman (Eds.), *The crime drop in America* (pp. 164-206). New York: Cambridge University Press.

Krauss, C. (1995, July 23). Crime lab: Mystery of New York, the suddenly safer city. *The New York Times,* sec. 4, p. 1.

Lane, R. (1999). Murder in America: A historian's perspective. In M. Tonry (Ed.), *Crime and justice: An annual review of research* (Vol. 25, pp. 191-224). Chicago: University of Chicago Press.

Laub, J. H. (1983). Urbanism, race, and crime. *Journal of Research in Crime & Delinquency, 20,* 183-198.

Lee, G. W. (1984). Are crime rates increasing? A study of the impact of demographic shifts on crime rates in Canada. *Canadian Journal of Criminology, 26,* 29-41.

Levin, J. (1999, May 7). An effective response to teenage crime is possible. *Chronicle of Higher Education,* p. 35.

Massey, D. S. (1995). Getting away with murder: Segregation and violent crime in urban America. *University of Pennsylvania Law Review, 143,* 1203-1232.

Maxson, C. (1999). Gang homicide: A review and extension of the literature. In D. Smith & M. Zahn (Eds.), *Homicide: A sourcebook of social research* (pp. 239-254). Thousand Oaks, CA: Sage.

Murphy, L. (1996, May 14). Statement before the Congressional Black Caucus Brain Trust on Juvenile Justice. *Congressional Record.* Washington, DC: Government Printing Office.

Nagin, D. S., Farrington, D. P., & Moffitt, T. E. (1995). Life-course trajectories of different types of offenders. *Criminology, 33,* 111-140.

Nagin, D. S., & Land, K. C. (1993). Age, criminal careers, and population heterogeneity: Specification and estimation of a nonparametric, mixed poisson model. *Criminology, 32,* 327-362.

Office of Program Policy Analysis and Government Accountability. (1996). *Review of prison population forecasting in Florida.* Tallahassee, FL: Author.

Pampel, F. C., & Williams, K. R. (2000). Intimacy and homicide: Compensating for missing data in the SHR. *Criminology, 38,* 661-680.

Parker, K. F., & McCall, P. L. (1999). Structural conditions and racial homicide patterns: A look at the multiple disadvantages in urban areas. *Criminology, 37,* 447-478.

President's Commission on Law Enforcement and the Administration of Justice. (1967). *Task force report: Crime and its impact—An assessment.* Washington DC: U.S. Government Printing Office.

Reiss, A. J., & Roth, J. A. (1993). *Understanding and preventing violence.* Washington, DC: National Academy Press.

Sagi, P. C., & Wellford, C. F. (1968). Age composition and patterns of change in criminal statistics. *Journal of Criminal Law, Criminology & Police Science, 59,* 29-36.

Sampson, R. J. (1987). Urban black violence: The effect of male joblessness and family disruption. *American Journal of Sociology, 93,* 348-382.

Sampson, R. J., & Wilson, W. J. (1995). Toward a theory of race, crime, and urban inequality. In J. Hagan & R. D. Peterson (Eds.), *Crime and inequality* (pp. 37-54). Stanford, CA: Stanford University Press.

Spelman, W. (1994). *Criminal incapacitation.* New York: Plenum.

Spelman, W. (2000). The limited importance of prison expansion. In A. Blumstein & J. Wallman (Eds.), *The crime drop in America* (pp. 97-129). New York: Cambridge University Press.

Steffensmeier, D. J., & Harer, M. D. (1991). Did crime rise or fall during the Reagan presidency? The effects of an "aging" U.S. population on the nation's crime rate. *Journal of Research in Crime & Delinquency, 28,* 330-359.

Steffensmeier, D. J., & Harer, M. D. (1999). Making sense of recent U.S. crime trends, 1980 to 1996/1998: Age composition effects and other explanations. *Journal of Research in Crime & Delinquency, 36,* 235-274.

Wellford, C. F. (1973). Age composition and the increase in recorded crime. *Criminology, 11,* 61-70.

Zimring, F. (1998). *American youth violence.* New York: Oxford University Press.

[25]

Firearm Use by Offenders

Survey of Inmates in State and Federal Correctional Facilities

By Caroline Wolf Harlow, Ph.D.
BJS Statistician

Approximately 203,300 prisoners serving a sentence in a State or Federal prison in 1997 were armed when they committed the crime for which they were serving time. An estimated 18% of State prison inmates and 15% of Federal inmates reported using, carrying, or possessing a firearm during the crime for which they were sentenced. In 1991, 16% of State inmates and 12% of Federal inmates said they were armed at the time of their offense.

Among all inmates in 1997, 9% of those in State prisons and 2% of those in Federal prisons said they fired a gun while committing their current offense. Of violent offenders, 18% of State inmates and 9% of Federal inmates discharged a firearm. Less than 2% of inmates serving time for a drug, property, or public-order offense fired a gun during the crime that resulted in their prison sentence.

Among prisoners who carried a firearm during the offense for which they were serving time in 1997, 14% had bought or traded for the gun from a store, pawnshop, flea market, or gun show. The 1997 percentage who had acquired their firearm at a retail outlet represented a significant drop from 21% in 1991. The percentage of inmates receiving their gun from family or friends rose from 34% in 1991 to 40% in 1997.

Highlights

Type of firearm	Percent of prison inmates	
	State	Federal
Total	18.4%	14.8%
Handgun	15.3	12.8
Rifle	1.3	1.3
Shotgun	2.4	2.0

Characteristic of inmates who carried firearms	Percent of prison Inmates possessing a firearm	
Offense	State	Federal
Violent	30.2%	35.4%
Property	3.1	2.9
Drug	8.1	8.7
Public-order	19.1	27.3
Gender		
Male	19.1%	15.5%
Female	7.3	6.2
Age		
24 or younger	29.4%	19.1%
25-34	16.5	15.5
35 or older	14.8	13.6
Criminal history		
First-time offender	22.3%	9.5%
Recidivist	17.2	18.4

Source of gun	Percent of State inmates possessing a firearm	
	1997	1991
Total	100.0%	100.0%
Purchased from –	13.9	20.8
Retail store	8.3	14.7
Pawnshop	3.8	4.2
Flea market	1.0	1.3
Gun show	0.7	0.6
Friends or family	39.6	33.8
Street/illegal source	39.2	40.8

Use of firearm	Percent of prison inmates possessing a firearm	
	State	Federal
Total	100.0%	100.0%
Fired	49.1	12.8
Killed/injured victim	22.8	5.0
Other	26.3	7.8
Brandished to –	73.2	46.2
Scare someone	48.6	29.3
Defend self	41.1	24.9

• During the offense that brought them to prison, 15% of State inmates and 13% of Federal inmates carried a handgun; about 2% had a military-style semiautomatic gun or machine gun.

• Among inmates in prison for homicide, a sexual assault, robbery, assault or other violent crime, 30% of State offenders and 35% of Federal offenders carried a firearm when committing the crime. Almost a fourth of State inmates and almost a third of Federal inmates serving a sentence for a violent crime had carried a handgun during the offense.

• 29% of State inmates under age 25 at the time of the survey were carrying a gun when they committed their current offense compared to 15% of those 35 or older.

• In 1997 among State inmates possessing a gun, fewer than 2% bought their firearm at a flea market or gun show, about 12% from a retail store or pawnshop, and 80% from family, friends, a street buy, or an illegal source.

• On average, State inmates possessing a firearm received sentences of 18 years, while those without a weapon had an average sentence of 12 years.

• Among prisoners carrying a firearm during their crime, 40% of State inmates and 56% of Federal inmates received a sentence enhancement because of the firearm.

Data for this report are based primarily on personal interviews with large nationally representative samples of State and Federal prison inmates. In the 1997 and 1991 Surveys of Inmates in State and Federal Correctional Facilities, inmates were questioned about any firearms they may have used when committing a crime and asked to specify the type of weapon, its source, and its use in committing crimes. In addition, inmates were queried about the types of both current and past offenses for which they were sentenced, including any weapons offenses.

Almost a fifth of prison inmates carried a gun during their crime

An estimated 18% of State prison inmates and 15% of Federal inmates reported that they used, carried, or possessed a firearm when they committed the crime for which they were serving a sentence to prison (table 1).[1]

When asked if they had ever been armed while committing a crime, about a quarter of State prison inmates and a fifth of Federal inmates reported that they had carried a gun while committing at least one crime.

Almost half of both State and Federal inmates said that they had owned or possessed a firearm at some time in their lives. Equivalent measures for lifetime gun ownership among adults in the general population are difficult to find. Personal or telephone interviews and polls provide estimates for persons in the general population owning a firearm at the time of the survey. An estimated 25% to 29% of the adult population reported currently owning a firearm when surveyed.[2] According to public opinion polls, members of 4 in every 10 U.S. households have access to a gun.

Less than 2% of inmates reported carrying a fully automatic or military-style semiautomatic firearm

Fewer than 1 in 50 State and Federal inmates used, carried, or possessed a

[1]For definitions of firearms, see *Methodology* on pages 14 and 15.
[2]Phillip J. Cook and Jens Ludwig, *Guns in America: Summary Report*, Washington, DC, Police Foundation, 1996, table 2.3.

2   *Firearm Use by Offenders*

military-style semiautomatic gun or a fully automatic gun during their current offense (table 2). These guns, as used in the questions and definitions for the personal interviews with prison inmates, include the following:

• *military-style semiautomatic pistol* — similar to a conventional semiautomatic pistol except that the magazine or clip is visible[3]

• *military-style semiautomatic rifle* — a semiautomatic rifle with military features such as a pistol grip, folding stock, flash suppressor, or bayonet mount

• *military-style semiautomatic shotgun* — a semiautomatic shotgun with military features such as a pistol grip, folding stock, flash suppressor, or bayonet mount

• *machine gun* — a fully automatic gun which, if the trigger is held down, will fire rapidly and continuously.

[3]The survey interview included in the operational definition of a military-style semiautomatic pistol the phrase "can hold more than 19 bullets."

Some examples of these firearms are the UZI, TEC-9, and MAC10 for handguns; the AR-15 and AK-47 for rifles; and the "Street Sweeper" for shotguns. Possession of these models meeting criteria specified in Federal statutes can be unlawful.

To be understood by inmate respondents who were asked about their gun use, the questions and definitions in the survey reflect terminology commonly used by prisoners to describe types of weapons. If questioned by respondents, interviewers read to them the definitions included on pages 14 and 15 of this report. Of necessity, this language is similar in concept but may differ in wording from technical descriptions in Federal statutes pertaining to firearms.

The Violent Crime Control and Law Enforcement Act of 1994 made it unlawful, with certain exceptions, to manufacture, transfer, or possess military-style semiautomatic weapons,

Table 1. Possession of firearms by State and Federal prison inmates, by type of firearm, 1997

| | Percent of prison inmates — | | | | | |
| | Armed during current offense | | Ever armed while committing offense | | Ever used or possessed firearm | |
Type of firearm	State	Federal	State	Federal	State	Federal
Total	100.0%	100.0%	100.0%	100.0%	100.0%	100.0%
Firearm	18.4%	14.8%	25.1%	20.0%	46.9%	48.9%
Handgun	15.3	12.8	21.3	17.2	36.0	38.6
Rifle	1.3	1.3	2.0	1.9	12.4	14.6
Shotgun	2.4	2.0	3.5	3.0	13.7	15.6
Other	0.5	0.6	1.1	0.9	2.7	2.3
No firearm	81.6%	85.2%	74.9%	80.0%	53.1%	51.1%

Note: Detail do not add to total because inmates may have had more than one firearm.

Table 2. Possession of firearms by State and Federal prison inmates, by whether the firearm was single shot, conventional semiautomatic, or military-style semiautomatic or fully automatic, 1997

| | Percent of prison inmates — | | | | | |
| | Armed during current offense | | Ever armed while committing offense | | Ever used or possessed firearm | |
Specific type of firearm	State	Federal	State	Federal	State	Federal
Single shot	9.9%	7.3%	14.2%	10.6%	31.0%	31.4%
Conventional semiautomatic	7.9	7.7	10.9	9.8	22.6	26.0
Military-style semiautomatic or fully automatic	1.5	1.7	2.5	2.3	5.6	5.6

Note: Columns do not add to total percent with firearms because inmates may have possessed more than one firearm. See text above and pages 14 and 15 for definitions.

if not lawfully possessed on September 13, 1994.[5]

Of inmates who carried a firearm during their offense, 8 in 10 had a handgun

Inmates reported that a handgun was their preferred firearm; of those carrying a firearm, 83% of State inmates and 87% of Federal inmates said that they carried a handgun during the offense for which they were serving their longest sentence. About 8% of State inmates who had carried a firearm during the commission of their crime reported having a military-style semiautomatic (7%) or fully automatic (2%) firearm, with some carrying both.

Type of firearm	Percent of prison inmates carrying a firearm during current offense State	Federal
Handgun	83.2%	86.7%
Rifle	7.3	8.9
Shotgun	13.1	13.7
Single shot	53.9%	49.2%
Conventional semiautomatic	43.2	51.8
Military-style semiautomatic	6.8	9.3
Fully automatic	2.4	3.8
Number of inmates	190,383	12,936

Note: Inmates could report carrying more than one type of firearm. For definitions of weapon categories, see pages 2, 14, and 15.

Firearm use during crimes increased from 1991 to 1997

Over the 6 years between surveys of inmates, 1991-97, possession of a firearm during a crime increased from 16% to 18% of State inmates and from 12% to 15% of Federal inmates (table 3). Because of the growth in the prison population, the estimated number of inmates carrying a firearm increased dramatically — from 114,100 in 1991 to 190,400 in 1997 in State prisons and from 6,300 in 1991 to 12,900 in 1997 in Federal prisons. These estimates were based on inmates who reported carrying a firearm during the offense for which they received their longest sentence.

[5]See P.L. 103-22 and *Commerce in Firearms in the United States*, Department of the Treasury, Bureau of Alcohol, Tobacco and Firearms, February 2000, page C-5.

Table 3. Possession of firearms, by type of offense, by State and Federal prison inmates, 1997 and 1991

	Prison inmates			
	1997		1991	
Current offense	Number	Percent who possessed a firearm during current offense	Number	Percent who possessed a firearm during current offense
State				
All inmates	1,037,241	18.4%	700,050	16.3%
Violent offense	483,713	30.2	323,653	29.1
Property offense	227,726	3.1	171,749	3.2
Drug offense	213,974	8.1	148,743	4.1
Public-order offense	99,396	19.1	47,001	16.1
Federal				
All inmates	87,466	14.8%	53,348	11.8%
Violent offense	12,604	35.4	9,113	38.0
Property offense	5,811	2.9	7,011	2.1
Drug offense	54,561	8.7	30,788	3.9
Public-order offense	12,708	27.3	4,964	28.5

Table 4. Firearm possession during current offense, by type of offense, for State and Federal prison inmates, 1997

	Prison inmates			
	State		Federal	
Current offense	Number	Percent who possessed a firearm during current offense	Number	Percent who possessed a firearm during current offense
Violent offense	483,713	30.2%	12,604	35.4%
Homicide	135,493	42.9	1,273	39.3
Sexual assault	87,687	2.9	679	0.0
Robbery	145,318	34.5	8,554	40.3
Assault	95,756	31.2	1,108	26.0
Other violent	19,459	27.1	989	22.4
Property offense	227,726	3.1%	5,811	2.9%
Burglary	111,198	4.0	279	10.1
Other property	116,528	2.3	5,531	2.5
Drug offense	213,974	8.1%	54,561	8.7%
Possession	91,511	7.8	9,959	7.0
Trafficking	116,578	8.6	39,769	9.1
Other drug	5,885	3.1	4,834	8.7
Public-order offense	99,396	19.1%	12,708	27.3%
Weapons	25,257	64.9	5,905	51.9
Other public-order	74,139	3.5	6,803	5.9

8% of drug offenders and 3% of property offenders armed while committing their crimes

Fewer than 1 in 10 offenders serving a sentence for selling or carrying illegal drugs and 1 in 30 inmates in prison for a property crime — burglary, larceny, fraud, or destruction of property — had a firearm with them while committing their current offense (table 4).

Inmates who had been sentenced for violent crimes used firearms more often than other prisoners. They were more likely than property, drug, or public-order offenders to have used or possessed a gun during their crime. An estimated 30% of violent offenders in State prisons and 35% in Federal prisons had a firearm at the time of the offense.

Offenders sentenced for homicide or for robbery reported the most extensive use of firearms. Among inmates sentenced for homicide, about 43% in State prisons and 39% in Federal prisons said they were carrying a firearm when they committed the offense. About 35% serving time for robbery in State prisons and 40% in Federal prison had a gun.

Table 5. Possession of a firearm during current offense, by selected characteristics for State and Federal prison inmates, 1997

	Prison inmates			
	State		Federal	
Selected characteristic	Number	Percent who possessed a firearm during current offense	Number	Percent who possessed a firearm during current offense
Gender				
Male	972,572	19.1%	81,102	15.5%
Female	64,669	7.3	6,364	6.2
Race/Hispanic origin				
White	346,188	14.8%	25,977	16.7%
Black	482,302	21.1	33,100	17.7
Hispanic	176,089	17.6	24,040	8.1
Other	32,662	19.3	4,349	17.9
Age				
20 or younger	61,663	35.5%	935	23.0%
21-24	143,533	26.8	6,865	18.6
25-34	396,166	16.5	31,970	15.5
35-44	305,765	13.3	26,636	12.8
45-54	100,133	17.4	14,393	15.3
55 or older	29,980	21.7	6,667	13.0
Educational attainment				
Some high school or less	445,479	16.8%	25,642	13.9%
GED	260,743	23.6	17,150	19.2
High school diploma	190,805	16.7	21,292	14.5
Some college	110,122	16.5	15,233	15.1
College graduate	27,649	12.1	7,963	8.3
Citizenship				
United States	983,876	18.5%	71,307	16.9%
Latin America	47,257	14.5	14,638	5.7
Other	4,609	22.0	1,376	2.4
Military service				
Served	129,913	16.4%	12,746	17.2%
Did not serve	907,142	18.6	74,676	14.4

Male inmates and young inmates carried firearms

Male State and Federal offenders were more likely than their female counterparts to have carried a firearm when committing their offense. About 19% of men in State prison and 16% in Federal prison reported using or possessing a firearm when committing their most serious offense, compared to 7% of women in State prison and 6% in Federal prison (table 5).

An estimated 21% of black non-Hispanic inmates in State prison, 18% of Hispanics, and 15% of white non-Hispanics said they had a gun with them while committing their most serious offense. About 18% of black and white inmates in Federal facilities and 8% of Hispanics had carried a firearm.

Young State inmates were more likely than older inmates to use firearms. About 29% of inmates under the age of 25 at the time of the survey were carrying a gun when they committed their current offense, compared to 15% of those 35 or older. Among Federal inmates, about 19% under age 25 and 14% age 35 or older said they had a gun with them.

Weapon offenses and offenders

Weapon offenses include unlawful distribution, sale, manufacture, alteration, transport, possession, or use of a deadly or dangerous weapon or accessory. In 1998 an estimated 195,000 persons were arrested by State or local law enforcement or referred to a U.S. attorney for prosecution for a weapon offense — counting only the most important offense and no secondary offenses. Over 35,000 persons were convicted of a weapon offense. About 49,000 persons were in a local jail or State or Federal prison for a weapon offense in 1998. An additional 100,000 were serving a sentence in the community on probation, parole, or supervised release.

An estimated 12% of State prison inmates and 19% of Federal inmates were either currently serving a sentence for a weapon offense or had been sentenced for a weapon offense in the past.

Weapons as the most serious offense or charge in the criminal justice system, 1998

	Number	Percent of total
State/local jurisdictions		
Arrested	190,600	1.3%
Defendants at initial filing	--	2.8
Convicted of a felony	31,904	3.4
In local jails	13,630	2.3
In State prisons	26,730	2.4
On probation/parole	100,440	2.3
Federal jurisdiction		
Received by U.S. attorneys as suspects	4,907	4.3%
Prosecuted	3,347	5.1
Convicted	3,413	5.6
In Federal prison	8,742	8.0
On probation/supervised release/parole	4,038	4.4

Note: The weapon offense is the offenders' most serious offense. Statistics on persons in Federal jurisdiction are for fiscal year 1998.
--Not available.

Sources: Data on weapon offenders come from the FBI's *Crime in the United States, 1998*, table 29; from BJS' *Compendium of Federal Justice Statistics, 1998;* from BJS' Survey of Inmates in Local Jails, 1996, and Survey of Inmates in State and Federal Correctional Facilities, 1997, and from the following BJS reports available through <www.ojp.usdoj.gov/pubalp2.htm>: *Felony Defendants in Large Urban Counties, 1998; Felony Sentences in the United States, 1998; Prisoners in 1999;* and the press release for probation and parole surveys 2000.

Current and past sentences for a weapon offense, for State and Federal prison inmates, 1997

Any current or past offense	Percent of prison inmates	
	State	Federal
Total	100.0%	100.0%
Current or past weapon offense	12.2%	18.6%
Current and past weapon offenses	1.3	2.2
Current weapon/past other offenses	4.1	8.5
Current weapon/no past offenses	1.1	2.7
Current other/past weapon offenses	5.8	5.1
Other current and/or past offenses	87.8%	81.4%

Table 6. State and Federal prison inmates possessing a firearm during their most serious offense, by characteristics of their family and background, 1997

| Inmates' family of origin and other background characteristics | Prison inmates | | | |
| | State | | Federal | |
	Number	Percent who possessed a firearm during current offense	Number	Percent who possessed a firearm during current offense
Lived with growing up				
Both parents	455,313	16.3%	47,279	13.2%
Single parent	438,741	19.7	30,146	16.2
Other	137,253	20.7	9,452	18.8
Parent ever incarcerated	188,166	22.7%	9,843	18.0%
Parent never incarcerated	833,005	17.4	76,382	14.5
Parent received welfare	374,340	20.8%	20,328	20.0%
Parent did not receive welfare	634,795	17.0	65,146	13.2
Inmate lived in public housing	186,847	21.1%	11,807	17.9%
Inmate did not live in public housing	835,540	17.8	74,656	14.5
Parent abused alcohol or drugs	327,404	18.5%	18,041	17.6%
Alcohol	241,521	16.6	14,541	17.8
Drugs	18,618	27.5	735	17.7
Both	66,986	22.9	2,752	17.0
Parent did not abuse alcohol or drugs	698,716	18.3	68,424	14.1
Peers engaged in illegal activity while growing up	780,234	19.6%	49,941	19.0%
Used drugs	688,497	19.7	42,764	18.5
Damaged/stole/sold property*	616,874	21.1	33,793	22.6
Drug trafficking	395,042	24.3	20,731	22.4
Robbery	203,745	30.4	8,400	32.5
Peers did not engage in any illegal activity	249,739	14.6	36,718	9.3

*Includes vandalism, shoplifting, stealing motor vehicles or parts, selling stolen property, and breaking and entering.

inmates living in some other arrangement while growing up (table 6).

A higher percentage of State inmates with a parent who had served a sentence to incarceration carried a gun (23%) than those whose parents had never been in prison or jail (17%). For Federal inmates, 18% of inmates who had incarcerated parents and 15% of those who did not carried a firearm.

Inmates who lived in families receiving welfare or living in publicly-subsidized housing while growing up were more likely than those who did not live under these types of government programs to be carrying a weapon. About 1 in 5 inmates whose family received welfare or who lived in publicly financed housing carried a firearm. About 1 in 6 State inmates and 1 in 7 Federal inmates whose parents were not receiving welfare benefits or living in publicly-financed housing had a gun.

A quarter of State inmates who said they had a parent who had abused drugs reported that they were carrying a gun while committing their current offense. In contrast, less than a fifth of those whose parents did not abuse substances had a firearm.

About 20% of State and Federal inmates whose friends while growing up used or traded drugs, stole, destroyed or damaged property, broke or entered private property, or robbed someone reported that they had a firearm with them when they committed their controlling offense. An estimated 15% of State inmates and 9% of Federal inmates who did not have friends involved in illegal activities

Background characteristics account for relatively small differences in firearm use

When inmates were interviewed for the 1997 Surveys, they were asked about their family background and experiences they had when growing up. Characteristics about which the inmates reported include parental upbringing, parental incarceration, welfare assistance to their family, parental use of alcohol and drugs, and peer participation in criminal behavior.

Inmates who grew up living with both parents were less likely to be using or carrying a firearm than those who grew up primarily living with one parent, grandparents, other relatives, friends, or a foster family. An estimated 16% of State inmates and 13% of Federal inmates living with both parents had a gun with them, compared to 20% of State inmates and 17% of Federal

Inmates who had ever been shot at

As one measure of violence in inmates' lives, inmates were asked if they had ever been shot at. This experience could have been at any time in their lives, including when they were committing the crime for which

| | State prison inmates | | Federal prison inmates | |
	Number	Percent carrying a firearm	Number	Percent carrying a firearm
Ever shot at with a gun	516,194	24.6%	30,064	24.0%
Wounded	213,429	26.7	12,933	24.4
Shot at but not wounded	302,765	23.1	17,131	23.6
Never shot at	514,676	12.1	56,679	10.1

they were in prison. About half of State prisoners reported that in the past they had been shot at by someone, and more than a fifth had actually been wounded by gunfire. A quarter of State and Federal inmates who had been shot at were carrying a firearm during their current offense, compared to a tenth of those who had never been shot at.

used or possessed a firearm during their current offense.

Violent recidivists were as likely as first time violent offenders to have carried a gun

Recidivism does not appear to be related to whether inmates were carrying guns when the type of current offense is taken into account. Violent offenders who had served a prior sentence and first time violent offenders were about equally likely to be carrying a firearm when committing their current offense — about 30% of violent offenders in State prisons carried a firearm (table 7). About a third of violent Federal offenders, whether recidivist or first time, carried a firearm.

Less than 10% of both first time and repeat State offenders serving time for property, drug, and public-order offenses carried a gun. Drug offenders who were recidivists were more likely to be carrying a firearm than first-time drug offenders (9% versus 6% of State inmates and 11% versus 5% of Federal inmates).

Inmates who had served prior sentences as a juvenile were more likely to have had a gun than those who did not have a juvenile record. For State offenders 22% who had a juvenile record and 13% with only an adult record had a firearm while committing their current offense; for Federal offenders 27% with a juvenile record and 14% with only an adult record possessed a firearm.

Inmates' retail purchase of firearms fell between 1991 and 1997

In 1997, 14% of State inmates who had used or possessed a firearm during their current offense bought or traded for it from a retail store, pawnshop, flea market, or gun show (table 8). Nearly 40% of State inmates carrying a firearm obtained the weapon from family or friends. About 3 in 10 received the weapon from drug dealers, off the street, or through the black market. Another 1 in 10 obtained their gun during a robbery, burglary, or other type of theft.

From 1991 to 1997 the percent of State inmates with guns who acquired them at a retail outlet fell from 21% to 14%. At the same time the percentage reporting that they used firearms furnished by family or friends increased from 34% to 40%. Between the two surveys the Brady Handgun Violence Prevention Act of 1993 was enacted. The act requires background checks for persons purchasing firearms from federally licensed firearm dealers. Changes in how inmates obtained firearms, when the two surveys are compared, may or may not reflect the requirements in the Brady Act. Inmates may have procured their firearm or entered prison before the Brady Act became effective in 1994.

Table 8. Source of firearms possessed during the current offense of State prison inmates, 1997 and 1991

Source of firearms	Percent of State prison inmates who possessed a firearm during current offense	
	1997	1991
Total	100.0%	100.0%
Purchased or traded from retail outlet	13.9%	20.8%
Retail store	8.3	14.7
Pawnshop	3.8	4.2
Flea market	1.0	1.3
Gun show	0.7	0.6
Family or friend	39.6%	33.8%
Purchased or traded	12.8	13.5
Rented or borrowed	18.5	10.1
Other	8.3	10.2
Street/illegal source	39.2%	40.8%
Theft or burglary	9.9	10.5
Drug dealer/off street	20.8	22.5
Fence/black market	8.4	7.8
Other	7.4%	4.6%

Table 7. Possession of firearm during current offense, by criminal history, prior sentences, and criminal justice status at arrest, for State and Federal prison inmates, 1997

	Prison inmates			
	State		Federal	
Criminal justice characteristic	Number	Percent who possessed a firearm during current offense	Number	Percent who possessed a firearm during current offense
Criminal history				
No previous sentence	247,287	22.3%	33,731	9.5%
Current offense				
Violent	155,195	31.1	3,952	31.8
Drug	44,744	5.8	20,425	4.8
Other	47,347	9.1	9,354	10.2
Recidivists	783,178	17.2	52,619	18.4
Current offense				
Violent	360,564	28.4	9,866	38.4
Drug	177,922	9.0	32,706	11.2
Other	244,692	6.5	10,047	22.3
Prior sentences				
Juvenile only	66,742	34.4%	2,835	25.8%
Adult only	404,646	12.7	34,294	13.5
Both juvenile and adult	309,002	19.4	15,897	27.3
Criminal justice status at arrest				
New court commitment	543,238	21.8%	63,320	13.7%
On status	489,320	14.6	23,628	17.8
Probation	229,952	15.0	11,644	14.0
Parole	252,355	14.1	11,736	21.3
Escape	7,013	17.9	248	32.9

Victims of violent offenders possessing firearms

About 30% of State inmates and 35% of Federal inmates sentenced for a violent offense — homicide, sexual assault, robbery, or assault — used or possessed a firearm when committing their current offense. A quarter of violent State prisoners and almost a third of Federal prisoners carried a handgun. Fewer than 1 in 10, however, carried a long gun — a rifle or shotgun — or a military-style semiautomatic or fully automatic weapon.

Inmates serving time for violent crimes were more likely to use a firearm when their victims were male rather than female, 18 or older rather than under age 18, and strangers, known by sight, or known casually rather than persons the inmates knew well.

• About 40% of violent State offenders who victimized a male had a gun compared to 17% of offenders when the victim was female.

• 39% of violent State inmates with a black victim and 33% of those with a Hispanic victim used a firearm, significantly more than the 25% with a white victim.

Possession of a firearm, by type of firearm, for State and Federal prison inmates sentenced for a violent offense, 1997

Type of firearm	Percent of prison inmates who possessed a firearm during current violent offense	
	State	Federal
Total	100%	100%
Any firearm	30.2%	35.4%
Handgun	24.7	30.4
Rifle	2.0	2.4
Shotgun	4.1	3.6
Other	0.7	1.2
Type of firearm		
Single shot	17.0%	18.0%
Conventional semiautomatic	12.1	16.3
Military-style semi-automatic or fully automatic	2.1	4.0

• Less than 10% of those who victimized persons 17 or younger, compared to over 33% of those who victimized persons 18 or older, possessed a firearm.

• Over a third of violent offenders used guns when their victims were strangers and casual acquaintances, compared to a fifth who used guns against persons they knew.

• 27% of offenders who victimized a current or former spouse, boyfriend, or girlfriend were armed while committing the crime. About 8% used guns against other relatives, including children, siblings, and other family members.

Characteristics of victims of violent crime, by whether the State prison inmate possessed a firearm, 1997

Characteristics of victim	Percent of violent State prison inmates who possessed a firearm during current offense
Gender	
Male	39.8%
Female	16.8
Race/Hispanic origin	
White	25.4%
Black	38.6
Hispanic	32.8
Other	29.1
Age	
17 or younger	8.2%
18-24	40.9
25-34	37.0
35 or older	33.8
Relationship to offender	
Stranger	35.6%
Known by sight or casually	36.2
Well known	20.6
Intimate*	27.0
Other relative	8.2
Friend	26.3
Other	23.9

*Includes spouse, ex-spouse, boyfriend, girlfriend, ex-boyfriend, and ex-girlfriend.

Recidivists less likely than first timers to buy their gun from a retail establishment

Although existence of a prior record did not change inmates' likelihood of having carried a gun while committing their current crime, it did influence where they acquired their gun. Recidivists were less likely than those who were first time offenders to have purchased their gun from a retail store, pawnshop, flea market, or gun show. About a tenth of recidivists and a fifth of first timers purchased their gun from a retail establishment (table 9).

A larger percentage of recidivists than first time offenders obtained their weapon through illegal activities or from the street or a black market source — 42% of recidivists and 31% of first timers.

Recidivists with firearms were as likely as first time offenders to obtain their gun from a family member or friends in 1997— about 40% acquired their guns from either family or friends.

The percentage of inmates who purchased or traded from a retail outlet, such as a store or pawnshop, fell during this period for both those with prior sentences and those without them. For repeat offenders, purchasing from retail fell from 17% to 11%, and for first time offenders from 33% to 20%.

For recidivists the percentage of inmates with firearms who obtained them from family or friends rose from 1991 to 1997 — for recidivists from 33% in 1991 to 39% in 1997 and for first timers from 36% in 1991 to 41% in 1997.

Table 9. Source of firearms possessed during current offense, by criminal history, for State prison inmates, 1997 and 1991

| Source of firearms | Percent of State prison inmates possessing a firearm who were — | | | |
| | First timers | | Recidivists | |
	1997	1991	1997	1991
Total	100.0%	100.0%	100.0%	100.0%
Purchased or traded from a retail outlet	20.1%	32.9%	11.4%	16.8%
Retail store	14.2	25.5	6.0	11.0
Pawnshop	4.2	5.4	3.7	3.9
Flea market	0.9	1.0	1.1	1.4
Gun show	0.8	1.0	0.7	0.4
Family or friend	40.5%	36.1%	39.2%	33.1%
Purchased or traded	11.0	11.5	13.5	14.0
Rented or borrowed	20.0	12.9	17.9	9.3
Other	9.5	11.6	7.8	9.9
Street/illegal source	30.9%	26.7%	42.4%	45.7%
Theft or burglary	7.6	4.7	10.9	12.4
Drug dealer/off street	15.7	14.7	22.8	25.2
Fence/black market	7.6	7.3	8.8	8.1
Other	8.5%	4.4%	6.9%	4.3%
Number of prison inmates	51,152	22,444	127,664	70,728

Victim, police, and inmate reports of gun use during violent crime

The FBI reports that over two-thirds of homicide victims were killed with a firearm. About 4 in 10 inmates serving a sentence for murder or manslaughter in State and Federal correctional facilities said that they had used a gun in committing the crime.

About 23% of robbery victims and 28% of aggravated assault victims told the National Crime Victimization Survey that the offender used a gun.

Possession of firearms during violent crime, as reported by victims, police, and prison inmates, 1997

| Violent crime | Percent of victimizations in the National Crime Victimization Survey | Percent of offenses in the FBI's Supplemental Homicide Reports/ Uniform Crime Reports | Percent of offenders possessing a firearm during a violent crime | |
			Survey of Inmates in State Correctional Facilities	Survey of Inmates in Federal Correctional Facilities
Homicide		67.8%	42.9%	39.3%
Sexual assault	2.4%		2.9	0.0
Robbery	23.0	39.7	34.5	40.5
Aggravated assault	28.4	20.0	31.2	26.0

Table 10. Source of firearms possessed during current offense,
by whether the firearm was single shot, conventional semiautomatic, or military-
style semiautomatic or fully automatic, for State prison inmates, 1997

Source of firearms	Percent of State prison inmates who possessed a firearm		
	Military-style semiautomatic or fully automatic	Conventional semiautomatic	Single shot
Total	100.0%	100.0%	100.0%
Purchased or traded from a retail outlet	19.3%	16.5%	12.2%
Retail store	10.6	9.2	7.5
Pawnshop	6.7	4.7	3.4
Flea market	0.0	1.2	0.9
Gun show	1.9	1.4	0.4
Family or friend	25.2%	35.6%	43.8%
Purchased or traded	11.1	13.0	12.7
Rented or borrowed	10.6	15.7	21.5
Other	3.5	6.9	9.5
Street/illegal sources	48.5%	42.1%	36.4%
Theft or burglary	9.8	8.0	11.4
Drug dealer/off street	23.4	23.6	18.4
Fence/black market	15.4	10.6	6.7
Other	7.0%	5.8%	7.6%
Number of prison inmates	14,896	79,031	96,531

Note: See note on table 2 and definitions on page 14.

Table 11. Source of firearms possessed during current offense,
by gender and age, for State prison inmates, 1997

Source of firearms	Percent of State prison inmates who possessed a firearm during their current offense, by gender and age				
	Male	Female	24 or younger	25-34	35 or older
Total	100.0%	100.0%	100.0%	100.0%	100.0%
Purchased or traded from a retail outlet	13.8%	16.5%	6.6%	12.7%	21.9%
Retail store	8.3	10.6	2.6	7.0	15.0
Pawnshop	3.8	5.5	2.9	4.0	4.5
Flea market	1.0	0.4	0.1	0.9	1.9
Gun show	0.8	0.0	0.9	0.8	0.4
Family or friend	39.4%	46.4%	40.1%	38.9%	39.8%
Purchased or traded	12.9	5.9	13.0	12.1	13.3
Rented or borrowed	18.3	28.4	20.3	18.8	16.6
Other	8.2	12.1	6.8	8.1	9.9
Street/illegal sources	39.4%	30.5%	46.8%	41.2%	29.9%
Theft or burglary	9.9	13.1	10.0	9.8	10.1
Drug dealer/off street	21.0	13.0	27.8	22.9	12.1
Fence/black market	8.5	4.3	9.0	8.6	7.8
Other	7.4%	6.6%	6.5%	7.1%	8.5%
Number of prison inmates	174,488	4,421	57,194	60,818	60,897

1 in 5 military-style semiautomatic or fully automatic guns bought from retail store

About a fifth of inmates with a military-style semiautomatic or fully automatic weapon bought it retail — at a store, flea market, or gun show (table 10). About a sixth of inmates with a conventional semiautomatic weapon and an eighth with a single-shot gun also had made a retail purchase.

While family and friends provided a quarter of military-style semiautomatic or fully automatic firearms, they gave inmates over a third of the conventional semiautomatic weapons and just under half of the single-shot guns.

Almost half of inmates possessing military-style semiautomatic or fully automatic weapons, about two-fifths of those with conventional semiautomatic firearms, and over a third of offenders having single-shot guns had got their firearm in a theft or burglary, or from a drug dealer, fence, or black market.

Young offenders less likely than older ones to have bought a firearm from a retail source

Young offenders were less likely than older inmates to have bought their gun from a retail outlet (table 11). About 7% of inmates 24 or younger and 22% of those 35 or older obtained their gun from a retail outlet.

About half of inmates who were 24 or younger, compared to less than a third of those 35 or older, acquired their gun through illegal activities, a drug dealer, or a black market.

Among those possessing a firearm during their current offense, an estimated 17% of women and 14% of men purchased their guns from a retail establishment. About 3 in 10 women offenders and 4 in 10 male inmates acquired their firearms from a theft, burglary, drug dealer, fence, or black market. Family and friends provided guns to about 46% of female inmates with firearms and 39% of male inmates.

Federal law may have disqualified over 8 in 10 inmates from buying a firearm

The Gun Control Act of 1968, as amended, and other Federal statutes list conditions which disqualify an individual from possessing a firearm or purchasing it from a licensed dealer. Some of these conditions include a prior felony conviction or indictment, current illegal drug use or addiction, dishonorable discharge from the Armed Forces, or being a fugitive from justice, a mental incompetent, or a nonresident alien. The Brady Act,

effective in 1994, mandated that federally licensed firearm dealers obtain background checks of potential purchasers, based on the conditions of eligibility.

A slightly lower percentage of State prisoners who had a gun, compared to those who did not, reported having a characteristic which may have disqualified them, as defined by Federal law. About 84% of State inmates who had possessed a gun and 88% who did not have a gun may have met at least one of the conditions, as measured in the inmate survey (table 12).

Among State inmates, those with and without guns answered differently on only two conditions. About 50% of those with a firearm and 56% without had a prior sentence to incarceration; about 37% with a gun and 49% without were on probation or parole. On other factors, about the same percentages reported meeting a condition that could have made them ineligible to purchase a firearm. Almost 6 in 10 said they had used illegal drugs before their controlling offense, about 1 in 10 had stayed in a mental health facility overnight, and 1 in 20 was a noncitizen.

Higher percentages of Federal inmates with guns than without them reported meeting at least one of the conditions of the Federal laws. About 83% with a firearm and 78% without one may have been disqualified from purchasing a gun. Higher percentages of inmates using guns compared to those without a gun had a prior incarceration (55% versus 37%), were on probation or parole when arrested (32% versus. 26%), or had used illegal drugs shortly before committing their current offense (56% versus 43%).

9% of all State prison inmates and 2% of all Federal inmates shot a gun while committing their current offense

In total, about 1 in 10 State inmates and 1 in 50 Federal inmates fired their gun while committing their current offense (table 13). Among inmates serving a sentence for a single violent crime incident, 18% of State inmates and 9% of Federal inmates said they fired the gun they were carrying.

Table 12. Selected characteristics that may make a gun purchase illegal under Federal law, by possession of firearm during current offense, for State and Federal prison inmates, 1997

| | Percent of inmates during current offense | | | |
| | State inmates | | Federal inmates | |
Selected characteristic	Possessed firearm	Did not possess firearm	Possessed firearm	Did not possess firearm
Total meeting at least one condition which may have made inmates ineligible to purchase a firearm	84.1%	87.7%	83.1%	77.7%
Prior incarceration for serious offense	49.8	55.9	55.1	36.9
On probation or parole when arrested	37.0	48.9	32.0	26.0
On escape when arrested	0.7	0.7	0.6	0.2
Illegal drug use in month before or at time of offense	58.8	56.3	56.0	43.0
Ever treated overnight in mental health facility	10.7	10.7	6.7	4.2
Not a U.S. citizen	5.2	6.0	7.8	22.6
Dishonorable discharge from U.S. military	0.3	0.3	0.7	0.2

Table 13. Extent of weapon use during current offense, for State and Federal prison inmates, 1997

| | Percent of prison inmates | | | | | |
| | All inmates | | Violent offenders | | Other offenders | |
Firearm use	State	Federal	State	Federal	State	Federal
Total	100.0%	100.0%	100.0%	100.0%	100.0%	100.0%
Used firearm	20.4%	8.9%	38.5%	35.1%	4.3	3.5
Discharged	8.9	2.0	17.7	8.5	1.1	0.6
Did not discharge	11.5	6.9	20.7	26.6	3.2	2.9
Possessed but did not use	3.6	8.2	3.0	7.2	4.1	8.4
Possessed other weapon	1.0	0.5	1.4	2.7	0.6	0.1
Did not possess weapon	75.0	82.4	57.2	55.0	91.0	88.0
Number	993,305	71,325	468,757	12,249	515,532	58,266

Note: Table excludes prison inmates serving a sentence for multiple incidents.

Table 14. Extent of firearm use during current offense for State and Federal prison inmates possessing a firearm, 1997

Firearm use	Percent of prison inmates possessing a firearm	
	State	Federal
Total	100.0%	100.0%
Used firearm	80.2%	48.6%
Discharged	49.1	12.8
Killed victim	14.6	3.0
Injured victim	15.4	3.5
Neither killed nor injured	26.3	7.8
Brandished/displayed	73.2	46.2
To scare someone	48.6	29.3
To defend self	41.1	24.9
To "get away"	18.9	11.6
Did not actively use firearm	19.8%	51.4%
Number	178,646	11,250

Note: Percents of subtotals do not add to totals because inmates may have used a firearm in more than one way. Table excludes prison inmates serving a sentence for multiple incidents.

About 1% of inmates serving a sentence for a single property, drug, or public-order incident discharged a gun.

Fewer than 1 in 20 State inmates and 1 in 10 Federal inmates, regardless of type of offense, said they possessed a firearm but did not use it. Another 2% reported they had another weapon, including a knife, scissors, ax, rock, club or other sharp or blunt object.

Table 15. Extent of firearm use during current offense, for State prison inmates possessing a firearm, 1997

Firearm use	Percent of State prison inmates possessing a firearm		
	Military-style semiautomatic or fully automatic	Conventional semiautomatic	Single-shot
Total	100.0%	100.0%	100.0%
Used firearm	74.6%	78.9%	80.8%
Discharged	42.9	46.3	50.6
Killed victim	11.2	13.5	15.7
Injured victim	14.2	15.1	15.3
Neither killed nor injured	23.4	24.0	27.3
Brandished/displayed	70.5	72.1	73.2
To scare someone	45.3	48.0	49.6
To defend self	39.7	42.4	39.9
To "get away"	20.4	18.5	18.7
Did not actively use firearm	25.4%	21.1%	19.2%
Number	14,280	76,010	96,810

Note: Percents of subtotals do not add to totals because inmates may have used a firearm in more than one way. Table excludes prison inmates serving a sentence for multiple incidents. See pages 2, 14, and 15 for definitions of firearms.

About half of inmates carrying a gun during their offense fired it and half of those injured or killed someone

If inmates carried a firearm, they tended to use it. Among inmates possessing a firearm and committing only one incident, four-fifths of State inmates and half of Federal inmates either fired the weapon or brandished or displayed it while committing the crime (table 14).

An estimated 23% of State inmates and 5% of Federal inmates with a gun either killed or injured their victim. Another 26% of State inmates and 8% of Federal inmates with a gun discharged the gun but did not injure or kill anyone with it.

Besides firing their weapon, inmates used their guns for other purposes. About half of State inmates said they used it to scare someone, about two-fifths to defend themselves, and a fifth to "get away."

About 81% of State inmates with a single-shot gun, 79% with a conventional semiautomatic, and 75% with a military-style semiautomatic weapon or a fully automatic weapon either fired or brandished it (table 15). About 51% with a single-shot gun, 46% with a conventional semiautomatic firearm, and 43% with a military-style semiautomatic weapon or a fully automatic weapon discharged their firearm. About a fifth either injured or killed their victim, regardless of the type of firearm.

About a quarter of inmates carrying military-style semiautomatic weapon or a fully automatic weapon and a fifth of those with a conventional semiautomatic or single-shot weapon did not actively use the gun in any way, discharging it or displaying it to scare someone, defend oneself, or "get away."

Table 16. Sentence length and time to be served, by possession of a firearm and type of offense, for State prison inmates, 1997

| Current offense | Sentence length in months | | | | Time expected to be served | | | |
| | Possessed firearm | | Did not possess firearm | | Possessed firearm | | Did not possess firearm | |
	Mean	Median	Mean	Median	Mean	Median	Mean	Median
Total	220 mo	180 mo	150 mo	96 mo	126 mo	91 mo	83 mo	52 mo
Violent offense	252	240	216	180	147	115	126	87
Homicide	330	480	352	600	196	172	209	182
Sexual assault	444	480	232	180	212	206	131	97
Robbery	232	180	192	120	125	94	102	72
Assault	177	120	133	96	101	75	83	59
Property offense	177	120	123	72	87	72	64	44
Drug offense	143	108	107	60	60	48	49	36
Public-order offense	98	60	78	48	55	40	46	28

Possession of a firearm during an offense increased sentences and expected time served of inmates

On average, inmates possessing a firearm had longer sentences and expected to serve a longer time than those who had not used or possessed a firearm while committing their offense. Sentences for State inmates with firearms had an average of about 18 years, while those for inmates without a firearm were about 12 years (table 16). Those who had carried a firearm expected to serve about 10 years on their sentence, and those without a firearm, 7 years.

Violent offenders with firearms had on average a sentence of over 20 years and those without firearms, about 18

years. Violent offenders who had carried a gun also expected to serve 12 years on average and those who did not carry them, 10 years.

Significantly higher percentages of inmates who possessed firearms, compared to those who did not, received a sentence enhancement, generally for possessing a firearm. About 40% of State inmates who carried a firearm during their current offense and 6% who were not carrying a firearm were given an enhancement to their sentence because of a firearm offense (table 17). About 56% of Federal inmates who carried a firearm and 14% who did not carry one received a weapons offense enhancement.

Methodology

The U.S. Census Bureau conducted the 1997 Survey of Inmates in State Correctional Facilities (SISCF) for the Bureau of Justice Statistics (BJS) and the 1997 Survey of Inmates in Federal Correctional Facilities (SIFCF) for BJS and the Bureau of Prisons. From June through October, 1997, inmates were interviewed about their current offense and sentences, criminal histories, family and personal backgrounds, gun possession and use, prior drug and alcohol use and treatment, educational programs, and other services provided while in prison. Similar surveys of State prison inmates were conducted in 1974, 1979, 1986, and 1991. Federal inmates were surveyed for the first time in 1991.

Sample design

The samples for the SISCF and SIFCF were taken from a universe of 1,409 State prisons and 127 Federal prisons enumerated in the 1995 Census of State and Federal Adult Correctional Facilities or opened between completion of the census and June 30, 1996. The sample design for both surveys was a stratified two-stage selection; first, selecting prisons, and second, selecting inmates in those prisons.

In the first stage correctional facilities were separated into two sampling frames: one for prisons with male inmates and one for prisons with female inmates. Prisons holding both genders were included on both lists.

Table 17. Sentence enhancements, by possession of a firearm during current offense, for State and Federal prison inmates, 1997

| Enhancements to sentence | Percent of inmates during current offense | | | |
| | State inmates | | Federal inmates | |
	Possessed firearm	Did not possess firearm	Possessed firearm	Did not possess firearm
Total	100.0%	100.0%	100.0%	100.0%
No enhancement	49.6%	70.3%	31.1%	57.7%
Any enhancement	50.4%	29.7%	68.9%	42.3%
Firearm offense	39.9	5.5	55.7	13.7
2nd or 3rd strike	16.4	20.0	26.0	18.5
Type of drug offense*	7.0	9.8	23.3	25.7

*Type of drug offense includes type of drug, quantity of drug, or activity involved with the drug offense.

In the sampling of State facilities, the 13 largest male prisons and 17 largest female prisons were selected with certainty. The remaining 1,265 male facilities and 261 female facilities were stratified into 14 strata defined by census region (Northeast except New York, New York, Midwest, South except Texas, Texas, West except California, and California). Within each stratum facilities were ordered by facility type (confinement and community-based), security level (maximum, medium, minimum, and none), and size of population. A systematic sample of prisons was then selected within strata with probabilities proportionate to the size of each prison.

For the sample of Federal prisons, one male prison and two female prisons were selected with certainty. The remaining 112 male facilities were classified into 5 strata defined by security level (administrative, high, medium, low, and minimum). The 20 remaining female facilities were stratified into 2 strata by security level (minimum and not minimum). Within security level, facilities were ordered by size of population and then selected with probability proportionate to size.

For the State survey 280 prisons were selected, 220 male facilities and 60 female facilities. Of the 280 facilities 3 refused to allow interviewing and 2 closed before the survey could be conducted. Overall, 32 male facilities and 8 female facilities were selected for the Federal survey, and all participated.

In the second stage, inmates were selected for interviewing. For State facilities interviewers selected the sample systematically using a random start and a total number of interviews based on the gender of the inmates and the size of the facility. For Federal facilities, a sample of inmates was selected for each facility from the Bureau of Prisons central list, using a random start and predetermined sampling interval.

All selected drug offenders were then subsampled so that only a third were eligible for interview. As a result, approximately 1 in every 75 men and 1 in 17 women were selected for the State survey, and 1 in every 13 men and 1 in every 3 women were selected for the Federal survey.

A total of 14,285 interviews were completed for the State survey and 4,041 for the Federal survey, for overall response rates of 92.5% in the State survey and 90.2% in the Federal survey.

The interviews, about an hour in length, used computer-assisted personal interviewing (CAPI). With CAPI, computers provide questions for the interviewer, including follow-up questions tailored to preceding answers. Before the interview, inmates were told verbally and in writing that participation was voluntary and that all information provided would be held in confidence. Participants were assured that the survey was solely for statistical purposes and that no individual who participated could be identified through use of survey results.

Estimates of prisoner counts

Based on the completed interviews, estimates for the entire population were developed using weighting factors derived from the original probability of selection in the sample. These factors were adjusted for variable rates of nonresponse across strata and inmates' characteristics and offenses. The sample for the State survey was adjusted to midyear custody counts for June 30, 1997, from data obtained in the National Prisoner Statistics series (NPS-1A). The sample from the Federal facilities was weighted to the total known sentenced custody population at midyear 1997.

Excluded from the estimate of Federal inmates were unsentenced inmates and those prisoners under Federal jurisdiction but housed in State and private contract facilities. Those prisoners who were under State jurisdiction, yet held in local jails or private facilities, were excluded from the estimated number of State prisoners. As a result, the estimated prisoner counts do not match those in other BJS data series. The estimated prisoner counts vary according to the particular data items analyzed. Estimates are based on the number of prisoners who provided information on selected items.

Accuracy of the estimates

The accuracy of the estimates presented in this report depends on two types of error: sampling and nonsampling. Sampling error is the variation that may occur by chance because a sample rather than a complete enumeration of the population was conducted. Nonsampling error can be attributed to many sources, such as nonresponses, differences in the interpretation of questions among inmates, recall difficulties, and processing errors. In any survey the full extent of the nonsampling error is never known. The sampling error, as measured by an estimated standard error, varies by the size of the estimate and the size of the base population.

Estimates of the standard errors have been calculated for the 1997 surveys. (See appendix tables 1 and 2.) For example, the 95-percent confidence interval around the percentage of State inmates who carried a firearm during current offense is approximately 18.4% plus or minus 1.96 times 0.42% (or 17.6% to 19.2%).

These standard errors may also be used to test the significance of the difference between two sample statistics by pooling the standard errors of the two sample estimates. For example, the standard error of the difference between violent or drug offenders carrying firearms when committing their current offense would be 1.0% (or the square root of the sum of the squared standard errors for each group). The 95%-confidence interval around the difference would be 1.96 times 1.0% or 1.9%. Since the difference, 2.1% (30.2% - 8.1%) is greater than 1.9%, the difference would be considered statistically significant.

The same procedure can be used to test the significance of the difference between estimates from the two surveys. For example, the standard error of the difference between Federal and State prison inmates carrying a firearm would be 0.9%. The 95-percent confidence interval around the difference would be 1.96 times .9% (or 1.7%). Since the difference of 3.6% (18.4% minus 14.8%) is greater than 1.6%, the difference would be considered statistically significant.

All comparisons discussed in this report were statistically significant at the 95-percent confidence level.

Definitions

The survey questionnaire used the following definitions in language and terms familiar to the respondents. Interviewers read the definitions to the inmates when needed.

Handguns include both pistols and revolvers. They are firearms held and fired with one hand and include the following:

— *Revolver* is a handgun with a revolving cylinder with several cartridge chambers. The chambers are successively lined up with the barrel and then discharged. (Classified as *single shot* for analysis.)

— *Derringer* is a short-barreled, single shot pocket pistol. A pistol has a chamber integral with the barrel. (Classified as *single shot* for analysis.)

— A *conventional semiautomatic pistol* uses a shell which is ejected and the next round of ammunition is loaded automatically from a magazine or clip internal to the pistol grip or handle. The trigger must be pulled for each shot.[5] (Classified as *conventional semiautomatic* for analysis.)

— *Military-style semiautomatic pistol* is similar to a conventional semiautomatic pistol except that the magazine or clip is visible.[5] Primary examples are the UZI, TEC-9, and MAC-10.

[5]The survey interview included in the operational definition of a conventional semiautomatic pistol "can hold a maximum of 19 bullets" and of a military-style semiautomatic pistol "can hold more than 19 bullets."

(Classified as *military-style semiautomatic* for analysis.)

A **rifle** is a firearm intended to be shot from the shoulder. It has a long barrel which shoots bullets. Types include:

— *Bolt-action, pump-action, lever-action, or single-shot rifles* require physical movement by the operator of some part of the rifle — a bolt, lever, or pump — to reload. A single shot rifle must be loaded after each shot. (Classified as *single shot* for analysis.)

— *Semiautomatic hunting-style rifle* is a rifle in which a shell is ejected and the next round of ammunition is loaded automatically from a magazine or clip. The trigger must be pulled for each shot. (Classified as *conventional semiautomatic* for analysis.)

— *Semiautomatic military-style rifle* has the characteristics of a semiautomatic hunting-style rifle. It also has military features such as a pistol grip, folding stock, flash suppressor, and bayonet mount. (Classified as *military-style semiautomatic* for analysis.)

A **shotgun** is a firearm intended to be shot from the shoulder with either a single- or double-barrel for firing shot

---

Appendix table 1. Standard errors for type of firearm during current offense, for State and Federal prison inmates, 1997

Type of firearm	Standard error for estimated percent armed during current offense	
	State	Federal
Any firearm	0.42%	0.75%
Handgun	0.39	0.70
Rifle	0.12	0.24
Shotgun	0.17	0.29
Single shot	0.33	0.55
Semiautomatic		
Conventional	0.30	0.56
Military-style	0.13	0.27

Note: See tables 1 and 2 for survey estimates.

Appendix table 2. Standard errors for firearm possession during current offense, for State and Federal prison inmates, 1997

Current offense	Standard error for estimated percent armed during current offense	
	State	Federal
Violent offense	0.74%	2.66%
Homicide	1.50	8.52
Sexual assault	0.63	0.00
Robbery	1.39	3.31
Assault	1.67	8.21
Other violent	3.55	8.26
Property offense	0.41%	1.37%
Burglary	0.66	11.23
Other property	0.49	1.31
Drug offenses	0.65%	0.73%
Possession	0.98	1.59
Trafficking	0.90	0.86
Other drug	2.52	2.52
Public-order offenses	1.39%	2.46%
Weapons	3.35	4.05
Other public-order	0.75	1.78

Note: See table 4 for survey estimates.

(a concentration of small pellets) at short ranges. Types include:

— *Bolt-action, pump-action, lever-action, or single shot shotgun* requires physical movement by the operator of some part of the shotgun — a bolt, lever, or pump — to reload. A single shot shotgun must be loaded after each shot. (Classified as *single-shot* for analysis.)

— *Semiautomatic hunting-style shotgun* is a shotgun in which a shell is ejected and the next round of ammunition is loaded automatically from a magazine or clip. The trigger must be pulled for each shot. (Classified as *conventional semiautomatic* for analysis.)

— *Semiautomatic military-style shotgun* has the characteristics of a semiautomatic hunting-style shotgun.

In addition, the shotgun has military features, such as a pistol grip, folding-stock, and detachable magazine or clip. It looks like a semiautomatic military-style rifle. (Classified as *military-style semiautomatic* for analysis.)

A **semiautomatic gun** is a firearm in which a shell is ejected and the next round of ammunition is loaded automatically from a magazine or clip. The trigger must be pulled for each shot. Semiautomatic guns may be classified as handguns, rifles, or shotguns.

A **machine gun** is an automatic gun which, if the trigger is held down, will fire rapidly and continuously. It is not a semi-automatic gun for which the trigger must be pulled for each shot. (Classified as *fully automatic* for analysis.)

A **BB gun** shoots a single pellet, using air rather than an explosive to propel the pellet. (Excluded from analysis, as were toy guns.)

This report in portable document format and in ASCII, its tables, and related statistical data are available at the BJS World Wide Web Internet site:
http://www.ojp.usdoj.gov/bjs/

The data for this report may be obtained from the National Archive of Criminal Justice Data at the University of Michigan. The archive may be accessed through the BJS website.

The Bureau of Justice Statistics is the statistical agency of the U.S. Department of Justice. Lawrence A. Greenfeld is the acting director.

BJS Special Reports address a specific topic in depth from one or more datasets that cover many topics. Caroline Wolf Harlow wrote this report.

Tom Bonczar and Lara Reynolds provided statistical assistance and verification. Terry Austin, Chief, National Tracing Center Division of the Bureau of Alcohol, Tobacco and Firearms, provided comments. Tom Hester and Tina Dorsey edited the report. Jayne Robinson administered final production.

November 2001, NCJ 189369

Part IV
Stitching Up the Pieces:
Firearm Injury Trauma
from Criminal Offending

[26]

Firearm Injury and Death from Crime, 1993-97

By Marianne W. Zawitz and Kevin J. Strom
BJS Statisticians

Highlights

Firearm injuries from crime include those caused by interpersonal violence regardless of whether the injured party was the intended target or even a perpetrator. Such injuries can be fatal (homicides) or nonfatal (assaults). Incidents resulting in firearm injury may involve other crimes like robbery and burglary but are referred to as assaults. While injuries other than gunshot wounds can result from crimes involving a firearm, this report focuses on gunshot wounds.

No single source of data completely measures firearm injury and deaths from crime. Several sources cover only fatalities while others cover nonfatal injury. For example, the National Crime Victimization Survey (NCVS) does not include data about victims who died. In addition, while the NCVS provides a wealth of information about crime and victims, it does not capture enough cases involving gunshot wounds to provide annual estimates of many of the characteristics of such events. Hospital emergency department surveillance systems are able to collect additional cases and details about victims of nonfatal gunshot wounds but do not collect information about victims who do not seek treatment in hospitals (about 20% of all victims of nonfatal gunshot wounds, according to the NCVS).

• Of serious nonfatal violent victimizations, 28% were committed with a firearm, 4% were committed with a firearm and resulted in injury, and less than 1% resulted in gunshot wounds.

• Of all nonfatal firearm-related injuries treated in emergency departments, 62% were known to have resulted from an assault. For firearm-related fatalities, 44% were homicides.

• The number of gunshot wounds from assaults treated in hospital emergency departments fell from 64,100 in 1993 to 39,400 in 1997, a 39% decline. Homicides committed with a firearm fell from 18,300 in 1993 to 13,300 in 1997, a 27% decline.

• Four out of five of the victims of both fatal and nonfatal gunshot wounds from crime were male.

• Almost half of the victims of both fatal and nonfatal gunshot wounds from crime were black males. About a quarter were black males ages 15 to 24.

• Over half the victims of nonfatal gunshot wounds from crime were younger than 25. Older victims were more frequent in the homicide statistics.

• Over half of the victims of nonfatal firearm injury from crime who went to an emergency room were subsequently hospitalized overnight.

To describe firearm injury and death from crime, this report uses data from victim surveys, hospital emergency departments, death certificates, and law enforcement reports on homicides. (See the box on page 5 and the *Methodology* for additional discussion of sources of data concerning firearm injury.)

How much crime involves firearms and gunshot wounds?

The BJS National Crime Victimization Survey (NCVS) data for 1993-97 show that of the 19.2 million incidents of nonfatal violent crime, excluding simple assault —
• 28% were committed with a firearm
• 4% were committed with a firearm and resulted in injury
• less than 1% resulted in gunshot wounds.

According to the FBI's Uniform Crime Reports, 30% of the murders, robberies, and aggravated assaults reported to police from 1993 to 1997 involved firearms. Of these violent crimes, 1% were murders. Of all murders from 1993 to 1997, 69% were committed with firearms.

How many people are injured by firearms and how many of these injuries are the result of crime?

According to the National Hospital Ambulatory Medical Care Survey conducted by the Centers for Disease Control and Prevention (CDC), 0.4% of all injury visits to hospital emergency departments from 1992 to 1995 were caused by firearms (4 of every 1,000 visits.)[1] This estimate includes all causes of firearm injury and may include visits for patients seeking follow-up care and patients who died at the hospital.

Estimates from the CDC Firearm Injury Surveillance Study show that from 1993 through 1997, about 412,000 nonfatal firearm-related injuries were treated in U.S. hospital emergency departments.

	Firearm injury from all causes
1993-97 Total	411,800
1993	104,200
1994	89,600
1995	84,200
1996	69,600
1997	64,200
Percent change	-38%

Source: Centers for Disease Control and Prevention, Firearm Injury Surveillance Study, 1993-97.

Of the total nonfatal firearm injuries —
• 62% resulted from assaults
• 17% were unintentional
• 6% were suicide attempts
• 1% were legal interventions
• 13% were from unknown causes.

---

[1] C.W. Burt and L.A. Fingerhut. "Injury visits to hospital emergency departments: United States, 1992-95," National Center for Health Statistics, *Vital Health Statistics*, 13:131, 1998.

While most nonfatal firearm-related injuries are from crime, most firearm-related deaths are suicides. According to the Vital Statistics, 180,533 firearm deaths occurred from 1993 through 1997: 51% were suicides, 44% homicides, 1% legal interventions, 3% unintentional incidents, and 1% were of undetermined causes.

The number of nonfatal assaults and homicides from firearms declined from 1993 to 1997

From 1993 to 1997 nonfatal firearm injuries from crime declined 39% and firearm-related homicides fell 27%. Firearm injury and deaths from other causes also declined over the period. Firearm injuries resulting from suicide attempts declined 45%, and those from unintentional causes declined 39%. Unintentional deaths from firearms fell by 36% and suicides fell by 7%. (For more detailed data, see *Appendix.*)

	Nonfatal and fatal firearm injuries	
	Nonfatal assaults	Homicides
1993-97 Total	257,200*	78,620
1993	64,100	18,253
1994	61,200	17,527
1995	53,400	15,551
1996	39,200	14,037
1997	39,400	13,252
Percent change	-39%	-27%

*95% confidence interval estimates the number to be between 160,300 to 353,700. See *Methodology.*

Sources: Centers for Disease Control and Prevention, Firearm Injury Surveillance Study, 1993-97 and the Vital Statistics of the United States, 1993-97.

The ratio of nonfatal to fatal gunshot injuries varies by intent

From 1993 through 1997 there were 3.3 nonfatal gunshot injuries from assault treated in hospital emergency departments for every firearm-related homicide. For gunshot injuries sustained unintentionally, there were 11.4 nonfatal injuries for every gunshot fatality. Firearm-related suicide

attempts were the most likely to result in a fatality, as there were 0.3 firearm-related attempted suicides for every completed suicide.[2]

Most victims of gunshot injury and death from crime were male; almost half were black males

From 1993 to 1997—
• Eighty-nine percent of the victims of nonfatal gunshot wounds from crime were male; 84% of firearm homicide victims were male, according to the FBI's Supplementary Homicide Reports (SHR).

• Blacks made up 54% of the victims of nonfatal gunshot wounds from crime and 54% of the homicide victims.

• Almost 1 in 5 victims of nonfatal gunshot wounds from crime were Hispanic. Equivalent data for homicide victims are not available in the SHR. According to the Vital Statistics, 18% of the homicide victims were Hispanic.

	Percent of victims of nonfatal gunshot wounds from crime
Black male	49 %
Hispanic male	17
White male*	15
Black female	6
White female*	3
Other male	3
Hispanic female	2
Other female	...
Unknown**	5

... Less than .05%.
*Represents white, non-Hispanic.
**Males of unknown race represented 4.2% of the victims, and females of unknown race were 0.5%.
Source: Centers for Disease Control and Prevention, Firearm Injury Surveillance Study, 1993-97.

Black males ages 15 to 24 made up 26% of all the victims of nonfatal gunshot wounds from crime and 22% of the homicide victims.

While the majority of victims of nonfatal and fatal gunshot wounds from crime

---

[2] V. Beaman, J.L. Annest, J.A. Mercy, M. Kresnow, and D.A. Pollock, "Lethality of firearm-related injuries in the United States population," *Annals of Emergency Medicine*, 35:258-266, 2000.

Different sources of data on firearm injury from crime show consistent demographic patterns

A comparison of two sources of firearm homicide data to the CDC's data on nonfatal firearm injury from crime shows similar demographic patterns among victims. Black males are the most frequent victims of firearm homicide and nonfatal firearm injury from crime. Young people are also more frequently victims in all three sources. One explanation of why older victims are more frequent in the homicide statistics is that they are less able than younger victims to recover from gunshot wounds.

Although these sources have different population coverage (see *Methodology*), the homicide victims in the Vital Statistics and the FBI's Supplementary Homicide Reports appear to be very similar. Some of the differences between these sources and the firearm injury study are due to differences in population coverage or to the estimation procedures used with the firearm injury surveillance sample.

	Firearm homicides, 1993-97		Nonfatal firearm injury from assault
	Vital statistics*	FBI's Supplementary Homicide Reports	
Race and gender			
White male	36 %	34 %	33 %**
White female	9	9	5 **
Black male	46	47	49
Black female	6	7	6
Other	3	2	4
Age			
0-14	3 %	2 %	3 %
15-19	17	17	26
20-24	22	22	25
25-34	29	29	26
35-44	17	16	12
45 and older	13	13	7
Unknown	0	1	0

*Includes legal intervention homicides.
**For comparison, Hispanics who were included in the other racial category in the original data were included in the white racial category. Hispanic origin is not sufficiently reported in the Supplementary Homicide Reports to allow comparison.
Sources: Vital Statistics of the United States, Centers for Disease Control and Prevention National Center for Health Statistics, 1993-97; FBI, Uniform Crime Reports, Supplementary Homicide Reports, 1993-97; and Centers for Disease Control and Prevention, National Center for Injury Prevention, Firearms Injury Surveillance Study, 1993-97.

were black, most victims of unintentional firearm injury and death and suicides and suicide attempts with firearms were white.

Many victims of nonfatal and fatal gunshot wounds from crime were juveniles and young adults

	Victims of firearm injury		Firearm homicide offenders
Age	Nonfatal assault	Homicide	
14 and under	3%	2%	2%
15-17	13	8	15
18-20	19	14	24
21-24	19	17	19
25 and older	45	58	40

Note: May not total to 100%. Data on persons of unknown age are not presented.
Sources: Centers for Disease Control and Prevention, Firearm Injury Surveillance Study, 1993-97, and FBI, Uniform Crime Reports, Supplementary Homicide Reports, 1993-97.

Juveniles (persons under age 18) accounted for 16% of the victims of nonfatal gunshot wounds from crime and 10% of the firearm homicide victims. Thirty-five percent of the victims of nonfatal gunshot wounds from crime and 24% of the homicide victims were under 21 years of age.

Homicide offenders are also likely to be young. According to the Supplementary Homicide Reports from 1993 to 1997, 60% of the offenders who used a firearm to commit murder were younger than 25; 17% were juveniles and 24% were between ages 18 and 20. (The Youth Handgun Safety Act of 1994 prohibits possession of handguns by anyone under 18, and under the Gun Control Act of 1968 it is unlawful for federally licensed firearms dealers to sell handguns to persons under 21.)

How did the victims of nonfatal firearm assaults get to the hospital?

Mode of transport to the hospital	Percent of gunshot wound victims
EMS/Rescue/Ambulance	66 %
Private vehicle	19
Walk-in	6
Police	3
Unknown	3
Air transport	3

Source: Centers for Disease Control and Prevention, Firearm Injury Surveillance Study, 1993-97.

About two-thirds of the victims of gunshot wounds from crime who were treated in emergency departments were taken to the emergency department by an emergency medical service, ambulance, or rescue squad.

Victims of unintentional firearm injury differ from gunshot victims from crime in that a higher percentage come to hospital by private vehicle than any other means.

Firearm Injury and Death from Crime, 1993-97 3

Where were victims of nonfatal gunshot assaults wounded?

Data from the CDC study of nonfatal firearm injury show that almost half of the victims shot as a result of an assault received wounds to the extremities (arms, hands, legs, or feet). Over a third of firearm assault victims were shot in their trunk, and the remainder were shot in their head or neck.

By contrast, over two-thirds of the victims of unintentional gunshot wounds were shot in their arms, legs, or feet, while two-thirds of the people who attempted suicide were shot in their head, neck or upper trunk.

Most victims of nonfatal firearm assaults who are treated in an emergency room are subsequently hospitalized

The CDC data show that 53% of the victims of nonfatal gunshot wounds from assaults (an estimated 137,000) were hospitalized at least overnight after their initial treatment in an emergency room. (95% confidence interval estimates the number to be between 84,900 to 189,000. See *Methodology*.) The remainder (46%) were released after being treated or transferred. An earlier CDC firearms study estimated that about 92% of the victims hospitalized for firearm injury were discharged from the hospital alive.[3]

Data from the NCVS on nonfatal firearm crimes for 1993-97 show that over half of the victims of gunshot wounds who sought treatment were treated and released.

Other characteristics of the events involving gunshot wounds from crime

For many victims of nonfatal and fatal gunshot wounds from crime, little is

---

[3] J.L. Annest and others, "National Estimates of Nonfatal Firearm-Related Injuries: Beyond the Tip of the Iceberg," *Journal of the American Medical Association*, 273, 22:1749-54, June 14, 1995

How often are police officers injured in assaults with firearms?

In 1998, over 400 police officers were injured in firearm assaults and 58 police officers were killed by a firearm while responding to a crime. The firearm injury rate for police officers declined in the early 1980's and began climbing again after 1987. In the late 1990's, firearm injury rates fell to the lowest levels recorded during the 1978-98 period.

The greatest decline in the number of officers killed by firearms occurred in the early 1980's. The number of officers injured by firearms during an assault rose during the late 1980's and early 1990's and declined sharply after 1992. As a result, the ratio of those injured to killed from firearm assaults has been decreasing.

Source: FBI, Uniform Crime Reports, Law Enforcement Officers Killed and Assaulted, 1978-98.

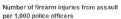
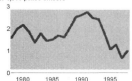

Number of firearm injuries from assault per 1,000 police officers

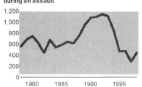

Number of police officers injured by firearms during an assault

Number of police officers killed by firearms during an assault

---

known about the event. For nonfatal injuries covered in the CDC study, much of this information is unavailable in hospital emergency departments. For fatalities, the police may not know or may not report any information about the event other than it was a homicide. This section outlines the details about events involving gunshot wounds from crime from one or more of the sources used.

Type of firearm

For 59% of the victims of nonfatal gunshot wounds from crime in the CDC study, the type of firearm used was unknown. Where the firearm type was known, 82% of the victims were shot by handguns, 14% by shotguns, and 4% by rifles.

In the Supplementary Homicide Reports from 1993 through 1997, 81% of those killed with firearms were killed

---

with a handgun, 6% with shotguns, 5% with rifles, and 7% with unspecified firearms. The SHR does not collect additional detail about the firearm.

Criminal circumstances

Information about whether the injury resulted from another crime, such as a robbery or from a physical fight, was recorded for about a third of the cases in the CDC study.

Of the victims of firearm homicide included in the Supplementary Homicide Reports from 1993 through 1997—
• 28% were killed because of an argument
• 19% were killed during the commission of another crime, including 11% during a robbery and 7% during a drug law violation
• 7% died as a result of a juvenile gang killing.

What information is available about firearm injury and death from crime and interpersonal violence?

Firearm homicide data from several sources have been available for many years including:
• Vital Statistics of the United States, which collects data from death certificates filed throughout the Nation
• Supplementary Homicide Reports, which include data reported to the FBI's Uniform Crime Reporting Program by State and local law enforcement agencies on a voluntary basis.

Both can provide State and local data as well as national data. Both systems also have limitations. (See additional discussion of these sources in the *Methodology*.) Neither collects any information from medical examiners or crime laboratories.

Little data on nonfatal firearm injuries were available until recently. While many jurisdictions have laws mandating the reporting of gunshot wounds to law enforcement, there is no national registry of such injuries.

CDC initiated the Firearms Injury Surveillance Study in June 1992. As discussed in the *Methodology*, this study collects data about gun-related

injuries treated at hospital emergency departments through the Consumer Product Safety Commission's National Electronic Injury Surveillance System. This study produces national estimates from a sample of hospital emergency departments.

Much of the firearm injury information relevant in the criminal justice context, like data about the offender and the circumstances, is not well reported in a hospital-based collection. Emergency department personnel are primarily concerned with treating victims. In addition, victims may be unable or unwilling to share information about the incident.

The National Crime Victimization Survey provides a detailed picture of crime incidents, victims, and trends occurring each year in the United States. Because firearm crime and resulting injury are relatively rare when compared to all types of crime, the NCVS provides limited information about gunshot injuries from crime. No local data are available from the NCVS.

The Federal Bureau of Investigation is currently implementing an improved crime reporting system, the National Incident-based Reporting System (NIBRS), which has the potential to provide detailed statistics about crime, including crimes committed with firearms that result in either nonfatal or fatal injury. Currently, 40 States are in some stage of development or implementation of NIBRS.

NIBRS covers those incidents where victims of firearm crime are known to the police. The information from NIBRS about the type of injuries incurred or the type of firearm used is limited.

Additional sources of data concerning firearm injury not specifically related to crime also exist. For a comprehensive discussion of all these sources, see J.L. Annest and J.A. Mercy, "Use of National Data Systems for Firearm-Related Injury Surveillance" in "Firearm-Related Injury Surveillance," R.M. Ikeda, J.A. Mercy, and S.P. Teret, eds., *American Journal of Preventive Medicine*, 15, 3S, October 1998.

Location of the assaults that resulted in gunshot wounds

The CDC study found that the location of the assault was —
• unknown by hospital staff in half the incidents
• a street or highway in 23%
• a home, apartment, or condominium in 14%
• other property, including schools or recreation areas, in 13%.

In 2% of the cases, the assault was reported to have occurred when the victim was on the job. In the text descriptions provided by hospital staff, the term "drive-by" was used to describe what happened to 12% of the victims of nonfatal gunshot injury from assaults. Similar data are not available from the SHR.

Relationship of injured victims to their attackers

In more than half of the cases in the CDC study, the victim's relationship to the offender was not reported. When relationship was reported, 49% of the victims were attacked by strangers and 28% did not see who shot them.

Victim-offender relationship	Percent of victims of nonfatal gunshot wounds from crime
Relationship unknown	56 %
Stranger	22
Did not see offender	12
Friend/acquaintance	8
All other known	3

Source: Centers for Disease Control and Prevention, Firearm Injury Surveillance Study, 1993-97.

Data from the BJS 1994 Study of Injured Victims of Violence (SIVV) show that intentional gunshot cases were less likely to contain information about the person who inflicted the injury than incidents involving intentional injuries not caused by a firearm. Among cases of nonfatal violent injuries treated in U.S. emergency departments in 1994, 55% of gunshot cases did not include information about the relationship of the victim to the offender compared to 27% of the cases involving non-gunshot injuries.

The relationship to the offender was unknown in 41% of the firearm homicides in the Supplementary Homicide Reports from 1993 through 1997. The killer was a stranger to the victim in 15% of the homicides. In 44% of the homicides during the period, the killer was known to the victim including —

• 31% in which the victim and offender were friends or acquaintances
• 12% in which the killer was a relative or intimate of the victim.

Methodology

CDC Firearms Injury Surveillance Study — These data were compiled through the U.S. Consumer Product Safety Commission's (CPSC) National Electronic Injury Surveillance System (NEISS). The CPSC established NEISS in 1972 to track product-related injuries. NEISS collects data from hospitals selected as a representative sample of the approximately 6,000 hospitals with emergency departments in the United States. From 1993 through 1996, 91 hospitals were in the sample; in 1997 the number of hospitals increased to 101. The system includes very large inner-city hospitals with trauma centers, as well as other types of urban, suburban, and rural hospitals. Data from the NEISS hospitals are weighted to provide national estimates about injuries treated in U.S. hospital emergency departments.

Through an agreement with CDC, NEISS was used to collect data on nonfatal gun-related injuries at all participating hospitals beginning in June 1992. NEISS personnel abstracted information from medical records on each case identified. Further information about the study can be found in J.L. Annest and others, "National Estimates of Nonfatal Firearm-Related Injuries: Beyond the Tip of the Iceberg," *Journal of the American Medical Association*, June 14, 1995.

The CDC data for 1993 through May 1997 consists of 13,402 unweighted cases. This report focuses on the 8,988 unweighted cases coded as assaults that involved nonfatal gunshot wounds caused by any weapon that uses a powder charge to fire a projectile. Injuries from undetermined intent were not included. Therefore, the estimates presented here may not be

the same as those previously published.

Because the CDC data are based on nonfatal firearm injuries treated at a nationally representative sample of U.S. hospital emergency departments, the estimates that are derived from the data are subject to sampling error. To measure the precision of national estimates obtained from the data, CDC estimated the generalized standard errors for estimates of selected sample size as follows:

Estimate	Standard error	Relative sampling error in percent	95% confidence interval
1,000	309	31%	394-1,606
5,000	1,200	24%	2,648-7,352
10,000	2,230	22%	5,629-14,371
25,000	5,225	21%	14,759-35,241
50,000	10,050	20%	30,302-69,698
100,000	19,600	20%	61,584-138,416
150,000	29,100	19%	92,964-207,036
257,000	49,344	19%	160,286-353,714

The Bureau of Justice Statistics also used NEISS to collect information about both firearm and nonfirearm intentional interpersonal injury. The BJS Study of Injured Victims of Violence (SIVV) collected data from 31 hospitals in the NEISS sample during 1994. The information on intentional firearm injury in the BJS study comes from the CDC firearm injury data. A BJS special report, *Violence-Related Injuries Treated in Hospital Emergency Departments,* (August 1997, NCJ-156921) presents findings from this study.

The National Hospital Ambulatory Medical Care Survey (NHAMCS) — Conducted by the National Center for Health Statistics of the Centers for Disease Control and Prevention, this survey is designed to collect data on the utilization and provision of ambulatory care services in hospital emergency and outpatient departments. Findings are based on a national sample of visits to the emergency departments and outpatient departments of non-institutional general and short-stay hospitals, exclusive of Federal, military, and Veterans Administration hospitals, in the 50 States and the District of Columbia.

The survey uses a four-stage probability design with samples of geographically defined areas, hospitals within these areas, clinics, hospitals, and patient visits within clinics. Annual data collection began in 1992.

National Crime Victimization Survey— The NCVS is the Nation's primary source of information on criminal victimization. The survey provides a detailed picture of crime incidents, victims, and trends occurring each year in the United States. The survey collects information on the frequency and nature of the crimes of rape, sexual assault, personal robbery, aggravated and simple assault, household burglary, theft and motor vehicle theft utilizing a nationally representative sample of approximately 43,000 households (about 80,000 persons).

The survey provides information about victims (such as age, gender, and race), offenders (age, gender, and race) and the crimes (use of weapons, nature of injury, etc.). From 1993 through 1997, the NCVS recorded 43 unweighted cases of gun shot injury from crime.

Firearm homicide data — Firearm homicide data come from two primary sources:
• Vital Statistics of the United States, which collect data from death certificates filed throughout the Nation
• Supplementary Homicide Reports, which include data reported to the Uniform Crime Reporting Program of the FBI by State and local law enforcement agencies on a voluntary basis.

The Vital Statistics information includes the demographic characteristics of firearm homicide victims and is thought to be an accurate count of the number of such deaths. It does not contain information about the circumstances surrounding the death, the type of firearm used, or suspected offenders. The Supplementary Homicide Reports provide such detailed information. However, not all agencies report, and not all reports are complete.

Appendix. Number of nonfatal gunshot injuries and firearm-related deaths

	Total	Assault or homicide	Legal intervention	Suicide attempts/ Suicide	Uninten-tional	Undeter-mined
Nonfatal gunshot injury						
1993-97	411,800	257,200	5,100 *	23,400	70,900	55,200
1993	104,200	64,100	1,300 *	5,600	18,200	15,100
1994	89,600	61,200	1,100 *	5,700	13,600	8,000
1995	84,200	53,400	1,000 *	5,000	14,300	10,400
1996	69,600	39,200	700 *	4,000	13,600	12,000
1997	64,200	39,400	900 *	3,100	11,100	9,700
Percent change	-38%	-39%	-31% *	-45%	-39%	-36%
Firearm-related deaths						
1993-97	180,533	78,620	1,501	91,940	6,217	2,255
1993	39,595	18,253	318	18,940	1,521	563
1994	38,505	17,527	339	18,765	1,356	518
1995	35,957	15,551	284	18,503	1,225	394
1996	34,040	14,037	290	18,166	1,134	413
1997	32,436	13,252	270	17,566	981	367
Percent change	-18%	-27%	-15%	-7%	-36%	-35%
Injury deaths**						
1993-97	737,650	112,877	1,770	154,966	450,778	17,259

*Annual estimates for legal intervention injuries are presented for completeness but may be statistically unreliable because they are based on a small number of cases.
**Injury deaths include firearm-related deaths. The total represents only the categories presented here.
Sources: Centers for Disease Control and Prevention, Firearm Injury Surveillance Study, 1993-97 and the Vital Statistics of the United States, 1993-97.

Vital Statistics reported 78,620 firearm-related homicides from 1993 through 1997. Supplementary Homicide Reports covering this period include data on 67,459 firearm-related murders.

The homicide data from the Vital Statistics and the Uniform Crime Reports provide slightly different estimates of the number of homicides annually. Rokaw and others attributed this to differences in —

• coverage of the U.S. population
• practices or rules governing the reporting of homicides to NCHS and the FBI
• criteria used in defining a case as a homicide
• categories used and rules employed to classify people among demographic subgroups.

Additional information about the differences between the Vital Statistics and the Uniform Crime Reports estimates of homicide can found in the following:

Cantor, D. and L.E. Cohen. "Comparing Measures of Homicide Trends: Methodological and Substantive Differences in the Vital Statistics and the Uniform Crime Report Time Series (1933-1975)," *Social Science Research*, 9:121-145, 1980.

Hindelang, M.J. "The Uniform Crime Reports Revisited," *Journal of Criminal Justice*, 2:1-17, 1974.

Rand, M.R. "The Study of Homicide Caseflow: Creating a Comprehensive Homicide Dataset," paper presented to the meeting of the American Society of Criminology in New Orleans, Louisiana, November 1992.

Rokaw, W.M., J.A. Mercy, and C.C. Smith, "Comparing Death Certificate with FBI Crime Reporting Statistics on U.S Homicides," *Public Health Reports*, 105:447-455, 1990.

Rosenberg, M.L. and J.A. Mercy. "Homicide: Epidemiologic Analysis at the National Level," *Bulletin of the New York Academy of Medicine*, 62, 5:376-399, 1986.

Law Enforcement Officers Killed and Assaulted — This FBI series provides detailed information about duty-related deaths including those that result from felonious actions. Federal, State, and local agencies notify the FBI of line-of-duty deaths. Once notified, the FBI contacts the victim officer's employing agency for additional details surrounding the death.

In addition, State and local agencies report the number of assaults resulting in serious injury or instances where a weapon was used which could have caused serious injury or death. Other assaults are recorded only if they involved more than verbal abuse or minor resistance to arrest. Data are submitted monthly to the FBI.

Sources

Annest, J.L., J.A. Mercy, D.R. Gibson, and G.W. Ryan. "National Estimates of Nonfatal Firearm-Related Injuries: Beyond the Tip of the Iceberg," *Journal of the American Medical Association*. 273, 22: 1749-54, June 14,1995.

"BB and Pellet Gun-Related Injuries, United States, June 1992, May 1994," *Morbidity and Mortality Weekly Report*, Centers for Disease Control and Prevention. 44, 49:909-13, December 15, 1995.

Beaman V., J.L. Annest, J.A. Mercy, M. Kresnow, and D.A. Pollock. "Lethality of firearm-related injuries in the United States population," *Annals of Emergency Medicine*. 35:258-266, 2000.

BJS. National Crime Victimization Survey, 1993-97.

Burt, C.W. and L.A. Fingerhut. "Injury visits to hospital emergency departments: United States, 1992-95," National Center for Health Statistics. *Vital Health Statistics*. 13, 131, 1998.

Centers for Disease Control and Prevention, National Center for Health Statistics. *Advance Report of Final Mortality Statistics, 1992*, *Monthly Vital Statistics Report*. 43, 6, December 1994.

Centers for Disease Control and Prevention, National Center for Injury Prevention. Firearms Injury Surveillance Study, 1993-97.

FBI. Uniform Crime Reports, Law Enforcement Officers Killed and Assaulted, 1978-98.

FBI. Uniform Crime Reports, Supplementary Homicide Reports, 1993-97.

Fox, J.A. and M.W. Zawitz. "Homicide Trends in the United States," a section of the BJS website, *http://www.ojp.usdoj.gov/bjs/homicide/homtrnd.htm*

Ikeda, R.M., J.M. Mercy, and S.P. Teret, eds. "Firearm-related injury surveillance," *American Journal of Preventive Medicine.*15, 3S, October 1998.

"Nonfatal and Fatal Firearm-Related Injuries — United States, 1993-97," *Morbidity and Mortality Weekly Report,* Centers for Disease Control and Prevention. 48, 45:1029-1034, November 19, 1999.

Rand, M.R. "Violence-Related Injuries Treated in Hospital Emergency Departments," BJS Special Report. August 1997, NCJ-156921.

Rokaw, W.M., J.A. Mercy, and J.C. Smith. "Comparing Death Certificate Data with FBI Crime Reporting Statistics on U.S. Homicides," *Public Health Reports.* 105:447-455.

Strom, K.J. "Using Hospital Emergency Room Data to Assess Intimate Violence-related Injuries," *Justice Research and Policy.* 4, Spring 2000.

Zawitz, M.W. *Firearm Injury from Crime.* BJS Selected Findings. April 1996, NCJ-160093.

The data and the report, as well as others from the Bureau of Justice Statistics, are available through the Internet —
http://www.ojp.usdoj.gov/bjs/

Some of the data utilized in this report are available from the National Archive of Criminal Justice Data at the University of Michigan, *http://www.icpsr.umich.edu/NACJD/home.html.* See CDC Firearm Injury Surveillance Study, 1993-1997, ICPSR 3018 and Uniform Crime Reports Supplementary Homicide Reports, 1976-1998, ICPSR 2832.

The Bureau of Justice Statistics is the statistical arm of the U.S. Department of Justice. Jan M. Chaiken, Ph.D., is director.

Substantial assistance in preparing this report was provided by J. Lee Annest, Ph.D., Director, and George W. Ryan, Ph.D., Mathematical Statistician, Office of Statistics and Programming, National Center for Injury Prevention and Control, Centers for Disease Control and Prevention; Lois Fingerhut, National Center for Health Statistics, Centers for Disease Control and Prevention; and Michael Rand and Craig Perkins, BJS.

Verification and publication review were provided by Rhonda Keith and Tom Hester of the Bureau of Justice Statistics.

October 2000, NCJ 182993

[27]

Children Who Are Shot: A 30-Year Experience

By Danielle Laraque, Barbara Barlow, Maureen Durkin, Joy Howell, Franklyn Cladis, David Friedman,
Carla DiScala, Rao Ivatury, and William Stahl

New York, New York

● Three data sets describe the pattern of gunshot injuries to children from 1960 to 1993: The Harlem Hospital pediatric trauma registry (HHPTR), the northern Manhattan injury surveillance system (NMISS) a population-based study, and the National Pediatric Trauma Registry (NPTR). A small case-control study compares the characteristics of injured children with a control group. Before 1970 gunshot injuries to Harlem children were rare. In 1971 an initial rise in pediatric gunshot admissions occurred, and by 1988 pediatric gunshot injuries at Harlem Hospital had peaked at 33. Population-based data through NMISS showed that the gunshot rate for Central Harlem children 10 to 16 years of age rose from 64.6 per 100,000 in 1986 to 267.6 per 100,000 in 1987, a 400% increase. The case fatality for children admitted to Harlem Hospital (1960 to 1993) was 3%, usually because of brain injury, but the majority of deaths occurred before hospitalization. During the same period, felony drug arrests in Harlem increased by 163%. The neighboring South Bronx experienced the same increase in gunshot wound admissions and felony arrests from 1986 to 1993. The NPTR showed a similar injury pattern for other communities in the United States. In a case-control analysis, Harlem adolescents who had sustained gunshot wounds were more likely to have dropped out of school, to have lived in a household without a biological parent, to have experienced parental death, and to have known of a relative or friend who had been shot than community adolescents treated for other medical or surgical problems. Since 1990, the Harlem Injury Prevention Program formed a coalition of school and community organizations joined by the District Attorney's Office in collaboration with the Tactical Narcotic Team (to eliminate drug selling from the schools and playgrounds), to provide safe, supervised activities for children. Data from 1990 to 1992 show a moderate decline in the incidence of gunshot wounds to children. Gun control legislation in conjunction with the community violence prevention activities are needed to curb the epidemic of gunshot injuries.

INDEX WORDS: Injuries, gunshot, pediatric, trauma registry.

From the Divisions of Pediatrics and Pediatric Surgery, Harlem Hospital Medical Center, Columbia University College of Physicians & Surgeons; MEDTEP, Urban Health Institute at Harlem Hospital; the Harlem Center for Health Promotion and Disease Prevention; Gertrude H. Sergievsky Center, School of Public Health, Columbia University; Department of Surgery at Lincoln Hospital, New York Medical College; National Institute on Disability and Rehabilitation Research, New York, NY.

Supported in part by grants from the Robert Wood Johnson Foundation, Johnson and Johnson, New York State Department of Health, New York State Division of Juvenile Justice, the Centers for Disease Control (R49/CCR 202585 and R48/CCR 205055), the National Institute of Neurological Diseases and Stroke (R29 NS27971-03 and R29 NS27971-04), and the Agency for Health Care Policy Research (5UO1-HS07399).

Presented at the 1994 Annual Meeting of the Section on Surgery of the American Academy of Pediatrics, Dallas, Texas, October 21-23, 1994.

Address reprint requests to Danielle Laraque, MD, FAAP, Department of Pediatrics, Columbia University at Harlem Hospital Medical Center, 506 Lenox Ave, MLK 17-140, New York, NY 10037.

THIS ARTICLE describes the pattern of gunshot injuries to Harlem children from 1960 to 1993 and compares this experience with that of the neighboring community of the South Bronx and with trauma centers around the country. It is hypothesized that the absence of a parent or extracurricular activities or employment is associated with risk for gunshot injury.

MATERIALS AND METHODS

Harlem Hospital, located in Northern Manhattan, the only hospital in Central Harlem, is a Level I Trauma Center and provides care for the majority of the local residents. Central Harlem is an economically disadvantaged, predominantly African-American community with 29% of its inhabitants younger than 17 years of age.

The present study uses three data sources: (1) The Harlem Hospital Pediatric Trauma Registry (HHPTR) records medical and social data on all children up to 17 years of age admitted for injury, excluding ingestions, foreign bodies, and burns. This hospital registry began in 1970, and information for prior years was obtained through chart review. The Lincoln Hospital Trauma Registry, begun in 1986, was compared with the Harlem Hospital data. (2) The Northern Manhattan Injury Surveillance System (NMISS), started in 1983, provided on-going population-based surveillance of severe pediatric injuries for children under 17 years of age residing in Central and West Harlem. NMISS includes data on all pediatric injuries resulting in hospitalization and/or death. Using methods described by Davidson et al,[1] census data from 1980 and 1990 provide population estimates for computation of annual incidence rates. (3) The National Pediatric Trauma Registry (NPTR), founded in 1985, currently accepts trauma data from 61 general and children's hospital trauma centers around the country.[2,3]

In a case control study, during 1993 to 1994, outpatient and inpatient Harlem children who sustained gunshot wounds are compared with age- and gender-matched children who are seen in the medical clinic or are hospitalized for other injuries. Data on family structure, school attendance, job experience, participation in sports, prison history, exposure to violence, and urine toxicology are collected for cases and controls.

RESULTS

From 1960 to 1993, 372 children were admitted to Harlem Hospital for gunshot wound (Fig 1). Only 2 children were admitted from 1960 to 1969. From 1970 to 1979, 88 children were admitted; in 1980 to 1989,

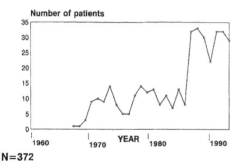

N=372

Fig 1. Pediatric gunshot wound admissions (ages 0 to 17 years) to Harlem Hospital for the years 1960 to 1993. Data from the Harlem Hospital Pediatric Trauma Registry.

Table 1. NMISS Gunshot Injury and Death Rates per 100,000 Central Harlem Children Aged 10 to 16 Years (1983 to 1992)

Year	Injury Rate per 100,000	Death Rate per 100,000
1983	101.9	0
1984	34.5	0
1985	20 1	8.4
1986	64.6	17.1
1987	267.6	26.1
1988	184.2	0
1989	217.8	18.0
1990	170.8	18.3
1991	152.5	0
1992	110.8	9.2

167 children; and from 1990 to 1993, 115 were admitted to the hospital. Of the hospitalized children, 302 (81%) were boys and 70 (19%) were girls. Eighty-three percent were between the ages of 10 and 16 years; the mean age was 13.8 years, the range 1 to 17 years. For the years 1970 to 1981, the nature and site of the injuries was reported by Barlow et al.[4] For the years 1982 to 1993, 257 children were hospitalized. As in the first series, the commonest site of injury was the extremity, and the most lethal, head injury (Fig 2). The case fatality for the 30-year period (1960 to 1991) is 3%.

The northern Manhattan injury surveillance system (1983 to 1992) showed that the gunshot injury rate for children 10 to 16 years of age rose from 64.6 per 100,000 in 1986 to 267.6 per 100,000 in 1987, a 400% rise (Table 1). During this period, 15 of the 18 child deaths (83%) of gunshot occurred before the child reached the hospital, and children 10 to 16 years represented 89% of all gunshot fatalities in Central

Harlem. For children 10 to 16 years of age, the death rate steadily increased, peaking in 1987 at 26.1 per 100,000, with an average rate for the 9 years of 9.7 per 100,000. Since 1990, the injury rate for this group has shown a moderate decline.

Lincoln Hospital in the South Bronx, an economically disadvantaged, predominantly Hispanic community, experienced a similar epidemic of childhood gunshot injuries, as noted in Fig 3.

From 1986 to 1993, the proportion of children injured by gunshot wounds for Harlem Hospital increased steadily, from an initial value of 4.7% in 1986 to 16.4% in 1992, and in the last 4 years (1989 to 1992) has averaged 14%. Data from the National Pediatric Trauma Registry were examined to determine if the Harlem experience was unique. These data show that the proportion of trauma admissions attributable to gunshot in both general and children's hospitals show a similar, if less dramatic, increase for the same period nationally. However, general hospitals, at a rate of 8%, cared for proportionally more gunshot wound victims than children's hospitals, at a rate of 4%. The case fatality for the 8 years for all

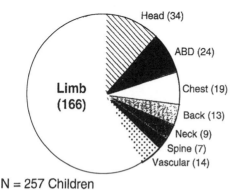

N = 257 Children

Fig 2. Pediatric gunshot wound injury sites for children admitted to Harlem Hospital from 1982 to 1993. The first series of children (1971 to 1981) was reported by Barlow et al.[4]

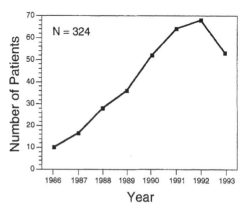

Fig 3. Pediatric gunshot wound admissions to Lincoln Hospital from 1986 to 1993. Data from the Lincoln Hospital Trauma Registry.

Table 2. Risk Factors for Adolescent Gunshot Injury in Central Harlem and Controls Seen for Medical Visits or Other Injuries

	Percentage	
	Gunshot Wound Patients (n = 26)	Controls (n = 34)
School drop-out	31	0*
Part-time job	4	21
Sports	15	35
Jail	12	0
Household		
Two-parent	19	32
One-parent	31	35
Nonparent	50	32
Parental death	38	12*

*$P < .05$.

centers exclusive of Harlem Hospital averaged 11.2%. For the same period the case fatality for Harlem Hospital was 3.2%.

Possible risk factors for injury were examined in the 1993 to 1994 case control study (Table 2). Initial results show that children who had been shot reported few extracurricular activities or work experiences compared with the control group of outpatient or inpatient children who had not been shot. School drop out and prior exposure to the criminal justice system were seen only in the gunshot wound group. Toxicology was performed only on hospitalized children. Sixty percent of gunshot-wounded children had positive toxicology (predominantly marihuana) compared with 20% of control children. Children who had been shot were less likely to live in either a two-parent or one-parent household and more likely to report living with a nonparent and to have experienced parental death.

Felony drug arrests from the Commissioner of Police were available for both the Central and South Bronx communities. Between 1986 and 1990, the data show a steady increase in drug arrests over the period corresponding to the escalation of pediatric gunshot wounds.

DISCUSSION

Three data sets, the Harlem Hospital pediatric trauma registry, the Northern Manhattan Injury Surveillance System providing population-based data, and the National Pediatric Trauma Registry are used to show the escalating national problem of gunshot injuries to children, especially adolescents. Gunshot injury, a rare event in children in Central Harlem before 1970, now represents over 15% of trauma admissions to Harlem Hospital and at least 5% of trauma admissions to 61 trauma centers around the United States. The Harlem experience is not unique and is shown in the adjacent community of the South Bronx. These experiences are in sharp contrast to the

available NPTR data from Toronto, Canada, for the years 1986 and 1992, with less than ½% of trauma admissions attributable to gunshot.[2] The contrast in the rates of crime, assaults, and homicides in two cities, Vancouver and Seattle, with differing handgun regulations, has been used to strongly support gun control as effective in the primary prevention of gunshot injuries and deaths.[5]

The pattern of injury to children indicates a stable case fatality of 3% for hospitalized Central Harlem children over the 30-year period. Head injury is responsible for most of the fatalities. This case fatality is lower than the overall case fatality for hospitalized children as reported through the National Pediatric Trauma Registry. Availability of population-based data through the Northern Manhattan Surveillance System shows, similar to the findings reported by Cooper et al,[6] that 83% of Central Harlem child deaths from gunshot occurred before hospitalization and therefore are not represented by either the hospital trauma registry or the National Pediatric Trauma Registry. Eighty-nine percent of deaths occurred to adolescents aged 10 to 16 years. From the Harlem data, because head injury was the predominant cause of death from gunshot, it is unlikely that prehospital care will impact on the death rate. Instead these data strongly suggest that only primary prevention through gun control will reduce child deaths.

Nationally, general hospitals with trauma centers have born the brunt of this epidemic with approximately 8% of trauma admissions attributable to gunshot as compared with less than 4% for children's hospitals.

An increase in felony drug arrests in Harlem and the South Bronx parallels the increase in gunshot injuries to children in these communities. In 1982, Barlow et al[4] and colleagues suggested that the 1973 New York State drug possession law that imposed mandatory sentences for adults offered an explanation for the recruitment of children 12 to 16 to sell drugs on the street. Knowledge of a range of risk factors for injured children is important in suggesting interventions. The present data support the hypothesis of the protective effects of a parental figure, school, and extracurricular activities, as has been suggested by other studies.[7,8] The current sample size for our case control study is small; more data are needed to confirm these initial results.

The current approach to violence in the Central Harlem community through the Harlem Hospital Injury Prevention Program includes the development of youth programs that promote safe activities and provide a safe environment.[9,10] HHIPP is addressing violence prevention in collaboration with groups such as Juvenile Justice, the Tactical Narcotic Task Force, the District Attorney's community outreach program, schools, and community-based organizations. The antiviolence program is being evaluated using the trauma registries and the NMISS, as well as case follow-up.

ACKNOWLEDGMENT

The authors thank Jamal Naqvi. Susan Weeks, Dana String, Beatrice Clanton, and Edward Eustaquio for trauma registry abstraction, and Aissatou Bey-Grecia, Theresa Thompkins. Ellen Colyer, and the staff of the Harlem Hospital Injury Prevention Program who work tirelessly to prevent injury to community children. We would also like to thank Dr Margaret Heagarty for reviewing the manuscript and for her support.

REFERENCES

1. Davidson LL, Durkin MS, O'Connor P, et al: The epidemiology of severe injuries to children in northern Manhattan: Methods and incidence rates. Paediat Perinat Epidemiol 6:153-165, 1992
2. National Institute on Disability and Rehabilitation Research, Pediatric Trauma Registry—Phase 2, 1994
3. Tepas JJ, Ramenosfsky M, Barlow B, et al: National Pediatric Trauma Registry. J Pediatr Surg 24:156-158, 1989
4. Barlow B, Niemirska M, Gandhi R, et al: Ten years experience with pediatric gunshot wounds. J Pediatr Surg 17:927-932, 1982
5. Sloan JH, Kellerman AI, Reay DT, et al: Handgun regulations, crime, assaults, and homicide: A tale of two cities. N Engl J Med 39:1256-1262, 1988
6. Cooper A, Barlow B, Davidson L, et al: Epidemiology of pediatric trauma: Importance of population based statistics. J Pediatr Surg 27:149-154, 1992
7. Davidson LL, Durkin MS, Kuhn L, et al: The impact of the safe kids/healthy neighborhoods injury prevention program in Harlem 1988-1991. Am J Public Health 84:580-586, 1994
8. Children's Defense Fund. The State of America's Children 1991, p 101; source: Search Institute, The Troubled Journey: A Portrait of 6th-12th Grade Youth, 1990
9. Laraque D, Barlow L, Davidson LL, et al: The Central Harlem Playground Injury Prevention Project A model for change. Am J Public Health 84:1691-1692, 1994
10. Laraque D, Barlow B, Durkin M, et al: Injury prevention in an urban setting: Challenges and successes. Bull N Y Acad Med (in press)

Discussion

M. Hirsch (Pittsburgh, PA): I want to thank Drs Laraque and Barlow for the opportunity to review this manuscript and applaud the efforts of Harlem Hospital Medical Center to chronicle this population-based study of 30 years of gunshot wound experience in children.

Despite the quality of these data, I think there are some dangers inherent in suppositions about the reasons for some of the fluctuation in the gunshot wound incidence.

The manuscript that you provided indicated that there was a supposition about an increase in violence related to a New York gun control law that was instituted in the early 1970s that might have pushed drug running into the hands of the pediatric population, and then the crack epidemic that you chronicle in the late 1980s as another reason for an increase in gunshot wounds was also listed as a contribution. In the injury rate that you described from the northern Manhattan project, there was also at least a supposition made that perhaps some of the violence prevention programs you mentioned might have been related to the diminution in the injury rate.

In order to make those kinds of suppositions we have to at least be sure that some of the phenomena you are describing are not just redistribution to other parts of the city. I know that some of the data from Lincoln Hospital is encouraging that it is not strictly that, but I wonder if the authors could comment on some city-wide data that does not just show that your injury prevention programs have pushed some of this violence to other parts of the city.

The other inference that you make very good use of is that gunshot wound fatality cannot really be affected by better trauma systems because most of these deaths occur before the kids ever enter the trauma systems.

Looking at some of the sociodemographic data of the gunshot wound victims in your manuscript it seems like a Herculean task when you look at all the children that might fit the profile of the kid that's likely to get shot, the child who has lost a parent or is out of school, has no employment, or is a victim of abuse. Because you are only really reporting kids who have been admitted or potentially killed, I think you are also only looking at the tip of the iceberg. There are a lot of kids out there who are at risk.

I wonder if you might comment a little bit more in detail about what combinations of prevention programs other than just gun control efforts you're using. Is this gun control, gun safety, conflict resolution, peer mediation? And what ages are you targeting for kids to get these prevention programs?

D. Laraque (response): Thank you for all your comments; you point to some important issues.

First of all, one of the advantages of using population-based data and comparing them with hospital admissions is exactly what you say, that you may falsely conclude that you have either a decrease or an increase based on your own hospital if you do not look at population-based data. Population-based injury rates reflect all gunshot injuries regardless of where the child is hospitalized. Trends can be derived and conclusions made of the effectiveness of particular interventions in a community.

Davidson and colleagues looked at the impact of the injury prevention program, Safekids/Healthy Neighborhood, a coalition of community organizations with Harlem Hospital Injury Prevention Program as the lead agency, and documented the effect of this intervention compared with a control community. The authors did show a decrease in severe injuries to children in the central Harlem community as compared to the control community; however, there was some contamination of the intervention with kids involved in our program coming from the control community. So I think there are difficult issues that we will need to track with data. The advantage of having multiple data sets, as we described, is that it allows us to control for some of these difficulties.

In terms of the profile of which kids are at risk, I think you are absolutely right. This is a preliminary study that begins to look at what some of the risk factors might be. At Harlem we are very alert to the fact that we want to look at protective factors, and not only at what places a young person at risk for gunshot injuries. We want to better understand the circumstances of those children who are not shot. We know more or less the profile of kids who are shot. We do not know the profile of the kids who in fact are dead and do not arrive at our hospitals.

In terms of your question about violence prevention, it is multifaceted. It is a complex problem, and gun control is but one possible solution. There are other examples, an elegant paper by the Seattle group has looked at Vancouver and Seattle and compared them. And certainly gun legislation has had a major impact, but it is not the only answer.

When we look at children and the profile of risk and the number of problems that they face, we believe that the better informed we are by the data, the better we can develop a community violence prevention response. Educational programs may not have an impact right away, but we have to begin to look at long-term outcomes.

R. Solenberger (San Antonio, TX): We have a very thriving trauma business at our hospital. I wrote a letter to the Academy Newsletter 2 years ago in which we targeted specifically a subset of teenagers that are dealing drugs and are armed by the drug dealers who are wallowing in money.

Now, this started out with a 16-year-old who came to our institution in shock with six entrance and exit wounds who was accompanied by his homosexual lover, his common-law 13-year-old wife, his probation officer, and just about every other type of authority.

The question that I would have is, are you willing to admit there is a subset of teenagers that really are predators? Because in your presentation it appears as though the attitude is everybody can be brought around by education.

The second thing is that in your abstract you talked about an accompanying increase in felony convictions and arrests that is quite high. Could this by any chance be a lead-in toward part of the solution; and that is, more vigorous arrests and prosecution?

In San Antonio we have been able to break the power of the gangs by actually dedicating police teams that go after them for repeat offenders. That seems to be working. Would this also be a methodology that should be approached and backed by your institutions?

D. Laraque (response): Maybe I can answer the last part first. The felony arrests have paralleled the increase, so the hypothesis here is that it is because of the drug trade that we are seeing increasing gun use, and that this results in increased gunshot injuries and increased felony drug arrests.

Our paper simply documents that a rise in gunshot injuries has paralleled the increase in drug felony arrests. Whether the intervention this suggests is more arrests for drugs, I don't know. I think that this is certainly not primary prevention. We have to look at the broader issues of drug use, drug selling, and the most appropriate interventions. Punitive interventions at the community level may not be the most effective in the final analysis.

I think your first question had to do with whether or not there is a subset of adolescents that may not be amenable to change. Yes, sure. We had 15 of our 18 deaths before hospitalization and we never reached those kids. An alternatives-to-violence program can impact only in a small way unless we begin to look at the complex problem of interpersonal/societal violence and address it with better communication, safe activities, and more opportunities for young people to stay out of trouble before they get into trouble.

[28]

Assaultive Violence in the Community:

Psychological Responses of Adolescent Victims and Their Parents

KATHY SANDERS-PHILLIPS, Ph.D.

Purpose: This article presents an overview of psychological responses to injuries due to assaultive violence, particularly gunshot wounds, in adolescents and parents.

Methods: Reviews were conducted of the psychological, medical, and public health literature to identify studies of violent injury in adolescent populations. Studies reviewed in this article include those reporting levels of gunshot and other violent injuries among pediatric patients in urban hospitals and those examining psychological responses of children and parents to violent injury and parental responses to potential death of a child.

Results: Existing literature indicates that the number of adolescent victims of assaultive violence is increasing. Adolescent victims of assaultive violence and their parents may experience significant psychological distress including school difficulties, guilt and fears of subsequent injury, and changes in risk behaviors and perceptions of life.

Conclusion: Greater awareness of the psychological repercussions of injury due to assaultive violence for adolescents and their families is needed among medical professionals. Hospital based interventions, which may include psychological support for adolescents and their parents and referrals for academic evaluation and assistance, should be developed for adolescent trauma victims and their families.

KEY WORDS:

Adolescents
Trauma
Violence prevention
Gunshot wounds

From the Department of Pediatrics, UCLA School of Medicine, Los Angeles, California 90056.

Address reprint requests to: K. Sanders-Phillips, Ph.D., Department of Pediatrics, UCLA School of Medicine, 101 North La Brea Avenue, Suite 403, Los Angeles, CA 90301.

Manuscript accepted June 23, 1997.

In 1985, the Surgeon General of the United States concluded that violence in this country is a public health problem of significant magnitude that exacts a tremendous toll on the population in terms of injuries and subsequent deaths (1). The conceptualization of violence as a public health problem, rather than primarily one of law enforcement, has focused attention on the importance of health providers in the prevention and care of victims of violence (1–4). Since the health care system is often a first place of encounter for victims of violence, it may play a critical role in addressing the psychological needs of victims and their families. While health care staff are prepared to provide medical management for victims of violence, many are unprepared to evaluate and manage the complex psychological and emotional consequences of violence for victims and their families (3). Thus, there is a need to increase awareness among medical professionals of the psychological repercussions of violence for children and their parents.

This article provides an overview of injuries owing to violence among adolescents in urban hospitals and identifies symptoms associated with violent injury among adolescent trauma victims during their hospitalization and after discharge. The primary focus is on the psychological impact of nonfatal injuries to adolescents resulting from assaultive violence in urban communities. Assaultive violence is defined as nonfatal and fatal interpersonal violence in which physical force or other means is used by one person with the intent of causing harm, injury, or death to another (5). Assaultive violence involving handguns is most common in the adolescent age group (6), and adolescents are most likely to be victimized by friends or acquaintances, most often in their neighborhood or community outside of the home (7–9). Accordingly, this article specifically examines psychological responses to injuries associated with gunshot wounds occurring as a result of community violence. Community violence is violence outside of the home, such as in the neighborhood or at school, that may be perpetrated by strangers or unrelated acquaintances (10,11). Given the disproportionate impact of violence on low-income, ethnic minority adolescents and findings that they are less likely than other groups of adolescents to receive psychological assistance after victimization (4), responses of low-income, ethnic minority children to violent injuries are emphasized in this review.

A review of literature on psychological responses of parents to injuries resulting from community violence in adolescent victims is presented in the second half of the article. Examination of parents' responses to adolescent trauma victims is important since parents' reactions to their child's injury may influence the child's psychological functioning and well-being. Therefore, the symptoms and psychological responses that can be anticipated in parents of adolescent trauma victims are discussed.

Conduct of the Literature Review

The primary purpose of the literature review was to document levels of violent injury, particularly gunshot wounds related to community violence, among pediatric populations, and identify psychological responses of adolescents and parents to these injuries. A computer-assisted literature search was conducted of the psychological, medical, and public health literature to identify studies of the incidence of childhood injuries owing to community violence and the psychological repercussions of violent injuries for adolescents and their parents. The databases searched included PsychLIT, Medline, Social Citation Index, Sociofile, and Social Work Abstracts, using adolescents, trauma, abuse, violence, and gunshots as key words. All databases were reviewed for the years 1980–1996. Although literature searches within each area were not exhaustive, studies reporting levels of gunshot and other violent injuries among pediatric patients in urban hospitals and those examining psychological responses of children and parents to violent injury as well as parental responses to potential death of a child were selected for review in this article.

Exposure to Community Violence Among Adolescents

Homicide and firearm-related injuries are the leading causes of death for adolescent males (1). Although a significant number of childhood homicides occur in the victim's home at the hands of a relative or friend (12), adolescents are more likely to be victimized outside of the home and firearms are most often involved (7–9). Current statistics indicate that the number of firearm injuries in adolescents resulting from community violence is increasing (7,13–15).

There has been a disproportionate impact of homicide and other types of community violence on low-income, ethnic minority children and neighborhoods. Homicide is a major cause of death among African-American males and females aged 15–24 years, and firearm-related homicides account for more than 80% of deaths among African-American males (16,17). Nationally, young African-American males are six times more likely to be murdered than African-American females, nine times more likely to be murdered than white males, and 26 times more likely to be murdered than white females (16). Age-adjusted rates of homicide among Latinos are approximately three to four times higher than those for white males (18,19). Foreign-born Latinos are at significantly higher risk for homicide than native-born Latinos (20).

Although more difficult to document than homicides, nonfatal injuries have been estimated to be at least 100 times more frequent than homicides (21). Statistics from the National Crime Survey (22) indicate that approximately 1.2 million crimes of violence against adolescents are not reported to law enforcement. Episodes of assaultive violence among adolescents are estimated to be approximately three times greater than indicated by arrest records (23). Studies of nonfatal injuries among adolescents in Massachusetts indicated that 1 in 60 adolescents and 1 in every 42 adolescent boys were victims of assaultive violence (24). Male adolescents are twice as likely to be victims of assaultive violence as girls, and their injuries are more serious (25,26). Like homicide, nonfatal assaultive violence is higher among low-income, ethnic minority youth. Young African-American males have higher rates of injury owing to assaultive violence than other male groups and outnumber African-American female victims three to one (25). Latino adolescent males have the second highest rates of injury owing to assaultive violence (25–27).

358 SANDERS-PHILLIPS   JOURNAL OF ADOLESCENT HEALTH Vol. 21, No. 6

The rising rates of assaultive violence are thought to be related to increasing community violence associated with street gang activities (14,28,29). Adolescent gang members tend to commit more violent crime than their non-gang counterparts and street gangs are more common among ethnic minority youth (28,30). Firearms are the weapon of choice among gang members and gang violence is more likely than not to involve victims who have no prior contacts with their assailants (14).

Violent Injuries in Urban Pediatric Populations

The high rates of injury owing to community violence are clearly evident on pediatric wards in urban hospitals. Approximately 1–3% of all adolescent victims may require medical care after an assault (24). As a result, pediatricians are increasingly treating patients who have been victims of violence. These patients frequently report previous exposure to community violence including hearing gunshots in their neighborhoods, witnessing shootings at school, and having a family member who is a victim of or involved in violence (31).

While the number of pediatric gunshot cases is increasing, ages of victims are decreasing (13,32–34). For example, in a study at one urban hospital in Los Angeles, the mean age of the 2000 patients with gunshot wounds was 19 years (13). The mean age of those 255 patients under the age of 15 years was 14.4 years, with most patients falling between the ages of 11 and 14 years. The majority were African American (83.5%), with smaller numbers of Latinos (16.1%) and others (0.4%). A total of 223 of these patients were admitted to the pediatric service. Major pathology resulting in serious morbidity, mortality or surgery was high and included the central nervous system, head, neck, chest, abdomen, and cardiovascular and musculoskeletal systems. Approximately 80% of these gunshot cases were related to gang shootings.

Several investigators have documented increasing rates of gunshot wounds and other violent injuries in pediatric populations (33–35) and concluded that the most urgent current problems in pediatrics result from behavioral factors such as violence (36). Despite evidence that injuries owing to violence are physically and psychologically debilitating for adolescents and parents, little effort has been made by most health care facilities to address the psychological and developmental sequelae of violence in pediatric populations and to assist parents of children who are victims of community violence.

Exposure to Community Violence: A Precursor to Violent Injury

Community violence may take many forms, but it generally includes homicide, rape, other types of sexual assault, aggravated assault, burglary, and robbery (10,11). Exposure to community violence is defined as frequent and continued exposure to the use of guns, knives, and drugs, and random violence (37). Although specific definitions and measures of community violence vary from one study to another, there is agreement that community violence that involves serious injury to an individual or fear of being killed can precipitate extreme psychological distress (10,11,38).

Increasing numbers of children in urban neighborhoods are exposed to high levels of community violence (36,37). In many low-income, ethnic minority communities, violence has become a stressor that is unpredictable, often occurs in public places, and affects innocent bystanders (10,11,38–41). High levels of community violence may result in perceptions of chronic danger among adults and children that affect daily social functioning (41). Danger is a judgment about one's degree of risk and recognition of liability to injury or negative consequences, and chronic danger is regular and persistent attacks of violence that disrupt day-to-day life (41). The psychological impact of living under conditions of chronic danger has been contrasted with the psychological repercussions of acute danger occurring in a normally safe community. Living under conditions of chronic danger requires significant adjustments in personality and behavior that allow for interpretation of the danger and accommodation to the realities of community life (38,40–42). Exposure to chronic danger has pervasive effects on cognitive, psychological, and behavioral processes, and affects day-to-day and long-term functioning in community adults and children (42).

Psychological Responses to Assaultive Injuries in Adolescents

In addition to exposure to high levels of violence in their neighborhoods, many adolescents become victims of community violence. Victimization is defined as harms that occur to individuals because of other human actors behaving in ways that violate social norms (8). Victimization owing to community violence has a potential for traumatic impact that is different from other stresses and trauma such as accidents, illness, bereavement, and natural disasters. Victimization involves issues of malevolence, betrayal, injustice, and morality to a much greater extent than other stressors or trauma and may involve social institutions such as police, courts, and social service agencies that are not involved in other types of trauma (8).

For adolescents, the experience of victimization may have profound effects on subsequent psychological adjustment and functioning. For example, the approximately 5% of adolescent gunshot cases with closed-head injuries may experience cognitive deficits or difficulties in learning subsequent to injury (43). Many also experience high levels of stress, impaired judgment, reduced attention span, irritability, short-term memory loss, and ongoing memory deficits during recovery. More extensive follow-up and educational intervention may be required for adolescent trauma victims with closed-head injuries than for adults, and the extent of recovery for adolescents is significantly influenced by the needs and developmental stage of the adolescent (43).

Experiences of illness and hospitalization are also stressful for adolescents and their families. Hospitalization, which involves isolation from peers, dependency on others for care, and loss of privacy, often conflicts with the adolescent's need to interact with a peer group, retain personal privacy, and feel independent (43). Illness and hospitalization during adolescence can also influence body image, self-esteem, and the relationship between the adolescent and parents (43). The adolescent trauma victim and his or her family are faced with a host of physical, psychological, social, and educational problems that may require attention and/or intervention on the part of health care staff.

Children and adolescents who have been victims of community violence may show a range of psychological symptoms including those associated with post-traumatic stress disorder (2,17,35,44–47). Diagnostic criteria for post-traumatic stress disorder include emotional and physiological hyperarousal, intrusive and frightening thoughts, feelings, and images of the trauma, and the numbing of emotional responses (8). In general, symptoms of post-traumatic stress disorder are more common among victimized girls and youth who do not have males living with them in the home (36), though all adolescent victims are at risk for development of the disorder.

The experience of victimization also commonly results in symptoms such as depression that reflect a generalized stress response (8). Since reactions may also include the betrayal of trust or sense of power-lessness and the violation of expectations of justice or fairness, feelings of anger, increased wariness or unwillingness to trust, and fearfulness of the recurrence of the event are often observed in victims of violence (8,46).

Many children who have been victims of violence report a sense of futurelessness characterized by a belief that they will not reach adulthood (19,48). These reactions may be accompanied by feelings of vulnerability, hopelessness, self-blame, and retaliation (42,49). Acting out, risk taking, and self-destructive behaviors are particularly common among adolescents who have been victims of community violence, as are high levels of passivity, emotional withdrawal, and difficulties in learning (50,51). Behaviors such as running away, attempting suicide, using illegal drugs, and increased sexual activity may be behavioral responses to victimization among adolescents (52,53). Repeated exposure to community violence may result in desensitization to the threat and consequences of violence and children may pursue opportunities for risk taking and confrontation with danger (42,49,54). Conversely, victimization during childhood may also increase the potential for future victimization or perpetration of violence by fostering a sense of helplessness or supporting conclusions that victimization is normative (8). Thus, childhood victims of violence are at greater risk of future victimization (55) and of becoming future perpetrators of violence (56,57).

Although adolescents may have more effective coping strategies than younger children for responding to the anxiety, fear, and anger related to victimization (58), they may not benefit from some of the coping mechanisms available to younger children. Adolescents may inhibit their emotions and, consequently, fail to profit from expressing their feelings regarding the victimization (8). In addition, adolescents may be more likely to mistrust or feel alienated from parents, and therefore fail to use parents as a source of support. Finally, since assumptions and perceptions regarding fairness and justice are more established for adolescents, it may be more difficult for them to adapt to the victimization by modifying their worldviews (8).

Ethnic and gender differences may exist in the degree of exposure, victimization, and psychological responses to violence (2,46). Girls are more likely to witness violence and experience depression in response to community violence, while boys are more likely to be victims and experience higher levels of distress (2,42). Black children are at higher risk than other groups of witnessing the death or murder of a relative or friend (19,20).

Impairments in cognitive functioning resulting from the physical injuries of victimization may coexist with psychological symptoms, especially characteristics of post-traumatic stress disorder and grief reactions that are also associated with victimization. Thus, it can be difficult to distinguish psychological symptoms that are related to the injury from symptoms associated with the experience of victimization, grief, or with the developmental tasks of adolescence (43,49). This is a continuing and important problem in the treatment of adolescent victims and their families since the establishing the etiology of a symptom may influence methods of treatment or remediation of the problem (43). Although post-traumatic stress disorder has been defined primarily in terms of its affective dimensions and closed-head injuries in terms of cognitive effects, similar symptoms may exist in both conditions, and symptoms of closed-head injury such as poor judgment or irritability may exacerbate psychological symptoms such as depression or affect developmental milestones such as peer relationships in adolescent trauma victims (8,43). In addition, post-traumatic stress disorder may complicate the grieving process by interfering with an adolescent's efforts to address his or her losses and adapt to subsequent life changes (49). These interactive relationships may form the basis for a matrix of psychological and cognitive symptoms that significantly influence the adaptation and recovery of adolescents and their families from the trauma of victimization (49).

Responses of Parents to Violent Injury in Their Children

Parents of children who have been victims of violence also show a range of psychological symptoms and responses. Symptoms of post-traumatic stress disorder are frequent and often accompanied by extreme fears of recurrence (59,60). Fears for their personal safety as well as the safety of other family members are pervasive (59,60). Subsequent to the injury of their child, parents must reconcile the selective nature of the assault, belief in the world as a meaningful and comprehensible place, and helplessness and frustration with their inability to protect their child (37,60,61).

Parents may also express considerable anxiety regarding their child's medical condition (43). These reactions may be followed by concern and frustra-

tion about deficits the child may experience as a result of the injury. Much of the frustration may stem from the parents' inability to alter their behavioral and/or academic expectations for their child, particularly if there have been closed-head injuries that may be associated with cognitive or behavioral deficits (43).

The parents' frustration and concern regarding limitations the child may experience subsequent to the injury are often exacerbated by guilt regarding their inability to protect their child from injury (14,59). Parental distress may be particularly high when parents blame themselves for the child's injury or conclude that their behaviors may have contributed to the child's injury (62). Conversely, parents may react to adolescent injuries by blaming the adolescent. In general, adolescents are more likely to be blamed for their own victimization than younger children (63,64). These reactions may occur because of beliefs that teenagers have more skills to avoid and resist victimization, or perceptions that adolescents voluntarily engage in risky behaviors, and because adults tend to take less responsibility for adolescents (8).

Parents must also cope with the ongoing threat of violence in their communities and the fear of repeated injury to their child. Parental adaptations to dangerous environments may result in child-rearing strategies that impede normal development. They may have difficulty in establishing a balance between circumventing community danger and encouraging adolescents to explore opportunities (43,47). As a result, they may overprotect or underprotect the adolescent, both of which may conflict with adolescent needs for independence and result in poorer adolescent outcomes (65). It is common for parents of adolescents who have been injured to place excessive restrictions on the adolescent's activities, including the choice of peers (43). Parents may also resort to the use of punitive styles of discipline, including physical assault, to protect the child from dangers in the neighborhood (47). Unfortunately, parental overprotection, underprotection, or use of punitive discipline in response to violence in the community may be related to subsequent problems such as early sexual activity and childbearing and/or increased aggression that may result in an adolescent's participation in the very gang activities that parents fear and are trying to avoid (47,65).

In summary, parents of adolescent victims of violence are faced with the challenge of reassuring and protecting their child, while coping with their own fears and trauma resulting from the child's injury (47). These stressors may decrease the extent to which the families of adolescent victims of violence may be able to provide the care and support to children both during and after hospitalization that is necessary for optimal recovery (42).

Critique of the Existing Literature

Despite increasing rates of injury owing to assaultive violence among adolescents, relatively few studies of the psychological effects of injuries on adolescents and parents have been conducted. As a result, the range of psychological effects on the adolescent and his or her parents has not been fully explored and is not completely understood.

Existing studies are limited by small sample sizes and restriction of samples to specific groups of adolescents such as those most likely to be treated in urban hospitals. The potential impacts of gender and ethnicity on adolescents' and parents' psychological responses and behaviors subsequent to injury have not been adequately examined. Given previous evidence that responses to trauma may vary by ethnicity and gender (66,67), it is important to assess the degree to which gender and ethnicity may mediate relationships between injuries owing to assaultive violence and later psychological functioning and adjustment.

There have also been no longitudinal studies of adolescents who have been victims of community violence. Consequently, we know little about possible long-term consequences of injury during adolescence. Longitudinal studies of adolescent victims may be important for several reasons. First, they may provide data regarding the importance of factors such as the timing of the injury or the circumstances of the injury on subsequent psychological functioning. For example, based on current findings, it is difficult to determine whether younger adolescents respond differently to victimization than older adolescents or whether the circumstances surrounding the injury may influence an adolescent's psychological responses.

Second, longitudinal studies may identify the extent to which subsequent psychological functioning and adjustment are affected in adolescents who have been victims of violent injury. The period of adolescence is characterized by several developmental milestones including identity formation, identification with peers, development of abstract thinking, and academic achievement (68,69,70). Unfortunately, few studies have examined the impact of injury

during adolescence on the attainment of these developmental milestones. For example, the degree to which identity formation may be influenced by injury during adolescence has not been assessed. Since early trauma, particularly physical trauma, may be related to poorer self-esteem and self-concept (71), the extent to which identity development may be affected by injury during adolescence should be explored. Similarly, influences on peer relationships, which are known to be affected by victimization (8), and cognitive skills, which are affected by both exposure to violence (50) and the nature of the injury to the adolescent (43), should be examined in future studies. The impact of victimization on the development of aggression or withdrawal, academic achievement, sexual functioning, and styles of coping with anxiety should also be assessed in future studies (8).

Both longitudinal and cross-sectional comparisons of adolescents may be needed to determine the specific psychological consequences of victimization owing to community violence versus family violence, particularly when the two types of victimization coexist. Although there have been numerous studies of the impact of intrafamilial versus extrafamilial sexual abuse of children, there have been few comparable comparisons of the impact of intrafamilial versus extrafamilial physical assault (8). The experience of adolescent victimization owing to violence outside of the home may result in different psychological sequelae than victimization in the home. The impact of victimization depends on many factors including an awareness of social norms regarding violence, the nature of peer relationships, and community and institutional (e.g., schools, police, courts, media) reactions to violence and victimization (8). Each of these factors may differ in cases of intrafamilial versus extrafamilial violence and for sexual versus physical assault. Data regarding the specific effect of assault owing to extrafamilial violence may be extremely important to our understanding of critical factors influencing development in adolescents in urban communities experiencing high levels of violence.

The potential impact of experiences of victimization on adolescent health behaviors has also not been examined despite evidence that exposure to community violence is an important predictor of health behaviors in adults and adolescents. High levels of community violence are associated with negative feelings about health among African-American and Latino community residents (72). Exposure to community violence is also related to poorer health behaviors such as higher levels of smoking and

362 SANDERS-PHILLIPS   JOURNAL OF ADOLESCENT HEALTH Vol. 21, No. 6

alcohol consumption in African-American women and Latinas, lack of a regular health care provider, and delays in seeking care (67,73,74). Exposure to violence among adolescents has been associated with greater use of illegal drugs, alcohol, and tobacco, as well as increased sexual activity and involvement in high-risk sexual behaviors (75–79). Since adolescent risk behaviors such as early sexual activity and tobacco and illegal drug use may covary and appear to be related to an underlying factor or factors (80–82), findings that exposure to violence is related to poorer health behaviors suggest that victimization may be a central factor related to adolescent risk behaviors.

Finally, there is limited understanding of the mechanisms by which exposure to violence and experiences of victimization may result in behavioral outcomes such as risk taking or aggressive behavior. Previous findings suggest that exposure to violence and victimization is associated with feelings of hopelessness, powerlessness, and alienation that precipitate a sense of despair (67). Increased risk taking and aggressive behavior in adolescent victims of violence are common responses of children to trauma (56,57) and may represent an attempt to compensate for the powerlessness and hopelessness engendered by the victimization and gain a sense of mastery over the trauma and the environment.

Summary and Recommendations for Future Research and Practice

This overview of psychological responses of adolescents and parents to violent injury in the community indicates that increasing numbers of adolescents are being victimized. Both adolescents and their parents may suffer significant psychological symptoms subsequent to the adolescent's injury. The psychological reactions of adolescents and parents may affect immediate recovery of the adolescent as well as subsequent psychological functioning in the adolescent victim.

Several issues should be addressed in future research and program development for adolescent victims of violence and their families. First, the considerable attention given to adolescent perpetrators of violence must be balanced by an equal or greater understanding of adolescent victims of violence (8).

The lack of attention to ethnic minority adolescent victims of violence is compounded by a similar lack of awareness of the cumulative impact of multiple

victimizations on development in ethnic minority children. In addition to physical injury owing to violence, ethnic minority children are at greater risk of previous exposure to violence and crime and experiences of racism and oppression (83,84). Garbarino (47) concluded that the impact of community violence on children must be understood in the larger context of domestic violence, poverty, and minority group status. The cumulative impact of victimization owing to poverty and oppression, exposure to community violence, and victimization on psychological functioning has not been examined in previous studies. The extent to which previous victimizations may precipitate or exacerbate psychological responses to subsequent victimization in ethnic minority children is not clear and should be assessed in future studies.

Childhood victimization must also be examined and understood within a developmental context (8). That is, we must begin to evaluate the effect of victimization on children and understand how the impact of victimization changes over the course of childhood and adolescence. For example, Finkelhor and Kendall-Tackett (8) suggested that the effect of childhood victimization may be mediated by four factors including the child's appraisal of the victimization and its implications, current developmental tasks, coping strategies, and available environmental buffers. In general, children at different developmental stages will appraise or interpret victimization differently, different developmental tasks will be affected, different coping strategies will be used, and different family and social contexts will have an impact on the effects of the victimization. For example, one could hypothesize that victimization during adolescence is most likely to be interpreted relative to the adolescent's self-concept or self-esteem, the developmental milestone of identity formation may be affected, coping strategies might include potentially hazardous and unhealthy behaviors such illegal drug use and increased sexual activity, and family support may not be readily sought or available (8). These factors may affect the adolescent's immediate responses to the victimization, which in turn may influence adult development and functioning (70). Our knowledge of the developmental needs and importance of the adolescent period and its relationship to adult development, in conjunction with the increased vulnerability of adolescents to victimization, should foster concern regarding both the short- and long-term impact of victimization during adolescence.

Finally, few attempts have been made to develop

hospital-based intervention programs for adolescent trauma victims and their families. In addition, several investigators and public health officials have expressed concern regarding the lack of training for medical staff in violence prevention and intervention (36,85). As Murray-Garcia (36) noted, the training of physicians and other medical staff in appropriate intervention with victims of violence may be particularly important in hospitals serving predominantly low-income, ethnic minority populations of children and adolescents. For these groups, violence prevention and the alleviation of psychological distress subsequent to injury should be critical components of patient care.

In summary, rates of violent injury owing to community violence in pediatric populations have prompted considerable interest in the role of medical professionals in violence prevention and intervention and in educating medical staff in the psychological repercussions of violent injury for adolescents and their parents. Our growing understanding of the psychological needs and challenges faced by adolescent victims of violence and their parents reinforces the conclusion that health professionals must be more aware of the psychological impact of victimization on adolescents, and hospital-based programs providing psychological support should be developed for adolescent victims and their families.

References

1. Report of the Secretary's Task Force on Black and Minority Health. Homicide, Suicide and Unintentional Injuries, Vol 5. U.S. Department of Health and Human Services, August, 1985.

2. Satcher D. Violence as a public health issue. Bull NY Acad Med 1995;72:46–56.

3. Sayre JW. Gunshot violence in the United States: A growing threat to all. A physician's personal view. Bull NY Acad Med 1995;72:31–45.

4. Gladstein J, Rusonis EJ, Heald FP. A comparison of inner-city and upper-middle class youths' exposure to violence. J Adolesc Health 1992;13:275–80.

5. Rosenberg M, Mercy J. Assaultive violence. In: Rosenberg M, Mercy J, eds. Violence in America: A public health approach. New York: Oxford University Press, 1991:14–50.

6. Rodriquez J. Childhood injuries in the United States. Am J Dis Child 1990;144:627–46.

7. Messner SF, Tardiff K. The social ecology of urban violence: An application of the "routine activities" approach. Criminology 1985;23:241–67.

8. Finkelhor D, Kendall-Tackett K. A developmental perspective on the childhood impact of crime, abuse and violent victimization. In: Cicchetti D, Toth S, eds. The Effects of Trauma on the Developmental Process (in press).

9. Finkelhor D, Dziuba-Leatherman J. Victimization of children. Am Psychol 1994;49:173–83.

10. Resnick H, Falsetti S, Kilpatrick D, Freedy J. Assessment of rape and other civilian trauma-related post-traumatic stress disorder: Emphasis on assessment of potentially traumatic events. In: Miller TW, ed. Theory and Assessment of Stressful Life Events. Madison, CT: International Universities Press, 1996:235–71.

11. Resnick H, Kilpatrick D, Dansky B, Saunders B, Best C. Prevalence of civilian trauma and posttraumatic stress disorder in a representative national sample of women. J Consult Clin Psychol 1993;61:984–91.

12. Mercy J, Goodman R, Rosenberg M, et al. Patterns of homicide victimization in the city of Los Angeles, 1970–79. Bull NY Acad Med 1986;62:427–45.

13. Ordog GJ, Prakash A, Wasserberger J, et al. Pediatric gunshot wounds. J Trauma 1987;27:1272–8.

14. Klein MW, Maxon CL. Street gang violence. In: Weiner NA, Wolfgang ME, eds. Violent Crime, Violent Criminals. Newbury Park: Sage, 1989:198–237.

15. Maxson CL, Gordon MA, Klein MW. Differences between gang and non gang homicides. Criminology 1985;23:209–22.

16. Centers for Disease Control. Homicide among black males—United States, 1978–1987. MMWR 1990;39:869–73.

17. Hammond WR, Yung B. Psychology's role in the public health response to assaultive violence among young African-American men. Am Psychol 1993;48:142–54.

18. Smith J, Mercy J, Rosenberg M. Suicide and homicide among Hispanics in the Southwest. Pub Health Rep 1986;101:265–70.

19. Tardiff K, Gross E. Homicide in New York City. Bull NY Acad Med 1986;62:413–26.

20. Sorenson S, Shen H. Homicide risk among immigrants in California, 1970 through 1992. Am J Public Health 1996;86:97–100.

21. O'Carroll PW. Homicides among black males 15–24 years of age, 1970–1984. MMWR 1988;37:53–60.

22. Christofel KK. Violent death and injury in U.S. children and adolescents. Am J Dis Child 1990;144:697–706.

23. U.S. Department of Justice. Criminal victimization, 1990. (Special report no. NCJ-122743). Washington, DC: Bureau of Justice Statistics, 1991.

24. Elliot D, Huizinga D, Morse B. Self-reported violent offending: A descriptive analysis of juvenile violent offenders and their offending careers. J Interpersonal Violence 1986;1:472–513.

25. Guyer B, Lescohier I, Gallagher SS, et al. Intentional injuries among children and adolescents in Massachusetts. New Engl J Med 1989;321:1564–89.

26. Harlow C. Female victims of violent crime (Bureau of Justice Statistics, Special report no. NCJ-126826). Washington, DC: U.S. Department of Health and Human Services, 1991.

27. Sumner B, Mintz E, Brown P. Interviewing persons hospitalized with interpersonal violence-related injuries: A pilot study. In: Report of the Secretary's Task Force on Black and Minority Health. Vol. 5. Washington, DC: U.S. Department of Health and Human Services, 1986:267–311.

28. Klein MW. Street gang cycles. In: Wilson JQ, Petersilia J, eds. Crime. San Francisco: ICS Press, 1995:217–36.

29. Felkenes GT, Becker HK. Female gang members: A growing issue for policy makers. J Gang Res 1995;2:1–10.

30. Block CR. Specification of patterns over time in Chicago homicides: Increases and decreases, 1965–1981. Chicago, IL: Criminal Justice Information Authority, 1985.

31. Groves BM, Zuckerman B, Marans S, et al. Silent victims: Children who witness violence. JAMA 1993;269:262–4.

32. Ordog GJ, Wasserberger J, Schatz I, et al. Gunshot wounds in children under 10 years of age: A new epidemic. Am J Dis Child 1988;142:618–22.

364 SANDERS-PHILLIPS   JOURNAL OF ADOLESCENT HEALTH Vol. 21, No. 6

33. Rivara FP, Stapleton FB. Handguns and children: A dangerous mix. Dev Behav Pediatr 1982;3:35–8.

34. Paulson JA, Rushford NB. Violent death in children in a metropolitan county: Changing patterns of homicide, 1958 to 1982. Pediatrics 1986;78:1013–20.

35. Chatman L, Billups M, Bell C, et al. Injury: A new perspective on an old problem. J Nat Med Assoc 1991;83:43–8.

36. Murray-Garcia J. African-American youth: Essential prevention strategies for every pediatrician. Pediatrics 1995;96:132–7.

37. Osofsky J. The effects of exposure to violence on young children. Am Psychol 1995;50:782–8.

38. Sonnenberg S. Victims of violence and post-traumatic stress disorder. Psychiatr Clin North Am 1988;11:581–90.

39. Bell CC, Jenkins EJ. Traumatic stress and children. J Health Care Poor Underserved 1991;2:175–88.

40. Sluzki C. Toward a model of family and political victimization: Implications for treatment and recovery. Psychiatry 1993;56:178–87.

41. Garbarino J, Kostelny K, Dubrow N. What children can tell us about living in danger. Am Psychol 1991;46:376–83.

42. Lorion RP, Salzman W. Children's exposure to community violence: Following a path from concern to research to action. Psychiatry 1993;56:55–65.

43. Jacobson M, Rubenstein E, Bohannon W, et al. Follow-up of adolescent trauma victims: A new model of care. Pediatrics 1986;77:236–41.

44. Singer MI, Anglin TM, Song L, et al. Adolescents' exposure to violence and associated symptoms of psychological trauma. JAMA 1996;273:477–82.

45. Davidson J, Smith R. Traumatic experiences in psychiatric outpatients. J Traumatic Stress 1990;3:459–75.

46. Fitzpatrick KM, Boldizar JP. The prevalence and consequences of exposure to violence among African American youth. J Am Acad Child Adolesc Psychiatry 1993;32:424–30.

47. Garbarino J. Children's responses to community violence: What do we know? Infant Mental Health J 1993;14:103–15.

48. Hughes H. Psychological and behavioral correlates of family violence in child witnesses and victims. Am J Orthopsychiatry 1988;58:77–90.

49. Pynoos RS, Steinberg AM, Goenjian A. Traumatic stress in childhood and adolescence: Recent developments and current controversies. In: van der Kolk BA, McFarlane AC, Weisaeth L, eds. Traumatic Stress: The Effects of Overwhelming Experience on Mind, Body, and Society. New York: Guilford Press, 1996:331–58.

50. Gardner GE. Aggression and violence—the enemies of precision learning in children. Am J Psychiatry 1971;128:77–82.

51. Barker RG. Habitats, Environments, and Human Behavior. San Francisco: Jossey-Bass, 1978.

52. Kendall-Tackett KA, Williams LM, Finkelhor D. Impact of sexual abuse on children: A review and synthesis of recent empirical studies. Psychol Bull 1993;113:164–80.

53. Mowbray CT. Post-traumatic therapy for children who are victims of violence. In: Ochberg FM, ed. Post-Traumatic Therapy and Victims of Violence. New York: Brunner/Mazel, 1988:196–212.

54. Garbarino J, Kostelny K, Dubrow N. What children can tell us about living in danger. Am Psychol 1991;46:376–83.

55. Russell DEH. Sexual Exploitation: Rape, Child Sexual Abuse, and Workplace Harassment. Beverly Hills: Sage, 1984.

56. Paperny D, Deisher R. Maltreatment of adolescents: The relationship to a predisposition toward violent behavior and delinquency. Adolescence 1983;18:499–506.

57. Rivera B, Widom C. Childhood victimization and violent offending. Violence Victims 1990;5:19–35.

58. Pynoos RS, Steinberg AM, Wraith R. A developmental model of childhood traumatic stress. In: Cichetti D, Cohen D, eds. Manual of Developmental Psychopathology, Vol. 2: Risk, Disorder, and Adaptation. New York: John Wiley, 1995:72–95.

59. Rinear E. Psychological aspects of parental response patterns to the death of a child by homicide. J Trauma Stress 1988;1:305–22.

60. Janoff-Bulman R. The aftermath of victimization: Rebuilding shattered assumptions. In: Figley C, ed. Trauma and Its Wake: The Study and Treatment of Post-traumatic Stress Disorder. New York: Brunner/Mazel, 1985:15–35.

61. Orbach CE. The multiple meaning of the loss of a child. Am J Psychotherapy 1977;13:906–15.

62. Downey G, Silver R, Wortman CB. Reconsidering the attribution-adjustment relation following a major negative event: Coping with the loss of a child. J Personal Soc Psychol 1990;59:925–40.

63. Isquith PK, Levine M, Scheiner J. Blaming the child: Attribution of responsibility to victims of child sexual abuse. In: Goodman GS, Bottoms BL, eds. Child victims, Child Witnesses: Understanding and Improving Testimony. New York: Guilford Press, 1993:203–28.

64. Nightingale NN. Juror reactions to child victim witnesses. Law Hum Behav 1993;17:679–94.

65. Henley J. The significance of social context: The case of adolescent childbearing in the African American community. J Black Psychol 1993;19:461–77.

66. Sanders-Phillips K, Moisan P, Wadlington S, et al. Ethnic differences in psychological functioning among black and Latino sexually abused girls. Child Abuse Neglect 1995;19:691–706.

67. Sanders-Phillips K. The ecology of urban violence: Its relationship to health promotion behaviors in low income black and Latino communities. Am J Health Promot 1996;10:308–17.

68. Piaget J. Intellectual evolution from adolescence to adulthood. Hum Dev 1972;15;1–12.

69. Erikson EH. Childhood and Society. New York: Norton, 1950.

70. Seidman E. Growing up the hard way: Pathways of urban adolescents. Am J Commun Psychol 1991;19:173–205.

71. McCann L, Sakheim DK, Abrahamson DJ. Trauma and victimization: A model of psychological adaptation. Counsel Psychol 1988;16:531–94.

72. Cohen P, Struening E, Muhlin G, et al. Community stressors, mediating conditions and well-being in urban neighborhoods. J Commun Psychol 1982;10:377–91.

73. Sanders-Phillips K. Correlates of health promotion behaviors in low-income, black women and Latinas. Am J Prevent Med 1996;12:450–8.

74. Rask KJ, Williams MV, Parker RM, et al. Obstacles predicting lack of a regular provider and delays in seeking care for patients at an urban public hospital. JAMA 1994;271:1931–3.

75. Amaro H, Russo N, Johnson J. Family and work predictors of psychological well-being among Hispanic women professionals. Psychol Women Q 1987;11:505–21.

76. Joshi N, Scott M. Drug use, depression, and adolescents. Pediatr Clin North Am 1988;35:1349–64.

77. Berenson A, San Miguel V, Wilkinson G. Violence and its relationship to substance use in adolescent pregnancy. J Adolesc Health 1992;13:470–4.

78. Orpinas P, Basen-Engquist K, Grunbaum J, et al. The co-morbidity of violence-related behaviors with health-risk be-

haviors in a population of high school students. J Adolesc Health 1995;16:216–225.

79. Lemp G, Hirozawa A, Givertz D, et al. Seroprevalence of HIV and risk behaviors among young homosexual and bisexual men: The San Francisco Berkeley young men's survey. JAMA 1994;272:449–54.

80. Jessor R. Risk behavior in adolescence: A psychosocial framework for understanding and action. J Adolesc Health 1991;12: 597–605.

81. Sussman S, Dent C, Stacy A, et al. Psychological predictors of health risk factors in adolescents. J Pediatr Psychol 1995;20: 91–108.

82. Donovan J, Jessor R. Structure of problem behavior in adolescence and young adulthood. J Consult Clin Psychol 1985;53: 890–904.

83. Wyatt GE. Sexual abuse of ethnic minority children. Identifying dimensions of victimization. Profess Psychol Res Practice 1990;21:338–43.

84. Shakoor BH, Chalmers D. Co-victimization of African American children who witness violence: Effects on cognitive, emotional, and behavioral development. J Nat Med Assoc 1991;83:233–8.

[29]

Gunshot injuries to the extremities: experience of a U.K. trauma centre

I.J. Persad*, R. Srinivas Reddy, M.A. Saunders, J. Patel

Kings College Hospital, Denmark Hill, London, U.K.

Accepted 9 August 2004

KEYWORDS
Gunshot injuries;
Extremities;
Limb injuries

Summary

Background: The Metropolitan Police figures suggest an increase in the incidence of injuries related to gun crime. We conducted a retrospective analysis of extremity gunshot injuries over a five-year period. Our aim is to report on our (1) incidence, (2) complications and (3) experience in treating these injuries.
Methods: Over a five-year period (1998—2002), 70 extremity gunshot injuries in 61 patients were identified from a trauma register and case notes reviewed retrospectively. The following were identified and analysed: type of injury (low or high-energy transfer), treatment (early/late), complications, patient demographics and compliance.
Results: There was a four-fold increase in incidence. Our incidence correlated well with The Metropolitan Police figures ($r = 0.93$). One-third of our injuries were managed non-operatively and on an outpatient basis. Complications were as follows: eight wound infections, one fracture non-union, one compartment syndrome, one vascular injury and five nerve injuries. Compliance was excellent for high-energy transfer injuries.
Conclusion: Extremity gunshot injuries are on an increase in the United Kingdom highlighting the need for trauma surgeons' knowledge of the management of these injuries. Complications can be reduced to a minimum if the basic principles of management are strictly adhered to.

Introduction

Gunshot injuries have become increasingly common in most countries particularly the United States of America.[5] In the United Kingdom there has been an approximately 30% increase in firearm associated crime over the period 1998—2002 as reported by the

* Corresponding author. Present address: Ian J. Persad, 14 Jephson Street, London SE58SZ, U.K. Tel.: +07748777689.
E-mail address: ian_persad@hotmail.com (I.J. Persad).

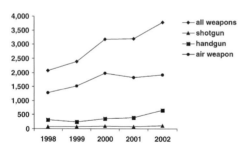

Scheme 1 Crimes reported in England and Wales, in which firearms were reported to have caused injury by type of principal weapon Source: Metropolitan Police Performance Information Bureau.

Metropolitan Police (Scheme 1). Firearm crimes and associated injuries are given liberal media coverage in the U.K. leading to the perception of an increase in the incidence of cases of firearm injuries an orthopaedic surgeon might see. Numerous papers are found in the literature concentrating on gunshot injuries to the extremities but almost all of these originate in the U.S.A.[1,2,4,6,7,9]

The complications associated with these injuries tend to be related to the degree of energy transfer[3] and include wound infection, neurovascular injury, compartment syndrome, delayed union and non-union of fractures.

In the U.S.A. gunshot-related injuries are the leading cause of death in male African-American teenagers.[1] In the United Kingdom it is a commonly held preconception that these injuries tend to predominate among the Afro-Caribbean population and that the management of these patients is challenging due to non-compliance to treatment.

Our aim is to report on (i) the yearly incidence of gunshot injuries to the extremity over a five-year period, (ii) complications seen using a basic treatment algorithm, and (iii) our experience in treating the victims of gunshot injuries to the extremity from a U.K. centre treating a multicultural urban population in South East London.

Patients and methods

Patients presenting with extremity gunshot wounds to our hospital were routinely referred for an orthopaedic assessment by the Accident and Emergency department. Over a five-year period (1998–2002) all cases of extremity gunshot wounds were identified from an orthopaedic trauma register and case notes were reviewed retrospectively.

The yearly incidence of gunshot injuries was correlated with Metropolitan Police figures.

To identify the type of injury and associated complications, the following data were analysed: type of weapon, victim-assailant distance, wound location, early/late treatment, antibiotic administration and associated complications. The injuries were divided into high- and low-energy transfer based on a combination of history, clinical assessment of the wound and X-ray findings.

To determine the patient demographics and patients' compliance to treatment, the age, cultural type, sex distribution of the victims and non-attendance at clinic follow-up were recorded.

The majority of cases were seen within six hours of the injury and tetanus toxoid was administered if the patient was unsure or had not received a booster over the last 10 years. Antibiotics were administered to all patients.

Management for low-energy transfer wounds involved minimal wound excision and cleansing. Associated fractures were managed as if they were closed injuries[6]. In general, high-energy wounds were surgically explored; skin edges and wound track were excised. Necrotic soft tissues were debrided[10] and associated fractures managed as if they were open with external fixation being the mainstay of fracture stabilisation. Surgical exploration was performed for wounds with associated neurovascular injuries.

Follow-up time in out patient clinics ranged from 7 to 105 days (mean = 22 days) for low-energy transfer injuries. High-energy transfer follow-up times ranged from 16 to 584 days (mean = 86 days).

Results

A total of 70 gunshot wounds in 61 patients were seen during the five-year period. Sex distribution was 49 male and 12 female patients. The ages of the patients ranged from 9 to 45 years (mean 26.7; S.D. 7.5).

The ethnic distribution of the victims is shown in Scheme 2a. This is compared to the distribution of our age-matched catchment population (Scheme 2b).

Of the 61 cases the victim—assailant distance was recorded in 46 cases and of these no wounds were inflicted from more than 20 feet and the majority (28 cases) were less than 10 feet.

There was an approximately four-fold increase in incidence of reported cases over the last 2 years as compared to the first 2 years (Scheme 3). There was good correlation ($r = 0.93$) with our recorded incidence (Scheme 3) and the metropolitan police

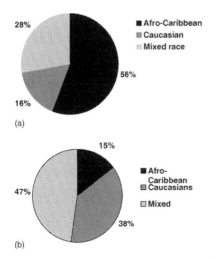

(a)

(b)

Scheme 2 (a) Ethnic distribution of gunshot victims. (b) Distribution of age matched 'catchment' population (distribution of catchment population that is of similar age distribution as our victims) Source: Business Intelligence Unit, Kings College Hospital.

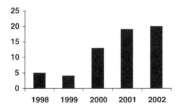

Scheme 3 Yearly distribution of gunshot injuries (excluding cases involving head, neck and torso).

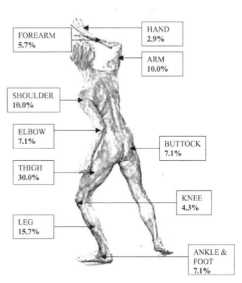

Figure 1 Anatomic locations of 70 gunshot wounds (excluding cases involving head, neck and torso).

reported incidence if all weapons were considered (Scheme 1).

There were 65 (92.9%) low-energy transfer injuries and 5 (7.1%) high-energy transfer injuries.

The anatomic distribution of the 70 gunshot injuries is shown on (Fig. 1)

Twenty-three of the 70 (33%) wounds were managed non-operatively (21 low-energy and 2 high-energy transfer), where the wound was simply cleaned and dressed in the Accident and Emergency department. These wounds were not associated with fractures. One of these, high-energy injuries developed a superficial wound infection which settled with conservative treatment (intravenous antibiotics). The other 22 cases had an uneventful outcome with no complications. The results are summarised in Table 1.

Five of the patients with low-energy transfer fractures had extensive soft tissue injuries and had wound debridement and external fixation (two forearm fractures, one tibial fracture and two femoral fractures). One comminuted femoral fracture initially treated by external fixation did not unite after four months and was subsequently treated with open reduction and internal fixation (ORIF) and bone grafting. There was one reported pin site infection and all of these fractures eventually united.

Two patients, one with a distal humeral fracture (low-energy transfer) and one with a proximal femoral fracture (high-energy transfer), had open reduction and internal fixation of their fractures. The proximal femur fracture was caused by a shotgun and developed a wound infection after initial wound debridement. ORIF was performed after the wound infection settled and both patients had an uncomplicated post-operative period.

Of all 70 wounds the missile was removed in 14 cases only. All of the wound infections (5/56) were superficial and settled with antibiotic treatment.

Three out of the five high-energy transfer wounds developed infection. One of these was treated by wound excision and cleansing under local anaesthetic in the Accident and Emergency department.

Five cases of nerve injury were seen, all in low-energy transfer injuries, one involving complete division of the posterior tibial nerve and one radial

Table 1 Summary of results

	Low energy	High energy
Number of injuries	65 (92.9%)	5 (7.1%)
Oral antibiotics	28.6%	0%
Intravenous antibiotics	71.4%	100%
Associated fracture	19 (33.9%)	2 (40%)
Cleaned and dressed in A&E	21 (32.3%)	2 (40%)
Wound debridement	44 (67.7%)	3 (60%)
ORIF	4 (21.1% of fractures)	1 (50% of fractures)
EX.-FIX	4 (21.1% of fractures)	1 (50% of fractures)
Plaster of paris only	9 (47.4% of fractures)	0 (0% of fractures)
Compliance to treatment	93%	100%

nerve injury both requiring nerve grafting. The others were neurapraxias and made full functional recovery.

There was one arterial injury associated with a femoral fracture (low-energy transfer), which required vascular grafting. Only one case of compartment syndrome was seen, again associated with a femoral fracture and due to a low-energy transfer injury.

Intra-articular involvement was seen in only one case where a bullet (low-energy) was lodged within the knee joint. This was treated by arthroscopic removal of the bullet and joint debridement and lavage.

One of the patients with a shotgun injury and proximal humerus fracture developed avascular necrosis of the humeral head and is presently awaiting an elective shoulder hemi-arthroplasty.

Follow-up at out patient clinics was excellent for patients sustaining high-energy transfer injuries and none of these cases were lost to follow-up. Of our 56 patients with low-energy transfer injuries one patient self-discharged and did not return and two were lost to follow-up (93% attendance at out patient clinics for low-energy injuries).

Discussion

The incidence of gunshot injuries and gun related crime appears to be increasing in the United Kingdom. This is the perception given by the media, "Police fear they are losing control of gun-crazy Britain"-The Observer-5th Oct. 03. These gun-crime-related headlines are not unusual in our daily newspapers at present. In addition, gunshot injuries are being reported in areas where this was previously unheard of, e.g., Nottingham.

We have seen a nearly four-fold increase in the incidence over the last 2 years. Our incidence (Scheme 3) correlates well with the police-reported figures (Scheme 1) if all weapons were considered (correlation coefficient = 0.93). While the police reported an 80% nationwide increase in incidence, we have seen an approximately 200% increase in incidence over five years locally.

The ethnic distribution of our victims was significantly different from the distribution of our catchment population (Scheme 2a and b). This could be due to the fact that our catchment population was only age matched. We were unable to match our victims to a similar employment status or social class population.

Low-energy transfer injuries generally predominate in civilian practice [2], and we have found the same with 88% of our injuries being low-energy. In a similar study by Billings et al.[2] in the U.S.A., 44 civilian gunshot injuries were reported, of which 9 cases were high-energy transfer. It is quite likely that the Americans see relatively more civilian high-energy transfer injuries because of easier availability of firearms.[8]

Based on experience in the U.S.A. these injuries can be managed on an outpatient basis provided there is no associated fracture or neurovascular injury.[7] One-third of our low-energy transfer injuries were managed as outpatients (Table 1) with no complications. Although antibiotic prophylaxis is not recommended in this group of patients,[9] all of our patients with low-energy injuries that were managed conservatively were started on oral antibiotics. We recognise that this may represent over treatment on our part.

Our complication rate in general was relatively low in comparison to similar American studies[2,11] with only five nerve injuries, one vascular injury and one compartment syndrome. Previously reported civilian studies[2,11] did not separate their complications into those due to high-and low-energy transfer as we have done. It is possible that higher complication rate may be due to relatively greater numbers of high-energy transfer injuries in those series[2,11] (Table 2).

Table 2 Complications over 5 years

	Low energy (n = 65)	High energy (n = 5)
Wound infection	5 (8.9%)	3 (60%)
Comp. syndrome	1 (1.8%)	0 (0%)
Nerve injury	5 (8.9%)	0 (0%)
Vascular injury	1 (1.8%)	0 (0%)
Non-union	1 (1.8%)	0 (0%)
Avascular necrosis	0 (0%)	1 (1.8%)

Our infection rate in general was very high. An infection rate of less than 4% has been reported for low-energy transfer injuries. Our rate of 8.9% for low-energy transfer injuries and 60% for high-energy transfer injuries despite routine antibiotic administration reflects a need for greater attention to wound care. Three out of five of our high-energy transfer injuries were complicated by infections. One of these cases was managed non-operatively and deserves particular attention. This foot injury was caused by a shotgun with multiple pellets seen on radiographs and was managed non-operatively and subsequently developed a superficial infection. In retrospect and in keeping with the general principles of management of high-energy injuries[2], this wound should have been explored and debrided on admission.

External fixation was our method of fracture fixation in 50% of operatively treated fractures. This management appears to be satisfactory as the vast majority of our low-energy transfer fractures united. There was one non-union with avascular necrosis of the humeral head. This was due to a shotgun wound to the shoulder at close range with radiographs on admission showing almost complete destruction of the humeral head. Compliance with treatment is usually poor[2,11] in reported reviews of gunshot injuries. We have found that contrary to popular belief compliance was excellent in our series. It may be that these patients are more amenable to treatment requiring patient compliance than was previously thought.

Conclusion

Based on our experience, we have shown that:
(1) The incidence of gunshot injuries is on the increase in the United Kingdom.
(2) The complications associated with these injuries can be reduced to a minimum if the basic principles of management are strictly adhered to.

References

1. Bartlett CS, Helfet DI, Hausman MR, Strauss E. Ballistics of gunshot wounds: effects on musculoskeletal tissues. J Am Acad Orthop Surg 2000;8(1):21–36.
2. Billings JB, Zimmerman MC, Aurori B, et al. Gunshot wounds to the extremities. Experience of a level 1 trauma centre. Orthop Review 1991;20(6):519–24.
3. Bowyer GW, Rossiter ND. Management of gunshot wounds of the limbs. J Bone Joint Surg Br 1997;79B(6):1031–6.
4. Deitch EA, Grimes WR. Experience with 112 shotgun wounds of the extremities. J Trauma 1984;24(7):600–3.
5. Hull JB. Management of Gunshot Fractures of the Extremities. J Trauma 1996;40(3 Suppl.):S193–7.
6. Marcus NA, Blair WF, Shuck JM, Omer Jr GE. Low-velocity gunshot wounds to extremities. J Trauma 1980;20(12):1061–4.
7. Ordog GJ, Wasserberger J, Balasubramanium S, Shoemaker W. Civilian gunshot wounds-outpatient management. J Trauma 1994;36(1):106–11.
8. Simpson BM, Grant RE. A synopsis of urban firearm ballistics: Washington, DC model. Clin Orthop 2003;408:12–6.
9. Simpson BM, Wilson RH, Grant RE. Antibiotic therapy in gunshot wound injuries. Clin Orthop 2000;408:82–5.
10. Stewart MP, Kinninmonth A. Shotgun wounds of the limbs. Injury 1993;24(10):667–70.
11. Tikka S, Bostman O, Marttinen E, Makitie I. A retrospective analysis of 36 civilian gunshot fractures. J Trauma 1996;40(Suppl. 3):S212–6.

Name Index

Abelson, Robert 52
Adams, Bonnie 371
Adams, Joseph M. 163
Adler, F. 425, 426
Adler, Patricia A. 134
Agar, Michael H. 161,
Ageton, Suzanne S. 188
Akers, Ronald L. 160, 405
Alarid, L.F. 427 passim, 433 passim
Alario, A.J. 98
Aldrich, John H. 416
Alex, N. 239
Allan, E. 426
Allen, J. xvi
Alwin, D.F. 395
Ander, R. 112
Anderson, Elijah xviii, xx, 5, 7, 23, 51, 52, 166,
        175, 189, 269, 272 passim, 370, 371, 372,
        381, 385, 386, 390, 401, 441 passim, 445,
        451
Andrade, Xavier 137
Annest, J 112
Anselin, Luc 377, 378
Archer, J. 254
Armstrong, B. 85
Arthur, J.A. 401
Atkinson, A.B. 394
Atkinson, Paul 138
Augustine, Michelle Campbell 438, 443, 444,
        445
Austin, C. 255
Austin, Harland 412
Austin, J. 272, 479
Ayres, M. 217

Bailey, Kenneth B. 139
Baily, W.C. 393
Baker, J. 113
Baldwin, D. 250
Ball, John C. 163
Ball, R.A. 38
Baller, Robert D. 377, 378
Barker, P. 215

Barlow, Barbara 517–21
Baron, Stephen 175, 177, 272, 279
Bartusch, Dawn Jeglum 87, 371, 376, 377
Baskin, Deborah R. 189, 427 passim
Baumeister, Roy 13
Baumer, Eric 438, 439, 443, 444, 447, 474
Baxi, H.R.S. 346
Bayatpour, M. 98
Beck, A. 217
Becker, Howard S. xxi, 160
Beckett, Katherine 438, 441, 442
Belknap, J. 426 passim
Bellesiles, M.A. xv
Bencivengo, M. 438
Bennett, Trevor xx, 177, 215–30
Bennett, W.J. 479
Benoit, M. 98
Berger, Peter 7
Bergstein, J. 112
Berk, Richard A. 163
Berkowitz, Leonard 319, 341, 406
Bernard, Thomas J. 405
Best, K.M. 99, 107
Biden, J. 474
Biernacki, Patrick 190
Birkbeck, C. 113, 114, 127
Bishop, V. 98, 106
Bjerregaard, Beth 5, 8, 33, 35, 111, 112, 113,
        125, 417
Black, Donald 371, 390, 439, 444, 459
Blake, A. 254
Blau, J. 279, 280, 393, 394, 401
Blau, P.M. 279, 280, 393, 394, 401
Block, C.R. xvi, 34, 35, 36, 39, 112, 418
Block, Richard xvi, 112, 317, 323, 418
Blumer, Herbert 46–7
Blumstein, Alfred xv, 5, 20, 34, 85, 112, 269,
        270, 347 passim, 357, 358, 361, 362, 437
        passim, 438, 439, 440 passim, 443, 445,
        451, 463, 469, 470, 474, 475, 476, 481,
Boland, Barbara 283
Bordua, David J. 409, 410
Bottoms, Anthony 160

Bourdieu, Pierre 169
Bowker, Lee xxii, 5
Boyen, M. 113, 120
Braga, Anthony xvi, 12, 27, 33, 34, 35, 36, 39, 85, 86, 113
Braithwaite, John 186, 401
Brame, R. 89
Bray, Timothy M. 34, 35, 41, 376
Brearly, H.C. 409
Brehm, J. 401
Brennan, P. 279
Brewer, V. 113
Briar, Scott 174
Brill, S. 113. 409
Broidy, L. 426
Brookman, F. 216
Brown, J.D. 272
Brown, William 28
Brownfield, B. 271
Brownstein, H.H. 346, 348, 349, 350–53 *passim*, 360
Bruce, Marino A. 369, 370, 372
Brunson, Rod 5
Bryk, Anthony S. 450
Buka, S.L. 86
Bullington, Bruce 137
Bullock, K. 218
Bunch, B.J. 427
Bursik, R. 37, 272
Burton, V.S. 427 *passim*
Buss, Arnold H. 319
Butterfield, F. 475
Butts, J.A. 85
Bynum, T.S. 347
Bynum, Timothy S. 85–95, 345–68

Cadenhead, Chris 97–110
Cairns, R. 113
Caldwell, A. xvi, 35, 85, 94
Callahan, Charles M. 98, 113, 416
Callero, Peter 8
Cameron, A. 91
Campbell, Anne 187, 188
Cancino, J.M. 348, 363
Capaldi, D.M. 93
Carpenter, Cheryl 161, 191
Carter, T.J. 98
Caruso, R. 112
Casciani, D. 215
Casey, John J. 136, 137
Caspi, A. 87, 88
Cavaiola, A.A. 98

Centerwall, B.S. 98
Cernkovich, S.A. 429
Chaiken, Jan M. 163
Chaiken, Marcia R. 163
Chalmers, D. 98
Chambliss, William J. 160
Champion, H.E. 85, 86
Chermak, S. 364
Cherry, D 112
Chesney-Lind, Meda 186, 187, 189
Chilton, Roland 445, 470
Chin, Ko-Lin xvi, 133, 348, 350
Cladis, Franklyn 517–21
Clarke, Ronald V. 160, 272, 319
Clear, Todd R. 460
Clemmer, D. 272
Cloward, Richard A. xvii, 41, 160, 279
Cohen, Albert K. 160
Cohen, Dov 372, 385
Cohen, J. xvi, 34, 35, 85, 86, 269, 270, 358, 444, 475
Cohen, Lawrence E. xvi, 271, 320, 376, 470
Cohen, P. 86
Cohen, R.L. 479
Colbus, D. 102
Cole, T 112, 124
Coleman, J.S. 394
Collins, Randall 439
Colvin, Mark 160
Conklin, John 163, 269, 270, 271
Conly, C. 33
Cook, Philip J. xv, xxi, 41, 85, 86, 87, 111, 112, 318, 322, 393, 395, 402, 408, 409, 410, 418, 469, 472, 476
Cooney, Mark 388, 439
Cork, D. 35, 357, 358, 443, 460, 475
Cork, P. 112
Cornish, Derek B. 160, 272, 319
Corynyn, John 135
Cothern, L. 126
Covey, Herbert C. 133
Crawford, Elizabeth M. 188, 189, 428, 429
Cressey, Donald R. xviii, 98, 106, 160, 161
Cronin, J. 348, 349, 353
Crumbaugh, J.C. 102
Crutchfield, R.D. 401
Culbertson, R.G. 280
Cullen, F.T. 426 *passim*
Cummings, Peter 412
Cunningham, L.C. xvi, xvii
Curry, G. David xvii, 27, 33–42

Curtis, Richard 187, 188, 189, 361
Cuvelier, S.J. 427 *passim*

D'Alessio, S. 123, 124
D'Angelo, L. 98, 106
Dahlberg L.L. xvi, 86
Daly, Kathleen 186, 187, 188, 189, 417, 427
Davidson, L.L. 521
Davies, Garth 372
Davis, James A. 394, 413
Davis, Peter 170
Dean, C. 89
Deane, Glenn 378
Decker, Scott H. xvi, xvii, xix, 5, 6, 7, 8, 33–42,
        85, 87, 94, 113, 114, 124, 125, 136, 161,
        163, 175, 177, 190–92 *passim*, 194, 218,
        225, 229, 269–80 *passim*, 349–50, 363,
        376, 417, 447
Deitch, E.A. xxv
DeLone, Miriam 410 *passim*
Derzon, J.H. 88
Deutschberger, Paul 6
Di Maio, V. 116, 123, 124
Dickson, N. 88
DiIulio, J.J. 479
DiScala, Carla 517–21
Dodd, T. 217
Dodge, Richard W. 329
Doerner, William G. 338
Dolan, Edward F. 135
Dollard, John 319
Doyle, Daniel 49, 370
Drass, Kriss A. 443, 445
Dunlap, E. 470
Dunworth, Terence 28
DuRant, Robert H. xvii, 97–110
Durkin, Maureen 517–21

Earls, Felton 151, 460
Earp, J. 113
Ebaugh, H.R.F. 272
Eckenrode, J. 98
Edwards, S. 347
Egley, H.A. Jr. 34. 35, 41, 376
Ekblom, P. 255
Ekland, W.R. 271
Ekland-Olson, Sheldon 177, 271
El Gato 150
Elis, Lori 186, 187
Ellickson, P.L. 86
Elliott, Delbert S. 163

Ellsworth, T. 280
Emerson, J. 248
Empey, LaMar T. 174
Engberg, J. 35, 358
Enger, C. 122
Esbensen, F.A. 100

Fackler, M. 117
Fagan, Jeffrey xvi, xvii, 34, 43–77, 86, 112, 135,
        271, 348, 350, 361, 370, 371, 372, 417,
        438
Farrington, David P. xix, xxi, 4, 5, 85, 86, 87,
        93, 178, 270, 272, 470, 486
Farrow, J. 113
Feeney, Floyd 163, 254
Feldman, J.J. 85, 98, 112
Felson, Marcus 160, 177, 271
Felson, Richard B. xxi, 49, 317–43, 370, 371
Fenley, M.A. 98
Fenstermaker, Sarah 186 *passim*
Ferdinand, T.N. 470
Fergusson, D.M. 93
Ferracuti, Franco 369
Figlio, R.M. 85, 88, 89
Fingerhut, L.A. 85, 98, 112, 124, 393
Finkelhor, D. 529
Finney, Shan 135
Fischer, Claude S. 320
Fisher, Joseph C. 409
Fleisher, Mark S. 163, 165, 175, 177, 178 *passim*
Flewelling, R.L. 362, 363, 446
Flood-Page, C. 216
Foley, L.A. 427
Forde, D.R. 271
Forgatch, M.S. 87, 93
Fox, James Alan xxii, 469–89, 438, 445, 446,
        470, 472, 473, 474, 479
Fox, R.J. 38
Francisco J.T.
Frankel, Martin 327
Franzese, Robert J. 133
Freud, Sigmund 425
Friedman, David 517–21
Froehike, R. 98, 105
Fulginiti, V.A. 98, 107
Funk, T. 111

Gabor, Thomas 163, 269–72 *passim*
Gainer, P.S. 85, 86
Garbarino, J. 529
Garmezy, N. 99, 107

Gerken, E.A. 98, 106
Gerrard, Nathan 4
Gersten, J.C. 98
Gertz, Marc 405, 410
Getts, Alan G. 97–110
Gibbons, Donald L. 174
Giddens, Anthony 370
Giglio, Greg 135
Gilfus, M. 425
Gill, M. 254
Giordano, P.C. 429
Gladstein, J. 98
Glaser, Barney 11
Glasgow, D.G. 280
Glassner, Barry 161, 191
Gleason, Debra K. 133, 136, 151
Goetting, A. 425
Goffman, Erving 9, 13, 14, 26, 47, 235, 236
Golden, Reid M. 443, 445
Goldstein, Paul J. 140, 346, 349, 350–53 *passim*,
        360–61 *passim*, 438, 439, 440, 443, 444
        passim, 451, 454, 457, 458
Golub, A. 470
Gomez, Pio 149–50 *passim*
Goode, W. 232
Gordon, M.A. 35
Gordon, Rachel 4, 5
Gorman, D.M. 438
Gorman-Smith, D. 86, 87, 88
Gottfredson, Michael F. 174 *passim*, 270
Graham, Nanette 371
Grasmick (1993) 37
Greene, William H. 450
Greenfeld, L.A. 426, 427, 433
Greenwood, C. 254
Greenwood, P.W. 269
Grimes W.R. xxv
Grogger, J. 471
Groves, W. Byron 160, 175
Gubrium, Jaber 13
Gujarati, Damodar 448
Gupta, Vanita 393–403
Guttridge, P. 279
Guyer, B. 98

Hagan, John 174–77 *passim*, 441
Hagedorn, John M. 37, 41, 134, 135, 136, 153
Hales, Gavin xvii, 79–84
Hammersly, Martyn 138
Hammett, M. 393

Hammond, W. 270
Hamowy, Ronald 439
Hamparian, D. 270 *passim*
Hanushek, Eric A. 328
Haran, J.F. 254
Harding, R. 254
Harer, Miles D. 443, 445, 469, 470
Harlow, Caroline Wolf 491–505
Harries, Keith D. 318
Harrington, H. 87
Harry, Joseph 177
Hartnagel, Timothy 175, 177, 272, 279
Hauser, R.M. 395
Hawkins, Gordon 86, 443 *passim*, 445, 448, 451,
        456, 458, 459, 460, 461, 462
Hayward, P. 217
Heckathorn, Douglas D. 161
Heimer, Karen 369
Hemenway, D., 113, 114
Henslin, James M. 162
Heumann, Milton 418
Hewitt, John 7, 21, 24
Hibberd, M. 255
Hickman, C. Addison 22
Hill, Gary D. 188, 189, 428, 429
Hindelang, M.J. 86, 407
Hinduja, S. 347
Hirsch, M. 520
Hirschi, Travis 86, 160, 174 *passim*, 270
Hobs, Dick 12
Hodgson, James F. 175
Hoffman, P. 273
Hofstadter, R. xv
Hogan, Michael xxii, 405–23
Holford, S. 98
Holloway, Katy xx, 215–30
Holmes, S.K. 98, 101
Holstein, James 13
Honaker, D. xix
Honaker, David xix, 165, 166, 168, 170, 175,
        176
Horai, J. 231
Horney, Julie 450
Hornsby, R. xx, xxvi
Hornstein, Harvey A. 320
Horowitz, Ruth xvi, 8, 370, 371, 372, 381, 385
Horwood, L.J. 93
Howard, G.J. 86, 93, 94, 112, 127
Howell, James C. xvi, 6, 85, 86, 93, 94, 112,
        125, 133, 136, 151

Howell, Joy 517–21
Hsieh, C.C. 393, 400
Huang, W.S. 371
Huebner, B. 347
Huff, C. R. xvii
Huff-Corzine, L. xvii
Hughes, Lorine 7
Hugo, Victor 393
Huizinga, David 87, 100, 126, 163
Hunt, Dana E. 136
Hunt, Jennifer 209
Hunter, P. 217
Hutson, H.R. xvi

Inciardi, J.A. xvi, xvii
Ingram, D.D. 85, 98, 112
Irwin, J. 272
Ivatury, Rao 517–21

Jackson, J. 426
Jackson, John E. 328
Jackson, R.K. 33
Jacob, Herbert 371
Jacobs, Bruce A. xvii, xix, 159–83, 269, 274
Jacobs, James B. 135
Jankowski, Martín Sánchez 136
Jara, D. 112
Jarvis, J.P.
Jensen, G.F. 271
Jessor, R. 99, 107
Joe, Karen A. 187
Johnson, Bruce D. 134, 470
Jonas, Steven 442
Jones, R.S. 272, 273, 279
Jurik, N.C. 428 *passim*, 433

Kagan, J. 99
Kaiza, P. 79, 84
Kalb, L. 126
Kanter, Rosabeth 16, 21
Kapardis, A. 254
Kasarda, John D. 137
Kasen, S. 86
Katz, Jack xv, xix, 6, 160, 166, 167, 174, 186, 187, 198, 254, 269, 272, 384
Kawachi, Ichiro 393–403
Kawai, Kriko 4, 5
Kazdin, A.E. 102
Keene, L. 127
Keiser, R. Lincoln 56

Kellermann, Arthur L. xxii, 393, 402, 405, 406, 410–12 *passim*, 414, 416 *passim*, 417 *passim*, 419
Kelley, Liz 185
Kempf, K.L. 270, 271
Kendall-Tackett, K. 529
Kennedy, Bruce P. xxii, 112, 393–403
Kennedy, David M. xvi, 12, 27, 33, 34, 35, 36, 39, 85, 113, 114, 125, 127
Kennedy, L.W. 271
Kennedy, Randall 371
Killias, Martin 409
Kilmer, B. 347, 442
Kim, J. 361
Kleck, Gary xv, xxii, 254, 405–23, 116, 120, 318, 325–26 *passim*
Klein, A.E. 102
Klein, D. 426
Klein, Malcolm W. xvi, xvii, xix, 5, 28, 34, 35, 36, 37, 39, 41, 134, 135, 136, 140, 151, 177
Klinger, David 371
Knox, G. 123
Koch, G.G. 86
Kochanek K.D.
Koons-Witt, Barbara A. xxii, 425–35
Koop, C.E. 98, 105
Kopel, D 112, 113, 115, 122, 254
Koper, C. 112, 113, 116, 120, 122
Kornhauser, Ruth 370
Kovacs, M. 102
Kowalski, Robin M. 185, 187
Krahn, H. 393
Kresnow, M. 112
Krivo, L.J. 280, 373, 383
Krohn, Marvin 4, 8, 14, 86, 87, 93, 94, 112, 127
Krug, Alan S. 409
Kruttschnitt, C. 426 *passim*, 429
Kubrin, Charis E. xxi, 3, 369–92
Kuhn, Manford 22

LaFree, Gary 437, 443, 445
Lahey, Benhamin 4, 5
Land, Kenneth 376, 378, 393, 470, 482
Landis, J.R. 86
Lane, R. 469
Langan, P.A. xix, xxi, 470
Laraque, Danielle xxiv, 517–21
Lasley, J.R. 271
Lattimore, P.K. 347

Laub, John H. 85, 86, 87, 112, 160, 188, 189, 429, 469, 470, 472, 476
Lauderbeck, David 136
Lauritsen, J.L. 271, 279, 474
Lawrence, H. 122, 124
LeBlanc, M. 86, 87, 93
LeCompte, Margaret D. 138
Lee, G.W. 470
Lee, Matthew R. 437–68
Leiter, J. 347
LeJeune, R. 239
Lemert, Edwin 167, 173, 176
Leonard, C.C. xv, xxi, xxv
Leonard, I.M. xv, xxi, xxv
Lester, D. 395, 409
Letkemann, Peter 177, 325, 339
Levin, Jack 438, 471
Liebow, Eliot 175
Lilienfeld, Abraham M. 411
Lilienfeld, David E. 411
Limber, S. 113
Lindesmith, Alfred 7
Lipsey, M.W. 88
Lipton, Douglas S. 136
Little, R. 113, 120
Lizotte, Alan 4, 5, 8, 14, 33, 35, 63, 86, 87, 93, 94, 111, 112, 113, 125, 126, 127, 410, 417 *passim*, 418, 419, 440
Lochner, Kimberly 393–403
Loeber, Rolf 4, 5, 85, 87, 126
Lofland, John 11, 172, 173
Lofland, Lyn H. 11
Loftin, Colin 418
Logan, Charles H. 321
Lombroso 425
Luckenbill, David F. xx, 49, 52, 370, 382, 384, 388, 406, 407
Lundberg, G.D. 98, 105
Lynam, D.R. 87
Lynch, Michael J. 160, 175

McBride, W.D. 33
McCall, George 15, 161, 165
McCall, Patricia L. 369, 370, 372, 376, 443, 445, 449, 484
McCarthy, Bill 174–77 *passim*
McCarthy, J.F. 85
McCleary, R.M. 272
McCluskey, Cynthia Perez xviii, 85–95

McCluskey, John D. 85–95, 345–68
McCorkle, Richard 5
MacCoun, R. 347, 349, 442, 451
McDermott, M. Joan 188, 189, 429
McDevitt, J. xvi
MacDonald, J.M. 270
McDowall, David 409, 410, 418
McDowell, D. 393, 402
McElrath, Karen xv, 325, 410, 416
McGarrell, E. 125, 364
McGee, Z.T. 98, 106
McGonigal, M. 112
McGrady, G.A. 85, 86
McGuigan, K.A. 86
McHorney, C. 98
McKay, Henry D. 160, 370, 394, 400
McNulty, Thomas L. 375, 376
Magaddino, Joseph P. 409, 410
Maguire, Kathleen 442
Maguire, M. 216
Maher, Lisa 163, 187–90 *passim*, 193, 209, 427
Maholick, L.T. 102
Maier, P.E. 271
Mann, Coramae Richey 188
Markowitz, Fred E. 371
Marquart, J.W. 427 *passim*
Marquis, Kent H. 417
Marrow, C. 85,86
Marshall, E. 117, 120
Marshall, Ineke H. 450
Martin J.M. 254
Martinez, P. 98, 101
Martinez, R. Jr. 269, 270, 271, 279, 348
Marvell, Thomas B. 418
Mason, J.98, 105
Massey, D.S. 484
Masters, A.S. 99, 107
Matthews, R. 254
Maupin, J. 126
Maxson, C.L. xvi, xvii, 34, 35, 36, 39, 41, 475
May, D. 127
May, Tim 12
Mays, G. Larry xviii, 111–32
Mazerolle, P. 89
Mead, G. 231
Medoff, Marshall H. 409, 410
Menard, Scott 133
Mercy, J.A. 98, 112
Merton, Robert K. 160

Messerschmidt, James W. 186 *passim*
Messner, Steven F. xxi, 317–43, 377, 393, 401, 443, 445
Michener, H. 250
Mickelwright, J. 394
Mieczkowski, Thomas 136
Miethe, Terance 5
Miles-Doan, Rebecca 376, 377
Miller, Jody xix, xxii, 5, 6, 185–214, 428 *passim*, 433
Miller, L. 126
Miller, M. xvi
Miller, N. 231
Miller, W.B. 34, 160, 272
Milne, B.J. 87
Miniño, A.M. xxiv
Minor, W. William 177
Moffitt, T.E. 87, 88, 89, 93
Monteforte, J.R. 438
Moody, Carlisle E. 418
Moore, J.W. xvi
Moore, Joan 5, 7, 133, 135, 137, 151
Morales, Armando T. 134, 139,
Morenoff, Jeffrey D. 151, 378
Morrison, S. xx, 219, 255
Morrison, Shona 253–68
Mueller, C.A. 85, 86
Murphy, Linda R. 329, 479, 480
Murray, Douglas R. 409
Murray-Garcia, J. 530
Mustaine, E. 271
Myers, G.P. 85, 86

Nadelmann, Ethan A. 439
Nagin, Daniel S. 93, 418, 470, 482
Neaigus, Alan 137, 138
Nelson, Forrest D. 416
Newburn, Tim 186
Newton, George D. 409
Nisbett, Richard E. 372, 385
Novello, A.C. 98, 105

O'Carroll, P.W. 98, 105
O'Donnell, Ian xx, 219, 254, 253–68
Oakley, Annie 163
Ohlin, Lloyd E. xvii, 41, 160, 279
Oliver, William 6, 189
Ordog, G.J. xxv
Osgood, Wayne D. 377, 450

Ousey, Graham C. xxii, 437–68

Padilla, Felix, M. xvi, 35, 134, 135, 136,
Page, Bryan 139
Pagliocca, P. 113
Pampel, F.C. 357, 446, 472, 473
Parenti, Christian 390
Parker, Karen F. 375, 377, 443, 445, 449, 484
Parks, Roger 371
Pastore, Ann L. 442
Patchin, Justin W. 345–68
Patel, J. 533–37
Paternoster, R. 89
Patillo-McCoy, Mary 390, 440
Patterson, Britt 409, 410
Patterson, G.R. 87, 93
Paulter, N. 127
Pauly, John 160
Pedhazur, E.J. 395
Pendergast, R.A. 98, 99, 100, 102, 103, 105, 106, 107
Pennell, Susan xvi, 35, 85, 94, 218, 225, 417
Perkins, Craig xxi, 305–16
Perry, D. 217
Persad, I.J. xxv, 533–37
Petersilia, J. 270
Peterson, R.D. 280, 373, 383
Peterson-Lynsky, D. 126
Pettiway, L.E. 271, 427 *passim*, 428, 433
Phillips, Llad 409
Piehl, Anne Morrison xvi, 12, 27, 33, 34, 35, 36, 39, 85, 113
Pierce, G.L. xvi
Pileggi, Nicholas, 171
Piliavin, Irving 174
Piquero, Alex R. xxii, 86, 89, 469–89
Poe-Yamagata, E. 112
Pogrebin, Mark R. xvii, 3–32
Pollack, I. 126, 127
Pollock, D. 112
Pollock, J.M. 426 *passim*, 433
Polsky, Ned 161, 163
Povey, D. 79, 84
Powell, K.E. 98, 105
Powers, J.L. 98
Preble, Edward 136, 137
Proctor, R. 98, 105
Prodzinski J.
Prothrow-Stith, Deborah 98, 99, 112, 393–403

Pruitt, Matthew V. 375, 377
Pugh, M.D. 393, 400
Putnam, R.D. 394

Quinney, Richard 160

Rafferty, Ann P. 411, 417
Rahn, W. 401
Raudenbush, Stephen W. 450
Regoeczi, W.C. 357, 365
Reidel, Marc 318, 327, 329, 357, 365
Reisig, Michael 371
Reiss, A.J. 393, 395, 469
Reuter, P. 347, 442
Rice, D.P. 393
Richters, J.E. 98, 101
Ricketts, Erol R. 377
Riggs, S. 98
Riley, K.J. 347, 444
Rivara F.P. 98, 113, 416
Rivera, C. 86, 87, 93
Rix, B. 218
Robins, L.N. 98, 101
Rodgers, A. 102
Rogan, D. 125, 364
Roncek, D.E. 271
Roscigno, Vincent J. 369,370, 372
Rose, Dina R. 460
Rosenberg, M.L. 98, 105
Rosenfeld, R. 34, 35, 41, 94, 113, 114, 347, 348,
    351 *passim*, 353, 360, 376, 437, 447, 469,
    474–76 *passim*, 447, 469, 474, 475, 476
Rossi, Peter H. 8, 123, 255, 417
Roth, J.A. 85, 86, 393, 395, 469, 475
Ruddell, Rick xviii, 111–32
Runyan, C.W. 98, 106
Rushforth N.B.
Rutter, M. 88, 99, 107
Ryan, P.J. 346

Sadowski, L. 113, 114
Sagi, P.C. 470
Sampson, Robert J. xxiii, 151, 160, 168, 187,
    192, 271, 279, 369, 371, 376, 377, 378,
    394, 460, 484
Sanchez, L. 425
Sanchez, Mark xvi, xvii, 144–46 *passim*, 150
Sanchez-Jankowski, M.S.
Sanders, William B. xvi, 8, 9, 137

Sanders-Phillips, Kathy xxiv, 523–32
Sanow, E. 117, 120
Sante, Luc 54
Sasson, Theodore, xxi, 438, 441, 442
Saunders, M.A. 533–37
Sawhill, Isabel V. 377
Sayles, Susan 410
Scales, B. 113
Schatzman, Leonard 11
Scheff, T. 231, 232
Schein, O. 122, 124
Schelling, T. 231
Schensul, Jean J. 138
Schiff, M. 98
Schlesselman, James J. 411, 417
Schmid, T.J. 272, 273, 279
Schram, Pamela J. xxii, 425–35
Schwaner, Shawn L. 269–82
Schwartz, S. 401
Seidman, Robert 160
Sellin, T. 85, 89
Serpe, Richard 8
Shakoor, B.H. 98
Shapland, J. 255
Shasky, J 98, 105
Shaw, Clifford R. 160, 370, 394, 400
Shaw, J.W. 125
Shelden, Randall G. 28, 189
Sheley, Joseph F. 8, 62, 85, 86, 94, 98, 106, 113,
    114, 416, 417
Sheppard, D. 86, 87, 125, 126
Sherif, Muzafer 18
Shermak, S. 125
Sherman, L.W. xv, 124, 125, 126, 364
Shibadeh, Edward S. 375
Shibutani, Tomatsu 7, 14, 231
Shine, E. 111
Short, J. Jr. xvii, 36, 37
Short, James 6, 7, 28
Shover, Neal xix, 165–68 *passim*, 170, 171, 175,
    176, 177
Sickmund, M. 112
Sifanek, Stephen J. xix, 133–56
Sikes, Gini 186
Silva, P.A. 87, 88
Silverstone, Daniel xvii, 79–84
Simcha-Fagan, O. 98
Simmel, G. 231
Simmons, Jerry 15

Simon, R.J. 425, 426
Simpson, S.S. 428, 429
Simpson, Sally 185, 186–88 *passim*, 208
Singer, J. 250
Singer, S. 271
Sirpal, Suman K. 5
Skolnick, Jerome H. xvii, 136
Slater, E.J. 98
Smailes, E. 86
Smith, C. xvi
Smith, Carolyn 4, 8, 14
Smith, D.L. 98
Smith, Douglas 371, 372, 410
Smith, J. 219
Smith, Tom W. 394, 413
Snell, T.L. 426, 427, 433
Snipes, Jeffrey B. 405
Snyder, H.N. 85, 112
Solenberger, R. 521
Sommers, I. 427 *passim*
Speir, John C. 338
Spelman, W. 470
Spergel, Irving A. 27, 34, 35, 37, 133, 135, 151,
      152, 155
Spielberger, A. 470
Spitz, W.U. 438
Spivak, H.R. 98, 99
Spunt, Barry 136
Srinivas Reddy, R. 533–37
Stack, Carol B. 193
Stafford, Marck C. 174
Stahl, William 517–21
Stanko, Elizabeth A. 186
Stanton, W. 88
Steadman, Henry J. 49, 320, 370
Stear, D. 270
Steffensmeier, Darrell J. 189, 375, 426, *passim*,
      427, 443, 445, 469, 470
Stein, Michael 165
Stokes, Randall 21
Stolley, Paul D. 411
Stolzenberg, L. 123, 124
Stone, Gregory 7
Stoolmiller, M. 87, 93
Stouthamer-Loeber, Magda 4,5
Straus, M.A. 101
Strauss, Anselm 7, 15, 11, 22
Stretesky, Paul B. xvii, 3–32
Strodtbeck, Fred 6

Strom, Kevin J. xxiv, 509–16
Stryker, Sheldon 8
Suffredini, B.R. 124
Sullivan, Mercer L. 136
Sundermann, C. 126, 127
Susser, M. 401
Sutherland, E.H. xviii, 98, 106, 160, 161, 174
Sutherland, Edwin 174
Swan, K. 112
Swift, S. xvi
Swistounoff, V. 124
Sykes, G. 272

Taubes, Gary 411
Taylor, Carl 135, 136, 153
Taylor, I. xx
Taylor, J. 216
Tedeschi, James 48, 231, 250, 319 *passim*, 339
Terry, Robert 189
Tesoriero, James M. 8, 86
Tewkesbury, R. 271
Thomas, P. 87, 88, 93, 272
Thornberry, Terence P. 4, 8, 86, 87, 93, 127
Thrasher, Frederick xvii, 6, 33
Tice, Dianne 13
Tielsch, J. 122
Tiezzi, L. 85
Tilley, N. 218
Tita, G.E. 34, 35, 358
Tittle, Charles R. 159, 160, 173, 174 *passim*,
      321
Tobin, Kimberley 4, 8, 14, 86, 93, 94, 112
Toch, Hans 410
Tolan, P.E. 86, 87, 88, 93
Tonry, Michael 442, 445
Torres, Jose 135
Tracy, P.E. 85, 88
Tracy, Sharon 28
Trivedi, P. 91
Trudeau, J. 347
Tunnell, Kenneth D. 163, 177
Turner, Anthony G. 329
Turner, Ralph 17
Turner, S. 270

Uchida, Craig D. 410
Urbina, S.P. 427

Valdez, Avelardo xix, 133–56

Valentine, B. xvii
Van Dine, S. 269
Van Maanen, M. 117
Van Stelle, K.R. 279
Van Winkle, Barrik xvi, xvii, xix, 5, 6, 7, 8, 34, 36, 37, 39, 125, 136, 190, 229
Varano, Sean P. xxi, 345–68
Vaughn, Michael 371
Vaughn, R.D. 85
Velez, Maria B. 371, 387
Venkatesh, Sudhir A. xvi, 135
Vigil, Diego 151
Vigil, James D. 5, 7, 8, 37
Vila, B. 37
Visher, C.A. 85,86, 94, 475
Vold, George B. 405

Wachtel, J. 113, 122, 128
Waldorf, Dan 135, 136, 172
Walker, A. xxi
Walker, D. 218
Walker, N. 270
Wallman, Joel 34, 41, 437, 470
Walsh, Dermot 176
Walter, J.H. 85
Walters, Glenn 167, 177
Walters, J.P. 479
Walters, L.H. 102
Ward, D.A. 427
Ward, J. 218
Ward, R.E. 427
Waschbusch, D.A. 87
Wasserman, G. 126
Waterman, P.D. 85
Watters, John 190
Weaver, G.S. xv, xxv
Weber, Dee 445
Webster, D.W. 85, 86
Weiber, A.W. 100
Weil, A. 346
Weinstein, Eugene 6
Weis, J.G. 86
Weiss, A. 125, 364
Weitzer, Ronald xxi, 369–92
Wellford, C. 348, 349, 353, 470
Wells, R.D. 98
Welniak, E. 394

Welsh, B.C. 85
Weppner, Robert 161
Werner, E.E. 99, 107
West, Candace 186 *passim*, 209
West, D.J. 270
White, Helen Raskin 438
White, Jacquelyn 185, 187
Widom, C.S. 98
Wiebel, Wayne 138
Wiles, Paul 160
Wilkinson, Deanna L. xvi, xvii, 43–77, 112, 370, 371
Wilkinson, Richard G. 400
Williams K.R. 357, 446, 472, 473
Williams, K.B. 362, 363
Williams, T. xvi, 136
Wilson, J. 364
Wilson, James Q. 127, 283
Wilson, Milbourne 18
Wilson, William Julius xxiii, 36, 169, 187, 189, 192, 369, 370, 373, 394, 401, 460, 484
Winfree, L.T. Jr. 126
Winn, R. 428 *passim*, 433
Wintemute, G. 86, 112, 113, 116, 122, 124, 128
Wolfgang, M.E. xxiii, 85, 88, 89, 269, 270 *passim*, 350, 369, 406
Woods, Elizabeth R. 97–110
Woodward, L. 98, 106
Wright, J. 123
Wright, James D. xv, 8, 62, 85, 86, 87, 98, 106, 113, 114, 255, 417
Wright, Richard T. xvii, xix, 159–83, 161, 163, 175, 177, 190–92 *passim*, 194, 269–80 *passim*, 349–50
Wrong, D. 232

Yablonsky, Lewis xvii, 4, 163
Yin, Zenong 137
Yoerger, K.L. 87, 93

Zahn, Margaret A. 438
Zatz, Margaret 418
Zawitz, Marianne W. xxiv, 509–16
Zimmerman, Don H. 186 *passim*, 209
Zimring, Franklin E. 86, 112, 122, 229, 317, 361, 406, 409, 410, 443 *passim*, 445, 448, 451, 456, 458, 459, 460, 461, 462, 471